DOS 5: A Developer's
Advanced Programming Guide to DOS
. . . .

DOS 5: A Developer's Guide
Advanced Programming Guide to DOS
. . . .

Al Williams

M&T Books
A Division of M&T Publishing, Inc.
501 Galveston Drive
Redwood City, CA 94063

© 1991 by M&T Publishing, Inc.

Printed in the United States of America

All rights reserved. No part of this book may be reproduced or transmitted in any form or by any means, electronic or mechanical, including photocopying, recording, or by any information storage and retrieval system, without prior written permission from the Publisher. Contact the Publisher for information on foreign rights.

Limits of Liability and Disclaimer of Warranty
The Author and Publisher of this book have used their best efforts in preparing this book and the programs contained in it. These efforts include the development, research, and testing of the theories and programs to determine their effectiveness.

The Author and Publisher make no warranty of any kind, expressed or implied, with regard to these programs or the documentation contained in this book. The Author and Publisher shall not be liable in any event for incidental or consequential damages in connection with, or arising out of, the furnishing, performance, or use of these programs.

Library of Congress Cataloging-in-Publication Data

Williams, Al –
    DOS 5: A Developer's Guide: advanced programming guide to DOS / Al Williams
        p.   cm.
    Includes bibliographical references and index.
    ISBN 1-55851-177-6 (book only)
    ISBN 1-55851-179-2 (book/disk)
    1. MS-DOS (computer operating system)   2. Systems programming (computer science)   I. Title.
QA76.76.O63W55   1991
005.4'46—dc20
                                                            90-32020
                                                                   CIP

94 93 92 91   4 3 2 1

All products, names, and services are trademarks or registered trademarks of their respective companies.

Project Editor: Linda Comer   **Technical Editor:** Ray Valdes
Cover Art: Lauren Smith Design

*To Pat and Patrick, but especially to my father,
who taught me to learn*

Contents

PREFACE

WHY THIS BOOK IS FOR YOU 1

INTRODUCTION 3
What You'll Need 4
Conventions 5

PART I: BASIC MS-DOS PROGRAMMING

CHAPTER 1: THE PC HARDWARE: AN OVERVIEW 9
Basic Addressing 9
Types of Memory 10
Registers 11
Addressing Revisited 18
Ports 19
Hardware Interrupts 20
The Timer 23
General I/O 23
The Keyboard 24
Video 26
Disks 27

CHAPTER 2: THE APPLICATION ENVIRONMENT 29
Types of DOS Applications 30
The DOS Interrupts 35
The BIOS Interrupts 37
BIOS Variables 38

The PSP	38
Memory Allocation in Detail	42
Summary	43

CHAPTER 3: C AND ASSEMBLY FOR DOS ... 45

More About Addressing	45
Accessing the Environment	50
Input and Output	50
Interrupts	51
Servicing Interrupts	58
Assembly Routines for C	59

CHAPTER 4: PROGRAMS AT LAST! ... 61

ESCAPE	61
SPACE	64
EDISP	66
PRTSCRN	68
SPYS	69

CHAPTER 5: DOS SERVICES ... 77

The Simple I/O Services	79
Disk Control Operations	87
File Operations	97
FCB File Services	102
Handle Services	102
Directory Operations	115
Date and Time Operations	118
Process Operations	120
Memory Operations	126
IOCTL Operations	130
Miscellaneous Operations	136
Other DOS Interrupts	145

CHAPTER 6: ROM BIOS SERVICES 153
  The Video Services 153
  The Equipment Configuration Service 163
  Reading the Size of Conventional Memory 163
  The Disk Services 164
  The Serial Port Services 171
  The Keyboard Services 175
  Printer Services 177
  The Clock Services 179
  BIOS Variables 180

CHAPTER 7: DIRECT ACCESS TECHNIQUES 183
  Writing Text to Screen Memory 183
  Interrupt Rules 188
  Managing Hardware Interrupts 190
  Direct Keyboard Access 191
  Interacting with DOS Memory Allocation 199
  Timing and Sound Generation 202
  The AT's Real-Time Clock 212
  Using Joysticks 212
  The Parallel Port 217
  The Serial Port 221

CHAPTER 8: THE COPROCESSOR 239
  Multiprocessing 240
  Data Types and Formats 241
  Coprocessor Operation 244
  Coprocessor Instructions 247
  Coprocessor Emulation 252
  A Simple Coprocessor Program 253
  A Four-Function Calculator 254
  Final Notes 267

PART II: ADVANCED MS-DOS PROGRAMMING

CHAPTER 9: BUILDING ROBUST APPLICATIONS 271
Handling Break Exceptions 273
Handling Critical Errors 279
Which Language is Best? 286
Multitasking Considerations 287
A High-Performance Application in C 298

CHAPTER 10: GRAPHICS PROGRAMMING 317
Mode Selection 319
Pixel Representation 323
Setting the Colors 335
Putting it Together 338
Improving Graphics Performance 354

CHAPTER 11: OF MICE AND MEN 357
Mouse Modes 358
The Mouse Screen 358
The Mouse Cursor 359
Mouse Sensitivity 359
Important Mouse Variables 360
Basic Mouse Commands 360
A Basic Mouse Library in C 371
Polling the Mouse 378
Event-Driven Programming 391
Using the Mouse with Graphics 408

CHAPTER 12: EXPANDING HORIZONS: EMS 411
How EMS Works 412
Detecting EMS 414
Select EMS Commands 415

Maintaining Compatibility	437
The CEMS Library	438
Using CEMS: DUP	442
Executing Code in EMS	455

CHAPTER 13: DEVICE DRIVERS 461

Device-Driver Components	461
Loading the Driver	466
Types of Drivers	466
Character-Driver Commands	466
Block-Driver Commands	472
Optional Commands	478
Putting It All Together	479
Sample Drivers	487
A Block Driver	493
Debugging	504
More Fun with Drivers	506

CHAPTER 14: TSR PROGRAMMING 507

TSR Architecture	507
Live and Let Live	508
A Simple Interceptor	509
WASTE1: The Next Step	513
WASTE: The Final Version	516
INTASM: A Development Environment for Interceptors	525
Controlling Cursor Size	540
More Fun with Interceptors	543
Pop-Up Fundamentals	544
DOS Access	545
Critical Sections	545
Context Management	546
TSRASM: A Pop-up Development Environment	547

Some Sample Pop-ups 579
If Your TSR Doesn't Work 594

PART III: PROTECTED-MODE TECHNIQUES

CHAPTER 15: 80386 PROTECTED MODE 599
The Benefits 600
Privileged Segments 602
Multitasking 611
Code Segments Revisited 614
Exceptions 615
Memory Management 618
Living in the Past: Real and V86 Modes 621
Handling Interrupts in V86 Mode 623
Switching to Protected Mode 624
Protected Mode on a PC 627

CHAPTER 16: USING EXTENDED MEMORY 629
BIOS Calls 629
Allocating Extended Memory 631
The CEXT Library 633
Other Ways to Access Extended Memory 641

CHAPTER 17: 80386 DEBUGGING 643
Hardware Debugging 643
The Exact Bits and Other Flags 645
Task-Switch Breakpoints 646
BREAK386 646
Detailed Program Operation 676
Advanced Interrupt Handlers in C 684

CHAPTER 18: ACCESSING 4 GIGABYTES IN REAL
      MODE..691
The Plan 691
Some Assembly Required 705
Using the SEG4G Library 706
Some Examples 706

CHAPTER 19: DOS EXTENDERS..713
About PROT 713
Using PROT 715
Putting It Together 722
Dynamic Link Mode 724
Debugging 731
What Went Wrong? 733
Multitasking 734
Under the Hood 735
The Seven-Percent Solution 738
Hardware Interrupts 739
Sixteen-Bit Tools in a 32-Bit World 739
Sample Programs 740
The Future 741
Commercial DOS Extenders 742

APPENDIX A: GLOSSARY..885
APPENDIX B: IBM PC CHARACTER SET..........................889
APPENDIX C: IBM PC LINE-DRAWING CHARACTERS.......893
APPENDIX D: IBM PC SCAN CODES..................................895
APPENDIX E: ANNOTATED BIBLIOGRAPHY......................899
INDEX 905

Preface

The question people most often ask me about this project is "Why another book on DOS?" On the surface, this seems like a legitimate question. After all, the PC thrust MS-DOS into the limelight in late 1981; surely enough has been written about it since then.

These statements overlook one important point: DOS is a moving target. Hardly a month goes by without an announcement of a new protected-mode standard or some extension or change to DOS. You have to struggle to keep up with it all, especially if you develop commercial software.

Many of the "standard" DOS books have become dated. Some attempt to keep up with new topics via hasty revisions. This book will take you on a grand tour of the DOS programming environment as it exists today, following the release of version 5.

Part 1 covers the basic PC hardware, along with BIOS and DOS functions. Unlike in many books, they are grouped here by function. After all, that's how you use them. I've even included the undocumented calls that I've found most useful.

Part 2 will teach you the more advanced tricks of the trade. Here you'll find solid programs to help you build resident programs and device drivers. You'll see how to add mouse support and graphics to your programs and how to use expanded memory to break the 640K limit.

The final section covers the exciting techniques possible with the 80286, 386, and 486 processors. We'll look at protected-mode debugging and extended memory, then dissect a complete 386 DOS extender.

Publisher's Note: Readers familiar with the first printing of this book may notice that Listing 9-4, formerly called DSCOPE.C, is now called COMLOOK.C. The name DSCOPE is used as a trademark by Harrison Uhl of Princeton, New Jersey, developer of shareware and commercial programs similar in function to our Listing 9-4. The erroneous use of the name DSCOPE in the first printing of this book was not intentional.

If you have previous experience with DOS programming, you can skip around to the chapters that interest you most. If not, you'll find that each chapter builds on the ones before it.

Many of the examples in this book are in C; others are in assembly and even C++ (all the C++ examples have corresponding examples in C). No matter what language you use, you'll find the chapters on PC hardware and the application environment especially valuable. Those chapters focus on *concepts* so you can handle other languages when the need arises.

If you know C or assembler, but not both, don't worry. In Chapter 3, we'll look at how certain operations look in both languages and cover some of the non-ANSI extensions common among C compilers.

My goal in writing this book is to enable you to write powerful, professional programs. I'm always pleased when people tell me about programs they have written using techniques I shared with them. Of course, I learned many of these techniques from other programmers who have shared them with me in person or via books and articles.

Good luck!

Al Williams
June 1991

Why This Book is For You

DOS 5: A Developer's Guide is the complete guide to writing professional programs for all versions of MS-DOS. Each chapter builds on the ones before it to give you a solid understanding of the DOS programming environment. You'll learn how to write applications, resident programs, device drivers—any kind of program that can be written for DOS.

Included is more than half a megabyte of source code. These are powerful, practical tools that you can use as part of your programs. You'll examine:

- A high-speed serial line analyzer
- A virtual-memory disk-copy program
- A mouse-based sketch program
- A toolkit for writing TSR programs
- A complete 386 protected-mode DOS extender.

DOS 5: A Developer's Guide won't lock you into a specific compiler or assembler. Every C program in the book will compile with Microsoft C and Borland's Turbo C. Most will also compile with the inexpensive Power C from Mix Software.

If you're an engineer, you'll learn how DOS works from the inside out. Toolkits make tackling low-level TSRs and device drivers a snap.

If you're a software developer, you'll discover the latest features DOS has to offer in version 5. You'll learn how to use extra memory, graphics, and protected-mode techniques in your applications.

And if you're a student, you'll see real programs developed in the real world, not contrived textbook examples.

Tired of Manual File Entry?
Save Yourself Some Time and Trouble...
Order the DOS 5: A Developer's Guide Source Code Disk

Why bother manually typing in the book's source code when all the information you need is **ready to use** on disk? Code examples are used throughout the text, and this book's optional disk (PC/MS-DOS format) contains the source code for all the programming examples listed. Useful functions can now be applied immediately! Only $20 postage-paid!

To order with your credit card, call **TOLL FREE 1-800-533-4372 (in CA 1-800-356-2002)**. Or mail your order with payment to M&T Books, 501 Galveston Drive, Redwood City, CA 94063. California residents please add applicable sales tax.

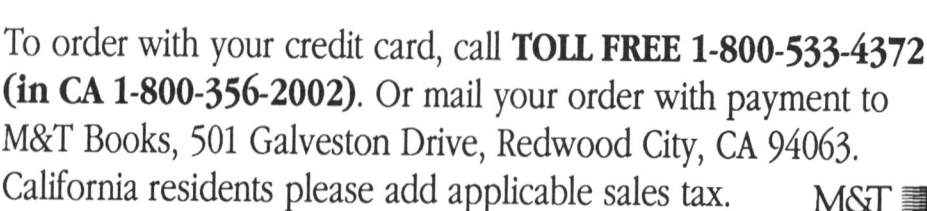

Note: Disks damaged in transit may be returned for a replacement. No credit or refund given.

Introduction

MS-DOS is somehow both constant and ever-changing. This venerable operating system has fostered a whole new generation of computer users and remained dominant since the IBM PC/XT's introduction in 1983. However, as many DOS users have upgraded to more powerful hardware, their demand for performance has increased. This has caused DOS to be peeked, poked, stretched, and extended over the years.

One of the first limitations to be tackled was DOS's inability to access more than a megabyte of memory. At least six standards allow you to use more than 1 Mbyte for data.

Several vendors offer multitasking shells that allow users to run more than one program concurrently. Even Microsoft, the manufacturer of DOS, offers Windows, a multitasking shell.

More recently, programmers wanted access to the special features of the 286, 386, and 486 chips used in many PCs. This has led to the appearance of DOS extenders, which give programs access to some or all of those special features. This powerful technique has breathed new life into DOS.

While other operating systems—including AT&T Bell Laboratories' Unix and IBM/Microsoft's OS/2—can do more than DOS, the fact remains that the DOS market is still the biggest game in town. Why? Some users don't want another operating system; they have become comfortable with DOS. More importantly, taking advantage of a new operating system's benefits requires you to buy all new application software—an expensive proposition, assuming you can find comparable software for the new system. Finally, DOS has modest hardware requirements. Unix and OS/2 offer more features, but at the cost of disk space and memory.

For whatever reasons, DOS will be around for a long time to come.

DOS 5: A DEVELOPER'S GUIDE

What You'll Need

The programs in this book assume that you have a PC-compatible computer running MS-DOS or PC-DOS version 2.0 or higher (though 3.0 or higher is preferred). *DOS* refers to either MS-DOS or PC-DOS. MS-DOS versions below 2.0 are no longer supported and are not discussed in this book.

Most of the programs in Part 3 require a 386 or 486 processor, though one chapter also works with a 286.

You'll also need a C compiler and an assembler. The code examples work with the following languages:

- Borland International's Turbo C, version 2.0 or higher
- Borland Turbo C++ (or Borland C++), version 1.0 or higher
- Mix's Power C, version 2.0 or higher
- Microsoft C, version 5.0 or higher
- Microsoft Assembler, version 5.0 or higher
- Borland Turbo Assembler, version 1.0 or higher.

Because the programs in this book work with many C compilers and assemblers, they may not take advantage of the special features available in the languages you use.

Chapters that deal with certain topics will require additional hardware. The chapter that covers mouse techniques, for instance, requires a mouse. You can safely skip any such chapters if they don't interest you.

PC programs call DOS functions to perform I/O and other tasks. Many programs also call BIOS functions to do I/O at a lower level. While this book covers the most common and useful DOS and BIOS calls, it doesn't present all of them—there are entire reference books on that subject alone. You would do well to buy one of the pocket references on DOS and BIOS calls, most of which are available for less than $10. However, you can easily work through this book without any other material.

INTRODUCTION

Conventions

In the following chapters, we will be talking about many types of computers. The term *PC* will refer to any member of the IBM PC family, including the original IBM PC, the XT, the AT, 386- and 486-based PCs, and the PS/2 series. The term *XT* will be reserved exclusively for PCs with 8088 and 8086 processors. The term *AT* will refer to 286-, 386-, and 486-based machines. Computers that use 386 and 486 processors are referred to as *386s* (for the purposes of this book, the 386 and 486 are equivalent).

Any features specific to or absent from the PS/2 will be noted as they occur. The only exceptions are PS/2 Models 25 and 30, which are considered here to be equivalent to the XT; any discussion of PS/2s in this book does not include these models unless stated explicitly.

In this book, an *H* follows hexadecimal numbers (as in assembler). Alternatively, a *0x* may precede a hexadecimal number (as in C and C++). Numbers separated by colons (B800:0000, for example) are also in hex. All other numbers are in decimal.

A byte is eight bits, a word is 16 bits, and a long or double word contains 32 bits. This follows the assembly-language conventions of *BYTE*, *WORD*, and *DWORD*. A paragraph is 16 consecutive bytes of memory starting at an address evenly divisible by 16. By convention, bit 0 of a binary number is the least significant bit. This means that bit 7 is the top bit of a byte; bit 15 is the top bit of a word.

Words that appear in the text in italics are names of variables or labels from a program. The character ƀ represents a blank (in those cases where blanks have significance).

5

PART I

Basic MS-DOS Programming

CHAPTER 1

The PC Hardware: An Overview

It may seem odd that the first chapter in a book about software concerns hardware. To program a PC effectively, however, we need to understand something about its hardware. In the following sections, we will review some basic architectural features of the 8086 and related processors and look at the PC hardware in more detail. If you program in a high-level language that hides many of these details from you, you'll find the first few sections especially helpful.

Basic Addressing

In 8086-type processors, memory is organized into eight-bit bytes. When dealing with quantities larger than eight bits, the 8086 stores the least significant byte in the lowest address. While that sounds logical, it's confusing when you're reading listings or memory dumps because the numbers seem backwards. For instance, the computer stores the word B800H as two bytes: 00H followed by B8H.

The Intel family of processors uses a memory-addressing technique known as *segmentation*. Simply put, a segment is a region of memory. The computer can handle multiple segments. In real mode—the one in which DOS runs—each segment is exactly 64 kilobytes (Kbytes) long, and there are 65,536 possible segments. The segments overlap so that each starts 16 bytes after the one before it. This is why DOS cannot address more than 1 Mbyte directly (65,536 x 16 = 1,048,576 bytes, or 1 Mbyte). The 8086 and 8088 (the processors used in XT-class machines) can only address 1 Mbyte anyway. The 286, 386, and 486 processors can accommodate much more memory, but DOS cannot access it directly.

Segments are numbered from 0000H to FFFFH. Since each segment is 64 Kbytes long, we use a value, called an *offset*, to specify the byte we want to address. A complete 8086 address always contains a segment and an offset. If the segment is 0040H and the offset is 0102H, we write 0040:0102. Because segments overlap every 16 (10H) bytes, address 0000:0010 is identical to address 0001:0000. Likewise, 0040:0000 is the same as 0000:0400, which is the same as 0020:0200. The computer also stores segmented addresses "backwards." For instance, 0040:1234 appears like this in the computer's memory (displayed in hex):

```
34 12 40 00
```

Programs form addresses with combinations of constant values and registers. For this reason, we'll return to addressing after we examine the processor's registers in more detail.

Types of Memory

Your programs can use several varieties of memory. As we just saw, the XT-class machines can only address 1 Mbyte of memory. This is called c*onventional memory*. An XT may contain up to 640 Kbytes of RAM; I/O devices, the BIOS ROM, and other system resources use the remaining 384 Kbytes.

When programs began running out of room, Lotus, Intel, and Microsoft joined forces to create the Expanded Memory Specification. You'll often see this with a version number, like EMS 3.2 or EMS 4.0 (the most current as of this writing). Most EMS systems consist of one or more EMS cards and a software program known as a *driver*. Your programs can request EMS memory from the driver; however, only 64 Kbytes of this memory are accessible at one time. The EMS driver places this 64-Kbyte block in the upper part of the 1-Mbyte address space, usually just under the BIOS. By making requests of the driver, your programs can map 16-Kbyte "pages" of EMS memory into the 64-Kbyte block.

THE PC HARDWARE: AN OVERVIEW

Even though EMS can handle up to 32 Mbytes, programs can only access a limited number of 16-Kbyte pages at a time. While this is cumbersome, expanded memory is the only kind of extra memory an XT-class machine can use. If your programs use other types of extra memory, they won't be able to run on 8088/8086-based machines.

EMS can also be simulated with disk memory. This requires no extra hardware but is very slow compared to hardware EMS systems.

On the 286, 386, and 486, 1 Mbyte isn't the end of the story. The 286 can address up to 16 Mbytes; the 386 and 486 can address up to 4,096 Mbytes (four gigabytes, or Gbytes). Technically, this extended memory is only accessible in protected mode. However, the BIOS provides a function to move data back and forth between any two addresses, including data in extended memory.

An Extended Memory Specification (XMS) driver allows programs to access almost 64 Kbytes of extended memory using a clever addressing technique that we'll explore later. It's important to note that protected mode makes no distinction between conventional and extended memory—extended memory simply begins at 1 Mbyte. Software is available to convert extended memory to expanded memory. On the 286, this isn't very efficient, and not all the EMS features can be emulated. However, with the 386's or 486's powerful memory-management capability, EMS can be completely and efficiently implemented in software.

Registers

The 8086 has four general-purpose registers, a flags register, four segment registers, two index registers, a stack segment register and pointer, a base register, and an instruction pointer register. Figure 1-1 shows these registers along with the additional registers found on the 286. Figure 1-2 shows the registers found on the 386 and 486. Note that the 286, 386, and 486 have a variety of special registers. These usually aren't very useful under DOS, but we'll see some of them when we look at protected-mode extensions to DOS.

DOS 5: A DEVELOPER'S GUIDE

General-Purpose Registers

AH	AL	
80	01	AX
15	7	0

BH	BL	
11	9F	BX
15	7	0

CH	CL	
4B	2C	CX
15	7	0

DH	DL	
21	3A	DX
15	7	0

00	00	SI
15	7	0

00	00	DI
15	7	0

FF	EF	BP
15	7	0

FF	70	SP
15	7	0

Figure 1-1. 8088/8086/80286 registers.

THE PC HARDWARE: AN OVERVIEW

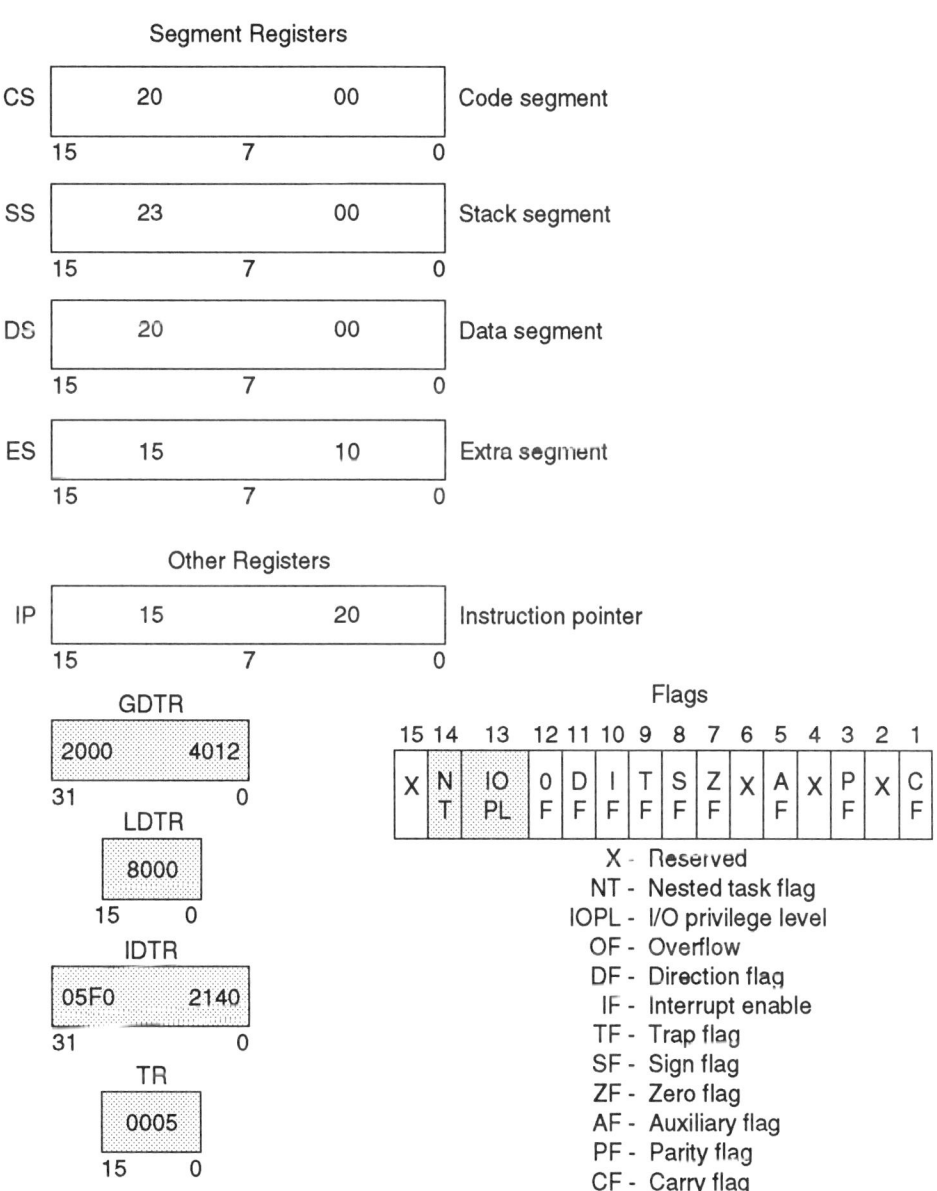

Figure 1-1. 8088/8086/80286 registers (continued).

Other Registers

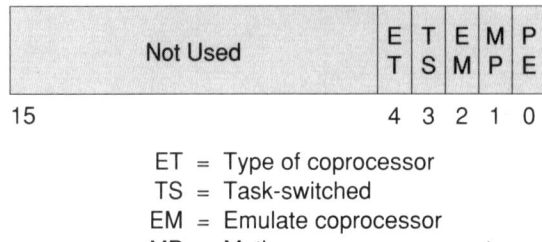

ET = Type of coprocessor
TS = Task-switched
EM = Emulate coprocessor
MP = Math coprocessor present
PE = Protected-mode enable

Figure 1-1. 8088/8086/80286 registers (continued).

AX, BX, CX, and DX are the general-purpose registers:

- AX is sometimes known as the *accumulator*; used in arithmetic operations.

- BX is the only general-purpose register that can participate in forming addresses in real mode.

- CX holds counts in loops and repeated operations.

- DX specifies I/O addresses, especially those greater than 0FFH. It also works with AX during multiply and divide instructions.

Each can hold a 16-bit number. Alternatively, you may elect to use any of them as two 8-bit registers. For instance, AH and AL are actually the two halves of the AX register. In Figure 1-1, AX contains 8001H, which means AH=80H and AL=01H. The 386 and 486 have the same general-purpose registers except that each is 32 bits wide. The 32-bit registers start with the letter *E*. If EAX contains 72018001H, as in Figure 1-2, then AX=8001H, AH=80H, and AL=01H. You cannot directly access just the top 16 bits of a 32-bit register.

THE PC HARDWARE: AN OVERVIEW

General-Purpose Registers

		AX		
72	01	AH 80	AL 01	EAX
31	23	15	7 0	

		BX		
23	98	BH 11	BL 9F	EBX
31	23	15	7 0	

		CX		
00	10	CH 21	CL 3A	ECX
31	23	15	7 0	

		DX		
00	00	DH 21	DL 3A	EDX
31	23	15	7 0	

		SI		
10	15	00	00	ESI
31	23	15	7 0	

		DI		
31	20	00	00	EDI
31	23	15	7 0	

		BP		
F0	11	FF	EF	EBP
31	23	15	7 0	

		SP		
3F	29	FF	70	ESP
31	23	15	7 0	

Figure 1-2. 80386/80486 registers.

DOS 5: A DEVELOPER'S GUIDE

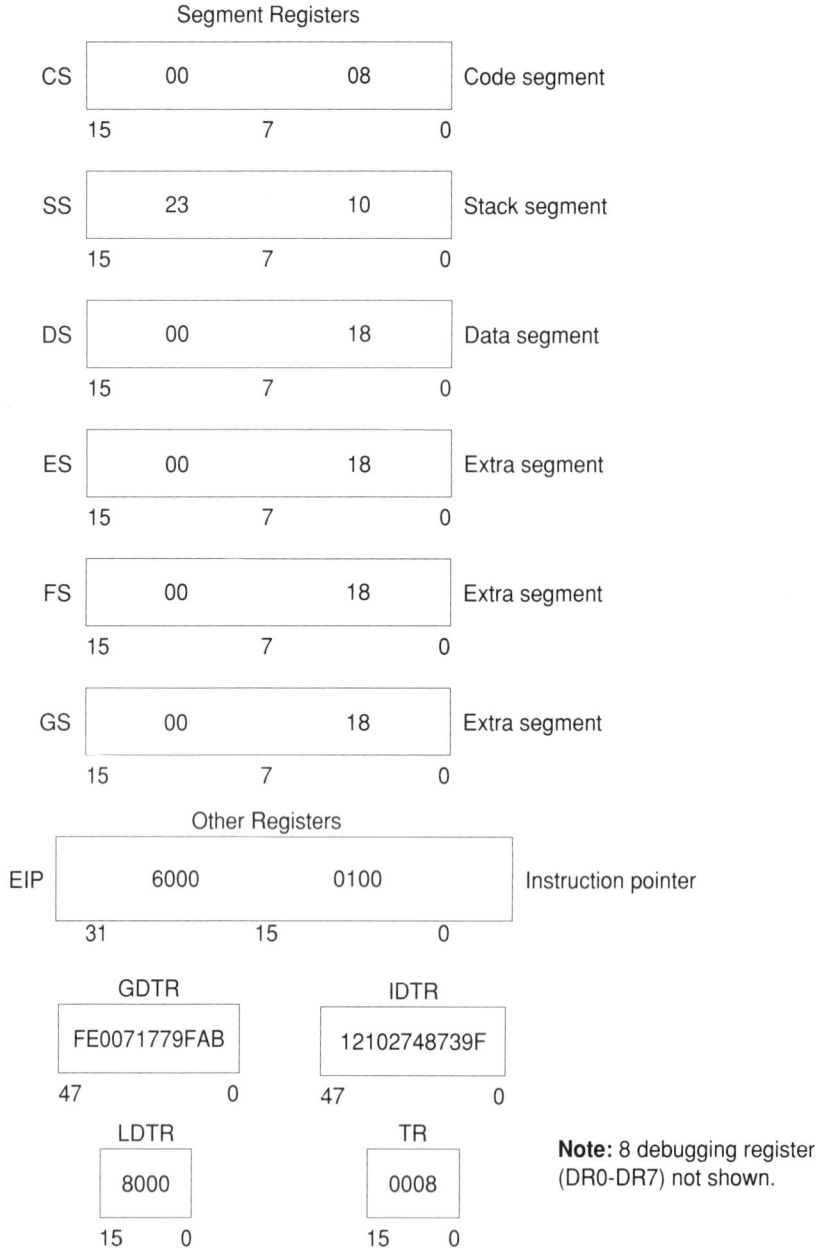

Figure 1-2. 80386/80486 registers (continued).

THE PC HARDWARE: AN OVERVIEW

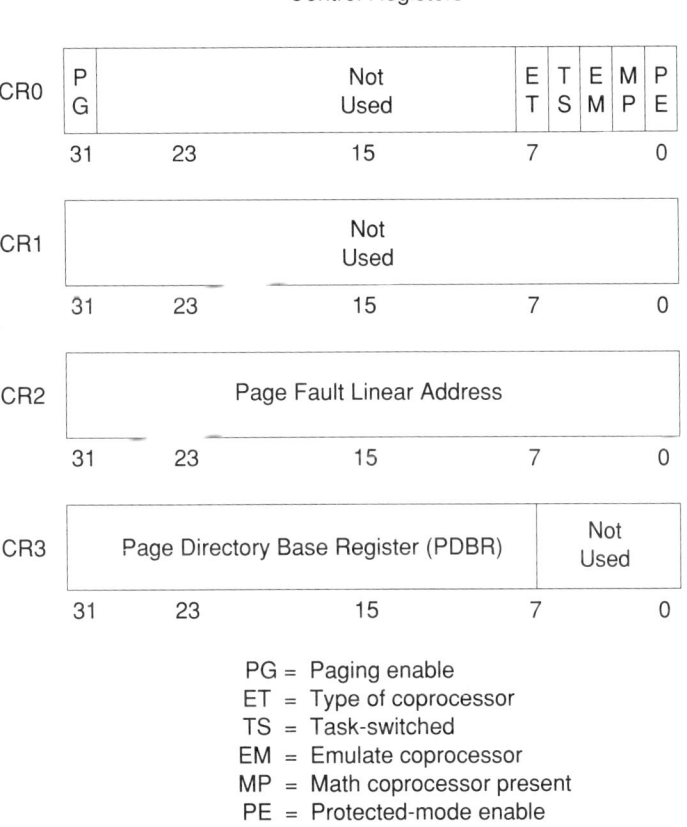

Figure 1-2. 80386/80486 registers (continued).

In theory, the general-purpose registers can be used for anything. However, each register has certain special functions. Sometimes you must use a register for a particular function; in other cases, one register may be more efficient than another.

The segment registers (CS, DS, SS, and ES) point to the current segments for code (CS), data (DS), and the stack (SS). ES is an extra segment that helps transfer data between segments. These segments participate in address calculations, as described below. The 386 and 486 processors have two additional extra segment registers, FS and GS.

The two index registers, SI and DI, participate primarily in forming addresses. Unlike the general-purpose registers, they cannot be split in half. On the 386 and 486, you can use ESI and EDI for 32-bit addresses or SI and DI for 16-bit addresses.

The 8086 family provides a stack for its own use and for the programmer. The stack serves as a temporary holding area for data and plays an important role in calling subroutines and interrupt functions. The stack segment (SS) register and the stack pointer (SP, or ESP on the 386/486) point to the top of the stack. To locate the current top of the stack, use the SS register as a segment value and the SP register as an offset.

The base register, BP (EBP on the 386/486), points to items on the stack. It is similar to the SI and DI registers in most respects. The difference will become apparent when we take another look at addressing.

The instruction pointer register, IP, is the offset in the code segment of the next instruction. You never modify IP directly, although jumps and subroutine calls do. Of course, on the 386 and 486, 32-bit modes use EIP.

The flags register contains a series of bits that determine the status of the processor. One bit shows whether the last arithmetic operation overflowed; another controls the processor's response to external events, or *interrupts*. Programs usually manipulate this register with special instructions to set and clear bits.

Addressing Revisited

In real mode, the 8086 family of processors can only form addresses using certain combinations of values. To form a complete address, we must compute an offset and decide which segment to use.

The following table shows how offsets are formed. In each column, you either pick one of the choices or skip to the next column. Add all these values together to obtain the offset.

THE PC HARDWARE: AN OVERVIEW

Base Register	Index Register	Constant
BX	SI	8-bit constant
BP	DI	16-bit constant

For example, SI, 20, BX, BX+DI, BX+SI+5, and BX+10 are all valid offsets. BX+SI+DI is not, since it requires two values from the index register column. Constants may be negative, so BX-10 is also a legal value.

Now that we know the offset, what segment value will the CPU use? Usually, unless the offset calculation uses the BP register, the segment is the value of the DS register. When the offset calculation uses BP, the CPU uses the SS register. However, a special prefix can force a particular segment register to be used, as shown in the following examples.

Instruction	Word at this address is loaded into AX	Notes
MOV AX,[BX+10]	DS:[BX+10]	DS default
MOV AX,[BP]	SS:[BP]	SS default
MOV AX,ES:[BP]	ES:[BP]	ES override
MOV AX,CS:[102H]	CS:[102]	CS override
MOV AX,DS:[BP]	DS:[BP]	DS override

Some string instructions (such as *MOVS*) use DS:SI and ES:DI implicitly. For these instructions, an override only affects SI; they always use ES and DI for one address.

Ports

The 8086 family provides I/O ports to connect devices to the CPU. Special instructions can read data from and write data to these ports. However, not all I/O devices use ports. The video adapters, for instance, use a block of memory addresses to represent the screen. They do use I/O ports for certain control functions, however.

The most common way to access the CPU's I/O ports is via the *IN* and *OUT* instructions. For example,

```
IN AL,20H
```

reads the value of I/O port 20H into the AL register. The meaning of the value depends on the hardware device at that address. The instruction

```
OUT 20H,AL
```

writes the value in AL to port 20H. This instruction's effect depends on the hardware device. We will explore various devices and their port assignments in great detail in later chapters.

Hardware Interrupts

A hardware interrupt is a special signal from an I/O device to the computer. This signal informs the computer that the I/O device requires attention. The processor will normally stop whatever it is doing to service the interrupt. When the interrupt completes, the processor resumes execution where it left off.

The 8086 family of processors can respond to 256 different interrupts. Starting at location 0000:0000 is a table of addresses for each interrupt (Figure 1-3). Each entry in this interrupt vector table is four bytes long, enough for a segment and an offset. If the processor receives interrupt 2 (INT 2), for example, it saves the flags and the current values of CS and IP on the stack. It then obtains the address stored at location 0000:0008 (F000:0103 in Figure 1-3) and executes the interrupt service routine at that address. An *IRET* instruction in the ISR signals the end of the interrupt and causes the processor to resume what it was doing before the interrupt.

Interrupts can come from many sources. For example, every time you press or release a key on the keyboard, you generate an interrupt. Other interrupts originate from the clock, printer, serial port, disk drives, and so on. The processor itself causes some interrupts. INT 0, for instance, occurs when a program attempts to divide by

THE PC HARDWARE: AN OVERVIEW

zero. These are all hardware interrupts. In a later chapter, we'll see how programs can cause software interrupts.

An 8259 programmable interrupt controller on the motherboard manages all hardware interrupts. The PC/XT class of computers has only one PIC, whereas ATs have two. These controllers take interrupt signals from various devices and convert them to specific interrupts for the processor.

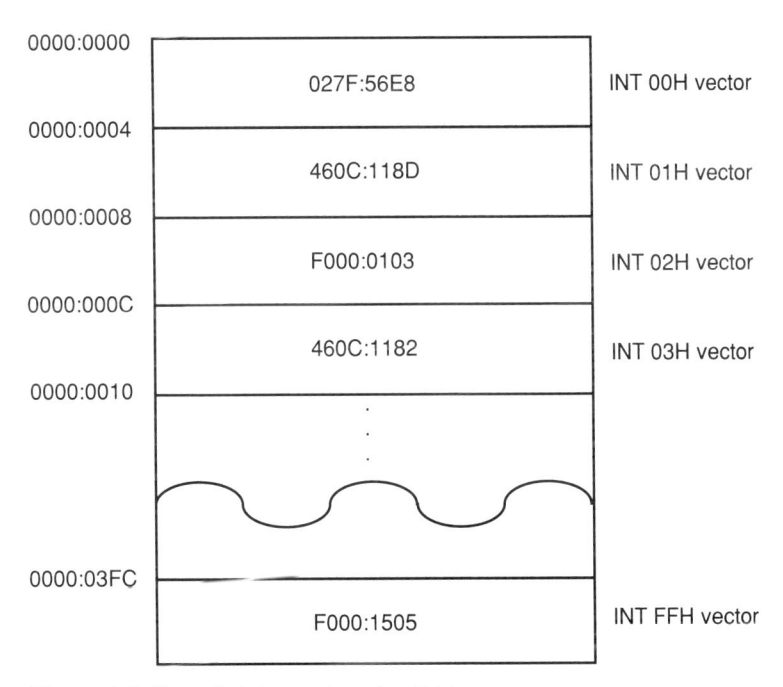

Address	Value	Vector
0000:0000	027F:56E8	INT 00H vector
0000:0004	460C:118D	INT 01H vector
0000:0008	F000:0103	INT 02H vector
0000:000C	460C:1182	INT 03H vector
...	...	...
0000:03FC	F000:1505	INT FFH vector

Figure 1-3. Sample interrupt vector table.

Table 1-1 shows the hardware interrupts with their corresponding PIC interrupt request inputs (known as *IRQ lines*). Be careful not to confuse IRQ numbers with interrupt numbers. For example, the keyboard connects to IRQ 1, which sends INT 9 to the CPU. The PICs can be reprogrammed to generate different interrupt numbers for each IRQ, but you won't often do that unless you work with the protected-mode techniques discussed in Part III.

DOS 5: A DEVELOPER'S GUIDE

The PICs also control the priority of interrupts. For example, the clock (on IRQ 0) has a higher priority than the keyboard (IRQ 1). If the processor is servicing a clock interrupt, the PIC won't generate an interrupt for the keyboard until the clock's ISR resets the PIC. On the other hand, the clock can interrupt the keyboard's ISR. The PICs can be programmed to use a variety of priority schemes, but this is rarely, if ever, seen in PC programming.

The AT's extra PIC connects to IRQ 2 of the first PIC. Therefore, the extra PIC's IRQs (8 through 15) have the same priority as IRQ 2. Disabling IRQ 2 disables all of the second PIC's interrupts.

Offset	Interrupt	IRQ	Machine	Description
0000H	00H		All	Divide by zero or divide overflow
0008H	02H		All	NMI (see text)
0010H	04H		All	Overflow (generated by INTO)
0020H	08H	0	All	System timer
0024H	09H	1	All	Keyboard
0028H	0AH	2	XT	General I/O
0028H	0AH	2	AT+	Interrupt from second PIC
002CH	0BH	3	All	COM2
0030H	0CH	4	All	COM1
0034H	0DH	5	XT	Hard disk
0034H	0DH	5	AT	LPT2
0034H	0DH	5	PS/2	General I/O
0038H	0EH	6	All	Floppy disk
003CH	0FH	7	All	LPT1
01C0H	70H	8	AT+	Real-time clock
01C4H	71H	9	AT+	General I/O (same as IRQ 2)
01C8H	72H	10	AT+	General I/O
01CCH	73H	11	AT+	General I/O
01D0H	74H	12	AT	General I/O
01D0H	74H	12	PS/2	Pointing device (mouse)
01D4H	75H	13	AT+	Coprocessor
01D8H	76H	14	AT+	Hard disk
01DCH	77H	15	AT+	General I/O

Note: AT+ means AT, 386/486, or PS/2.

Table 1-1. Hardware interrupts and their corresponding IRQ lines.

THE PC HARDWARE: AN OVERVIEW

You can stop interrupts from disturbing an important section of code in several ways. The *CLI* instruction disables all external interrupts except the nonmaskable interrupt. The NMI, which does not go through a PIC, can be disabled with circuitry on the motherboard. In addition, the PICs can be programmed to turn off specific interrupts.

DOS and the PC rely heavily on interrupts. Because understanding them is the key to understanding the PC, we will return to this subject throughout the book.

The Timer

All motherboards have a timer chip (an 8253 on the XT, an 8254 on the AT). This timer has three separate clocks, or *channels*. Random-access memory, or RAM, uses one channel to time the refresh period. (This channel is not very interesting to programmers.) Another channel keeps the time-of-day clock running. About 18 times per second, this timer generates INT 8 (IRQ 0), the highest-priority interrupt. Disk operations use the output from this channel to correct the time-of-day clock after disk operations.

The remaining channel is the most interesting to the programmer. Not only is it free for us to use, the output from this spare channel can optionally be routed to a speaker to create basic sound effects and music.

General I/O

The XT has an 8255 peripheral interface adapter that serves several functions. Though the AT doesn't have this PIA, it duplicates most of the functions of one, and our software can't tell the difference. The PIA provides three I/O ports to communicate with the keyboard, read the motherboard switches, and control the speaker.

Of course, the AT can't read motherboard switches because it doesn't have any. Instead, it uses a SETUP program to write configuration data to memory in its real-time-clock chip. A battery powers the real-time clock, so you only have to run SETUP when your battery dies or you change the configuration. The port that controls the real-time clock also enables and disables NMI. (The XT uses a different port to control NMI.)

23

The PC motherboard also contains an 8237A direct memory access (DMA) controller. This chip allows certain devices, like the hard disk, to transfer data rapidly to the computer's memory without CPU intervention. By design, the 8237A works with computers that use 16-bit address buses (like the old 8080). The motherboard has several DMA page registers to adapt the chips to the 8088/8086. When DMA is used, these registers hold the top four bits of the address. Consequently, the DMA chips can address the entire 1-Mbyte address space but may only access 64 Kbytes at a time. One DMA channel also handles dynamic memory refresh under control of the timer chip. This has no real effect on the way we write programs, however.

Many other I/O cards can connect to the PC. Parallel ports are available for printers; serial ports can connect with a wide variety of devices. Game ports, network cards, CD-ROM—every day, manufacturers produce new cards for connecting new devices. It's impossible to keep up with them all. Luckily, once you understand how to program for one device, the others won't seem so intimidating.

The Keyboard

The PC keyboard, which has its own CPU, interfaces with the XT via the 8255 PIA. While the AT doesn't have a PIA as such, our software can't tell the difference when communicating with the keyboard.

The keyboard's function might seem obvious, but the AT's does have a few tricks. For instance, its keyboard can accept commands. It can reset the computer, test itself, control a memory address line, and do other miscellaneous duties.

Each time the user presses a key, the PIA generates an IRQ 1 via the system PIC. This causes the processor to receive an INT 9. If the processor is accepting interrupts, the ISR reads a scan code from the keyboard. Actually, the keyboard causes this interrupt when you press or release a key. Each key generates two scan codes: one for a press and another for a release. However, the keyboard doesn't know about shifted letters. For instance, A, a, and Alt-A generate the same scan code because each code represents one physical key. Even keys that don't have ASCII codes, like Alt and Shift, generate scan codes.

THE PC HARDWARE: AN OVERVIEW

The BIOS processes each IRQ 1 to determine what action to take. Some keys and key combinations cause immediate results (a good example is Control-Alt-Delete). The BIOS maintains the status of the keyboard in memory and updates it when a change in keys (such as Shift and Alt) is detected. If it's a "regular" key, the BIOS translates the scan code into ASCII according to the current shift status and places both codes in the keyboard buffer. Programs read the keyboard buffer using the BIOS INT 16H function. The AT and PS/2 keyboards can generate special scan codes or XT-compatible scan codes.

Earlier we saw that the 8086 limits DOS to 1 Mbyte of memory. However, the 286 can address up to 16 Mbytes of memory, while the 386 and 486 can go up to 4 Gbytes (4,096 Mbytes). The AT keyboard controller helps us access this memory. In an XT-type 8088 machine, addresses above 1 Mbyte wrap around. That is, address FFFF:0010 refers to the same memory location as address 0000:0000; FFFF:0020 is the same as 0000:0010. This is because the 8088 only has 20 address lines (A0 through A19). The 286, 386, and 486 processors have more than 20 lines, so an address of FFFF:0010 is valid in extended memory. In fact, XMS drivers use this technique to allow DOS programs to use almost 64K of extended memory.

We normally want the AT to wrap addresses around like an XT would. Anticipating this, the AT motherboard designers routed the A20 line through the keyboard controller. Ordinarily, the controller blocks A20 from reaching the memory chips. A special command to the keyboard controller can unblock A20, and another command will block it again later. This so-called A20 gate is essential to accessing extended memory.

Programs usually read the keyboard by using DOS or BIOS services. The BIOS services return the ASCII code and scan code for each keystroke. The DOS services, and most C input routines, return only the ASCII code. If the key is a special one (like a function key) or an Alt (such as Alt-X), these services return a zero. This signals that the next input call will return the scan code of this key. The BIOS keyboard functions return a word that contains the ASCII code (zero for a special key) and the scan code.

Video

Perhaps the most familiar component of the PC is the video monitor. Several common video adapters are available:

- Monochrome Display Adapter (MDA)—A black-and-white, text-only card.

- Hercules Graphics Adapter (HGA)—Another black-and-white card that can act exactly like an MDA but can also do high-resolution, black-and-white graphics. This is the only common video card that IBM did not originate.

- Color Graphics Adapter (CGA)—Displays color text and very low-resolution graphics.

- Enhanced Graphics Adapter (EGA)—A superior color text and graphics card.

- Video Gate Array (VGA)—The premium color display card in common use, providing crisp color text and high-resolution graphics.

While each card is different, they have basic similarities. They all use a block of memory to represent the screen, for example, and all appear to use a 6845 display controller (even if they don't). The block of memory that represents the screen image is the video RAM. On monochrome-only systems, this memory starts at B000:0000. Color adapters' memory usually starts at B800:0000, although VGA and EGA can begin as low as A000:0000 in some graphics modes. This RAM is resident on the video card. The card accesses it directly to determine what to display on the screen.

Many adapters support multiple pages in some modes. This allows a program to prepare a page without displaying it and later switch to it. The new page displays almost instantaneously.

In text modes, each character takes two bytes—an ASCII code and a byte to determine such attributes as the character's color. Chapter 9 discusses the contents of video RAM in more detail.

THE PC HARDWARE: AN OVERVIEW

In graphics mode, one or more bits represent each point on the screen. Monochrome graphics, for instance, only need one bit per point, or *pixel*. A 16-color display would take four bits per pixel. In some graphics modes, representing the image requires more memory than the PC allocates for the display adapter. In that case, a program can command the adapter to switch banks of memory to the same address. We'll study this in more detail in the chapter on graphics programming.

A variety of specialty adapters are also available. IBM's 8514/A is a high-performance card that has dedicated graphics hardware on board. Competing in this arena are a variety of boards built around Texas Instruments' 340X0 graphics coprocessor. These boards have their own 32-bit processors to handle graphics. While such video systems are fascinating, they are expensive and only used in specialized applications. If you become familiar with the standard video hardware, you'll have no difficulties with these more advanced systems if you need to tackle them in the future.

Disks

The PC usually uses one interface adapter to operate floppy disks and another to operate hard disks. Some PCs use special disk controllers (like SCSI host adapters). DOS provides a full suite of services to allow file I/O with disks. Both DOS and the BIOS offers calls to read and write particular sectors. Unless you're writing very arcane programs, you won't need to work with the disk at the sector level.

The PC BIOS organizes disks using sides, tracks, and sectors. Floppy disks often have two usable sides; hard disks may have many sides because they often have several platters. The BIOS numbers sides starting at zero.

Data is stored on a disk in concentric rings, which are the disk's tracks. The first track is 0. Each track contains multiple sectors; each sector contains a fixed amount (usually 512 bytes) of data. The first sector on a track is number 1. A cylinder consists of the tracks from all the sides. For instance, cylinder 0 on a two-sided floppy contains the first track on side 0 of the disk and the first track on side 1.

27

DOS treats the disk as a series of sectors. Each sector is numbered (the first sector is 0). DOS groups sectors into clusters, each containing one or more sectors of data. On any one disk, all the clusters contain the same number of sectors.

To reduce the size of certain system tables, DOS only allocates disk space in units of clusters. For instance, if a disk has four sectors per cluster, a small file might have four, eight, or 12 sectors. If the file were only one byte in length, four sectors would be needed to store it. The number of sectors per cluster, and most of the other numbers, can vary from disk to disk. Later, we'll learn how to make DOS tell us these important disk parameters.

CHAPTER 2

The Application Environment

When DOS is loaded from a bootable disk, it usually places itself into the lowest memory locations available (although DOS 5 may load portions of itself into high memory). Device drivers, a special type of DOS program, load next. Finally, COMMAND.COM (or another program specified by the *SHELL* command in the CONFIG.SYS file) is loaded. The remaining memory is free for user programs.

A large portion of the command interpreter, COMMAND.COM, loads in the highest part of memory. This is the transient portion. (The rest, which loads in low memory, is the resident portion.) The transient portion may be overlaid by a user program requiring additional memory. When this happens, the resident portion of COMMAND.COM reloads the transient portion after the user program exits. Figure 2-1 shows the system memory map in detail.

It is important to realize that DOS may load a program into any free memory location as long as it is on a segment boundary. In other words, the starting address's offset must be 0000, but its segment can be any value. The location may be different each time the program loads and will almost certainly differ depending on the machine. Different types of programs handle this problem in various ways.

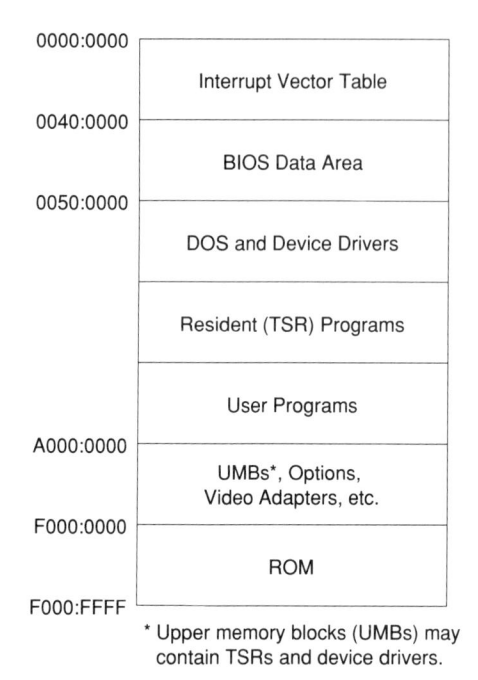

```
0000:0000 ┌─────────────────────────┐
          │  Interrupt Vector Table │
0040:0000 ├─────────────────────────┤
          │     BIOS Data Area      │
0050:0000 ├─────────────────────────┤
          │  DOS and Device Drivers │
          ├─────────────────────────┤
          │  Resident (TSR) Programs│
          ├─────────────────────────┤
          │      User Programs      │
A000:0000 ├─────────────────────────┤
          │     UMBs*, Options,     │
          │   Video Adapters, etc.  │
F000:0000 ├─────────────────────────┤
          │           ROM           │
F000:FFFF └─────────────────────────┘
           * Upper memory blocks (UMBs) may
             contain TSRs and device drivers.
```

Figure 2-1. System memory map.

Types of DOS Applications

DOS programs fall into four categories: .EXE files, .COM files, device drivers, and terminate-and-stay-resident (TSR) programs. A .COM, .EXE, or TSR program in memory is sometimes called a *process*. Each type of program has a set of rules you must follow when writing them, and each works best for certain tasks.

.EXE Files. .EXE files, the most natural application model for DOS programs, may contain multiple code and data segments. Since a segment can only be 64 Kbytes long, this is an important feature when building large programs.

An .EXE file consists of three parts. The first is a header, shown in Table 2-1, that contains information about the program. Among other things, the header tells DOS how much memory the program needs, where to start the program, and the location of the data segment.

THE APPLICATION ENVIRONMENT

Offset	Length	Description
00H	word	.EXE file magic number (405AH)
02H	word	Length of last sector
04H	word	Size of file, including header (512-byte pages)
06H	word	Number of relocation table items
08H	word	Size of header (paragraphs)
0AH	word	Minimum # of paragraphs needed above program (paragraphs)
0CH	word	Maximum # paragraphs allowed above program (paragraphs)
0EH	word	Displacement of stack segment (paragraphs)
10H	word	Contents of SP register on entry
12H	word	Checksum
14H	word	Contents of IP register on entry
16H	word	Displacement of code (paragraphs) relative to start of program
18H	word	Offset to first relocation table entry (byte)
1AH	word	Overlay number (0 for main program)

Table 2-1. .EXE header.

The second part of an .EXE file is the relocation table. This table contains segment fix-ups, which point to places in the file that explicitly reference segments. DOS adds the two-byte number at each fix-up location to the segment address where the .EXE file loads, then copies the resulting number into memory.

The final part of the .EXE file is the data to be loaded into the computer. Except for the segment references just mentioned, DOS copies these bytes into memory as is. Figure 2-2 shows a symbolic representation of an .EXE file and how DOS would load it into memory. In this example, the first free segment is at 4010H.

.COM Files. This is the simplest application model: The program receives all available memory. The data segment is the same as the code segment, which also equals the stack segment. .COM files always load and begin execution at offset 100H in their code segments. DOS doesn't process a .COM file in any way, so such a file can't contain explicit references to segments as an .EXE file can. .COM files have no headers—they only contain the data to load into memory.

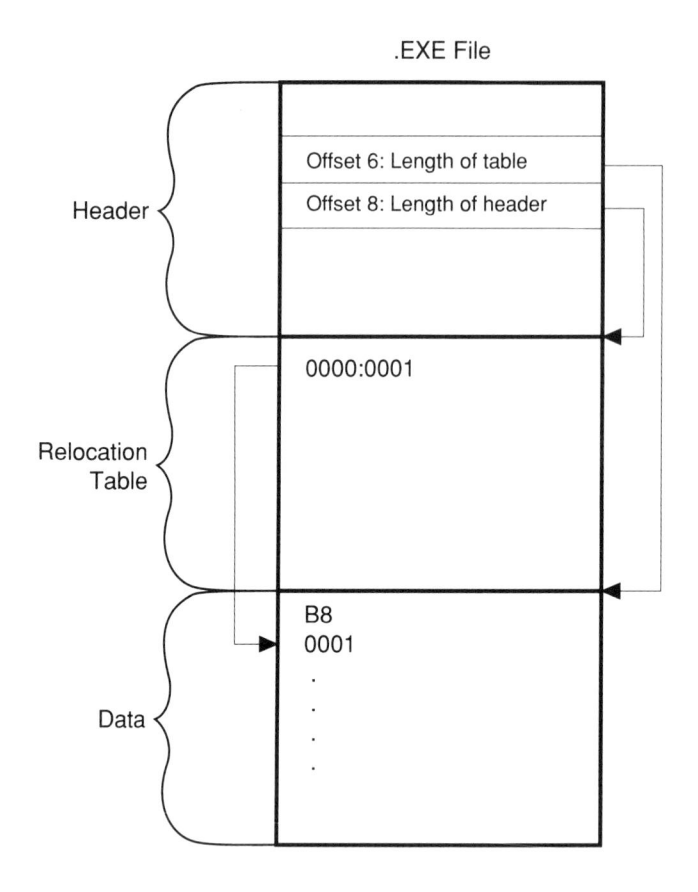

```
                              .EXE File
                    ┌──────────────────────┐
           ┌        │                      │
           │        ├──────────────────────┤
           │        │ Offset 6: Length of table │
   Header ─┤        ├──────────────────────┤
           │        │ Offset 8: Length of header │
           │        ├──────────────────────┤
           └        │                      │
                    ├──────────────────────┤
                    │ 0000:0001            │
           ┌        │                      │
 Relocation│        │                      │
    Table ─┤        │                      │
           │        │                      │
           └        │                      │
                    ├──────────────────────┤
                    │ B8                   │
                    │ 0001                 │
           ┌        │  .                   │
           │        │  .                   │
     Data ─┤        │  .                   │
           │        │  .                   │
           └        │  .                   │
                    └──────────────────────┘
```

Memory at segment 4010H:

0	1	2
B8	11	40	. . .

MS-DOS adds 4010H + 0001H = 4011H

Figure 2-2. .EXE file load.

.COM files are a good choice for simple programs. They load faster than .EXE files, and an unpacked .EXE file is slightly larger than a .COM file of the same length. However, because a .COM file has only one segment, its length cannot exceed

THE APPLICATION ENVIRONMENT

64 Kbytes. Of course, a .COM file program can use more memory if the programmer resorts to special techniques. If you need more than 64 Kbytes of memory, you should use the .EXE format.

TSR Programs. TSRs are not really different kinds of programs; they may be .COM files or .EXE files. After an ordinary .COM or .EXE program completes, however, DOS removes it from memory before continuing. A TSR program, on the other hand, leaves a portion of itself in memory after exiting. It usually hooks itself into one or more interrupt routines so that when an interrupt occurs the TSR can process it. It may or may not pass the interrupt to the original interrupt handler. This is useful in at least three instances:

1. When installing new interrupt handlers. For instance, we might want to handle keyboard interrupts and translate or disallow certain keys.

2. When providing library programs that other programs can share. For example, instead of linking a library with each of our programs to manage a custom display, we could place the routines in a TSR. Other programs would then call this library via interrupts. TSR mouse drivers and other commercial programs use this approach.

3. When creating pop-up programs. These are programs that can be activated, usually with an unusual sequence of keys, at any time. Borland's SideKick, for instance, allows you to pop up a notepad, calculator, calendar, and other tools while working with another program. Since this constitutes a limited form of multitasking and DOS isn't multitasking, these programs are probably the most challenging to write and debug under DOS.

A well-designed TSR program shouldn't interfere with other TSR programs, though some do. Most TSR programs can be removed from memory with a special command. There are even special utility programs to remove TSRs that can't remove themselves.

Like COMMAND.COM, TSRs have resident and transient portions. The transient portion executes just like a normal .COM or .EXE file, while the resident portion stays behind.

Device Drivers. Device drivers are special programs that communicate between DOS and one or more devices. DOS provides default device drivers for the standard devices (such as PRN, LPT1, and CON) and disk drives. It loads device drivers right after itself during the boot sequence. Like TSRs, these drivers remain in memory after they exit; unlike TSRs, you cannot remove them, nor can you install them without rebooting the system.

There are two types of device drivers: character and block. Character drivers have names like *LPT1* and *CON* (or any other name you assign them, up to eight characters). DOS automatically assigns letters to block drivers (for instance, A:, B:, and C:).

Each type of driver has a specific format and must contain the routines that DOS prescribes. From that perspective, drivers are easy to write; however, because the routines to interface with some devices are difficult—and since device drivers are very hard to debug—most programmers consider them a challenge. Device drivers have many special considerations, so we will defer discussion of them until later in the book.

Some drivers don't actually control a physical device. DOS's RAMDRIVE is a good example. This driver creates a RAM disk, a simulated disk drive in RAM.

Occasionally a device driver doesn't control a device at all. Such drivers run a program at boot time, or they load an interrupt handler that the user can't remove or that other device drivers require. The program that provides EMS memory, for instance, is a device driver. This allows it to be loaded before other device drivers that may wish to use EMS memory.

THE APPLICATION ENVIRONMENT

The DOS Interrupts

DOS provides several software interrupts for application programs. Since DOS might be loaded at any memory location, this provides a sure, simple way for applications to call it.

INT 21H: This is by far the most common DOS interrupt. By using function codes in the AH register, this interrupt invokes dozens of services for a user program. For example, if AH=4CH, the program will exit. If AH=2CH, DOS will return the time of day in the CX and DX registers.

INT 20H: This interrupt terminates a running program. The CS register must be set to the value of the program segment prefix (we will discuss the PSP shortly). This call can't return an exit code, does minimal shutdown processing, and is difficult to call from .EXE files. INT 21H, function 4CH, is much more practical. New programs should use it in lieu of INT 20H.

INT 27H: This interrupt is similar to INT 20H. TSR programs use it to exit to DOS; the interrupt tells DOS the program should remain in memory. INT 27H suffers from the same problems as INT 20H, so use INT 21H, function 31H, instead.

INT 22H: DOS stores the program's terminate address in this interrupt. When a program exits, this is the address to which DOS returns control. If the program ran from the DOS prompt, this address is somewhere inside COMMAND.COM. If another program started it, the address is inside the other program. You will rarely, if ever, use this address in your programs.

INT 23H: DOS generates this interrupt when the user presses Control-Break or Control-C on the keyboard. By changing the address of the interrupt, you can ignore or trap these keys in your program. Be aware, however, that the BIOS gets the first crack at handling Control-Break via INT 1BH. Interestingly, Control-2 and Alt-3 (the 3 on the numeric keypad) also produces a break. We will return to the subject of break-handling in Chapter 9.

INT 24H: This address is similar to INT 23H except that it occurs when DOS detects a critical error. Critical errors occur because of conditions that DOS can't correct without outside help. If you have ever tried to use a disk drive that didn't have a floppy in it, you have seen a critical error. The default routine generates the well-known "Abort, Retry, Ignore" message. Like INT 23H, a user program can change this interrupt to gain control when such an event occurs. Chapter 9 will discuss critical-error trapping in detail.

INT 25H and INT 26H: These interrupts allow a program to arbitrarily read and write DOS disk sectors. This is dangerous stuff, so be careful if you feel the urge to experiment. If you do, beware: these interrupts leave the caller's flags on the stack when they return. You must pop one word off the stack or your program is likely to crash soon thereafter.

INT 2EH: This undocumented call causes COMMAND.COM to execute a command. While this is sometimes useful, not many third-party COMMAND.COM replacements support it. If you use this interrupt in commercial software, you'll get complaints from users of these alternative interpreters.

INT 2FH: DOS versions 3.0 and above define this interrupt, which controls some TSR programs. With it, you can determine whether PRINT, ASSIGN, SHARE, or APPEND is active. INT 2FH can also sends commands to PRINT. You can use this call, known as the *multiplex interrupt*, for your own TSR programs (see Chapter 14).

INT 33H: While DOS does not reserve this interrupt, it is commonly used for the mouse driver. Programs issue INT 33H to configure and query the mouse.

INT 60H–67H: These are not really DOS interrupts per se; DOS reserves them for user programs. Avoid using INT 67H, which is automatically used by EMS drivers.

The BIOS Interrupts

Every PC motherboard contains a BIOS ROM. The BIOS provides functions to control the PC hardware at a lower level than DOS functions do.

The BIOS provides interrupts in much the same fashion as DOS. Many of them take function codes in the AH register, just like INT 21H. Of course, the BIOS is specific to the PC, so using BIOS functions will make your program incompatible with DOS machines that are not fully PC-compatible. However, very few DOS machines are not PC-compatible, so this shouldn't be a major concern. One compatibility note: None of the BIOS screen routines will work with a Hercules monochrome graphics adapter in graphics mode.

The BIOS functions generally operate at a lower level than the DOS functions, and using them requires more work. However, they pay off by providing more control over the machine. The video functions, for example, allow color displays, cursor control, and other hardware-specific features. BIOS output can't be redirected, however, because that is a DOS function. Likewise, the BIOS disk functions read and write arbitrary disk sectors—not DOS files.

INT 5: This service dumps a text screen to a standard printer attached to LPT1. The PrtSc key, located on most keyboards, automatically invokes INT 5. User programs can also use INT 5 to print the screen. This interrupt only prints characters, even if the monitor is in graphics mode. INT 5 doesn't work for Hercules monochrome graphics cards in graphics mode.

INT 10H–1AH: These interrupts provide a wealth of services that will be covered in detail later. Programs access all the BIOS video, keyboard, disk, and other services via these interrupts and their subfunctions.

INT 1BH: This interrupt occurs when the BIOS detects the Control-Break key. It is similar to DOS's INT 23H except that this routine simply sets a flag when the break occurs and then returns. Of course, we can replace this interrupt to cause any action we want.

DOS 5: A DEVELOPER'S GUIDE

INT 1CH: This interrupt runs when the timer tick (IRQ 0) occurs. A program can replace or intercept INT 1CH without worrying about hardware details necessary for INT 8 (the actual timer-tick interrupt).

INT 1DH: This isn't a real interrupt; it points to a table of video parameters.

INT 1EH: Another pointer to a table, this one containing disk parameters.

INT 1FH: Yet another table pointer. This interrupt points to a table of graphic characters used by the BIOS in certain modes.

BIOS Variables

In addition to interrupts, the BIOS communicates with other programs via a special region of memory at segment 40H. Since many of these variables can be read and written using BIOS interrupts, only a few are useful. By reading them, you can determine information about the keyboard, video, disks, printers, and serial ports. For example, bit 2 in the byte at 0040:0017 is set if the Control key is held down.

You may find some programs that access the BIOS memory area as if it were at segment 0. Keep in mind that 0000:0417 is the same address as 0040:0017. For that matter, 0020:0217 is also the same address. Many programmers use segment 0 because clearing a segment register is somewhat easier than loading 0040H into it.

The PS/2 has an additional BIOS data area at the top of conventional memory. Since the location of this area varies, a BIOS interrupt reports the address of this extended area if it is present.

The PSP

For all .COM and .EXE programs, including TSRs, DOS creates a 256-byte area known as the *PSP*. The PSP is a prefix because it immediately precedes the program in memory. It allows access to a myriad of data about the program's operating context.

THE APPLICATION ENVIRONMENT

Table 2-2 shows the layout of the PSP and contains capsule descriptions of all the fields. Some of the entries are no longer in common use; they simplified the porting of CP/M programs to DOS. Note that the values stored in the PSP for INTs 23H and 24H are the values DOS restores to those interrupts after the running program terminates. Only very unusual programs modify these values.

Offset	Length	Description
00H	word	INT 20H (terminate)
02H	word	End of memory allocation block
04H	byte	RESERVED
05H	5 bytes	FAR CALL to DOS function dispatcher
0AH	dword	INT 22H terminate address
0EH	dword	INT 23H Control-Break handler address
12H	dword	INT 24H critical error handler address
16H	word	Parent process's PSP
18H	20 bytes	Handle table
2CH	word	Environment block address
2EH	dword	RESERVED
32H	word	Handle table size
34H	dword	Handle table address
38H	23 bytes	RESERVED
50H	word	INT 21H DOS CALL
52H	byte	FAR RET
53H	9 bytes	RESERVED
5CH	36 bytes	Default unopened file control block #1
6CH	20 bytes	Default unopened file control block #2
80H	byte	Length of command-line arguments
81H	127 bytes	Arguments from command line; also default DTA

Table 2-2. PSP layout.

The Command Line. An interesting PSP field is the command line stored at location 81H (its length is at offset 80H). This is the entire command line the user entered after the program name, with no redirection or piped commands. For example:

39

```
PGM1 This is a command
```

becomes

```
♭This♭is♭a♭command
```

where ♭ denotes a blank. As another example:

```
PGM1 Command<file1| PGM2 option
```

becomes

```
♭Command
```

The DTA. DOS uses a special memory area, known as the *disk transfer area*, for certain disk operations. The default DTA is at location 80H in the PSP, directly on top of the command line. You must either copy the command line before doing disk I/O or change the DTA using INT 21H, function 1AH.

The Parent PSP. The field at offset 16H contains the segment address of the PSP for the program that started the current program. This is useful for chaining backward to your caller's program. However, COMMAND.COM sets its own segment address in this field, even if it isn't the original shell. This is a good way to detect COMMAND.COM, but it's a dead end if you're backtracking. Of course, some COMMAND.COM replacements or other programs may behave the same way.

The Environment. When any program (including COMMAND.COM) starts another program, DOS gives the new program a duplicate set of the first program's environment variables. A program's environment block starts at the segment address stored in offset 2CH of its PSP. This block consists of strings that end with a zero byte. The last entry ends with two zero bytes. In DOS 3.0 and later, the word following the two trailing zeros will be 0001H (two bytes), followed by the full name of the program and a zero byte. A program named *CC* might have the following name in the environment block:

THE APPLICATION ENVIRONMENT

```
C:\TOOLS\BIN\CC.EXE
```

The entire name need not be uppercase.

Usually, strings in the environment are of the form

```
VAR=VALUE
```

where any uppercase string can take the place of *VAR* and any string can be *VALUE*. By searching the environment or using the C function *getenv()*, our programs can learn about the current *PATH* or any other defined environment variables. However, the strings don't have to follow this format; they simply have to end with a zero byte. When we start a new program, it gets a copy of the current program's environment, even if that program has changed it. On the other hand, changes a program makes to its environment block aren't copied to the parent program when the current program exits.

In versions of DOS before 3.3, the first copy of COMMAND.COM didn't have a pointer to an environment block—the pointer was zero. The environment was, by default, in the next memory block. Other programs still have environment pointers in these early versions of DOS.

File Handles. Another interesting field appears at offset 34H: a pointer to a table of file handles (the process file table, or PFT). DOS stores the length of this table in offset 32H and the default table of 20 handles at offset 18H.

DOS predefines the first five entries of the PFT for each process. Table 2-3 shows these handles and their purpose. Each entry in the PFT is an index into the system file table (SFT). The *FILES=* statement in the CONFIG.SYS file sets the length of the SFT. DOS sets unused PFT entries to 0FFH.

Handle Number	Device Assignment	Default Device
0	Standard input	Keyboard
1	Standard output	Display
2	Standard error	Display
3	Auxiliary device	COM1:
4	Printer output	LPT1:

Table 2-3. Standard handles.

Many PFT entries may point to the same entry in the SFT. It is common, for instance, for STDIN, STDOUT, and STDERR to point to the same device (the console). Each open file or device only has one entry in the SFT, however, even if it is used more than once or by more than one process.

In the event that a program needs more than 20 file handles, the program can reserve a larger area, copy the old PFT to the new area, and change the PSP fields to reflect the new area and its length.

Memory Allocation in Detail

We have determined *when* DOS allocates memory; now we'll look at *how* it does so.

A 16-byte data structure precedes each block of memory controlled by DOS. This structure is the arena header, also known as a memory control block (MCB). The first byte of the arena header can be a 4DH, indicating a normal memory block, or a 5AH, indicating the last memory block. The next two bytes contain the PSP segment address of the process that owns it. When a process terminates, DOS automatically frees any memory the process owns. If the block is available, DOS sets the owner's PSP field to 0000H. The next two bytes contain the length of the memory block in paragraphs (recall that a paragraph is 16 bytes). This length doesn't include the arena header itself.

THE APPLICATION ENVIRONMENT

DOS 5 uses the last eight bytes of the header to store the file name associated with the owner of the block. This is either the file name identifying the owner (without the extension), *SC* for system code, or *SD* for system data. If the name is fewer than eight bytes long, it will end with a hex 0. This field is only valid when DOS loads a program into a block. Versions of DOS prior to 5 don't use this field.

Because we have the length of the block, we can always scan forward from one memory block to the next. However, there's no easy way to go backward. Luckily, as we will see later, an undocumented call gets the first arena header in the system. Once we have this address, we can scan forward through all the memory blocks.

DOS 5 supports upper memory blocks, blocks of memory that lie above 640K and below 1 Mbyte. A device driver normally uses special hardware (like that built into the 386 or a special card for the 286) to create UMBs. DOS 5 can supply UMBs (with EMM 386), or a third-party package (like Quarterdeck Office Systems' QEMM or Qualitas' 386MAX) can provide them.

While third-party packages can create UMBs for most versions of DOS, DOS 5 fully integrates UMB support. For example, it can load most of its own code into high memory, leaving more memory available for user programs.

For compatibility with older programs, DOS doesn't normally include the UMBs in the chain of memory arenas. However, a special function call can make these available just like ordinary memory blocks. In addition, the commands *DEVICEHIGH* and *LOADHIGH* can load device drivers and programs (especially TSRs) into UMBs.

Summary

Each .COM or .EXE file starts with two memory blocks. One contains its PSP, code, and data; the other contains a block of environment variables (and the program name in DOS version 3.0 or greater). When building a PSP for a .COM file, DOS assumes the program requires all available memory. For an .EXE file, the header provides information about how much memory the program requires and other important parameters. Figure 2-3 contains a sample memory map of an .EXE file that in turn loads and runs a .COM file. DOS uses the segment address of the PSP to refer to a program. When used this way, the PSP address is often called the *process identifier*, or PID.

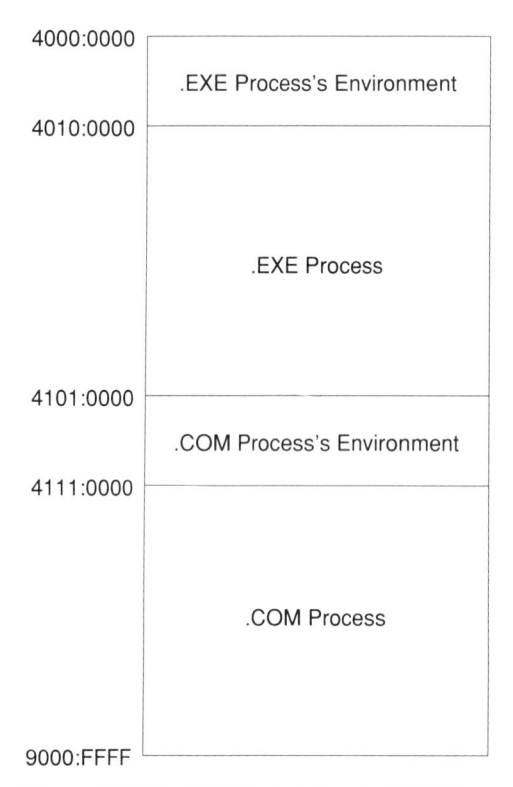

```
4000:0000 ┌─────────────────────────────┐
          │                             │
          │   .EXE Process's Environment│
4010:0000 ├─────────────────────────────┤
          │                             │
          │                             │
          │                             │
          │        .EXE Process         │
          │                             │
          │                             │
          │                             │
4101:0000 ├─────────────────────────────┤
          │   .COM Process's Environment│
4111:0000 ├─────────────────────────────┤
          │                             │
          │                             │
          │                             │
          │        .COM Process         │
          │                             │
          │                             │
          │                             │
9000:FFFF └─────────────────────────────┘
```
Figure 2-3. An .EXE file loading a .COM file.

MS-DOS loads .COM files into one 64-Kbyte segment. The CS, DS, ES, and SS registers are all equal. The PSP is at offset 0, and IP is set to 100H. DOS places data from the .COM file at offset 100H. The stack pointer starts at FFFFH, the top of the 64-Kbyte segment. .EXE files start with CS, DS, and SS set to the code, data, and stack segments, respectively. The PSP is at ES:0. The .EXE header controls the setting of IP and SP.

CHAPTER 3

C and Assembly for DOS

So far we have talked about interrupts, I/O, and memory access. Assembly-language programmers will have no difficulty programming these operations; assembly handles them directly. Many C programmers, however, are unfamiliar with the mechanisms C uses for these operations. This chapter examines several useful techniques and shows the C methods that perform these operations.

More About Addressing

C uses pointers to reference arbitrary locations in memory. Intel's infamous segmentation scheme complicates pointers on the PC. Contemporary PC C compilers have two types of pointers: near and far. Near pointers, which are 16 bits long, can address up to 64 Kbytes of memory. Far pointers, which contain a 16-bit segment and a 16-bit offset, can work with the entire 1 Mbyte of memory.

Here are some typical pointer declarations:

```
char far * screen;
int near *p;
char *default_pointer;
```

In these examples, what type of pointer is *default_pointer*? The answer depends on the memory model selected. C compilers support different models that control the default size of pointers. However, regardless of the model, you can always override a pointer with *near* or *far*. The following table summarizes the common memory models supported by popular C compilers.

DOS 5: A DEVELOPER'S GUIDE

Name	Maximum Code Size	Maximum Data Size	Size of Code Ptr	Size of Data Ptr	Notes
Tiny	64K*	64K*	16 bits	16 bits	For COM files Borland and Microsoft (6.0 or above) only
Small	64K	64K	16 bits	16 bits	
Medium	1M	64K	32 bits	16 bits	
Compact	64K	1M	16 bits	32 bits	
Large	1M	1M	32 bits	32 bits	No one data item > 64K
Huge	1M	1M	32 bits	32 bits	Data items > 64K OK

*Total code and data must not exceed 64K.

Table 3-1. Common memory models.

The programs we will examine in this book use far pointers extensively. Rather than depend on a particular compiler model, the programs declare these pointers explicitly.

Declaring a far pointer, such as the *screen* pointer in the above example, is simple enough. To be useful, however, a pointer must be set to some address. The *FP_SEG* and *FP_OFF* macros, defined in the compiler's DOS.H header, helps us use far pointers. These macros can be used to set or read the segment or offset values:

```
FP_SEG(screen)=0xB800;        /* Set segment to B800. */
FP_OFF(screen)=0;
printf("%x",FP_SEG(screen));  /* Print segment value. */
```

For example, programs that use far pointers to access the PSP use the *_psp* variable. This global variable, declared in STDLIB.H, contains the segment address of the program's PSP. The following program prints out the command line exactly as it was entered:

C AND ASSEMBLY FOR DOS

```c
#include <stdio.h>
#include <dos.h>
main()
   {
   int len;               /* length of command line */
   char far *cmd_line;    /* pointer to command line */
   FP_SEG(cmd_line)=_psp;
   FP_OFF(cmd_line)=0x80; /* offset of command line in PSP */
   len=*cmd_line++;       /* Read length. */
   while (len--) putchar(*cmd_line++); /* Print command line. */
   putchar('\n');
   }
```

Before C places the arguments in *argv[]*, it strips blanks and tabs and processes quotes and other characters. By accessing the PSP directly, you can bypass this default processing.

Turbo C and Power C also have an *MK_FP* macro. COMPAT.H, seen in Listing 3-1, endows this macro to Microsoft C as well. COMPAT.H smooths out many differences among Microsoft C, Borland Turbo C, and Mix's Power C. In the above program, *cmd_line* could have been set with one line instead of two by using the following line:

```c
screen=MK_FP(_psp,0x80);
```

Listing 3-1. COMPAT.H header file.

```
/*****************************************************************
 *                                                                *
 * File: compat.h                                                 *
 *                                                                *
 * Description:                                                   *
 * Header file for compatibility between compilers                *
 * plus some general equates, etc.                                *
 *                                                                *
 *****************************************************************/

#ifndef COMPATHEADER
```

DOS 5: A DEVELOPER'S GUIDE

```
#define COMPATHEADER

#ifdef __POWERC
#define cls clrscrn()
#define INTREGS unsigned Rbp, unsigned Rdi, unsigned Rsi, \
    unsigned Rds, unsigned Res, unsigned Rdx, unsigned Rcx, \
    unsigned Rbx, unsigned Rax, unsigned Rip, unsigned Rcs, \
    unsigned Rfl
#define int86fx(a,b,c,d) (int86x(a,b,c,d),(c)->x.flags)
#define int86f(a,b,c) (int86(a,b,c),(c)->x.flags)
#define __FAR

#else
#define FARNULL (void far *)0
#define __FAR far
#endif

#define NEARNULL (void near *)0

#ifndef __TURBOC__
#ifndef __POWERC
#define cls _msc_cls()
#define INTREGS unsigned Res, unsigned Rds, unsigned Rdi,\
    unsigned Rsi, unsigned Rbp, unsigned Rsp, unsigned Rbx, \
    unsigned Rdx, unsigned Rcx, unsigned Rax, unsigned Rip, \
    unsigned Rcs, unsigned Rfl
#define enable() _enable()
#define disable() _disable()
#define getvect(x) _dos_getvect(x)
#define setvect(x,y) _dos_setvect(x,y)
#define bioskey(a) _bios_keybrd(a)
#define MK_FP(s,o) ((void far *)((((unsigned long)(s))<<16) | \
    ((unsigned long) (o))))

/* Microsoft must link with int86fx.asm if int86fx or int86f
    is used. */
#define int86f(a,b,c) int86fx(a,b,c,NULL)

/* Use BIOS to clear screen. */
#ifndef NOCLSFUNC
```

```c
void _msc_cls()
   {
   union REGS r;
/* Clear screen. */
   r.x.ax=0x0600;
   r.h.bh=0x7;
   r.x.cx=0;
   r.x.dx=24*256+79;
   int86(0x10,&r,&r);
/* Get video page. */
   r.h.ah=0xf;
   int86(0x10,&r,&r);
/* Set cursor. */
   r.x.dx=0;
   r.h.ah=2;
   int86(0x10,&r,&r);
   }
#endif

#endif
#endif

#ifdef __TURBOC__
#define cls clrscr()
#ifndef __BORLANDC__
#define inp(n) inportb(n)
#define outp(p,n) outportb(p,n)
#endif
#define INTREGS unsigned Rbp, unsigned Rdi, unsigned Rsi, \
   unsigned Rds, unsigned Res, unsigned Rdx, unsigned Rcx, \
   unsigned Rbx, unsigned Rax, unsigned Rip, unsigned Rcs, \
   unsigned Rfl
#define int86fx(a,b,c,d) (int86x(a,b,c,d),(c)->x.flags)
#define int86f(a,b,c) (int86(a,b,c),(c)->x.flags)
#endif

/* end of header */
#endif
```

Accessing the Environment

The environment segment is accessible from C in several ways. The functions *getenv()* and *putenv()* manipulate the environment in an easy, portable fashion. The following program sets an environment variable, *PAT*, then prints the *PATH* and *PAT* variables:

```
#include <stdio.h>
#include <stdio.h>
main()
    {
    putenv("PAT=Test Entry");
    printf("%s - %s\n",getenv("PATH"),getenv("PAT"));
    }
```

Most compilers offer a variable, similar to *_psp*, that points to the environment. Turbo C, for example, has a global *environ*. Most compilers can also pass an environment pointer to *main()*, right after the *argv* argument. The details of these pointers vary slightly from compiler to compiler, so consult the manuals before using them.

The method used most often in this book is brute force. By using far pointers to address the PSP, a program can locate and use the environment. This approach is very general and, while not as portable as the *putenv()* and *getenv()* functions, has the advantage of being directly translatable to assembly language. Although this helps illustrate points in a book, it's less important in the real world; you're better off using *putenv()* and *getenv()* in your own programs.

Of course, the program's name from the end of the environment block is always available in *argv[0]*. This is the easiest way to get that information in C.

Input and Output

Input and output from C are straightforward. Turbo C uses the *inportb()* and *inport()* functions to read a byte or word from a port. Microsoft C uses *inp()* to read a byte from a port, while Power C has all three functions. For example:

```
n=inp(0x61);
```

C AND ASSEMBLY FOR DOS

sets *n* to the eight-bit value of I/O port 61H. DOS.H contains the declarations for these functions.

Output is similar. Microsoft uses the *outp()* function to write a byte to a port. Borland's library has an *outportb()* call for bytes and an *outport()* call for words. Power C has all three. The call

```
outp(0x20,0x22);
```

writes 22H to port 20H. Again, DOS.H declares these functions. The programs presented in this book use *inp()* and *outp()*, and COMPAT.H translates for your compiler.

Interrupts

Working with interrupts involves three operations: generating interrupts, servicing interrupts, and managing the interrupt vector table.

Generating interrupts is easy. In fact, there are many ways to generate interrupts from C. For our programs, we will be interested in two of the methods (you can look up the others in your C compiler's library reference; most of them are variations of these two).

To use interrupts, you must read and write the processor's registers directly from C. Once again, DOS.H declares the things you need. It starts by declaring the *REGS* union, which contains two structures representing the word-length and byte-length registers. A structure named *x* contains the word-length registers (AX, BX, and so on). The *h* structure contains the byte-length registers. These structures are defined differently depending on the compiler. Here is a typical declaration:

```
struct WREGS
    {
    unsigned int ax, bx, cx, dx, si, di, cflags, flags;
    };
```

```
struct BREGS
    {
    unsigned char al, ah, bl, bh, cl, ch, dl, dh;
    };

union REGS
    {
    struct WREGS x;
    struct BREGS h;
    };
```

Notice that even though the BP register has special significance to the C compiler, it may not be included. Luckily, most DOS and BIOS calls don't use BP.

The following program fragment sets the AX register to 0200H:

```
union REGS r;
r.x.ax=0x200;
```

Setting AL to 50H and BH to 22H requires the following code:

```
r.h.al=0x50;
r.h.bh=0x22;
```

If you use the Microsoft compiler, you'll notice that its *REGS* union does not contain the complete flags register. Power C, Microsoft C, and Turbo C all contain the *cflag* member, the status of the carry flag.

Of course, these structures don't actually modify the register's contents; certain functions use them as arguments to represent the registers. For example, the following code calls INT 21H, function 2, which displays a character in DL to the console:

```
#include <dos.h>
main()
    {
```

```
union REGS rin,rout;
rin.h.ah=0x2;              /* function number */
rin.h.dl='A';              /* Print letter A. */
int86(0x21,&rin,&rout);    /* Just do it. */
}
```

The *int86()* function takes three arguments: the interrupt number, a pointer to the registers to send to the interrupt routine (*rin*, in the example), and a pointer that stores the interrupt routine's response (*rout*). You will often make the *rin* and *rout* pointers the same. The *int86()* function returns the value of AX; it also stores this value in the *x.ax* member of *rout*.

This method only works for interrupts that don't use segment registers. Many interrupts do require segment registers for input or output, and that's when *int86x()* comes into play. This function is identical to *int86()* except that it uses a fourth argument: a pointer to an *SREGS* structure. This argument points to the segment registers that go in and out of the interrupt routine. The structure contains entries for four segment registers, as shown in the following code, but *int86x()* only uses DS and ES.

```
struct SREGS
   {
   unsigned int es, cs, ss, ds;
   };
```

If an interrupt returns information in flags other than the carry flag, you won't be able to call it from Microsoft C using these functions. Listing 3-2 shows a routine, *int86fx()*, that works just like *int86x()* except that it returns the value of the flags instead of AX. If the *SREG* pointer is null, the routine works like *int86()*, again returning the flags. In the interest of compatibility, programs in this book that read the flags register use *int86fx()* or *int86f()* (defined in COMPAT.H). COMPAT.H defines these functions as macros for Turbo C and Power C. Microsoft C users will need to link INT86FX.OBJ (created from INT86FX.C) to their programs that use either function.

DOS 5: A DEVELOPER'S GUIDE

Many common interrupts have special routines in the C library to call them specifically. Chapter 5 shows these equivalent calls where they exist.

Listing 3-2. INT86FX.ASM.
```
;****************************************************************
;*                                                              *
;* File: INT86FX.ASM                                            *
;*                                                              *
;* Provides C function similar to int86x(), but the flags       *
;* register is returned to the calling program.                 *
;*                                                              *
;****************************************************************

; Change this line to reflect the model you are using.
MODEL       SMALL,C

; register structure
WR          STRUC
RAX         DW      ?
RBX         DW      ?
RCX         DW      ?
RDX         DW      ?
RSI         DW      ?
RDI         DW      ?
CFLAG       DW      ?
WR          ENDS

; segment register structure
SR          STRUC
RES         DW      ?
RCS         DW      ?
RSS         DW      ?
RDS         DW      ?
SR          ENDS

            PUBLIC int86fx

.CODE
; These variables are in the code segment so we can access them
; even when DS has been changed to execute the interrupt.
```

C AND ASSEMBLY FOR DOS

```
; space for interrupt vector address
VECTOR  EQU     THIS DWORD
VECT0   DW      ?
VECT1   DW      ?

; storage for bp,dsx
OLDBP   DW      ?
OLDDS   DW      ?
NEWDS   DW      ?

; Store interrupt number here so we can test for INT 25H or 26H
; right after the interrupt completes.
INTNO   DB      ?

; Load a pointer (far or near depending on model).
LOADP   MACRO   P1
        IF      @DataSize
        LDS     BX,P1
        ELSE
        MOV     BX,P1
        ENDIF
        ENDM

int86fx PROC    INO:WORD, INPTR:PTR WR, OUTPTR:PTR WR, SEGS:PTR SR
        PUSH    SI
        PUSH    DI
        PUSH    DS
; Ask DOS for interrupt vector.
        MOV     AX,INO
; Put it away for later.
        MOV     CS:[INTNO],AL
        MOV     AH,35H
        INT     21H
; Store it away.
        MOV     CS:[VECT0],BX
        MOV     CS:[VECT1],ES
; Save BP.
        MOV     CS:[OLDBP],BP
; Save DS.
        MOV     CS:[OLDDS],DS
```

55

```
; Get REGS and transfer them to most real registers.
        LOADP   INPTR
        MOV     AX,[BX].CFLAG
        ROR     AX,1
        PUSHF
        MOV     AX,[BX].RBX
        PUSH    AX
        MOV     AX,[BX].RAX
        PUSH    AX
        MOV     CX,[BX].RCX
        MOV     DX,[BX].RDX
        MOV     SI,[BX].RSI
        MOV     DI,[BX].RDI
; Get SEGS; if null don't mess with segment registers.
        LOADP   SEGS
IF      @DataSize
        MOV     AX,DS
        OR      AX,BX
ELSE
        OR      BX,BX
ENDIF
        JZ      NOSEG
; Store segment values (DS, ES).
        MOV     AX,[BX].RDS
        PUSH    AX
        MOV     ES,[BX].RES
        POP     DS
NOSEG:
        POP     AX
        POP     BX
        POPF
        PUSHF
; Simulate interrupt (note PUSHF above).
        CALL    CS:[VECTOR]
; Save flags and DS for later examination.
        PUSHF
        CMP     CS:[INTNO],25H
        JZ      REMFLAG
        CMP     CS:[INTNO],26H
        JNZ     NOREMF
```

C AND ASSEMBLY FOR DOS

```
; INT 25H and 26H leave old flags on the stack, so remove them.
REMFLAG:
        POPF
NOREMF:
        PUSH    DS
        POP     CS:[NEWDS]
; Restore BP.
        MOV     BP,CS:[OLDBP]
        PUSH    AX
; Read registers to *OUTPTR.
        LAHF
        ROL     AL,1
        AND     AL,1
        PUSH    BX
        MOV     AX,CS:[OLDDS]
        LOADP   OUTPTR
        MOV     [BX].CFLAG,AX
        POP     AX
        MOV     [BX].RBX,AX
        POP     AX
        MOV     [BX].RAX,AX
        MOV     [BX].RCX,CX
        MOV     [BX].RDX,DX
        MOV     [BX].RSI,SI
        MOV     [BX].RDI,DI
; See if SEGS were used. If so, restore them.
        LOADP   SEGS
IF      @DataSize
        MOV     AX,DS
        OR      AX,BX
ELSE
        OR      BX,DX
ENDIF
        JZ      NOSEG1
        MOV     [BX].RES,ES
        MOV     AX,CS:[NEWDS]
        MOV     [BX].RDS,AX
NOSEG1:
        POP     AX
        POP     DS
        POP     DI
```

```
        POP     SI
        RET
int86fx ENDP

        END
```

Servicing Interrupts

Writing an ISR in C is simple. The following statements declare an interrupt routine in Microsoft C 5.0:

```
void interrupt far isr(   unsigned Res, unsigned Rds,
                          unsigned Rdi, unsigned Rsi,
                          unsigned Rbp, unsigned Rsp,
                          unsigned Rbx, unsigned Rdx,
                          unsigned Rcx, unsigned Rax)
   {
   /* interrupt service routine */
   }
```

The formal parameters in the interrupt function contain the value of the registers when the interrupt occurred. *Rax*, for instance, contains the AX register's value. If the function modifies *Rax*, AX will receive that value when the interrupt returns.

All the major C compilers use the same technique for interrupt functions. However, the order of the register parameters varies from compiler to compiler. For simplicity, interrupt functions in this book will appear as follows:

```
void interrupt far func(INTREGS);
```

INTREGS, a macro defined in COMPAT.H (Listing 3-1), declares the registers in the proper format using the naming convention shown above.

Interrupt functions can be called just like regular functions. However, arguments can't be passed to them. Often, you will write an ISR that replaces an existing one, then calls the original ISR before or after processing the interrupt. This is known as *hooking an interrupt.*

C AND ASSEMBLY FOR DOS

After writing an interrupt function, you need to modify the interrupt vector table to point to the function. You'll also want to read the interrupt vector table. You should always read the existing interrupt vector before modifying it. When your program exits, the original vector must be restored. You'll often want to call the old vector, too.

The *setvect()* and *getvect()* calls write and read interrupt vectors in Turbo C and Power C. Microsoft C uses *_dos_setvect()* and *_dos_getvect()*, which are equivalent. COMPAT.H allows us to write *setvect()* and *getvect()* regardless of the compiler used. The following call points INT 60H to a user-defined interrupt handler named *user()*:

```
setvect(0x60,user);
```

C allows the interrupts to be enabled or disabled. The calls *enable()* and *disable()* act like the *STI* and *CLI* instructions, respectively. Microsoft uses *_enable()* and *_disable()*, but COMPAT.H comes to the rescue once again.

Assembly Routines for C

Many of the C programs in this book call assembly-language functions. When you assemble the latter, be sure to specify the */Ml* option. This prevents the assembler from forcing all symbols into uppercase. If you don't use this option, the linker won't be able to find the assembly-language function.

59

CHAPTER 4

Programs at Last!

Because we haven't yet covered all the functions we need for complex assembly programs, most of the programs in this chapter are in C. They illustrate most of the techniques we covered in Chapters 2 and 3.

ESCAPE

ESCAPE is an assembly-language program that sends escape codes to the screen or the printer. This is handy if ANSI.SYS is installed and you want to send commands to it or control printer modes from the command line.

This program uses two DOS interrupts: INT 21H, function 2, and INT 21H, function 4CH. Function 2 simply displays the character in the DL register to the screen. Function 4CH exits the program. Chapter 5 will cover these calls, along with many others, in greater detail.

If you don't know assembly language, read Listing 4-1 carefully. This will help you follow the assembly code that appears later.

Listing 4-1. ESCAPE.ASM.
```
;*****************************************************************
;*                                                               *
;* File. ESCAPE.ASM                                              *
;*                                                               *
;* This program sends escape codes to STDOUT.                    *
;* This is useful for sending print codes to the printer.        *
;* For example:                                                  *
;*    ESCAPE [ >LPT1                                             *
;* or                                                            *
;*    ESCAPE 2kP >LPT1                                           *
```

DOS 5: A DEVELOPER'S GUIDE

```
;*                                                                *
;* You can also send codes to ANSI.SYS. Example:                  *
;*    ESCAPE [1;40m                                               *
;*                                                                *
;* ESCAPE by itself sends only an escape character. Leading       *
;* blanks and tabs are ignored. That is:                          *
;*    ESCAPE    2K                                                *
;* is the same as:                                                *
;*    ESCAPE 2K                                                   *
;*                                                                *
;******************************************************************
;

; Set up memory model.
.MODEL      SMALL

; Set up a stack.
.STACK 100H

; Start code segment.
.CODE

ESCAPE      EQU     1BH             ; escape code
BLANK       EQU     ' '             ; blank
TAB         EQU     9               ; tab

; one and only procedure (function)
MAIN        PROC
            MOV     AX,ES           ; Make ds=es address PSP.
            MOV     DS,AX
            MOV     CL,DS:[80H]     ; PSP:80H is length of command line.
            MOV     DL,ESCAPE       ; Print escape using INT 21H fn 2.
            MOV     AH,2
            INT     21H
            XOR     BX,BX           ; BX=0

; Loop here until blanks are gone.
BLANKS:     OR      CL,CL           ; If length is zero, end of line...
            JZ      SHORT DONE      ; so jump to done.
            MOV     DL,[BX+81H]     ; Get character from PSP:(BX+81H).
            DEC     CL              ; count--
            INC     BX              ; BX++
```

PROGRAMS AT LAST!

```
                CMP     DL,BLANK    ; If blank...
                JZ      BLANKS      ; skip.
                CMP     DL,TAB      ; If tab...
                JZ      BLANKS      ; skip.
; Print characters to end of command line.
PRINTIT:        MOV     AH,2        ; Use INT 21H fn 2.
                INT     21H
                MOV     DL,[BX+81H] ; Get next character
                INC     BX          ; BX++
                DEC     CL          ; count--
                JNS     PRINTIT     ; If count>=0 keep printing.

; Use INT 21H fn 4CH to quit.
DONE:           MOV     AH,4CH
                INT     21H
MAIN            ENDP                ; end of function
                END     MAIN        ; end of program--start at main
```

The main procedure sets DS equal to the segment address of the PSP. DS is the default data segment, making data from the PSP easier to read. The CL register receives the length of the command line, and the program prints an escape character using INT 21H, function 2.

Since BP, BX, SI, and DI are the only registers that can form address offsets, we should use one of them to loop through the command line. BP references the SS segment by default, so using that register would be too much trouble. ESCAPE uses BX to point to the current character; SI or DI could also have been used.

The first loop starts at label *blanks*. Here we skip leading any spaces and tabs in the command line. If the command line is empty or contains only blanks, a jump to *done* ends the program.

The next loop begins at *printit*. This loop uses INT 21H, function 2, to print the characters one at a time until CL is less than zero (*JNS* stands for "Jump if No Sign"). When CL is negative, the code at label *done* terminates the program.

63

To see ESCAPE in action, try these commands while ANSI.SYS is active:

```
ESCAPE [37;44m    Set screen color.
ESCAPE [2J        Clear screen.
ESCAPE [0m        Reset screen.
```

You can send ESCAPE codes to the printer using redirection. For example:

```
ESCAPE m>LPT1
```

SPACE

This program is a good example of using low-level access to bypass a limitation in standard C. Its purpose is to print the number of blanks sent to it via the command line (Listing 4-2). For instance:

```
SPACE▒A▒Line
```

prints:

```
A Line has 2 spaces.
```

It would be difficult, if not impossible, to write this program without accessing the PSP. When the C start-up code places the command line in the *argv* array, it breaks it into tokens that don't contain white space. Of course, you could quote the string, but that would be cheating.

The pointer *cmdline* contains the address of the command line, much as the BX register did in ESCAPE. The *len* variable corresponds to the CL register. With these variables set, the program is trivial; it uses the library call *isspace()* to determine which characters are blanks.

PROGRAMS AT LAST!

Listing 4-2. SPACE.C.
```
/****************************************************************
*                                                                *
* File: space.c                                                  *
*                                                                *
* Description:                                                   *
* This program uses direct access to the PSP to count the        *
* number of blanks (as defined by isspace()) in the command      *
* line.                                                          *
*                                                                *
* You couldn't write this program using conventional methods     *
* because C usually provides the command line in the argv[]      *
* array and is stripped of spaces.                               *
*                                                                *
****************************************************************/

#include <stdio.h>
#include <dos.h>
#include <ctype.h>
#include <stdlib.h>

main()
    {
/* far pointer to command line */
    char far *cmdline;
    int len;                  /* length of command line */
    int blanks=0;             /* number of blanks */
/* Set far pointer to point to PSP:80H. */
    FP_SEG(cmdline)=_psp;
    FP_OFF(cmdline)=0x80;
/* Get length and bump pointer to 81H. */
    len=*cmdline++;
    putchar('"');
    while (len--)             /* for each character... */
        {
/* If blank, count it. */
        if (isspace(*cmdline)) blanks++;
        putchar(*cmdline++);  /* Print it out. */
        }
/* Print results. */
    printf("\" has %d blanks.\n",blanks);
    }
```

EDISP

The EDISP program (Listing 4-3) reads the environment block, displaying the environment much as the *SET* command does from the DOS prompt. In addition, EDISP displays its own name from the environment block, if it's available. C compilers provide several methods of accessing that block but this method is the most general.

EDISP uses two pointers: *eblock* points to the environment data, while *eptr* points to the segment address of the environment block (field 2CH in the PSP). This value sets the segment of *eblock*.

The first *do* loop ends when it finds two 0 bytes in a row; the second terminates at the end of each string. After EDISP finds the two 0 bytes, it checks for a 0001H. Note that *eblock*, a character pointer, must be cast to a far integer pointer to check for both bytes in one test.

Replacing

```
if (*(int far *)++eblock==1)
```

with

```
if (*(int *)++eblock==1)
```

would work in models with far data pointers (large and compact) but would fail for small and medium models. By explicitly using the *far* keyword, EDISP works in any model. It uses the "%Fs" format in the *printf* statement for the same reason. In the small and medium models, *printf* would expect a near pointer and would print garbage if sent a far pointer.

PROGRAMS AT LAST!

Listing 4-3. EDISP.C.
```
/************************************************************
*                                                            *
* File: edisp.c                                              *
*                                                            *
* Description:                                               *
* Displays all environment variables plus the program's      *
* name from the environment block.                           *
*                                                            *
************************************************************/

/* NOTE: many C compilers send main() a pointer to the environment
   if you specify it. For instance:
      main(int argc, char *argv[], char far *envp);
   EDISP doesn't use this method; it directly accesses the PSP to
   obtain the environment address. */

#include <stdio.h>
#include <dos.h>
/* MSC doesn't define _psp in DOS.H. */
#include <stdlib.h>

main()
    {
/* pointer to segment address of environment block */
    unsigned int far *eptr;
    char far *eblock;           /* pointer into environment */
/* Get segment address of block. */
    FP_SEG(eptr)=_psp;
    FP_OFF(eptr)=0x2c;
/* Put it in segment of eblock. */
    FP_SEG(eblock)=*eptr;
    FP_OFF(eblock)=0;           /* Environment block starts at 0. */
    do {
       do {
/* If not zero, print it. */
          if (*eblock) putchar(*eblock);
          else putchar('\n');   /* else new line */
          } while (*eblock++);  /* Do until end of line. */
       } while (*eblock);       /* Do until end of block. */
```

67

DOS 5: A DEVELOPER'S GUIDE

```
/* Print name if present. */
/* Note the %Fs in the printf. This specifies a far pointer.
   It is redundant in models with large data (i.e., large, compact)
   but mandatory in small and medium models. */

   if (*(int far *)++eblock==1)
      printf("My name is %Fs.\n",eblock+2);
   else printf("Name not present.\n");
   }
```

PRTSCRN

PRTSCRN (Listing 4-4) displays statistics on the screen and shows how the BIOS print screen interrupt (INT 5) is called from within a C program. Press P to print the screen and exit. Any other key simply exits.

INT 5 neither requires nor returns registers. Because *int86()* requires a *REGS* union, however, the program must supply one.

Listing 4-4. PRTSCR.C.
```
/***************************************************************
*                                                               *
* File: prtscr.c                                                *
*                                                               *
* Description:                                                  *
* Call the print screen interrupt (INT 5) from C.               *
*                                                               *
****************************************************************/

#include <stdio.h>
#include <dos.h>
#include <conio.h>
#include "compat.h"

main()
   {
   int c;
/* Generate some output. */
   cls;
```

PROGRAMS AT LAST!

```
   printf("Results of survey:\n");
   printf("   For ........ 30%\n");
   printf("   Against ..... 68%\n");
   printf("   Undecided ... 2%\n");
   printf(
      "\nPress <P> to print and quit, any other key to quit.\n");
/* Wait for a key. */
   c=getch();
/* if function key */
   if (!c) getch();                /* Ignore. */
/* If P then print. */
   else if (c=='P'||c=='p') printscreen();
   }

/* Routine to print the screen using INT 5. This is in a separate
   function, so the details of it are hidden from main(). */

printscreen()
   {
/* dummy variable--no registers needed */
   union REGS r;
/* interrupt 5--BIOS printscreen */
   int86(5,&r,&r);
   return 0;
   }
```

SPYS

This whimsical program (Listing 4-5) displays the number of secret agents on the payroll. Since this is classified data, it wouldn't do for a counteragent to print the screen using the PrtSc key.

Since PrtSc generates an INT 5, SPYS traps INT 5 and sets a flag when it occurs. This flag triggers a warning to the user. INT 5 requires no register manipulations, so the register names don't appear in the parameter list in the *prtsc()* function.

SPYS also captures INT 23H, the DOS break interrupt, preventing the user from pressing Control-C or Control-Break to exit the program. This serves two purposes.

DOS 5: A DEVELOPER'S GUIDE

First, the user can't break out to DOS and print the screen. Second, SPYS must restore the print screen vector before returning to DOS. If the user exited without allowing SPYS to do that important task, the next PrtSc operation would very likely crash the machine.

The *onbreak()* function does nothing, but it prevents the default break handler from executing. C gives us several other ways to trap the break keys (as we will see later in Chapter 8), but SPYS uses this one.

When you're writing interrupt routines like *onbreak()* and *prtsc()*, call library routines carefully. Any function that makes a DOS call cannot itself be called safely. When *prtsc()* gets control, for example, the processor could be running any code—including DOS. Since DOS isn't reentrant, a system call would cause a crash. Every compiler's library is different, and there are no easy rules to determine which routines are safe. Your compiler manual should shed some light on this subject.

Run the SPYS program and press Control-Break. Notice that a ^C appears on the screen. The BIOS INT 1BH detects Control-Break and signals DOS, which prints the ^C to the screen before calling INT 23H. SPYS1 (Listing 4-6) is identical to SPYS except that it catches 1BH, the BIOS break interrupt. Run SPYS1 and notice that the ^C is no longer displayed.

By catching interrupt 1BH and using BIOS keyboard input, you make ^C just another key. Chapter 8 covers break handling in more detail.

Listing 4-7 shows the *prtsc()* routine written in assembly language. You could link it with SPYS or SPYS1 if you replaced the existing *prtsc()* function with the following line:

```
void far interrupt prtsc();
```

Notice that interrupt routines must be declared far and end with an *IRET* instruction. It's important that an interrupt routine restore any registers it has

PROGRAMS AT LAST!

modified to their original values. An interrupt automatically preserves CS, IP, and the flags; the programmer is responsible for all other registers. Some software interrupts (like INT 21H) return values in registers and the flags. This is acceptable because programs call a software interrupt and know their registers will be modified. An interrupt like INT 5, however, can occur anytime during any program.

Listing 4-5. SPYS.C.
```
/****************************************************************
 *                                                                *
 * File: spys.c                                                   *
 *                                                                *
 * Description:                                                   *
 * Displays "classified" data. Disables break and printscreen.    *
 *                                                                *
 ****************************************************************/

#include <stdio.h>
#include <dos.h>
#include <conio.h>
#include "compat.h"

/* global flag--set when PrtSc is pressed */
int printscreen=0;

/* storage for old interrupt routine */
#ifdef __POWERC
void interrupt (far *old5)();
#else
void (interrupt far *old5)();
#endif


/* Print screen interrupt. */
void far interrupt prtsc()    /* no registers required */
    {
    printscreen=1;            /* Set flag. */
    }
```

71

DOS 5: A DEVELOPER'S GUIDE

```c
/* break interrupt */
void far interrupt onbreak()   /* no registers required */
    {
/* Don't do anything. Ignore the break. */
    }

main()
    {
    cls;
/* Capture printscreen interrupt... */
    old5=getvect(5);
    setvect(5,prtsc);
/* and ^C interrupt. */
    setvect(0x23,onbreak);
/* Generate some output. */
    printf("WARNING -- Secure data\n");
    printf("Number of friendly spies on payroll:     132\n");
    printf("Number of friendly spies not on payroll: 50\n");
    printf("Number of enemy spies on payroll:        12\n\n");
    printf("Total spies:                             194\n\n\n");
    printf("Press any key to exit\n");
/* Wait for a key--this function returns 0 if no key is waiting. */
    while (!kbhit())
        {
/* If printscreen was pressed... */
        if (printscreen)
            {
            printscreen=0;      /* Reset flag. */
            printf("You are not allowed to print this screen.\n");
            }
        }
/* Read key pressed and discard. */
    if (!getch()) getch();
    cls;
/* Restore interrupts. */
/* DOS restore INT 23H */
    setvect(5,old5);
    }
```

PROGRAMS AT LAST!

Listing 4-6. SPYS1.C.
```
/****************************************************************
 *                                                              *
 * File: spys1.c                                                *
 *                                                              *
 * Description:                                                 *
 * Displays "classified" data. Disables break and printscreen.  *
 *                                                              *
 * If using Microsoft C, link with int86fx.asm.                 *
 *                                                              *
 ****************************************************************/

#include <stdio.h>
#include <dos.h>
#include <bios.h>
#include <conio.h>
#include "compat.h"

/* global flag--set when PrtSc is pressed */
int printscreen=0;


/* storage for old interrupt routines */
#ifdef __POWERC

void interrupt (far *old5)();
void interrupt (far *old1b)();

#else

void (interrupt far *old5)();
void (interrupt far *old1b)();

#endif

/* Print screen interrupt. */
void far interrupt prtsc()              /* no registers required */
    {
    printscreen=1;                      /* Set flag. */
    }
```

73

DOS 5: A DEVELOPER'S GUIDE

```
/* break interrupt */
void far interrupt onbreak()        /* no registers required */
    {
/* Don't do anything. Ignore the break. */
    }

main()
    {
    cls;
/* Capture printscreen interrupt... */
    old5=getvect(5);
    setvect(5,prtsc);
/* and ^Break interrupt. */
    old1b=getvect(0x1b);
    setvect(0x1b,onbreak);
    setvect(0x23,onbreak);          /* just in case */
/* Generate some output. */
    printf("WARNING -- Secure data\n");
    printf("Number of friendly spies on payroll:     132\n");
    printf("Number of friendly spies not on payroll: 50\n");
    printf("Number of enemy spies on payroll:        12\n\n");
    printf("Total spies:                             194\n\n\n");
    printf("Press any key to exit\n");
/* Wait for a key--function returns a 0 if no key is waiting. */
    while (!key_fmbios(1))
        {
/* If printscreen was pressed... */
        if (printscreen)
            {
            printscreen=0;          /* Reset flag. */
            printf("You are not allowed to print this screen.\n");
            }
        }
/* Read key pressed and discard. */
/* If we read this with a DOS call, it might trigger a ^C. */
    key_fmbios(0);
    cls;
/* Restore interrupts. */
    setvect(5,old5);
    setvect(0x1b,old1b);
    }
```

PROGRAMS AT LAST!

```c
key_fmbios(int cmd)
   {
   union REGS r;
   int f;
   r.h.ah=cmd;
   f=int86f(0x16,&r,&r);
   if (cmd==1)
      return (f&0x40)?0:1;          /* key status */
   return r.x.ax;
   }
```

Listing 4-7. PRTSC.ASM.

```
;***********************************************************
;*                                                         *
;* File: PRTSC.ASM                                         *
;*                                                         *
;* Replacement prtsc() function for SPYS and SPYS1.        *
;*                                                         *
;***********************************************************

        .MODEL   SMALL,C           ; Change to correct model.

        .DATA
                 EXTRN   printscreen:WORD

        .CODE
                 PUBLIC  prtsc
prtsc            PROC    FAR
                 PUSH    AX          ; Save registers.
                 PUSH    DS
                 MOV     AX,@Data    ; address data segment
                 MOV     DS,AX
                 MOV     AX,1        ; Store 1 to print screen.
                 MOV     PRINTSCREEN,AX
                 POP     DS          ; Restore registers.
                 POP     AX
                 IRET                ; Return from interrupt
prtsc            ENDP

                 END
```

CHAPTER 5

DOS Services

This chapter details the most useful services DOS provides for user programs. Some of the more esoteric calls, those that were only in effect for one or two versions of DOS, are not covered.

For each call, the description includes the closest equivalent C function, if any. In some cases, the C function provides a slightly different service from the DOS call; check your manual. Even between compiler vendors, differences can crop up. For example, *putch()* is similar to INT 21H, function 2, in the Microsoft and Mix compilers. With Turbo C, however, *putch()* is closer to the BIOS functions that write to the screen (it allows colors, for example).

Many DOS functions return with the carry flag set if an error occurs. These functions also leave an error code in the AX register. Table 5-1 shows these error codes.

DOS 5: A DEVELOPER'S GUIDE

Error Code	Meaning	DOS Version
01H	Invalid function number	2.0+
02H	File not found	2.0+
03H	Path not found	2.0+
04H	No handles available	2.0+
05H	Access denied (e.g., file is read-only or directory)	2.0+
06H	Invalid handle	2.0+
07H	Memory control blocks damaged	2.0+
08H	Insufficient memory	2.0+
09H	Invalid memory block address	2.0+
0AH	Invalid environment	2.0+
0BH	Invalid format	2.0+
0CH	Invalid file access byte	2.0+
0DH	Invalid data	2.0+
0FH	Invalid drive	2.0+
10H	Can't remove current directory	2.0+
11H	Not same device	2.0+
12H	No more files match wildcard	2.0+
13H	Can't write to write-protected disk	2.0+
14H	Unknown unit	2.0+
15H	Drive not ready	2.0+
16H	Command not recognized	2.0+
17H	CRC (checksum) error	2.0+
18H	Invalid request structure length	2.0+
19H	Disk seek error	2.0+
1AH	Unknown media type	2.0+
1BH	Sector not found	2.0+
1CH	Out of paper (printer)	2.0+
1DH	Error while writing	2.0+
1EH	Error while reading	2.0+
1FH	General error	2.0+
20H	Sharing violation	3.0+
21H	Lock violation	3.0+
22H	Invalid disk change	3.0+
23H	FCB unavailable	3.0+
24H	Sharing buffer overflow	3.3+
25H	Bad code page	4.0+
26H	Handle EOF	4.0+
27H	Handle disk full	4.0+
32H	Not supported	3.1+
33H	Not listening	3.1+
34H	Duplicate name	3.3+
35H	Bad network path	3.3+
36H	Network busy	3.3+
37H	Non existent device	3.3+
38H	Too many commands	3.3+
39H	Adapter error	3.3+
3AH	Bad network response	3.3+
3BH	Network error	3.3+

Table 5-1. MS-DOS error codes.

DOS SERVICES

Error Code	Meaning	DOS Version
3CH	Adapter incompatible	3.3+
3DH	Print queue full	3.3+
3EH	No spool space	3.3+
3FH	Print cancelled	3.3+
40H	Network name deleted	3.3+
41H	Network access denied	3.3+
42H	Bad device type	3.3+
43H	Bad network name	3.3+
44H	Too many names	3.3+
45H	Too many sessions	3.3+
46H	Sharing paused	3.3+
47H	Request not accepted	3.3+
48H	Redirection pause	3.3+
50H	File exists	3.3+
51H	Duplicate FCB	3.3+
52H	Can't make directory	4.0+
53H	Critical error (INT 24H) failure	3.3+
54H	Out of structures	3.3+
55H	Already assigned	3.3+
56H	Invalid password	3.3+
57H	Invalid parameter	3.3+
58H	Network write error	3.3+
5AH	Comp not loaded	5.0+

Table 5-1. MS-DOS error codes (continued).

The Simple I/O Services

Most DOS programmers have abandoned the simple I/O services. These 12 functions mimic calls to CP/M, an old 8080 operating system. I/O via handles (as discussed in Chapter 2) is normally more useful, though simple I/O can also be useful in some programs. In the examples in Chapter 4, for instance, we used one of these functions (function 2) to write characters to the console.

Handle I/O is better because it's more flexible. A program can redirect handles and test them for errors. Calls can determine whether the handle is a file, a local device, or a network device. Simple I/O doesn't allow any of these operations, and every available function can be duplicated by handle calls. Still, programmers often take advantage of the simple calls' ease of use in short programs with modest I/O needs.

DOS 5: A DEVELOPER'S GUIDE

Input character with echo   **Function 01H**

Description:

> Inputs a character from STDIN, which is the console if no redirection is in effect. This function checks for Control-C from the console and generates an INT 23H if it is detected. If a character isn't ready, function 1 waits for one. DOS displays the character read on the STDOUT device. Like all DOS input calls, special keys (like Alt-X and F10) return a zero. This signals that the next input call will return the scan code of the key.

Input:

> AH=01H

Output:

> AL=character read

Equivalent C functions:

> `getche()`

DOS versions:

> All

Input character without echo   **Function 08H**

Description:

> Identical to function 1 except that the character read does not appear on STDOUT.

Input:

> AH=08H

Output:

> AL=character read

Equivalent C functions:

`getch()`

DOS versions:

All

Direct input character without echo   **Function 07H**

Description:

Resembles function 8. The difference is that this function ignores Control-C.

Input:

AH=07H

Output:

AL=character read

Equivalent C functions:

No direct equivalent.

DOS versions:

All

Direct I/O   **Function 06H**

Description:

This is one of DOS's odder functions. It can write any character except 0FFH directly to STDOUT. If the output is 0FFH, DOS generates no output. Instead, it reads a character from STDIN without checking for breaks.

Input:

AH=06H

DL=character to output or 0FFH for input

Output:

> if DL=0FFH
> AX=input character if available
> zero flag set if no input available

Equivalent C functions:

> No direct equivalent.

DOS versions:

> All

Line input   **Function 0AH**

Description:

> Reads one line of input. DOS uses this function to read the command line at its own prompt. It reads an entire line at a time and allows editing similar to what you get at the DOS prompt. Function 0AH requires a buffer of the following format:

Max. read length	# characters read	Buffer for input
(1 byte)	(1 byte)	(as long as first field indicates)
set by programmer	set by DOS	set by DOS—ends with 0DH

Input:

> AH=0AH
> DS:DX=pointer to buffer (see above)

Output:

> None

Equivalent C functions:

> `cgets()`

DOS SERVICES

DOS versions:

All

Flush keyboard and call function   Function 0CH

Description:

Discards any keystrokes waiting in the keyboard buffer. If AL is equal to an input function number (1, 6, 7, 8, or 0AH), that function is called immediately after the buffer flush operation.

Input:

AH=0CH
AL=function number (1, 6, 7, 8, or 0AH)
Other registers as appropriate for function in AL

Output:

As appropriate for function specified

Equivalent C functions:

No direct equivalent.

DOS versions:

All

Check for input   Function 0BH

Description:

Determines whether a character is waiting to be read from STDIN. Since most of the input functions wait for a key if one isn't available, this function is essential if you want to do processing while waiting for a key. Look at the following code fragment:

```
WLOOP:
  MOV AH,0BH
  INT 21H            ; Check for key.
```

83

DOS 5: A DEVELOPER'S GUIDE

```
    OR AL,AL
    JNZ KEYPRESS      ; If key pressed, jump.
    CALL MUSIC        ; Play a note of music; still waiting.
    JMP WLOOP
KEYPRESS:
    MOV AH,1
    INT 21H           ; Read character.
```

The IOCTL functions (discussed later) can perform this same service on any file, including STDIN.

Input:

    AH=0BH

Output:

    AL=0FFH if character available

    AL≠0FF if character not available

Equivalent C functions:

```
kbhit()
```

DOS versions:

    All

Character output   Function 02H

Description:

    Sends the ASCII character in the DL register to the STDOUT device (usually the screen).

Input:

    AH=02H

Output:

    DL=character

DOS SERVICES

Equivalent C functions:

`putch()`

DOS versions:

All

Print string   Function 09H

Description:

Another CP/M throwback, function 9 prints a string to the STDOUT device. That sounds like a good idea until you find that the string must end with a dollar sign ($). This means strings containing dollar signs can't be printed with this function. However, it is useful for printing titles and help messages from programs. You shouldn't use this function to print strings the user has input—they could contain dollar signs.

Input:

AH=09H

DS:DX=string

Output:

None

Equivalent C functions:

No direct equivalent.

DOS versions:

All

Input from STDAUX   Function 03H

Description:

   Reads a character from the primary serial device (COM1). Serious serial port work, like terminal emulators, requires more sophisticated methods than DOS provides, so this function is of limited use. Function 03H waits for a character if one is not available.

Input:

   AH=03H

Output:

   AL=input character

Equivalent C functions:

   No direct equivalent.

DOS versions:

   All

Output to STDAUX   Function 04H

Description:

   Output a character to STDAUX (usually COM1).

Input:

   AH=04H
   DL=character

Output:

   None

Equivalent C functions:

   No direct equivalent.

DOS SERVICES

DOS versions:

All

Output to STDPRN   Function 05H

Description:

This function outputs a character to the printer (usually PRN or LPT1).

Input:

AH=05H
DL=character

Output:

None

Equivalent C functions:

No direct equivalent.

DOS versions:

All

Disk Control Operations

Reset disk   Function 0DH

Description:

Flushes all file buffers. Because this call doesn't update the directory, however, it isn't very useful under most circumstances.

Input:

AH=0DH

Output:

None

DOS 5: A DEVELOPER'S GUIDE

Equivalent C functions:

No direct equivalent.

DOS versions:

All

Change current disk   **Function 0EH**

Description:

Changes the current drive. DOS indicates the drive numerically (A=0, B=1, and so on). DOS versions 3.0 and later return the value of the *LASTDRIVE* command in CONFIG.SYS. If no *LASTDRIVE* command appears in CONFIG.SYS, DOS returns the default value (5). In earlier versions of DOS, this call returns the number of logical drives (at least two) available.

Input:

AH=0EH
DL=drive

Output:

AL=number of logical drives

Equivalent C functions:

```
_dos_setdrive()    (Microsoft)
setdisk()          (Borland, Mix)
```

DOS versions:

All

DOS SERVICES

Return current disk   Function 19H

Description:

    The converse of function 0EH, this call returns the current drive using the same notation.

Input:

    AH=19H

Output:

    AL=current disk

Equivalent C functions:

```
_dos_getdrive()    (Microsoft)
getdisk()          (Borland, Mix)
```

DOS versions:

    All

Set DTA address   Function 1AH

Description:

    Changes the DTA address. This is important because the default DTA overlays the command line in the PSP. We will also use this function when programming TSRs.

Input:

    AH=1AH
    DS:DX=new DTA address

Output:

    None

DOS 5: A DEVELOPER'S GUIDE

Equivalent C functions:

setdta() (Borland, Mix)

DOS versions:

All

Return DTA address   **Function 2FH**

Description:

A relative of function 1AH, this call returns the current address of the DTA.

Input:

AH=2FH

Output:

ES:BX=pointer to current DTA

Equivalent C functions:

getdta() (Borland, Mix)

DOS versions:

All

Get disk information   **Function 1BH**

Description:

Returns a variety of data about the current disk. The media ID byte may be one of the following:

F0H = 3.5-inch double-sided, 18 sectors/track or unknown

F8H = fixed disk

F9H = 5.25-inch double-sided, 15 sectors/track, or 3.5-inch double-sided, nine sectors/track

FCH = 5.25-inch single-sided, nine sectors/track

FDH = 5.25-inch double-sided, nine sectors/track

DOS SERVICES

FEH = 5.25-inch double-sided, eight sectors/track

FFH = 5.25-inch double-sided, eight sectors/track

Input:

AH=1BH

Output:

AL=number of sectors/cluster
DS:BX=pointer to copy of media ID byte
CX=number of bytes/sector
DX=number of clusters

Equivalent C functions:

`getfatd()` (Borland, Mix)

DOS versions:

All

Get specified disk information   Function 1CH

Description:

Identical to function 1BH except that it returns information about the drive specified numerically. If the drive specified is 0, DOS uses the default drive. Otherwise, 1 represents drive A, 2 is drive B, and so on.

Input:

AH=1CH
DL=drive number (see above)

Output:

AL=number of sectors/cluster
DS:BX=pointer to copy of media ID byte
CX=number of bytes/sector
DX=number of clusters

Equivalent C functions:

```
getfat()   (Borland, Mix)
```

DOS versions:

All

Return disk free space   **Function 36H**

Description:

Returns most of the information returned by function 1CH but also includes the amount of free space remaining. The only information not included is the media ID byte, which identifies the drive's type.

Input:

AH=36H
DL=drive number (as in function 1CH)

Output:

if drive is invalid
    AX=FFFFH
if drive is valid
    AX=number of sectors/cluster
    BX=number of free clusters
    CX=number of bytes/sector
    DX=total number of clusters on drive

Equivalent C functions:

```
_dos_getdiskfree()   (Microsoft)
getdfree()           (Borland, Mix)
```

DOS versions:

2.0 and above

DOS SERVICES

Set/clear verify flag Function 2EH

Description:

Controls DOS's verify flag. If this flag is set, a disk read follows each disk write to check that the sector is readable. Unfortunately, the data read isn't compared to the data written, so this is of little utility unless you want to slow your disk access by one half.

Input:

AH=2EH
AL=set code (0=off, 1=on)

Output:

None

Equivalent C functions:

`setverify()` (Borland, Mix)

DOS versions:

All

Return verify flag Function 54H

Description:

Reads the state of the verify flag.

Input:

AH=54H

Output:

AL=verify flag (0=off, 1=on)

Equivalent C functions:

`getverify()` (Borland, Mix)

DOS 5: A DEVELOPER'S GUIDE

DOS versions:

2.0 and above

Locate default disk information block **Function 1FH**

Description:

Returns a pointer to a table with detailed information about the current drive. The table contains the following:

Bytes	Description
0	Drive number (0=A, 1=B, etc.)
1	Driver unit number
2–3	Bytes/sector
4	Sectors/cluster-1
5	Cluster to sector shift
6-7	Number of boot sectors
8	Number of file allocation tables (FATs)
9–10	Number of root directory entries
11–12	Sector number of first data sector
13–14	Last cluster number
15	Sectors for FAT
16–17	Sector of root directory
18–21	Address of device header
22	Media ID (see function 1BH)
23	Set to zero if disk has been accessed
24–27	Address of next disk block (or FFFFH if last one)
28–29	Last allocated cluster
30–31	Number of free clusters

DOS SERVICES

Input:

　　AH=1FH

Output:

　　DS:BX=pointer to table

Equivalent C functions:

　　No direct equivalent.

DOS versions:

　　All (undocumented)

Locate disk information block　　　　　　　　　　　　　　**Function 32H**

Description:

　　Identical to function 1FH except that a particular drive may be specified.

Input:

　　AH=32H
　　DL=drive number (0=default, 1=A, 2=B, and so on)

Output:

　　AL=status (0=drive exists, FFH=bad drive number)
　　DS:BX=pointer to table

Equivalent C functions:

　　No direct equivalent.

DOS versions:

　　2.0 and above (undocumented)

Set/get volume information   Function 69H

Description:

Returns the volume information for the specified drive. The data buffer contains the following:

Bytes	Description
0	Reserved
2	Serial number
6	Volume name (11 bytes)
17	FAT string (ASCII characters 'FAT16' or 'FAT12')

If AL=1, the serial number from the buffer is written to the disk.

Input:

AH=69H
AL=subfunction (0=read buffer, 1=write serial number)
DS:DX=pointer to 25-byte buffer

Output:

DS:DX=see above

Equivalent C functions:

No direct equivalent.

DOS versions:

4.0 and above (undocumented)

DOS SERVICES

File Operations

The file operations work with files specified by name. The file name, which may include a drive letter and directories, must be an ASCII string terminated by a zero byte. These strings, known as *path names*, can be a maximum of 66 characters long (67 including the zero byte).

Delete file   Function 41H

Description:

  Delete a file. This call does not accept wildcards.

Input:

  AH=41H
  DS:DX=pointer to path name

Output:

  if carry=1
      AX=error code

Equivalent C functions:

  `unlink(), remove()`

DOS versions:

  2.0 and above

Change file attributes   Function 43H

Description:

  Sets or clears the read-only, hidden, system, and archive bits associated with each file. The file name may not contain wildcards. The attributes byte has the following format:

DOS 5: A DEVELOPER'S GUIDE

7	6	5	4	3	2	1	0	Bit
Not Used	Not Used	Archive	Subdir	Volume	System	Hidden	Read-Only	

Input:

    AH=43H
    AL=subfunction (00H to read attribute, 01 to set attribute)
    DS:DX=pointer to path name
    if AL=01H
        CX=new attribute (CH is always 0)

Output:

    if carry flag set
        AX=error code
    if subfunction 00
        CL=attribute

Equivalent C functions:

```
_dos_setfileattr(), _dos_setfileattr()   (Microsoft)
_chmod()                                 (Borland)
chmod()                                  (Mix)
```

DOS versions:

    All

Find first file   Function 4EH

Description:

Works with function 4FH to find files that match a given file name. The name may contain wildcards. When this function receives a file name (such as A*.*), it returns the first file that matches (if any) and stores special information in the DTA. Remember, the default DTA coincides with the command line in the PSP, so be careful. Either change the DTA address or read the command line before using this function. The DTA contains the following data:

DOS SERVICES

Bytes	Description
0–20	Reserved
21	Attribute
22–23	File time
24–25	File date
26–29	File size
30–42	File name (ends with 0)

The attribute byte uses the same bit pattern used with function 43H. If we specify the volume attribute bit, only files with that bit set are returned. Otherwise, DOS only compares the hidden, system, and subdirectory flags with the attribute specified. In other words, if we search for files with the subdirectory flag set, this function also returns normal files that match the wildcard. An attribute of zero matches only normal files.

The date and time are in this format:

15	14	13	12	11	10	9	8	7	6	5	4	3	2	1	0	Bit
\multicolumn{5}{c}{hours}			\multicolumn{6}{c}{minutes}			\multicolumn{5}{c}{seconds/2}	

15	14	13	12	11	10	9	8	7	6	5	4	3	2	1	0	Bit
\multicolumn{7}{c}{year-1980}			\multicolumn{4}{c}{month}			\multicolumn{5}{c}{day}	

An error code of 12H from this function (or function 4FH) simply indicates that no more files match the wildcard specified.

Input:

  AH=4EH
  CX=attribute
  DS:DX=path name (with wildcards)

99

DOS 5: A DEVELOPER'S GUIDE

Output:

    if carry set
        AX=error code

Equivalent C functions:

```
_dos_findfirst()   (Microsoft)
findfirst()        (Borland)
```

DOS versions:

    2.0 and above

Find next file　　　　　　　　　　　　　　　　　　　　　　　**Function 4FH**

Description:

Once function 4EH has returned the first matching file name, this function returns the subsequent files, one at a time, using the same format. The data that function 4EH leaves in the first 21 bytes of the DTA tells this function which file to return. See the description of function 4EH for the contents of the DTA following a call to this function.

Input:

    AH=4FH

Output:

    if carry set
        AX=error code

Equivalent C functions:

```
_dos_findnext()   (Microsoft)
findnext()        (Borland, Mix)
```

DOS versions:

    2.0 and above

DOS SERVICES

Rename file   Function 56H

Description:

Renames a file. The new file must be on the same disk as the original file. The path name may not contain wildcards.

Input:

AH=56H
DS:DX=pointer to path name
ES:DI=pointer to new path name

Output:

if carry set
    AX=error code

Equivalent C functions:

```
rename()
```

DOS versions:

2.0 and above

Qualify file name   Function 60H

Description:

Resolves a file name into a complete path name. It decodes any references to paths changed by the *SUBST*, *JOIN*, or *ASSIGN* command.

Input:

AH=60H
DS:SI=pointer to path name (ends with 0)
ES:DI=pointer to new path-name buffer

Output:

    if carry set
        AX=error code
    if carry clear
        ES:DI=fully qualified name

Equivalent C functions:

    No direct equivalent.

DOS versions:

    3.0 and above (undocumented)

FCB File Services

Early versions of DOS used file control blocks to control access to files. As subdirectories and other features were added, FCBs became impractical, and DOS added handle I/O functions to support all I/O.

You shouldn't use FCBs in your programs. They cannot operate on files outside the current directory. Programs that use FCBs also pose difficulties when running with networks.

Handle Services

File handles, an idea borrowed from the Unix operating system, provide a consistent way to access files and I/O devices. You can use one of the predefined handles (STDIN, STDOUT, STDERR, STDAUX, or STDPRN) or open new handles to files and devices. DOS returns these handles to your program, and you use them to indicate which file you want to work with when calling DOS.

A file name to handle calls is a series of ASCII bytes ending with a zero. The string can contain up to 66 characters, not including the ending zero byte.

DOS SERVICES

Create a file   Function 3CH

Description:

Create a file and return its handle. When creating a file, you can specify that the file be read-only, hidden, or system, if you desire. If the file name already exists, the new file destroys the old file and takes its place. The attribute byte is identical to the one in function 43H.

Input:

AH=3CH
CX=attributes
DS:DX=pointer to path name

Output:

if carry set
    AX=error code
if carry clear
    AX=file handle

Equivalent C functions:

```
_dos_creat()    (Microsoft)
creat()         (Borland, Mix)
```

DOS versions:

2.0 and above

Create a new file   Function 5BH

Description:

Identical to function 3CH except that this function fails if the file already exists.

Input:

AH=5BH
CX=attribute
DS:DX=pointer to path name

Output:

    if carry set
        AX=error code
    if carry clear
        AX=file handle

Equivalent C functions:

```
_dos_creatnew()   (Microsoft)
creatnew()        (Borland)
```

DOS versions:

    3.0 and above

Open file   Function 3DH

Description:

This call opens an existing file and returns a handle to it. The open-mode byte uses the following format:

7	6	5	4	3	2	1	0	Bit
Inherit flag	\multicolumn{3}{c}{Share mode}	0	\multicolumn{3}{c}{Access mode. 000= read 001=write, 010=r/w}	

Share mode, available in DOS 3.0 and above, sets rules about how a file may be shared on a network. Normal programs set this three-bit field to 0. The inherit flag is also unique to DOS 3.0 and above. If this bit is clear, the file will be open for any new programs started by the current program.

Input:

    AH=3DH
    AL=open mode
    DS:DX=pointer to path name

DOS SERVICES

Output:

> if carry set
> > AX=error code
>
> if carry clear
> > AX=file handle

Equivalent C functions:

```
_dos_open()  (Microsoft)
_open()      (Borland)
```

DOS versions:

> 2.0 and above (3.0 and above for share and inherit flags)

Close file   Function 3EH

Description:

> Closes an open file handle. All processing ends, and DOS writes all buffered data to disk. It's a good idea to close any open file when you're done with it. When your program exits, DOS automatically closes open file handles.

Input:

> AH=3EH
> BX=file handle

Output:

> if carry set
> > AX=error code

Equivalent C functions:

```
_dos_close()  (Microsoft)
_close()      (Borland)
```

DOS versions:

> 2.0 and above

Change file position **Function 42H**

Description:

Similar to the *fseek()* function in the standard C library, this call determines which bytes of a file will be read or written next. You may set the current byte of the file relative to the beginning, end, or current position in the file. The return value is a 32-bit offset relative to the start of the file. You can learn the size of a file by calling function 42H to seek to the end of the file; the return value will equal the file's size. When you open a file, DOS sets the file's position so that the first read or write occurs at the beginning of the file. Each subsequent read or write advances the position by the number of bytes read or written. Using this function, you can alter this default behavior. Notice that the offset can be negative.

Input:

AH=42H
AL=origin of move (0=start of file, 1=current location, 2=end of file)
BX=file handle
CX:DX=offset to move relative to origin (32 bits, signed)

Output:

if carry set
    AX=error code
if carry clear
    DX:AX=new location relative to beginning of file

Equivalent C functions:

```
lseek()
```

DOS versions:

2.0 and above

DOS SERVICES

Read from handle   **Function 3FH**

Description:

Reads bytes from a handle opened for read or read/write access. It returns the number of bytes read, or zero for end of file. If the carry flag is set, an error occurred. With most character input devices (for example, the console), no more than one line of data is returned for each call. In this case, the number of bytes read may be less than requested. For other types of handles, if the number of bytes read does not agree with the number of bytes requested, a problem has occurred. Often, the file simply runs out of bytes (end of file). The carry flag is clear for this type of error.

Input:

AH=3FH
BX=file handle
CX=number of bytes to read
DS:DX=pointer to buffer

Output:

if carry set
    AX=error code
if carry clear
    AX=number of bytes read

Equivalent C functions:

```
_dos_read()  (Microsoft)
_read()      (Borland)
```

DOS versions:

2.0 and above

Write to file handle — Function 40H

Description:

Whereas function 3FH reads from an open handle, this function writes to one. Of course, the handle must be open for write or read/write access. Writing a zero-length buffer to the file will cause it to be truncated to the current position. If the current position is past the end of the file, the file will be extended to the new position instead.

Function 40H returns the number of bytes actually written. If this value is less than the number you asked it to write, an error has occurred even if the carry flag is clear.

Input:

AH=40H
BX=file handle
CX=number of bytes to write
DS:DX=pointer to buffer

Output:

if carry set
    AX=error code
if carry clear
    AX=number of bytes read

Equivalent C functions:

```
_dos_write()    (Microsoft)
_write()        (Borland)
```

DOS versions:

2.0 and above

DOS SERVICES

Duplicate handle   **Function 45H**

Description:

    Duplicates an open handle. The new handle refers to the same file as the original handle. The file's current position is the same for both handles. This is useful if we want to close a handle (so that its information is updated on disk) but continue using the handle: Rather than closing the handle and reopening it, we can simply duplicate the handle and close the duplicate. In DOS 3.3 or later, we could also do this with function 68H (discussed below).

Input:

    AH=45H
    BX=file handle

Output:

    if carry set
        AX=error code
    if carry clear
        AX=new file handle

Equivalent C functions:

```
dup()
```

DOS versions:

    2.0 and above

Redirect file handle   **Function 46H**

Description:

    Similar to function 45H; programs often use both functions together. Function 46H redirects one handle to another. For example, DOS defines handle 1 as STDOUT. What if a program wanted to redirect its output to the printer (handle 4)? This function would close handle 1, then make handle 1 a copy of handle 4. Now all output to STDOUT would go to STDPRN. If the program later

DOS 5: A DEVELOPER'S GUIDE

wanted to restore STDOUT, it should have used function 45H to duplicate STDOUT before it called function 46H. When the time came to restore the old STDOUT handle, it would be a simple matter of redirecting the duplicate handle back to handle 1. The following code shows the operations required:

```
    MOV AH,45H
    MOV BX,1
    INT 21H              ; Duplicate original STDOUT.
    MOV STDOUT_SAVE,AX   ; Save it away.
    MOV CX,4
    MOV AH,46H           ; BX still equals 1 from above.
    INT 21H              ; Redirect STDOUT to STDPRN.
; Program's output now goes to printer.
    .
    .
    .
; Reset STDOUT.
    MOV AH,46H
    MOV BX,STDOUT_SAVE
    MOV CX,1
    INT 21H
```

Input:

    AH=46H
    BX=file handle
    CX=redirected handle

Output:

    if carry set
        AX=error code

Equivalent C functions:

```
dup2()
```

DOS versions:

    2.0 and above

DOS SERVICES

Read/set file's date and time   **Function 57H**

Description:

    With this function, a program can read or modify the date and time DOS associates with each file. Any changes take effect when the file is closed, even if your program writes to the file after using this call.

    DOS uses this format for the time and date:

15	14	13	12	11	10	9	8	7	6	5	4	3	2	1	0	Bit
hours					minutes						seconds/2				

15	14	13	12	11	10	9	8	7	6	5	4	3	2	1	0	Bit
year-1980							month				day				

Input:

    AH=57H
    AL=subfunction (0=read time/date, 1=set time/date)
    BX=file handle
    if subfunction is 1
        CX=new time
        DX=new date

Output:

    if carry set
        AX=error code
    if carry clear and subfunction=0
        CX=file's time
        DX=file's date

Equivalent C functions:

```
_dos_getftime(), _dos_setftime()   (Microsoft)
getftime(), setftime()             (Borland, Mix)
```

DOS versions:

2.0 and above

Create temporary file   **Function 5AH**

Description:

Creates a temporary file in any directory you specify. The string indicating the path to the file should be followed by at least 13 empty bytes. DOS fills these bytes with the file name and returns a handle to the open file. The program that creates a temporary file is responsible for deleting it.

Input:

AH=5AH
CX=attribute (see function 43H)
DS:DX=pointer to drive and path name (end with '\')

Output:

if carry set
    AX=error code
if carry clear
    AX=file handle
    DS:DX=full path name

Equivalent C functions:

`creattemp()` (Borland)

DOS versions:

3.0 and above

DOS SERVICES

Set handle count   Function 67H

Description:

Sets the maximum number of open file handles for the calling process. Each process starts with space for 20 handles. This call does not affect the systemwide limit set by the *FILES* command in CONFIG.SYS.

Input:

AH=67H
BX=number of handles (20-65,535)

Output:

if carry set
    AX=error code

Equivalent C functions:

No direct equivalent.

DOS versions:

3.3 and above

Commit file   Function 68H

Description:

This call effectively closes a handle, though the handle is still available for use after the call. This is a much simpler way to flush the buffers than outlined above for function 45H.

Input:

AH=68H
BX=file handle

Output:

> if carry set
> > AX=error code

Equivalent C functions:

> No direct equivalent.

DOS versions:

> 3.3 and above

Extended file open/create   **Function 6CH**

Description:

> Another call to open or create files. This one gives the programmer much greater control over the operation than the other calls. The attribute is only used when creating a file. The action word's lower eight bits look like this:

7 6 5 4	3 2 1 0	Bit
If file doesn't exist, 0000=fail, 0001=create	If file exists, 0000=fail, 0001=open, 0010=destroy/create	

> The upper eight bits are always zero.
>
> The file can be opened in auto commit mode, in which each write is automatically followed by a commit (see function 68H).

Input:

> AH=6CH
> BL=open code (see function 3DH)
> BH=control word (40H=auto commit, 20H=return critical errors, 60H=both)
> CX=attribute (see function 43H)
> DX=action word (see above)
> ES:SI=pointer to path name

DOS SERVICES

Output:

    if carry set
        AX=error code
    if carry clear
        AX=file handle
        CX=action taken (1=file opened, 2=file created, 3=file destroyed)

Equivalent C functions:

    No direct equivalent.

DOS versions:

    4.0 and above

Directory Operations

Make directory   Function 39H

Description:

    Make a directory.

Input:

    AH=39H
    DS:DX=pointer to path name of directory

Output:

    if carry set
        AX=error code

Equivalent C functions:

    `mkdir()`

DOS versions:

    2.0 and above

Remove directory   Function 3AH

Description:

> Remove a subdirectory. The subdirectory must not contain files and must not be the current working directory. In a network environment, be careful not to remove someone else's working directory.

Input:

> AH=3AH
> DS:DX=pointer to path name of directory

Output:

> if carry set
> > AX=error code

Equivalent C functions:

> `rmdir()`

DOS versions:

> 2.0 and above

Change working directory   Function 3BH

Description:

> Changes the current working directory.

Input:

> AH=3BH
> DS:DX=pointer to path name of directory

Output:

> if carry set
> > AX=error code

Equivalent C functions:

```
chdir()
```

DOS versions:

2.0 and above

Return current working directory **Function 47H**

Description:

Returns the current working directory without the drive letter or the first backslash. The name ends with a zero byte. Since the leading backslash doesn't appear, this function only returns a zero byte if the working directory is the root directory.

Input:

AH=47H
DL=drive (0=current drive, 1=A, 2=B, etc.)
DS:DI=pointer to buffer for directory name

Output:

if carry set
AX=error code
if carry clear
DS:SI=pointer to path name

Equivalent C functions:

```
getcwd()
```

DOS versions:

2.0 and above

Date and Time Operations

Return date   Function 2AH

Description:

    Returns the current date. The year 0 is actually 1980; year 1 is 1981, and so on.

Input:

    AH=2AH

Output:

    AL=day of week (0=SUN, 1=MON, etc.)
    CX=year-1980
    DH=month
    DL=day

Equivalent C functions:

```
_dos_getdate()  (Microsoft)
getdate()       (Borland, Mix)
```

DOS versions:

    All

Set date   Function 2BH

Description:

    Sets the date. On AT computers with later versions of DOS, this call sets not only the DOS date but also the real-time clock, which keeps the time and date (even when the computer is off).

Input:

    AH=2BH
    CX=year-1980
    DH=month
    DL=day

DOS SERVICES

Output:

> if supplied date invalid
> > AL=FFH
>
> if date OK
> > AL=0

Equivalent C functions:

```
_dos_setdate() (Microsoft)
setdate()      (Borland, Mix)
```

DOS versions:

> All

Return time　　　　　　　　　　　　　　　　　　　　　　　　**Function 2CH**

Description:

> Allows programs to read the current time of day. Although DOS returns the time to 1/100th of a second, it is only accurate to about 1/20th of a second.

Input:

> AH=2CH

Output:

> CH=hour
> CL=minutes
> DH=seconds
> DL=1/100th seconds

Equivalent C functions:

```
_dos_gettime() (Microsoft)
gettime()      (Borland, Mix)
```

DOS versions:

> All

Set time   **Function 2DH**

Description:

Sets the time. Like function 2BH, this call sets the AT's real-time clock.

Input:

AH=2DH
CH=hours
CL=minutes
DH=seconds
DL=1/100th seconds

Output:

if supplied time invalid
    AL=FFH
if time OK
    AL=0

Equivalent C functions:

```
_dos_settime()  (Microsoft)
settime()       (Borland, Mix)
```

DOS versions:

All

Process Operations

These functions control the current program and allow one program to load or execute a new program. Functions 00H (exit program) and 26H (create PSP) are obsolete, so don't use them.

DOS SERVICES

Exit program   Function 4CH

Description:

The preferred method of exiting a non-TSR program. This function frees all memory owned by a process, closes file handles, and restores the Control-C and critical error handlers.

Input:

AH=4CH
AL=return code

Output:

None

Equivalent C functions:

```
exit()
```

DOS versions:

2.0 and above

Load or execute another program   Function 4BH

Description:

Function 4BH has four subfunctions. Subfunction 0, the most common, loads and executes another program. Subfunction 1 loads another program and switches the PSP context to that program, then returns to the calling program. Subfunction 3 loads overlays, which are incomplete fragments of a program. Interestingly, few commercial programs use subfunction 3 to manage overlays.

Subfunctions 0, 1, and 3 require a parameter block. This block returns data about the loaded program after a subfunction 1 call. The format of the parameter block is shown in Table 5-2. If the specified environment pointer is 0000H, DOS copies the calling program's environment for the new program.

Before calling subfunction 0 or 1, DOS must have enough memory free to load the program. For .COM programs and most .EXE programs, this entails freeing some of the memory owned by the program.

The new program inherits any handles opened by the parent (except files from DOS 3.0 and later that were opened with the inherit bit set—see function 3DH). Often a program will redirect STDIN and STDOUT, then call a program to perform some task on its behalf.

Programs should not load other programs without using this function. This is especially important for programs running under DOS 5 because it takes some special steps when loading programs. If you must load another program without using one of the above subfunctions under DOS 5, call subfunction 5 of this function with the parameter block shown in Table 5-2. After DOS returns, you must jump directly to the new program without making any further DOS or BIOS calls. In practice, you will rarely, if ever, need to load a program without using one of the other subfunctions.

Programs can use subfunction 0 to execute any program, including COMMAND.COM. Subfunction 1, which DOS doesn't document, is useful for writing debuggers and other special programs.

Input:

AH=4BH
AL=subfunction (0=execute, 1=load program, 3=load overlay, 5=set exec state)
if subfunction 5
    DS:DX=pointer to program's parameter block
if not subfunction 5
    ES:BX=pointer to control block
    DS:DX=pointer to program's (or overlay's) path name

DOS SERVICES

Subfunctions 0 and 1

Offset	Size (Bytes)	Description
00H	2	Segment address of new environment. If 0, the original environment is copied.
02H	4	Far pointer to command line *
06H	4	Far pointer to FCB1
0AH	4	Far pointer to FCB2
0EH	2	Child's SP
10H	2	Child's SS
12H	2	Child's IP
14H	2	Child's CS

Notes: *Command line consists of a count byte, followed by the command's arguments, followed by a carriage return (which is not included in the count). Usually, the first character is a blank.
Subfunction 0 uses offsets 00H-0DH only.
Subfunction 1 returns information in offsets 0EH-15H.

Subfunction 3

Offset	Size (Bytes)	Description
00H	2	Segment address for overlay code
02H	2	Relocation offset. This is usually the same as the segment address unless you plan to load the overlay and then move it somewhere else.

Subfunction 5

Offset	Size (Bytes)	Description
00H	2	Reserved
02H	2	Type flag (1 = Exe, 2 = Overlay)
04H	4	Far pointer to program path name
08H	2	New program's PSP segment
0AH	2	New program's IP
0CH	2	New program's CS
0DH	4	Program size (including PSP)

Table 5-2. INT 21H, function 4BH parameter block.

Output:

> if carry set
> > AX=error code
> if carry clear
> > BX=size of new program (in paragraphs; subfunction 1 only)
> if DOS version 2.X
> > destroys all registers except CS and IP

Equivalent C functions:

> `spawn(), exec()`

DOS versions:

> 2.0 and above (subfunction 5; DOS 5 and above)

Read exit code   **Function 4DH**

Description:

> Returns the exit code of a program run with function 4BH. The exit code is destroyed once the program reads it; you may only call this function once for each call to function 4BH.

Input:

> AH=4DH

Output:

> AH=exit type (0=normal, 1=Control-Break, 2=critical error, 3=TSR)
> AL=return code

Equivalent C functions:

> No direct equivalent.

DOS versions:

> 2.0 and above

DOS SERVICES

Terminate and stay resident   Function 31H

Description:

Instead of INT 27H, programs should use this call to exit as a TSR. We will examine this call in much greater detail when we study TSR programming.

Input:

AH=31H
AL=return code
DX=number of paragraphs to remain resident

Output:

None

Equivalent C functions:

```
_dos_keep()  (Microsoft)
keep()       (Borland, Mix)
```

DOS versions:

2.0 and above

Return PSP address   Function 51H/62H

Description:

Returns the current PSP address. This is often handy, particularly for TSR programming. (See function 5D06H for information on using function 51H with DOS 2.0.)

Input:

AH=62H or AH=51H

Output:

BX=current PSP segment

125

Equivalent C functions:

`getpsp()`, `getpid()` (Borland, Mix)

DOS versions:

3.0 and above (function 51H, DOS 2.0 and above—undocumented)

Set PSP address   **Function 50H**

Description:

Tells DOS to use a new PSP. This is valuable for TSR programming. (See function 5D06H for information on using function 50H with DOS 2.0.)

Input:

AH=50H
BX=new PSP

Output:

None

Equivalent C functions:

No direct equivalent.

DOS versions:

2.0 and above (undocumented)

Memory Operations

These calls control DOS's memory management. Most .EXE programs and all .COM programs ask DOS for all available memory when they load. If the program then wishes to start another program, it must release some of its memory. Remember that DOS only allocates conventional memory. Memory-allocation functions always deal with 16-byte chunks (paragraphs).

DOS SERVICES

Allocate memory Function 48H

Description:

Programs can use function 48H to allocate memory from DOS. A request for FFFFH paragraphs will always fail but will return the number of paragraphs available.

Input:

AH=48H
BX=number of paragraphs to allocate

Output:

if carry set
AX=error code
BX=size of largest free block (in paragraphs)
if carry clear
AX=segment address of allocated block

Equivalent C functions:

```
_dos_allocmem()    (Microsoft)
allocmem()         (Borland, Mix)
```

DOS versions:

2.0 and above

Free memory Function 49H

Description:

Frees memory allocated using function 48H. Since DOS allocates the environment block using that function, TSR programs commonly use function 49H to release the block.

Input:

> AH=49H
> ES=segment address of block

Output:

> if carry set
>   AX=error code

Equivalent C functions:

> `_dos_freemem()` (Microsoft)
> `freemem()`   (Borland, Mix)

DOS versions:

> 2.0 and above

Resize block   **Function 4AH**

Description:

> Changes the size of an existing block of memory. This is especially useful when a program owns all memory but later wants to return some of it. A program's memory block begins with its PSP, and that block can be resized to reflect the actual memory usage. Of course, the block can also grow if memory is available. If you shrink a program's memory allocation, make sure the stack is inside the new block of memory. This is especially troublesome with .COM programs, so be careful.

Input:

> AH=4AH
> BX=new number of paragraphs
> ES=segment address of block

Output:

> if carry set
> AX=error code
> BX=maximum possible size of block

Equivalent C functions:

```
_dos_setblock()    (Microsoft)
setblock()         (Borland, Mix)
```

DOS versions:

> 2.0 and above

Control memory allocation strategy   **Function 58H**

Description:

> Controls the way DOS searches for free memory. With the default first-fit strategy, DOS allocates memory from the first block it finds that is big enough. The last-fit strategy works the same way, but it begins at the top of memory and works its way down. The best-fit method uses the block that is closest in size to the memory request. Very few application programs require control over the allocation strategy.
>
> With DOS 5, this call also controls the allocation of UMBs, the memory between 640 Kbytes and 1 Mbyte. If bit 7 of the strategy code is on, DOS loads programs into UMBs first. Since some older programs may not work correctly with UMBs, DOS usually ends the DOS memory chain at the 640-Kbyte boundary. Using subfunctions 2 and 3, a program can add the UMBs to the DOS memory chain. DOS calls then allocate UMBs if they are present. If your programs alter the UMB state with this call, return it to its original setting before relinquishing control.
>
> UMBs are only available if you specify the *,UMB* option on the *DOS=* line in the CONFIG.SYS file. If you omit this option, any attempt to link the UMBs or load high will return an error code.

Input:

AH=58H

AL=subfunction (0=read strategy, 1=set strategy, 2=get UMB state, 3=set UMB state)

BX=strategy code (if AL=1: 0=first fit, 1=best fit, 2=last fit; if bit 7 set, load UMBs first; if bit 6 set, search only UMBs) (if AL=3: 0=unlink UMBs, 1=link UMBs)

Output:

if carry set
    AX=error code
if carry clear and subfunction = 0
    AX=strategy code
if carry clear and subfunction = 2
    AL=link code (1=linked)

Equivalent C functions:

No direct equivalent.

DOS versions:

3.0 and above (undocumented)

IOCTL Operations

The IOCTL functions communicate directly with device drivers. They all have a function code of 44H. The function numbers referred to below in boldface type are actually subfunction numbers placed in AL. The Borland and Mix libraries have an *ioctl()* function to call these routines.

Some of the information sent and received via IOCTL channels depends on the device and is not covered here. The double-byte character support added in DOS version 4.0 is also omitted. The more useful calls appear below.

DOS SERVICES

Get device information **Subfunction 00H**

Description:

Returns a word containing information about files or devices. If bit 7 is set, the handle refers to a device. Otherwise, the handle maps to a file. The word returned has one of the following formats:

File information word

15 14 13 12 11 10 9 8	7	6	5 4 3 2 1 0	Bit
reserved	0	D	Drive code	

D is set if file has been written to
Drive code is 0 for drive A, 1 for drive B, etc.

Device information word

15	14	13 12 11 10 9 8	7	6	5	4	3	2	1	0	Bit
XX	II	reserved	1	EOF	R	XX	CK	NL	SO	SI	

XX is reserved
II is 1 if device supports IOCTL read and write control data function
EOF is 0 if input device is at end of file
R is 1 if device is in raw mode (in other words, no special action taken on
    ^C, ^S, ^P, ^Z, carriage return)
CK is 1 if device is the clock device
NL is 1 if device is the NUL device
SO is 1 if device is the STDOUT device
SI is 1 if device is the STDIN device

Input:

AH=44H
AL=00H
BX=file handle

Output:

    if carry set
        AX=error code
    if carry clear
        DX=information word

Equivalent C functions:

    No direct equivalent.

DOS versions:

    2.0 and above

Set device information   **Subfunction 01H**

Description:

    Sets bits in the device information word (see subfunction 00H). This call does not apply to handles that refer to files. The word in DX duplicates the word returned by subfunction 00H for devices and only uses bits 0 through 7.

Input:

    AH=44H
    AL=01H
    BX=file handle
    DX=information word

Output:

    if carry set
        AX=error code

Equivalent C functions:

    No direct equivalent.

DOS versions:

    2.0 and above

DOS SERVICES

Check input status Subfunction 06H

Description:

Determines whether a handle is ready for input. A file is ready if it is not at EOF.

Input:

AH=44H
AL=06H
BX=file handle

Output:

if carry set
AX=error code
if carry clear
AL=status (0=not ready, FFH=ready)

Equivalent C functions:

No direct equivalent.

DOS versions:

2.0 and above

Check output status Subfunction 07H

Description:

Determines whether a handle is ready for output. Files never fail this test.

Input:

AH=44H
AL=07H
BX=file handle

DOS 5: A DEVELOPER'S GUIDE

Output:

>if carry set
>>AX=error code
>
>if carry clear
>>AL=status (0=not ready, FFH=ready)

Equivalent C functions:

>No direct equivalent.

DOS versions:

>2.0 and above

Check for removable block device   **Subfunction 08H**

Description:

>Determines whether a block device (a floppy disk, for example) is removable.

Input:

>AH=44H
>AL=08H
>BL=drive number (0=default, 1=A, 2=B, etc.)

Output:

>if carry set
>>AX=error code
>
>if carry clear
>>AL=status (0=removable, 1=not removable)

Equivalent C functions:

>No direct equivalent.

DOS versions:

>3.0 and above

DOS SERVICES

Check for remote block device   **Subfunction 09H**

Description:

   Determines whether a block device (a network drive, for instance) is remote.

Input:

   AH=44H
   AL=09H
   BL=drive number (0=default, 1=A, 2=B, etc.)

Output:

   if carry set
       AX=error code
   if carry clear
       DX=device attribute word (bit 12 is set if device is remote)

Equivalent C functions:

   No direct equivalent.

DOS versions:

   3.1 and above

Check for remote file handle   **Subfunction 0AH**

Description:

   Determines whether a handle refers to a network file or device.

Input:

   AH=44H
   AL=0AH
   BX=file handle

Output:

> if carry set
> > AX=error code
>
> if carry clear
> > DX=attribute word (bit 15 is set if remote)

Equivalent C functions:

> No direct equivalent.

DOS versions:

> 3.1 and above

Miscellaneous Operations

Set interrupt vector   Function 25H

Description:

> Sets the specified interrupt vector. This is easier than modifying the interrupt table directly. In addition, some multitasking DOS extensions won't work if you directly modify the interrupt vectors. These extensions will correctly handle a call to this function.

Input:

> AH=25H
> AL=interrupt number
> DS:DX=address of ISR

Output:

> None

Equivalent C functions:

```
_dos_setvect()  (Microsoft)
setvect()       (Borland, Mix)
```

DOS SERVICES

DOS versions:

All

Return interrupt vector   **Function 35H**

Description:

Returns the address of the ISR for the specified interrupt. See function 25H for a discussion of why this may be preferable to modifying the interrupt table directly.

Input:

AH=35H
AL=interrupt number

Output:

ES:BX=address of ISR

Equivalent C functions:

```
_dos_getvect()  (Microsoft)
getvect()       (Borland, Mix)
```

DOS versions:

2.0 and above

Return DOS version number   **Function 30H**

Description:

Returns the major and minor version numbers for the running copy of DOS. For example, DOS 3.1 has a major version of *3* and a minor version of *1*. All versions before version 2.0 return a major version number of *0* and no minor version number.

Starting with DOS 5, the value this function returns may not reflect the actual version number. The *SETVER* command can be used to force DOS to report a different version number to a specific program. (See function 33H to locate the actual version number.)

Input:

AH=30H
AL=subfunction (0=get OEM number, 1=get version flag; DOS 5 only)

Output:

AL=major version number
AH=minor version number
BL:CX=optional serial number
if subfunction=0
    BH=OEM number
if subfunction=1
    BH=version flag (if DOS in ROM BH=8; otherwise BH=0)

Equivalent C functions:

No direct equivalent, but C stores these values in two global variables: *_osmajor* and *_osminor*.

DOS versions:

All (1.x doesn't return useful values)

Control break flag/return boot disk   Function 33H

Description:

In DOS versions below 4.0, returns or changes the DOS break flag. If the flag is clear, DOS only checks for Control-C or Control-Break when executing functions 01H through 0CH. If the flag is set, DOS checks for break characters during any I/O. This flag is global in scope—it affects all programs in the system. DOS does not restore it when a program exits.

DOS SERVICES

In DOS 4.0 and above, subfunction 5 returns a number corresponding to the drive from which the system was booted. This code is usually 1 (drive A) or 3 (drive C).

DOS 5 uses subfunction 6 to return the actual DOS version number (without regard to *SETVER*—see function 30H).

Input:

AH=33H
AL=subfunction (0=read, 1=set, 5=read boot drive, 6=read version information)
DL=flag (if subfunction=1: 0=off, 1=on)

Output:

if subfunction=0 or 1
    DL=flag
if subfunction=5
    DL=drive code (1=A, 2=B, etc.)
if subfunction=6
    BL=major version number
    BH=minor version number
    DL=revision number (0–7)
    DH=version flag (if 0BH then DOS in ROM; if 10H then DOS in HMA)

Equivalent C functions:

setcbrk(), getcbrk() (Borland, Mix)

DOS versions:

2.0 and above

Get extended error information　　　　　　　　　　　　　　　　　**Function 59H**

Description:

Returns more detailed information about an error that occurred from another INT 21 function. It destroys the CL, DX, SI, BP, and DS registers in addition to the output registers. ES and DI may be destroyed even if DOS doesn't use them for output. This service is useful primarily in critical error handlers (see Chapter 9).

Input:

AH=59H
BX=version code (0 for DOS 3.0-compatible information)

Output:

AX=extended error code (see Table 5-1)
BH=error class (see Table 5-3)
BL=action suggested (see Table 5-4)
CH=error location (see Table 5-5)
if AX=22H
　　ES:DI=pointer to volume name

Equivalent C functions:

```
dosexterr()
```

DOS versions:

3.0 and above

DOS SERVICES

Value in BH	Description of Class
01H	Out of a resource
02H	Temporary situation
03H	Authorization problem
04H	Internal error in system software
05H	Hardware failure
06H	System software failure
07H	Application program failure
08H	Item not found
09H	Invalid format or type
0AH	Interlocked item
0BH	Media problem
0CH	Already exists
0DH	Unknown

Table 5-3. Error classes.

Value in BL	Description of Suggested Action
01H	Retry, then prompt user
02H	Retry after a brief pause
03H	If user entered item, prompt for it again
04H	Terminate after closing files
05H	Terminate immediately; don't close files
06H	No action; error was informational only
07H	Prompt the user to perform an action (e.g., change disk)

Table 5-4. Suggested actions.

Value in CH	Probable Location of Error
01H	Unknown to DOS
02H	Random access device
03H	Network
04H	Character device
05H	Memory

Table 5-5. Error locations.

141

Set extended error information   **Function 5D0AH**

Description:

Sets extended error information for function 59H. This undocumented call is useful for writing TSRs; the TSR must save the error information and restore it when it's done. This function has other obscure subfunctions that COMMAND.COM uses internally. The data area has the following format:

Byte address	Contents
0	AX
2	BX
4	CX
6	DX
8	SI
10	DI
12	DS
14	ES
15	0
.	.
.	.
.	.
20	0

Input:

    AX=5D0AH

    DS:DX=pointer to 22-byte data area

Output:

    None (may destroy CX and DX)

Equivalent C functions:

    No direct equivalent.

DOS SERVICES

DOS versions:

3.1 and above (undocumented)

Locate critical error flag   Function 5D06H

Description:

Locates the critical error flag. If you set this flag under DOS 2.X, functions 50H and 51H use a different stack from the one they normally use. This allows TSRs to call them. If you don't write TSRs for DOS 2, you probably don't need this flag. Setting it also allows TSRs to call DOS functions 0CH and below.

Input:

AX=5D06H

Output:

DS:SI=pointer to critical error flag

Equivalent C functions:

No direct equivalent.

DOS versions:

2.0 and above (undocumented)

Return busy flag   Function 34H

Description:

Returns a pointer to a flag that is nonzero when it is not safe to use DOS. However, it is safe to call DOS when it executes INT 28H even if the busy flag is set. TSR programs use this function extensively.

Input:

AH=34H

Output:

> ES:BX=pointer to busy flag

Equivalent C functions:

> No direct equivalent.

DOS versions:

> 2.0 and above

Control switch character   **Function 37H**

Description:

> Controls the DOS switch character, which introduces options to DOS commands. The default character is '/' (as in *DIR* /w /p).

Input:

> AH=37H
> AL=subfunction (0=read, 1=set)
> DL=switch character (if subfunction 1)

Output:

> if error
>   AL=0FFH
> if no error
>   DL=switch character

Equivalent C functions:

> No direct equivalent.

DOS versions:

> 2.X, 3.X (undocumented in some versions). DOS 4.0 and 5 support this function, but it has no effect.

DOS SERVICES

Get DOS internal information   **Function 52H**

Description:

Returns a pointer to the second entry of a table containing internal DOS information. This data differs slightly between versions 2.X and 3.X of DOS. The table below is for DOS 3.X; the data in locations 16 and beyond is not the same for DOS 2.X. While none of this data is very useful, the word immediately preceding the table is the segment address of the first memory block (a very useful thing to know).

Input:

AH=52H

Output:

ES:BX=table address (subtract two to find segment of first block)

Equivalent C functions:

No direct equivalent.

DOS versions:

2.0 and above

Other DOS Interrupts

So far we have examined INT 21H. As we learned in Chapter 2, DOS uses other interrupts as well. That chapter describes INTs 20H, 22H, and 23H, so they aren't included here.

Critical error interrupt   **INT 24H**

Description:

DOS issues this interrupt in the event of a critical error. The interrupt handler receives a status byte in the following format:

7	6	5	4	3	2	1	0	Bit
0=disk 1=other	unused	Ignore allowed	Retry allowed	Fail allowed	00=DOS, 01=FAT, 10=DIR, 11=Data		0=read 1=write	
Error location		Allowed responses			Area affected		Attempted operation	

A program should never issue INT 24H. However, programs can revector this interrupt to a routine to handle the critical error in special ways. An error code occupies the lower half of DI. DOS does not define the upper portion. (See Chapter 9 for additional details regarding error codes.)

Input:

AH=status

BP:SI=pointer to device header of driver

DI=error code

Output:

AL=return code (0=ignore, 1=retry, 2=abort, 3=fail)

Equivalent C functions:

No direct equivalent.

DOS versions:

2.0 and above

Absolute disk read　　　　　　　　　　　　　　　　　　　　　　　　**INT 25H**

Description:

Reads an absolute disk sector via DOS. This call has two forms: one works with all versions of DOS for files that contain less than 32 Mbytes; another, for version 4.0 and above, can work with files larger than 32 Mbytes.

Both forms of this interrupt leave the original flags on the stack. This value must be removed from the stack after the interrupt completes. If you don't want to restore the flags, you may discard them by adding two to the stack pointer.

DOS SERVICES

If a program attempts to access a large disk partition using the first form, the function returns 0207H as the error code in AX. The second form requires a parameter block of the following format:

Bytes	Description
0–3	Beginning sector
4–5	Number of sectors
6–9	Pointer to data buffer

Input:

    AL=drive number (0=A, 1=B, etc.)
    if first form (<32 Mbytes)
        DS:BX=pointer to buffer for data
        CX=number of sectors to read
        DX=beginning sector
    if second form (>32 Mbytes)
        DS:BX=pointer to parameter block
        CX=-1

Output:

    if carry set
        AL=error code (see Table 5-6)
        AH=error cause (see Table 5-7)

Equivalent C functions:

    No direct equivalent.

DOS versions:

    All

Error Code	Description
00H	Disk is write-protected
01H	Invalid drive number
02H	Drive not ready
04H	CRC error
06H	Seek error
07H	Unknown disk format
08H	Sector not found
0AH	Write error
0BH	Read error
0CH	General error
0FH	Invalid disk change

Table 5-6. Critical error codes.

Error Code	Description
02H	Bad sector ID
03H	Write-protected
04H	Bad sector
08H	DMA failure
10H	Bad CRC
20H	Bad controller
40H	Bad seek
80H	Time-out

Table 5-7. Disk read/write error codes.

Absolute disk write INT 26H

Description:

Writes an absolute disk sector via DOS. This call has two forms: One works with all versions of DOS for files that contain less than 32 Mbytes; another, for version 4.0 and above, can work with files larger than 32 Mbytes. The second form takes a parameter block identical to the one used by INT 25H.

Both forms of this interrupt leave the original flags on the stack. This value must be removed from the stack after the interrupt completes. If you don't want to restore the flags, you may discard them by adding two to the stack pointer.

DOS SERVICES

Input:

    AL=drive number (0=A, 1=B, etc.)
    if first form (<32 Mbytes)
        DS:BX=pointer to data buffer
        CX=number of sectors to write
        DX=beginning sector
    if second form (>32 Mbytes)
        DS:BX=pointer to parameter block
        CX=-1

Output:

    if carry set
        AL=error code (see Table 5-6)
        AH=error cause (see Table 5-7)

Equivalent C functions:

    No direct equivalent.

DOS versions:

    All

Terminate and stay resident   **INT 27H**

Description:

    This is an obsolete call used in TSR programs. Use INT 21H, function 31H, instead.

Input:

    CS=PSP address
    DX=first nonresident segment address

Output:

    None

Equivalent C functions:

No direct equivalent.

DOS versions:

All

DOS safe interrupt   **INT 28H**

Description:

Your programs normally won't call this interrupt, but TSR programs will often intercept it. When DOS issues an INT 28H, it is safe to use DOS functions even if the busy flag is set (see INT 21H, function 34H). If you write TSR programs, they should issue INT 28H when they are active but idle.

Input:

None

Output:

None

Equivalent C functions:

No direct equivalent.

DOS versions:

All (undocumented)

Favored driver output   **INT 29H**

Description:

This interrupt must be supplied by console output drivers. It allows DOS to write characters to the console quickly. You can also output characters using this interrupt. Warning: These characters go directly to the console—redirection and other DOS features don't apply.

DOS SERVICES

Input:

AL=character

Output:

None

Equivalent C functions:

No direct equivalent.

DOS versions:

All (undocumented)

COMMAND.COM back door   INT 2EH

Description:

This interrupt causes COMMAND.COM to execute a string as if it were typed at the DOS prompt. This can be useful, but many COMMAND.COM replacements don't support it. For this reason, it shouldn't be used in commercial software. Programs that own all memory must release some before executing this interrupt.

The command line's first byte is its total length. The command string follows, ending with a carriage return (0DH) that counts when determining the length. You can't depend on this interrupt to preserve any registers, not even SS:SP.

Input:

DS:SI=command string

Output:

None

Equivalent C functions:

No direct equivalent.

DOS versions:

All (undocumented)

Multiplex interrupt (idle signal) INT 2FH

Description:

> DOS uses the multiplex interrupt for a variety of purposes. Its primary function is to communicate with TSR programs (PRINT, for example). It can also be used to signal a variety of conditions. We'll talk about this interrupt in great detail in the chapter on TSR programming.
>
> Sometimes it's useful to know when an application isn't busy. Microsoft Windows 3.0, for example, can time-slice in enhanced mode. If the program is waiting for some slow event (like a keystroke), it may be advantageous to signal Windows that the program doesn't need many time slices at the moment. In addition, DOS 5 can provide power management to extend the life of laptop batteries, an easier task if it knows when a program is idle.
>
> Starting with DOS 5, a multiplex interrupt function is available to inform DOS that the program is in a wait loop. Typically, a program checks for some event (perhaps a keystroke). If the test succeeds, the program proceeds. If it fails, the program issues this interrupt function. When the interrupt returns, the process repeats. Windows-specific applications should not issue this interrupt; that environment can tell when a Windows application is idle.

Input:

> AX=1680H

Output:

> if function supported
>   AL=0
> if function not supported
>   AL=80H

Equivalent C functions:

> No direct equivalent.

DOS versions:

> 5.0 and above (the multiplex interrupt is available starting with DOS 3.0)

CHAPTER 6

ROM BIOS Services

Programs communicate with the BIOS primarily through software interrupts, much like the DOS services. The BIOS also makes certain variables available to programs. This chapter covers the most common BIOS calls and the most useful BIOS variables.

The Video Services

INT 10H provides all BIOS video services. Many video adapters have their own BIOS chips on the video card; these BIOS chips replace or supplement the default INT 10H services. This section covers only the BIOS functions that work with all IBM video adapters. The chapter on graphics programming in Part 2 will touch on some of the more specialized functions.

Set video mode   **Function 00H**

Description:

> Sets the video mode. Color cards generally use mode 2 or 3 to display text, while monochrome cards use mode 7 (see Table 6-1). When the BIOS sets the mode, it also clears the screen. On ATs, PS/2s, and any machine with an EGA or VGA installed, adding 128 to the mode's number will prevent the screen from clearing.

DOS 5: A DEVELOPER'S GUIDE

Mode Number	Type	Maximum Colors	Text Format	Graphics Format	Maximum Pages	Buffer Segment
00H	Text	6	40X25	---	8	B800H
01H	Text	16	40X25	---	8	B800H
02H	Text	16	80X25	---	4^a $8^{b,c}$	B800H
03H	Text	16	80X25	---	4^a $8^{b,c}$	B800H
04H	Graphics	4	40X25	320X200	1	B800H
05H	Graphics	4	40X25	320X200	1	B800H
06H	Graphics	2	80X25	640X200	1	B800H
07H	Text	Mono	80X25	---	1^d 8^c	B000H
0DH	Graphics	16	40X25	320X200	8	A000H
0EH	Graphics	16	80X25	640X200	4	A000H
0FH	Graphics	Mono	80X25	640X350	2	A000H
10H	Graphics	16	80X25	640X350	2	A000H
11H	Graphics	2	80X25	640X480	1	A000H
12H	Graphics	16	80X25	640X480	1	A000H
13H	Graphics	256	40X25	320X200	1	A000H

Notes: [a] CGA
       [b] EGA
       [c] VGA
       [d] MDA

Table 6-1. Display modes.

Input:

    AH=00H

    AL=mode (see Table 6-1)

Output:

    None

Equivalent C functions:

```
_setvideomode()    (Microsoft)
_setgraphmode()    (Borland)
_setvmode()        (Mix)
```

ROM BIOS SERVICES

Set cursor   **Function 01H**

Description:

Sets the text-mode cursor size. By default, the BIOS sets the start line at 6 and the ending line at 7 for color adapters. The monochrome cards use 11 and 12. Setting CX to 2020H will cause most adapters to hide the cursor.

Input:

AH=01H
CH=cursor's starting line
CL=cursor's ending line

Output:

None

Equivalent C functions:

```
_setcursortype()                              (Borland)
curson(), cursoff(), cursblk(), curslin()     (Mix)
```

Move cursor   **Function 02H**

Description:

Moves the text cursor on the specified page. Each video page has a separate cursor that moves independently of the others. The BIOS considers the top left corner of the screen to be row 0, column 0. Moving the cursor to a position that is off the screen causes the cursor to disappear. Table 6-1 shows the screen size for each mode.

Input:

AH=02H
BH=page
DH=row
DL=column

155

DOS 5: A DEVELOPER'S GUIDE

Output:

None

Equivalent C functions:

```
_settextposition()    (Microsoft)
gotoxy()              (Borland)
poscurs()             (Mix)
```

Read cursor   Function 03H

Description:

Returns the text cursor's position and size for the specified page.

Input:

AH=03H
BH=page

Output:

CH=cursor's start line
CL=cursor's end line
DH=row
DL=column

Equivalent C functions:

```
_gettextposition()    (Microsoft)
wherex(), wherey()    (Borland)
curscol(), cursrow()  (Mix)
```

Set current page   Function 05H

Description:

Selects the page to display. This does not disturb other pages in any way. Using other BIOS functions, a program can write text to any page regardless of which one is current. See Table 6-1 to determine how many pages each mode supports.

Input:

>AH=05H
>AL=page

Output:

>None

Equivalent C functions:

```
_setvisualpage()   (Microsoft)
setvisualpage()    (Borland)
setvpage()         (Mix)
```

Scroll window up   **Function 06H**

Description:

> Scrolls a specified screen region up a specified number of lines. All text in the window moves up. The BIOS discards lines that would move above the window and fills the area at the bottom of the window with blanks. If the number of lines is zero or is greater than the height of the window, the BIOS clears the entire window.

Input:

>AH=06H
>AL=number of lines (or 0 to clear)
>BH=attribute for blanks
>CH=window's upper left row
>CL=window's upper left column
>DH=window's lower right row
>DL=window's lower right column

Output:

>None

Equivalent C functions:

No direct equivalent.

Scroll window down   Function 07H

Description:

Identical to function 06H except that the text moves down in the window, leaving a blank space at the top.

Input:

AH=07H
AL=number of lines (or 0 to clear)
BH=attribute for blanks
CH=window's upper left row
CL=window's upper left column
DH=window's lower right row
DL=window's lower right column

Output:

None

Equivalent C functions:

No direct equivalent.

Read character at cursor   Function 08H

Description:

Returns the character and attribute at the current cursor position on the specified page.

Input:

AH=08H
BH=page

ROM BIOS SERVICES

Output:

    AH=attribute
    AL=ASCII character

Equivalent C functions:

```
gettext()            (Borland)
readch(), readattr() (Mix)
```

Write character and attribute   Function 09H

Description:

Writes one or more characters to the screen, starting at the cursor position on the specified page. An attribute for text mode or a color for graphics mode controls the appearance of the character. This function does not recognize control codes, nor does the cursor move after this function is called. In graphics mode, be careful not to write more characters than the line can hold; overwriting the end of the line won't work and may corrupt your display. Another graphics-mode quirk: setting bit 7 of the color value will cause the pixels to be exclusive *OR*ed with the current colors on the screen.

Input:

    AH=09H
    AL=character
    BH=page (background color for mode 13H)
    BL=attribute (text mode) or color (graphic mode)
    CX=repeat count

Output:

    None

Equivalent C functions:

```
writechs() (Mix)
```

DOS 5: A DEVELOPER'S GUIDE

Write character   Function 0AH

Description:

Identical to function 09H except that it uses the existing screen color in text mode. In graphics mode, it is identical to function 09H.

Input:

AH=0AH
AL=character
BH=page (background color for mode 13H)
BL=color (graphics modes only)
CX=repeat count

Output:

None

Equivalent C functions:

`writech()` (Mix)

Write pixel   Function 0CH

Description:

Draws a pixel (dot) at the specified graphic location. If the color value has bit 7 set, it is exclusive *OR*ed with the current color at that location.

Input:

AH=0CH
BH=page
DX=row
CX=column

Output:

None

ROM BIOS SERVICES

Equivalent C functions:

    `_setpixel()` (Microsoft)
    `putpixel()` (Borland)
    `setpixel()` (Mix)

Read pixel   **Function 0DH**

Description:

Returns the color of the specified pixel.

Input:

AH=0DH
BH=page
CX=column
DX=row

Output:

AL=pixel's color

Equivalent C functions:

    `_getpixel()` (Microsoft)
    `getpixel()` (Borland, Mix)

Write Teletype Character   **Function 0EH**

Description:

Writes a single character to the specified video page. Unlike the other video output functions, this one recognizes the bell (07H), backspace (08H), line-feed (0AH), and carriage-return (0DH) characters and acts on them accordingly. The service updates the cursor's position. It does not, however, support color in text modes—the character appears in whatever color was at that position.

Input:

AH=0EH
AL=character
BH=page
BL=color (graphics modes only)

Output:

None

Equivalent C functions:

putch() (Borland)

Return video information   **Function 0FH**

Description:

Returns the current video mode, page, and number of text columns available.

Input:

AH=0FH

Output:

AH=number of text columns
AL=display mode (see function 00H above)
BH=current page

Equivalent C functions:

_getvideoconfig() (Microsoft)
getvconfig()   (Mix)

ROM BIOS SERVICES

The Equipment Configuration Service

Description:

INT 11H returns a word in the AX register reporting the hardware found by the BIOS start-up routines.

Input:

None

Output:

AX=configuration word
- Bits 15-14=number of printer adapters installed
- Bit 12=1 if game port installed
- Bits 11-9=number of serial ports found
- Bits 7-6=number of floppies - 1
- Bits 5-4=initial mode: 1=40-column color, 2=80-column color, 3=80 column monochrome
- Bit 2=1 if pointing device installed (PS/2 only)
- Bit 1=1 if coprocessor installed
- Bit 0=1 if any floppies installed

Equivalent C functions:

```
_bios_equiplist()  (Microsoft)
biosequip()        (Borland, Mix)
```

Reading the Size of Conventional Memory

Description:

INT 12H returns the size of conventional memory (in Kbytes) in the AX register.

Input:

None

Output:

AX=memory size

Equivalent C functions:

`_bios_memsize()` (Microsoft)

The Disk Services

INT 13H supplies all the BIOS disk services. These provide facilities for reading and writing disks at the sector level. They also have extensive support for formatting disks. However, the methods used to format disks vary widely from the XT to the AT to the PS/2. Only the functions you can count on having available on all machines are covered in this section. Be careful when experimenting with these services—one wrong move can ruin your whole disk, to say nothing of your day.

The BIOS disk services take a disk number. The first floppy disk is drive 0, the second is drive 1, and so on. The hard disk drives start at 80H and go up from there.

None of the BIOS disk services wait for the floppy drives to spin up. When a program encounters an error on a floppy disk, IBM recommends that it reset the controller (see below) and try again. If the operation fails three times in a row, it is safe to assume this is a real error.

The programmer specifies the function code as an argument to the call.

Reset disk controller   **Function 00H**

Description:

Resets the floppy controller or the hard and floppy controllers. Programs usually call this function after a disk operation fails. Resetting a particular drive resets its controller, along with all the drives attached to that controller. Resetting a hard disk controller also resets the floppy controller. Table 6-2 shows the possible errors returned.

ROM BIOS SERVICES

Error Code	Meaning
00H	No error
01H	Invalid command
02H	Address mark not found
03H	Write-protected*
04H	Sector not found
05H	Reset error**
06H	Floppy removed*
07H	Invalid parameter table**
08H	DMA overrun*
09H	DMA > 64K
0AH	Bad sector flag**
0BH	Bad track**
0CH	Invalid media type*
0DH	Invalid number of sectors on format**
0EH	Control data address mark detected**
0FH	Out-of-range DMA arbitration level**
10H	Invalid CRC or ECC error
11H	ECC corrected data error**
20H	Controller failure
40H	Seek failed
80H	Time-out
AAH	Drive not ready**
BBH	Unknown error**
CCH	Write fault**
E0H	Status register error**
FFH	Sense operation failed**

* Floppy disk only
**Hard disk only

Table 6-2. BIOS disk errors.

Input:

AH=00
DL=drive number 00H-7FH (floppy), 80H-FFH (hard)

165

DOS 5: A DEVELOPER'S GUIDE

Output:

   if carry=1
      AH=error code
   if carry=0
      AH=00H

Equivalent C functions:

   No direct equivalent.

Reset hard disk　　　　　　　　　　　　　　　　　　　**Function 0DH**

Description:

   Identical to function 00H except that this function does not affect the floppy controller.

Input:

   AH=0DH
   DL=drive number 80H-FFH

Output:

   if carry=1
      AH=error code
   if carry=0
      AH=00H

Equivalent C functions:

   No direct equivalent.

Report disk status　　　　　　　　　　　　　　　　　　**Function 01H**

Description:

   Returns the status of the most recent disk operation for the specified drive. Table 6-2 shows the possible errors returned.

ROM BIOS SERVICES

Input:

    AH=01H
    DL=drive

Output:

    AH=00H
    AL=status code (see Table 6-2)

Equivalent C functions:

    No direct equivalent.

Read sectors   **Function 02H**

Description:

    Reads a given number of sequential sectors from the specified side of a track. On hard disks, the program must store the top two bits of the 10-bit track number in the top two bits of CL. The remaining six bits of CL hold the sector number.

Input:

    AH=02H
    AL=number of sectors
    CH=track
    CL=sector/track (see above)
    DH=side
    DL=drive
    ES:BX=address of buffer for data

Output:

    if carry=1
        AH=error (see Table 6-2)
    if carry=0
        AH=00
        AL=number of sectors

DOS 5: A DEVELOPER'S GUIDE

Equivalent C functions:

No direct equivalent.

Write sectors   Function 03H

Description:

Writes sectors to the disk. In all other respects, it is identical to function 02H.

Input:

AH=03H
AL=number of sectors/track (see function 02H)
CH=track
CL=sector/track (see function 02H)
DH=side
DL=drive
ES:BX=address of data buffer

Output:

if carry=1
    AH=error (see Table 6-2)
if carry=0
    AH=00
    AL=number of sectors

Equivalent C functions:

No direct equivalent.

Verify sectors   Function 04H

Description:

This service is similar to function 02H except that no data transfer occurs. The BIOS verifies that the sectors exist and that the CRC (cyclic redundancy check, a sophisticated checksum) is correct. In theory, the buffer is unnecessary, but some older BIOSs do require that ES:BX point to a valid buffer.

Input:

> AH=04H
> AL=number of sectors
> CH=track
> CL=sector
> DH=side
> DL=drive
> ES:BX=address of data buffer

Output:

> if carry=1
> > AH=error (see Table 6-2)
> if carry=0
> > AH=00
> > AL=number of sectors

Equivalent C functions:

> No direct equivalent.

Return drive parameters   **Function 08H**

Description:

> Returns data about the specified drive. The XT doesn't support this function for floppy disk drives, nor does it return the drive type in the BL register.

Input:

> AH=08H
> DL=drive

Output:

> if carry=1
> > AH=error code (see Table 6-2)
>
> if carry=0
> > BL=drive type (1=360K, 2=1.2M, 3=720K, 4=1.44M)
> > CH=lowest eight bits of highest track number
> > CL=bits 7-6: first two bits of highest track number
> > > bits 5-0: highest track number
> >
> > DH=maximum side number
> > DL=number of physical drives
> > ES:DI=pointer to disk parameter table

Equivalent C functions:

> No direct equivalent.

Seek   **Function 0CH**

Description:

> Positions a hard disk's head to a specified track. No data transfer occurs. This function does not work for floppy drives.

Input:

> AH=0CH
> CH=lowest eight bits of track number
> CL=upper two bits of track in bits 7-6
> DH=side
> DL=drive

Output:

> if carry=1
> > AH=error code (see Table 6-2)
>
> if carry=0
> > AH=00

ROM BIOS SERVICES

Equivalent C functions:

No direct equivalent.

Return drive status   Function 10H

Description:

Tests the specified hard disk drive to ensure that it is operational. This function does not work for floppy drives.

Input:

AH=10H
DL=drive

Output:

if carry=1
   AH=error code (see Table 6-2)
if carry=0
   AH=00H

Equivalent C functions:

No direct equivalent.

The Serial Port Services

INT 14H provides crude serial communication services. The services do not buffer data and do no handshaking. This makes them unsuitable for anything more sophisticated than driving a serial printer or some other mundane task. C makes all these functions available with the _bios_serialcom() (Microsoft) and bioscom() (Borland and Mix) calls.

Initialize COM port **Function 00H**

Description:

Initializes the serial port specified. The configuration byte has this format:

7 6 5	4	3	2	1 0	Bit
Baud Rate	Parity O/E	Parity Enable	Stop Bits	Word Length	

where:

Baud Rate = 0 for 110 baud
　　　　　　1 for 150 baud
　　　　　　2 for 300 baud
　　　　　　3 for 600 baud
　　　　　　4 for 1,200 baud
　　　　　　5 for 2,400 baud
　　　　　　6 for 4,800 baud
　　　　　　7 for 9,600 baud

Parity O/E= 1 for even parity, 0 for odd parity (if Parity Enable is set)
Parity Enable= 1 to enable parity, 0 to disable parity
Stop Bits= 0 for one stop bit, 1 for two stop bits
Word Length= 2 for seven bits, 3 for eight bits

The port status byte has this format:

7	6	5	4	3	2	1	0	Bit
Time Out	XMIT SR Empty	XMIT HR Empty	Break Detect	Frame Error	Parity Error	Overrun Error	Data Ready	

The modem status byte has the following format:

7	6	5	4	3	2	1	0	Bit
CD	Ring Indic.	DSR	CTS	Delta CD	Falling Ring	Delta DSR	Delta CTS	

Input:

AH=00H
AL=configuration byte
DX=COM port number (0=COM1, 1=COM2, etc.)

Output:

AH=port status byte
AL=modem status byte

Equivalent C functions:

No direct equivalent.

Send character   **Function 01H**

Description:

Sends a character over the specified COM port and checks the Time-Out bit in the port status word to determine if the operation was successful.

Input:

AH=01H
AL=character
DX=COM port number (0=COM1, 1-COM2, and so on)

Output:

AH=port status (see function 00H)

Equivalent C functions:

No direct equivalent.

DOS 5: A DEVELOPER'S GUIDE

Read character   Function 02H

Description:

Reads a character from the specified COM port and checks the error bits in the port status word to determine if the operation was successful.

Input:

AH=02H
DX=COM port number (0=COM1, 1=COM2, etc.)

Output:

AH=port status (see function 00H)
AL=character

Equivalent C functions:

No direct equivalent.

Return COM port status   Function 04H

Description:

Returns the status of the specified COM port.

Input:

AH=04H
DX=COM port number (0=COM1, 1=COM2, etc.)

Output:

AH=port status (see function 00H)
AL=modem status (see function 00H)

Equivalent C functions:

No direct equivalent.

ROM BIOS SERVICES

The Keyboard Services

The BIOS provides a simple interface via INT 16H for accessing the keyboard. The actual characters don't come from the keyboard, but rather the type-ahead buffer. The AT and PS/2 have a few additional calls related to the enhanced keyboard that this section will not cover. C makes all these functions available with the _bios_keybrd() (Microsoft) and bioskey() (Borland and Mix) calls.

Read keyboard character   Function 00H

Description:

> Waits for a character and returns it. This function forces the duplicate keys on the AT's and PS/2's enhanced keyboards to appear the same as the PC's keys. It will not return the F11 and F12 keys found on these keyboards. Function 10H is identical to function 0 except that the enhanced keys are available.

Input:

> AH=00H

Output:

> AH=scan code
> AL=ASCII character

Equivalent C functions:

> No direct equivalent.

Check keyboard   Function 01H

Description:

> Returns with the zero flag set if no key is waiting to be read. If a key is waiting, the program can read its value from the AX register. It remains in the buffer, however—function 0 must be used to clear it. This service treats the enhanced keyboard just like function 0 does. Use function 11H, which is identical to this function, to return codes for the extended keys.

Input:

AH=01H

Output:

if zero flag=0
AH=scan code
AL=ASCII character

Equivalent C functions:

No direct equivalent.

Return shift status   **Function 02H**

Description:

Returns the status of the keyboard's shift keys. The returned byte is in the following format:

7	6	5	4	3	2	1	0	Bit
Insert On	Cap Lock	Num Lock	Scroll Lock	Alt key pressed	Ctl key pressed	Left Shift	Right Shift	

Input:

AH=02H

Output:

AL=flags

Equivalent C functions:

No direct equivalent.

Printer Services

INT 17H provides communications to the PC's parallel printer ports. These services require the program to specify the port it wants in the DX register. DX should be set to 0, 1, or 2 for LPT 1, 2, or 3, respectively. C makes all these functions available with the _bios_printer() (Microsoft) and biosprint() (Borland and Mix) calls.

Write to printer   **Function 00H**

Description:

Sends a character to the specified printer. The returned status has the following format:

7	6	5	4	3	2	1	0	Bit
Not Busy	Ack	No Paper	Select	I/O Error	Not Used		Time-Out	

Your program should check bits 5, 3, and 0 to make sure the operation was successful.

Input:

AH=00H
AL=character
DX=printer number

Output:

AH=status

Equivalent C functions:

No direct equivalent.

Reset printer port   Function 01H

Description:

   Resets the printer port and returns a status byte identical to the one returned by function 00H.

Input:

   AH=01H
   DX=printer number

Output:

   AH=status (see function 00H)

Equivalent C functions:

   No direct equivalent.

Return printer status   Function 02H

Description:

   Returns the status of the specified printer.

Input:

   AH=02H
   DX=printer number

Output:

   AH=status (see function 00H)

Equivalent C functions:

   No direct equivalent.

ROM BIOS SERVICES

The Clock Services

The BIOS provides access to the time-of-day counter via INT 1AH. The timer ticks 18.2 times per second. The original PC (with no hard disk) doesn't support any of these services. The AT and PS/2 also use INT 1AH functions to manipulate the real-time clock. C makes these functions available with the _bios_timeofday() (Microsoft) and *biostime()* (Borland) calls.

Return ticks since midnight   Function 00H

Description:

Returns the number of ticks since midnight. The maximum value is 1,573,040. When midnight occurs, the BIOS sets a flag that this call returns and clears.

Input:

AH=00H

Output:

AL=midnight flag (if nonzero, midnight has passed since last call)
CX:DX=ticks since midnight (32 bits)

Equivalent C functions:

No direct equivalent.

Set ticks   Function 01H

Description:

Sets the BIOS time-of-day counter to an arbitrary value. This call uses the same format as function 00H and clears the midnight flag as well.

Input:

AH=01H
CX:DX=ticks

179

DOS 5: A DEVELOPER'S GUIDE

Output:

None

Equivalent C functions:

No direct equivalent.

BIOS Variables

The BIOS uses variables in memory to communicate with programs. Many of these variables duplicate information available via the interrupts. Most programs should use the interrupts. However, some interrupt routines may not be able to call other interrupts and may need to access these variables directly. The following list, while not complete, includes the more useful variables.

- 0040:0000 - The BIOS stores the base I/O addresses of COM1 through COM4 in these eight bytes. COM1 is at 0000H, COM2 is at 0002H, and so on. Any COM ports not installed have addresses of 0000H.

- 0040:0008 - This is a table of I/O addresses for LPT1 through LPT4, similar to the above table for COM ports.

- 0040:0017 - This byte holds the status of the keyboard's shift keys. This is the same byte that INT 16H, function 02H, returns. If you change bits in this byte, you can fool the BIOS. Setting Caps Lock on, for instance, has the same effect as pressing the Caps Lock key on the keyboard.

- 0040:0018 - This byte holds more information about the keyboard's state. It has the following format:

7	6	5	4	3	2	1	0	Bit
Insert Press	Cap Lck Press	Num Lck Press	Scr Lck Press	Pause	Sys Req Press	L. Alt Press	L. Ctl Press	

In general, it's best not to change these bits. One exception is bit 3, the Pause bit. Pressing the Pause or Control-NumLock key causes the BIOS to stop

ROM BIOS SERVICES

most programs from running. Interrupts still run, however. If a program can't tolerate a pause, it can set up a timer interrupt routine and reset this bit on each tick. That way, the program couldn't be paused for more than 1/18th of a second at a time.

- 0040:001A - These two bytes point to the head of the BIOS keyboard buffer.

- 0040:001C - These two bytes point to the tail of the BIOS keyboard buffer.

- 0040:001E - This is the default keyboard buffer (16 two-byte words).

- 0040:0049 - This byte stores the current video mode. The notation is the same as INT 10H, function 0.

- 0040:004A - These two bytes indicate the number of characters per row the current video mode allows.

- 0040:004C - This word holds the number of bytes required to store one screenful of data.

- 0040:004E - This word stores the offset for the current video page.

- 0040:0050 - This is a table of 8 two-byte words that contain the current cursor position for each page. The first byte is the column; the second byte is the row.

- 0040:0060 - This byte holds the ending scan line for the cursor.

- 0040:0061   This byte holds the starting scan line for the cursor.

- 0040:0062 - The BIOS stores the current video page number in this byte.

- 0040:006C - These four bytes contain the number of timer ticks since midnight. This is the same value returned by INT 1A, function 00H.

- 0040:0070 - This byte contains the midnight flag used by INT 1AH.

181

DOS 5: A DEVELOPER'S GUIDE

- 0040:0071 - The top bit of this byte is set when the BIOS detects a Control-Break. The PC's system software never clears this bit.

- 0040:0078 - This table of four bytes contains the time-out value for each LPT port.

- 0040:007C - This table of four bytes contains the time-out value for each COM port.

- 0040:0080 - This word points to the beginning of the keyboard type-ahead buffer, which must be somewhere within segment 0040H. By default, this location is 001EH. Some BIOS clones don't use this address themselves; they only provide it for your programs to examine. However, many BIOS chips (including the IBM BIOS) allow programs to change this address.

- 0040:0082 - This word points to the end of the keyboard buffer (see 0040:0080 for more details).

- 0040:00F0 - The PC and AT reserve the 16 bytes starting at this address for communications between different programs. Very few programs use this area, however, since there is no standard method for accessing it. If you use it, a different program may also use it and change the data you expect to find there later. You should put some fixed-byte sequence, or signature, in part of the memory. If this sequence is absent when you read the data, you can assume another program is using the same memory. A checksum probably wouldn't hurt, either. The PS/2 manual doesn't document this memory region.

- 0050:0000 - This byte contains the status of the print screen command (INT 05H). If it is 0, the last print screen was successful. If it is FFH, an error occurred. If the byte is 1, a print screen is in progress. Curiously, if you set this byte to 1, the print screen key won't work because the BIOS will think a print screen is already in progress. This is a handy way to disable that key.

CHAPTER 7

Direct Access Techniques

The DOS and BIOS functions provide a simple, portable way to write programs. There is, however, a penalty for this convenience: reduced speed. Programs that directly manipulate the PC hardware are much faster than those that use DOS and BIOS services. Even if speed doesn't concern you, you'll still need to access the PC hardware to overcome certain limitations in the PC's system software. For example, you can't use DOS or the BIOS to create different tones from the PC's speaker.

Writing Text to Screen Memory

One area in which the DOS and BIOS services are especially slow is video output. Many programs write text directly to screen memory because it is much faster than using the normal DOS and BIOS functions. To access screen memory, you need to determine the address, determine the value needed, and store that value at the address.

Calculating a screen address requires knowledge of the type of adapter in use and the current video page. For text modes, if the video mode reported by INT 10H, function 0FH, is 7, a monochrome adapter is in use. Otherwise, a color card of some type is active. The monochrome card's buffer starts at segment B000H. Color text modes start at B800H.

INT 10H, function 0FH, also reports the active video page and the number of columns on the screen. If you're trying to place a character at column x and row y of the current page, the following formula calculates the offset:

```
offset=page * pagesize + 2 * y * maxcolumns + 2 * x
```

DOS 5: A DEVELOPER'S GUIDE

where:

- *page* is the current page number

- *pagesize* is 2,048 for 40-column modes or 4,096 for 80-column modes. Each page only requires 2,000 or 4,000 bytes; the adapter does not use the excess memory.

- *maxcolumns* is the number of columns per row (40 or 80)

- *x* is the column number (0–39 or 0–79)

- *y* is the row number (0–24).

Of course, if you have computed this offset once, you can increment it by two to point to the next character. As a simplification, you can set the mode to 80 columns using INT 10H, function 0, then force the page to 0 using INT 10H, function 5. This reduces the preceding equation to:

```
offset=160*y+2*x
```

This offset combines with the segment address of the card (B000H or B800H) to yield the complete address required.

What goes at this address? Figure 7-1 shows text stored in video RAM. Each character requires two bytes. The most significant byte is the attribute, and the least significant one is the actual character to display. The attribute controls the character's color and appearance. On monochrome systems, characters can be bold, blinking, underlined, reversed (white on black), or normal. For instance, a capital *A* is ASCII 41H. When displaying a white-on-black *A*, the video RAM contains 0741H. Each position on the screen has its own pair of bytes.

DIRECT ACCESS TECHNIQUES

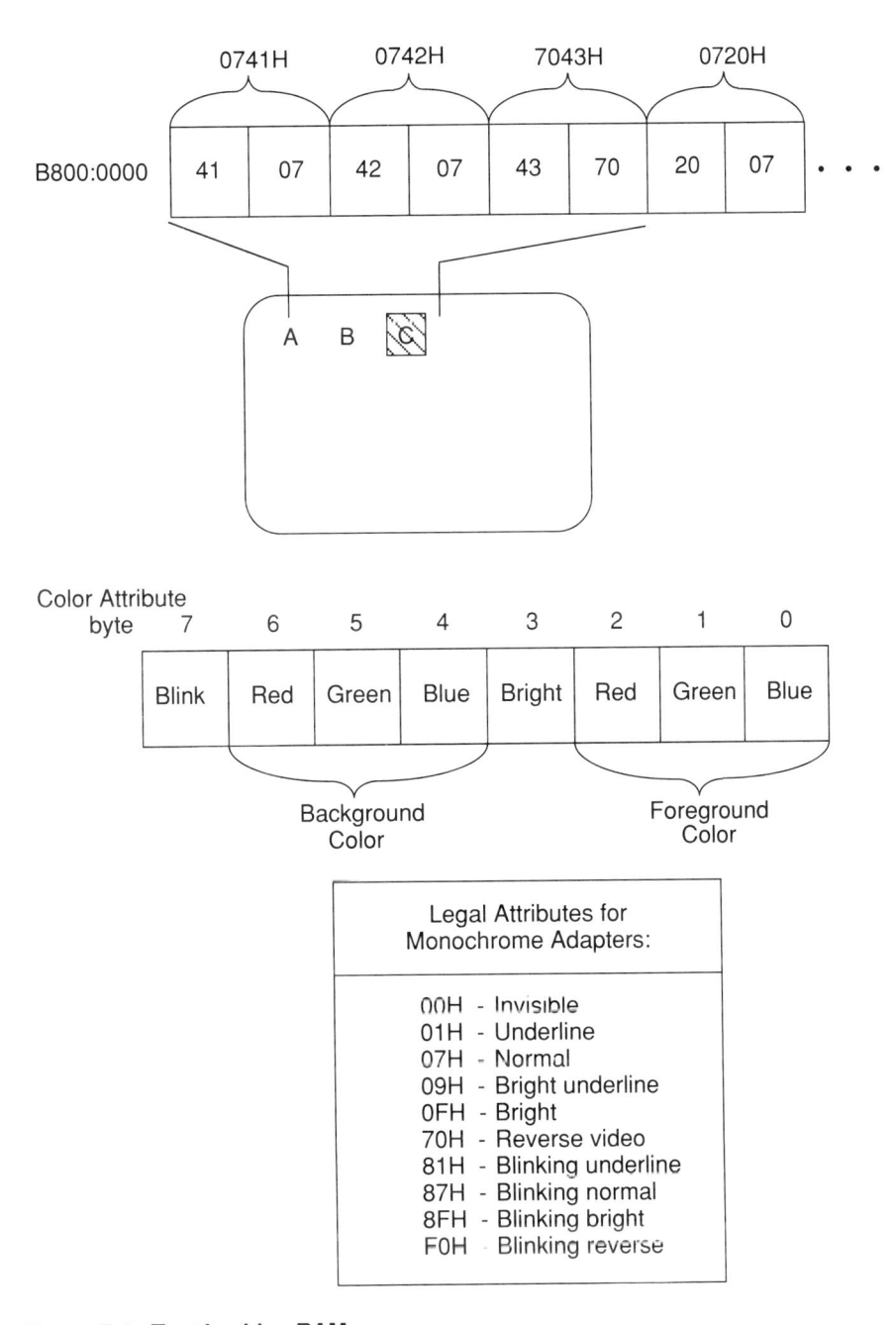

	0741H	0742H	7043H	0720H	
B800:0000	41 | 07	42 | 07	43 | 70	20 | 07	. . .

A B C

Color Attribute byte

7	6	5	4	3	2	1	0
Blink	Red	Green	Blue	Bright	Red	Green	Blue

Bits 6–4: Background Color
Bits 2–0: Foreground Color

Legal Attributes for Monochrome Adapters:

00H - Invisible
01H - Underline
07H - Normal
09H - Bright underline
0FH - Bright
70H - Reverse video
81H - Blinking underline
87H - Blinking normal
8FH - Blinking bright
F0H - Blinking reverse

Figure 7-1. Text in video RAM.

When individual characters are written, memory access is straightforward. However, when you're operating on many characters at once, it can be advantageous to use the 8086's string move instructions or C's *movedata()* function. Consider the code in Listing 7-1. This simple program uses the *movedata()* function to save and restore the screen and a pointer to place individual characters on the screen.

Many CGA adapters produce snow when a program uses direct screen access. This effect isn't harmful to the monitor but is hard on the user's eyes. The snow occurs when the video adapter and the CPU access the screen memory at once. To prevent this, you can write to the screen only when bit 0 or 3 of port 3DAH is set to one. During these times, the monitor is retracing and the adapter won't access memory. In Listing 7-1, the main loop might look like this:

```
/* Fill screen with inverse blanks. */
for (i=0;i<screensize;i++)
   {
   int retrace;
   do {
      retrace=inp(0x3DA);
      } while ((retrace&9)==0);   /* Wait for retrace. */
   *(screen+i)=0x7020;             /* Screen is int pointer. */
   }
```

Because this technique slows down screen access, you should make the users enable it if they have this problem. Many installation programs display some text on the screen and ask the users if they saw snow. Other programs require the users to set a command-line option or an environment variable if the adapter requires snow suppression.

DIRECT ACCESS TECHNIQUES

Listing 7-1. LIST71.C.
```
/*******************************************************************
 *                                                                 *
 * File: list71.c                                                  *
 *                                                                 *
 * Description:                                                    *
 * Example of direct screen access.                                *
 * Stores screen - whites screen out - restores old screen.        *
 *                                                                 *
 *******************************************************************/

#include <stdio.h>
#include <dos.h>
#include <conio.h>
#include "compat.h"

int buffer[2048];              /* place to store screen */

main()
   {
   int far *screen;
   unsigned bufseg;
   unsigned bufoff;
   union REGS r;
   int i,screensize;
   void far *buffad;
   buffad=(void far *)buffer;
/* Determine video parameters. */
   r.h.ah=0xF;
   int86(0x10,&r,&r);
   screensize=r.h.ah==80?4096:2048;
/* Compute top left corner of screen address. */
/* offset for 40- or 80-column */
   screen=MK_FP(r.h.al==7?0xB000:0xB800,r.h.bh*screensize);
/* Save old screen. */
   bufseg=FP_SEG(buffad);
   bufoff=FP_OFF(buffad);
   movedata(FP_SEG(screen),FP_OFF(screen),bufseg,bufoff,
       screensize);
/* Fill screen with inverse blanks. */
/* Screen is int. * */
```

```
   for (i=0;i<screensize/2;i++) *(screen+i)=0x7020;
/* Wait for a key. */
   if (!getch()) getch();   /* Throw away function keys. */
/* Restore old screen. */
   movedata(bufseg,bufoff,FP_SEG(screen),FP_OFF(screen),
      screensize);
   }
```

Interrupt Rules

The three golden rules of interrupts are:

1. Any non-TSR program that modifies the interrupt vector table must restore it to its original condition before exiting.

2. A program that wants to use one of the user interrupts (60H through 67H) must make sure the interrupt is not being used by another program. DOS initially sets these interrupt vectors to 0000:0000.

3. Hardware interrupts must restore all registers before completing.

As we have seen in earlier examples, rule 1 must apply even if the program terminates with a critical error or break or for any other reason. In C++, interrupts can be managed with a class (see Listing 7-2). This hides most of the processing required to satisfy rule 1. If your C++ compiler always calls destructors when the program exits (even for a Control-Break or critical error), the class in Listing 7-2 is all you need. Otherwise, you must trap those exits and call the destructor explicitly. Chapter 9 covers exit trapping in more detail.

Programming techniques often require one or more of the PC's interrupts to be hooked. To hook an interrupt, a program replaces an ISR with one of its own. The new routine may elect to call the old one under certain conditions.

DIRECT ACCESS TECHNIQUES

Listing 7-2. INTHOOK.CPP.

```cpp
/*****************************************************************
 *                                                               *
 * File: inthook.cpp                                             *
 *                                                               *
 * Description:                                                  *
 * Hooks an interrupt vector and automatically restores it       *
 * using a C++ class.                                            *
 *                                                               *
 *****************************************************************/

#include <dos.h>

#define DEMO 1        /* Set to 1 for DEMO main(). */

/* main class */
class hook
    {
    void far interrupt (*oldf)(...);
    int intn;
public:
    hook(int n,void far interrupt (*f1)(...));
    ~hook();
    };

/* Constructor: store old vector, set new one. */
hook::hook(int n, void far interrupt (*f1)(...))
    {
    intn=n;
    oldf=getvect(n);
    setvect(n,f1);
    }

/* Destructor: restore old interrupt vector. */
hook::~hook()
    {
    setvect(intn,oldf);
    }

#if DEMO
#include <iostream.h>
```

189

```
int looping=1;

void far interrupt abfunc(...)
   {
   looping=0;
   }

main()
   {
   hook prtsc(5,abfunc);
   cout << "Press <SHIFT-PrtSc> to abort\n";
   while (looping) cout<<'X';
   cout<<"Abort detected";
   }

#endif
```

Managing Hardware Interrupts

PICs form the backbone of the PC's interrupt system. Because they are highly programmable, we will only examine some of their more important capabilities.

The AT has an extra PIC to handle IRQ lines 8 through 15. The interrupt output of this PIC connects to IRQ 2 of the primary PIC. The BIOS forces IRQ 9 to act like the original IRQ 2.

PICs prioritize interrupts—once one occurs, lower-priority interrupts are blocked and must wait for the higher-priority interrupt to complete. This remains true until the PIC receives an end-of-interrupt (EOI) signal. Programs send a 20H to I/O port 20H to signal an EOI for IRQs 0 through 7. IRQs 8 through 15 (only on AT-class machines) require the service routine to send a 20H to I/O ports A0H and 20H.

The PIC contains a mask register at port 21H (A1H for IRQs 8 through 15). Each bit, when set, prevents the corresponding IRQ line from generating an interrupt. For instance, if bit 0 of this register is set, the PIC disables IRQ 0 or IRQ 8 depending on which PIC's mask register you use. On the AT, if a program disables IRQ 2, it is also disabling IRQs 8 through 15.

DIRECT ACCESS TECHNIQUES

Of course, all hardware interrupts can be disabled with a *CLI* instruction or the *disable()* call from C. To reenable them, use *STI* or *enable()*. The Microsoft C library uses *_enable()* and *_disable()*, but COMPAT.H (Listing 3-1) allows you to write *enable()* or *disable()* regardless of which compiler you use.

The only external interrupt not controlled by the PICs and the *CLI* instruction is the NMI. The NMI line usually signals some catastrophic event. Memory errors, for example, generate an NMI. By definition, the 8086 can't mask the NMI. The motherboard, however, does have the circuitry to prevent an NMI from occurring. You will rarely need to disable the NMI. On the PC, the motherboard controls it with I/O port A0H. Clearing bit 7 of this port will cut off NMI. The same method works for the AT, but it uses port 70H.

Direct Keyboard Access

You will rarely have a reason to replace the BIOS keyboard routine that handles the INT 9 signals generated by each keystroke. However, you may want to intercept INT 9, check for a particular key, and act on it before (or after) the INT 9 function has a chance to process it.

Each key generates a scan code that a program can read from port 60H. The keyboard must be reset before another scan code can be sent. The following C code reads a scan code and resets the keyboard:

```
scancode=inp(0x60);        /* Read code. */
temp=inp(0x61);            /* Read keyboard status. */
outp(0x61,temp|0x80);      /* Set bit 7 and write. */
outp(0x61,temp);           /* Write again--bit 7 clear. */
outp(0x20,0x20);           /* Reset PIC. */
```

Presumably, this code is in an interrupt routine hooked to INT 9. The last line resets the PIC so that other interrupts can occur. As an example, suppose we want to set a global flag if the user presses Control-5. Further, we only want the 5 on the numeric keypad to set this flag. Listing 7-3 shows a simple program to do just that.

191

Listing 7-3. LIST73.C.

```c
/******************************************************************
 *                                                                *
 * File: list73.c                                                 *
 *                                                                *
 * Description:                                                   *
 * Intercepts keyboard interrupt (9) to detect                    *
 * Control-5 on the numeric keypad.                               *
 *                                                                *
 ******************************************************************/

#include <stdio.h>
#include <dos.h>
#include "compat.h"


/* Set when control-numeric 5 is pressed. */
int ctl5flag=0;


#ifdef __POWERC
void interrupt (far *oldkb)();
#else
void (interrupt far *oldkb)();
#endif
/* Take no action on ^C. */
void interrupt far onbreak()
    {
    }

void interrupt far newkb()
    {
    int scancode,temp;
    char far *bios_keyflag;
    scancode=inp(0x60);            /* Read code. */
    if (scancode!=0x4C)            /* Scan code for numeric 5. */
        {
/* Wasn't numeric 5--let it pass. */
        oldkb();
        return;
        }
```

DIRECT ACCESS TECHNIQUES

```
    bios_keyflag=MK_FP(0x40,0x17);
/* If control key is down, eat the scan code and don't let old
   ISR take control. */

    if (((*bios_keyflag&4)==4)
        {
        temp=inp(0x61);              /* Read keyboard status. */
        outp(0x61,temp|0x80);        /* Set bit 7 and write. */
/* Write again--bit 7 clear. */
        outp(0x61,temp);
        outp(0x20,0x20);             /* Reset PIC. */
        ctl5flag=1;
        return;
        }
    oldkb();
    return;
    }

main()
    {
    int k;
/* Ignore breaks. */
    setvect(0x23,onbreak);
    oldkb=getvect(9);
    setvect(9,newkb);
    printf("Press <Esc> to quit\n");
    do {
/* If regular keystroke, echo it--ignore function keys. */
        if (kbhit())
            {
            if (!(k=getche())) getch();
            if (k=='\r') putch('\n');
            }
/* Check for flag. */
        if (ctl5flag)
            {
            printf("\nControl-5 Pressed\n");
            ctl5flag=0;
            }
        } while (k!=27);             /* Escape. */
    setvect(9,oldkb);                /* Reset interrupt vector. */
    }
```

As you may recall from Chapter 6, the BIOS maintains a status word at 0040:0017 that stores the state of the shift keys, including the Control key. Each keyboard interrupt starts the program's interrupt handler, *newkb( )*. It checks to see if the key is the 5 on the numeric keypad. If it is, the handler examines the shift state to see if the Control shift is active. If both conditions are true, it sets a flag (*ctl5flag*) for the main program. If either condition is false, the handler calls the original keyboard handler (stored in *oldkb*). Appendix D is a table of scan codes generated by the keyboard. These codes aren't always reported by the BIOS; for example, the numeric keypad's 5 key isn't active unless Num-Lock is on.

Another way of manipulating the keyboard is via the type-ahead buffer. The buffer begins at the offset specified by 0040:0080 and ends at the location specified by 0040:0082. The default buffer starts at 0040:001E and ends at 0040:003D. You should be able to change the buffer's location by altering the offsets at 0040:0080 and 0040:0082, but not all BIOS ROMs allow it.

The first character, known as the *buffer's head*, can be found via the offset stored at 0040:001A. This is the next character that will be read by an INT 16H call. A pointer to the last character is at 0040:001C. If these two pointers are equal, the buffer is empty. If the tail is two bytes less than the head, the buffer is full. The buffer is circular; that is, when a pointer moves past the end of the buffer, it wraps around to the beginning.

With this knowledge, you can insert characters in the buffer or peek at keys without reading them. Listing 7-4 shows a program that places the string *"DIR\r"* in the type-ahead buffer. When it exits, DOS executes a directory command.

The AT and PS/2 keyboard controllers can accept a variety of commands (see Figure 7-2). When writing directly to the command port at I/O address 64H, you should always read port 64H and wait for bit 1 until it is clear. One command to the keyboard controller enables and disables the A20 line of the processor. Listing 7-5 shows a C function that switches A20. The PS/2 should use the same method to switch the A20 line. However, some older PS/2s won't switch A20 with the keyboard controller. Listing 7-5 also shows a method that works with all PS/2s. Not all PC compatibles use the same method to switch A20.

DIRECT ACCESS TECHNIQUES

Command	Description
20H	Read command byte (see below)
60H	Write command byte (see below)
AAH	Self test (55H in output buffer if passed)
ABH	Interface test (000H in output buffer if passed)
ADH	Disable keyboard (sets bit 4 of command byte)
AEH	Enable keyboard (clears bit 4 of command byte)
C0H	Read input port
D0H	Read output port
D1H	Write output port
F0-FEH	Pulse output bits*
FFH	No operation

* This command causes bits 0-3 of the output port to pulse low. The last four bits of the command determine which bits to pulse. If the command bit is 0, the corresponding output bit goes low. If the bit is 1, the output bit is unchanged. For example, FEH causes bit 0 of the command port to pulse low.

Keyboard Input Port

7	6	5	4	3	2	1	0
Keyboard enable	Monochrome display	Reserved	0=512K RAM 1=256K RAM	Not used			

Keyboard Output Port

7	6	5	4	3	2	1	0
Data out	Clock out	Input buffer empty	Output buffer full	Not used		Gate A20	Reset CPU

Keyboard Status Port (64H)

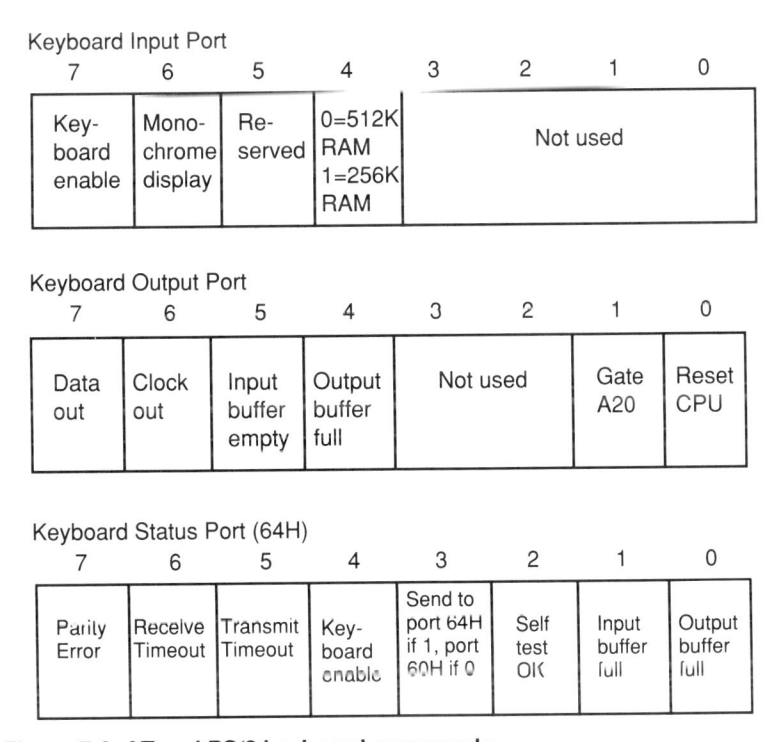

7	6	5	4	3	2	1	0
Parity Error	Receive Timeout	Transmit Timeout	Keyboard enable	Send to port 64H if 1, port 60H if 0	Self test OK	Input buffer full	Output buffer full

Figure 7-2. AT and PS/2 keyboard commands.

Listing 7-4. LIST74.C.

```c
/****************************************************************
 *                                                              *
 * File: list74.c                                               *
 *                                                              *
 * Description:                                                 *
 * Places "DIR\r" directly in the keyboard buffer.              *
 *                                                              *
 * Notes:                                                       *
 *   1) Scan codes are not placed in the buffer.                *
 *      This isn't a problem for most programs.                 *
 *                                                              *
 *   2) This routine doesn't check for overflow                 *
 *      of the keyboard buffer.                                 *
 *                                                              *
 ****************************************************************/

#include <stdio.h>
#include <dos.h>
#include "compat.h"

char *s="DIR\r";

main()
   {
   stuff(s);
   }

/* routine to do the work */
stuff(char *string)
   {
   unsigned far *bufbegin;
   unsigned far *bufend;
   unsigned far *buftail;
   unsigned far *buffer;
/* Set up buffer pointers. */
   FP_SEG(bufbegin)=FP_SEG(bufend)=FP_SEG(buftail)=FP_SEG(buffer)
      =0x40;
   FP_OFF(bufbegin)=0x80;
   FP_OFF(bufend)=0x82;
```

DIRECT ACCESS TECHNIQUES

```c
   FP_OFF(buftail)=0x1C;
   disable();                          /* no interrupts */
   FP_OFF(buffer)=*buftail;
/* for each character */
   while (*string)
      {
      *buffer++=*string++;             /* Store in buffer. */
/* Wrap around buffer. */
      if (FP_OFF(buffer)>=*bufend) FP_OFF(buffer)=*bufbegin;
      }
   *buftail=FP_OFF(buffer);            /* Set new buffer tail. */
   enable();                           /* Allow interrupts again. */
   }
```

Listing 7-5. A20.C.
```c
/****************************************************************
 *                                                              *
 * File: a20.c                                                  *
 *                                                              *
 * Description:                                                 *
 * Turns A20 on or off based on value of flag.                  *
 * if flag==0, turn A20 off else turn A20 on.                   *
 *                                                              *
 * This routine is hardware specific; it will work for ATs      *
 * and 100% compatible machines or PS/2s.                       *
 ****************************************************************/

/* Set this to 1 for a PS/2 machine.

The PS/2 should work like an AT, but some older models do not
properly switch A20 with the AT code. Newer ones do, but all
will work with the PS2 routine shown below.
*/

#define PS2 0
```

197

DOS 5: A DEVELOPER'S GUIDE

```c
/* You will want to define your own time-out routine. */
timeout()
    {
    printf("Timeout\n");
    exit(1);
    }

void a20(int flag)
    {
#if PS2
    unsigned int timect=0;
/* Switch bit 1 of port 92H. */
    outp(0x92,flag?(inp(0x92)|2):(inp(0x92)&~2));
/* Wait for change to be reflected. */
    while(((inp(0x92)&2)>>1)!=flag)
    if (!++timect)
        timeout();
    return;
#else
    if (keywait()) timeout();
    outp(0x64,0xD1);                    /* Send output command. */
    if (keywait()) timeout();
    outp(0x60,flag?0xDF:0XDD);          /* Output A20 line switch. */
    if (keywait()) timeout();
    outp(0x64,0xFF);                    /* No operation--delay. */
    if (keywait()) timeout();
#endif
    }

/* Wait keyboard controller...times out after 64K tries. */
keywait()
    {
    unsigned int timeout=0;
    while (inp(0x64)&2)
        {
        if (!++timeout) return 1;
        }
    return 0;
    }
```

DIRECT ACCESS TECHNIQUES

Interacting with DOS Memory Allocation

Chapter 2 touched on DOS's MCBs, and Chapter 5 covered the undocumented INT 21H, function 52H, which returns the first MCB. This data is all we need to print a memory map of the system. Program PS.C (Listing 7-6) does just that.

The *int86x()* call uses INT 21H, function 52H, to determine the segment address of the first MCB in the system. *MK_FP()* sets the *mcbptr* pointer to this segment.

The main loop executes until it processes the last block (marked by a *5AH*). PS gets the owner and size information directly from the MCB. Since the size is in paragraphs, PS multiplies that value by 16 to obtain the byte size.

If the first data word of the memory block is 20CDH, the block is most likely a PSP. If it is, PS extracts and displays the parent PID word from it.

PS moves the *mcbptr* pointer to the next MCB by adding the size of the block to the MCB's segment address. The loop repeats for the new block.

If PS runs under DOS 5, it links the UMBs into DOS memory using INT 21H, function 58H (assuming they are present). Any program that does this should take care to restore the UMB status before exiting.

Listing 7-6. PS.C.
```
/****************************************************************
 *                                                              *
 * File: ps.c                                                   *
 *                                                              *
 * Description:                                                 *
 * A "Process Status" command for MS-DOS.                       *
 * Displays all MCBs in the system along with sizes, etc.       *
 *                                                              *
 * Note: For Power C, set far heap size to 0. If you don't,     *
 *       PS will consume all free memory for itself, which      *
 *       will result in a misleading display.                   *
 *                                                              *
 ****************************************************************/
```

DOS 5: A DEVELOPER'S GUIDE

```c
#include <stdio.h>
#include <stdlib.h>
#include <dos.h>
#include "compat.h"

/* pointer to MCB */
union
   {
   char far *byte;
   unsigned far *word;
   } ptr;

/* break interrupt */
void far interrupt onbreak()         /* no registers required */
   {
/* Don't do anything. Ignore the break. */
   }

main()
   {
   int umbactive;
   union REGS r;
   struct SREGS s;
/* pointer to read addresses */
   unsigned far *peekptr;
   char far *mcbptr;                 /* pointer to MCBs */
   int blockid=0;
/* No break--if program exits with DOS 5, UMBs will be left in.
*/
   setvect(0x23,onbreak);
/* Check for DOS 5 or later. If so, enable UMBs. */
   if (_osmajor>=5)
       {
       r.x.ax=0x5802;
       int86(0x21,&r,&r);
       umbactive=r.h.al;
       r.x.ax=0x5803;
       r.x.bx=1;
       int86(0x21,&r,&r);
       }
```

DIRECT ACCESS TECHNIQUES

```c
/* Get magic address. */
   r.h.ah=0x52;
   int86x(0x21,&r,&r,&s);
/* Get pointer to segment of 1st MCB. */
   peekptr=MK_FP(s.es,r.x.bx-2);
/* Make pointer to MCB. */
   mcbptr=MK_FP(*peekptr,0);
   printf("SEG.  OWNR.  SIZE (hex)  SIZE (decimal) PARENT\n" );
/* Loop until last block. */
   do {
      unsigned seg;                /* segment of MCB */
      unsigned owner;              /* owner of block */
      unsigned size;               /* size of block */
/* parent process (if MCB is PSP) */
      unsigned ppid;
      unsigned long bytesize;      /* size in bytes */
      ptr.byte=mcbptr;
      seg=FP_SEG(mcbptr)+1;        /* Get MCB #. */
      blockid=*ptr.byte++;         /* Get block id. */
      owner=*ptr.word++;           /* Get owner. */
      size=*ptr.word++;            /* Get size. */
      printf("\n%04X   ",seg);
/* Print owner's PID or FREE. */
      if (owner) printf("%04X ",owner);
      else printf("FREE ");
/* Convert to size in bytes and print. */
      bytesize=(unsigned long) size*16;
      printf("%05lX         %7lu",bytesize,bytesize);
/* Skip to actual memory block. */
      ptr.byte+=11;
/* PSPs start with INT 20 (CD 20)...data block might start
   with the same bytes, but it is unlikely. */

/* probably a PSP */
      if (*ptr.word==0x20CD)
         {
         ppid=ptr.word[11];
         printf("          %04X",ppid);
         }
```

201

DOS 5: A DEVELOPER'S GUIDE

```c
/* Find next MCB. */
    mcbptr=MK_FP(FP_SEG(mcbptr)+size+1,0);
    } while (blockid!=0x5A);
  putchar('\n');
/* If DOS 5 or later, restore UMB link state. */
  if (_osmajor>=5)
    {
    r.x.bx=umbactive;
    r.x.ax=0x5803;
    int86(0x21,&r,&r);
    }
  exit(0);
  }
```

Timing and Sound Generation

In Chapter 2, we learned two ways to generate sound: toggling the speaker bit on and off and programming the PC's timer chip (see Listings 7-7 through 7-10). The simplest method, toggling the speaker bit, involves setting and resetting bit 1 of I/O port 61H. This directly drives the speaker. How often you switch the bit between 1 and 0 determines the frequency of the note. Since bit 0 of this port places the timer output on the speaker, you must clear it when making sounds using this method.

Listing 7-7 uses this simple method to make a tone. One limitation of this technique is that a faster machine will produce a higher-pitched note than a slower machine. Also, unless the program disables interrupts, the timer tick will modulate the note with an 18.2-Hz subtone. Try removing the *disable()* statement and notice the difference.

Listing 7-7. LIST77.C.

```
/***************************************************************
*                                                               *
* File: list77.c                                                *
*                                                               *
* Description:                                                  *
* A very simple tone generator.                                 *
*                                                               *
***************************************************************/
```

DIRECT ACCESS TECHNIQUES

```
#include <dos.h>
#include "compat.h"

main()
   {
   int bits,delay,d,i;
   disable();
   bits=inp(0x61)&0xfc;          /* Turn off bits 0,1. */
   for (delay=10;delay<300;delay+=20)
      {
      for (i=0;i<200;i++)
         {
         bits^=2;                /* Toggle bit 1 on and off. */
         outp(0x61,bits);        /* speaker on and off */
         for (d=0;d<delay;d++) dummy();
         }
      }
   outp(0x61,bits&0xfc);         /* Turn off speaker. */
   enable();                     /* Enable interrupts. */
   }

/* dummy function to prevent some optimizers from killing
   the delay loop */
dummy()
   {
   }
```

Listing 7-8 uses the timer to start a tone that continues while the processor works. It continues until the program calls *tone_stop()*. Another call, *tone_tone()*, makes short tones. This call doesn't return until the tone completes. Listings 7-9 and 7-10 contain a short C program to call the tone-generating function.

Listing 7-8. TONE.ASM.

```
;****************************************************************
;*                                                              *
;* File: TONE.ASM                                               *
;*                                                              *
;* Provides C functions to create tones.                        *
;* See TONE.H for functions and TONETEST.C for examples.        *
;*                                                              *
;****************************************************************

        .MODEL    SMALL,C              ; Change to correct model.

; macro to load word reg with argument
CARG            MACRO     R,N
                IF        @CodeSize    ;; large/med/huge
                MOV       R,[BP+6*N]
                ELSE
                MOV       R,[BP+4*N]   ;; small/compact
                ENDIF
                ENDM

        .CODE
                IF        @CodeSize
ARGOFF1         EQU       6
ARGOFF2         EQU       8
ARGOFF3         EQU       10
ARGOFF4         EQU       12
ARGOFF5         EQU       14
                ELSE
ARGOFF1         EQU       4
ARGOFF2         EQU       6
ARGOFF3         EQU       8
ARGOFF4         EQU       10
ARGOFF5         EQU       12
                ENDIF

; speaker bit definitions
CNTLWORD        EQU       0B6H
PORT1           EQU       043H
PORT2           EQU       042H
PORTB           EQU       061H
```

DIRECT ACCESS TECHNIQUES

```
            PUBLIC  tone_begin, tone_stop, tone_tone

; tone_begin(int freq);
tone_begin  PROC
            PUSH    BP
            MOV     BP,SP
            MOV     AL,CNTLWORD     ; program timer
            OUT     PORT1,AL
            IN      AL,PORTB        ; Enable speaker.
            OR      AL,3
            OUT     PORTB,AL
            CARG    AX,1            ; Get frequency.
            OUT     PORT2,AL
            MOV     AL,AH
            OUT     PORT2,AL
            POP     BP
            RET
tone_begin  ENDP

; tone_stop();
tone_stop   PROC
            IN      AL,PORTB        ; Disable speaker.
            AND     AL,0FCH
            OUT     PORTB,AL
            RET
tone_stop   ENDP

; Call tone_begin, wait for duration time ticks,
; and call tone_stop.
; tone_tone(freq,dur);
tone_tone   PROC
            PUSH    BP
            MOV     BP,SP
            PUSH    [BP+ARGOFF1]
            CALL    tone_begin      ; Begin tone.
            POP     AX              ; Clear stack.
            XOR     AX,AX
            INT     1AH             ; Get time from BIOS.
; Add delay to current time.
            ADD     DX,[BP+ARGOFF2]
```

```
                ADC     CX,0
                MOV     BX,0B0H         ; Check for midnight overflow.
                MOV     AX,18H
                CMP     CX,AX
                JZ      TST1
                JB      PROCEED
SUBR:           SUB     DX,BX           ; Adjust for midnight rollover.
                SBB     CX,AX
                JMP     SHORT PROCEED
TST1:           CMP     DX,BX
                JGE     SUBR
PROCEED:                                ; CX:DX has adjusted time.
                MOV     BX,DX
                MOV     AX,CX
TLOOP:                                  ; Loop until time of day = new
                                        ; time.
                PUSH    AX
                INT     1AH             ; Get time of day.
                POP     AX
                CMP     AX,CX
                JB      TLOOP
                JG      TEXIT
                CMP     DX,BX
                JB      TLOOP
TEXIT:
                CALL    tone_stop       ; Stop tone.
                POP     BP
                RET
tone_tone       ENDP
                END
```

DIRECT ACCESS TECHNIQUES

Listing 7-9. TONETEST.C.
```c
/*******************************************************************
 *                                                                 *
 * File: tonetest.c                                                *
 *                                                                 *
 * Description:                                                    *
 * C program to test the tone_tone assembly language function.     *
 *                                                                 *
 *******************************************************************/

#include <stdio.h>
#include "tone.h"

main()
   {
   int n,f,d;
   for (f=500;f<3000;f+=100) tone_tone(f,5);
   for (;;)
      {
      printf("Frequency, duration? (-1,-1 to quit) ");
      n=scanf("%d %d",&f,&d);
      if (n!=2)
         {
/* Throw away bad input. */
         scanf("%*[^\n]");
            continue;
         }
      if (f==-1&&d==-1) exit(0);
      tone_tone(f,d);
      }
   }
```

207

Listing 7-10. TONE.H.

```c
/************************************************************
 *                                                          *
 * File: tone.h                                             *
 *                                                          *
 * Description:                                             *
 * This is the header for TONE.ASM.                         *
 *                                                          *
 ************************************************************/

#ifndef TONE_HEADER

#ifndef __POWERC
/* This starts a tone from the speaker of freq f. */
void tone_begin(unsigned int f);

/* This stops a tone started with tone_begin. */
void tone_stop(void);

/* This makes a tone of freq f, duration d
   (in 1/18-second units). */
void tone_tone(unsigned int f, unsigned int d);

#else
/* This starts a tone from the speaker of freq f. */
void _tone_begin(unsigned int f);

/* This stops a tone started with tone_begin. */
void _tone_stop(void);

/* This makes a tone of freq f, duration d
   (in 1/18-second units). */
void _tone_tone(unsigned int f, unsigned int d);

#define tone_begin(a) _tone_begin(a)
#define tone_stop _tone_stop
#define tone_tone(a,b) _tone_tone(a,b)

#endif

#define TONE_HEADER
#endif
```

DIRECT ACCESS TECHNIQUES

Most PC programming uses channel 2 in mode 3 of the 8253 timers. This method produces the same tone on different machines. Even better, a program can start a tone, then continue processing—the tone continues without further attention from the computer. The timer can also time events. The operation is the same, but the speaker is not connected to the timer's output.

In mode 3, the 16-bit timer register loads a number and begins counting down to zero. The timer subtracts two from the count on each clock pulse and sets its output high for the first count. When the count reaches zero, the timer reloads the original count and starts over with its output set low. This cycle repeats until the program issues new commands to the timer. (If the count is odd, the output is high for *(count+1)/2* counts and low for *(count-1)/2* counts.) The timer counts down once about every 838 microseconds (1.19318 MHz).

Reading or writing a channel requires access to two I/O ports. The command port at address 43H controls access to the channel. Each channel also has its own I/O port. Channel 0's port is at 40H, channel 1's is at 41H, and channel 2's is at 42H. The control port receives a byte that determines the operations to perform. You may also use the timer to keep track of times less than 1/18th of a second. Since most intervals of interest to programmers are longer than that, this feature has little value.

For sound or timing operations, you must enable channel 2's clock input by setting bit 0 of I/O port 61H (you can toggle this bit to modulate tones, if you wish). When generating sound, bit 1 must also be set. Remember, channel 0 controls the system clock interrupt (IRQ 0/INT 08H). When IRQ 0 occurs, the BIOS increments the time of day and issues an INT 1CH before allowing additional timer interrupts. By hooking INT 08H or INT 1CH, a program can take actions on each timer tick (18.2 times per second). If you replace INT 08H, be sure to reset the PIC (write a 20H to I/O port 20H). If you don't, all hardware interrupts will be disabled, locking the keyboard. The same warning applies if you create an INT 1CH routine and never return from it; that's because the INT 08H handler doesn't reset the PIC until the INT 1CH has completed.

Some programs that need better timing resolution may want to hook INT 08H and speed up the system clock. However, you must call the old INT 08H handler about 18 times per second. Usually a program will set the timer to some multiple of the usual clock rate. For example, if you speed up the clock by a factor of five (18.2 * 5 = 91 times per second), then every five times the new INT 08H handler runs it should call the old handler.

The control word for port 43H has the following format:

7 6	5 4	3 2 1	0	Bit
Channel number 0–2	Command (see text)	Mode number (0–5) (usually 3, see text)	Use BCD if 1	

The command bits in the control word can be:

00—latch current value of counter (so it can be read)

01—read/write high byte of counter

10—read/write low byte of counter

11—read/write high byte, then low byte of counter

To calculate a count value given a frequency in Hertz (cycles per second), use the following formula:

COUNT=1193180/Frequency

Table 7-1 shows several octaves of musical notes and their corresponding timer count value.

DIRECT ACCESS TECHNIQUES

Note	Timer Value	Note	Timer Value
C	72977	C#	4304
C#	68890	D	4063
D	65023	D#	3834
D#	61346	E	3619
E	57921	F	3416
F	54657	F#	3224
F#	51608	G	3043
G	48701	G#	2873
G#	45962	A	2711
A	43388	A#	2559
A#	40946	B	2415
B	38651	C	2280
C	72977	C#	2152
C#	68890	D	2031
D	65023	D#	1917
D#	61346	E	1809
E	57921	F	1708
F	54657	F#	1612
F#	51608	G	1521
G	48701	G#	1436
G#	45962	A	1355
A	43388	A#	1279
A#	40946	B	1207
B	38651	C	1140
C	18241	C#	1076
C#	17217	D	1015
D	16251	D#	958
D#	15340	E	898
E	14478	F	854
F	13666	F#	806
F#	12899	G	760
G	12175	G#	718
G#	11491	A	677
A	10847	A#	639
A#	10238	B	603
B	9663	C	570
C	9121	C#	538
C#	8609	D	507
D	8120	D#	479
D#	7670	E	452
E	7239	F	427
F	6833	F#	403
F#	6449	G	380
G	6087	G#	359
G#	5746	A	338
A	5423	A#	319
A#	5348	B	301
B	4831	C	285
C (Middle)	4560		

Table 7-1. Musical notes.

211

The AT's Real-Time Clock

The AT contains a CMOS clock and RAM chip that do several things:

- Maintain the time and date, even when the computer is off
- Store a variety of configuration data
- Help 286 processors switch from protected mode to real mode.

The RAM stores the current time and date along with other information (see Figure 7-3). Programs access the RAM using only two I/O ports. You write the RAM address for the required byte to I/O port 70H, then immediately read (or write) port 71H to obtain (or set) the value.

Using Joysticks

Many PCs have one or two game ports for joysticks. While the AT BIOS provides a service (INT 15, function 84H) tailored for joysticks, the PC machines don't have this function. Direct access is therefore often the best choice for joystick programs.

A maximum of two joysticks can be connected to a game port. Each has two analog channels, representing the X and Y axes of the stick, and two digital channels, one for each button. With the maximum number of devices connected, this works out to four analog channels and four digital channels. The channels share a single I/O port (201H).

The digital channels can be read at any time by examining bits 7 through 4 of port 201H. Bits 4 and 5 correspond to buttons 1 and 2 on the first joystick. Bits 6 and 7 represent buttons 1 and 2 on the second joystick. When you press a button, the game adapter sets the button's bit to zero. The bit remains at zero until you release the button.

DIRECT ACCESS TECHNIQUES

Address	Function
0H	Seconds
1H	Second alarm
2H	Minutes
3H	Minute alarm
4H	Hours
5H	Hour alarm
6H	Day of week
7H	Day in month
8H	Month
9H	Year
0AH	Status register A
0BH	Status register B
0CH	Status register C
0DH	Status register D
0EH	Diagnostic status byte
0FH	Shutdown status byte
10H	Disk drive type byte *
11H	Reserved
12H	Fixed drive type byte **
13H	Reserved
14H	Equipment byte
15H	Low-base memory byte
16H	High-base memory byte
17H	Low-expansion memory byte
18H	High-expansion memory byte
19H	Drive C extended byte
1AH	Drive D extended byte
1BH-2DH	Reserved
2EH-2FH	Checksum
30H	Low-expansion memory byte
31H	High-expansion memory byte
32H	Date century byte
33H	Information flags
34H-3FH	Reserved

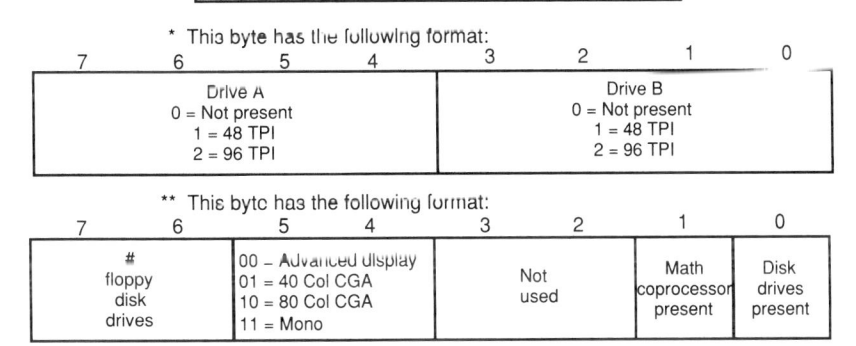

* This byte has the following format:

7 6 5 4	3 2 1 0
Drive A 0 = Not present 1 = 48 TPI 2 = 96 TPI	Drive B 0 = Not present 1 = 48 TPI 2 = 96 TPI

** This byte has the following format:

7 6	5 4	3 2	1	0
# floppy disk drives	00 = Advanced display 01 = 40 Col CGA 10 = 80 Col CGA 11 = Mono	Not used	Math coprocessor present	Disk drives present

Figure 7-3. AT real-time-clock RAM.

The analog channels use subterfuge to place four analog channels on four bits of the game port. Bits 0 and 1 of port 201H access the first joystick's *X* and *Y* position, while bits 2 and 3 do the same for the second joystick. How is this possible? The game port uses a technique that converts an analog quantity to a time interval. Because computers are good at keeping time (by counting), they can determine the analog position of the joystick.

To begin reading the analog channels, you must write a value to port 201H. Any value will do—the game port only requires that you write something. The game port will set bits 0 through 4 to one. Your program should immediately begin counting. When the bit in question becomes a zero, the program should cease counting. The value of the count will be relative to the joystick's position in the axis represented by the bit. The value has to be compared with other values read from the same joystick. That is, if the last *X* axis sample had a count of 400 and the next count is 210, the joystick moved to the left considerably. If it had been 330 instead of 400, the movement would have been less noticeable, but still to the left. A count of 500 would indicate movement to the right.

Joystick positions can't be determined precisely. No two joysticks are likely to yield the same readings for the same position. Indeed, some joysticks change values with temperature or a sharp rap on the table. If you count the analog values in software, a faster machine yields different values from a slow machine. You can time the value using the timer chip, of course, but you still won't know the exact position of the joystick.

Many commercial programs ask the user to center the joystick and press a button when the program starts. This way, the program can get a baseline count for later use.

Listings 7-11 and 7-12 show a simple program that uses one joystick. You might find the assembly function *joys()* useful in your own programs.

DIRECT ACCESS TECHNIQUES

Listing 7-11. JOYS.ASM.

```
;******************************************************************
;*                                                                *
;* File: JOYS.ASM                                                 *
;*                                                                *
;* C function to return joystick position and button status.      *
;* Use:                                                           *
;*     buttons=joys(int *x, int *y);                              *
;* Returns input from joystick port (see text).                   *
;*                                                                *
;* See JOY.C for example.                                         *
;*                                                                *
;******************************************************************
        .MODEL   SMALL,C

        .CODE
                PUBLIC joys
joys            PROC
                PUSH    BP
                MOV     BP,SP
                PUSH    DI
                PUSH    SI
                XOR     AX,AX
; joystick port
                MOV     DX,201H
                MOV     CX,AX
                MOV     BX,AX
                CLI
; Begin digitizing.
                OUT     DX,AL
JLP:            INC     SI
                CMP     SI,1024
                JZ      ART           ; time-out
; Read port.
                IN      AL,DX
                TEST    AL,1
                JZ      NOX
; Increment x counter if bit 0 high
                INC     BX
NOX:            TEST    AL,2
                JZ      NOY
```

DOS 5: A DEVELOPER'S GUIDE

```
; Increment y counter if bit 1 high.
            INC     CX
NOY:        TEST    AL,3
; Keep going until both x and y done.
            JNZ     JLP
ABT:        STI
; Store x and y coordinates.
            MOV     DI,[BP+06]
            MOV     [DI],CX
            MOV     DI,[BP+04]
            MOV     [DI],BX
            POP     SI
            POP     DI
            POP     BP
            RET
joys        ENDP
            END
```

Listing 7-12. JOY.C.

```
/****************************************************************
 *                                                              *
 * File: joy.c                                                  *
 *                                                              *
 * Description:                                                 *
 * Sample joystick program using JOYS.ASM.                      *
 *                                                              *
 ****************************************************************/

#include <conio.h>
#include <dos.h>
#include "compat.h"

/* Declare assembly-language function. */
#ifndef __POWERC
extern int joys(int *x,int *y);
#else
extern int _joys(int *x,int *y);
#define joys(a,b) _joys(a,b)
#endif
```

```
main()
   {
   cls;
   printf("Press any keyboard key to exit\n");
/* Do forever. */
   for (;;)
      {
      int b1,b2;                          /* status of buttons */
/* button input, x and y input */
      int in,x,y;
      if (kbhit())
         {
         if (!getch()) getch();    /* Eat key. */
         exit(0);
         }
      in=joys(&x,&y);
      if (in&0x10) b1=0;
      else b1=1;
      if (in&0x20) b2=0;
      else b2=1;
      cprintf(
         "Button A is %3s    Button B is %3s    X=%06u    Y=%06u\r",
         b1?"On ":"Off",b2?"On ":"Off",x,y);
      }
   }
```

The Parallel Port

PCs can support up to four parallel ports. Most computers only use these ports to communicate with printers. (In fact, the designation *LPT* is short for *line printer*.) Parallel ports are faster than serial ports because they send eight bits of data at once. They have some input capability, but it is difficult to use and rarely seen in PC programming.

The BIOS can support up to four ports, designated *LPT1* through *LPT4*. Each uses three I/O ports to communicate with the computer. The ports' addresses vary from machine to machine. Luckily, the BIOS stores the address of each adapter starting at 0040:0008. Each address takes one word, so LPT1's I/O address is at

DOS 5: A DEVELOPER'S GUIDE

0040:0008, LPT2's is at 0040:000A, and so on. If no adapter is installed for a given LPT port, its address is zero.

Each parallel port uses three consecutive I/O addresses. The first address is the data register, which contains data for the printer. The next port, which is read-only, reads the printer's status. The last port sends control signals to the printer. Figure 7-4 shows the three I/O registers.

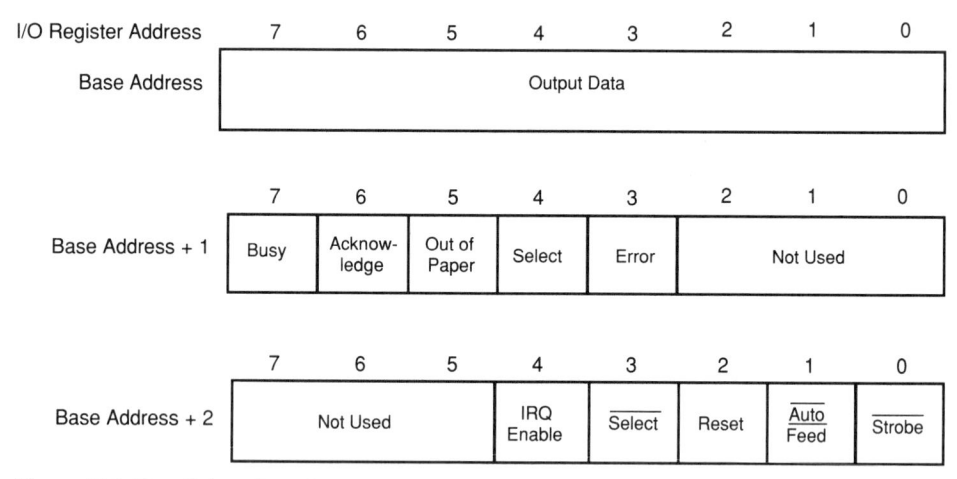

I/O Register Address	7	6	5	4	3	2	1	0
Base Address	\multicolumn{8}{c}{Output Data}
	7	6	5	4	3	2	1	0
Base Address + 1	Busy	Acknowledge	Out of Paper	Select	Error	\multicolumn{3}{c}{Not Used}
	7	6	5	4	3	2	1	0
Base Address + 2	\multicolumn{3}{c}{Not Used}	IRQ Enable	Select	Reset	Auto Feed	Strobe

Figure 7-4. Parallel port registers.

Programs should reset the printer port before using the printer. Doing so requires that the program write an 0CH to the third I/O register; this keeps the printer selected and resets the port. After waiting at least 1/20th of a second, the program should clear the reset bit (send an 8 to the port). If you want the port to send an interrupt when it is ready for more data, send an 18H instead of an 8. The PIC handles these interrupts. By convention, LPT1 uses IRQ 7. The AT uses IRQ 5 for LPT2. Of course, this doesn't have to be true—you should make your software configurable if it uses interrupt-driven parallel I/O. Cards vary, but most allow the user to select the IRQ line to be used.

DIRECT ACCESS TECHNIQUES

Always check the status port (the second I/O address) before writing to the printer. Sadly, different printers return different codes for error conditions. If bits 7, 4, and 3 are set and bit 5 is clear, it should be safe to write to the printer. If bit 5 is set, the printer is out of paper. If bits 7, 4, and 3 are clear, there's no telling what went wrong. In theory, bit 3 is turned on to show that the printer is off, bit 4 to show that it's deselected, and bit 7 to indicate that it's busy. In practice, printer manufacturers abuse these bits. It seems no matter which bits you test, at least one printer won't work with that combination.

If the printer is ready, simply write a byte to the data register and set bit 0 of the third I/O register to one. Immediately clear the bit, and the character will print.

Once you send a character, you can't send another until the port finishes with the first one. If the program enabled interrupts (by setting bit 4 of the control register), an interrupt will occur when the printer is ready. Most programs, however, monitor bit 7 of the status port. When the printer port sets that bit, it's clear to send again. While you check that bit, you can also check for errors. Listing 7-13 illustrates this technique.

Alternatively, the port will momentarily clear bit 6 of the status register as an acknowledgment. However, you could miss the acknowledgment because it only appears for a short time.

Any input to the port is *OR*ed with the output data. Therefore, to read input, you must write a zero to the data port and read from the data port. No control lines are used for input, making it difficult to know when the device has sent a new byte. In particular, you can't detect when the device sends two consecutive bytes with the same value. Whatever protocol you use must prevent this from occurring.

DOS 5: A DEVELOPER'S GUIDE

Listing 7-13. PRDEMO.C.

```c
/***************************************************************
 *                                                              *
 * File: prdemo.c                                               *
 *                                                              *
 * Description:                                                 *
 * Send a string directly to the printer.                       *
 *                                                              *
 ***************************************************************/

#include <dos.h>
#include <time.h>
#include "compat.h"

/* port address pointer */
unsigned far *peekad;

/* string to send */
char *string="DOS 5: A Developer's Guide.\r\n";

main()
   {
   clock_t tick;
/* point to port address of LPT1 */
   peekad=MK_FP(0x40,8);
   outp(*peekad+2,8);         /* Reset printer */
   tick=clock();
   while (clock()<tick+2);    /* Wait for 2 clock ticks. */
   outp(*peekad+2,0xC);       /* Printer should be ready. */
   tick=clock();
   while (clock()<tick+2);    /* Wait for 2 more clock ticks. */
   while (*string) lptchar(*string++);
   }

lptchar(int c)
   {
   int status;
   int errct=0;
   do {
      status=inp(*peekad+1)&0xb8;
```

220

```c
        if ((status&0x7f)!=0x18)    /* Check for error. */
          {
/* Wait for 10 consecutive errors. */
          if (++errct<10) continue;
          printf("Printer error\n");
          exit();
          }
       } while (!(status&0x80));    /* Wait for not busy. */
    outp(*peekad,c);                /* Write byte. */
    status=inp(*peekad+2);          /* control port */
    outp(*peekad+2,status&0xFE);    /* Send strobe. */
    outp(*peekad+2,status|1);       /* Reset strobe. */
    return 0;
    }
```

The Serial Port

A full discussion of data communications is beyond the scope of this book; entire books have been written on that subject alone. For now, we can get by with a quick overview of the subject.

PCs can, and often do, contain one or more serial or COM ports. These ports connect modems, printers, and other RS-232 devices to the PC. Luckily, most other serial adapters and modem cards emulate the standard IBM serial port, so if you know how to program that port the others shouldn't present a problem.

The BIOS works with up to four serial ports, COM1 through COM4. The PC uses an 8250 (or similar) chip to handle serial communications. This chip is one type of universal asynchronous receiver/transmitter (UART).

Unlike a parallel port, a serial port sends data one bit at a time. In particular, the serial ports that interest us are those that are self-clocking (asynchronous). This means that the sender starts each word with a start bit, sends the data (which may or may not contain a special parity bit), and sends one or more stop bits. The start and stop bits frame the data.

Serial-Port Parameters. The sender and receiver must agree on several parameters before transmission can succeed. The first parameter is the baud rate, the speed at which the data is sent. For our purposes, one baud is one bit per second.

Both parties must also agree on the number of bits in a word and the number of stop bits to send. The term *stop bit* is misleading. It is actually the minimum length of time the communication line must be idle between the transmission of two words. If the computer sends an *A* at 8:00 Monday morning and a *B* at 8:00 a.m. Tuesday, the stop bit was 24 hours long—much longer than one or two bits. In modern systems, one bit is almost always adequate. Older mechanical equipment may need extra time to get ready for the next character.

Another important decision concerns the use of parity. Parity comes in several flavors: none, odd, even, space, and mark. With odd or even parity, the UART sends an extra bit with each data word. The port selects the bit so that the total number of ones in the word is either odd or even. Mark parity is always a one, and space parity is always a zero. Parity helps detect any errors in the transmission of a word. It's not the best error-detection scheme, however; if two (or any even number) of bits are corrupt, a parity check will fail to detect it.

If we send data at 2,400 baud, eight bits, no parity, and one stop bit, does that mean we can send 300 (2,400÷8) data bytes per second? No. Since the start and stop bits are extra, we can send a maximum of 240 bytes per second.

Another parameter that must match on both sides is flow control. If a program is sending data to a printer at 9,600 baud, it is entirely possible that the printer will be unable to keep up. Even if it can print at that rate, what happens if it runs out of paper? The sender must be told to stop sending until the printer can catch up.

One common method of flow control is hardware handshaking. By using special signals, two devices can pace each other. This is most often seen in devices connected via a cable. Another common way to control flow is *XON/XOFF* handshaking. In this

DIRECT ACCESS TECHNIQUES

scheme, the receiver must determine when it will need the sender to stop. Just before that time, the receiver sends an *XOFF* character. The sender must stop as soon as it detects this character and must remain silent until the receiver sends an *XON* character. Many devices use this protocol, but it is especially useful when using modems. Some systems don't do flow control at all; they run slowly enough that they can always keep up.

While all these requirements might be intimidating, the programmer doesn't need to worry about them. The UART can convert bytes to serial format, frame them with start and stop bits, add parity, and so on, freeing us from having to think about these details.

The BIOS provides routines to manage the serial port. For simple tasks—say, writing to a printer—they are adequate. However, receiving characters from high-speed sources usually requires buffering and flow control. The BIOS doesn't provide either.

Direct UART Access. The UART has seven registers (see Figure 7-5) located at consecutive I/O ports. Like the parallel ports, the BIOS stores the start address for each COM port in a special location. COM1's base address is at 0040:0000, COM2's is at 0040:0002, and so on. Some BIOSs don't register COM3 or COM4 even if the hardware is present. If the BIOS doesn't think the COM port exists, its address is zero.

The first I/O register contains data going in and out of the port. You must be careful to read this register promptly when data is available. If you don't, an overrun error will occur. Likewise, you must not place data in this register until the UART sends the previous character. How do you know when it's safe to access the data register? Look at the sixth register, the one that contains status bits.

DOS 5: A DEVELOPER'S GUIDE

Port Address of Register: Base address:

Receive buffer/transmit holding register — Register 1

7	6	5	4	3	2	1	0
			Data in or out				

Base address + 1:

Interrupt enable register — Register 2

7	6	5	4	3	2	1	0
0	0	0	0	Modem status	Receive line status	Transmit holding register empty	Receive data available

Base address + 2:

Interrupt identification register — Register 3

7	6	5	4	3	2	1	0
0	0	0	0	0	110 = Line status / 100 = Received data / 010 = Trans. buffer empty / 000 = Modem status		

Base address + 3:

Line control register — Register 4

7	6	5	4	3	2	1	0
Divisor latch access bit	Send break	Parity 000 = none, 001 = odd, 011 = even, 010 = mark, 111 = space			Number of stop bits 0-1, 1-2	Word length 00-5, 01-6, 10-7, 11-8	

Base address + 4:

Modem control register — Register 5

7	6	5	4	3	2	1	0
0	0	0	Loop-back test	Out 2	Out 1	RTS	DTR

Base address + 5:

Line status register — Register 6

7	6	5	4	3	2	1	0
0	Trans. empty	Transmit holding reg. empty	Break detected	Framing error	Parity error	Overrun error	Receive data ready

Base address + 6:

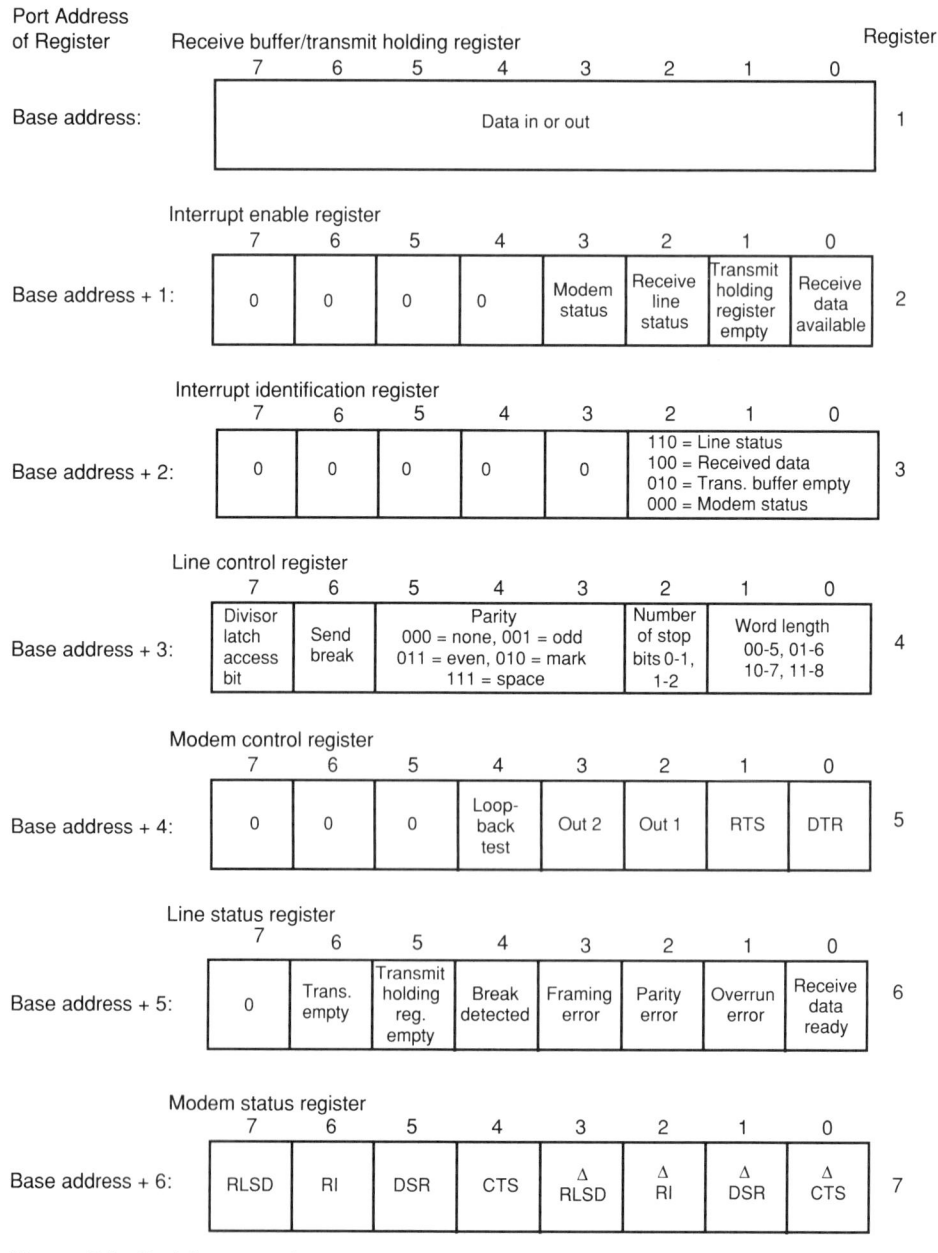

Modem status register — Register 7

7	6	5	4	3	2	1	0
RLSD	RI	DSR	CTS	Δ RLSD	Δ RI	Δ DSR	Δ CTS

Figure 7-5. Serial-port registers.

DIRECT ACCESS TECHNIQUES

It would be inconvenient to monitor the status of these bits constantly (that's how the BIOS works). Luckily, the UART can generate interrupts when it detects one of four conditions:

- An error (such as a parity error or a disconnect) has occurred
- A character is available
- The transmitter has finished sending a character
- The hardware handshaking lines change state.

Each interrupt can be disabled by clearing a bit in register 2 of the UART. In addition, unless the OUT2 bit in register 5 is set, the UART won't generate any interrupts. Of course, they can also be disabled like other hardware interrupts: with the *CLI* instruction or via the PIC.

COM1 usually uses IRQ 4 (IRQ 3 on the PC), and COM2 uses IRQ 3 on the AT and IRQ 4 on the PC. COM3 and COM4 have no standard IRQ number; programs that use them must be told which IRQ line to use. It's always a good idea to allow the user to set the IRQ line, anyway, because some machines don't follow this convention.

The first two registers also configure the baud rate for the UART. Writing to these two registers when bit 7 of the fourth register is high sets the baud rate. You can determine the correct number using the following formula:

UART value = 115200/Baud_rate

A Simple Terminal Emulator. Listings 7-14 and 7-15 show a complete interrupt-driven serial I/O library. The listings include a bare-bones terminal emulator. The first routine, *comint()*, handles all UART interrupts. Subordinate routines do all the processing. The *comint()* routine loops until it finds no more outstanding service requests.

A circular buffer, *rcvbuf[]*, holds incoming data until the main program asks for it. A similar buffer, *xmitbuf[]*, holds data on its way out of the terminal. A program may place characters in the outgoing buffer using *sio_put()*. If no room exists in the buffer, the call returns a one. As soon as the program accepts a character for output, it calls *xmit()*. If the UART is not ready for output, this does nothing (*xmit()* is called again when the UART is ready). If the UART was already idle, however, this call ensures that the character is sent.

Programs can use *sio_get()* to receive characters. This call waits for a character, so programs may wish to use *sio_charready()* to check the buffer's status.

The *sio_setup()* function initializes all UART parameters. Since this routine hooks an interrupt vector, you must call *sio_stop()* before exiting a program that calls *sio_setup()*.

While this simple terminal emulator is useful, it isn't complete. In the next chapter we'll learn what it takes to make a complete application.

Listing 7-14. SERIO.C.
```
/***************************************************************
 *                                                              *
 * File: serio.c                                                *
 *                                                              *
 * Description:                                                 *
 * A library for interrupt-driven serial I/O with a             *
 * simple terminal emulator demo program.                       *
 *                                                              *
 ***************************************************************/

#include <stdio.h>
#include <dos.h>
#include <time.h>
#include "compat.h"

/* Set to 0 for library, 1 for demo program. */
#define DEMO 1
```

DIRECT ACCESS TECHNIQUES

```c
static void xmit(void);
static void rcv(void);
static void msr(void);
static void linestat(void);

#define BUFFERLEN 1024

/* If <FILL bytes are free in rcvbuf, send XOFF. */
#define FILL 32

/* ticks to hold a break */
#define BRKTIME 5

/* base address of UART I/O */
static int basead;

/* IRQ and mask bit for PIC */
static int irqmask,irqnum;

#define XOFF 19
#define XON 17

/* global variables of interest to user's program */
int sio_error=0,sio_errct=0;     /* error words */

/* Set to 1 when break occurs. */
int sio_break=0;

int sio_linestat;                /* line status */

int sio_modemstat;               /* modem status */

int sio_doxoff=1;                /* Set xon/xoff mode on. */

/* If 1, sio_get() returns -1 if break occurred. */
int sio_brkmode=0;

#define DATA_REG 0
/* interrupt enable register */
#define IER 1
#define IIR 2                    /* interrupt id register */
```

```c
#define LCR 3                       /* line control register */
#define MCR 4                       /* modem control register */
#define LSR 5                       /* line status register */
#define MSR 6                       /* modem status register */

#define circinc(a,b) circadd(a,b,1)

#ifdef __TURBOC__
#pragma option-N-                   /* Turn off stack checking. */
#endif

#ifdef __POWERC
/* Power C's default is no stack check anyway. */
#pragma stackchk-
#endif

#ifndef __TURBOC__
#ifndef __POWERC
#pragma check_stack(off)
#endif
#endif

#ifdef __POWERC
static void interrupt (far *oldirq)();
#else
static void (interrupt far *oldirq)();
#endif

/* ISR for UART interrupt */
void far interrupt comint()
    {
    int intstat;
    intstat=inp(basead+IIR);
    if (intstat&1) oldirq();         /* No interrupt pending. */
    else while (!(intstat&1))
        {
        if (intstat==2) xmit();
        else if (intstat==4) rcv();
        else if (intstat==6) linestat();
        else msr();
```

DIRECT ACCESS TECHNIQUES

```
        intstat=inp(basead+IIR);
        }
    outp(0x20,0x20);                /* Reset PIC. */
    }

/* Handle Modem Status interrupts. */
static void msr()
    {
    sio_modemstat=inp(basead+MSR);
    }

/* Handle Line Status interrupts. */
static void linestat()
    {
    sio_linestat=inp(basead+LSR);
    if (sio_linestat&0x10) sio_break=1;
    }

/* Define two circular buffers. */
static char xmitbuf[BUFFERLEN];

static unsigned xmithead=0,xmittail=0;

static char rcvbuf[BUFFERLEN];

static unsigned rcvhead=0,rcvtail=0;

static int sentxoff=0,sendxoff=0,sendxon=0;

static int gotxoff=0;

/* Increment buffer pointer circularly. */
static unsigned circadd(unsigned ptr,unsigned max,unsigned offset)
    {
    ptr+=offset;
    while (ptr>=max) ptr-=max;
    return ptr;
    }
```

DOS 5: A DEVELOPER'S GUIDE

```c
/* Attempt to transmit character. */
static void xmit()
    {
    int c;
/* false alarm */
    if (!(inp(basead+LSR)&0x20)) return;
    if (sendxoff)
        {
        sendxoff=0;
        outp(basead+DATA_REG,XOFF);
        sentxoff=1;
        return;
        }
    if (sendxon)
        {
        sendxon=0;
        outp(basead+DATA_REG,XON);
        sentxoff=0;
        return;
        }
    if ((sio_doxoff&&gotxoff)||xmithead==xmittail) return;
    c=xmitbuf[xmittail];
    xmittail=circinc(xmittail,sizeof(xmitbuf));
    outp(basead+DATA_REG,c);
    }

/* Attempt to receive a character. */
static void rcv()
    {
    int tmp;
/* false alarm */
    if (!(inp(basead+LSR)&1)) return;
    tmp=circinc(rcvhead,sizeof(rcvbuf));
    if ((rcvhead>rcvtail&&tmp>rcvtail&&tmp<rcvhead) ||(rcvhead<
        rcvtail&&tmp>rcvtail))
        {
/* buffer overflow */
        sio_error=1;
        sio_errct++;
        return;
        }
```

DIRECT ACCESS TECHNIQUES

```c
    tmp=circadd(rcvtail,sizeof(rcvbuf),FILL);
    if ((rcvhead>rcvtail&&tmp>rcvtail&&tmp<rcvhead) ||(rcvhead<
       rcvtail&&tmp>rcvtail))
       {
       if (sio_doxoff)
          {
          sendxoff=1;
/* Wait for transmit buffer to empty. */
          while (!(inp(basead+LSR)&0x20));
          xmit();
          }
       }
    else
       {
       if (sentxoff)
          {
          sendxon=1;
/* Wait for transmit buffer to empty. */
          while (!(inp(basead+LSR)&0x20));
          xmit();
          }
       }
    rcvbuf[rcvhead]=inp(basead+DATA_REG);
    if (sio_doxoff)
       {
       if (rcvbuf[rcvhead]==XOFF) gotxoff=1;
       if (rcvbuf[rcvhead]==XON) gotxoff=0;
       }
    rcvhead=circinc(rcvhead,sizeof(rcvbuf));
    }

/* Reset stack checking to default */
#ifdef __TURBOC__
#pragma option -N.
#endif

#ifndef __TURBOC__
#ifndef  POWERC
#pragma check_stack()
#endif
#endif
```

DOS 5: A DEVELOPER'S GUIDE

```c
/* Power C's default is no stack check--
   since the PC compiler doesn't let us reset
   pragmas to the command-line state, we'll just
   leave it off. */

/* delay */
static t_delay(int ticks)
    {
    clock_t tick0;
    tick0=clock()+ticks;
    while (clock()<tick0);
    }

/* user interface routines */
/* Write a character. Returns 0 if successful. */
int sio_put(int c)
    {
    int tmp;
    tmp=circinc(xmithead,sizeof(xmitbuf));
/* Check for buffer overflow. */
    if ((xmithead>xmittail&&tmp>xmittail&&tmp<xmithead)||(
        xmithead<xmittail&&tmp>xmittail)) return 1;
    xmitbuf[xmithead]=c;
    xmithead=tmp;
/* Call xmit in case transmitter has been idle for
   a while. If transmitter is busy, xmit won't do
   anything. */

    xmit();
    return 0;
    }

/* Check for character available (1 means char ready). */
int sio_charready()
    {
    return rcvhead!=rcvtail;
    }
```

DIRECT ACCESS TECHNIQUES

```c
/* Wait for character and return it. Returns -1 for break. */
int sio_get()
   {
   int c;
   while (rcvhead==rcvtail) if (sio_brkmode&&sio_break)
       {
       sio_break=0;
       return-1;
       }
   c=rcvbuf[rcvtail];
   rcvtail=circinc(rcvtail,sizeof(rcvbuf));
   return c;
   }

/* baud rate table */
static unsigned int brtable[]=
   {
/* 110 baud */
   0x417,0x300,0x180,0x60,0x30,0x18,0xc,0x6
   };

/* Start up comport.
   You can specify the comport (1, 2, 3, 4) or a port address
   (i.e., 0x3f8). If you specify a port, you must specify irq.
   If you specify the comport and irq is zero, the default is
   used. */

sio_setup(int comport,int irq,int baud,int bits,int parity,int
   stops)
   {
   unsigned far *peekad;
   unsigned cntlword;
/* Point to table of COM addresses. */
   peekad=MK_FP(0x40,0);
   if (comport>=1&&comport<=4)
       {
       basead=peekad[--comport];    /* Get base address. */
       if (!basead) return 1;        /* not installed */
/* Set default IRQ. */
/* Set IRQ=4 for COM1/3, 3 for COM 2/4. */
       if (!irq) irq=(comport&1)==1?3:4;
```

233

DOS 5: A DEVELOPER'S GUIDE

```c
      }
   else
      {
/* Explicit I/O set must have IRQ. */
      if (!irq) return 1;
      basead=comport;
      }
   if (baud<0||baud>sizeof(brtable)/sizeof(int)) return 1;
   if (bits<5||bits>8) return 1;
   if (stops<1||stops>2) return 1;
   if (parity<0||parity>4) return 1;
   irqnum=irq;
/* Calculate irq mask bit for PIC. */
   irqmask=1<<irq;
   oldirq=getvect(irq+8);          /* Get old IRQ vector. */
   setvect(irq+8,comint);
   outp(basead+LCR,0x83);          /* none/8/1--DLAB set */
/* Set baud rate. */
   outp(basead+DATA_REG,brtable[baud]&0xFF);
   outp(basead+IER,brtable[baud]>>8);
/* Calculate control word for LCR. */
   cntlword=(2*parity-parity?1:0)<<4;
   cntlword|=2*(stops-1);
   cntlword|=bits-5;
   outp(basead+LCR,cntlword);
   outp(basead+MCR,0xF);           /* Enable interrupts. */
   outp(basead+IER,0xF);
   outp(0x21,inp(0x21)&~irqmask);
   return 0;
   }

/* CALL THIS FUNCTION BEFORE PROGRAM EXIT! */
void sio_stop()
   {
   outp(basead+IER,0);             /* Clear UART interrupts. */
   outp(basead+MCR,0);
   outp(0x21,inp(0x21)|irqmask);   /* Clear PIC. */
   setvect(irqnum+8,oldirq);       /* Restore interrupt vector. */
   }
```

DIRECT ACCESS TECHNIQUES

```c
/* Send a break. */
void sio_sendbreak()
   {
   outp(basead+LCR,inp(basead+LCR)|0x40);
   t_delay(BRKTIME);
   outp(basead+LCR,inp(basead+LCR)&~0x40);
   }

/* This is a very simple terminal emulator to demonstrate the
   library. */

#if DEMO

#include <conio.h>
#include <ctype.h>

void cmdlinehelp()
   {
   printf("SERIO - a bare-bones terminal emulator.\n\n"
      "usage: SERIO comport irq baud_rate bits parity stop_bits\n"
      "      if irq is 0, the default is used\n");
   printf("   baud_rate is:\n""    0 - 110\n"
      "              1 -   150\n""    2 - 300\n"
      "              3 -  1200\n""    4 - 2400\n");
   printf("              5 -  4800\n""    6 - 9600\n"
      "              7 - 19200\n\n""    parity is:\n"
      "                          0 - none\n""    1 - odd\n");
   printf("              2 - even\n""    3 - mark\n"
      "              4 - space\n\n"
      " or: SERIO port_address irq baud_rate bits parity \
stop_bits\n");
   printf("   port_address is the address of the COM board\n"
      "       irq must be specified\n");
   exit(0);
   }

void help()
   {
   cputs("\r\nSIO commands\r\n""ALT-B - send break\r\n"
```

235

DOS 5: A DEVELOPER'S GUIDE

```c
        "ALT-E - toggle duplex (echo)\r\n""ALT-H - help\r\n"
        "ALT-X - quit\r\n");
    }

/* Ignore breaks. */
void interrupt far onbreak()
    {
    }

main(int argc,char *argv[])
    {
    int c,k;
    int duplex=1;
    cls;
    if (argc<7) cmdlinehelp();
/* Ignore breaks. */
    setvect(0x23,onbreak);
    if (sio_setup(atoi(argv[1]),atoi(argv[2]),atoi(argv[3]),atoi(
        argv[4]),atoi(argv[5]),atoi(argv[6])))
        {
        printf("Error opening serial port\n");
        exit(1);
        }
    printf(
        "SIO V1.0 Bare-bones terminal emulator. Press ALT-H for \
help\n\n"
        );
    while (1)
        {
        if (kbhit())
            {
            k=getch();
            if (!k)
                {
                k=getch();
                if (k==45) break;     /* ALT-X */
/* Alt-E */
                else if (k==18) duplex=duplex?0:1;
/* Alt-B */
                else if (k==48) sio_sendbreak();
```

DIRECT ACCESS TECHNIQUES

```
/* Alt-H */
            else if (k==35) help();
            }
        else
            {
            if (!duplex&&isprint(k)) putch(k);
            if (!duplex&&k=='\r')
                {
                putch(k);
                putch('\n');
                }
            while (sio_put(k));
            }
        }
    if (sio_charready()) putch(sio_get());
    if (sio_break)
        {
        sio_break=0;
        puts("\r\n***BREAK***");
        }
    }
    sio_stop();
    exit(0);
    }

#endif
```

Listing 7-15. SERIO.H.
```
/****************************************************************
 *                                                              *
 * File: serio.h                                                *
 *                                                              *
 * Description:                                                 *
 * Header file for programs that use SERIO.C.                   *
 *                                                              *
 ****************************************************************/

#ifndef SERIOHEADER

#define SERIOHEADER
```

```c
/* Write a character. Returns 0 if successful. */
int sio_put(int c);

/* Check for character available (1 means char ready). */
int sio_charready(void);

/* Wait for character and return it. Returns -1 for break. */
int sio_get(void);

/* Start up comport.
   You can specify the comport (1,2,3,4) or a port address
   (i.e., 0x3f8). If you specify a port, you must specify irq.
   If you specify the comport and irq is zero, the default is
   used. */

sio_setup(int comport,int irq,int baud,int bits,int parity,int
   stops);

/* CALL THIS FUNCTION BEFORE PROGRAM EXIT! */
void sio_stop(void);

/* Send a break. */
void sio_sendbreak(void);

/* end of header */
#endif
```

CHAPTER 8

The Coprocessor

The goal of this chapter is to show you how to program the numeric coprocessor directly. The coprocessor makes complicated arithmetic computations fast and easy to code. Most C compilers have math libraries that use the coprocessor for floating-point operations. Even when using these libraries, you'll benefit from knowing how the coprocessor works. If you don't have a coprocessor but do have Turbo C and an assembler, you can still run the programs in this section.

Coprocessor instructions look just like regular 8086 instructions. Their assembler mnemonics all start with the letter *F*. Instead of executing these instructions, however, the CPU passes them to the coprocessor and decodes any address fields required.

Writing software routines to do floating-point arithmetic is difficult, and the resulting routines aren't very fast. Rather than extend the 8086 family to do floating point in hardware, Intel elected to use a coprocessor. There are several advantages to this approach. The primary benefit is that the coprocessor can be working on a calculation while the processor continues to execute the program. Of course, if the program needs the answer to continue, it must wait for the coprocessor to finish. With proper attention to the program's flow, however, a large degree of concurrency may be attained.

Because many systems don't have a coprocessor, most C compilers have emulation libraries. If these libraries don't detect a coprocessor, they emulate the coprocessor instruction. Though this isn't very fast, the advantage is that we can write software that works on all systems. The program will run faster on a machine with a coprocessor.

The sample programs given later in this chapter use assembly, but they start with a short C program (which simply calls the assembly routines) so that the emulation library can be used. This way, you can learn to use the coprocessor without owning one. Be careful if you use this technique yourself—not every library emulates every coprocessor instruction. In particular, the programs in this chapter won't work with Microsoft's emulation library.

Multiprocessing

Since the CPU's instructions don't work with floating-point numbers, they execute much faster than coprocessor instructions. Typically, the CPU can issue a coprocessor command and execute many instructions before the coprocessor is ready for a new command. The CPU must not try to send the coprocessor a command before the last coprocessor instruction has completed. A special instruction, *FWAIT*, will cause the CPU to wait until the coprocessor is ready for commands. It's common practice to precede each coprocessor command with *FWAIT* so that a program doesn't erroneously send commands to the coprocessor. You wouldn't want the *FWAIT* to follow every command; that would defeat the advantages of concurrent processing.

Because the *FWAIT* prefix is so common in coprocessor programming, both Turbo Assembler and Microsoft Assembler automatically insert this instruction in your code wherever it belongs. The only time you see the *FWAIT* command is while debugging your code.

Certain instructions can be coded with an *FN* prefix to disable *FWAIT* generation. The assembler then adds an *NOP* prefix to the instruction instead of an *FWAIT* (certain emulation techniques require the extra byte). For example, *FCLEX* becomes *FNCLEX*.

THE COPROCESSOR

Data Types and Formats

The coprocessor supports several data types (see Figure 8-1). It represents integer numbers as you would expect—using two's complement binary, just like the main CPU.

Floating-point numbers are different. They have three components: a sign, a mantissa (or significand), and a characteristic (or exponent). The size of the mantissa and characteristic varies among the available precisions (single, double, and extended). The sign, which is always one bit long, is set to 1 if the number is negative. The sign bit is all that differs between a positive and a negative number. Compare this to an integer value, where -1, for example, is FFFFH and +1 is 0001H.

The mantissa contains the significant digits of the floating-point value. The coprocessor assumes a decimal point (or radix point, if you prefer) that follows the first bit of the mantissa. For example, the numbers 1, 2, and 4 have the same binary mantissa. The difference is in the characteristic. In mathematical terms, $value = -1^{sign} * mantissa * 2^{characteristic}$.

To maximize precision, the coprocessor often normalizes numbers. This means it shifts the mantissa left until the most significant bit is a one. (Of course, zero can't be represented with a one in the mantissa; the coprocessor uses special encoding for zero.) This is so common that single- and double-precision numbers don't even store the first bit—it is assumed to be a one. The extended-precision format holds temporary results (those that might not be normalized), so it uses an explicit first bit.

The coprocessor also encodes the characteristic. It adds a bias, the value of which depends on the precision, to the characteristic before storing it. Because of this bias, an encoded characteristic of one represents the lowest value (say, -126), and a characteristic containing all ones is the highest value. (The characteristic zero is a special case.) The designers of the coprocessor used a biased characteristic to take advantage of special tricks for speeding floating point comparisons.

241

Coprocessor Data Types

Word integer

| 15 | Two's complement | 0 |

Short integer

| 31 | Two's complement | 0 |

Long integer

| 63 | Two's complement | 0 |

BCD

| 79 | S | Not Used | 72 | 18-digit BCD magnitude | 0 |

Single-precision

| 31 | S | Characteristic | 23 | Mantissa | 0 |

Double-precision

| 63 | S | Characteristic | Mantissa | 0 |

Extended-precision

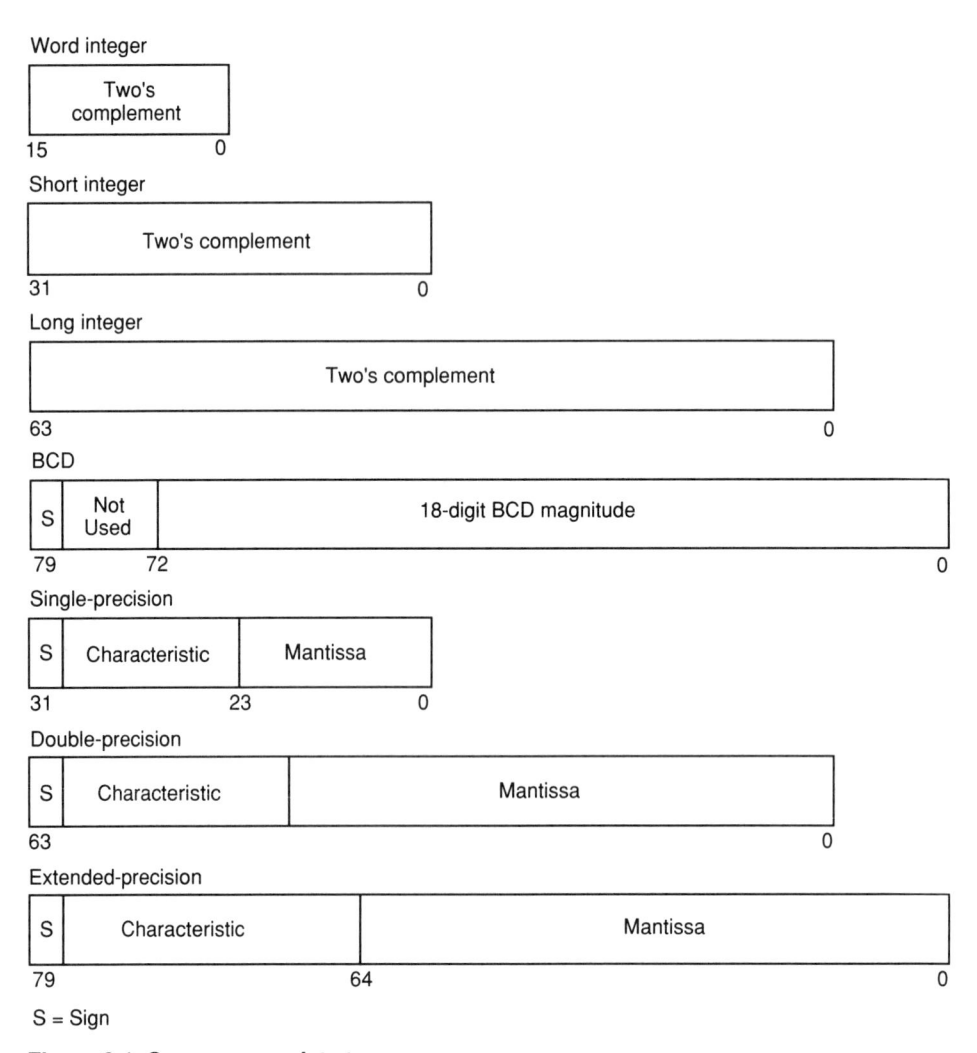

| 79 | S | Characteristic | 64 | Mantissa | 0 |

S = Sign

Figure 8-1. Coprocessor data types.

If the characteristic is zero, the coprocessor considers the mantissa to be denormal. Denormals represent numbers of such small magnitude that a normalized number cannot represent them. The assumed first digit is then zero instead of one. The coprocessor also assumes the characteristic to be one (the lowest characteristic) instead of zero, allowing the coprocessor to work with numbers of very small magnitude (including zero). As you might expect, the coprocessor represents zero with a mantissa and characteristic of zero. As you might not expect, the sign bit can be positive or negative. This is of little consequence except when dividing by zero and using the affine infinity mode, which we will learn about soon. When a calculation underflows, the result is a denormal number.

In the extended-precision format, you can have both unnormals and denormals. An unnormal's first bit is zero, not one. Other than that, an unnormal is just like a regular number. Since the other formats assume the first bit is a one, unnormals can't exist in those formats. Unnormals warn a program that its calculation may have lost precision. If the coprocessor operates on denormal numbers, in particular, the result will be an unnormal if it can't represent the result with a denormal.

When the result of a calculation is too large for the coprocessor to represent, it generates an infinite quantity. The affine and projective modes determine how the coprocessor treats infinity. Affine mode has two infinite representations, a positive infinity and a negative infinity. Projective mode doesn't distinguish between positive and negative infinity. The coprocessor represents infinity with a mantissa of zero and a characteristic of all ones. The sign determines whether it's positive or negative.

The coprocessor recognizes an illegal data value as a NAN (not a number). Any operation performed with a NAN will result in a NAN. In this way, NANs propagate through calculations: Using a NAN guarantees that the final answer is a NAN. NANs have a characteristic of all ones and can have any mantissa except zero. Because NANs can have many values, the programmer can define different NANs for different reasons. For example, at the beginning of a program each uninitialized variable could be set to a different NAN. If the program used one of these variables, the output would reflect the responsible variable.

One special NAN is the indefinite value, which the coprocessor generates for invalid operations (for example, calculating the square root of a negative number). The mantissa that represents the indefinite value varies depending on the format (see Figure 8-2). Only the programmer can create other NANs.

```
Integer:   1000...0000
Single:    1 111111111000...000
Double:    1 1111111111111000...000
Extended:  1 11111111111111111000...000
Decimal:   1111 1111 1111 1111 XXX...
```

X can represent either a 0 or a 1.

Figure 8-2. Indefinite representation.

The coprocessor also supports a packed binary coded decimal (BCD) format that uses four bits to represent each decimal digit in the number. This is handy for input and output purposes but has no provision for a decimal point—your program must scale the number after the coprocessor reads it. The coprocessor only stores the integer portion of the number for BCD output. Later we'll examine a program that uses the BCD format for all of its I/O.

Regardless of the data type, the coprocessor will convert it to extended precision before operating on it to help prevent inaccuracy. The extended-precision number can later be stored back into any data type.

Coprocessor Operation

The coprocessor organizes its general-purpose registers as a stack of eight extended-precision numbers. The STP field in the status register contains a number from zero through seven that indicates which register is the top of the stack. When the program pushes a number on the stack, STP is decremented and the indicated register (R(STP)) receives the pushed value. When the program pops a number, the reverse operation occurs. The stack wraps around at both ends; if STP is zero when a push occurs, the new STP will be seven.

If you're familiar with Hewlett-Packard calculators, the idea of a math stack won't be new to you. Programs push numbers on the stack, and the coprocessor operates on the first one or two numbers on the stack. For example, look at this pseudocode:

THE COPROCESSOR

```
PUSH 5
PUSH 25
+
```

This would add 5 and 25, removing both of them from the stack. The result, 30, would remain on the top of the stack.

The coprocessor can generate interrupts when certain events occur if the program asks it to do so. If the program doesn't want interrupts, the coprocessor takes a standard default action when these events happen. Figure 8-3 shows the various exception conditions that can cause interrupts. Ordinary programs can usually leave interrupts disabled and allow the coprocessor to take its usual action. The PC's coprocessor connects to NMI (INT 02H). The AT uses IRQ 13 (INT 75H), but the BIOS directs this interrupt to NMI for software compatibility.

Precision	This exception indicates that the coprocessor will have to round a result. By default, the coprocessor simply performs the rounding.
Underflow	Occurs when a calculation results in a number too small to represent as a normalized floating-point number. Ordinarily, the coprocessor uses the denormal form of the result.
Overflow	If the result of a calculation is too large to represent, the coprocessor generates this exception. Normally, the 8087 returns infinity. For integer and decimal formats, an invalid operation occurs instead (see below).
Divide by Zero	This happens when dividing a nonzero number by zero (0/0 generates an invalid operation). Ordinarily, this operation returns infinity.
Denormal	If an operation is attempted with a denormal, the coprocessor generates this exception. By default, the operation proceeds, and the result becomes an unnormal or denormal.
Invalid Operation	Results from any illegal operation. Example: $\infty * \infty$, or taking the square root of a negative number. Any operation involving a NAN also generates this exception. By default, this results in a NAN. If one or more NANs caused this exception, the coprocessor returns the one with the largest mantissa. Otherwise, it uses the indefinite NAN.

Figure 8-3. Coprocessor exceptions.

When an interrupt occurs, the program may wish to know what caused it. The *FLDENV* instruction will store, among other things, pointers to the current instruction and to the current operand. Our simple programs won't use interrupts; the coprocessor's default actions are very sensible.

Besides the stack, the coprocessor has several registers that control its operation. STP, for example, determines the top of the stack; it resides in a 16-bit status register (see Figure 8-4). This register also contains a busy flag, four condition bits, and the exception bits. Once the coprocessor sets an exception bit, it remains set until the programmer resets it with the *FCLEX* instruction or the coprocessor receives a hardware reset. We'll look at the condition flags in more detail when we discuss the instructions that use them.

15	14	13 12 11	10	9	8	7	6	5	4	3	2	1	0
B	C3	ST	C2	C1	C0	IR	X	PE	UE	OE	ZE	DE	IE

B = Busy
C3, C2, C1, C0 = Condition codes
ST = Top of stack
IR = Interrupt request
PE = Precision request
UE = Underflow exception
OE = Overflow exception
ZE = Zero divide exception
DE = Denormal exception
IE = Invalid operation exception
X = Not used

Figure 8-4. Coprocessor status register.

The coprocessor's operation depends on the settings in the control register (see Figure 8-5). It contains bits to set the infinity, rounding, and precision control. The precision control is only useful if you want to emulate some other computer's math processing. The rounding control bits are useful if you do esoteric computations. For instance, if you compute *1÷3* twice—once rounding toward positive infinity and once toward negative infinity—you'll get two numbers that straddle the real answer. This allows you to compute the maximum error caused by rounding. Rounding toward the nearest even, which is the default, is usually best.

THE COPROCESSOR

The interrupt masks (PM, VM, OM, ZM, DM, and IM) must be cleared to enable the coprocessor to interrupt the CPU when an exception occurs. The IEM bit disables all interrupts from the coprocessor. If an exception occurs while IEM=1, the coprocessor will remember that it wants to interrupt the CPU and will do so as soon as IEM is clear.

```
15 14 13 12 11 10  9  8  7  6  5  4  3  2  1  0
┌────────┬──┬──┬─────┬───┬──┬──┬──┬──┬──┬──┬──┐
│  Not   │IC│RC│ PC  │IEM│ X│PM│UM│OM│ZM│DM│IM│
│ Used   │  │  │     │   │  │  │  │  │  │  │  │
└────────┴──┴──┴─────┴───┴──┴──┴──┴──┴──┴──┴──┘
```

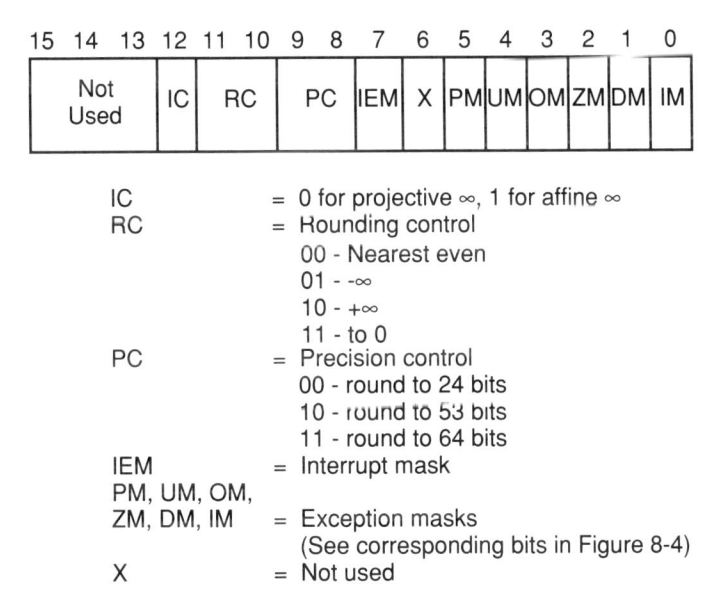

IC = 0 for projective ∞, 1 for affine ∞
RC = Rounding control
    00 - Nearest even
    01 - -∞
    10 - +∞
    11 - to 0
PC = Precision control
    00 - round to 24 bits
    10 - round to 53 bits
    11 - round to 64 bits
IEM = Interrupt mask
PM, UM, OM,
ZM, DM, IM = Exception masks
    (See corresponding bits in Figure 8-4)
X = Not used

Figure 8-5. Coprocessor control register.

Coprocessor Instructions

While complete coverage of every coprocessor instruction is beyond the scope of this book (your assembler manual should have a complete list), we can divide the instructions into five categories: load, store, compute, compare, and control. Figure 8-6 contains a brief instruction summary.

LOAD	FILD	- Load integer
	FLD	- Load real
	FBLD	- Load BCD
	FLDZ	- Load zero
	FLD1	- Load one
	FLDP1	- Load π
	FLDL2T	- Load $\log_2 10$
	FLDL2E	- Load $\log_2 e$
	FLDLG2	- Load $\log_{10} 2$
	FLDLN2	- Load $\log_e 2$
STORE	FST[P]	- Store real
	FIST[P]	- Store integer
	FBSTP	- Store BCD and pop
	FXCH	- Exchange stack register (0–7) with top of stack
COMPUTE	FADD[P]	- Add
	FIADD	- Add in-memory integer
	FSUB[P]	- Subtract
	FISUB	- Subtract in-memory integer
	FSUBR[P]	- Reverse subtract
	FISUBR	- Reverse subtract in-memory integer
	FMUL[P]	- Multiply
	FIMUL	- Multiply in-memory integer
	FDIV[P]	- Divide
	FIDIV	- Divide in-memory integer
	FDIVR[P]	- Reverse divide
	FIDIVR	- Reverse divide in-memory integer
	FABS	- Absolute value
	FCHS	- Change sign
	FRNDINT	- Round to integer
	FXTRACT	- Extract characteristic and mantissa
	FSQRT	- Square root
	FSCALE	- Scale
	FPREM	- Partial remainder
	FPTAN	- Partial tangent
	FPATAN	- Partial arctangent
	FYL2X	- $y * \log_2 x$
	FYL2XP1	- $y * \log_2(x+1)$
	F2XM1	- $2_x - 1$

Figure 8-6. Coprocessor instruction summary.

THE COPROCESSOR

COMPARE	FCOM[P]	- Compare stack's top two values and set C0 and C3
	FCOMPP	- Compare and pop top two values off stack
	FICOM[P]	- Compare stack top and in-memory integer
	FTST	- Compare top of stack with zero
	FXAM	- Examine top of stack and set C0-C3
CONTROL	FINIT	- Reset the coprocessor
	FENI	- Enable coprocessor interrupts
	FDISI	- Disable coprocessor interrupts
	FLDCW	- Loan control register
	FSTCW*	- Store control register
	FCLEX*	- Clear the exception flags
	FINCSTP	- Increment ST without changing data values
	FDECSTP	- Decrement ST
	FFREE	- Discard contents of register
	FNOP	- No operation
	FLDENV	- Load environment registers
	FSTENV*	- Store environment registers
	FSAVE*	- Save the coprocessor's state—useful in multitasking and debugging
	FRSTOR	- Restore the coprocessor's state
	FSTSW*	- Store status word

Note: [P] indicates the instruction will pop stack if the programmer adds a P to the end of the instruction.

*These instructions have a no-wait form (e.g., FNCLEX, FNSTCW).

Figure 8-6. Coprocessor instruction summary (continued).

The load instructions push values on the stack. These values can be any of the types discussed (integer, real, or BCD). In addition, the coprocessor can load several constants, such as zero, one, or π. You can also load another stack register onto the top of the stack. The assembler uses the notation *ST* or *ST(n)*, where *n* is a number from zero through seven, to refer to stack registers. *ST(0)* is equivalent to the top of the stack; *ST(1)* is the next register, and so on. For example, all of the following are legal:

```
FLD ST(4)      ;Load ST(4).
FLD ST(2)      ;Load ST(2).
FLD ST(7)      ;Load ST(7).
```

The assembler decides which size memory operation to use for coprocessor instructions based on the operands, just as it does for the CPU. For example:

```
.DATA
DATAWORD   DW   4
DBLDATA    DD   40000
.CODE
FILD             DATAWORD
FILD             DBLDATA
```

Notice that the same instruction loads a word or a double word on the stack depending on the size of the data. Of course, the coprocessor converts them both to extended precision as it loads them.

The store instructions reverse the operation of the load instructions. The instructions ending with a *P* (such as *FISTP*, *FSTP*, and *FBSTP*) remove the word they store from the top of the stack. The same instructions without the *P* suffix (which stands for *POP*) store the word at the top of the stack, but the word remains on the stack after the store completes. When a word is stored to a format other than extended precision, rounding takes place as determined by the control register.

Most compute instructions can operate on coprocessor registers or memory operands. Many use the first two stack registers, replacing the top of the stack with the result by default. When coprocessor registers are used, one of them must be ST. The first register gets the result. Memory operands always use ST as one operand and for storing the result. Look at the following examples:

```
FMUL ST,ST(3)           ; ST=ST*ST(3)
FMUL ST(3),ST           ; ST(3)=ST(3)*ST
FIMUL DWORD PTR [BX]    ; ST=ST*integer at [BX]
FDIV                    ; ST=ST(1)/ST
FRDIV                   ; ST=ST/ST(1)
FDIV ST,ST(2)           ; ST=ST(2)/ST
FDIV ST(2),ST           ; ST(2)=ST(2)/ST
FDIVR ST(2),ST          ; ST(2)=ST/ST(2)
```

THE COPROCESSOR

One special instruction is *FPREM*, which calculates the exact remainder when two numbers are divided. Since this can take a while, the coprocessor does it in iterations. When remainders are computed, C2 (in the status register) is clear if the instruction is complete; otherwise, the program must loop back to the *FPREM* instructions.

If you plan to use the transcendental functions (logarithm, exponent, and trigonometric), study the Intel documentation carefully. Many of these functions have limits on the values they can take as inputs. For example, *F2XM1*, which computes $2^{ST}-1$, only works for values greater than or equal to zero and less than or equal to 0.5. If your program needs to work with quantities outside this range, it will have to use special algorithms to compute the answer using several calls to *F2XM1*. Similarly, the coprocessor doesn't compute hyperbolics, common or natural logarithms, and other quantities, but it provides the primitive operations that allow you to implement these functions.

The compare instructions allow programs to test values and make decisions. When comparing, the coprocessor places a result code in C0 and C3 (see Table 8-1). The *FXAM* instruction determines the type of value in ST and returns the result in C3 through C0 (see Table 8-2). The program can examine these values by using the *FSTSW* instruction to write the status word to memory.

C3	C0	Result
0	0	ST > operand
0	1	ST < operand
1	0	ST = operand
1	1	Not comparable

Table 8-1. Comparison result codes.

C3	C2	C1	C0	Result
0	0	0	0	Positive unnormal
0	0	0	1	Positive NAN
0	0	1	0	Negative unnormal
0	0	1	1	Negative NAN
0	1	0	0	Positive normal
0	1	0	1	Positive infinity
0	1	1	0	Negative normal
0	1	1	1	Negative infinity
1	0	0	0	Positive zero
1	0	0	1	Empty
1	0	1	0	Negative zero
1	0	1	1	Empty
1	1	0	0	Positive denormal
1	1	0	1	Empty
1	1	1	0	Negative denormal
1	1	1	1	Empty

Table 8-2. FXAM condition codes.

The control instructions allow the program to save and restore the coprocessor's state, examine and change the control and status registers, and perform other useful operations.

Coprocessor Emulation

Many PCs don't have a coprocessor, but most C compilers have emulation libraries. In Turbo C, for example, you compile with the *-f* option to enable emulation. If a coprocessor is available, the program will use it; otherwise, the library emulates the coprocessor. Turbo Assembler and Microsoft Assembler have switches to allow the use of emulator libraries. However, the assemblers don't supply the libraries—you must have the C compiler as well.

The following sample programs use a C program to start the assembly-language portion of the code. The programs require a C *main()* because the emulation library needs certain initialization steps that the compiler performs automatically.

THE COPROCESSOR

A Simple Coprocessor Program

Listings 8-1 and 8-2 contain a program to compute $2*\pi*11.25$. The C *main()* function only calls the assembly-language coprocessor routine and prints the result. In C, functions that return floating-point values do so in ST.

Listing 8-1. COPROC.C.

```c
/*******************************************************************
*                                                                  *
* File: coproc.c                                                   *
*                                                                  *
* Description:                                                     *
* Dummy C program to call coprocessor routine and                  *
* print the results.                                               *
*                                                                  *
*******************************************************************/

main()
   {
   extern double comath();
   double d;
   d=comath();
   printf("%lf\n",d);
   }
```

Listing 8-2. COMATH.ASM.

```
;*******************************************************************
;*                                                                 *
;* File: COMATH.ASM                                                *
;*                                                                 *
;* Calculates 11.25*2*pi.                                          *
;* Uses COPROC.C for emulation library and to print result.        *
;*                                                                 *
;* Be sure to assemble with the /Ml option.                        *
;* If you are emulating the coprocessor, use the /e option.        *
;*                                                                 *
;*                                                                 *
;*******************************************************************
```

253

DOS 5: A DEVELOPER'S GUIDE

```
            .MODEL          SMALL,C

            .8087
            .DATA
    ; constants
    DATA1       DT      11.25
    TWO         DW      2

            .CODE
                PUBLIC      comath
    comath      PROC                ; Calculate 11.25*2*pi.
                FINIT               ; Reset coprocessor.
                FLDPI               ; Push PI on the stack.
                FILD        TWO     ; Push integer 2 on the stack.
                FMUL                ; Multiply (2*pi).
                FLD         DATA1   ; Push data1 on stack (11.25).
                FMUL                ; Multiply 11.25*(2*pi).
    ; Return--C takes value from top of stack.
                RET
    comath      ENDP

                END
```

A Four-Function Calculator

Listings 8-3 and 8-4 show CALC.C and $CALC.ASM, a simple four-function calculator. Of course, CALC.C is just a dummy C *main( )* function. You can enter real numbers in decimal, along with the four basic operators (+, -, *, and /). CALC displays the answer when you press the equal sign. To simplify matters, it acts on operators left to right (that is, 4+5*10=90, not 54). In addition, CALC's output routine shows many digits past the decimal point that are not significant.

At the top of $CALC.ASM, an equate defines the *ROUNDING* constant. If this is zero, CALC displays all digits in the answer. If it is not zero, CALC rounds the answer to double precision before displaying it. Try it both ways with the expression *123.456+0.544=*. Since binary numbers cannot exactly represent certain decimal numbers, a slight error is present.

THE COPROCESSOR

Listing 8-3. CALC.C.
```c
/*****************************************************************
 *                                                                *
 * File: calc.c                                                   *
 *                                                                *
 * Description:                                                   *
 * This is a dummy C program to call the assembly                 *
 * language coprocessor routine.                                  *
 *                                                                *
 *****************************************************************/

main()
    {
    extern void calc();
    calc();
    }
```

Listing 8-4. $CALC.ASM.
```
;*****************************************************************
;*                                                                *
;* File: $CALC.ASM                                                *
;*                                                                *
;* Coprocessor routine that operates like a simple four-func-     *
;* tion calculator. Requires CALC.C for emulation library.        *
;*                                                                *
;* Be sure to assemble with the /Ml option.                       *
;* If you are emulating the coprocessor, use the /e option.       *
;* If you have a coprocessor, this program will run as a          *
;* stand-alone program if you change the last line to:            *
;*    END calc                                                    *
;*                                                                *
;*****************************************************************

.MODEL    SMALL,C

.8087
```

DOS 5: A DEVELOPER'S GUIDE

```
; This equate determines if CALC rounds to double precison
; before displaying the answer. Rounding provides better answers
; for values that can't be represented exactly in binary.

ROUNDING     EQU    0           ; Set to zero for full precision.

.DATA
CTLWORD      DW     03BFH       ; normal control word
INTWORD      DW     0FBFH       ; control word to truncate integers

; buffer for BCD numbers
RESULT       DT     ?
ENDRES       EQU    $

; variables for input routine
COUNT        DW     0
DIGIT        DB     0

; constants
TEN          DT     10.0
; used to read fractions
FSCALEF      DT     1000000000000000000.0

; input buffer for numbers
NUMBUF       DB     20 DUP(?)
NUMEND       EQU    $

; current operator (+,-,*,/)
OP           DB     ?

; This variable provides the input routine with
; a capability similar to C's ungetc() function.
LASTCH       DB     0

; sign-on message
SOMSG        DB     'CALC 8087 calculator by Al Williams',13,10
             DB     'Press ^C to quit.',13,10,'$'

; error message
BADNUM       DB     13,10,'Bad number. Please reenter.',13,10,'$'
```

THE COPROCESSOR

```
; macro to duplicate top of stack (like ENTER on HP calculator)
FDUP        MACRO
            FLD   ST
            ENDM


IF          ROUNDING
; storage location to force rounding
ROUNDED     DQ    ?
ENDIF


.CODE
            PUBLIC calc
; MAIN routine
calc        PROC
            FINIT               ; Reset coprocessor.
            FLDCW CTLWORD       ; Load control word.
; Print sign on message.
            MOV   DX,OFFSET SOMSG
            MOV   AH,9
            INT   21H
; Begin calculation.
START:
            CALL  GETNUM        ; Get number.
; main loop
CLOOP:
            CALL  GETOP         ; If = return zero flag.
            JZ    START         ; When op is '=' start all over.
            CALL  GETNUM        ; Get number on stack.
            CALL  XEQ           ; Execute last operator.
            JMP   CLOOP
calc        ENDP

CLR         PROC                ; Clear result.
            XOR   AX,AX
            MOV   COUNT,AX
            MOV   DIGIT,AL
            MOV   BX,10
CLR1:
            MOV   BYTE PTR RESULT-1[BX],AL
            DEC   BX
```

DOS 5: A DEVELOPER'S GUIDE

```
                JNZ     CLR1
                RET
CLR             ENDP

STORE           PROC            ; Store digit in result buffer.
                PUSH    BX
                AND     AL,0FH
                MOV     AH,DIGIT
                SHR     AH,1
                JNC     STOOK
                SHL     AL,1
                SHL     AL,1
                SHL     AL,1
                SHL     AL,1
STOOK:          XOR     BX,BX
                MOV     BL,AH
                OR      BYTE PTR RESULT[BX],AL
                INC     DIGIT
                POP     BX
                RET
STORE           ENDP

; Read a number and leave it on the top of stack.
; The strategy is to read the number as an integer.
; The negative exponent is counted in count.
; The BCD integer is loaded, and 10^count is
; calculated and multiplied by the integer.
GETNUM          PROC
GETREDO:
                CALL    CLR
                MOV     BX,OFFSET NUMBUF
                JMP     SHORT GL0
GETLOOP:
                CALL    OUCH    ; echo space
GL0:
                CALL    INCH
                CMP     AL,' '
                JZ      GETLOOP ; Skip leading space.
                CMP     AL,'-'  ; leading minus sign
                JNZ     GETTRY0
                CALL    OUCH    ; echo character
```

THE COPROCESSOR

```
; Set sign.
            MOV     BYTE PTR RESULT[9],80H
            JMP     SHORT GETMORE
GETTRY0:
            CMP     AL,' '
            JZ      GETEND
            CMP     AL,'+'
            JZ      GETEND
            CMP     AL,'-'
            JZ      GETEND
            CMP     AL,'*'
            JZ      GETEND
            CMP     AL,'/'
            JZ      GETEND
            CMP     AL,'='
            JZ      GETEND
            CMP     AL,'.'
            JNZ     GETDIG
; Process dp.
; If count is not zero, then 2 dp's are in same number.
            CMP     COUNT,0
            JNZ     GETERR
            CALL    OUCH        ; echo
            DEC     COUNT       ; Keep exponent.
            JMP     GETMORE

GETDIG:
            CMP     AL,'0'
            JNB     GETTRY9
GETERR:
            MOV     AL,7
            CALL    OUCH
GETMORE:
            CALL    INCH
            JMP     GETTRY0
GETTRY9:
            CMP     AL,'9'
            JA      GETERR
            CMP     BX,OFFSET NUMEND
            JB      GETSTO
```

259

DOS 5: A DEVELOPER'S GUIDE

```
BADNO:
            MOV     AH,9
            MOV     DX,OFFSET BADNUM
            INT     21H
            JMP     GETREDO
GETSTO:
            CALL    OUCH
            MOV     [BX],AL
            INC     BX
            CMP     COUNT,0
            JZ      GETMORE
            DEC     COUNT
            JMP     GETMORE
; Here to convert number to binary and put on stack.
GETEND:
            CMP     BX,OFFSET NUMBUF
            JZ      BADNO
GETXFER0:
            MOV     LASTCH,AL    ; Unget character for next input.
GETXFER:
            DEC     BX
            CMP     BX,OFFSET NUMBUF
            JB      SHORT GETXDONE
            MOV     AL,[BX]
            CALL    STORE        ; Put digit in result buffer.
            JMP     GETXFER
GETXDONE:
; Load BCD number into coprocessor.
            FBLD    RESULT
; Get exponent.
            MOV     CX,COUNT
            OR      CX,CX
            JZ      GETINT       ; Integer input--do nothing.
            INC     CX
            CALL    EXP10        ; Compute 10^X.
            FMUL
GETINT:
            RET
GETNUM      ENDP
```

; Slow but easy method to compute 10^X (where X is an integer).

THE COPROCESSOR

```
; Just loop X times multipying by 10 each time.
EXP10       PROC
            PUSH    CX
; Treat negative exponent as positive for now.
            OR      CX,CX
            JNS     POSEXP
            NEG     CX
POSEXP:
            FLD1                ; Start with 1 (10^0).
EXPLOOP:
            JCXZ    EXPOUT
            FLD     TEN         ; * 10.0 for each time through
            FMUL
            DEC     CX
            JMP     EXPLOOP
EXPOUT:
            POP     CX
; If exponent was negative, take reciprocal.
            OR      CX,CX
            JNS     EXPX
            FLD1
            FDIVR
EXPX:       RET
EXP10       ENDP


; Get an operator (+,-,*,/,=).
; = displays the result.
GETOP       PROC
OPTOP:
; Read any leading blanks.
            CALL    INCH
            CMP     AL,' '
            JNZ     OPNONB
            CALL    OUCH
            JMP     OPTOP

OPNONB:
; Store +,-,*,/ -- goto equals for =.
            MOV     OP,AL
            CMP     AL,'+'
            JZ      OPOUT
```

DOS 5: A DEVELOPER'S GUIDE

```
                CMP     AL,'-'
                JZ      OPOUT
                CMP     AL,'*'
                JZ      OPOUT
                CMP     AL,'/'
                JZ      OPOUT
                CMP     AL,'='
                JZ      EQUALS
; Beep on error.
                MOV     AL,7
                CALL    OUCH
                JMP     OPTOP

EQUALS:
                CALL    OUCH
IF              ROUNDING
                FSTP    ROUNDED
                FLD     ROUNDED     ; Round to double precision.
ENDIF
                FDUP
                CALL    TRUNC       ; Get integer portion.
                FDUP
                FBSTP   RESULT      ; Convert to BCD.
; answer-integer_part = fractional_part
                FSUB
                XOR     CX,CX
                CALL    PRINTIT     ; Print integer part.
                MOV     AL,'.'      ; Print decimal point.
                CALL    OUCH
                FLD     FSCALEF     ; Load big number.
                FMUL                ; frac_part * big_number
; Part after decimal point is always positive;
; otherwise you'd get printouts like -1.-5.
                FABS
; frac_part, which is now a positive integer to BCD
                FBSTP   RESULT
; Wait for conversion to finish.
                FWAIT
; Print out fractional part.
                MOV     CL,1
                CALL    PRINTIT
```

THE COPROCESSOR

```
        ; Do CRLF.
                MOV     AL,13
                CALL    OUCH
                MOV     AL,10
                CALL    OUCH
                XOR     AX,AX
                RET

        ; Store ordinary operators.
        OPOUT:  CALL    OUCH
                MOV     AL,1
                OR      AL,AL
                RET
        GETOP   ENDP

        ; Truncate integer portion of float.
        ; CAUTION: resets control word.
        TRUNC   PROC
                FLDCW   INTWORD
                FRNDINT
                FLDCW   CTLWORD
                RET
        TRUNC   ENDP

        ; output character
        OUCH    PROC
                MOV     DL,AL
                MOV     AH,2
                INT     21H
                RET
        OUCH    ENDP

        ; input character
        INCH    PROC
                XOR     AL,AL
        ; Return unget character, if present.
                CMP     AL,LASTCH
                JZ      INCH0
                XCHG    AL,LASTCH
                RET
```

DOS 5: A DEVELOPER'S GUIDE

```
INCHO:
        MOV     AH,8
        INT     21H
        OR      AL,AL
        JNZ     INOUT
        MOV     AH,8        ; Ignore function keys.
        INT     21H
        JMP     INCHO
INOUT:  RET
INCH    ENDP

; Print result to screen.
; If cx is 0, skip leading zeros.
PRINTIT PROC
        MOV     BX,OFFSET RESULT+8
        MOV     AL,[BX+1]
        AND     AL,80H
        JZ      PLOOP
; Print sign if negative.
        MOV     AL,'-'
        CALL    OUCH
PLOOP:  CMP     BX,OFFSET RESULT
        JB      ENDPR
; Get digit.
        MOV     AL,[BX]
        DEC     BX
        PUSH    AX
        SHR     AL,1
        SHR     AL,1
        SHR     AL,1
        SHR     AL,1
        ADD     AL,'0'
        CMP     AL,'0'
        JNZ     PIT
; If cx is 0 and digit is 0, skip it.
        OR      CX,CX
        JZ      SKIP
PIT:
        CALL    OUCH        ; output character
        INC     CX          ; Don't suppress nonleading 0's.
```

THE COPROCESSOR

```
SKIP:
            POP     AX
            AND     AL,0FH
            ADD     AL,'0'
            CMP     AL,'0'
            JNZ     PIT1
            OR      CX,CX
            JZ      PLOOP
PIT1:
            CALL    OUCH
            INC     CX
            JMP     PLOOP
ENDPR:      RET
PRINTIT     ENDP

; Do operation specified.
XEQ         PROC
            MOV     AL,OP
            CMP     AL,'+'
            JNZ     NOTPLUS
            FADD
            RET
NOTPLUS:
            CMP     AL,'-'
            JNZ     NOTSUB
            FSUB
            RET
NOTSUB:
            CMP     AL,'*'
            JNZ     NOTMUL
            FMUL
            RET
NOTMUL:
            FDIV
            RET
XEQ                 ENDP

            END
```

265

The body of the program is quite simple. The *getnum* and *getop* routines do all the work. The *getnum* call reads a number into *numbuf*, keeping track of the number of digits past the decimal point. Actually, by counting down from zero, the count is the decimal exponent of the entered number. For example:

$123.45 \longrightarrow 12345 \times 10^{-2}$

Two digits after the decimal point give an exponent of -2.

The integral portion of the number is loaded as a BCD number on the coprocessor's stack. The program then calculates 10^{count} and multiplies it by the rest of the number. The last character read is not part of the number, and the program puts it back (like C's *ungetch( )* function) for *getop* to read or discard.

The *getop* subroutine does most of its work when the user presses the equal key. First, it calls *trunc* to remove the fractional portion of the top of the stack. Notice that the rounding control bits are set to 11. This prevents the integer part of the answer from being changed. If we didn't change the rounding control, 145.92 might print out as 146.92, an incorrect answer. The program writes the integer portion to the result variable (in BCD format) and subtracts it from the original number to obtain the fractional part.

The *printit* routine then prints out the integer portion. If the *FSUB* instruction didn't precede the call to *printit*, the program would have to use an *FWAIT* to ensure the coprocessor had written the data to the result buffer. Next, we have to convert the fraction to an integer by multiplying by 10^{18}. Since the sign is already accounted for with the integer portion, the *FABS* instruction makes sure this value is always positive. Again, the result buffer receives the BCD value, and *printit* prints the buffer.

THE COPROCESSOR

Final Notes

Accessing the coprocessor with C is easy once you know how it works. Most compilers provide a _control87() function to set the control word, _clear87() to reset the exception bits, and _status87() to read the status word. These functions vary slightly from compiler to compiler, so check your documentation.

This chapter cannot hope to provide a comprehensive treatment of the coprocessor. If you need to do some heavy number-crunching, consider obtaining a complete reference and some math books appropriate to the task at hand.

If you use a 287 or 387 coprocessor or the built-in coprocessor on the 486, be aware that there are some differences. For example, the 387 doesn't support projective infinity. If you're writing complex programs for these coprocessors, take the time to learn about the differences. For most basic math operations, however, the coprocessors are the same.

PART II

Advanced MS-DOS Programming

CHAPTER 9

Building Robust Applications

Most of the programs presented so far haven't been very robust. That is, they depend on the user to enter correct data and are intolerant of errors. That's fine for sample programs, but real programs must be bulletproof. They should also be easy to use and intuitive, though these issues are somewhat more subjective.

To be robust, a program must do at least the following:

- Detect and act on all errors
- Handle all possible inputs
- Respond appropriately to break keys
- React correctly to critical errors.

These are the four laws of applications. The first law is extremely dependent on the application. For example, if a program attempts to allocate memory, what action should it take if the attempt fails? There isn't one right answer; some programs have no choice but to abort with an error. Sometimes requesting less memory is appropriate; alternately, other memory may be released and the request attempted again. A program may deal with such errors in several ways depending on when the error occurs.

Users shouldn't lose their work when an error occurs. One famous product has a screen builder that breaks this law. After spending an hour and a half building a screen, the user could get a message that the system is out of memory and is aborting to DOS. This is unforgivable. The system should either allow users to save their work or automatically save it to a temporary file.

The sample programs in Chapters 4, 7, and 8 apply the second law to some degree. Many of them use the *getch()* function to read keystrokes. Suppose a program is waiting for the user to press any key. In C, we might write:

```
getch();
```

This is a mistake, however. If the user presses a function key (or any other extended ASCII key), this call will return a zero. The next keyboard input call will return the scan code of the function key. However, it will interpret the scan code as ASCII. The correct code is:

```
if (!getch()) getch();
```

Of course, the second law also applies in a much more general sense. If you ask for numeric input, make sure you get it. If the number must be within a certain range, check it. Don't forget to check input string lengths. Again, much of this depends on the type of programs you write.

When designing applications, you must give some thought to the third and fourth rules. DOS provides default actions for these conditions (or exceptions), and many programmers use them. These defaults can be sufficient; small programs that do simple screen output and don't do anything special can probably get away with the standard actions.

Other programs aren't so easy. Control-Break probably should not end a program that requires the user to enter 100 numbers. At the very least, the break key can be programmed to ask users if they want to quit. Some programs use the break key to stop a long operation prematurely.

BUILDING ROBUST APPLICATIONS

Both the default break handler and the critical error handler will affect your screen display. Some programs don't care, but pretty windows and other special formatting can easily be ruined.

All of the issues mentioned so far concern aesthetics. However, if your program modifies interrupt vectors or is a TSR program, don't allow Control-Break or critical errors to cause it to exit before you reset everything to its original state. Failure to do so will cause system crashes.

In short, a program may choose to:

- Accept the default exception handlers

- Disallow one or both exceptions

- Allow one or both exceptions but take special action before exiting

- Replace the default handlers with different ones (add a prompt or pop up a window with critical errors, for instance).

Handling Break Exceptions

To review, four keys can generate a break exception: Control-C, Control-Break, Control-2, and Alt-3 (the 3 on the numeric keypad). Of these, only Control-Break actually triggers a special interrupt (1BH). When this interrupt is triggered, the BIOS sets a special flag to inform DOS that a break occurred. On most system calls, DOS looks at this flag and checks to see if the keyboard buffer's next character is any of the other keys. If either condition is true, DOS prints a ^C and generates an INT 23H. The default INT 23H handler flushes all file buffers and terminates the program.

If your application doesn't create windows, you might not mind the appearance of the ^C. If that's the case, break handling is simple. Just replace INT 23H's vector with a pointer to your break handling routine. After doing any necessary processing, execute an *IRET* to ignore the break. If you want the program to terminate, set the

DOS 5: A DEVELOPER'S GUIDE

carry flag and end the handler with a *FAR RET*. This instruction is a signal to DOS to kill the current program. If you end the handler with a *FAR RET* and the carry flag is clear, the program will resume execution.

If a ^C destroys your screens, you have several options. If you write directly to the screen and never use the DOS or BIOS services for output, you can always move the BIOS cursor off the screen and not move it again. DOS will print the ^C, but it will be invisible.

A better approach is to intercept INTs 1BH and 16H or 9H (the keyboard interrupts). If the keyboard interrupt detects a break key or INT 1BH occurs, arrange to call your break handler. If the keyboard interrupt detects a break, don't pass the break codes back to the caller. Listing 9-1 shows an example of this technique.

Listing 9-1. BREAKS.ASM.

```
;***************************************************************
;*                                                              *
;* File: breaks.asm                                             *
;*                                                              *
;* Example of capturing ^C and preventing DOS's ^C display.     *
;*                                                              *
;***************************************************************
.MODEL          SMALL
.STACK          1024

.DATA
; current video page
VPAGE           DB      ?

;storage for old 1BH vector
OLD1BO          DW      ?
OLD1BS          DW      ?
```

BUILDING ROBUST APPLICATIONS

```
; string to print on break
BSTRING         DB      13,10,'--BREAK--',13,10,0

.CODE
; storage for old int 9 vector
; We will want to jump to this when DS != the data segment
; so it is in the code segment.
OLDKEY          DW      ?
OLDKEYS         DW      ?

; actual break handler
BRK             PROC    FAR
                PUSH    DS
                PUSH    AX
                PUSH    BX
; Get data addressability.
                MOV     AX,@Data
                MOV     DS,AX
                MOV     BX,OFFSET BSTRING
                MOV     AH,0EH
                MOV     BH,VPAGE
BLOOP:
                MOV     AL,[BX]
                INC     BX
                OR      AL,AL
                JZ      SHORT OUTBRK
                PUSH    BX
                INT     10H             ; Print break message.
                POP     BX
                JMP     BLOOP
OUTBRK:
                POP     BX
                POP     AX
                POP     DS
                IRET                    ; Return; don't terminate.
BRK             ENDP

; new keyboard (INT 16H) handler
```

DOS 5: A DEVELOPER'S GUIDE

```
; Here we catch functions 0,1 (10H, 11H), which are the
; same functions except that they are aware of the extended
; keyboard keys (like F11 and F12).
; We never allow a program (including DOS) to see a
; ^C (or Alt-numeric pad 3) or ^2.

NEWKEY          PROC    FAR
                CMP     AH,10H
                JZ      PKEY
                CMP     AH,11H
                JZ      PKEY2
                CMP     AH,1
                JZ      PKEY2
                OR      AH,AH
; Only worry about functions 0 and 1 10H & 11H.
                JZ      PKEY
; Continue with old handler (its IRET will return to caller).
                JMP     DWORD PTR CS:[OLDKEY]

; Handle functions 0,10H.
PKEY:           PUSH    AX
                JMP     SHORT PK1
; Call break routine when ^C detected.
PKEY1:          INT     1BH
PK1:            POP     AX
                PUSH    AX
                PUSHF                   ; Simulate old INT 16.
                CALL    DWORD PTR CS:[OLDKEY]
                CMP     AL,3
                JZ      PKEY1           ; Don't return ^C
                CMP     AX,0300H        ; or ^2.
                JZ      PKEY1
                ADD     SP,2            ; Remove AX off stack.
                IRET

; Handle functions 1,11H.
PKEY2:          PUSH    AX
                JMP     SHORT PK3
```

BUILDING ROBUST APPLICATIONS

```
; Call break when ^C detected.
PKEY3:          INT     1BH
PK3:            POP     AX
                PUSH    AX
                PUSHF                   ; Simulate old INT 16.
                CALL    DWORD PTR CS:[OLDKEY]
; No key waiting--report to caller.
                JZ      PKEY6
                CMP     AL,3
                JZ      PKEY4           ; Don't return ^C
                CMP     AX,0300H        ; or ^2.
                JNZ     PKEY5
PKEY4:
; "Eat" waiting key (don't care about fn 10H return).
                XOR     AH,AH
                PUSHF
                CALL    DWORD PTR CS:[OLDKEY]
                JMP     PKEY3

PKEY5:
                ADD     SP,2            ; Remove AX off stack.
                CMP     AX,0300H        ; Clear zero flag.
                RET     2               ; Return with flags.

PKEY6:
                ADD     SP,2            ; Remove AX off stack.
                CMP     AX,AX           ; Set zero flag.
                RET     2               ; Return with flags.


NEWKEY          ENDP

; Set up (or remove) interrupt handlers.
; If AX==0 install, else remove.
BREAK_SETUP     PROC
                PUSH    DS
                OR      AX,AX
                JNZ     CLEANUP
                MOV     AX,351BH        ; Get INT 1BH vector...
                INT     21H
                MOV     OLD1B0,BX
```

DOS 5: A DEVELOPER'S GUIDE

```
                MOV     BX,ES
                MOV     OLD1BS,BX
                MOV     AX,3516H        ; and INT 16 too.
                INT     21H
                MOV     CS:OLDKEY,BX
                MOV     BX,ES
                MOV     CS:OLDKEYS,BX
                MOV     AX,@Code
                MOV     DS,AX
                MOV     DX,OFFSET NEWKEY
                MOV     AX,2516H
                INT     21H             ; Set INT 16.
                MOV     DX,OFFSET BRK
                JMP     SHORT ENDSETUP
CLEANUP:
                PUSH    DS
                MOV     DX,CS:OLDKEY
                MOV     DS,CS:OLDKEYS
                MOV     AX,2516H        ; Reset 16H.
                INT     21H
                POP     DS
; Reset 1BH.
                MOV     DX,OLD1BO
                MOV     DS,OLD1BS
ENDSETUP:
                MOV     AX,251BH        ; Set or reset 1BH.
                INT     21H
                POP     DS
                RET
BREAK_SETUP     ENDP

; Main routine--echo characters until escape.
MAIN            PROC
                MOV     AX,@Data
                MOV     DS,AX
; Call break_setup to set break vectors.
                MOV     AX,0
                CALL    BREAK_SETUP
                MOV     AH,0FH          ; Get video page.
                INT     10H
```

```
                MOV     VPAGE,BH
KLOOP:          MOV     AH,8
                INT     21H             ; Get keystroke.
                CMP     AL,27           ; escape?
                JZ      SHORT XIT
                MOV     DL,AL
                MOV     AH,2
                INT     21H             ; Print character.
                CMP     DL,0DH          ; carriage return
                JNZ     KLOOP
                MOV     DL,0AH          ; If so, print line feed too.
                MOV     AH,2
                INT     21H
                JMP     SHORT KLOOP
; Leave program.
XIT:            MOV     AX,1            ; Call break_setup to reset.
                CALL    BREAK_SETUP
                MOV     AH,4CH
                INT     21H
MAIN            ENDP
                END     MAIN
```

ANSI C provides a simple, portable way to intercept break exceptions via the *signal()* call. However, this call usually allows the ^C printout to occur.

Handling Critical Errors

Critical errors occur when DOS detects a condition from which it can't recover by itself. The most common critical error occurs when you access a floppy disk drive that has no disk in it. DOS executes an INT 24H when such an error occurs. The default handler prints the famous "Abort, Retry, Ignore" message. By replacing INT 24H, you can process these errors as you see fit. For programs that don't do special screen output, the default handler is usually adequate. However, the default message will wreak havoc on windows and other screen layouts. Also, if you have moved the cursor from the screen to hide it, you should intercept INT 24H and at least put the cursor back on the screen. The default handler can then be called.

DOS 5: A DEVELOPER'S GUIDE

An application with windows might put an error window on the screen. Some programs, especially TSRs and real-time software, just ignore or fail all errors with no response from the user.

DOS passes a great deal of data to a critical error handler. The AX and DI registers contain the two most important pieces (see Figure 9-1). Actually, only the low-order byte of DI is significant. The stack contains all the registers as they were when the user's program called DOS. This can be useful in identifying exactly what operation caused the error. In DOS version 2.0 and above, BP:SI points to the header for the device driver that participated in the error.

AH register contains:

7	6	5	4	3	2	1	0
0=Disk 1=Character device or FAT	Not used	Ignore allowed	Retry allowed	Fail allowed	00=DOS area 01=FAT 01=Directory 11=Data		0=Read operation 1=Write operation

Low 8 bits of DI register contain:

```
00H - Disk is write-protected
01H - Invalid drive number
02H - Drive not ready
03H - Bad command
04H - CRC error
05H - Bad request packet
06H - Seek error
07H - Unknown disk format
08H - Sector not found
09H - Printer out of paper
0AH - Write error
0BH - Read error
0CH - General error
0FH - Invalid disk change
```

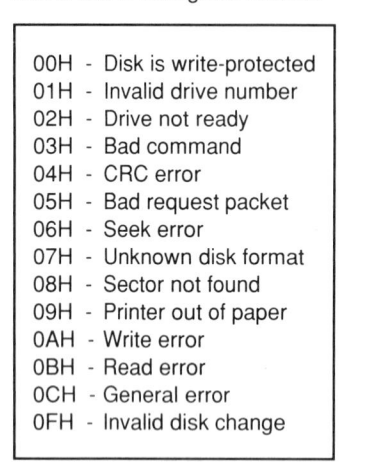

Stack at time of INT 24H:

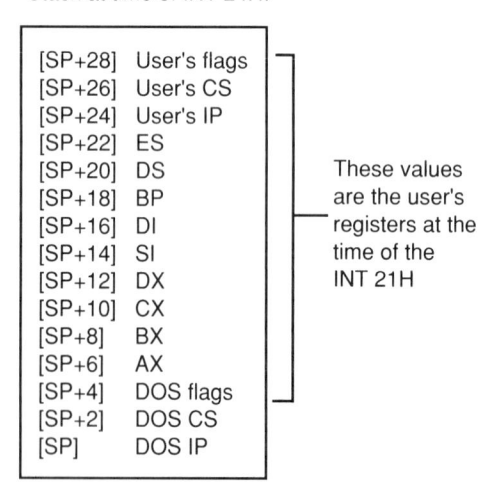

```
[SP+28]  User's flags
[SP+26]  User's CS
[SP+24]  User's IP
[SP+22]  ES
[SP+20]  DS
[SP+18]  BP
[SP+16]  DI
[SP+14]  SI
[SP+12]  DX
[SP+10]  CX
[SP+8]   BX
[SP+6]   AX
[SP+4]   DOS flags
[SP+2]   DOS CS
[SP]     DOS IP
```

These values are the user's registers at the time of the INT 21H

BP:SI = Pointer to device header

Figure 9-1. Critical error information.

BUILDING ROBUST APPLICATIONS

Since a critical error interrupt occurs inside DOS, you can't call most DOS functions. It is safe to call INT 21H, functions 01H through 0CH, 30H, and 59H. Of course, the handler can call the BIOS.

When your program returns to DOS, it places in the AL register a code that determines how DOS will proceed. All other registers must be preserved. The possible return codes are:

- 00H   Ignore
- 01H   Retry
- 02H   Abort
- 03H   Fail (DOS 3.1 and above).

Note that the byte passed to the handler in AL can disallow certain return codes. Your handler should not return illegal codes. If it does, DOS will probably abort the program (or fail the operation in DOS 3.3 and above). If you allow a return of 2 (abort), be sure to unhook the interrupt vectors and perform any other housekeeping.

Listing 9-2 shows a contrived program to generate and handle critical errors. Run the program with no disk in drive A to see how it works.

Listing 9-2. CRITERR.ASM.

```
;****************************************************************
;*                                                              *
;* File: criterr.asm                                            *
;*                                                              *
;* Example of capturing and handling critical errors.           *
;*                                                              *
;****************************************************************
.MODEL          SMALL

.STACK          512

.DATA
```

DOS 5: A DEVELOPER'S GUIDE

```
FHANDLE         DW      ?                  ; FILE HANDLE

; critical error messages
CERR0           DB      'Disk is write protected',0
CERR1           DB      'Invalid drive',0
CERR2           DB      'Drive not ready (is the drive door open?)',0
CERR3           DB      'Bad command',0
CERR4           DB      'CRC error',0
CERR5           DB      'Bad disk request',0
CERR6           DB      'Seek error'
CERR7           DB      'Unknown disk format',0
CERR8           DB      'Sector not found',0
CERR9           DB      'No paper in printer',0
CERRA           DB      'Write error',0
CERRB           DB      'Read error',0
CERRC           DB      'General error',0
CERRD           DB      '? ERROR',0   ; impossible error code
CERRE           DB      '? ERROR',0   ; impossible error code
CERRF           DB      'Invalid disk change',0

; table of critical error messages
CERRTBL         DW      OFFSET CERR0
                DW      OFFSET CERR1
                DW      OFFSET CERR2
                DW      OFFSET CERR3
                DW      OFFSET CERR4
                DW      OFFSET CERR5
                DW      OFFSET CERR6
                DW      OFFSET CERR7
                DW      OFFSET CERR8
                DW      OFFSET CERR9
                DW      OFFSET CERRA
                DW      OFFSET CERRB
                DW      OFFSET CERRC
                DW      OFFSET CERRD
                DW      OFFSET CERRE
                DW      OFFSET CERRF

CERRMSG         DB      '.',13, 10, 'Abort program (Y/N)? ',0
```

BUILDING ROBUST APPLICATIONS

```
FNAME           DB      'A:\$$AAW$$.JNK',0

.CODE

;   Note:
;   BIOS is used for I/O so messages appear on the screen even if
;   the output is redirected.
;
;   The INT 24H vector does not need to be reset before program
;   termination since DOS restores the vector from the PSP.

; Get a Y or an N. Return carry set for Y, clear for N.
; Destroys BX, AX, DX. Assumes DS addressability.
GETYN           PROC
REINPUT:
                XOR     AH,AH
                INT     16H             ; Get key.
                AND     AL,0DFH         ; Convert to uppercase.
                CMP     AL,'N'
                JZ      PROCESS
                CMP     AL,'Y'
                JNZ     REINPUT
PROCESS:
                PUSH    AX
                MOV     AH,0FH
                INT     10H             ; Get video page.
                POP     AX
                PUSH    AX
; Echo Y or N followed by CR/LF.
                MOV     AH,0EH
                INT     10H
                MOV     AL,0DH
                INT     10H
                MOV     AL,0AH
                INT     10H
                POP     AX
                SUB     AL,'Y'          ; Carry clear if yes, set if no.
                CMC                     ; Invert carry flag.
                RET
GETYN           ENDP
```

DOS 5: A DEVELOPER'S GUIDE

```
; Print a null-terminated string (DS:BX) to the screen with BIOS.
; Destroys AX,BX.
BIOSP           PROC
                PUSH    SI
                MOV     SI,BX
                MOV     AH,0FH
                INT     10H             ; Get page.
                MOV     AH,0EH

BPLOOP:         MOV     AL,[SI]
                OR      AL,AL
                JZ      BPXIT
                INC     SI
                INT     10H
                JMP     BPLOOP

BPXIT:
                POP     SI
                RET
BIOSP           ENDP

CRITICAL        PROC    FAR
                PUSH    DS
                PUSH    AX
                PUSH    DX
                PUSH    BX
; Get data addressability.
                MOV     AX,@Data
                MOV     DS,AX
; Look up error code from CERRTBL with DI.
                MOV     BX,DI
                AND     BX,0FFH
                SHL     BX,1            ; Each entry is two bytes.
                MOV     BX,CERRTBL[BX]
; Print error message.
                CALL    BIOSP
; Prompt for action.
                MOV     BX,OFFSET CERRMSG
                CALL    BIOSP
```

```
; Return carry for yes, no carry for no.
                CALL    GETYN
                POP     BX
                POP     DX
                POP     AX
                POP     DS
; Return code to DOS.
                MOV     AL,1
                JNC     ENDCR
                MOV     AL,2
ENDCR:          IRET
CRITICAL        ENDP

MAIN            PROC
; Install critical error handler.
                MOV     AX,SEG CRITICAL
                MOV     DS,AX
                MOV     DX,OFFSET CRITICAL
                MOV     AX,2524H
                INT     21H
; Open and close file on A drive.
                MOV     AX,@Data
                MOV     DS,AX           ; address data segment
; Get dummy file name.
                MOV     DX,OFFSET FNAME
                MOV     AX,3D00H        ; Open file for read.
                INT     21H
                MOV     BX,AX
                MOV     AH,3EH
                INT     21H             ; Close file.
EXIT:
                XOR     AL,AL           ; Exit with a 0 return code
                MOV     AH,4CH
                INT     21H
MAIN            ENDP

                END     MAIN
```

Most PC C compilers have a set of functions for dealing with critical errors. The program installs a handler via the *harderr()* or *_harderr()* call. The details vary slightly between compilers, so refer to your manual for more information.

Which Language is Best?

The PC supports many programming languages. This book uses primarily C (with some C++) and assembly. Of these, which is best? The answer, of course, depends largely on the type of programs you write.

C++ is essentially an object-oriented extension to C. There probably isn't anything you can do in C++ that you can't do in C, or vice versa. Objects simply make certain programs easier to write, maintain, or enhance. C++ also supports features to aid code readability (function overloading, operator definitions, and so on), but these don't actually add power to the language.

Assembly language can be very difficult to code, debug, and maintain. These can be important factors, particularly in commercial software development. However, assembly is essential for small code, fast code, and odd machine operations (the DOS extender that appears later in this book is a good example).

One utility available on bulletin boards fattens the cursor using INT 10H, function 1. Because it is written in a high-level language (Pascal), the .EXE file is longer than 3 Kbytes. The same code in assembly can be shorter than 10 bytes. If a high-level language's overhead is bigger than your whole program, consider using assembly.

Often you can write your code in C, identify the parts that consume the most time (or space), and rewrite those pieces in assembly. Similarly, you can often isolate time-critical or odd operations for assembly coding, using C for the remainder.

BUILDING ROBUST APPLICATIONS

Multitasking Considerations

With the advent of task-switching programs (like DOS 5's DOSSHELL) and multitasking software (like Windows 3.0 and Quarterdeck Office Systems' DESQview), your program may have to share certain resources. In general, common sense is a good guideline; for example, don't write to memory you don't own.

However, some situations deserve special consideration. If your application spends a great deal of time in an idle loop, it may take processor time that another task could use. Starting with DOS 5, programs have a standard way of informing the operating system that they are idle (see INT 2FH, function 1680H, in Chapter 5). As an added bonus, DOS 5 can use this information to conserve battery power for laptop computers.

A few types of programs may need to know about task-switching events. A terminal emulator, for example, may not want to let the user switch to another task. Also, some resident and device-driver programs must know which task is active at any given time to handle requests properly.

If you need this kind of interaction with the task-switching environment, you need to learn more about the task switcher in use. Microsoft documents DOS 5's task-switcher applications programming interface (API), and other products are likely to move in that direction. At this time, however, commercial task switchers have no standard protocol for communicating with users' programs.

Luckily, few programs must interact with these task switchers. If you find yourself writing this type of software, you need to talk to the task-switching program's vendor.

A Simple Program: HEXDUMP

Listing 9-3 shows a simple program written in assembler. HEXDUMP.ASM dumps a file in hexadecimal to the STDOUT device. It handles bad input (in the form of a command-line argument), input errors, breaks, and critical errors.

DOS 5: A DEVELOPER'S GUIDE

You'll notice that both exception handlers do I/O via BIOS calls. That way, even if the user redirects STDIN or STDOUT, the error messages will go to the console. The break handler could use a handle to STDERR or open the CON device, but the critical error handler can only make certain DOS calls.

Listing 9-3. HEXDUMP.ASM.

```
;****************************************************************
;*                                                               *
;* File: HEXDUMP.ASM                                             *
;*                                                               *
;* Displays a file in hex. Addresses > 64K wraparound.           *
;*                                                               *
;****************************************************************
.MODEL          SMALL

.STACK          512

.DATA

FHANDLE         DW      ?               ; FILE HANDLE

INBUFF          DB      512 DUP (?)

BUFFPTR         DW      ?

OBUFFER         DB      81 DUP (?)

LINENO          DW      0

; critical error messages
CERR0           DB      'Disk is write protected',0
CERR1           DB      'Invalid drive',0
CERR2           DB      'Drive not ready (is the drive door open?)',0
CERR3           DB      'Bad command',0
CERR4           DB      'CRC error',0
CERR5           DB      'Bad disk request',0
CERR6           DB      'Seek error'
CERR7           DB      'Unknown disk format',0
```

BUILDING ROBUST APPLICATIONS

```
CERR8           DB      'Sector not found',0
CERR9           DB      'No paper in printer',0
CERRA           DB      'Write error',0
CERRB           DB      'Read error',0
CERRC           DB      'General error',0
CERRD           DB      '? ERROR',0  ; impossible error code
CERRE           DB      '? ERROR',0  ; impossible error code
CERRF           DB      'Invalid disk change',0

; table of critical error messages
CERRTBL         DW      OFFSET CERR0
                DW      OFFSET CERR1
                DW      OFFSET CERR2
                DW      OFFSET CERR3
                DW      OFFSET CERR4
                DW      OFFSET CERR5
                DW      OFFSET CERR6
                DW      OFFSET CERR7
                DW      OFFSET CERR8
                DW      OFFSET CERR9
                DW      OFFSET CERRA
                DW      OFFSET CERRB
                DW      OFFSET CERRC
                DW      OFFSET CERRD
                DW      OFFSET CERRE
                DW      OFFSET CERRF

CERRMSG         DB      '.',13, 10, 'Abort program (Y/N)? ',0

ERRM1           DB      'Error on input file.',13,10
ERR1L           DW      $-ERRM1

ERRM2           DB      'Error on output file.',13,10
ERR2L           DW      $-ERRM2

HELPMSG         DB      'HEXDUMP - by Al Williams',13,10
                DB      'Dumps a file in hex format to STDOUT',13,10
                DB      'Usage: HEXDUMP filename',13,10
HELPLEN         DW      $-HELPMSG

BRKMSG          DB      'Quit (Y/N)? ',0
```

DOS 5: A DEVELOPER'S GUIDE

```
        .CODE

; Routines for handling ^Break & Critical errors.
; Note:
;    BIOS is used for I/O so messages appear on the screen even if
;    the output is redirected. This is important for critical
;    errors in particular since they can't use the handle I/O
;    calls.
;
;    The INT 23H and 24H vectors do not need to be reset before
;    program terminations since DOS restores these vectors from
;    the PSP.

; Get a Y or an N. Return carry set for Y, clear for N.
; Destroys BX, AX, DX. Assumes DS addressability.
GETYN           PROC
REINPUT:
                XOR     AH,AH           ; AH=0
                INT     16H             ; Get key.
                AND     AL,0DFH         ; Convert to uppercase.
                CMP     AL,'N'
                JZ      PROCESS
                CMP     AL,'Y'
                JNZ     REINPUT
PROCESS:
                PUSH    AX
                MOV     AH,0FH
                INT     10H             ; Get video page.
                POP     AX
                PUSH    AX
                MOV     AH,0EH
                INT     10H
                MOV     AL,0DH
                INT     10H
                MOV     AL,0AH
                INT     10H
                POP     AX
                SUB     AL,'Y'          ; Carry clear if yes, set if no.
                CMC                     ; Invert carry flag.
                RET
GETYN           ENDP
```

BUILDING ROBUST APPLICATIONS

```
; Print a null-terminated string (DS:BX) to the screen with BIOS.
; Destroys AX,BX.
BIOSP           PROC
                PUSH    SI
                MOV     SI,BX
                MOV     AH,0FH
                INT     10H             ; Get page.
                MOV     AH,0EH

BPLOOP:         MOV     AL,[SI]
                OR      AL,AL
                JZ      BPXIT
                INC     SI
                INT     10H
                JMP     BPLOOP

BPXIT:
                POP     SI
                RET
BIOSP           ENDP

; break handler
; Ask user to confirm exit.

ONBREAK         PROC    FAR
                PUSH    DS
                PUSH    AX
                PUSH    BX
                PUSH    DX
; Get data addressability.
                MOV     DX,@Data
                MOV     DS,DX
; Print message.
                MOV     BX,OFFSET BRKMSG
                CALL    BIOSP
; Ask yes or no (carry= yes, no carry=no).
                CALL    GETYN
                POP     DX
                POP     BX
                POP     AX
                POP     DS
```

```
                RET
ONBREAK         ENDP

; critical error handler
CRITICAL        PROC    FAR
                PUSH    DS
                PUSH    AX
                PUSH    DX
                PUSH    BX
; address data
                MOV     AX,@Data
                MOV     DS,AX
; Look up DI in error table.
                MOV     BX,DI
                AND     BX,0FFH
                SHL     BX,1
                MOV     BX,CERRTBL[BX]
; Print corresponding message.
                CALL    BIOSP
; Continue or not?
                MOV     BX,OFFSET CERRMSG
                CALL    BIOSP
; Return carry set for yes, clear for no.
                CALL    GETYN
                POP     BX
                POP     DX
                POP     AX
                POP     DS
; Return code to DOS.
                MOV     AL,1
                JNC     ENDCR
                MOV     AL,2
ENDCR:          IRET
CRITICAL        ENDP

; ***************************
; Main Program
; ***************************

MAIN            PROC
; INSTALL ^C HANDLER
```

BUILDING ROBUST APPLICATIONS

```
                MOV     AX,SEG ONBREAK
                MOV     DS,AX
                MOV     DX,OFFSET ONBREAK
                MOV     AX,2523H
                INT     21H
; Install critical error handler.
                MOV     AX,SEG CRITICAL
                MOV     DS,AX
                MOV     DX,OFFSET CRITICAL
                MOV     AX,2524H
                INT     21H
                MOV     AX,@Data
                MOV     DS,AX           ; address data segment
                MOV     CL,ES:[80H]     ; Get length of command line.
                OR      CL,CL
                JNZ     CONT1
                JMP     HELP            ; Empty command; get help.
CONT1:
                MOV     BX,80H
READNAME:
                INC     BX
; Skip blanks and tabs.
                CMP     BYTE PTR ES:[BX],' '
                JZ      READNAME
                CMP     BYTE PTR ES:[BX],9
                JZ      READNAME
                CMP     BYTE PTR ES:[BX],0DH
                JNZ     CONT2
                JMP     HELP            ; HELP if blank command string.
CONT2:
                MOV     DX,BX
; Find end of file name.
FINDEND:
                INC     BX
                CMP     BYTE PTR ES:[BX],0DH
                JNZ     FINDEND
; Terminate file name with 0.
                MOV     BYTE PTR ES:[BX],0
                MOV     AX,3D00H
; Save DS and set DS=ES.
; (File name is in PSP, which is segment ES:.)
```

DOS 5: A DEVELOPER'S GUIDE

```
                PUSH    DS
                PUSH    ES
                POP     DS
; Open file for read.
                INT     21H
                POP     DS              ; Restore old DS.
                JC      FERROR          ; file error
; Store file handle.
                MOV     FHANDLE,AX
; Read block in.
DOMORE:
                MOV     BX,FHANDLE
                MOV     AH,3FH
                MOV     CX,512
                MOV     DX,OFFSET INBUFF
                INT     21H             ; Read block from file.
                JC      FERROR          ; Error?
                OR      AX,AX           ; End of file?
                JZ      FEXIT
; set up output buffer
                MOV     DI,OFFSET OBUFFER
                MOV     SI,11H
                MOV     CX,AX
                MOV     BX,DX
                INC     CX
                CALL    PUTLNNO         ; Put line # in front.
MLOOP:
                DEC     CX
; If -, get new input block.
                JS      DOMORE
; If 0, print last line of block.
                JZ      WRITEIT
; SI counts--10H bytes/line.
                DEC     SI
                JNZ     OLDLINE
                MOV     SI,10H
                JMP     WRITEIT         ; Write complete line.

; Continue building line.
OLDLINE:
                MOV     AL,[BX]
```

BUILDING ROBUST APPLICATIONS

```
            SHR     AL,1
            SHR     AL,1
            SHR     AL,1
            SHR     AL,1        ; GET MSD
            CALL    CVT2HEX
            MOV     AL,[BX]
            CALL    CVT2HEX
            INC     BX
            MOV     BYTE PTR [DI],' '
            INC     DI
            JMP     MLOOP

; Write output.
WRITEIT:
            PUSH    CX
            PUSH    BX
            ADD     LINENO,10H  ; new line #
; End with CR/LF.
            MOV     BYTE PTR [DI],0DH
            MOV     BYTE PTR [DI+1],0AH
            INC     DI
            INC     DI
            MOV     CX,DI
            MOV     DX,OFFSET OBUFFER
; Compute # of bytes to write.
            SUB     CX,DX
; Write to STDOUT (handle 1).
            MOV     BX,1
            MOV     AH,40H
            INT     21H
            POP     BX
            POP     CX
            JC      OFERROR
            MOV     DI,DX       ; Reset output buffer.
            CALL    PUTLNNO
            JMP     OLDLINE

; here on file error
FERROR:     MOV     DX,OFFSET ERRM1
            MOV     CX,ERR1L
            JMP     SHORT ERRPRINT
```

DOS 5: A DEVELOPER'S GUIDE

```
; here on output file error
OFERROR:
            MOV     DX,OFFSET ERRM2
            MOV     CX,ERR2L
ERRPRINT:
            MOV     BX,2
            MOV     AH,40H
            INT     21H
            MOV     AL,1
            JMP     SHORT $EXIT

; Close file and exit Exit.
FEXIT:
            PUSH    AX
            MOV     BX,FHANDLE
            MOV     AH,3EH
            INT     21H             ; Close file.
            POP     AX
            JMP     SHORT $EXIT

EXIT:
            XOR     AL,AL           ; Exit with 0 return code.
$EXIT:
            MOV     AH,4CH
            INT     21H
MAIN        ENDP

; Convert number to hex and store in buffer.
CVT2HEX     PROC
            AND     AL,0FH
            MOV     AH,30H
            CMP     AL,9
            JLE     LE9
            MOV     AH,'A'-0AH
LE9:        ADD     AL,AH
            MOV     [DI],AL
            INC     DI
            RET
CVT2HEX     ENDP
```

BUILDING ROBUST APPLICATIONS

```
; Store line number in output buffer.
PUTLNNO         PROC
                MOV     AX,LINENO
                MOV     AL,AH
                SHR     AL,1
                SHR     AL,1
                SHR     AL,1
                SHR     AL,1
                CALL    CVT2HEX
                MOV     AX,LINENO
                MOV     AL,AH
                CALL    CVT2HEX
                MOV     AX,LINENO
                SHR     AL,1
                SHR     AL,1
                SHR     AL,1
                SHR     AL,1
                CALL    CVT2HEX
                MOV     AX,LINENO
                CALL    CVT2HEX
                MOV     AX,' :'
                MOV     [DI],AX         ; Remember ' :' is stored
                                        ; backwards.
                INC     DI
                INC     DI
                RET
PUTLNNO         ENDP

; Print help messages.
HELP            PROC
                MOV     DX,OFFSET HELPMSG
                MOV     AH,40H
                MOV     BX,2
                MOV     CX,HELPLEN
                INT     21H
                MOV     AL,1
                JMP     $EXIT
HELP            ENDP

                END     MAIN
```

A High-Performance Application in C

COMLOOK.C is a program that lets you view data communications between two RS-232 devices. One device connects to COM1 of the computer running COMLOOK, while the other connects to COM2. Any data received on either port is immediately sent to the other port. In addition, unless the user has paused the program, the screen displays the data in hex. Each port's data appears in a different color.

COMLOOK, the source code for which appears in Listing 9-4, uses GETOPT.C to process command-line options (see Listings 9-5 and 9-6). This general-purpose routine is modeled after the Unix call of the same name. The programs we will develop later use GETOPT.C.

Listing 9-4. COMLOOK.C.

```
/******************************************************************
 *                                                                *
 * File: comlook.c                                                *
 *                                                                *
 * Description:                                                   *
 * Connects COM1 to COM2 and displays data from both ports.       *
 *                                                                *
 ******************************************************************/

#include <bios.h>
#include <conio.h>
#include <dos.h>
#include <stdio.h>
#include <ctype.h>
#include "compat.h"
#include "getopt.h"

/* required prototype */
unsigned int far *dirwrite();

/* This macro writes the Pause message on the status line. */
#define put_pause() status=(unsigned int far *)(vidptr+0xf00);\
   dirwrite(status,LCOLOR,"Pause          ")
```

BUILDING ROBUST APPLICATIONS

```c
/* putch with color */
#define vputc(ch,clr) c=ch;color=clr;xvputc()

/* status line color */
#define LCOLOR 0x70

/* shorthand int 14H and int 10H calls */
#define int14(rset) int86(0x14,&rset,&dummy)
#define int10(rset) int86(0x10,&rset,&dummy)

union REGS rin,rout,r232A,r232B,dummy,CURMV;

long vidptr;

int statret,flag=0,ch,n,vidseg,far *key1,far *key2,page=0,c,color
   ,color1,color2,color3;

unsigned int far *status;

/* You can add or delete help messages by just changing this
   array, but be sure each string is exactly the same length as
   the existing strings. */

char *helpmsgs[]=
   {
   "P or Space to pause","Esc to quit      ",
   "1/! sets COM1 color","2/@ sets COM2 color",
   "3 set background ","C clears the screen"
   };

/* current help message */
int helpno=0;

/* Set to 1 for scrolling (only for slow speeds). */
int scroll=0;

int pcontig=0xE3;                /* default 9600,n,8,1 */

/* base address of COM ports */
int com1base,com2base;
```

DOS 5: A DEVELOPER'S GUIDE

```c
main(int argc,char *argv[])
   {
/* Set default colors. */
   color1=0x13;
   color2=0x12;
   color3=0x10;
/* Process options. */
/* -1 and -2 set colors 1 and 2. */
/* -b sets configuration (see table on help screen). */
/* -? gets help. */
   do {
       statret=getopt(argc,argv,"1:2:b:B:sS?");
       switch(toupper(statret))
           {

case 'S':
          scroll=1;
          break;

case '1':
          color1=atoi(optarg)&0x7F;
          break;

case '2':
          color2=atoi(optarg)&0x7F;
          break;

case 'B':
          pconfig=atoi(optarg)&0xFF;
          break;

case '?':
          help();
          break;
          }
       } while (statret!=-1);
/* Use key1 to get COM port base addresses. */
   FP_SEG(key1)=0;
   FP_OFF(key1)=0x400;
   com1base=key1[0];
```

```c
    if (!com1base)
        {
        printf("Error: COM1 not found\n");
        exit(1);
        }
    com2base=key1[1];
    if (!com2base)
        {
        printf("Error: COM2 not found\n");
        exit(1);
        }
/* Set up video pointers. */
    vidinit();
    _cls();
/* Write help message, etc. */
    curset();
/* Point to keyboard buffer pointers. */
    FP_SEG(key2)=0;                 /* key1 seg already 0 */
    FP_OFF(key1)=0x41a;
    FP_OFF(key2)=0x41c;
/* Configure COM port with BIOS call. */
    r232A.x.dx=0;
    r232A.x.ax=pconfig;
    int14(r232A);
    r232A.x.dx=1;                   /* Repeat for COM 2. */
    int14(r232A);
/* Set up BIOS calls for later. */
    rin.x.ax=0x0601;
    rin.x.cx=0;
    rin.x.dx=0x174f;                /* row=23, col=79 */
    r232A.h.ah=2;
    r232B.h.ah=1;
/* MAIN LOOP */

top:
/* dummy handshaking--you may need to change */
/* COM1's CTS=COM2's RTS and COM1's DSR=COM2's DTR & vice versa */
/* If CTS, set RTS. */
    if (inp(com1base+6)&0x10) outp(com2base+4,inp(com2base+4)|2);
/* else reset RTS */
    else outp(com2base+4,inp(com2base+4)&~2);
```

DOS 5: A DEVELOPER'S GUIDE

```c
/* If DSR, set DTR. */
   if (inp(com1base+6)&0x20) outp(com2base+4,inp(com2base+4)|1);
/* else reset DTR */
   else outp(com2base+4,inp(com2base+4)&~1);
   if (inp(com1base+5)&1)        /* if COM1 data ready */
      {
/* Write to COM2. */
      outp(com2base,ch=inp(com1base));
/* Flag is set when screen disabled. */
      if (!flag)
         {
/* Convert to hex and display. */
         n=ch>>4;
         if (n>9) n+='A'-10;
         else n+='0';
         vputc(n,color1);
         n=ch&0xf;
         if (n>9) n+='A'-10;
         else n+='0';
         vputc(n,color1);
         vputc(' ',color3);
         vputc(' ',color3);
         }
      }
/* dummy handshaking--you may need to change */
/* If CTS, set RTS. */
   if (inp(com2base+6)&0x10) outp(com1base+4,inp(com1base+4)|2);
/* else reset RTS */
   else outp(com1base+4,inp(com1base+4)&~2);
/* If DSR, set DTR. */
   if (inp(com2base+6)&0x20) outp(com1base+4,inp(com1base+4)|1);
/* else reset DTR */
   else outp(com1base+4,inp(com1base+4)&~1);
   if (inp(com2base+5)&1)        /* if COM2 data ready */
      {
/* Write to COM1. */
      outp(com1base,ch=inp(com2base));
/* Flag is set when screen disabled. */
      if (!flag)
         {
         n=ch>>4;                /* Print hex on screen. */
```

BUILDING ROBUST APPLICATIONS

```
            if (n>9) n+='A'-10;
            else n+='0';
            vputc(n,color2);
            n=ch&0xF;
            if (n>9) n+='A'-10;
            else n+='0';
            vputc(n,color2);
            vputc(' ',color3);
            vputc(' ',color3);
            }
        }
/* if keyboard data available */
    if (*key1!=*key2)
        {
/* Get commands, ignore function keys. */
        if (!(ch=getch())) getch();
        switch(ch)
            {

case 27:
            CURMV.h.ah=0x2;         /* Restore cursor. */
            CURMV.h.bh=0;
            CURMV.h.dh=24;
            CURMV.h.dl=15;
            int10(CURMV);
            exit(0);
            break;

case ' ':
case 'P':
case 'p':
            flag^=1;
/* Don't remove braces from if! */
            if (flag)
                {
                put_pause();
                }
            else
                {
                curset();
                }
            break;
```

```
    case 'c':
    case 'C':
            _cls();
            break;

    case '1':
            changefg(&color1,(unsigned int far *)(vidptr+0xf5c));
            break;

    case '2':
            changefg(&color2,(unsigned int far *)(vidptr+0xf6c));
            break;

    case '3':
            changebg(&color3,FARNULL);
            break;

    case '!':
            changebg(&color1,(unsigned int far *)(vidptr+0xf5c));
            break;

    case '@':
            changebg(&color2,(unsigned int far *)(vidptr+0xf6c));
            break;

    case '?':
            if (++helpno>=sizeof(helpmsgs)/sizeof(char *)) helpno=0;
            curset();
            break;
            }
        }
/* Keep going. */
   goto top;
   }

/* Write directly to screen. */
unsigned int far *dirwrite(unsigned int far *curptr,unsigned int
  color,char *string)
   {
   color<<=8;
```

BUILDING ROBUST APPLICATIONS

```c
   while (*string)*curptr++=color+*string++;
   return curptr;
   }

/* Change a foreground color. */
changefg(unsigned int *color,unsigned int far *screen)
   {
   if ((7&*color)==7)*color&=~7;
   else *color+=1;
   dirwrite(screen,*color,"FF");
   }

/* Change a background color. */
changebg(unsigned int *color,unsigned int far *screen)
   {
   if ((0x70&*color)==0x70)*color&=~0x70;
   else *color+=0x10;
   if (screen!=FARNULL) dirwrite(screen,*color,"FF");
   }

/* Clear screen. */
_cls()
   {
   int clear;
   int far *s;
   clear=0;
   s=(int far *) vidptr;
   while (clear++<1920)*s++=((color3)<<8)+' ';
   }

static int far *cursor;        /* current cursor */

static int far *tos;           /* top of screen */

/* number of characters output */
int count=0;

/* Initialize video parameters and pointers. */
vidinit()
   {
   union REGS r;
```

```
    r.h.ah=0xF;                         /* Get video mode. */
    int86(0x10,&r,&r);
    if (r.h.al!=2&&r.h.al!=3&&r.h.al!=7)
        {
        printf(
        "Error: You must use an 80 column text mode for DSCOPE.\n"
        );
        exit(1);
        }
    if (r.h.al==7)
        {
        vidseg=0xB000;
        vidptr=0xB0000000L;
        }
    else
        {
        vidseg=0xB800;
        vidptr=0xB8000000L;
        }
/* Force page 0. */
    r.x.ax=0x500;
    int10(r);
    FP_SEG(cursor)=FP_SEG(tos)=vidseg;
    FP_OFF(tos)=FP_OFF(cursor)=0;
/* Move BIOS cursor off screen. */
    CURMV.h.ah=0x2;
    CURMV.h.bh=0;
    CURMV.h.dh=25;
    CURMV.h.dl=15;
    int10(CURMV);
    }

/* Put character to screen. */
xvputc()
    {
    if (count==1920)                    /* full screen? */
        {
        if (!scroll)
            {
            count=0;
            cursor=tos;
```

BUILDING ROBUST APPLICATIONS

```c
/* Alternate high-intensity bit. */
        page^=8;
        }
    else
        {
        rin.h.bh=color3;
        int10(rin);
        count-=80;
        cursor=tos+(23*80);
        }
    }
count++;
*cursor++=((color|page)<<8)+c;
}

/* Write help message, etc. */
curset()
    {
    unsigned int far *s;
    s=(unsigned int far *)(vidptr+0xf00);
    s=dirwrite(s,LCOLOR,helpmsgs[helpno]);
    s=dirwrite(s,LCOLOR,"  ? for more help   COM1=");
    s=dirwrite(s,color1,"FF");
    s=dirwrite(s,LCOLOR," COM2=");
    s=dirwrite(s,color2,"FF");
    dirwrite(s,LCOLOR," (C) 1989 by A. Williams ");
    }

/* The following lines are split into multiple printf's due to
   Power C's string constant limitations. */

help()
    {
    printf("COMLOOK by Al Williams.\n"
    "Usage: COMLOOK [-1 color] [-2 color] [-s] [-b config]\n");
    printf("    -1 sets port 1's color (decimal number)\n"
    "    -2 sets port 2's color (decimal number)\n");
    printf(
    "    -s enables scrolling (use only for slow speeds)\n");
```

DOS 5: A DEVELOPER'S GUIDE

```
    printf(
    "     -b sets the serial port configuration as follows:\n"
    "        Baud rate   Word Length ParityStop bits\n");
    printf(
    "        0= 110    2=7 bits     0=None 0=One \n"
    "       32= 150    3=8 bits     8=Odd    4=Two \n"
    );
    printf(
    "       64= 300                48=Even\n"
    "       96= 600\n"
    "      128=1200\n"
    "      160=2400\n");
    printf("       192=4800\n"
    "             224=9600\n"
    "Add the numbers together to get the config parameter.\n"
    "Example: 9600 baud 8, even, 1 = 224+3+48+0=275\n");
    exit(1);
    }
```

Listing 9-5. GETOPT.C.

```
/****************************************************************
 *                                                              *
 * getopt  -  A C language command-line parser by Al Williams   *
 * Modeled after the Unix call of the same name                 *
 * (with some enhancements).                                    *
 *                                                              *
 * Usage:                                                       *
 * int n, argc;                                                 *
 * char **argv;                                                 *
 * char *argsel;                                                *
 * n=getopt(argc,argv,argsel);                                  *
 *                                                              *
 * argc and argv are the usual command-line variables.          *
 * argsel is a string containing option letters. If an option   *
 * letter is followed by a ':', the argument takes a            *
 * parameter. If a letter is  followed by  a '-', it takes an   *
 * optional parameter.                                          *
 * n returns the argument letter. A '?' is returned on unknown  *
 * arguments. A -1 is returned when no arguments are left to    *
 * process.                                                     *
```

BUILDING ROBUST APPLICATIONS

```
 *  Global variables (in getopt.h)                                *
 *     int optind     - first argument to process (default = 1)   *
 *     int opterr     - if 1, errors goto stderr (default), if 0, *
 *                      errors are discarded. Other values cause  *
 *                      errors to goto stdout.                    *
 *     char *optchar  - characters used to introduce options      *
 *                      (default="/-")                            *
 *     char *optarg   - parameter associated with argument. If no *
 *                      parameter is found, the char * is set to  *
 *                      NULL.                                     *
 *     char opttype   - character that introduced the current     *
 *                      option                                    *
 *                                                                *
 * Notes:                                                         *
 *    Options are case-sensitive (you can use forms like          *
 *    "aAbB").                                                    *
 *                                                                *
 *    Options can be mixed. That is, with the option string       *
 *    "abc:d:ef-" you could give arguments -ae -c parameter1 -b   *
 *    -dparameter2 -fparmameter3. You cannot use -f parameter3,   *
 *    however, since -f takes an optional parameter.              *
 *                                                                *
 *    The variable optind is set to the first argv element that   *
 *    your program should use as an argument. If you want a       *
 *    command like "CMD file [-a -b]" you could set optind to 2   *
 *    before your first call to getopt.                           *
 *                                                                *
 *    The special argument '--' (or whatever optchar is set to    *
 *    repeat) causes getopt to skip that argument and report      *
 *    that no more arguments remain. For example, in the          *
 *    "abc:d:ef-" example, CMD -acc param -- -f would ignore -f   *
 *    as an option, leaving the program free to read it.          *
 *                                                                *
 * See the main() program below for an example of using getopt.   *
 *                                                                *
 ****************************************************************/

#include <stdio.h>
#include <string.h>

#define DEBUG 0                         /* Include test main(). */
```

309

DOS 5: A DEVELOPER'S GUIDE

```c
/* first argument to process */
int optind=1;

/* Direct output to stderr(1), stdout(other), or nothing (0). */
int opterr=1;

/* default option character */
char *optchar="/-";

/* argument option, if any */
char *optarg=NULL;

/* Which character started argument? */
char opttype=0;

static void opterrp(char *s,char c)
    {
    if (opterr==1) fprintf(stderr,s,c);
    else if (opterr!=0) printf(s,c);
    }

int getopt(int argc,char **argv,char *opts)
    {
    int i;
    optarg=NULL;
    if (argc<=optind) return-1;        /* no arguments */
/* not an argument */
    if (!strchr(optchar,argv[optind][0])) return-1;
    opttype=argv[optind][0];
    if (!argv[optind][1])
        {
        opterrp("Invalid option '%c'\n",argv[optind][0]);
        optind++;
        return '?';
        }
    if (argv[optind][1]==opttype)       /* -- argument */
        {
        optind++;
        return-1;
        }
```

BUILDING ROBUST APPLICATIONS

```
/* Scan character options. */
   for (i=0;i<=strlen(opts);i++)
      {
      if (argv[optind][1]==opts[i]||opts[i]=='\0')
         {
         if (opts[i]&&opts[i+1]==':'||opts[i+1]=='-')
            {
            if (argv[optind][2]!='\0')
               {
               optarg=argv[optind++]+2;
               }
            else
               {
               if (opts[i+1]!='-')
                  {
                  optarg=argv[++optind];
                  if (optind>=argc) opterrp(
                  "Missing argument to option %c\n",opts[i]);
                  }
               optind++;
               }
            }
         else
            {
            if (!opts[i]) opterrp("Unknown argument: %c\n",argv[
            optind][1]);
/* Reposition arguments. */
            strcpy(argv[optind]+1,argv[optind]+2);
            if (!argv[optind][1]) optind++;
            }
         return opts[i]?opts[i]:'?':
         }
      if (opts[i+1]==':') i!!;
      }
   }

#if DEBUG
/* The remainder of this file consists of two demo programs.
   The first one takes options a b: c o- d e x: and prints them
   out with their arguments (if any). It then prints out the
   remaining portion of the command line.
```

The second demo takes four switches (a b c d) that can be
turned on (+a) or off (-a). It reports the state of each
switch listed on the command line. This is useful for programs
like Unix's CHMOD command.
*/

```c
/* Make this zero for demo #1 and 1 for demo #2. */
#define WHICHDEMO 0

#if WHICHDEMO

main(int argc,char *argv[])
    {
    int stat;
    do {
        stat=getopt(argc,argv,"ab:co-dex:");
        if (stat>0) printf("Got option %c: %s\n",stat,optarg);
        } while (stat!=-1);
    for (stat=optind;stat<argc;stat++)
        {
        printf("got: %s\n",argv[stat]);
        }
    }

#else

main(int argc,char *argv[])
    {
    int stat;
    optchar="-+";
    do {
        stat=getopt(argc,argv,"abcd");
        if (stat>0)
            {
            if (opttype=='+') printf("%c turned on\n",stat);
            else printf("%c turned off\n",stat);
            }
        } while (stat!=-1);
    }

#endif

#endif
```

Listing 9-6. GETOPT.H.

```
/****************************************************************
 *                                                                *
 * getopt  -  A C language command-line parser by Al Williams     *
 * Modeled after the Unix call of the same name                   *
 * (with some enhancements).                                      *
 *                                                                *
 * Usage:                                                         *
 * int n, argc;                                                   *
 * char **argv;                                                   *
 * char *argsel;                                                  *
 * n=getopt(argc,argv,argsel);                                    *
 *                                                                *
 * argc and argv are the usual command-line variables.            *
 * argsel is a string containing option letters. If an option     *
 * letter is followed by a ':', the argument takes a              *
 * parameter. If a letter is  followed by  a '-', it takes an     *
 * optional parameter.                                            *
 * n returns the argument letter. A '?' is returned on unknown    *
 * arguments. A -1 is returned when no arguments are left to      *
 * process.                                                       *
 *                                                                *
 * Global variables                                               *
 *    int optind     - first argument to process (default = 1)    *
 *    int opterr     - if 1, errors goto stderr (default); if 0,  *
 *                     errors are discarded. Other values cause   *
 *                     errors to goto stdout.                     *
 *    char *optchar  - characters used to introduce options       *
 *                     (default="/-")                             *
 *    char *optarg   - parameter associated with argument. If no  *
 *                     parameter is found, the char * is set to   *
 *                     NULL.                                      *
 *    char opttype   - character that introduced the current      *
 *                     option                                     *
 *                                                                *
 * Notes:                                                         *
 *   Options are case-sensitive (you can use forms like           *
 *   "aAbB").                                                     *
 *                                                                *
 *   Options can be mixed. That is, with the option string        *
 *   "abc:d:ef-" you could give arguments -ae -c parameter1 -b    *
```

DOS 5: A DEVELOPER'S GUIDE

```
 *      -dparameter2 -fparameter3. You cannot use -f parameter3,  *
 *      however, since -f takes an optional parameter.             *
 *                                                                 *
 *      The variable optind is set to the first argv element that  *
 *      your program should use as an argument. If you want a      *
 *      command like "CMD file [-a -b]" you could set optind to 2  *
 *      before your first call to getopt.                          *
 *                                                                 *
 *      The special argument '--' (or whatever optchar is set to   *
 *      repeat) causes getopt to skip that argument and report     *
 *      that no more arguments remain. For example, in the         *
 *      "abc:d:ef-" example, CMD -aec param -- -f would ignore -f  *
 *      as an option, leaving the program free to read it.         *
 *                                                                 *
 * See the main() program in getopt.c for an example of using      *
 * getopt.                                                         *
 *                                                                 *
 *****************************************************************/

#ifndef GETOPTHEADER

#define GETOPTHEADER


extern int optind;        /* starting argv member */
extern int opterr;        /* error-handling method */
extern char *optchar;     /* option character (default /- ) */
extern char *optarg;      /* argument to switch */
extern char opttype;      /* character used with this option */



/* main function prototype */
int getopt(int argc,char **argv,char *opts);


/* end of header */
#endif
```

314

BUILDING ROBUST APPLICATIONS

This is the kind of application you would expect to write in assembly using sophisticated interrupt techniques. However, by applying the direct-access techniques from Chapter 7, you can write the program in C using no interrupt functions. On an AT-type computer, the program should run fast enough to handle 9,600-baud transmissions.

The critical concern of COMLOOK is time. Whenever the computer isn't polling the COM ports, data loss is possible. This is obviously a debugging tool, so it should be as unobtrusive as possible to the other machines.

Scrolling the screen robs the program of most of its time. The solution is to stop scrolling the screen. When COMLOOK fills the screen, it simply starts over at the top. It toggles the intensity bit on both colors between "screens" so you can determine the location of the current data byte. While this method is unorthodox, it allows COMLOOK to work at baud rates much higher than you would expect without introducing unacceptable delays in the data stream. If the baud rate is low, you can make COMLOOK scroll with the *-s* switch.

COMLOOK contains many techniques for enhancing speed—look carefully at the listing and read the comments. For example, *key1* and *key2* point to the keyboard buffer's head and tail pointers. When those pointers are equal, the keyboard buffer is empty. The simple statement

```
if (*key1!=*key2)  /* Process keys. */
```

can replace a slower call to *keyhit()* or *bioskey()*. Since COMLOOK depends on the *int86()* call, it defines many *REGS* unions to speed up operation. Once the program initializes these unions, it reuses them over and over without having to set them up again.

At present, COMLOOK works with COM1 and COM2 and is difficult to configure for different baud rates. With *getopt()*, however, these modifications are simple. Give them a try.

CHAPTER 10

Graphics Programming

Graphics programs are especially difficult to write for the PC. The graphic aspect of these programs is no more challenging than on other computers; the difficulty lies in the bewildering number of video standards a program has to support. At present, the HGA, CGA, EGA, and VGA boards seem to be the leading standards. Extended Graphics Array (XGA), Memory Controller Gate Array (MCGA), PCJr, 8415/A, Texas Instruments Graphics Architecture (TIGA), and other cards also exist but in lesser numbers. Worse still, many EGA and VGA cards support enhanced modes that differ between manufacturers.

Faced with so many choices (and who knows how many more to come), what can you do? You have several options:

- Require a certain adapter for your program. This will hurt your market, although for some programs (maybe a CAD package) this is a reasonable choice.

- Use a graphics library from an outside vendor. This is always a good choice if you can afford the royalties and the library runs fast enough for you. It also assumes that the library provides the functions your program needs.

- Work through the BIOS. This is very slow, and not all boards and modes may have BIOS support. Hercules graphic cards, for example, don't have BIOS support because they aren't IBM products.

- Write your own direct-access graphic routines. If you do this, you'll want to isolate the code to ease modification or replacement when new video standards come along.

317

DOS 5: A DEVELOPER'S GUIDE

Naturally, this chapter focuses on the last option. In particular, we will discuss CGA, EGA, VGA, and HGA. Entire books have been written on graphics programming, so the intent of this chapter is only to whet your appetite.

Table 10-1 shows the standard video modes. Of course, you may not have every mode on your computer. Even if the video adapter supports them, your monitor may not. The CGA card supports graphics in modes 4, 5, and 6. Mode 5 is identical to mode 4 except that the CGA suppresses color output when a composite monitor is used (you'll rarely encounter such monitors). When using the more common red-green-blue (RGB) monitor, modes 4 and 5 are identical.

Mode	Adapters	Graphics Resolution	Text Format	Bytes/ Row	Number of Color	Bytes/ Page	Page 0 Segment
4	CGA+	320X200	40X25	40	4	-	B800H
5	CGA+	320X200	40X25	40	4	-	B800H
6	CGA+	640X200	80X25	80	2	-	B800H
-	HGA	720X348	-	90	2	32K	B000H
13	EGA+	320X200	40X25	40	16	8K	A000H
14	EGA+	640X200	80X25	80	16	16K	A000H
15	EGA+	640X350	80X25	80	2	32K	A000H
16	EGA+	640X350	80X25	80	16*	32K	A000H
17	VGA	640X480	80X30	80	2	-	A000H
18	VGA	640X480	80X30	80	16	-	A000H
19	VGA	320X200	40X25	320	256	-	A000H

* Four colors for 64K EGA

CGA+ means CGA, EGA, or VGA
EGA+ means EGA or VGA

Table 10-1. Graphic video modules.

The EGA works with all the CGA modes and supports modes 13 through 16. Your monitor might not support all four modes. Mode 15, for example, only works with a monochrome monitor.

The VGA does everything the EGA does and adds modes 17 through 19. The first two are similar to the EGA modes internally; they are just larger. Mode 19, however, is radically different from (and simpler than) the other modes.

GRAPHICS PROGRAMMING

If you own a non-IBM EGA or VGA, your card probably supports other modes as well. Programming these enhanced modes varies widely from card to card. Once you tackle the material in this chapter, you should be able to make sense of the technical documentation for your card if you need the extra resolution offered by nonstandard modes.

The programs in this chapter are in C. Be warned: For high-performance graphics, you should use assembly language to plot points. Well-written assembly-language graphic functions will be much faster than the C routines in this chapter. However, the C code is easier to understand and modify should you wish to experiment.

Mode Selection

If your program can use different adapters, it will have to determine which video card is present. The VGA and EGA support special BIOS calls. If these calls work, a VGA (or EGA) must be present. If the BIOS calls fail, the card must be a CGA, HGA, or nongraphic monochrome display adapter (MDA).

The HGA and MDA only use mode 7, while the CGA can't use mode 7. If the mode isn't 7, the video display is a CGA; if the mode is 7, we have an HGA or MDA. The HGA supplies a retrace input on the display status port (3BAH). This bit's state will change periodically. The MDA has no such input. If the bit fails to change state within a short time, the adapter is an MDA; otherwise, it's an HGA.

VIDDET.C, in Listing 10-1, uses the following strategy to determine the video adapter type:

1. Load the BX register with FFFFH.

2. Call INT 10H, function 10H, with AL=1AH. The VGA returns color page information in the BX register via this call. The other adapters don't use this function.

DOS 5: A DEVELOPER'S GUIDE

3. If BX is not equal to FFFFH, the display is a VGA. Locate and return the VGA information.

4. Call INT 10H, function 12H, with BL=10H. The EGA and VGA return configuration information in the BX and CX registers via this call. The other adapters don't use this function.

5. If BX is not equal to FFFFH, the display is an EGA. Return the EGA information.

6. Check the current video mode using INT 10H, function 0FH. If the mode is not 7, the display is a CGA. Return.

7. Check for the retrace signal from port 3BAH. If it is present, the display is an HGA; otherwise, it's an MDA. Return.

Listing 10-1. VIDDET.C.

```
/****************************************************************
*                                                                *
* File: viddet.c                                                 *
*                                                                *
* Description:                                                   *
* Routine to detect the attached video hardware.                 *
*                                                                *
****************************************************************/

#include <dos.h>

/* Set DEMO to 1 for a demo program. */
#define DEMO 0

/* Equates for video types. */
#define MDA 0
#define HGA 1
#define CGA 2
#define EGA 3
#define VGA 4
```

GRAPHICS PROGRAMMING

```c
/* EGA and VGA information */
int ega_mem=-1;
int ega_monitor=-1;

video_det()
    {
    union REGS r;
    int far *vmem,x,i;
/* Try VGA call. */
    r.x.bx=0xffff;
    r.x.ax=0x101a;
    int86(0x10,&r,&r);

/* If it worked... */
    if (r.x.bx!=0xffff)
        {
/* get VGA info and return. */
        r.h.ah=0x12;
        r.h.bl=0x10;
        int86(0x10,&r,&r);
        ega_monitor=r.h.bh;
/* may not show 512K/1024K VGA memory */
        ega_mem=64*(1+r.h.bl);
        return VGA;
        }
/* Try EGA call. */
    r.h.ah=0x12;
    r.h.bl=0x10;
    int86(0x10,&r,&r);

/* If it worked... */
    if (r.h.bh!=0xff)
        {
/* set EGA info and return. */
        ega_monitor=r.h.bh;
        ega_mem=64*(1+r.h.bl);
        return EGA;
        }

/* Check for mode 7. */
    r.h.ah=0xf;
    int86(0x10,&r,&r);
```

321

```
/* If not mode 7, must be CGA */
   if (r.h.al!=7) return CGA;

/* Check for HGA vertical retrace. */
   x=inp(0x3ba)&0x80;
   for (i=0;i<30000;i++) if (x!=(inp(0x3ba)&0x80)) return HGA;
   return MDA;
   }

#if DEMO

#include <stdio.h>

main()
   {
   int type;
   type=video_det();
   printf("%d %d %d\n",type,ega_monitor,ega_mem);
   }

#endif
```

It is usually best to let INT 10H, function 0, set the video card's mode. The HGA, of course, can't use this method. Setting the HGA's graphics mode requires you to copy some parameters into the HGA's 6845 video controller. Be careful to set the values exactly as recommended by the manufacturer—bad parameters can destroy the video monitor.

After programming the 6845, you have to set a few bits in the HGA's control registers. Programming the 6845 with another set of values and resetting the control bits will return the HGA to text mode. Later in this chapter we'll see the routine that does these operations.

Pixel Representation

The plotting routines in this chapter follow the standard convention for specifying points:

- A point (20,50) has an X coordinate of 20 and a Y coordinate of 50.

- The X axis starts at the top left of the screen and runs to the right.

- The Y axis begins at the top left and runs down.

- The top left corner of the screen is (0,0).

- The bottom right of the screen depends on the mode selected. For mode 4 (320 by 200), the bottom corner is (319,199).

CGA and HGA Pixel Addressing. All PC video adapters represent dots (pixels) as bits in memory. For CGA and HGA modes that only have two colors, each bit is a pixel. In the CGA's four-color mode, each pixel requires two bits. The value of the two bits (from 0 to 3) determines the color of the pixel. This is a linear organization (as opposed to the EGA's planar representation; see below). Figures 10-1 and 10-2 show the CGA and HGA memory organization.

Both the CGA and HGA alternate rows of pixels between two banks of memory. For the CGA, if the Y coordinate of the pixel is even, it's in bank 0; otherwise, it's in bank 1. The HGA has four banks of pixels. To change a pixel or determine its value, we need to know four things: its segment address, which bank it's in, which byte it's in, and which bit (or bits) represent the pixel.

The segment address is B800H for the CGA or B000H for the HGA. These segment values are for page 0 (the only fully supported page on the CGA). By adding the size of the page, in paragraphs, to the segment value, we can access either HGA page. Each HGA page is 32 Kbytes long (800H paragraphs).

DOS 5: A DEVELOPER'S GUIDE

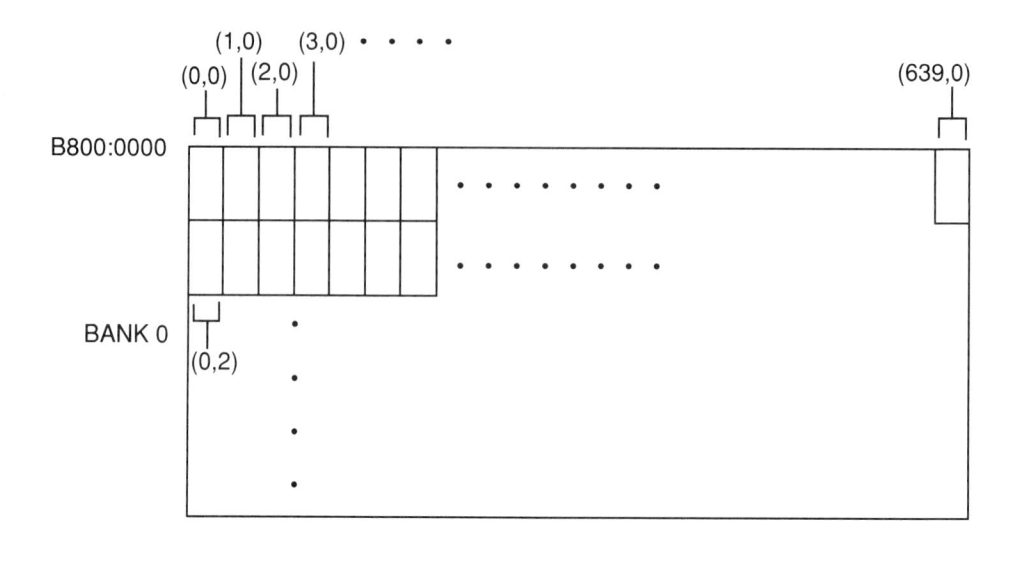

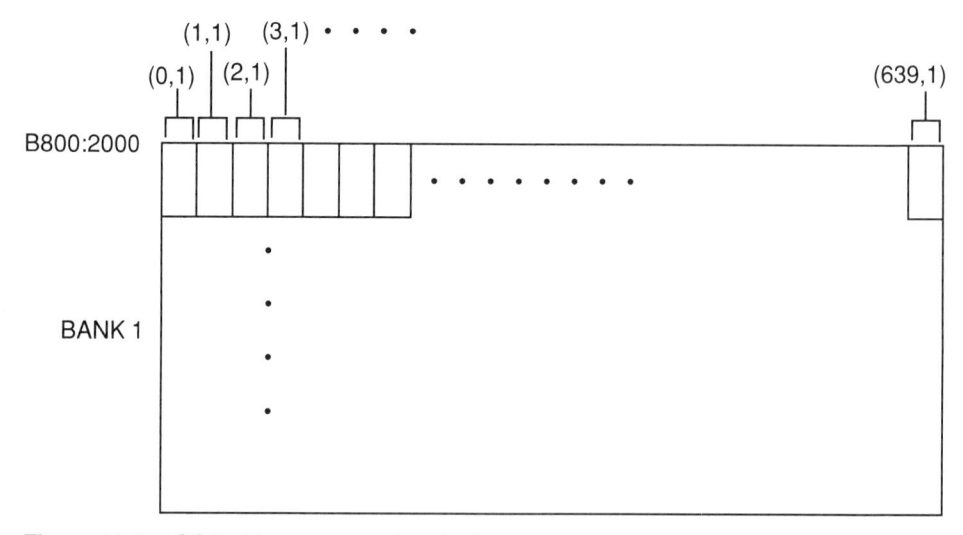

Figure 10-1a. CGA video memory (mode 6).

GRAPHICS PROGRAMMING

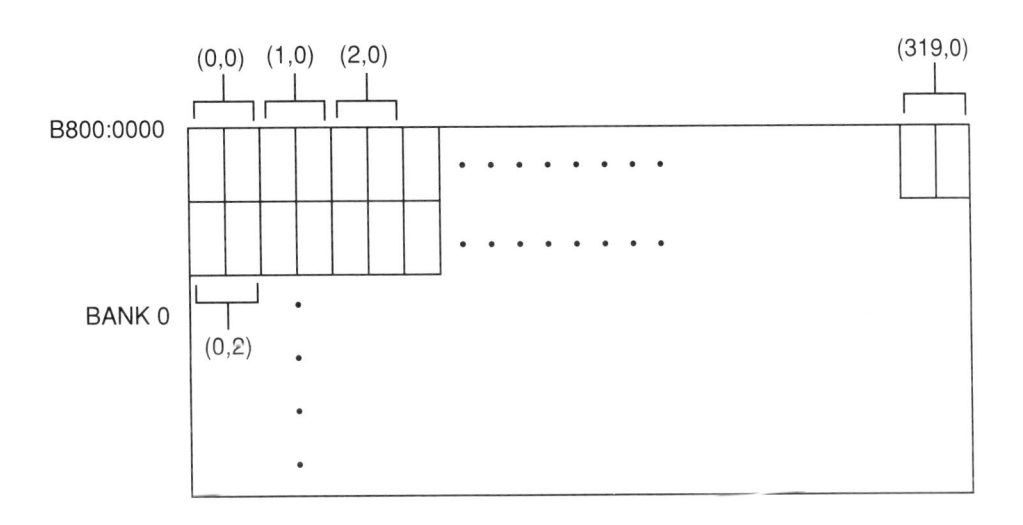

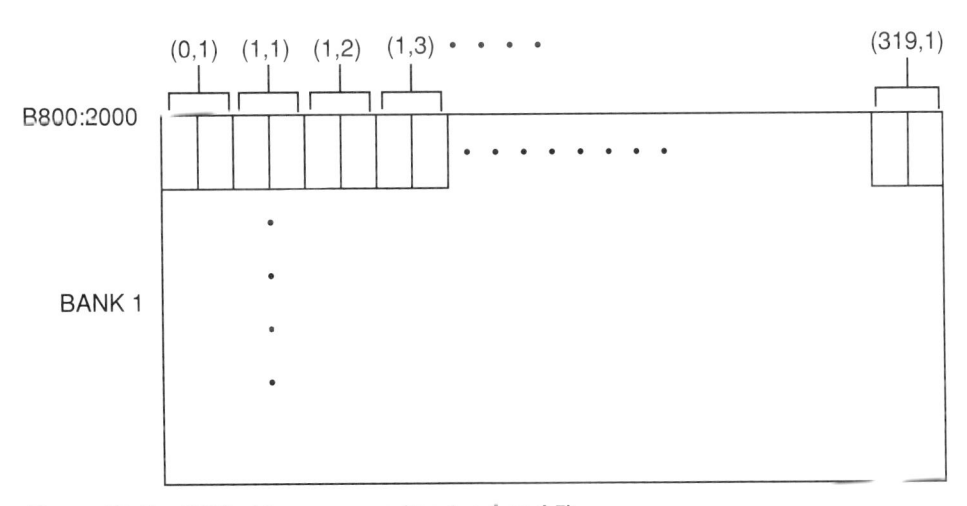

Figure 10-1b. CGA video memory (modes 4 and 5).

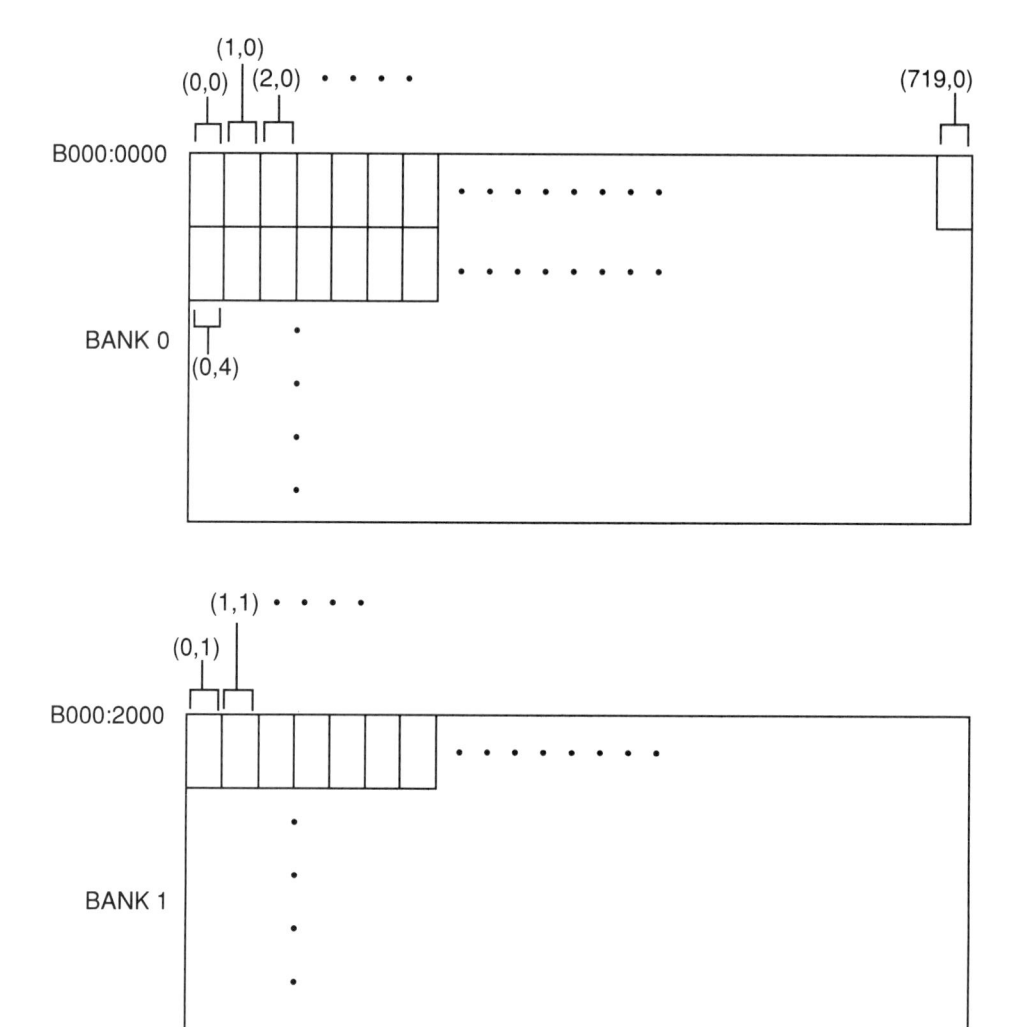

Figure 10-1c. HGA video memory.

GRAPHICS PROGRAMMING

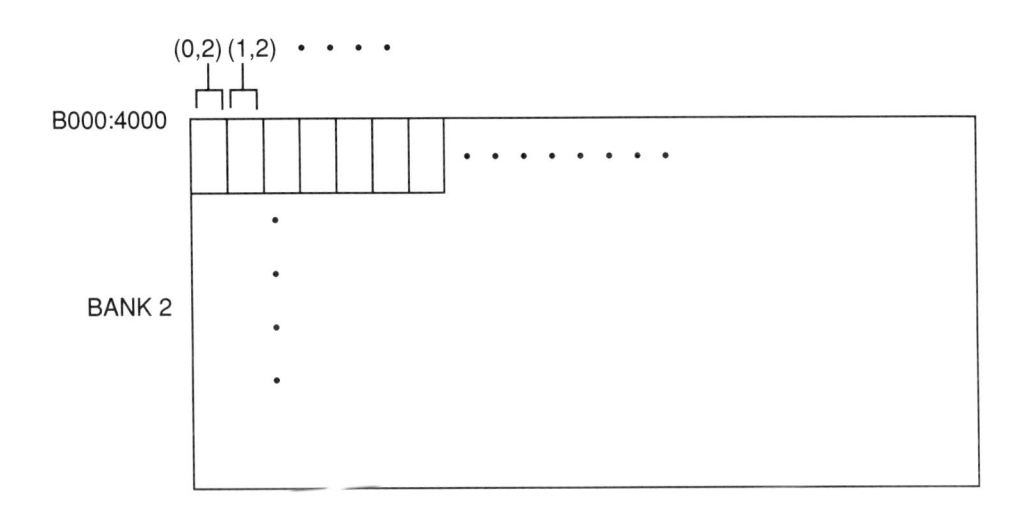

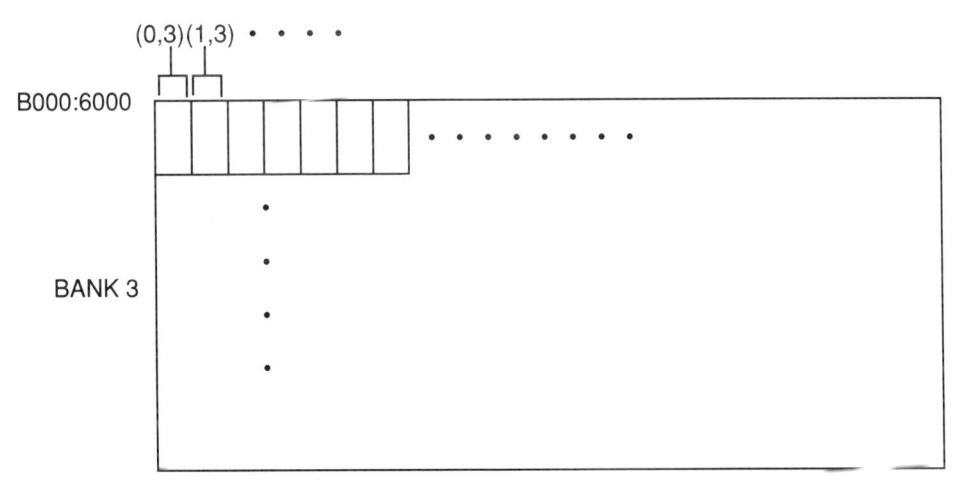

Figure 10-1c. HGA video memory (continued).

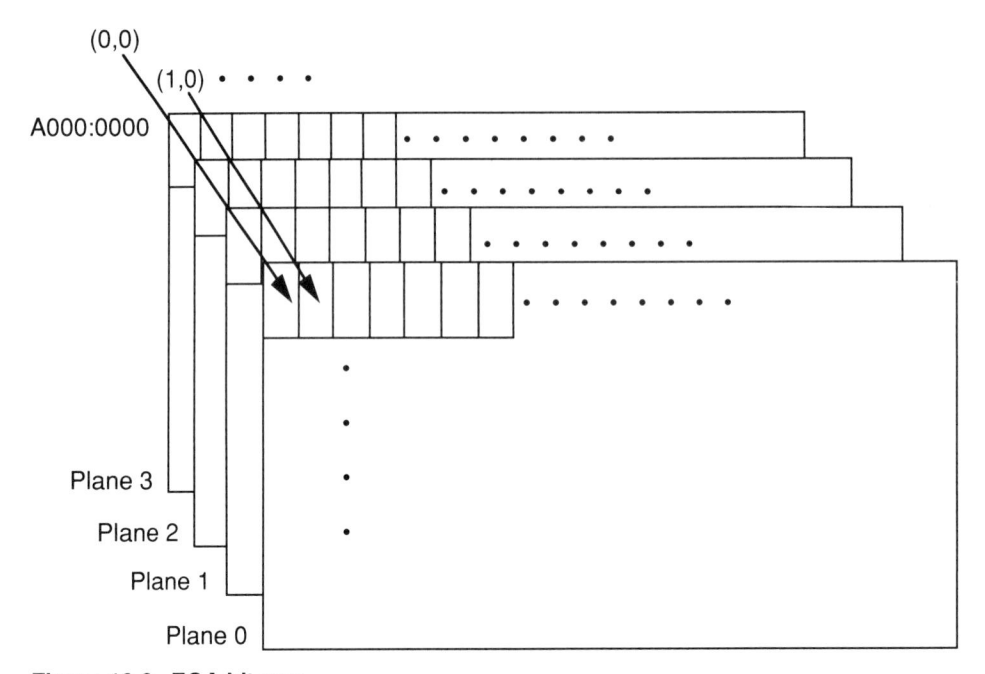

Figure 10-2. EGA bit map.

Determining the bank is simple. The following equation will do nicely:

```
bank = X % Number_of_banks;
```

Of course,

```
a % b
```

is the same as

```
a & (b-1)
```

when *b* is an integral power of two. Therefore:

```
bank = X & 1; (CGA)
bank = X & 3; (HGA)
```

GRAPHICS PROGRAMMING

For both cards, each bank is 8 Kbytes long. Therefore, the offset of the first pixel in each bank is

```
offset0 = bank * 8192;
```

or

```
offset0 = bank<<13;
```

Each bank stores pixels along the X axis together. That is, the CGA's bank 0 contains pixels at (0,0), (0,1), (0,2). To determine the specific byte that contains a pixel, you must calculate the starting address of its Y coordinate. This is simple if you know how many bytes each row contains. Each CGA mode has 80 bytes per row; the HGA has 90. Recall that each CGA bank has only half the original rows and the HGA has only one-fourth. Then:

```
row = Bytes_per_row * (Y/Number_of_banks);
row = 80 * (Y>>1); (CGA)
row = 90 * (Y>>2); (HGA)
```

Determining the byte inside the row is as simple as dividing the X coordinate by the number of pixels per byte. For the CGA in mode 6 or the HGA, each byte contains eight pixels. Modes 4 and 5 use four pixels per byte (two bits per pixel). Therefore:

```
column = X/Pixels_per_byte;
column = X>>2; (Modes 4 and 5)
column = X>>3; (Mode 6, HGA)
```

Putting it all together, we can find the offset of the pixel in question:

```
offset=offset0+row+column;
```

Now that we have the correct byte, the next step is to determine the bit or bits that control the pixel. The adapters store pixels backwards; bit 7 is the lowest X coordinate and bit 0 the highest. To determine the relevant bit number, use the following formulas:

```
bitno = (~X & 3)<<1; (Modes 4 and 5)
bitno = ~X & 7; (Mode 6, HGA)
```

The EGA. The EGA uses a radically different method of finding pixels: planar addressing. Planar addressing is simpler than linear in that it doesn't use banks. However, in other ways it is more complex. Modes 13 through 16 use planar addressing, as do modes 17 and 18 of the VGA. However, VGA mode 19 uses the much simpler method we'll be looking at next. Though the following discussion talks about the EGA, it applies equally to VGA modes 17 and 18.

The EGA has three write modes, and the VGA has four. We'll talk now about mode 0, the most versatile mode. After mastering it, we can easily understand the others.

Page 0 of the EGA modes always starts at segment A000H (you can compute the address of other pages the same way we did for the HGA). Each bit of EGA memory controls a pixel, which may be up to four bits long. How is this possible? Think of EGA memory as made up of planes, one for each bit of the pixel (see Figure 10-2). There are many ways to modify the bits of each plane, but you can't modify them all directly.

To access four bytes for the price of one, the EGA uses a set of four latch registers. These registers hold the contents of the last byte read from EGA memory. Each latch register contains a byte from one plane. When the processor writes to EGA memory, some bits come from the processor and others from the latch registers. Sometimes data from the processor and the latch register are combined before being written to memory. One consequence of this is that programs must read a byte of EGA memory before they can modify that byte. This loads the latch registers. If you write to a byte without loading the latch registers, the results will be unpredictable. Of course, once you read a byte, you may write to it more than once as long as you don't read another byte between the read and the write.

The EGA has an eight-bit-long bit-mask register. The BMR controls access to the pixels in a byte. If the BMR bit corresponding to a pixel is zero, that pixel will not change for any reason. This allows programs to work with one or more pixels without disturbing the other pixels.

GRAPHICS PROGRAMMING

Another important EGA register is the map-mask register. The four-bit MMR is similar to the BMR except that it controls access to planes. Each bit corresponds to one plane. If a bit is zero, processor data won't affect the corresponding plane. Instead, that plane's bits will come from the latch register. Note that the bit is never reset (or set)—it simply doesn't change, because the latch register contains the plane's original value.

Using only the BMR and MMR, we can plot points on the EGA. Finding the byte offset is only slightly different from finding the offset on the CGA. It's actually simpler because the EGA uses no banks:

```
offset = X/Bits_per_byte + Y * Bytes_per_row;
```

or:

```
offset = X>>3 + Y * Bytes_per_row;
```

The bit-number equation is the same as the HGA method already covered. However, in this case, we want to put a one in the pixel's bit so we can store the value in the BMR. To simplify:

```
mask = 0x80 >> (X & 7);
```

With all this set up, the following pseudocode will set the point at (X,Y) to the four-bit value of *color*:

1: mask -> BMR (select pixel)

2: Read EGA memory to load latch.

3: Write 0 to EGA memory (clear all planes of selected bit); this assumes MMR == 0xF (see below).

4: color -> MMR

5: Write mask to EGA memory (you could write 0xFF to memory instead; the only bit changed will be the one selected in the bit mask register, as long as the bit to change is set—the others don't matter).

6: Reset MMR and BMR.

The last step poses a problem. Ideally, the program returns these registers to their original state. However, most EGA registers are write-only (most VGA registers can be read). The BIOS assumes some default values, and almost all programs return the registers to these values. The BIOS expects the BMR to equal FFH and the MMR to equal 0FH. The pseudocode given above assumes the MMR will have that value in step 3.

The preceding routine modifies one pixel at a time. However, you can change up to eight pixels at once, if you desire. Of course, they will all be the same color. You can often increase your program's speed by setting as many pixels as possible with each write.

This routine isn't the only method that can do the job; the set/reset register (SRR) and the set/reset enable register (SRER) can also plot a point. Both registers are four bits long, each bit corresponding to a plane. If a plane's bit is set in the SRER, the entire plane will be forced to the value of its bit in the SRR. Of course, this only works for pixels enabled with the BMR. The SRER's default value is zero, which disables the SRR and SRER. The same routine, again in pseudocode, is:

1: 0xF -> SRER (enable all planes)

2: color -> SRR (force plane to color)

3: mask -> BMR (select pixel)

4: Read EGA memory (load latch registers).

5: Write to EGA memory (the value written doesn't matter).

6: Reset BMR, SRER (since resetting the SRER disables the SRR, you won't need to reset the SRR).

GRAPHICS PROGRAMMING

The first method required a read and two writes. This method only takes a read and a write—a big advantage. Remember that a zero in the SRR actually resets the bit in EGA memory, while a zero in the MMR (as in the first method) only prevents the bit from changing. Our routine still had to zero out the bit before writing the color.

One additional register affects plotting points: the data rotate register (Figure 10-3). In practice, it is easier to rotate data in the CPU; however, the DRR's *AND*, *OR*, and *XOR* (exclusive *OR*) settings allow us to plot points in these modes with no additional instructions. The default setting is zero.

7	6	5	4	3	2	1	0
Not Used			Plot Mode 00-normal 01-AND 10-OR 11-XOR		Rotation Count (0-7)		

Figure 10-3. Data rotate register.

The preceding discussion assumes the EGA is using write mode 0 (the default). You may change the write-mode register (WMR) and use modes 1 and 2 (and 3 on the VGA). Mode 1 is good for transferring one area of the screen to another (in animation, for example). In this mode the program reads a location, loading the latch registers. When the program writes to another location, the EGA copies the latch registers into the new location. The BMR doesn't do anything in this mode. The MMR is used to protect certain planes, if necessary.

Mode 2 is very similar to mode 0. The EGA copies the low-order four bits sent from the processor into each pixel whose BMR bit is set. This is an excellent way to fill the screen rapidly.

Mode 3, only available on the VGA, disables the SRER. Any pixel whose BMR bit is set will take on the color in the SRR.

DOS 5: A DEVELOPER'S GUIDE

Ordinarily, the value read from the EGA corresponds to the eight bits of plane 0. However, you can control which plane's data the latch register receives using the read map register (RMR). Of course, reading an entire pixel takes four reads—one for each plane. The RMR's default value is zero.

Accessing the EGA registers is simple. Figure 10-4 shows how. Note that each register requires you to send a command byte to one port and a data byte to the next port.

Register Name	Command Byte	Command Port	Data Port
Map-mask register (MMR)	2	3C4H	3C5H
Set/reset register (SRR)	0	3CEH	3CFH
Set/reset enable register (SRER)	1	3CEH	3CFH
Data rotate register (DRR)	3	3CEH	3CFH
Read-map register (RMR)	4	3CEH	3CFH
Write-mode register (WMR)	5	3CEH	3CFH
Bit-mask register (BMR)	8	3CEH	3CFH

To write to a register, send its command byte to the specified command port, then send the data to the data port.

Example:
   Set write mode to 2

```
outp(0X3CE,5);
outp(0X3CF,2);
```

Figure 10-4. Useful EGA registers.

The VGA 256-Color Mode. The VGA supports mode 19, a 256-color mode. Some striking effects are possible with this many colors, even at such low resolution (320 by 200). Luckily, this is the simplest graphics mode of all. Each pixel is a byte, and there are 320 bytes per row. Therefore:

```
offset = Y * 360 + X;
```

Once you have the offset, write a byte to pick a color or read the color directly. Oddly, the most powerful graphics mode is also the simplest!

Setting the Colors

So far we have plotted points of different colors, but what colors? The HGA, of course, is black or white (which may be green or amber on some monitors). From there it gets a little more complicated.

The color adapters make you choose a subset of colors to display from a larger set of possible colors. The CGA can display four colors out of 16; the VGA can display 256 colors out of 262,144. This subset of displayable colors is the adapter's palette. Each card manages the palette a little differently.

Changing the palette instantly changes the color of all pixels on the screen (unless, of course, their color didn't change in the palette). When the mode is set via the BIOS, the BIOS sets up a default palette appropriate to the mode. (You can use the VGA BIOS to disable this feature, but you'll rarely need to.)

CGA Colors. The CGA can display 16 colors, but not at the same time. INT 10H, function 0BH, sets the CGA color palette. For modes 4 and 5, you can select two fixed palettes (see Figure 10-5). The palette defines colors for pixels with a value of one, two, or three. You also can choose any of the 16 possible colors for the background, which shows for pixels with a zero value. Many programs clear the screen using one of the palette's colors, then draw with the zero pixel—this allows drawing with any of the 16 possible colors (but only one at a time). Figure 10-6 shows the format of this BIOS call.

The same call affects mode 6. On a CGA card, the zero pixel in mode 6 is always black. The background color is actually the color the CGA assigns to pixels that are in the ON state. However, on an EGA or VGA card in mode 6, the colors correspond to the first two (0 and 1) in the palette. Some VGA cards have a special CGA compatibility mode (set with a special program) that causes them to behave like a CGA card.

DOS 5: A DEVELOPER'S GUIDE

EGA Colors. The EGA displays as many as 16 colors simultaneously. Correspondingly, there are 16 palette registers—one for each possible pixel value. Each of these palette registers can hold a six-bit number. Figure 10-7 shows the format for each EGA palette register. By default, palette register 0 contains a zero (black), register 1 contains a one (blue), and so on. By changing the numbers, you can create different colors. The EGA, with six color bits, can display 64 colors (but not all at once). To set a color palette register, use INT 10H, function 10H (see Figure 10-8).

Palette	Color	Value
0	Green	1
	Red	2
	Yellow	3
1	Cyan	1
	Magenta	2
	White	3

Note: Background color determines color 0.

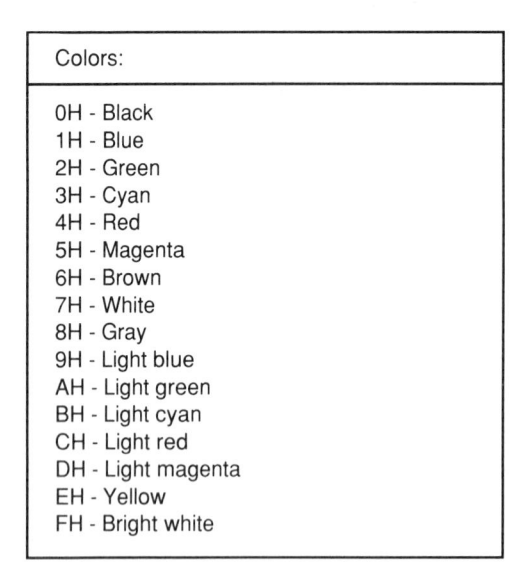

Colors:
0H - Black
1H - Blue
2H - Green
3H - Cyan
4H - Red
5H - Magenta
6H - Brown
7H - White
8H - Gray
9H - Light blue
AH - Light green
BH - Light cyan
CH - Light red
DH - Light magenta
EH - Yellow
FH - Bright white

Figure 10-5. CGA palettes and colors.

GRAPHICS PROGRAMMING

```
Interrupt 10H, Function 0BH.

    Set:

        AH=0BH
        BH=01H to set palette, 00H to set background color
        BL=Color or palette (see Figure 10-5)
```

Figure 10-6. Setting the CGA palette and background color.

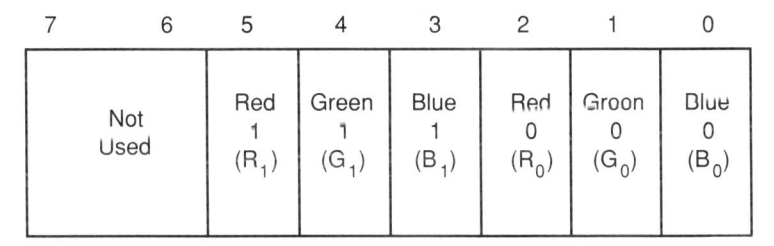

7	6	5	4	3	2	1	0
Not Used		Red 1 (R_1)	Green 1 (G_1)	Blue 1 (B_1)	Red 0 (R_0)	Green 0 (G_0)	Blue 0 (B_0)

Figure 10-7. EGA color register.

```
Interrupt 10H, Function 10H, Subfunction 00H.

    Set:

        AX=1000H
        BH=Color value (see Figure 10-7)
        BL=Palette register (0H-FH)
```

Figure 10-8. Setting the EGA palette registers.

VGA Colors. The VGA uses palette registers similar to the EGA's. However, each register holds eight bits. These bits select one of 256 color registers. Each color register has 18 bits—six bits each for red, blue, and green. With this scheme, the VGA can display 262,144 colors. By default, the first 16 color registers duplicate the 16 palette registers on the EGA. The remaining colors form a gray scale, and an equal number of colors spread from blue to green. You can program the color registers using INT 10H, function 10H (see Figure 10-9).

337

```
Interrupt 10H, Function 10H, Subfunction 10H.

Set:

    AX=1010H
    BX=Color register
    CH=Green value (0-63)
    CL=Blue value (0-63)
    DH=Red value (0-63)
```

Figure 10-9. Setting the VGA color registers.

In 16-color mode, you can change colors by changing the palette register to another color register or by reprogramming a color register. Of course, setting the palette register assumes that the color you want is already in one of the color registers.

In 256-color mode (mode 19), there are no palette registers. Each pixel (which is a byte long) selects one color register. Again, mode 19 is simpler than the other modes.

Putting it Together

Listings 10-2 and 10-3 contain CGRAPH, a simple graphics library in C. CGRAPH also uses VIDDET.C (Listing 10-1). Figure 10-10 shows the calls provided (set *DEMO* to 1 in Listing 10-3 to see CGRAPH in action). CGRAPH can plot points on the HGA, CGA, EGA, and VGA. It can plot regular points, or it can *OR*, *AND*, or *XOR* a color with the existing color. CGRAPH contains a function to manipulate the color palette and color registers.

A key data structure for CGRAPH is *video_info* (Table 10-2). This structure contains information for each supported video mode. Some of the data is for internal use, but much of it will also be useful for your programs.

Three separate routines plot points: *lplot()* (for HGA and modes 4, 5, and 6); *pplot()* (for modes 13 through 18); and *plot256()* (for mode 19). There are two versions of *pplot()*: one using the BMR/MMR method, the other using the SRR/

GRAPHICS PROGRAMMING

SRER method. Set the *EGA_PLOTTER* constant to zero for the BMR method or to one for the SRR/SRER method. All the routines support normal, *AND*, *OR*, and *XOR* plotting. The *pplot()* routines use the EGA's hardware support for these modes; the other plot routines handle them explicitly.

The *herc_init()* routine uses the *herc_graf[]* array to set the HGA for graphics. The *herc_text[]* array contains the data to switch back to text mode. The *herc_text()* function uses this array to reset the card.

g_plotmode(mode)	Sets plot mode to one of the following: PLOT_NORM PLOT_AND PLOT_OR PLOT_XOR
g_reset( )	Returns to normal text mode
g_init(mode,page)	Sets video mode and page. Returns 0 if successful, -1 if unsuccessful.
g_setpage(page)	Sets current video page
g_cls( )	Clears graphics screen
g_setcolors(SET_BACK, 0, color, 0, 0)	Sets CGA background color
g_setcolors(CGA_PAL, 0, palette, 0, 0)	Sets CGA palette
g_setcolors(EGA_PAL, register, color, 0, 0)	Sets EGA palette register
g_setcolors(VGA_COLOR, register, green, blue, red)	Sets VGA color register
g_plot(x, y, color)	Plots a point

Figure 10-10. CGRAPH functions.

339

Field Name	Contents
mode	Current video mode
maxcolors	Maximum number of colors
colormask	Value to AND with colors. Always one less than maxcolors
vidseg	Segment address of video memory
maxx	Maximum X coordinate + 1
maxy	Maximum Y coordinate + 1
bytesperrow	Number of bytes per row
whichplot	Plot routine to use for g_plot
parapage	Number of paragraphs per page

Table 10-2. video_info fields.

Listing 10-2. CGRAPH.H.
```
/***************************************************************
 *                                                              *
 * File: cgraph.h                                               *
 *                                                              *
 * Description:                                                 *
 * Header file for CGRAPH.C                                     *
 *                                                              *
 ***************************************************************/

/* plot modes */
#define PLOT_NORM 0
#define PLOT_OR   16
#define PLOT_AND  8
#define PLOT_XOR  24

/* setcolors() commands */
#define SET_BACK  0        /* Set background color. */
#define CGA_PAL   1        /* Set CGA palette. */
#define EGA_PAL   2        /* Set EGA palette registers. */
#define VGA_COLOR 3        /* Set VGA color registers. */
```

GRAPHICS PROGRAMMING

```c
/* adapter types */
#define MDA 0
#define HGA 1
#define CGA 2
#define EGA 3
#define VGA 4

extern struct _video_info
   {
   char mode;
   int maxcolors;
   int colormask;
   int vidseg;
   int maxx;
   int maxy;
   char bytesperrow;
   char whichplot;
   int paraperpage;
   } video_info;

int g_plotmode(int set);

void g_reset(void);

int g_init(int mode,int page);

void g_cls(void);

void g_setcolors(int cmd,int reg,int c1,int c2,int c3);

void g_setpage(int page);

void(*g_plot)(),

int video_det();

extern int ega_mem;

extern int ega_monitor;

extern int g_adapter;
```

341

DOS 5: A DEVELOPER'S GUIDE

Listing 10-3. CGRAPH.C.
```
/******************************************************************
 *                                                                *
 * File: cgraph.c                                                 *
 *                                                                *
 * Description:                                                   *
 * A simple graphics library in C. Supports VGA, EGA, CGA, HGA.   *
 *                                                                *
 ******************************************************************/

#include <stdio.h>
#include <dos.h>
#include "cgraph.h"

static void herc_init();
static void herc_reset();

/* Set DEMO to 1 for a demo program. */
#define DEMO 1

/* Set EGA_PLOTTER to 1 for SRR plotting, 0 for BMR plotting. */
#define EGA_PLOTTER 0

/* pointer to video RAM */
static unsigned char far *vidptr=NULL;

/* plotting mode */
static int plotmode=PLOT_NORM;

/* pointer to plot routine */
void(*g_plot)();

/* macros for EGA/VGA register access */
/* map mask register */
#define EGA_MAPMASK(val)(outp(0x3c4,2),outp(0x3c5,val))

/* set/reset register */
#define EGA_SR(val)(outp(0x3ce,0),outp(0x3cf,val))

/* set/reset enable register */
#define EGA_SRE(val)(outp(0x3ce,1),outp(0x3cf,val))
```

GRAPHICS PROGRAMMING

```c
/* rotate register */
#define EGA_DRR(val)(outp(0x3ce,3),outp(0x3cf,val))

/* read map register */
#define EGA_RDMAP(val)(outp(0x3ce,4),outp(0x3cf,val))

/* write-mode select */
#define EGA_WMODE(val)(outp(0x3ce,5),outp(0x3cf,val))

/* bit mask register */
#define EGA_BITMASK(val)(outp(0x3ce,8),outp(0x3cf,val))

/* video information structure */
struct _video_info video_info;

/* adapter type (-1 == unknown) */
int g_adapter=-1;

/* video info table for modes 4...19 */
static struct _video_info cfgtable[]=
    {
    { 4,4,3,0xb800,320,200,80,0,0x400 },
    { 5,4,3,0xb800,320,200,80,0,0x400 },
    { 6,2,1,0xb800,640,200,80,0,0 },
    { 7,2,1,0xb000,720,348,90,0,0 },    /* Hercules */
    { 8,0,0,0,0,0,-1,0 },               /* PCjr--not supported */
    { 9,0,0,0,0,0,-1,0 },
    { 10,0,0,0,0,0,-1,0 },
    { 11,0,0,0,0,0,-1,0 },              /* reserved modes */
    { 12,0,0,0,0,0,-1,0 },
    { 13,16,15,0xa000,320,200,40,1,0x200 },
    { 14,16,15,0xa000,640,200,80,1,0x400 },
    { 15,2,1,0xa000,640,350,80,1,0x800 },
    { 16,16,15,0xa000,640,350,80,1,0x800 },
    { 17,2,1,0xa000,640,480,80,1,0 },
    { 18,16,15,0xa000,640,480,80,1,0 },
    { 19,256,255,0xa000,320,200,320,2,0 }
    };
```

DOS 5: A DEVELOPER'S GUIDE

```c
/* Set plot mode--returns old value. */
g_plotmode(int set)
    {
    int ovalue=plotmode;
    plotmode=set;
    if (video_info.mode>=13&&video_info.mode<=18)
       {
       outp(0x3ce,3);
       outp(0x3cf,set);
       }
    return ovalue;
    }

/* Reset to text mode. */
void g_reset()
    {
    union REGS r;
    g_plotmode(PLOT_NORM);
/* Hercules is special case. */
    if (video_info.mode==7) herc_reset();
/* Set mode. */
    r.x.ax=video_info.mode==7?7:3;
    int86(0x10,&r,&r);
/* Set page. */
    r.x.ax=0x500;
    int86(0x10,&r,&r);
    }

/* linear plot for HGA, CGA modes */
static void lplot(unsigned int x,unsigned int y,int color)
    {
    unsigned mask;
    unsigned offset;
/* Compute offset. */
    offset=(y&(video_info.mode==7?3:1))<<13;
    offset+=video_info.bytesperrow*(y>>(video_info.mode==7?2:1));
    offset+=x>>(video_info.maxcolors==2?3:2);
/* Compute mask. */
    if (video_info.maxcolors==2) mask=~x&7;
    else mask=(~x&3)<<1;
```

```c
/* Set pointer. */
   FP_OFF(vidptr)=offset;
/* Make sure color is legal. */
   color&=video_info.colormask;
/* Shift color to proper bits. */
   color<<=mask;
/* Handle different plotmodes. */
   switch(plotmode)
       {

case PLOT_NORM:
       *vidptr&=~(video_info.colormask<<mask);
       *vidptr|=color;
       break;

case PLOT_OR:
       if (color)*vidptr|=color;
       break;

case PLOT_AND:
       *vidptr&=color|~(video_info.colormask<<mask);
       break;

case PLOT_XOR:
       if (color)*vidptr^=color;
       break;
       }
    return;
    }

#if EGA_PLOTTER==0

/* BMR/MMR plot method */
static void pplot(unsigned int x,unsigned int y,unsigned int
  color)
    {
    unsigned mask;
    int latch;
    unsigned offset;
```

DOS 5: A DEVELOPER'S GUIDE

```c
/* Calculate offset and mask. */
    offset=(x>>3)+y*video_info.bytesperrow;
    mask=0x80>>(x&7);
    FP_OFF(vidptr)=offset;
/* Set BMR. */
    EGA_BITMASK(mask);
/* Load latch registers. */
    latch=*vidptr;
/* Zero out pixel. */
    *vidptr=0;
/* Set MMR. */
    EGA_MAPMASK(video_info.colormask&color);
/* Set pixel. */
    *vidptr=mask;
/* Reset registers. */
    EGA_BITMASK(255);
    EGA_MAPMASK(15);
    return;
    }

#else

/* SRER/SRR method */
static void pplot(unsigned int x,unsigned int y,unsigned int
    color)
    {
    unsigned mask;
    int latch;
    unsigned offset;
/* Find offset and mask. */
    offset=(x>>3)+y*video_info.bytesperrow;
    mask=0x80>>(x&7);
    FP_OFF(vidptr)=offset;

/* Set BMR. */
    EGA_BITMASK(mask);
/* Set SRR. */
    EGA_SR(color);
/* Set SRER. */
    EGA_SRE(15);
```

GRAPHICS PROGRAMMING

```c
/* Load latch registers. */
   latch=*vidptr;
/* Write any value to EGA memory. */
   *vidptr=0xff;

/* Reset registers. */
   EGA_BITMASK(255);
   EGA_SRE(0);
   return;
   }

#endif

/* VGA mode 19 plot routine */
static void plot256(unsigned x,unsigned y,int color)
    {
    unsigned offset;
/* Compute offset. */
    offset=video_info.maxx*y+x;
    FP_OFF(vidptr)=offset;
/* Handle different plot modes. */
    switch(plotmode)
        {

case PLOT_NORM:
        *vidptr=color;
        break;

case PLOT_OR:
        if (color)*vidptr|=color;
        break;

case PLOT_AND:
        *vidptr&=color;
        break;

case PLOT_XOR:
        if (color)*vidptr^=color;
        break;
        }
    return;
    }
```

```c
/* Set mode and page. Returns 0 for success, -1 for failure. */
int g_init(int mode,int page)
    {
    int i;
    union REGS r;
/* Check for legal mode number. */
    if (mode<4||mode>19) return-1;
    if (g_adapter==-1) g_adapter=video_det();
    if (g_adapter==MDA) return-1;
    if (g_adapter==HGA&&mode!=7) return-1;
    if (g_adapter==CGA&&mode>6) return-1;
    if (g_adapter==EGA&&mode>16) return-1;
    if (g_adapter==EGA&&mode==15&&ega_monitor!=1) return-1;
    if (g_adapter==EGA&&ega_monitor==1&&mode!=15) return-1;
/* Check for unsupported mode. */
    if (cfgtable[mode-4].whichplot==-1) return-1;
/* HGA is a special case. */
    if (mode==7) herc_init(page,1);
    else
        {
/* Set mode. */
        r.x.ax=mode;
        int86(0x10,&r,&r);
        }
    video_info=cfgtable[mode-4];
/* Set page. */
    g_setpage(page);

/* Select plot routine. */
    if (video_info.whichplot==0) g_plot=lplot;
    else if (video_info.whichplot==1) g_plot=pplot;
    else if (video_info.whichplot==2) g_plot=plot256;

/* Set plot mode. */
    g_plotmode(PLOT_NORM);
    return 0;
    }

/* Set page. */
void g_setpage(int page)
    {
```

GRAPHICS PROGRAMMING

```c
    union REGS r;
    if (video_info.mode==7) herc_init(page,0);
    else
        {
/* Set page with BIOS. */
        r.x.ax=0x500|page;
        int86(0x10,&r,&r);
        FP_SEG(vidptr)=video_info.vidseg+page*
            video_info.paraperpage;
        }
    }

/* Clear graphics screen. */
void g_cls()
    {
    unsigned seg;
    if (video_info.mode==7)
        {
/* Clear HGA screen. */
        seg=FP_SEG(vidptr);
        vidptr[0]=vidptr[1]=0;
        movedata(seg,0,seg,2,0xFFFE);
        }
    else
        {
        union REGS r;
/* Change mode to clear color screens. */
        r.x.ax=video_info.mode;
        int86(0x10,&r,&r);
        }
    }

/* constants for herc init and herc reset */
static int herc_text[]=
    {
    0x61,0x50,0x52,0xf,0x19,0x6,0x19,0x19,2,0xd,0xb,0xc
    };

static int herc_graf[]=
    {
    0x35,0x2d,0x2e,7,0x5b,2,0x57,0x57,2,3,0,0
    };
```

DOS 5: A DEVELOPER'S GUIDE

```c
/* Set up HGA. */
static void herc_init(int page,int cls_flag)
    {
    int i;
/* Allow graphics mode and two-page access. */
    outp(0x3bf,3);
    for (i=0;i<sizeof(herc_graf)/sizeof(int);i++)
        {
        outp(0x3b4,i);
        outp(0x3b5,herc_graf[i]);
        }
/* Pick page. */
    outp(0x3b8,page?0xaa:0x2a);
    FP_SEG(vidptr)=page?0xb800:0xb000;
    FP_OFF(vidptr)=0;
    if (cls_flag) g_cls();
    }

/* Reset HGA. */
static void herc_reset()
    {
    int i;
    union REGS r;
    for (i=0;i<sizeof(herc_text)/sizeof(int);i++)
        {
        outp(0x3b4,i);
        outp(0x3b5,herc_text[i]);
        }
    outp(0x3b8,0x28);
/* Disallow graphics mode and two-page access. */
    outp(0x3bf,0);
    FP_SEG(vidptr)=0;
    }

/* palette handling */
/* C2 and C3 only required for VGA_COLOR command */
void g_setcolors(int cmd,int reg,int c1,int c2,int c3)
    {
    union REGS r;
    switch(cmd)
        {
```

GRAPHICS PROGRAMMING

```c
/* Set background color. */
case SET_BACK:
      if (video_info.mode>=4&&video_info.mode<=6)
          {
          r.h.ah=0xb;
          r.x.bx=c1;
          int86(0x10,&r,&r);
          }
      else
          {
          g_setcolors(EGA_PAL,0,c1,c2,c3);
          }
      break;

/* Set CGA palette. */
case CGA_PAL:
      r.h.ah=0xb;
      r.x.bx=0x100|c1;
      int86(0x10,&r,&r);
      break;

/* Set EGA palette. */
case EGA_PAL:
      r.x.ax=0x1000;
      r.h.bh=c1;
      r.h.bl=reg;
      int86(0x10,&r,&r);
      break;

/* Set VGA color register. */
case VGA_COLOR:
      r.x.ax=0x1010;
      r.x.bx=reg;
      r.h.ch=c1;
      r.h.cl=c2;
      r.h.dh=c3;
      int86(0x10,&r,&r);
      break;
      }
   }

#if DEMO
```

DOS 5: A DEVELOPER'S GUIDE

```c
/* DEMO PROGRAM - will pick best mode or use mode specified on
   command line. */

main(int argc,char *argv[])
   {
   int mo;
   mo=atoi(argv[1]);
   main1(mo);
   }

main1(int mode)
   {
   int x,y,j,c=0;
   if (!mode) setmode();
   else g_init(mode,0);
   j=video_info.maxx/video_info.maxcolors;
   for (y=0;y<video_info.maxy;y++)
      {
      if (kbhit()) kexit();
      c=0;
      for (x=0;x<video_info.maxx;x++)
         {
         if (x&&x%j==0) if (++c>=video_info.maxcolors) c=0;
         g_plot(x,y,c);
         }
      }
   g_plotmode(PLOT_XOR);
   for (y=0;y<video_info.maxy;y++)
      {
      if (kbhit()) kexit();
      for (x=0;x<video_info.maxx;x++)
         {
         g_plot(x,y,0xff);
         }
      }
   command();
   g_reset();
   }

kexit()
   {
```

```
    if (!getch()) getch();
    g_reset();
    exit();
    }
#include <ctype.h>

command()
    {
    int scan;
    if (video_info.mode==4||video_info.mode==5)
        {
        int loopct=500;
        do {
            int delayct=1400;
            if (loopct&1) g_setcolors(CGA_PAL,0,1,0,0);
            else g_setcolors(CGA_PAL,0,0,0,0);
            while (--delayct);
            } while (--loopct);
        return 0;
        }
    if (video_info.mode!=19)
        {
        for (scan=0;scan<256;scan++)
            {
            int delayct=1400;
            g_setcolors(EGA_PAL,0,scan,0,0);
            g_setcolors(EGA_PAL,15,scan,0,0);
            while (--delayct);
            }
        return 0;
        }
    for (scan=0;scan<256;scan++)
        {
        int delayct=1400;
        g_setcolors(VGA_COLOR,32,scan,scan/2,0);
        g_setcolors(VGA_COLOR,33,scan/2,scan,scan);
        g_setcolors(VGA_COLOR,34,0,scan,scan/2);
        while (--delayct);
        }
    return 0;
    }
```

```
setmode()
    {
/* Try VGA. */
    if (!g_init(19,0)) return 0;
/* Try EGA color. */
    if (!g_init(16,0)) return 0;
/* Try EGA mono. */
    if (!g_init(15,0)) return 0;
/* Try CGA color. */
    if (!g_init(4,0)) return 0;
/* Try HGA. */
    if (!g_init(7,0)) return 0;
    return 1;                       /* ??? */
    }

#endif
```

Improving Graphics Performance

If you use CGRAPH, keep the following performance issues in mind:

- The graphics routines would be faster in assembler.

- You can often use the EGA's special write modes to get better performance. For example, setting eight pixels at a time or using mode 1 for filling areas can significantly improve performance.

- On the EGA, the plot routines have a great deal of overhead for each call. If you're drawing a circle, for example, each call sets the BMR and MMR (if you're using that method). The call resets them, only to set them again on the next call. Routines to draw graphics primitives (such as lines, circles, and rectangles) can benefit from having their own plot codes to avoid this overhead. Alternatively, you could write *g_start_plot()* and *g_stop_plot()* routines to set up and reset the registers as required. However, don't exit the program or call another program without restoring all EGA registers to their default values.

GRAPHICS PROGRAMMING

- Often you can speed EGA or VGA graphics by using palette changes. Say we want to display a traffic light. Drawing and redrawing circles of red, yellow, and green could be time-consuming. Why not change colors with the palette registers? Then the following pseudocode routine would work and would be fast:

    1: Set palette registers 0 through 3 to black.

    2: Draw rectangle in color 0 (body of traffic light).

    3: Draw top circle in color 1 (red light).

    4: Draw middle circle in color 2 (yellow light).

    5: Draw bottom circle in color 3 (green light).

    6: Set color 1 to red.

    7: *old_color*=1

    8: Determine light's next state.

    9: If next state is green, do steps 10 through 13.

    10: Set old palette register (determined by *old_color*) to black.

    11: Set color 3 to green.

    12: *old_color*=3

    13: Go to step 8.

    (Steps 9 through 13 repeat for yellow and red.)

- The EGA and VGA have many specialized hardware features for scrolling, panning, and producing split screens. If you write software only for the EGA or VGA, consider using these features. Likewise, the EGA and VGA BIOS has many specialized calls for changing fonts, setting the palette, and so on. See the bibliography (Appendix E) if you would like to learn more about the special EGA and VGA capabilities.

CHAPTER 11

Of Mice and Men

Many commercial programs support a mouse-driven interface. Some programs use the mouse as an option; others require one for operations. Before you decide to incorporate mouse support in your programs, consider how the program will be used. Take, for example, a word-processing program. Many users will be touch typists and won't want to remove their hands from the keyboard to use a mouse. Mouse support might be worthwhile, but the user should have the option of not using one. What if some users don't have a mouse? Will this prevent them from using your program? Of course, for some programs the mouse makes so much sense that you may safely require one. It's hard to imagine a graphics paint program, for instance, that you would want to use without a mouse (or an equivalent pointing device).

A wide variety of mouse hardware is available for the PC: trackballs; two- and three-button mice; and optical, mechanical, and even wireless mice. Luckily, mice come with a special driver program that communicates with the hardware. All the drivers communicate with programs via INT 33H. Some have extra commands, but we can count on the drivers to support a standard set of commands. Some mouse drivers are TSR programs; others are true device drivers. It doesn't matter—all mouse communications use INT 33H.

The mouse-driver interface opens up many possibilities for emulating a mouse. For instance, you could write a driver to allow use of the arrow keys as a mouse when scroll lock is active. With special software, many special purpose devices (like graphics tablets) can serve as mice.

Mouse Modes

A program may interact with the mouse in two ways. It can poll the mouse; the mouse driver will then report the mouse's position and status on request. Alternatively, the program can arrange for the driver to call a special subroutine when a mouse event occurs. The program can decide which events will activate the subroutine. For example, a program might only want to know when the user presses the left button.

Polling is much simpler for programs to manage but requires more attention from the program. The event-driven mode is more difficult—it's similar to handling hardware interrupts—but better suits the natural operation of the mouse. The mouse is completely independent of the program, anyway. If a program turns the mouse cursor on, the cursor moves with the mouse without further action from the program. This is true regardless of which method the program uses to access the mouse.

The Mouse Screen

The mouse operates on a virtual screen that may have more pixels than the physical screen. When reset, the driver sets four variables that correspond to the minimum and maximum horizontal and vertical cursor positions. For example, in the CGA's medium-resolution mode (320 by 200 pixels), the mouse's screen is 640 by 200. Each virtual horizontal pixel will be even. The top left of the screen is at (0,0); the next pixel to the right is (2,0).

Text modes use the same 640-by-200 coordinate system, but each virtual pixel will be a multiple of eight in 80-by-25 modes. In 40-by-25 text modes, the horizontal virtual pixels will always be a multiple of 16, and the vertical pixels are multiples of eight. The first character on an 80-by-25 text screen is (0,0); the next character is (8,0); and the first character of the second line is (0,8).

For HGA graphics and the EGA and VGA modes (except mode 0DH), the virtual pixels match the physical pixels. The EGA's mode 0DH uses a virtual screen of 1,280 by 200 pixels. The virtual horizontal pixels are always multiples of four in this mode.

The Mouse Cursor

The driver maintains a mouse cursor, which may be different from the computer's normal cursor. Even when the cursor isn't visible, the driver keeps track of its location.

The mouse driver contains a variable that controls the cursor display. If the variable is zero, the cursor is visible. By default, the driver places the cursor in the middle of the screen and stores a -1 in the cursor-visibility variable to hide it.

The mouse driver can display three types of cursors. In text modes, the mouse can control the BIOS cursor directly. This is the mouse's hardware cursor mode. More commonly, the driver uses a software cursor in text modes. This cursor alters or replaces the character at the cursor location. For example, the software cursor could change that location to a red box with a white character in it.

In graphic modes, the driver allows you to program a bit-map that it displays as a cursor. By default, the cursor is an arrow. Graphic cursors have a hot spot that defines which pixel in (or near) the cursor is the one to report as the mouse position.

When a program is updating the screen, it must protect the area it modifies from the mouse cursor. Failure to do so can garble the screen. The simplest way to do this is to hide the cursor completely, though you can also protect portions of the screen.

Mouse Sensitivity

The mouse driver must translate mouse motion to screen coordinates. The mouse's sensitivity determines how much motion is needed to move the cursor. Common mice detect motion in 1/200-inch increments. This is the mouse's resolution. Some mice have higher or lower resolution, and some support multiple resolutions.

The units of mouse motion are called *mickeys*. A mouse with 1/200-inch resolution has 200 mickeys per inch. The mouse sensitivity determines how many mickeys the driver must see before advancing the cursor. By default, the driver uses one mickey per horizontal pixel and two mickeys per vertical pixel. Of course, as described above, these are virtual pixels.

Another parameter that controls the mouse's feel is the double-speed threshold (specified in mickeys per second), which provides nonlinear gain for mouse movement. When the mouse is moving faster than this value, the driver moves the mouse cursor twice as fast as it usually does.

Important Mouse Variables

Mouse drivers maintain several variables that our programs will use directly or indirectly. The driver sets these variables to a known state when it receives a reset command. Any program that uses the mouse should issue a reset command first. Not only does it reset these important variables, it allows the program to determine whether a mouse is present.

Upon receipt of a reset command, the driver hides the cursor (by storing a -1 in the cursor-visibility variable) and places the invisible cursor at the screen's center. The text cursor defaults to an inverse-box software cursor, and the graphic cursor defaults to an arrow. The driver assumes video page 0 is active and reverts to polling mode. It also makes the entire screen available for the mouse.

Basic Mouse Commands

This section lists the most useful mouse commands provided by the driver. The C function names included with each description refer to the CMOUSE library, presented later in this chapter. Most of these functions are usually included in mouse drivers. Since each mouse manufacturer provides its own mouse drivers, you can't be sure that a given mouse driver supports a given function. Also, many mouse drivers offer extra functions not widely available in other drivers. Programs access all mouse functions via INT 33H.

Reset mouse   **Function 00H**

Description:

   This function resets the mouse (see above). It also allows a program to determine whether the mouse exists and the number of buttons present.

Input:

   AX=0000H

Output:

   if mouse driver is present
      AX=FFFFH
      BX=number of buttons
   if mouse driver is absent
      AX=0000H

C function:

   `int mouse_init();`

   (Returns number of buttons, or 0 if driver not present.)

Show cursor   **Function 01H**

Description:

   Increments the cursor-visibility variable if it is nonzero. The driver displays the mouse cursor only when this variable is zero. (See function 02H below for details.) This allows subroutines to hide the cursor without affecting the calling program. As a side effect, this call resets the screen protection set with function 10H.

Input:

   AX=0001H

Output:

   None

C function:

> void mouse_show();

Hide cursor   **Function 02H**

Description:

> Decrements the cursor-visibility variable. If the cursor was visible, it will be hidden. Since this affects a counter, not a flag, a corresponding call to function 01H for each call to function 02H must occur before the cursor will reappear. This allows subroutines to hide the cursor without affecting the calling program. For example, imagine a program that hides the cursor and then calls a subroutine. The subroutine hides the cursor, does something, and calls function 01H to show the cursor. With a counter, the cursor is still invisible when the main program resumes. With a flag, the cursor would be unexpectedly visible.

Input:

> AX=0002H

Output:

> None

C function:

> void mouse_hide();

Poll mouse   **Function 03H**

Description:

> Returns the current mouse position and button status.

Input:

> AX=0003H

OF MICE AND MEN

Output:

    BX=button status
        Bit 2 = center button
        Bit 1 = right button
        Bit 0 = left button
    CX=current X coordinate
    DX=current Y coordinate

C function:

```
int mouse_show(int *x,int *y); (Returns BX.)
```

Set cursor position   **Function 04H**

Description:

    Forces the mouse cursor to a new location, specified in virtual pixels. The cursor will be displayed immediately at the new location unless the cursor-visible flag is not zero (see function 02H) or the new location lies in a protected region (see function 10H). If necessary, the position will be clipped to fit inside the limits specified by functions 07H and 08H. Some older mouse drivers won't show the cursor at the new location until the mouse moves. To rectify this, call function 02H (hide cursor) and function 01H (show cursor) after calling this function.

Input:

    AX=0004H
    CX=X coordinate
    DX=Y coordinate

Output:

    None

C function:

```
void mouse_set(int x,int y);
```

Button press info   Function 05H

Description:

> Determines how many times the specified button has been pressed and where its last press occurred. This function clears the button's count after reading it. (Function 00H also clears all button counts.) Function 05H also returns the entire button status, as in function 03H.

Input:

> AX=0005H
> BX=button (see function 03H)

Output:

> AX=button status (see function 03H)
> BX=button counter (0-32,767)
> CX=cursor's X position at last button press
> DX=cursor's Y position at last button press

C function:

```
int mouse_press();
```

Button release info   Function 06H

Description:

> Determines how many times the specified button has been released and where its last release occurred. This function clears the button's count after reading it. (Function 00H also clears all button counts.) Function 06H also returns the entire button status, as in function 03H.

Input:

> AX=0006H
> BX=button (see function 03H)

Output:

AX=button status (see function 03H)
BX=button counter (0-32,767)
CX=cursor's X position at last button release
DX=cursor's Y position at last button release

C function:
```
int mouse_release();
```

Set X limit   Function 07H

Description:

Restricts the mouse's movement to a range of X coordinates (specified in virtual pixels).

Input:

AX=0007H
CX=minimum X coordinate
DX=maximum X coordinate

Output:

None

C function:
```
void mouse_xlimit(int xmin,int xmax);
```

Set Y limit   Function 08H

Description:

Restricts the mouse's movement to a range of Y coordinates (specified in virtual pixels)

Input:

AX=0008H
CX=minimum Y coordinate
DX=maximum Y coordinate

Output:

None

C function:

```
void mouse_ylimit(int ymin,int ymax);
```

Set graphics cursor   **Function 09H**

Description:

Sets a graphics cursor bit-map. The function requires a buffer containing a 32-byte mask that is *AND*ed with the existing screen contents, followed by a 32-byte image that is *XOR*ed with the result of the *AND*. Besides the cursor's shape, this function sets the hot spot. Programs specify the hot spot relative to the top left corner of the cursor. The hot spot's X and Y coordinates must be between -16 and 16. The default graphics cursor is an arrow.

Input:

AX=0009H
BX=relative X coordinate for hot spot
CX=relative Y coordinate for hot spot
ES:DX=pointer to cursor image buffer

Output:

None

C function:

None

OF MICE AND MEN

Set text cursor   **Function 0AH**

Description:

Sets the mouse cursor used in text modes. When the software cursor is used, the driver *AND*s a bit mask with the existing character on the screen and *XOR*s another mask to the result. For example, to create an inverse block cursor (the default), the driver would *AND* with 77FFH (turn off blink and intensity) and *XOR* with 7700H (invert color, preserve character). For a black-on-white '+' cursor, the *AND* value would be 0000H and the *XOR* value would be 702BH.

Input:

AX=000AH
BX=0 for software cursor, 1 for hardware cursor
if BX=0
    CX=*AND* mask
    DX=*XOR* mask
if BX=1
    CX=cursor start line (see INT 10H, function 01H)
    DX=cursor end line (see INT 10H, function 01H)

Output:

None

C function:

```
void mouse_hwcursor(int start,int end);
void mouse_swcursor(int andmask,int xormask);
```

Set event handler   **Function 0CH**

Description:

Sets an address that the driver will call when certain events occur. This function also specifies which events will cause the call. The routine must not modify anything, shouldn't call DOS or the BIOS, and must end with a *FAR RET*. When called, the routine can expect the following data in its registers:

DOS 5: A DEVELOPER'S GUIDE

> AX=event flags (same as the event mask; see Figure 11-1 later in chapter)
> BX=button state (same as for function 03H)
> CX=current *X* coordinate
> DX=current *Y* coordinate
> SI=raw *Y* mickey counts
> DI=raw *X* mickey counts
> DS=driver's data segment

Input:

> AX=000CH
> CX=event mask (see Figure 11-1)
> ES:DX=address of handler

Output:

> None

C function:

```
void mouse_handler(int mask,void far *handler);
```
(Not exactly equivalent; see below)

Set sensitivity   Function 0FH

Description:

> Sets the number of mickeys required to move the cursor eight pixels in each direction. By default, the driver sets the *X* sensitivity to eight mickeys per eight pixels and the *Y* sensitivity to 16 mickeys per eight pixels.

Input:

> AX=000FH
> CX=number of mickeys per eight pixels in *X* direction
> DX=number of mickeys per eight pixels in *Y* direction

Output:

> None

C function:

```
void mouse_sense(int xsense,int ysense);
```

Protect area   Function 10H

Description:

Protects a portion of the screen from the mouse cursor. When the cursor moves into the protected area, it becomes invisible until moved from the area or until function 01H resets the protection.

Input:

AX=0010H
CX=upper left X coordinate
DX=upper left Y coordinate
SI=lower right X coordinate
DI=lower right Y coordinate

Output:

None

C function:

```
void mouse_protect(int leftx, int lefty, int rightx, int righty);
```

Set double-speed threshold   Function 13H

Description:

Determines the speed at which the driver will double the mouse cursor's movement. Programs can disable speed-doubling by setting the required value to an impossibly high value (say, 30,000 mickeys/second).

Input:

AX=0013H
DX=threshold speed (mickeys/second)

Output:

None

C function:

```
void mouse_thresh(int speed);
```

Mouse info   **Function 24H**

Description:

Returns information about the mouse and mouse driver. Older mouse drivers may not support this function. To be sure, load BX with FFFFH before calling function 24H. If BX is FFFFH upon return, the driver doesn't support this call (or the driver is not present; see function 00H).

Input:

AX=0024H

Output:

BH=major version number
BL=minor version number
CH=mouse type
- 1=bus mouse
- 2=serial mouse
- 3=InPort mouse
- 4=PS/2 mouse
- 5=HP mouse

CL=mouse IRQ (0 for PS/2)

C function:

```
int mouse_vers(int *major,int *minor,int *type,int *irq);
```

(Returns 0 if call was successful.)

A Basic Mouse Library in C

To make the mouse interface easier to use from C, you can write C functions that call the mouse functions. Listings 11-1 through 11-3 show the CMOUSE library used in this chapter. Many of the functions store data via pointers passed as arguments. These functions won't store data into a NULL pointer—if you don't want the value returned, simply pass a NULL for the pointer.

Listing 11-1. CMOUSE.H.
```
/****************************************************************
 *                                                              *
 * File: cmouse.h                                               *
 *                                                              *
 * Description:                                                 *
 * Header for CMOUSE.C                                          *
 *                                                              *
 ****************************************************************/

#ifndef CMOUSE_HEADER
#define CMOUSE_HEADER

#define LEFT_BUTTON 1
#define RIGHT_BUTTON 2
#define MID_BUTTON 3

extern int mouse_event;

extern void far *mouse_event_func;

int mouse_init(void);

void mouse_show(void);

void mouse_hide(void);

int mouse_poll(int *x, int *y);

void mouse_set(int x, int y);
```

DOS 5: A DEVELOPER'S GUIDE

```
int mouse_press(int which,int *times,int *x,int *y);

int mouse_release(int which,int *times,int *x,int *y);

void mouse_xlimit(int min_x,int max_x);

void mouse_ylimit(int min_y,int max_y);

void mouse_swcursor(int andmask,int xormask);

void mouse_hwcursor(int start,int end);

void mouse_protect(int x0,int y0,int x1,int y1);

void mouse_handler(int events,void far *f);

void mouse_sense(int xmicks,int ymicks);

void mouse_thresh(int speed);

int mouse_vers(int *major,int *minor,int *type,int *irq);
#endif
```

Listing 11-2. CMOUSE.C.
```
/****************************************************************
 *                                                              *
 * File: cmouse.c                                               *
 *                                                              *
 * Description:                                                 *
 * C Library for mouse access.                                  *
 * Link with CMOUSEA.ASM.                                       *
 *                                                              *
 ****************************************************************/

#include <stdio.h>
#include <dos.h>
#include <stdarg.h>
```

```c
/* shorthand call to mouse driver */
#define INT33(r) int86(0x33,&r,&r)

/* MIX doesn't use _ in front of names, so if using Mix
   adjust the name to match Microsoft/Borland names. */
#ifdef __POWERC
#define mouse_int _mouse_int
#define mouse_event_func _mouse_event_func
#endif

/* Current event flag and user's event function.
   CMOUSE always uses the mouse_int() function (from CMOUSEA.ASM)
   as the event handler. mouse_int() calls the function stored
   here in mouse_event_func. */

int mouse_event;
extern void far *far mouse_event_func;

/* Mouse start-up; returns # of buttons or 0 if not present. */
int mouse_init()
    {
    union REGS r;
    mouse_event=0;
    r.x.ax=0;
    INT33(r);
    return r.x.ax?r.x.bx:0;
    }

/* Show mouse cursor. */
void mouse_show()
    {
    union REGS r;
    r.x.ax=1;
    INT33(r);
    }

/* Hide mouse cursor. */
void mouse_hide()
    {
    union REGS r;
```

DOS 5: A DEVELOPER'S GUIDE

```c
   r.x.ax=2;
   INT33(r);
   }

/* Poll mouse. */
int mouse_poll(int *x,int *y)
   {
   union REGS r;
   r.x.ax=3;
   INT33(r);
   if (x)*x=r.x.cx;
   if (y)*y=r.x.dx;
   return r.x.bx;
   }

/* Set mouse cursor location. */
void mouse_set(int x,int y)
   {
   union REGS r;
   r.x.ax=4;
   r.x.cx=x;
   r.x.dx=y;
   INT33(r);
/* Compensate for bug in some older mouse drivers. */
   mouse_hide();
   mouse_show();
   }

/* Read button-press information. */
int mouse_press(int which,int *times,int *x,int *y)
   {
   union REGS r;
   r.x.ax=5;
   r.x.bx=which;
   INT33(r);
   if (times)*times=r.x.bx;
   if (x)*x=r.x.cx;
   if (y)*y=r.x.dx;
   return r.x.ax;
   }
```

```
/* Read button-release information. */
int mouse_release(int which,int *times,int *x,int *y)
    {
    union REGS r;
    r.x.ax=6;
    r.x.bx=which;
    INT33(r);
    if (times)*times=r.x.bx;
    if (x)*x=r.x.cx;
    if (y)*y=r.x.dx;
    return r.x.ax;
    }

/* Set mouse x-axis limits. */
void mouse_xlimit(int min_x,int max_x)
    {
    union REGS r;
    r.x.ax=7;
    r.x.cx=min_x;
    r.x.dx=max_x;
    INT33(r);
    }

/* Set mouse y-axis limits. */
void mouse_ylimit(int min_y,int max_y)
    {
    union REGS r;
    r.x.ax=8;
    r.x.cx=min_y;
    r.x.dx=max_y;
    INT33(r);
    }

/* Set software cursor. */
void mouse_swcursor(int andmask,int xormask)
    {
    union REGS r;
    r.x.ax=0xa;
    r.x.bx=0;
    r.x.cx=andmask;
```

```c
    r.x.dx=xormask;
    INT33(r);
    }

/* Set hardware cursor. */
void mouse_hwcursor(int start,int end)
    {
    union REGS r;
    r.x.ax=0xa;
    r.x.bx=1;
    r.x.cx=start;
    r.x.dx=end;
    INT33(r);
    }

/* Protect screen region. */
void mouse_protect(int x0,int y0,int x1,int y1)
    {
    union REGS r;
    r.x.ax=0x10;
    r.x.cx=x0;
    r.x.dx=y0;
    r.x.si=x1;
    r.x.di=y1;
    INT33(r);
    }

/* Set up event handler.
   Notice that CMOUSE always uses mouse_int() (from CMOUSEA.ASM)
   as a mouse handler. mouse_int() then calls the user's
   function. */
void mouse_handler(int events,void far *f)
    {
    extern void far mouse_int();
    union REGS r;
    struct SREGS rseg;
    void far *mscbug=(void far *)mouse_int;
    mouse_event=events;
    mouse_event_func=f;
    r.x.ax=0xc;
```

```c
    r.x.cx=events;
    r.x.dx=FP_OFF(mscbug);
    rseg.es=FP_SEG(mscbug);
    int86x(0x33,&r,&r,&rseg);
    }

/* Set mouse sensitivity. */
void mouse_sense(int xmicks,int ymicks)
    {
    union REGS r;
    r.x.ax=0xf;
    r.x.cx=xmicks;
    r.x.dx=ymicks;
    INT33(r);
    }

/* Set double-speed threshold. */
void mouse_thresh(int speed)
    {
    union REGS r;
    r.x.ax=0x13;
    r.x.dx=speed;
    INT33(r);
    }

/* Find mouse version. Returns -1 if unsuccessful or
   0 if information is valid. */
int mouse_vers(int *major,int *minor,int *type,int *irq)
    {
    union REGS r;
    r.x.bx=0xffff;
    r.x.ax=0x24;
    INT33(r);
    if (r.x.bx==0xffff) return-1;
    if (major)*major=r.h.bh;
    if (minor)*minor=r.h.bl;
    if (type)*type=r.h.ch;
    if (irq)*irq=r.h.cl;
    return 0;
    }
```

Listing 11-3. CMOUSEA.ASM.

```
;****************************************************************
;*                                                               *
;* File: cmousea.asm                                             *
;*                                                               *
;* Assembly-language hook for CMOUSE library event handler.      *
;* Assemble with /Ml switch.                                     *
;*                                                               *
;****************************************************************

; Adjust for proper memory model.
.MODEL SMALL,C

.CODE
      PUBLIC mouse_event_func,mouse_int

mouse_event_func DD ?

mouse_int PROC FAR
      PUSHF
      CALL CS:[mouse_event_func]
      RET
mouse_int ENDP

      END
```

Polling the Mouse

Programs poll the mouse using the functions *mouse_poll()*, *mouse_press()*, and *mouse_release()*. When using the *mouse_poll()* function to detect a button press, remember that the bit will remain high as long as the button remains pressed. Listing 11-4 contains a simple text-mode drawing program, ESKETCH, that uses *mouse_poll()* to poll the mouse. The main program initializes the mouse and makes the cursor visible. A loop detects buttons; the left button draws a block character, while the right button uses a space. When the keys are pressed at the same time, the menu bar at the bottom of the screen becomes active. ESKETCH uses the *getopt()* function from Chapter 9 to process command-line options.

OF MICE AND MEN

Listing 11-4. ESKETCH.C.
```
/****************************************************************
 *                                                              *
 * File: esketch.c                                              *
 *                                                              *
 * Description:                                                 *
 * Simple sketch program using CMOUSE.C.                        *
 * Uses polling to detect mouse events.                         *
 *                                                              *
 ****************************************************************/

#include <stdio.h>
#include <dos.h>
#include <conio.h>
#include "cmouse.h"
#include "getopt.h"
#include "stdarg.h"
#include "compat.h"

/* screen colors */
int backcolor=0x10;
int forecolor=0xf;

/* Ignore breaks (just in case). */
void interrupt far onbreak()
    {
    }

main(int argc,char *argv[])
    {
    int x,y,stat;
/* mouse sensitivity */
    int xsense=40,ysense=40;
/* default cursor */
    int curand=0x77ff,curxor=0x7700;
/* Check for mouse. */
    if (!mouse_init())
        {
        printf("ESKETCH requires a mouse\n");
        exit(1);
        }
```

DOS 5: A DEVELOPER'S GUIDE

```c
/* Disable break--there shouldn't be any chance of DOS
   seeing a break in this program, but better safe than
   sorry. */
   setvect(0x23,onbreak);

/* Process options with getopt(). */
   do {
       stat=getopt(argc,argv,"x:X:y:Y:aA");

/* Set x and y sensitivity. */
       if (stat=='x'||stat=='X') xsense=atoi(optarg);
       if (stat=='y'||stat=='Y') ysense=atoi(optarg);

/* Set alternate cursor. */
       if (stat=='a'||stat=='A')
           {
           curand=0;
           curxor=0xf00|'+';
           }

/* help */
       if (stat=='?') help();
       } while (stat!=-1);

/* Set up mouse parameters. */
   mouse_sense(xsense,ysense);
/* Protect menu bar. */
   mouse_ylimit(0,23<<3);
/* Set up for drawing routines. */
   draw_init();
/* Select and show cursor. */
   mouse_swcursor(curand,curxor);
   mouse_show();
/* Goto main loop. */
   mainloop();
   }

/* last x and y positions */
int x0=-1,y0=-1;
```

OF MICE AND MEN

```
mainloop()
    {
    int stat,x,y;
    while (1)
        {
/* Poll for mouse. */
        while (!(stat=mouse_poll(&x,&y)));
/* Delay in case right and left button press-- you can't count on
   these coming at the exact same time. */
        bios_delay();
/* Update button status--if it was left and right, there has
   been enough time by now. */
        stat=mouse_poll(NULL,NULL);
/* Convert to screen coordinates. */
        x>>=3;
        y>>=3;
/* If both down, do menu. */
        if ((stat&LEFT_BUTTON)&&(stat&RIGHT_BUTTON)) { stat=0;
do_menu(); }
/* If left...draw. */
        if (stat&LEFT_BUTTON)
            {
            x0=x;
            y0=y;
/* Draw 1st point. */
            draw(x,y,219);
/* while button down */
            while ((stat=mouse_poll(&x,&y))&LEFT_BUTTON)
                {
/* Convert to screen coordinates. */
                x>>=3;
                y>>=3;
/* Connect the dots! */
                if (x0!=x||y0!=y) lineto(x,y,219);
                }
            continue;
            }
```

381

DOS 5: A DEVELOPER'S GUIDE

```c
/* If right button, draw. */
      if (stat&RIGHT_BUTTON)
          {
          x0=x;
          y0=y;
/* Draw 1st point. */
          draw(x,y,' ');
/* while button down */
          while ((stat=mouse_poll(&x,&y))&RIGHT_BUTTON)
              {
/* Convert to screen coordinates. */
              x>>=3;
              y>>=3;
/* Connect the dots! */
              if (x0!=x||y0!=y) lineto(x,y,' ');
              }
          }
      }
   }

/* video page */
static int vpage=0;

/* Set up for draw routines. */
draw_init()
    {
    union REGS r;
/* Clear screen. */
    r.x.ax=0x0600;
    r.h.bh=backcolor;
    r.x.cx=0;
    r.h.dh=24;
    r.h.dl=79;
    int86(0x10,&r,&r);
/* Get page number. */
    r.h.ah=0xf;
    int86(0x10,&r,&r);
    vpage=r.h.bh;
/* Draw menu bar. */
    draw_menu();
    }
```

```
/* Goto x,y coordinate on screen. */
goxy(int x,int y)
    {
    union REGS r;
    r.h.bh=vpage;
    r.h.ah=2;
    r.h.dh=y;
    r.h.dl=x;
    int86(0x10,&r,&r);
    }

/* Draw ch at (x,y). */
draw(int x,int y,int ch)
    {
    union REGS r;
/* Hide mouse cursor before update. */
    mouse_hide();
/* Move cursor. */
    goxy(x,y);
/* Write character. */
    r.x.ax=0x900|ch;
    r.h.bl=backcolor|forecolor;
    r.h.bh=vpage;
    r.x.cx=1;
    int86(0x10,&r,&r);
/* Redisplay mouse cursor. */
    mouse_show();
    }

/* General-purpose menu function.
    x0,y0 - x1,y1 defines the box the menu lies inside.
    num is the number of items present.
    For each item, you need four arguments that specify
    the box the mouse has to click in to select an item.
    m_menu scans them in order, so you can specify a bigger
    box that surrounds a smaller box and distinguish between them.

    Returns number 0 to num-1 or -1 if right button pressed.

    All x's and y's are in BIOS cursor locations for 80X25. */
```

DOS 5: A DEVELOPER'S GUIDE

```c
int m_menu(int x0,int y0,int x1,int y1,int num,...)
    {
    va_list items;
    int i,press,x,y,oldx,oldy;

/* Reset press counters. */
    mouse_press(0,NULL,NULL,NULL);
    mouse_press(1,NULL,NULL,NULL);
    while (mouse_poll(NULL,NULL));   /* Wait for buttons up. */

/* Reset release counters. */
    mouse_release(0,NULL,NULL,NULL);
    mouse_release(1,NULL,NULL,NULL);
/* Convert screen coordinates to mouse coordinates. */
    x0<<=3;
    y0<<=3;
    x1<<=3;
    y1<<=3;

/* Get old X,Y position. */
    mouse_poll(&oldx,&oldy);

/* Hide cursor. */
    mouse_hide();

/* Limit cursor to menu rectangle. */
    mouse_xlimit(x0,x1);
    mouse_ylimit(y0,y1);

/* Show mouse. */
    mouse_show();

/* Loop. */
    while (1)
        {
/* Get press for left key. */
        mouse_press(0,&press,&x,&y);
        if (press)
            {
```

```
/* If pressed, scan items to see if one matches. */
        va_start(items,num);
        do {
/* Wait for release. */
            mouse_release(0,&press,NULL,NULL);
            } while (!press);
/* Convert pixels to screen pixels. */
        x>>=3;
        y>>=3;
/* for each item */
        for (i=0;i<num;i++)
            {
            int t1,t2,t3,t4;
/* Get bounding box coordinates. */
            t1=va_arg(items,int);
            t2=va_arg(items,int);
            t3=va_arg(items,int);
            t4=va_arg(items,int);
/* See if click was in range. */
            if ((x>=t1&&x<=t3)&&(y>=t2&&y<=t4))
                {
/* Yes! Reset mouse parameters and return item # (0 to num-1). */
                mouse_ylimit(0,23<<3);
                mouse_xlimit(0,79<<3);
                mouse_set(oldx,oldy);
                va_end(items);
                return i;
                }
            }
        va_end(items);
        }
/* Check left key. */
    mouse_press(1,&press,&x,&y);
    if (press)
        {
/* Wait for release. */
        do {
            mouse_release(1,&press,NULL,NULL);
            } while (!press);
```

DOS 5: A DEVELOPER'S GUIDE

```c
/* Reset mouse and return -1. */
        mouse_ylimit(0,23<<3);
        mouse_xlimit(0,79<<3);
        mouse_set(oldx,oldy);
        return -1;
        }
    }
}

/* Do menu function. */
do_menu()
    {
    int ans;
/* Call m_menu. */
    ans=m_menu(0,24,79,24,4,0,24,5,24,9,24,18,24,22,24,26,24,75,24,
        78,24);
/* If right button, cancel. */
    if (ans==-1) return 0;
/* foreground color menu */
    if (ans==0)
        {
        ans=color_menu(16);
        if (ans!=-1) forecolor=ans;
        return 0;
        }
/* background color menu */
    if (ans==1)
        {
        ans=color_menu(8);
        if (ans!=-1) backcolor=ans<<4;
        return 0;
        }
/* Clear screen. */
    if (ans==2)
        {
        mouse_hide();
        draw_init();
        mouse_show();
        return 0;
        }
```

```
/* Any other...exit. */
   mouse_init();
   exit(0);
   }

/* menu text */
static char *menubar=
   "Colors   Background   Clear         (Press both mouse"
   " buttons for menu)      Quit";

/* Clear menu bar in inverse color. */
set_menu()
   {
   union REGS r;
   goxy(0,24);
   r.x.ax=0x0920;
   r.h.bh=vpage;
   r.h.bl=0x70;
   r.x.cx=80;
   int86(0x10,&r,&r);
   }

/* Draw menu from menubar[] text. */
draw_menu()
   {
   union REGS r;
   char *s=menubar;
   mouse_hide();
   set_menu();
   while (*s)
      {
      r.h.ah=0xe;
      r.h.al=*s++;
      r.h.bh=vpage;
      int86(0x10,&r,&r);
      }
   mouse_show();
   }
```

DOS 5: A DEVELOPER'S GUIDE

```c
/* Handle the color menus. */
color_menu(int max)
    {
    union REGS r;
    int i;
    mouse_hide();
    set_menu();
/* Display 8 or 16 colors (background or foreground). */
    for (i=0;i<max;i++)
        {
        goxy(i*5,24);
        r.x.ax=0x900|219;
        r.h.bh=vpage;
        r.h.bl=0x70|i;
        r.x.cx=3;
        int86(0x10,&r,&r);
        }
    mouse_show();

/* Call m_menu to pick a color.
   This is a lot of stack space--for a real program, you might
   want to rewrite m_menu to take an array pointer.  */
    i=m_menu(0,24,79,24,max,0,24,2,24,5,24,7,24,10,24,12,24,15,24,
        17,24,20,24,22,24,25,24,27,24,30,24,32,24,35,24,37,24,40,24,
        42,24,45,24,47,24,50,24,52,24,55,24,57,24,60,24,62,24,65,24,
        67,24,70,24,72,24,75,24,77,24);
/* Redraw main menu. */
    draw_menu();
    return i;
    }

/* Delay from 1/18 to 2/18 of a second. */
bios_delay()
    {
    int dxct;
    union REGS r;
    r.h.ah=0;
    int86(0x1a,&r,&r);
    dxct=r.x.dx&1;
```

```c
    do {
        r.h.ah=0;
        int86(0x1a,&r,&r);
        } while ((r.x.dx&1)==dxct);
    do {
        r.h.ah=0;
        int86(0x1a,&r,&r);
        } while ((r.x.dx&1)!=dxct);
    }

/* Quick Signum and Absolute Value for INT */
#define SGN(a) (a>0?1:(a==0?0:-1))
#define ABS(a) (a<0?-a:a)
#define XLEN (ABS(deltax)+1)
#define YLEN (ABS(deltay)+1)

/* Interpolate line from x0,y0 to x,y. */
lineto(int x,int y,int ch)
    {
    int deltax,deltay,xt,yt,xinc,yinc,xtinc,ytinc;
    deltax=x-x0;
    deltay=y-y0;
    if (ABS(deltax)<=1&&ABS(deltay)<=1)
        {
        draw(x,y,ch);
        }
    else
        {
        if (ABS(deltax)<=ABS(deltay))
            {
            ytinc=YLEN/XLEN*SGN(deltay);
            yt=deltax?ytinc+y0:-1;
            xt=-1;
            xinc=0;
            yinc=SGN(deltay);
            }
        else
            {
            xinc=SGN(deltax);
            xtinc=XLEN/YLEN*SGN(deltax);
```

DOS 5: A DEVELOPER'S GUIDE

```
            yt=-1;
            xt=deltay?xtinc+x0:-1;
            yinc=0;
            }
         while (x!=x0||y!=y0)
            {
            if (x!=x0) x0+=xinc;
            if (y!=y0) y0+=yinc;
            if ((y0==yt&&x0!=x)||(!xinc&&x0!=x&&y0==y))
               {
               if (x!=x0) x0+=SGN(deltax);
               yt+=ytinc;
               }
            if ((x0==xt&&y0!=y)||(!yinc&&deltay&&x0==x))
               {
               if (y!=y0) y0+=SGN(deltay);
               xt+=xtinc;
               }
            draw(x0,y0,ch);
            }
         x0=x;
         y0=y;
         return 0;
         }
      }

/* command-line help */
help()
      {
      printf("ESKETCH by Al Williams\n");
      printf("Options:\n");
      printf(" -A        use alternate cursor\n");
      printf(" -X n      set X sensitivity\n");
      printf(" -Y n      set Y sensitivity\n");
      exit(1);
      }
```

OF MICE AND MEN

It's possible for the user to move the mouse faster than the driver can respond. You can't count on seeing each pixel that the mouse has moved through. For this reason, ESKETCH doesn't plot points directly when it detects a button. Instead, it draws a line segment between the mouse's last two points. The *lineto()* function provides the required logic. When the mouse moves one physical pixel at a time, *lineto()* simply plots points using the *draw()* function. If the mouse cursor jumps several pixels, *lineto()* interpolates a line from the last position to the new position.

Notice that the main loop has to convert the virtual pixels from the mouse driver to real cursor locations for the BIOS. ESKETCH assumes an 80-by-25 screen, so the conversion is simple:

```
x>>=3;
y>>=3;
```

Decreasing the mouse sensitivity can make drawing easier or harder, depending on your personal preferences. Experiment with different mouse sensitivities (via ESKETCH's -*X* and -*Y* options). One interesting function in ESKETCH is *m_menu()*. You may want to use this function in your own programs. It allows you to treat rectangles within a region of the screen as menu selections. Using *m_menu()*, you can easily write bar menus (like ESKETCH's) and drop-down menus. Since *m_menu()* uses rectangles for menu targets, you can even select icons placed on the screen.

Event-Driven Programming

Function 0CH lets the program ask the driver to call a special function when an event happens. Figure 11-1 shows the event mask word sent to function 0CH. For each event you want to intercept, place a one in the corresponding bit of the event mask.

Only one event handler can be active. The driver calls the handler with a *CALL FAR* instruction; the handler must end with a *RET FAR*. Although the handler doesn't end with an *IRET*, you must write it as if it were a hardware interrupt handler. You can't change any registers or make DOS or BIOS calls from within the handler. For programs using CMOUSE, a special assembly-language routine (Listing 11-3) calls a C interrupt function to handle events. This simplifies the handler because the compiler saves and restores all registers automatically.

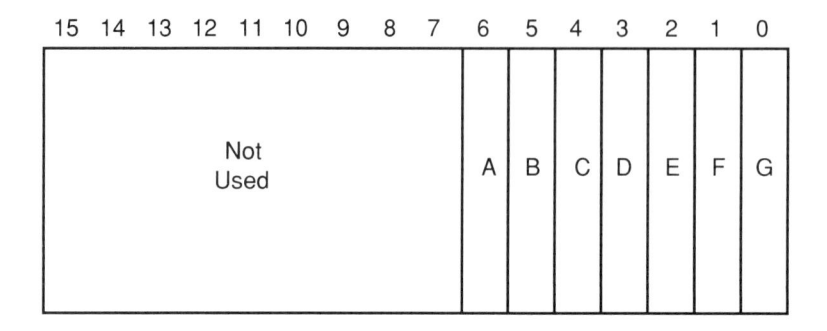

```
15 14 13 12 11 10 9 8 7   6   5   4   3   2   1   0
┌─────────────────────┬───┬───┬───┬───┬───┬───┬───┐
│                     │   │   │   │   │   │   │   │
│       Not           │ A │ B │ C │ D │ E │ F │ G │
│       Used          │   │   │   │   │   │   │   │
│                     │   │   │   │   │   │   │   │
└─────────────────────┴───┴───┴───┴───┴───┴───┴───┘
```

BIT DEFINITIONS
A - Center button released
B - Center button pressed
C - Right button released
D - Right button pressed
E - Left button released
F - Left button pressed
G - Motion

Figure 11-1. Mouse event flags.

When the driver calls the handler, it passes information about the mouse in the registers (see Figure 11-2). Notice that the event flag word looks the same as the event mask word. The handler shouldn't assume that only one bit in the event flag word will be set. The bits will reflect all current events, even those the handler didn't ask to see. Of course, at least one bit that the handler did ask for will be on.

It's important to clear the event mask before exiting the program in any way (including divide-by-zero and critical errors). It's usually best to reset the mouse using *mouse_init()* or function 00H before leaving the program, anyway. This resets everything, including the event mask.

OF MICE AND MEN

Listing 11-5 shows an event-driven draw program, ESKETCH1. Instead of polling for mouse events, the main loop takes drawing instructions from a queue. The event driver, *event( )*, puts the commands in the queue based on mouse events.

Register	Contents
AX	Mouse event flags (Figure 11-1)
BX	Button status (see below)
CX	X - axis coordinate
DX	Y - axis coordinate
SI	Y - axis raw mickeys
DI	X - axis raw mickeys
DS	Driver's data segment

Button status word

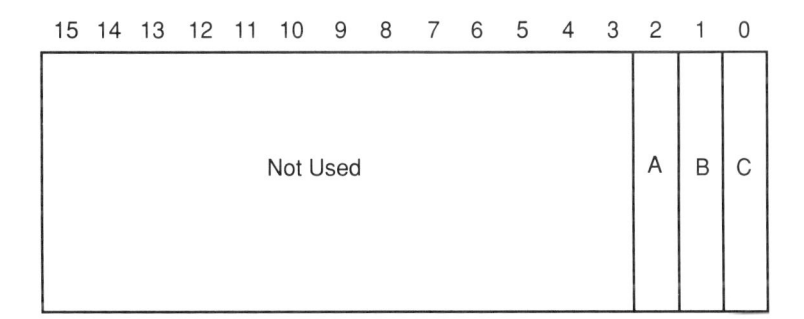

```
 15  14  13  12  11  10  9  8  7  6  5  4  3  2  1  0
┌─────────────────────────────────────────┬───┬───┬───┐
│                                         │   │   │   │
│               Not Used                  │ A │ B │ C │
│                                         │   │   │   │
└─────────────────────────────────────────┴───┴───┴───┘
```

BIT DEFINITIONS
A - Center button down
B - Right button down
C - Left button down

Figure 11-2. Parameters passed to event handler.

DOS 5: A DEVELOPER'S GUIDE

Listing 11-5. ESKETCH1.C.

```c
/****************************************************************
 *                                                              *
 * File: esketch1.c                                             *
 *                                                              *
 * Description:                                                 *
 * Simple sketch program using CMOUSE.C                         *
 * Uses event-driven mouse handling.                            *
 *                                                              *
 ****************************************************************/

#include <stdio.h>
#include <dos.h>
#include <conio.h>
#include "cmouse.h"
#include "getopt.h"
#include "stdarg.h"
#include "compat.h"

/* screen colors */
int backcolor=0x10;
int forecolor=0xf;

/* Ignore breaks (just in case). */
void interrupt far onbreak()
    {
    }

/* mouse event handler */
void interrupt far on_int();

main(int argc,char *argv[])
    {
/* general x,y, and button status */
    int x,y,stat;
/* mouse sensitivity */
    int xsense=16,ysense=32;
/* default cursor */
    int curand=0x77ff,curxor=0x7700;

/* Check for mouse. */
```

```
    if (!mouse_init())
        {
        printf("ESKETCH1 requires a mouse\n");
        exit(1);
        }

/* Disable break--there shouldn't be any chance of DOS
   seeing a break in this program, but better safe than
   sorry. */
    setvect(0x23,onbreak);

/* Process options with getopt(). */
    do {
        stat=getopt(argc,argv,"x:X:y:Y:aA");

/* Set x and y sensitivity. */
        if (stat=='x'||stat=='X') xsense=atoi(optarg);
        if (stat=='y'||stat=='Y') ysense=atoi(optarg);

/* Select alternate cursor. */
        if (stat=='a'||stat=='A')
            {
            curand=0;
            curxor=0xf00|'+';
            }

/* help */
        if (stat=='?') help();
        } while (stat!=-1);

/* Set up mouse parameters. */
    mouse_sense(xsense,ysense);
    mouse_ylimit(0,23<<3);        /* Protect menu bar. */
/* Set up for drawing routines. */
    draw_init();
/* Select and show cursor. */
    mouse_swcursor(curand,curxor);
    mouse_show();
/* Goto main loop. */
    mainloop();
    }
```

DOS 5: A DEVELOPER'S GUIDE

```c
/* queue for mouse events */
#define QSIZE 256           /* Should be power of 2. */
#define QAND (QSIZE-1)

struct _cmd
    {
    int cmd;
    int x;
    int y;
    } cmdqueue[QSIZE];

/* head and tail of queue */
int cmdhead=0;
int cmdtail=0;

/* Set button status from command packet. */
setstat(struct _cmd cmd,int stat)
    {
    if (cmd.cmd==2) stat|=LEFT_BUTTON;
    else if (cmd.cmd==4) stat&=~LEFT_BUTTON;
    else if (cmd.cmd==8) stat|=RIGHT_BUTTON;
    else if (cmd.cmd==16) stat&=~RIGHT_BUTTON;
    return stat;
    }

/* last x and y coordinates */
int x0=-1,y0=-1;

mainloop()
    {
    int stat=0,x,y;
    struct _cmd cmd,peek;
/* Ask for mouse events. */
    mouse_handler(0x1f,(void far *)on_int);

/* Do forever. */
    while (1)
        {
/* Wait for event. */
        while (cmdhead==cmdtail);
```

```
/* Get command packet. */
      cmd=cmdqueue[cmdtail];
      cmdtail=(cmdtail+1)&QAND;
/* Convert mouse pixels to screen pixels. */
      x=cmd.x>>3;
      y=cmd.y>>3;
/* If button command, update stat. */
      if (cmd.cmd!=1) stat=setstat(cmd,stat);
/* If it was a button-down command, wait awhile and see if
   we have a chord (both buttons down). */
      if (cmd.cmd==2||cmd.cmd==8)
         {
         if (cmdhead==cmdtail) bios_delay();
         if (cmdhead!=cmdtail)
            {
            peek=cmdqueue[cmdtail];
/* If next command was button down, we have a chord. */
            if (peek.cmd==2||peek.cmd==8)
               {
/* Consume command and update stat. */
               stat=setstat(peek,stat);
               cmdtail=(cmdtail+1)&QAND;
               }
            }
         }

/* If chord detected, call do_menu(). */
      if ((stat&LEFT_BUTTON)&&(stat&RIGHT_BUTTON))
         {
         stat=0;
         do_menu();
         }

/* If left button, draw dot and register x and y position.
   Motion will cause calls to line_to until button released. */
      if (stat&LEFT_BUTTON)
         {
         draw(x,y,219);
         x0=x;
         y0=y;
         }
```

DOS 5: A DEVELOPER'S GUIDE

```c
/* Wait for button up. */
      while (stat&LEFT_BUTTON)
          {
          while (cmdhead==cmdtail);   /* Wait for event. */
          cmd=cmdqueue[cmdtail];
          cmdtail=(cmdtail+1)&QAND;
/* Convert pixels. */
          x=cmd.x>>3;
          y=cmd.y>>3;
/* If not motion command, update stat. */
          if (cmd.cmd!=1) stat=setstat(cmd,stat);
/* Draw line */
          lineto(x,y,219);
          }

/* If right button, draw dot, and register x and y position.
   Motion will cause calls to line_to until button released. */
      if (stat&RIGHT_BUTTON)
          {
          draw(x,y,' ');
          x0=x;
          y0=y;
          }

/* Wait for button up. */
      while (stat&RIGHT_BUTTON)
          {
          while (cmdhead==cmdtail);   /* Wait for event. */
          cmd=cmdqueue[cmdtail];
          cmdtail=(cmdtail+1)&QAND;
/* Convert pixels. */
          x=cmd.x>>3;
          y=cmd.y>>3;
/* If not motion command, update stat. */
          if (cmd.cmd!=1) stat=setstat(cmd,stat);
          lineto(x,y,' ');
          }
      }
   }
```

```c
/* Add packet to queue. */
#define enqueue(a,b,c)  \
   {cmdqueue[cmdhead].cmd=a;cmdqueue[cmdhead].x \
   =b;cmdqueue[cmdhead].y=c;cmdhead=(cmdhead+1)&0xff;}

/* mouse event handler */
void far interrupt on_int(INTREGS)
    {
    int stat,state=1;
    stat=Rax&0x1F;
/* Generate separate command for each bit set in event flags. */
    while (stat)
        {
        if (stat&1) enqueue(state,Rcx,Rdx);
        stat>>=1;
        state<<=1;
        }
    }

/* video page */
static int vpage=0;

/* Clear screen and register video page for other routines. */
draw_init()
    {
    union REGS r;
    r.x.ax=0x0600;
    r.h.bh=backcolor;
    r.x.cx=0;
    r.h.dh=24;
    r.h.dl=79;
    int86(0x10,&r,&r);
    r.h.ah=0xf;
    int86(0x10,&r,&r);
    vpage=r.h.bh;
/* Draw menu bar. */
    draw_menu();
    }
```

```c
/* Move cursor to x,y. */
goxy(int x,int y)
    {
    union REGS r;
    r.h.bh=vpage;
    r.h.ah=2;
    r.h.dh=y;
    r.h.dl=x;
    int86(0x10,&r,&r);
    }

/* "Draw" the character at x,y. */
draw(int x,int y,int ch)
    {
    union REGS r;
/* Hide mouse cursor. */
    mouse_hide();

/* Move BIOS cursor. */
    goxy(x,y);

/* Draw character. */
    r.x.ax=0x900|ch;
    r.h.bl=backcolor|forecolor;
    r.h.bh=vpage;
    r.x.cx=1;
    int86(0x10,&r,&r);
    mouse_show();
    }

/* General-purpose menu function.
    x0,y0 - x1,y1 defines the box the menu lies inside.
    num is the number of items present.
    For each item, you need four arguments that specify
    the box the mouse has to click in to select an item.
    m_menu scans them in order, so you can specify a bigger
    box that surrounds a smaller box and distinguish between them.

    Returns number 0 to num-1 or -1 if right button pressed.
```

```
   All x's and y's are in BIOS cursor locations for 80X25. */
int m_menu(int x0,int y0,int x1,int y1,int num,...)
   {
   va_list items;
   int i,press,x,y,oldx,oldy;

/* Disable mouse events. */
   mouse_handler(0,(void far *)on_int);

/* Reset press counters. */
   mouse_press(0,NULL,NULL,NULL);
   mouse_press(1,NULL,NULL,NULL);
   while (mouse_poll(NULL,NULL));    /* Wait for buttons up. */

/* Reset release counters. */
   mouse_release(0,NULL,NULL,NULL);
   mouse_release(1,NULL,NULL,NULL);
/* Convert screen coordinates to mouse coordinates. */
   x0<<=3;
   y0<<=3;
   x1<<=3;
   y1<<=3;

/* Get old X,Y position. */
   mouse_poll(&oldx,&oldy);

/* Hide cursor. */
   mouse_hide();

/* Limit cursor to menu rectangle. */
   mouse_xlimit(x0,x1);
   mouse_ylimit(y0,y1);

/* Show mouse. */
   mouse_show();

/* Loop. */
   while (1)
      {
```

DOS 5: A DEVELOPER'S GUIDE

```c
/* Get press for left key. */
    mouse_press(0,&press,&x,&y);
    if (press)
        {
/* If pressed, scan items to see if one matches. */
        va_start(items,num);
/* Wait for release. */
        do {
            mouse_release(0,&press,NULL,NULL);
            } while (!press);
/* Convert pixels to screen pixels. */
        x>>=3;
        y>>=3;
/* for each item */
        for (i=0;i<num;i++)
            {
            int t1,t2,t3,t4;
/* Get bounding box coordinates. */
            t1=va_arg(items,int);
            t2=va_arg(items,int);
            t3=va_arg(items,int);
            t4=va_arg(items,int);
/* See if click was in range. */
            if ((x>=t1&&x<=t3)&&(y>=t2&&y<=t4))
                {
/* Yes! Reset mouse parameters and return item # (0 to num-1). */
                mouse_ylimit(0,23<<3);
                mouse_xlimit(0,79<<3);
                mouse_set(oldx,oldy);
                va_end(items);
                mouse_handler(0x1f,(void far *)on_int);
                return i;
                }
            }
        va_end(items);
        }
/* Check left key. */
    mouse_press(1,&press,&x,&y);
    if (press)
        {
```

OF MICE AND MEN

```c
/* Wait for release. */
        do {
            mouse_release(1,&press,NULL,NULL);
            } while (!press);
/* Reset mouse and return -1. */
        mouse_ylimit(0,23<<3);
        mouse_xlimit(0,79<<3);
        mouse_set(oldx,oldy);
        mouse_handler(0x1f,(void far *)on_int);
        return -1;
        }
    }
}

/* Do menu function. */
do_menu()
    {
    int ans;
/* Call m_menu. */
    ans=m_menu(0,24,79,24,4,0,24,5,24,9,24,18,24,22,24,26,24,75,24,
        78,24);
/* If right button, cancel. */
    if (ans==-1) return 0;
/* foreground color menu */
    if (ans==0)
        {
        ans=color_menu(16);
        if (ans!=-1) forecolor=ans;
        return 0;
        }

/* background color menu */
    if (ans==1)
        {
        ans=color_menu(8);
        if (ans!=-1) backcolor=ans<<4;
        return 0;
        }
```

```c
/* Clear screen. */
   if (ans==2)
      {
      mouse_hide();
      draw_init();
      mouse_show();
      return 0;
      }

/* Any other...exit. */
   mouse_init();   /* Reset mouse. */
   exit(0);
   }

/* menu text */
static char *menubar=
  "Colors   Background   Clear        (Press both mouse"
  " buttons for menu)      Quit";

/* Clear menu bar in inverse color. */
set_menu()
   {
   union REGS r;
   goxy(0,24);
   r.x.ax=0x0920;
   r.h.bh=vpage;
   r.h.bl=0x70;
   r.x.cx=80;
   int86(0x10,&r,&r);
   }

/* Draw menu from menubar[] text. */
draw_menu()
   {
   union REGS r;
   char *s=menubar;
   mouse_hide();
   set_menu();
   while (*s)
      {
```

```c
        r.h.ah=0xe;
        r.h.al=*s++;
        r.h.bh=vpage;
        int86(0x10,&r,&r);
        }
    mouse_show();
    }

/* Handle the color menus. */
color_menu(int max)
    {
    union REGS r;
    int i;
    mouse_hide();
    set_menu();
/* Display 8 or 16 colors (background or foreground). */
    for (i=0;i<max;i++)
        {
        goxy(i*5,24);
        r.x.ax=0x900|219;
        r.h.bh=vpage;
        r.h.bl=0x70|i;
        r.x.cx=3;
        int86(0x10,&r,&r);
        }
    mouse_show();

/* Call m_menu to pick a color. */
/* This is a lot of stack space--for a real program, you might
   want to rewrite m_menu to take an array pointer.  */
    i=m_menu(0,24,79,24,max,0,24,2,24,5,24,7,24,10,24,12,24,15,24,
        17,24,20,24,22,24,25,24,27,24,30,24,32,24,35,24,37,24,40,24,
        42,24,45,24,47,24,50,24,52,24,55,24,57,24,60,24,62,24,65,24,
        67,24,70,24,72,24,75,24,77,24);
/* Redraw main menu. */
    draw_menu();
    return i;
    }
```

DOS 5: A DEVELOPER'S GUIDE

```c
/* Delay from 1/18 to 2/18 of a second. */
bios_delay()
   {
   int dxct;
   union REGS r;
   r.h.ah=0;
   int86(0x1a,&r,&r);
   dxct=r.x.dx&1;
   do {
      r.h.ah=0;
      int86(0x1a,&r,&r);
      } while ((r.x.dx&1)==dxct);
   do {
      r.h.ah=0;
      int86(0x1a,&r,&r);
      } while ((r.x.dx&1)!=dxct);
   }

/* Quick Signum and Absolute Value for INT */
#define SGN(x)(x>0?1:(x<0?-1:0))
#define ABS(x)(x>=0?x:-x)
#define XLEN (ABS(deltax)+1)
#define YLEN (ABS(deltay)+1)

/* Interpolate line from x0,y0 to x,y. */
lineto(int x,int y,int ch)
   {
   int deltax,deltay,xt,yt,xinc,yinc,xtinc,ytinc;
   deltax=x-x0;
   deltay=y-y0;
   if (ABS(deltax)<=1&&ABS(deltay)<=1)
      {
      draw(x,y,ch);
      }
   else
      {
      if (ABS(deltax)<=ABS(deltay))
         {
         ytinc=YLEN/XLEN*SGN(deltay);
         yt=deltax?ytinc+y0:-1;
```

```c
            xt=-1;
            xinc=0;
            yinc=SGN(deltay);
            }
        else
            {
            xinc=SGN(deltax);
            xtinc=XLEN/YLEN*SGN(deltax);
            yL=-1;
            xt=deltay?xtinc+x0:-1;
            yinc=0;
            }
        while (x!=x0||y!=y0)
            {
            if (x!=x0) x0+=xinc;
            if (y!=y0) y0+=yinc;
            if ((y0==yt&&x0!=x)||(!xinc&&x0!=x&&y0==y))
                {
                if (x!=x0) x0+=SGN(deltax);
                yt+=ytinc;
                }
            if ((x0==xt&&y0!=y)||(!yinc&&deltay&&x0==x))
                {
                if (y!=y0) y0+=SGN(deltay);
                xt+=xtinc;
                }
            draw(x0,y0,ch);
            }
        x0=x;
        y0=y;
        return 0;
        }
    }

/* command-line help */
help()
    {
    printf("ESKETCH by Al Williams\n"),
    printf("Options:\n");
    printf("  -A          use alternate cursor\n");
    printf("  -X n        set X sensitivity\n");
```

```
printf("  -Y n         set Y sensitivity\n");
exit(1);
}
```

ESKETCH1 is similar to ESKETCH. The *mainloop()* function is very different, however; it must read commands from the queue instead of from the mouse. In addition, *m_menu()*, which polls the mouse, has to override the event handler and restore it before exiting.

Of course, ESKETCH1 doesn't take full advantage of the queued mouse commands. It waits for mouse events with the line

```
while (cmdhead==cmdtail);
```

However, if ESKETCH1 had something else to do while waiting, it could use the following code:

```
while (cmdhead==cmdtail) background();
```

Here, the *background()* function would do any other tasks that needed attention.

Using the Mouse with Graphics

Using the mouse with graphics is much the same as using it with text modes. A problem arises if you program the EGA registers directly, however. The mouse driver modifies the EGA registers as it draws the mouse cursor. Since most EGA registers are write-only, the mouse driver can't tell how to reset them. To rectify this, the mouse driver provides extensions to the BIOS INT 10H services. These extensions allow programs (including the mouse driver) to change the EGA registers. Besides changing the registers, the driver also records the values and provides functions to read them (Figure 11-3).

OF MICE AND MEN

Call all functions via interrupt 10H

Read EGA register   Function F0H

Read an EGA register's contents

Input: AH = F0H
            BX = Register number
            DX = Group ID (See below)

Output: BL = Contents of register

Write EGA register   Function F1H

Write a value to an EGA register

Input: AH = F1H
            BL = Register number
            BH = Register value
            DX = Group ID (See below)

Output: None

Check for EGA register functions   Function FAH

Determine if the mouse driver supplies the above functions

Input: AH = FAH
            BX = 0

Output: BX = Nonzero if functions available

Group ID	EGA Registers
00H	CRT Controller (3D4H)
08H	Sequencer (3C4H)
10H	Graphics Controller (3CEH)
18H	Attribute Controller (3C0H)
20H	Output Register (3C2H)
28H	Feature Control Register (3DAH)
30H	Graphics 1 Position (3CCH)
38H	Graphics 2 Position (3CAH)

Figure 11-3. Partial list of mouse driver EGA register calls.

CHAPTER 12

Expanding Horizons: EMS

The Lotus-Intel-Microsoft Expanded Memory Specification (LIM EMS, or just EMS) defines a convention for allowing DOS to access additional memory. This memory is usually on a special EMS board. The specification defines a software protocol for programs to communicate with an EMS driver. The driver takes care of details that vary from board to board. Because EMS is simply a software protocol, drivers can be written to emulate EMS memory by using disk storage, extended memory, or special boards not originally designed to accommodate EMS (for example, certain PS/2 memory cards).

The first widely supported EMS version was 3.2, which allows access to a maximum of 8 Mbytes of memory. EMS 4.0 builds on 3.2 but is more flexible, especially for designers of operating environments like Windows and DESQview. It also allows programs to access up to 32 Mbytes of EMS. This chapter will show how code and data are stored in EMS 3.2 and 4.0 memory; we won't delve into the more esoteric features of EMS 4.0.

Even if you don't need the more unusual features of EMS 4.0, you should get a copy of the EMS 4.0 reference and toolkit. Both are free for the asking; call Intel at (800) 538-3373 or (503) 629-7354. This is the definitive reference for EMS, and the toolkit has helpful libraries and examples on disk.

EMS isn't the only way to expand your program's memory capacity—programs can use extended memory for the same purpose. However, any PC can accommodate EMS hardware. Even without extra hardware, EMS can be emulated. Extended memory requires an AT or above, and there's no easy way to simulate it. As we will see, EMS deals with memory in 16-Kbyte logical pages. Your program must manage its use of these pages. Creating and destroying many small objects dynamically is difficult in EMS. Most programs that use EMS use it for static data, large tables and arrays, screen images, text, and so on.

How EMS Works

Programs access EMS memory through a 64-Kbyte block of memory. This block is the *page frame*. Most drivers place the page frame above 640 Kbytes, usually just under the BIOS ROMs. However, it can be anywhere in the first megabyte of memory. The page frame can hold up to four EMS pages (16 Kbytes each). When a program needs data from an EMS page, the driver maps a logical page into one of the four slots (or physical pages) in the page frame.

The driver decides how it will accomplish this memory mapping. Disk- and 286-based emulators physically copy the memory in and out of the page frame. Drivers that support EMS boards and the 386 remap addresses, a much more efficient approach.

EMS 4.0 may map EMS to pages other than the page frame. In theory, it can map EMS pages to any address below 1 Mbyte (the hardware may limit this somewhat). For storing data, this usually isn't useful. For executing code or writing operating systems, however, it can be very handy.

The EMS software is usually installed in CONFIG.SYS so that other device drivers may use it. However, programs communicate with the driver via INT 67H—not using device I/O as a true driver would.

When a program wants to use EMS, it asks the driver for the number of pages it requires. Assuming the driver can comply, it returns a handle. The program uses this handle for each call to the EMS driver. Like a file handle, this one has no intrinsic meaning; it simply identifies a block of EMS memory. A program can ask for multiple handles or increase and decrease the number of pages an existing handle contains.

Since EMS memory is separate from DOS memory, programs must be sure to free it before exiting. You must handle possible exits caused by critical errors, Control-Break, or divide by zero. If your program exits without freeing its EMS memory, the memory will be lost until you reboot the computer.

If an interrupt routine or device driver uses EMS, special rules apply. These programs must save the EMS context before using any EMS memory. The interrupted program may have pages mapped in, and your routine must restore the context before returning. This is also true when your program can execute another program that might use EMS. When your program regains control, it won't be able to depend on the state of the EMS unless you save the state before calling the other program. The EMS driver provides several ways to save and restore the EMS context.

In summary, a program that uses EMS must do the following:

1. Determine if EMS is present on the system.
2. Allocate one or more EMS handles.
3. Map EMS pages into physical pages as needed.
4. Access code and data in the page frame as needed.
5. Free the EMS handle when done.

If you use EMS from inside an interrupt handler, a TSR, or a device driver, you must preserve the state of the EMS driver before mapping pages. The next two sections explain the techniques programs use to perform these tasks. We will then develop a simplified C library to handle EMS access and use it in some practical programs.

Detecting EMS

Before using EMS, a program must make sure the driver is present. The EMS driver's name is always EMMXXXX0. If you can open this device, the driver is present. For example:

```
FILE *fp;
fp=fopen("EMMXXXX0","r");
if (!fp)    /* no EMS */;
else        /* EMS */;
```

Device drivers and some TSR programs can't call DOS to open a file. These programs can detect the EMS driver using a different method. If the EMS driver is present, the segment address of the INT 67H vector will be its starting segment. Because of the way device drivers are constructed, a driver's name will start in the 10th byte of its starting segment. The following code fragment detects the EMS driver using this method:

```
char *emmname="EMMXXXX0";
char far *p;
/* Point to INT 67H vector. */
FP_SEG(p)=0;
FP_OFF(p)=0x67*4;
p=*(char far **)p;         /* p may now point to device driver. */
if (memcmp(p,emmname,8))   /* no EMS */;
else                       /* EMS */;
```

In assembly, the *REP CMPS* instruction can take the place of the *memcmp()* call. Of course, this code assumes *memcmp()* will accept a far pointer (in other words, you're using the compact, large, or huge model). If it won't, you may have to code the comparison by hand. For example:

```
while (*emmname)
    {
    if (*emmname++!=*p++)
        {
        /* no EMS */
        return;
        }
    }
/* EMS present */
```

EXPANDING HORIZONS: EMS

Select EMS Commands

This section discusses the most useful EMS commands. Programs access EMS functions via INT 67H. The C functions listed in the descriptions refer to the CEMS library that appears later in the chapter.

Notice that every EMS call returns an error status in the AH register (the error codes appear in Table 12-1). This makes it simple to check each EMS call for errors.

Always check to make sure the EMS driver is present (as discussed in the preceding section) before calling EMS functions. Other programs may use INT 67H, causing unpredictable results. Worse, if no programs are using INT 67H, the computer will crash if you attempt an EMS call.

Return status   Function 40H

Description:

    Returns a zero if the EMS hardware and software are present and functioning properly. If there is a problem, the function returns an error code.

Input:

    AH=40H

Output:

    if successful

        AH=0

    else

        AH=error code (see Table 12-1)

Minimum EMS version:

    3.0

C function:

```
ems_present()   (calls this function as part of its task)
```

Error Code	Description
80H	Internal error in EMS driver
81H	EMS hardware error
82H	EMS driver is busy
83H	Invalid handle
84H	Undefined function
85H	No more handles available
86H	Error while saving or restoring context
87H	Allocation request exceeds total amount of memory available
88H	Allocation request exceeds amount of free memory available
89H	Cannot allocate 0 pages
8AH	Logical page number out of range
8BH	Bad physical page number
8CH	Out of room in context save area
8DH	Handle already used for context save
8EH	Context save area does not contain entry for this handle
8FH	Undefined subfunction
90H	Undefined attribute
91H	Unsupported feature
92H	Source and destination regions overlap (informational; move was successful)
93H	Specified length exceeds allocated length
94H	Conventional memory region and EMS region overlap
95H	Offset out of range
96H	Region greater than 1 Mbyte
97H	Can't exchange overlapping regions
98H	Undefined memory type
9AH	Supports alternate map or DMA register sets, but not alternate register sets
9BH	Supports alternate map or DMA register sets, but none are currently available
9CH	Alternate map or DMA register sets not supported
9DH	Alternate register set is not defined or allocated
9EH	Dedicated DMA channels not supported
9FH	Specified DMA channel not supported
A0H	Handle name not found
A1H	Handle name in use
A2H	Memory address wraps around 1-Mbyte boundary
A3H	Invalid pointer or corrupt array
A4H	Access denied by operating system

Table 12-1. EMS error codes.

Return page frame   Function 41H

Description:

Returns the segment address of the page frame. With EMS 4.0, EMS memory can map to addresses other than the page frame.

Input:

AH=41H

Output:

if successful
    AH=0
    BX=segment address of page frame
else
    AH=error code (see Table 12-1)

Minimum EMS version:

3.0

C function:

```
ems_pfa()
```

Return number of pages   Function 42H

Description:

Returns the number of free EMS pages and the total number of pages in the system.

Input:

AH=42H

DOS 5: A DEVELOPER'S GUIDE

Output:

> if successful
>> AH=0
>> BX=number of free pages
>> DX=total number of pages
>
> else
>> AH=error code (see Table 12-1)

Minimum EMS version:

> 3.0

C function:

```
ems_pages(int *total)
```

Allocate EMS   Function 43H

Description:

> Allocates an EMS handle and assigns it a specified number of pages. The number of pages may not be zero. EMS 4.0 has a function that allows zero-page handle allocation.

Input:

> AH=43H
> BX=number of pages

Output:

> if successful
>> AH=0
>> DX=EMS handle
>
> else
>> AH=error code (see Table 12-1)

EXPANDING HORIZONS: EMS

Minimum EMS version:

3.0

C function:

```
ems_alloc(int pages)
```

Map page   **Function 44H**

Description:

Causes the EMS driver to map a logical page into a physical page in the page frame. If BX is FFFFH, the driver renders the specified physical page inaccessible. For EMS 3.X, the physical page number ranges from 0 to 3. EMS 4.0 may have many physical pages. However, the first four pages still correspond to the four page-frame slots.

Input:

AH=44H
AL=physical page
BX=logical page
DX=EMS handle

Output:

if successful
    AH=0
else
    AH=error code (see Table 12-1)

Minimum EMS version:

3.0

C function:

```
ems_map(int handle, int p_page, unsigned int l_page)
```

419

DOS 5: A DEVELOPER'S GUIDE

Free memory   **Function 45H**

Description:

Releases a handle's memory, allowing other programs to use it. The specified handle becomes invalid.

Input:

AH=45H
DX=EMS handle

Output:

if successful
    AH=0
else
    AH=error code (see Table 12-1)

Minimum EMS version:

3.0

C function:

```
ems_free(int handle)
```

Return version   **Function 46H**

Description:

Returns the EMS version number the driver supports. The return value is in BCD format. For example, an EMS 3.2 driver will return 32H; a 4.0 driver will return 40H.

Input:

AH=46H

EXPANDING HORIZONS: EMS

Output:

    if successful

        AH=0

        AL=BCD version number

    else

        AH=error code (see Table 12-1)

Minimum EMS version:

    3.0

C function:

```
ems_vers()
```

Save page map   Function 47H

Description:

    Saves the mapping context for the first four physical pages in an internal save area. The driver associates the context with the caller's EMS handle. Note that this call only saves the state of the EMS 3.X page frame; programs that use EMS 4.0's additional pages must use function 4EH or 4FH. Be especially alert for error 8CH, which occurs when the internal save area is full.

Input:

    AH=47H

    DX=EMS handle

Output:

    if successful

        AH=0

    else

        AH=error code (see Table 12-1)

Minimum EMS version:

3.0

C function:

None

Restore page map   Function 48H

Description:

Restores the mapping context saved via function 47H.

Input:

AH=48H
DX=EMS handle

Output:

if successful
    AH=0
else
    AH=error code (see Table 12-1)

Minimum EMS version:

3.0

C function:

None

Save page map   Function 4E00H

Description:

Saves the entire mapping context in a user-supplied buffer. Function 4E03H will return the size of the buffer required.

Input:

AX=4E00H
ES:DI=pointer to buffer

Output:

if successful
AH=0
else
AH=error code (see Table 12-1)

Minimum EMS version:

3.2

C function:

None

Restore page map   **Function 4E01H**

Description:

Restores the entire mapping context using a buffer created by function 4E00H.

Input:

AX=4E01H
DS:SI=pointer to buffer

Output:

if successful
AH=0
else
AH=error code (see Table 12-1)

Minimum EMS version:

3.2

C function:

None

Save/restore page map — Function 4E02H

Description:

Combines the action of functions 4E00H and 4E01H. The driver saves the mapping context, then loads a new one from a different buffer.

Input:

AX=4E02H
ES:DI=pointer to buffer for old map context
DS:SI=pointer to buffer for new map context

Output:

if successful
    AH=0
else
    AH=error code (see Table 12-1)

Minimum EMS version:

3.2

C function:

None

Page map size — Function 4E03H

Description:

Returns the size, in bytes, of the buffer that functions 4E00H through 4E02H require.

Input:

AX=4E03H

EXPANDING HORIZONS: EMS

Output:

> if successful
>> AH=0
>> AL=buffer size (bytes)
>
> else
>> AH=error code (see Table 12-1)

Minimum EMS version:

> 3.2

C function:

> None

Save partial page map   Function 4F00H

Description:

> Saves the specified physical pages' mapping context in a user-supplied buffer. Function 4F02H returns the size of the buffer the save requires.

Input:

> AX=4F00H
> DS:SI=pointer to map list (see Figure 12-1)
> ES:DI=pointer to buffer

Output:

> if successful
>> AH=0
>
> else
>> AH=error code (see Table 12-1)

Minimum EMS version:

> 4.0

C function:

> None

Offset	Contents
0000	Number of entries in list
0002	Segment address
0004	Segment address

Figure 12-1. Partial page map list.

Restore partial page map Function 4F01H

Description:

　Restores the context saved by function 4F00H.

Input:

　AX=4F01H
　DS:SI=pointer to buffer

Output:

　if successful
　　AH=0
　else
　　AH=error code (see Table 12-1)

Minimum EMS version:

　4.0

C function:

　None

EXPANDING HORIZONS: EMS

Partial page map size   Function 4F02H

Description:

Returns the size, in bytes, of a partial page map buffer.

Input:

AX=4F02H
BX=number of pages to save

Output:

if successful
    AH=0
    AL=size in bytes

else
    AH=error code (see Table 12-1)

Minimum EMS version:

4.0

C function:

None

Map multiple pages   Function 50H

Description:

Maps multiple logical pages into multiple physical pages. If AL is zero, the program specifies physical pages by number (as in function 44H). If AL is one, the program specifies the actual segment addresses of each physical page. The DS:SI register pair points to a buffer that contains a 32-bit entry for each page to map. The first 16-bit word of the entry is the logical page number, and the following word is the physical page number (or segment address). As with function 44H, a logical page number of FFFFH will unmap the corresponding physical page. You must never map pages below 640 Kbytes unless you have allocated them from DOS first.

Input:

AH=50H
AL=0 for numbered pages, 1 for segment-addressed pages
CX=number of pages to map
DX=EMS handle
DS:SI=pointer to buffer

Output:

if successful
    AH=0
else
    AH=error code (see Table 12-1)

Minimum EMS version:

4.0

C function:

None

Reallocate EMS   **Function 51H**

Description:

Changes the number of EMS pages associated with an EMS handle. The program can request an allocation of zero pages with this function. This frees all memory but leaves the handle available for use.

Input:

AH=51H
BX=new number of pages
DX=EMS handle

EXPANDING HORIZONS: EMS

Output:

    if successful
        AH=0
        BX=new number of pages
    else
        AH=error code (see Table 12-1)
        BX=old number of pages

Minimum EMS version:

    4.0

C function:

    None

Map and jump   **Function 55H**

Description:

    Remaps the specified pages, as function 50H does, then jumps to an address. This call only returns if the driver detects an error before jumping. When execution resumes at the new address, the AH register will be zero.

Input:

    AH=55H
    AL=0 for numbered pages, 1 for segment-addressed pages
    DX=EMS handle
    DS:SI=pointer to buffer (see Figure 12-2)

Output:

    if successful
        AH=0
    else
        AH=error code (see Table 12-1)

DOS 5: A DEVELOPER'S GUIDE

Minimum EMS version:

4.0

C function:

None

Jump Buffer

Offset	Contents
0000H	Target address
0004H	Number of pages to map
0005H	Pointer page map list

Page Map List

Offset	Contents
0000H	Logical page #1
0002H	Physical page #1
0004H	Logical page #2
0006H	Physical page #2

Note: The length of the map list is determined by the byte at offset 0004H in the jump buffer.

Figure 12-2. Jump buffer.

Map and call   **Function 56H**

Description:

Remaps the specified pages, as function 50H does, then does a far call to the specified address. If the called routine executes a far return, the driver remaps the pages, as specified in another buffer, and returns to the caller. The caller should allow extra stack space for this function's overhead (see function 5602H).

Input:

AH=56H
AL=0 if numbered pages, 1 if segment-addressed pages
DX=EMS handle
DS:SI=pointer to buffer (see Table 12-2)

Offset	Contents
0000H	Target address
0004H	New page map length
0005H	Pointer to new page map list (see Figure 12-2)
0009H	Old page map length
000AH	Pointer to old page map list (see Figure 12-2)
000EH	8-byte buffer (the EMS driver uses this buffer)

Table 12-2. Call buffer.

Output:

    if successful
        AH=0
    else
        AH=error code (see Table 12-1)

Minimum EMS version:

    4.0

C function:

    None

Map and call stack space   **Function 5602H**

Description:

    Returns the amount of stack space, in bytes, that function 56H requires.

Input:

    AX=5602H

Output:

    if successful
        AH=0
        BX=stack size (bytes)
    else
        AH=error code (see Table 12-1)

Minimum EMS version:

    4.0

C function:

    None

EXPANDING HORIZONS: EMS

Memory move   **Function 5700H**

Description:

Moves up to 1 Mbyte of data from any conventional or EMS memory location to any other conventional or EMS memory location. This call does not disturb the current mapping context. An error code of 92H indicates that the source and destination addresses overlapped. The driver moves the data in such a way that the results will be correct even if the memory overlaps.

Input:

    AX=5700H
    DS:SI=pointer to buffer (see Table 12-3)

Offset	Contents
0000H	Length of region
0004H	Type of source region*
0005H	Source handle (or 0 for conventional memory)
0007H	Source start offset of source region**
0009H	Starting segment of conventional or logical page (EMS)
000BH	Type of destination region*
000CH	Destination handle (or 0 for conventional memory)
000EH	Starting offset of destination memory**
0010H	Destination start segment (conventional) or logical page (EMS)

* 0=Conventional memory   ** Must be in range 0-3FFFH if
   1=EMS   region type is EMS

Table 12-3. Move/exchange buffer.

DOS 5: A DEVELOPER'S GUIDE

Output:

    if successful
        AH=0
    else
        AH=error code (see Table 12-1)

Minimum EMS version:

    4.0

C function:

    None

Memory exchange   **Function 5701H**

Description:

    Exchanges two blocks of conventional or EMS memory. The block length may be up to 1 Mbyte. This function does not disturb the current mapping context.

Input:

    AX=5701H
    DS:SI=pointer to buffer (see Table 12-3)

Output:

    if successful
        AH=0
    else
        AH=error code (see Table 12-1)

Minimum EMS version:

    4.0

C function:

None

Get mappable pages   **Function 5800H**

Description:

Returns a table of segment addresses and physical page numbers for each mappable page. The driver sorts the entries in the table by ascending segment address. Note that pages 0 through 3 always correspond to the page-frame address. Function 5801H returns the number of mappable pages; use it to determine how big the buffer should be.

Input:

AX=5800H
ES:DI=pointer to buffer (see Figure 12-3)

Output:

if successful
    AH=0
    CX=number of entries in table
else
    AH=error code (see Table 12-1)

Minimum EMS version:

4.0

C function:

None

DOS 5: A DEVELOPER'S GUIDE

Offset	Contents
0000H	Segment address
0002H	Page #
0004H	Segment address
0006H	Page #

EXAMPLE:

Offset		
00H	9000H	04H
04H	9400H	05H
08H	E000H	00H
0CH	E400H	01H
10H	E800H	02H
14H	EC00H	03H

Rows 08H–14H: Page frame

Figure 12-3. Physical page map.

Number of mappable pages   **Function 5801H**

Description:

    Returns the number of mappable pages.

Input:

    AX=5801H

Output:

    if successful
        AH=0
        CX=number of pages
    else
        AH=error code (see Table 12-1)

Minimum EMS version:

    4.0

C function:

    None

Maintaining Compatibility

For most applications using EMS for data storage, EMS 3.2 is adequate. Even though EMS 4.0 offers some convenience (like functions 5700H and 5701H), it probably isn't worth the loss of compatibility to use it in a commercial product. Of course, if you know your programs will only run with EMS 4.0, by all means use the new functions. The extra pages can also help speed EMS access.

If you want to run code in EMS memory, version 3.2 is more limiting; the "EMS" code must be 64 Kbytes or less in length. Also, it may be difficult to jump from one EMS code segment to another. EMS 4.0 solves these problems. If you want to run code in EMS, consider making version 4.0 a requirement.

The CEMS Library

The CEMS library (Listings 12-1 and 12-2) provides a suite of calls for EMS 3.2 memory. Of course, the calls work just as well with EMS 4.0 but are unable to access all of EMS 4.0's special features.

Listing 12-1. CEMS.H.

```
/*****************************************************************
 *                                                               *
 * File: cems.h                                                  *
 *                                                               *
 * Description:                                                  *
 * Header for CEMS.C.                                            *
 *                                                               *
 *****************************************************************/

#ifndef CEMS_HEADER
#define CEMS_HEADER

extern int ems_errno;

int ems_present(void);

int ems_present2(void);

int ems_pfa(void);

int ems_pages(int *total);

int ems_alloc(int pages);

int ems_map(int handle,int p_page,unsigned int l_page);

int ems_free(int handle);

int ems_version(void);

#endif
```

EXPANDING HORIZONS: EMS

Listing 12-2. CEMS.C.
```
/******************************************************************
 *                                                                *
 * File: cems.c                                                   *
 *                                                                *
 * Description:                                                   *
 * C functions to access basic EMS commands.                      *
 *                                                                *
 ******************************************************************/

#include <stdio.h>
#include <dos.h>

int ems_errno=0;

#define INT67(r) ems_errno=(int86(0x67,&r,&r)&0xFF00)>>8

static char *emmname="EMMXXXX0";

/* Returns 1 if EMS present and functional, else 0.
   If EMS driver not preset, ems_errno==-1. */
int ems_present()
    {
    union REGS r;
    FILE*fp;
    ems_errno=-1;
    fp=fopen(emmname,"r");
    if (fp)
        {
        close(fp);
        r.h.ah=0x40;
        INT67(r);
        }
    return fp?r.h.ah==0:0;
    }

/* Alternate EMS detection--use for ISRs, TSRs, and drivers. */
int ems_present2()
    {
    union REGS r;
```

439

DOS 5: A DEVELOPER'S GUIDE

```c
    char far *emm;
    char *emcmp=emmname;
    ems_errno=-1;
/* Point emm to start of driver (maybe). */
    FP_SEG(emm)=0;
    FP_OFF(emm)=0x67*4;
    emm=*(char far * far *) emm;
/* Point to driver name. */
    FP_OFF(emm)=0xa;
/* Compare name with EMM name. */
    while (*emcmp) if (*emcmp++!=*emm++) break;
    if (*emcmp) return 0;
/* Driver preset... */
    r.h.ah=0x40;
    INT67(r);
    return r.h.ah==0;
    }

/* Returns page frame segment address or zero if error. */
int ems_pfa()
    {
    union REGS r;
    r.h.ah=0x41;
    INT67(r);
    return r.h.ah?0:r.x.bx;
    }

/* Returns pages available or -1 if error.
   If total is not null, *total gets the total number of pages
   in the system. */
int ems_pages(int *total)
    {
    union REGS r;
    r.h.ah=0x42;
    INT67(r);
    if (r.h.ah) return-1;
    if (total)*total=r.x.dx;
    return r.x.bx;
    }
```

EXPANDING HORIZONS: EMS

```c
/* Allocate a handle--return handle or -1 if error. */
int ems_alloc(int pages)
    {
    union REGS r;
    r.h.ah=0x43;
    r.x.bx=pages;
    INT67(r);
    return r.h.ah?-1:r.x.dx;
    }

/* Map page--return 0 if ok, 1 if error. */
int ems_map(int handle,int p_page,unsigned int l_page)
    {
    union REGS r;
    r.h.ah=0x44;
    r.h.al=p_page;
    r.x.bx=l_page;
    r.x.dx=handle;
    INT67(r);
    return r.h.ah!=0;
    }

/* Free handle--return 0 if ok, 1 if error. */
int ems_free(int handle)
    {
    union REGS r;
    r.h.ah=0x45;
    r.x.dx=handle;
    INT67(r);
    return r.h.ah!=0;
    }

/* Return version number or 0 if error. */
int ems_version()
    {
    union REGS r;
    r.h.ah=0x46;
    INT67(r);
    return r.h.ah?0:r.h.al;
    }
```

CEMS provides a C call for each EMS function it supports. The exceptions are *ems_present()* and *ems_present2()*. The *ems_present()* function checks for an EMS driver using the *fopen()* method and calls function 40H. The *ems_present2()* function scans the INT 67H vector to detect the EMS driver, then calls function 40H. You will use only one of these functions in your programs.

Each CEMS call returns an error indication. CEMS stores the last EMS driver error code in the global variable *ems_errno*. Programs should always check the return value from each CEMS call; if an error occurs, they can check *ems_errno* to find the cause.

Using CEMS: DUP

The DUP program (Listings 12-3 and 12-4) uses the CEMS library for data storage. DUP copies a floppy disk into EMS memory and writes it to as many floppies as desired. For a 360-Kbyte floppy, a program like DUP could use conventional memory. For 720-Kbyte, 1.2-Mbyte, and 1.44-Mbyte floppies, conventional memory is impractical.

Listing 12-3. DUP.C.
```
/****************************************************************
 *                                                              *
 * File: dup.c                                                  *
 *                                                              *
 * Description:                                                 *
 * A simple disk duplication program.                           *
 * DUP uses a VM_ module (VM_EMS, VM_DISK) to handle            *
 * virtual memory for it. It also requires GETOPT.C.            *
 *                                                              *
 * Warning: If you use Mix C, you must use large model for DUP. *
 *                                                              *
 ****************************************************************/

/* Must be large model for MIX. */
#include <stdio.h>
#include <stdlib.h>
```

EXPANDING HORIZONS: EMS

```c
#include <dos.h>
#include <conio.h>
#include <ctype.h>
#include "compat.h"
#include "getopt.h"

/* Define VM page size. */
#define PAGESIZE 16384

#define STR(x)#x

/* drive to work with */
int drive=0;

/* format program and options */
char fmtpgm[129]="FORMAT";
char fmtopt[129]="";

/* verify option */
int verify=0;

/* buffer for verify option */
char vbuff[PAGESIZE];

/* disk parameters */
int nrsec,bytespersect;

/* prototypes for VM package */
extern int vm_alloc(unsigned long size);
extern char far *vm_map(unsigned long size);
extern int vm_commit(void);
extern void vm_free(void);

/* break handler */
void interrupt far onbreak()
    {
    int c;
    printf("\nDo you really want to quit (Y/N)? ");
    do {
        c=getche();
```

DOS 5: A DEVELOPER'S GUIDE

```c
        c=toupper(c);
        } while (c!='N'&&c!='Y');
    if (c=='N') return;
    vm_free();
    exit(10);
    }

/* Critical error handler. DUP fails all errors so it can detect
   if a disk needs formatting. */

void interrupt far onerror(INTREGS)
    {
/* Fail errors (requires DOS 3+). */
    Rax=Rax&0xFF00|3;
    return;
    }

main(int argc,char *argv[])
    {
    int c;
    unsigned long adr;
    union REGS r,r1;
    struct SREGS s;
    char far *buff;
    unsigned int nrsects,secno;
    int secperpage;
/* Check for DOS 3.0 or better. You could use DUP with lower
   version of DOS if you don't have any unformatted disks. */
    if (_osmajor<3)
        {
        printf("DUP requires MSDOS 3.0 or above\n");
        exit(20);
        }
/* Hook break and critical ints. */
    setvect(0x23,onbreak);
    setvect(0x24,onerror);
/* Parse options. */
    while ((c=getopt(argc,argv,"VvF:f:O:o:"))!=-1)
        {
        switch(toupper(c))
            {
```

```c
        case 'V':                         /* verify */
                verify=1;
                break;

        case 'F':                         /* format program */
                strcpy(fmtpgm,optarg);
                break;

        case 'O':                         /* format options */
                strcpy(fmtopt,optarg);
                break;

        case '?':                         /* help */
                help();
                }
        }
/* If drive letter specified, parse it too--default A:. */
    if (argc>1&&argc>=optind) drive=toupper(*argv[optind])-'A';
/* Get source disk. */
    printf("DUP V1.0\nPlease insert source disk in drive %c: and"
         " press <Enter>:",drive+'A');
/* Wait for enter. */
    while ((c=getche())!='\r') if (c==EOF) break;
    if (c==EOF) exit(1);
    printf("\nReading disk...\n");
/* Get disk parameters. */
    r.h.ah=0x36;
    r.h.dl=drive+1;
    int86(0x21,&r,&r);
    if (r.x.ax==0xffff)
        {
        printf("%c: does not contain a valid disk.\n",drive+'A');
        exit(2);
        }
/* Compute number of sectors. */
    nrsec=nrsects=r.x.ax*r.x.dx;
/* Compute number of bytes. */
    bytespersect=r.x.cx;
    adr=(unsigned long) nrsects*bytespersect;
    secperpage=PAGESIZE/r.x.cx;
```

DOS 5: A DEVELOPER'S GUIDE

```c
    if (!secperpage)
        {
        printf("Disk's sector size >"STR(PAGESIZE)"\n");
        exit(3);
        }
    if (vm_alloc(adr))
        {
        printf(
            "Insufficient virtual memory is available to copy this "
            "disk.\n");
        exit(4);
        }
    adr=0L;
    secno=0;
    r.h.al=drive;
    r.x.cx=secperpage;
/* Copy all sectors to EMS. */
    while (nrsects)
        {
        buff=vm_map(adr);
        if (nrsects<secperpage) r.x.cx=nrsects;
        r.x.dx=secno;
        s.ds=FP_SEG(buff);
        r.x.bx=FP_OFF(buff);
#ifndef __POWERC

        int86x(0x25,&r,&r1,&s);
#else

        r1.x.cflag=absread(drive,r.x.cx,r.x.dx,buff);
#endif

        if (r1.x.cflag)
            {                         /* ERROR */
            printf("Error reading source disk\n");
            vm_free();
            exit(6);
            }
        secno+=r.x.cx;
        nrsects-=r.x.cx;
```

EXPANDING HORIZONS: EMS

```
            adr+=PAGESIZE;
            }
/* Prompt for destination disk. */
    while (1)
        {
        r.x.cx=secperpage;
        printf(
            "Insert destination disk. Press <ENTER> to duplicate"
            " or <Q> to quit:\n");
/* Wait for Enter or Quit. */
        while ((c=getche())!='\r')
            {
            if (c==EOF||toupper(c)=='Q')
                {
                vm_free();
                exit(0);
                }
            }
/* Check for legit dest disk (continue if not). */
        if (prep(drive,0))
            {
            printf("Incorrect or bad destination disk.\n");
            continue;
            }
        printf("Writing disk....\n");
        adr=0L;
        secno=0;
        nrsects=nrsec;
/* Write each EMS page out to disk. */
        while (nrsects)
            {
            buff=vm_map(adr);
            if (nrsects<secperpage) r.x.cx=nrsects;
            r.x.dx=secno;
            s.ds=FP_SEG(buff);
            r.x.bx=FP_OFF(buff);
#ifndef __POWERC

            int86x(0x26,&r,&r1,&s);
#else
```

447

DOS 5: A DEVELOPER'S GUIDE

```
            r1.x.cflag=abswrite(drive,r.x.cx,r.x.dx,buff);
#endif

            if (r1.x.cflag)
                {                          /* ERROR */
                printf("Error writing to destination disk\n");
                continue;
                }
            secno+=r.x.cx;
            nrsects-=r.x.cx;
            adr+=PAGESIZE;
            }
/* If user wants a verify, do it now. */
        if (verify)
            {
            int i,totbytes;
            printf("Verifying disk....\n");
            r.x.cx=secperpage;
            adr=0L;
            secno=0;
            nrsects=nrsec;
/* Read each page of sectors into vbuff; compare with EMS page. */
            while (nrsects)
                {
                buff=vm_map(adr);
                if (nrsects<secperpage) r.x.cx=nrsects;
                r.x.dx=secno;
                s.ds=FP_SEG(vbuff);
                r.x.bx=FP_OFF(vbuff);
#ifndef __POWERC

                int86x(0x26,&r,&r1,&s);
#else

                r1.x.cflag=absread(drive,r.x.cx,r.x.dx,vbuff);
#endif

                if (r1.x.cflag)
                    {                      /* ERROR */
                    printf("Error verifying disk\n");
```

EXPANDING HORIZONS: EMS

```c
                continue;
                }
/* Compare buffers here. */
            totbytes=r.x.cx*bytespersect;
            for (i=0;i<totbytes;i++)
                {
                if (vbuff[i]!=buff[i])
                    {
                    i=0;
                    break;
                    }
                }
            if (!i)
                {
                printf("Error verifying disk\n");
                break;
                }
            secno+=r.x.cx;
            nrsects-=r.x.cx;
            adr+=PAGESIZE;
            }
        if (i) printf("Verification complete\n");
        }
      }
    }

/* help! */
help()
    {
    printf("DUP Version 1.0 by Al Williams.\n");
    printf("DUP is a simple file duplicator\n\n");
    printf("usage: DUP [options] [drive]\n");
    printf("Options:\n");
    printf("-v        Verify duplicated disk\n");
    printf("-f pgm    Use pgm to format blank disks\n");
    printf("-o optsOptions for format program\n\n");
    printf(
        "If the argument to -o contains spaces, you must quote"
        " it as in:\n");
    printf("  DUP -o \"/N:9 /T:40\"\n");
```

DOS 5: A DEVELOPER'S GUIDE

```c
   exit(1);
   }

/* Prep a disk--if the disk is OK return a 0, else return a 1.
   If flag is 0, prep() will attempt to format an otherwise bad
   disk. */

prep(int drive,int flag)
   {
   union REGS r;
   unsigned int bpt,ns;
/* Get parameters. */
   r.h.ah=0x36;
   r.h.dl=drive+1;
   int86(0x21,&r,&r);
   if (r.x.ax==0xffff)
      {
      if (!flag)
         {
         format(drive);
         return prep(drive,1);
         }
      return 1;
      }
/* Compute number of sectors. */
   ns=r.x.ax*r.x.dx;
/* Compute number of bytes. */
   bpt=r.x.cx;
   if (bpt!=bytespersect||ns!=nrsec)
      {
      if (flag)
         {
         format(drive);
         return prep(drive,1);
         }
      return 1;
      }
   return 0;
   }
```

EXPANDING HORIZONS: EMS

```c
/* Format the indicated drive.
   You should check for errors from the system() call below, but
   the return value of system isn't portable between compilers. */

format(int drive)
    {
    char cmd[129];
    printf("Formatting...\n");
    sprintf(cmd,"%s %c: %s",fmtpgm,drive+'A',fmtopt);
    system(cmd);
    }
```

Listing 12-4. VM_EMS.C.
```c
/**************************************************************
 *                                                            *
 * File: vm_ems.c                                             *
 *                                                            *
 * Description:                                               *
 * EMS-based virtual memory functions.                        *
 *                                                            *
 **************************************************************/

#include <stdio.h>
#include <dos.h>
#include "cems.h"

#define PAGESIZE 16384

/* EMS page/handle/pfa segment */
static int vmpage=-1;
static int vmpfa;
static int vmhandle=-1;

/* Free VM memory. */
void vm_free()
    {
    ems_free(vmhandle);
    vmhandle=-1;
    }
```

451

DOS 5: A DEVELOPER'S GUIDE

```c
/* Allocate VM memory. */
int vm_alloc(unsigned long size)
    {
    int pages;
    if (!ems_present()) return 1;
    if (vmhandle!=-1)
        {
        vm_free();                  /* Free old VM handle. */
        }
    vmpfa=ems_pfa();
    pages=size/PAGESIZE;
    if (size%PAGESIZE) pages++;
    vmhandle=ems_alloc(pages);
    return vmhandle==-1;
    }

/* Map in EMS page. VM_EMS only uses page 0 for simplicity. */
char far *vm_map(unsigned long offset)
    {
    int page;
    char far *rval=(char far *)0;
    page=offset/PAGESIZE;
/* If page is already mapped in, fine; else map the page in. */
    if (page!=vmpage)
        {
        if (ems_map(vmhandle,0,page)) return rval;
        vmpage=page;
        }
/* Compute pointer to correct byte. */
    FP_SEG(rval)=vmpfa;
    FP_OFF(rval)=0;
    return rval;
    }

/* Commit page function--not required for EMS, but needed for
   VM_DISK and VM_EXT. Provided here for consistency. This causes
   a page to be written back out to the VM device. */

int vm_commit()
    {
    }
```

EXPANDING HORIZONS: EMS

DUP uses the functions in VM_EMS.C (Listing 12-4) to access EMS memory. By isolating the EMS calls, you can use other methods to store the data. VM_DISK.C (Listing 12-5), for example, uses a hard disk instead of EMS to store the disk data. (Note: Don't run DUP from a floppy drive if you use VM_DISK.C—it creates the temporary storage file on the current drive.) In a later chapter we'll create VM_EXT.C so that DUP can access extended memory.

Listing 12-5. VM_DISK.C.

```
/****************************************************************
 *                                                              *
 * File: vm_disk.c                                              *
 *                                                              *
 * Description:                                                 *
 * Disk-based virtual memory functions.                         *
 *                                                              *
 ****************************************************************/

#include <stdio.h>
#include <dos.h>

#define PAGESIZE 16384

/* file handle and name */
static FILE*vmfile=NULL;
static char *vmfilename="VM$$$.@@@";

/* buffer and page # in buffer */
static int vmpage=-1;
static char vmbuffer[PAGESIZE];

/* Allocate vm space with given number of bytes. */
int vm_alloc(unsigned long size)
   {
   if (vmfile)                    /* Dispose of old file. */
      {
      fclose(vmfile);
      unlink(vmfilename);
      }
```

DOS 5: A DEVELOPER'S GUIDE

```c
/* Open file. */
    vmfile=fopen(vmfilename,"w+b");
    if (!vmfile) return 1;
/* Compute number of pages. */
    if (size%PAGESIZE) size=(size/PAGESIZE+1)*PAGESIZE;
/* Write to last page. This prevents out-of-space errors later. */
    if (fseek(vmfile,size-1,SEEK_SET)) return 1;
    putc(0,vmfile);
    return ferror(vmfile);
    }

/* Free VM. */
void vm_free()
    {
    fclose(vmfile);
    unlink(vmfilename);
    vmfile=NULL;
    }

/* Map a vm page and return address to byte. */
char far *vm_map(unsigned long offset)
    {
    int page;
    char far *rval=(char far *)0;
    char far *mixbug=(char far *) vmbuffer;
/* Compute page. */
    page=offset/PAGESIZE;
/* If page isn't in buffer, read it in... */
    if (page!=vmpage)
        {
/* but first swap out old page. */
/* Performance would be better if you made the app
   mark a dirty bit when it wrote to the VM page. */

        if (vm_commit()) return rval;
        if (fseek(vmfile,(long) page*PAGESIZE,SEEK_SET)) return
            rval;
        fread(vmbuffer,1,sizeof(vmbuffer),vmfile);
        vmpage=page;
        if (ferror(vmfile)) return rval;
        }
```

EXPANDING HORIZONS: EMS

```
/* Get pointer to byte. */
   FP_SEG(rval)=FP_SEG(mixbug);
   FP_OFF(rval)=offset-(long) page*PAGESIZE+FP_OFF(mixbug);
   return rval;
   }

/* Write page back out to disk. */
int vm_commit()
   {
   if (vmpage==-1) return 0;
   if (fseek(vmfile,(long) vmpage*PAGESIZE,SEEK_SET)) return 1;
   fwrite(vmbuffer,1,sizeof(vmbuffer),vmfile);
   return ferror(vmfile);
   }
```

DUP's operation is quite straightforward. It analyzes the source disk and copies it, sector by sector, to EMS using DOS INT 25H. INT 26H later reverses the process, placing data on the destination disk.

Note that the Mix C compiler's *int86x()* routine doesn't properly clean up the stack after an INT 25H (or 26H). If you use this compiler, DUP uses Mix's *absread()* and *abswrite()* functions instead of *int86x()*. Therefore, you must use Mix's large model to accommodate the pointer to the EMS page frame. Other compilers can call INTs 25H and 26H using *int86x()*, allowing DUP to compile in any model. DUP is careful to free EMS memory before exiting. The *onbreak()* function captures Control-Break events and frees EMS before terminating. DUP fails critical errors so that it can detect an unformatted disk. Because a critical error won't terminate the program, the critical error handler doesn't need to free EMS memory. This program should never generate divide-by-zero or floating-point errors, but if it did these would also have to free EMS memory.

Executing Code in EMS

Code never actually executes in EMS; it resides in EMS and executes in mappable memory (the page frame or another mapped page, for example). With EMS 3.2, the code must fit in the page frame, and the code must be mapped in and

DOS 5: A DEVELOPER'S GUIDE

out explicitly. With EMS 4.0, functions 55H and 56H make it easier to pass control to EMS code. Of course, EMS 4.0 also makes it possible to map more than 64 Kbytes (if the hardware supports it).

Listing 12-6 shows how code is run in EMS. This simple example copies a short program (and some data) into pages 0 and 1 of an EMS handle. The program calls the routine in page 0, then maps in page 2 (presumably to work with some data there). Finally, the program calls the routine in page 1 and remaps page 2.

Listing 12-6. EMSEXEC.C.

```
/****************************************************************
 *                                                              *
 * File: emsexec.c                                              *
 *                                                              *
 * Description:                                                 *
 * Simple example of EMS code execution.                        *
 *                                                              *
 * WARNING: IF YOU ARE USING MICROSOFT C YOU MUST USE THE /ZP1  *
 * OPTION. IF YOU DO NOT, THE CHAR's IN alttbl WILL TAKE UP TWO *
 * BYTES AND CONFUSE THE EMS DRIVER.                            *
 *                                                              *
 ****************************************************************/

#include <stdio.h>
#include <dos.h>
#include "cems.h"
#include "compat.h"

char dispstring[]="I'm running in EMS!\r\n$";

char string2[]="Me too!\r\n$";

char code[]=
   {
   0x1E,              /* PUSH DS */
   0x0E,              /* PUSH CS */
   0x1F,              /* POP DS */
   0xBA,0,1,          /* MOV DX,100 (changed by C code) */
   0xB4,0x09,         /* MOV AH, 9 */
```

EXPANDING HORIZONS: EMS

```
    0xCD,0x21,       /* INT 21H */
    0x1F,            /* POP DS */
    0xCB             /* RETF */
    };

int handle;

void interrupt far onbreak()
    {
    }

main()
    {
    int i;
    char far *emsptr;
    union REGS r,r1;
    struct SREGS s;
    struct maptable
        {
        unsigned int lpage;
        unsigned int ppage;
        } mt1,mt2;
    void far *mscbug;
    struct altertable
        {
        void far *addr;
        char newmaplen;
        struct maptable far *newmt;
        char oldmaplen;
        struct maptable far *oldmt;
        char resvd[8];
        } altthl;
    if (!ems_present())
        {
        printf("This program requires EMS memory.\n");
        exit(1);
        }
    setvect(0x23,onbreak);          /* Ignore break. */
    handle=ems_alloc(3);
    if (handle==-1) err(ems_errno);
    if (ems_map(handle,0,0)) err(ems_errno);
```

457

```
    FP_SEG(emsptr)=ems_pfa();
    FP_OFF(emsptr)=0;
/* Load code into EMS and fix up. */
    for (i=0;i<sizeof(code);i++) emsptr[i]=code[i];
    for (i=0;i<sizeof(dispstring);i++) emsptr[0x100+i]=dispstring[
        i];
    if (ems_map(handle,0,1)) err(ems_errno);
    for (i=0;i<sizeof(code);i++) emsptr[i]=code[i];
    for (i=0;i<sizeof(string2);i++) emsptr[0x100+i]=string2[i];
/* Set up mapping tables. */
    mt2.ppage=mt1.ppage=mt1.lpage=0;
    mt2.lpage=2;
    alttbl.addr=emsptr;
    alttbl.newmaplen=1;
    alttbl.oldmaplen=1;
    alttbl.newmt=(void far *)&mt1;
    alttbl.oldmt=(void far *)&mt2;
/* Get ready to run code. */
    r.x.ax=0x5600;
    r.x.dx=handle;
    mscbug=(void far *)&alttbl;
    r.x.si=FP_OFF(mscbug);
    s.ds=FP_SEG(mscbug);
/* Map in page 0, call, then map in page 2 upon return. */
    int86x(0x67,&r,&r1,&s);
    if (r1.h.ah) err(r1.h.ah);
    mt1.lpage=1;
    mt2.lpage=2;
/* Map in page 1, call, then map in page 3 upon return. */
    int86x(0x67,&r,&r1,&s);
    if (r1.h.ah) err(r1.h.ah);
    ems_free(handle);
    exit(0);
    }

err(int code)
    {
    printf("EMS error %02X\n",code);
    if (handle!=-1) ems_free(handle);
    exit(1);
    }
```

EXPANDING HORIZONS: EMS

In a real program, the code would load from disk and fill the 16-Kbyte page. This technique is especially useful for TSRs and other programs in which space is at a premium.

Programs must never place their stacks in EMS. If they do, an interrupt routine that changes the EMS mapping will crash the machine.

You can map one logical page into more than one physical page simultaneously. This technique, known as *aliasing*, may be useful in certain applications. However, not all EMS drivers—especially those that emulate EMS—support aliasing. If your program depends on this technique, you must verify that the driver supports it. Simply map a page into two physical pages, change a byte in the first physical page, and look at the second physical page. If the byte changed in both pages, aliasing is available.

EMS 4.0 offers many advanced features. You can learn more about them in the EMS 4.0 reference. For example, handles can have names. Programs that want to share data can do so via named EMS handles. Another EMS 4.0 feature allows EMS memory to retain its contents through a warm-boot (if the hardware can support it). With the right hardware, EMS 4.0 can even support smaller page sizes.

CHAPTER 13

Device Drivers

Starting with version 2.0, DOS supports installable device drivers. These drivers allow DOS to communicate with practically any device. DOS establishes rigid guidelines for device drivers; they must contain certain data and routines. This makes them easy to write. However, most device drivers deal with complex hardware – that's the difficult part. In addition, DOS device drivers are extremely difficult to debug.

DOS device drivers—an idea borrowed from other operating systems—help keep DOS from becoming obsolete. Manufacturers can use them to interface anything to DOS (such as optical disks, terminals, high-capacity magnetic disks, and tapes). Without device drivers, these manufacturers would have to provide custom interfaces for their devices. Worse, they might have to wait for Microsoft to support them directly. Imagine your program had to know about hundreds of disk drives and how to control them directly. Device drivers hide this complexity from our programs.

Keep in mind that device drivers don't always support physical devices. A RAM disk driver, for example, supports a virtual disk drive in the PC's memory.

Device-Driver Components

Every device driver consists of three distinct parts: the header, the strategy routine, and the interrupt routine. It may also contain code specific to the device it controls.

In practice, a driver's .ASM file looks like one for a .COM file. However, the driver source code must begin with an *ORG 0* statement. In addition, you don't specify a start address for the driver. After linking, the EXE2BIN program (supplied

DOS 5: A DEVELOPER'S GUIDE

by Microsoft with DOS) converts the .EXE file to a driver file. Driver files may have any extension; many use .SYS. Don't use .EXE or .COM as an extension—device drivers must not be executed from the DOS prompt.

The header, located in the first part of the file (see Figure 13-1), defines the driver to DOS. The definition includes the name, the type of device, and other items that we will cover shortly. Two important fields in the header point to the strategy and interrupt routines.

DOS calls the strategy routine with a pointer to a request packet. This packet is a variable-length data structure containing commands to the driver. The driver also returns data in the packet. The strategy routine should simply save the address of the packet and return. DOS will immediately call the interrupt routine.

While the format of the request packet varies from command to command, the first four bytes of the packet are always the same. The first byte (*PACKET*+0) is the length of the packet. The third byte (*PACKET*+2) is always the DOS driver command. The driver returns status information in the fourth word of the packet (*PACKET*+3).

In the status word (see Figure 13-2), the DONE bit (bit 8) is always set when the driver returns to DOS. If the ERR bit (bit 15) is on, an error occurred. Bits 7 through 0 contain the error code when ERR is set. Only certain commands use bit 9, the BUSY bit. DOS expects a status word each time it calls the driver.

The interrupt routine should retrieve the address of the packet and perform the commands. For no apparent reason, DOS uses two routines instead of one—perhaps Microsoft's designers were planning to accommodate features that were never implemented.

Drivers must respond to certain commands—the number of commands depends on the driver. Typical commands initialize the driver, obtain status information, and perform I/O. For a list of driver commands, see Table 13-1.

DEVICE DRIVERS

Offset	Contents
0H	Pointer to next driver*
4H	Attribute (see below)
6H	Offset of strategy routine
8H	Offset of interrupt routine
AH	8-byte device name (character drivers only). Name is left-justified and blank-padded. -or- Number of units supported (1 byte; block drivers only).

* Set to FFFFFFFFH if last (or only) device in file. Other devices place offset of next driver in first two bytes. MS-DOS places full pointer to next driver in this field at run time.

```
15  14  13  12  11  10   9   8   7   6   5   4   3   2   1   0
```

| C H R | I O C T L | N O N I B M / O T B | N E T W O R K | O C R M | Not Used | Q U E R Y | G I O C T L | X | S P E C L | C L O C K | N U L | S T D O U T / B I G | S T D I N |

BIT DEFINITIONS

X   = Not used
CHR   = 1 for character device, 0 for block device
IOCTL = 1 if driver supports IOCTL
OCRM[1] = 1 if driver supports OPEN DEVICE, CLOSE DEVICE, and REMOVABLE MEDIA calls
GIOCTL[3] = 1 if driver supports GENERIC IOCTL call
QUERY[4] = 1 if driver supports IOCTL query

FOR CHARACTER DEVICES

SPECL = 1 if CON device supports INT 29H
CLOCK = 1 if CLOCK device
NUL   = 1 if NUL device
STDOUT = 1 if STDOUT device
STDIN = 1 if STDIN device
OTB[2] = 1 if driver supports output until busy

FOR BLOCK DEVICES

NONIBM   = 1 if driver is for non-IBM block driver
NETWORK[2] = 1 if driver is for a network block driver
BIG[5]   = 1 if driver supports 32-bit sector addresses

[1] MS-DOS version 3.00 or later
[2] MS-DOS version 3.10 or later
[3] MS-DOS version 3.20 or later
[4] MS-DOS version 4.0 or later
[5] MS-DOS version 5.0 or later

Figure 13-1. Device header.

15	14 13 12 11 10	9	8	7 6 5 4 3 2 1 0
E R R	Not used	B U S Y	D O N E	Error code if bit 15 is set

Error Codes:

Code	Error
0H	Write-protect
1H	Unknown unit
2H	Not ready
3H	Unknown command
4H	CRC error
5H	Bad request packet
6H	Seek error
7H	Unknown media
8H	Sector not found
9H	Out of paper (printer)
AH	Write error
BH	Read error
CH	General error
FH	Invalid disk change (DOS 3.0 and above)

Figure 13-2. Status word.

DOS provides a trapdoor for programs to communicate with device drivers via the *IOCTL INPUT* and *IOCTL OUTPUT* commands. These functions allow programs to send arbitrary data to the device driver. Ordinarily this data is sent to the driver, not the device. For example, a program might send a command to a printer driver (via *IOCTL OUTPUT*) telling it to expect input for an Epson printer. Perhaps the driver converts the codes to drive a different printer. Another *IOCTL OUTPUT* command would disable the translation. DOS doesn't care what strings you send or receive via IOCTL—the meaning is between the program and the device driver. Drivers don't have to support the IOCTL functions.

DEVICE DRIVERS

Character Drivers

Command	Function	Corresponding Attribute Bit	Notes
00H	INIT		Required
03H	IOCTL INPUT	IOCTL	
04H	INPUT		Required
05H	INPUT (NO WAIT)		Required
06H	INPUT STATUS		Required
07H	INPUT FLUSH		Required
08H	OUTPUT		Required
09H	VERIFY OUTPUT		Required
0AH	OUTPUT STATUS		Required
0BH	OUTPUT FLUSH		Required
0CH	IOCTL OUTPUT	IOCTL	
0DH	DEVICE OPEN	OCRM	DOS 3.0 and above
0EH	DEVICE CLOSE	OCRM	DOS 3.0 and above
10H	OUTPUT UNTIL BUSY	OTB	DOS 3.1 and above
13H	GENERIC IOCTL	GIOCTL	DOS 3.2 and above
19H	IOCTL QUERY	QUERY	DOS 5.0 and above

Block Drivers

Command	Function	Corresponding Attribute Bit	Notes
00H	INIT		Required
01H	MEDIA CHECK		Required
02H	BUILD-BPB		Required
03H	IOCTL INPUT	IOCTL	
04H	INPUT		Required
08H	OUTPUT		Required
09H	VERIFY OUTPUT		Required
0CH	IOCTL OUTPUT	IOCTL	
0DH	DEVICE OPEN	OCRM	DOS 3.0 and above
0EH	DEVICE CLOSE	OCRM	DOS 3.0 and above
0FH	REMOVABLE MEDIA CHECK	OCRM	DOS 3.0 and above
13H	GENERIC IOCTL	GIOCTL	DOS 3.2 and above
17H	GET LOGICAL	GIOCTL	DOS 3.2 and above
18H	SET LOGICAL	GIOCTL	DOS 3.2 and above
19H	IOCTL QUERY	QUERY	DOS 5.0 and above

Table 13-1. Driver commands.

Loading the Driver

DOS loads device drivers shortly after it boots up. The CONFIG.SYS file names these drivers with the *DEVICE=* command. Once a driver loads, you must reboot the computer with a new CONFIG.SYS file to remove it.

Because device drivers can't be unloaded, they always consume memory. Users' programs compete for the same memory, so it is imperative that drivers use no more memory than is absolutely necessary. For this reason, drivers should be written in assembly language. They can be written in C but will take up more space than a well-written assembly-language driver.

Types of Drivers

Drivers come in two flavors: character and block. Character drivers support devices that create or accept data in streams. DOS uses character drivers (some of which are built in) to control the screen, keyboard, printers, and COM ports. For example, the ANSI.SYS installable driver controls the screen and keyboard. All character drivers have a name, something like a simple, eight-character file name with no extension. This name has nothing to do with the driver's file name. For instance, ANSI.SYS uses the name *CON*.

Block drivers control disk or disklike devices. DOS imposes the idea of sectors and a file system on block drivers. A block driver must report information about its device's format and status and transfer sectors of data from memory to disk and vice versa. DOS assigns block drivers letters instead of names. If the first driver controls two disks, it receives the letters *A* and *B*. A block driver receives a letter for each disk it controls. The letters are always consecutive.

Character-Driver Commands

All character drivers must support nine commands: *INIT, INPUT, OUTPUT, VERIFY OUTPUT, INPUT (NO WAIT), INSTATUS, INFLUSH, OUTSTATUS,* and *OUTFLUSH*. The driver also may elect to implement the *IOCTL INPUT, IOCTL OUTPUT, DEVICE OPEN, DEVICE CLOSE,* and *GENERIC IOCTL* commands.

DEVICE DRIVERS

INIT. DOS starts each driver with an *INIT* command. Table 13-2 shows the *INIT* command's packet. In a character driver, the primary function of *INIT* is to tell DOS how much memory the driver wishes to reserve. Since this command only runs once, it usually resides at the end of the driver. When the driver reserves memory, it does not reserve the space occupied by the code for the *INIT* command. DOS then reuses the space. Other drivers use the memory consumed by the *INIT* code for other purposes after *INIT* has finished.

Offset	Contents	Length (Bytes)	Type
00H	Length of packet	1	In
02H	Command byte (00H)	1	In
03H	Status word	2	Out
0DH	Number of units	1	Out
0EH	End of available memory*	4	In
0EH	End address	4	Out
11H	Error message flag**	1	Out
12H	Pointer to command line	4	In

* MS-DOS 5.0 and above
** MS-DOS 4.0 and above

Table 13-2. INIT request packet for character drivers.

The *INIT* routine must return the end address (segment and offset) in *PACKET*+0EH. It also places a one in the byte at *PACKET*+0DH to indicate a single-character device (character drivers may only control one logical device). If the driver doesn't want to load—perhaps it couldn't find its device—it must return zero in *PACKET*+0DH and make its end address equal to CS:0000.

The *INIT* command has two other peculiarities. First, it is the only device-driver command that can call DOS. The routine must only call INT 21H, functions 01H through 0CH and function 30H. These functions can print copyright messages and error messages or request input from the user. In addition, function 30H allows the driver to determine the current DOS version. This is important because some driver features may require a certain version of DOS.

The other interesting feature of *INIT* is its ability to read the command line. The packet contains a four-byte address at *PACKET*+12H that points to the first character following the *DEVICE=* command in the CONFIG.SYS file. This is useful for accepting configuration information from the command line. Notice that the first characters in the command line are the name of the driver's file; you have to skip the file name before parsing parameters. The command line is placed in an internal buffer and should be considered read-only.

With DOS 4.0 and above, the byte at *PACKET*+17H controls error messages. If the driver aborts (by setting the number of units to zero) and sets the byte at this location to a nonzero value, DOS (4.0 or later) will issue an error message.

INPUT, OUTPUT, and VERIFY OUTPUT. These three commands are similar: All transfer data to or from the device. The address of the data is in *PACKET*+0EH, and the number of bytes to transfer is at *PACKET*+12H. Table 13-3 shows the packet format for these commands.

Offset	Contents	Length (Bytes)	Type
00H	Length of packet	1	In
02H	Command (4 = input, 8 = output, 9 = verify output)	1	In
03H	Status word	2	Out
0EH	Pointer to buffer	4	In
12H	Number of bytes to transfer	2	I/O

Table 13-3. I/O request packet for character drivers.

The *INPUT* command transfers the specified number of bytes from the device to the buffer specified by the address at *PACKET*+0EH. The *OUTPUT* and *VERIFY OUTPUT* commands transfer the data from the buffer to the device. The *VERIFY OUTPUT* should also verify the data transfer if that is possible with the given device.

DEVICE DRIVERS

If not enough data is available to satisfy an input request, the driver may return fewer bytes than requested. When doing so, it must place the actual number of bytes transferred into the count field of the packet (*PACKET*+12H). Some drivers wait for the data before returning to DOS; others wait up to some time-out limit. A driver may also return a device-not-ready error if data isn't available.

If the device can't accept more characters on output, the driver should wait for a time-out period. If the device still can't accept characters when this period expires, the driver can return a device-not-ready error. If the driver transfers less than the requested length, it should update the byte count at *PACKET*+12H to reflect the correct value.

DOS can handle character devices in raw (binary) or cooked (line-disciplined) mode. Devices start in cooked mode, in which DOS only reads data up to a carriage return. DOS also treats certain control characters (such as a backspace) as special characters. In binary mode, DOS passes all input characters directly to your program. You can change the mode with INT 21H (function 44H, subfunction 01H). As long as the handle used to access the device is in cooked mode, *INPUT* commands will always request one byte of data. This allows DOS to evaluate each character and decide whether it should request another.

INPUT (NO WAIT). The *INPUT (NO WAIT)* command allows DOS to peek at a character if one is available. If a character is waiting when DOS calls this command, the driver returns it to DOS in *PACKET*+0DH. The driver should not discard the character, however. A subsequent *INPUT* or *INPUT (NO WAIT)* call will return the same character. If no input is available from the device, the driver returns with the BUSY bit set in the status return. Table 13-4 shows the request packet for this call.

Offset	Contents	Length (Bytes)	Type
00H	Length of packet	1	In
02H	Command (05H)	1	In
03H	Status word	2	Out
0DH	Character waiting	1	Out

Table 13-4. INPUT (NO WAIT) request packet for character drivers.

INSTATUS and OUTSTATUS. The *INSTATUS* and *OUTSTATUS* commands allow DOS to check the status of the device. Some drivers buffer characters to and from the device in a queue. When the device generates an interrupt, the driver receives (or sends) characters without intervention from DOS. For these drivers, the status commands return the state of the queue. *INSTATUS* sets the BUSY flag if no characters are waiting; *OUTSTATUS* sets the BUSY flag if the output queue is full.

If there is no output queue, the *OUTSTATUS* command returns the status of the device directly. If the input is not interrupt-driven and buffered, the driver always returns with the BUSY flag set. Otherwise, DOS would never initiate an input operation.

INFLUSH and OUTFLUSH. Only drivers that buffer characters use these commands. Other drivers can immediately set the DONE bit in the status return word and return. Buffered drivers should discard any characters waiting in the input queue (for *INFLUSH*) or output queue (for *OUTFLUSH*).

IOCTL INPUT and IOCTL OUTPUT. These commands allow the driver to send and receive control strings, as discussed above. The format of the request packet is almost identical to the *INPUT* and *OUTPUT* commands (see Table 13-5). Of course, the command byte is different. Many drivers don't implement these commands; those that do must set bit 14 in their headers' attribute words.

DEVICE DRIVERS

Offset	Contents	Length (Bytes)	Type
00H	Length of packet	1	In
02H	Command (03H = IOCTL Input, 0CH = IOCTL Output)	1	In
03H	Status word	2	Out
0EH	Pointer to buffer	4	In
12H	Number of bytes to transfer	2	I/O

Table 13-5. IOCTL request packet.

These commands act exactly like the *INPUT* and *OUTPUT* commands except that the data is for the driver, not the device. The driver inspects the input buffer for commands and acts on them. It may return information, if desired, on the next *IOCTL OUTPUT* command call.

DEVICE OPEN and DEVICE CLOSE. Most character drivers don't use the *DEVICE OPEN* and *DEVICE CLOSE* commands. As their names imply, they occur when a program opens or closes the device via a file handle. If the driver wants DOS to call these commands, bit 11 must be set in the attribute word.

A sophisticated printer driver, for example, might use *DEVICE OPEN* to print a banner page on the printer. Then, when it received the *DEVICE CLOSE* command, it could form-feed and reset the printer.

These functions are of limited use with the CON, AUX, and PRN devices, which DOS always keeps open.

GENERIC IOCTL. The *GENERIC IOCTL* command allows programs to send additional commands to the device driver. Unlike the other IOCTL commands, DOS defines the generic command's meanings. For character devices, this command involves switching code pages—not a very interesting topic for the average programmer. Because this is such a specialized topic, we won't cover it in this chapter. If you need to write drivers that support multiple code pages, read the MS-DOS Programmer's Reference.

Block-Driver Commands

All block drivers support six commands: *INIT, MEDIA CHECK, BUILD BPB, INPUT, OUTPUT,* and *VERIFY OUTPUT*. They may also support the *IOCTL INPUT, IOCTL OUTPUT, DEVICE OPEN, DEVICE CLOSE, REMOVABLE MEDIA CHECK, GENERIC IOCTL, GET LOGICAL*, and *SET LOGICAL* commands.

Writing a block driver requires intimate knowledge of the DOS file system and the disk device in question. You should understand how DOS organizes disks before attempting to write your own block drivers. Later in this chapter, we will look at a fully functional floppy-disk driver that will help you get started.

DOS supplies the *GENERIC IOCTL, GET LOGICAL*, and *SET LOGICAL* commands primarily for specialized applications. Because they are of limited interest, we won't cover them in this chapter. If you need these functions, read the MS-DOS Programmer's Reference.

Notice that block drivers use many of the same commands used by character drivers. Be careful; many of the commands have a slightly different format when used with block devices. The first part of the request packet is the same for block devices as for character devices, with one exception: The second byte of the packet (*PACKET*+01H) contains the unit number affected by the operation. All block commands except *INIT* use this field.

INIT. For block devices, the *INIT* command is only slightly different from the character device's version. The request packet (see Table 13-6) is almost identical to the character device packet except that:

DEVICE DRIVERS

- Block drivers can control more than one unit by placing the number of units in *PACKET*+0DH. Each unit is a separate drive letter (A:, B:, C:, and so on).

- Block drivers must return a pointer to a table of pointers, which in turn point to BIOS parameter blocks (BPBs) in *PACKET*+12H (the same location as the command-line pointer).

- DOS (3.10 and above) places a one-byte drive number in *PACKET*+16H for the driver to examine. Zero is drive A:, 1 is drive B:, and so on.

Offset	Contents	Length (Bytes)	Type
00H	Length of packet	1	In
02H	Command (00H)	1	In
03H	Status word	2	Out
0DH	Number of units	1	Out
0EH	End of available memory *	4	In
0EH	End address	4	Out
12H	Pointer to command line	4	In
12H	Pointer to table of BPB pointers	4	Out
16H	Device number**	1	In
17H	Error message flag***	1	Out

* DOS 5.0 and above
** DOS 3.1 and above
*** DOS 4.0 and above

Table 13-6. INIT request packet for block drivers.

The BPB contains the information DOS needs to know about the disk. With DOS 2.0 and above, disks store the BPB in their boot records. This is handy because the boot record also contains information the driver needs. Table 13-7 shows the boot record and BPB of a DOS-format disk. The boot record is always in the first sector. If you're reading non-DOS or DOS 1.x disks, you'll need to generate the BPB information yourself based on the disks' characteristics.

473

DOS 5: A DEVELOPER'S GUIDE

Offset	Length (Bytes)	Contents
00H	3	Jump to bootstrap loader
03H	8	OEM name
0BH	2	Number of bytes per sector
0DH	1	Number of sectors per cluster
0EH	2	Number of reserved sectors
10H	1	Number of FATs
11H	2	Number of root directory slots
13H	2	Total number of sectors [a]
15H	1	Media description
16H	2	Number of sectors per FAT
18H	2	Number of sectors per track
1AH	2	Number of heads
1CH	2 [b]	Number of hidden sectors
20H	4	Total number of sectors
24H	1	Physical drive number [c]
25H	1	Reserved [c]
26H	1	Signature (29H) [c]
27H	4	Volume serial number [c]
2BH	11	Volume label [c]
36H	8	File system type ('FAT12' or 'FAT16')

[a] If this word is zero, the actual count is stored at offset 20H (DOS 4.0 and above)
[b] Four bytes for DOS 4.0 and above
[c] Optional; for DOS 4.0 and above only

Table 13-7. Disk boot record.

Notice that DOS 4 and 5 define extensions to the boot record, allowing them to handle disk partitions larger than 32 Mbytes.

DOS expects the *INIT* command to return a pointer to a table of pointers. Each pointer in the table points to a BPB. Each unit the driver supports must have its own BPB. Even if the driver supports only one unit, you must return a pointer to the BPB's pointer.

MEDIA CHECK. Before accessing a disk, DOS ensures that the user did not put a different disk in the drive since the last time it checked. The *MEDIA CHECK* command asks the driver to determine this. The driver must inform DOS whether or

DEVICE DRIVERS

not the disk is different. If the driver doesn't know, it can return an indeterminate status to DOS; DOS assumes the disk has changed unless it has data to write to the disk.

How can a driver determine this information? Obviously, if it supports a disk that isn't removable, the driver can always reply negatively. Removable disks are trickier. On the AT and PS/2, the BIOS has a call to determine whether the user opened the disk door. This doesn't prove the disk is different, but it's sufficient for DOS's purposes.

Another clue is to reread the BPB of the disk. If the media descriptor byte changed, the disk changed. For the driver's convenience, the request packet (see Table 13-8) contains the last known media descriptor.

Offset	Contents	Length (Bytes)	Type
00H	Length of packet	1	In
01H	Unit number	1	In
02H	Command (01H)	1	In
03H	Status word	2	Out
0DH	Media description	1	In
0FH	Media status (FFH = changed, 0 = unknown, 1 = not changed)	2	Out
0FH	Pointer to volume name*	4	Out

* Only returned when OCRM bit is on and media status=FFH.

Table 13-8. Request packet for MEDIA CHECK command.

Depending on your hardware, other methods may be available to determine disk changes. On an XT-type machine, you probably don't want to reread the BPB very often. An alternative is to store the time of the last successful disk access. If the next one is very soon thereafter (Microsoft says less than two seconds), you can assume the disk hasn't changed. You can also check the volume ID in the root directory (another inconclusive test).

If you decide the disk changed, place an FFFFH in *PACKET*+0EH. If the disk didn't change, put a one in the same word. If all else fails, place a zero in *PACKET*+0EH to tell DOS you don't know one way or the other. You should only do this as a last resort—always returning a zero will slow your disk-read accesses considerably (DOS will keep rereading the disk's BPB).

If bit 11 is set in the driver's attribute word (indicating support for *DEVICE OPEN*, *DEVICE CLOSE*, and *REMOVABLE MEDIA CHECK*), the driver has to return more information when it decides the disk has changed. A pointer to the new disk's volume name goes in *PACKET*+0FH.

BUILD BPB. When DOS decides the disk has changed, it asks the driver for the new disk's BPB via the *BUILD BPB* command. DOS places some information in the request packet (see Table 13-9), but it is of little use. The driver will usually determine the BPB (see the *INIT* command above) and return a pointer to it in *PACKET*+12H. Note that this is a pointer to the BPB, not a pointer to a pointer as in the *INIT* command. The unit field of the request packet determines which BPB pointer to return.

INPUT, OUTPUT, and VERIFY OUTPUT. The character driver's *INPUT*, *OUTPUT*, and *VERIFY OUTPUT* commands are similar to those for a block driver. Even the request packet is similar (see Table 13-10). However, the transfer-count field (at *PACKET*+12H) is in sectors, not bytes. In addition, *PACKET*+14H tells the driver which sector to start with. *PACKET*+0DH contains the media descriptor byte as a convenience for the driver. If bit 11 is set in the attribute byte, the driver should store a pointer to the current volume name at *PACKET*+16H if it returns with an invalid disk change error (error code 0FH).

DEVICE DRIVERS

Offset	Contents	Length (Bytes)	Type
00H	Length of packet	1	In
01H	Unit number	1	In
02H	Command (02H)	1	In
03H	Status word	2	Out
0DH	Media description [a]	1	In
0EH	Pointer to FAT or buffer [b]	4	In
12H	Pointer to BPB	4	Out

[a] This value is of little use. The new BPB's media description value supersedes this one.

[b] If non-IBM bit is set, this field points to a temporary buffer. If the bit is clear, the field points to the old disk's FAT—do not modify the old disk's FAT.

Table 13-9. Request packet for BUILD BPB command.

Offset	Contents	Length (Bytes)	Type
00H	Length of packet	1	In
01H	Unit number	1	In
02H	Command (4 = Input, 8 = Output, 9 = Verify output)	1	In
03H	Status word	2	Out
0DH	Media description	1	In
0EH	Pointer to buffer	4	In
12H	Number of sectors to transfer	2	I/O
14H	Starting sector [a]	2	In
16H	Long starting sector [a]	4	In
16H	Pointer to volume name [b]	4	Out

[a] With DOS 4.0 and above, if the field at offset 14H contains FFFFH, the starting sector is in the field at offset 16H.

[b] Returned only when invalid disk change error occurs (DOS 3.0 and above).

Table 13-10. Block I/O request packet.

The operation of these commands is almost identical to their character-driver counterparts. One difference stems from an optimization that DOS uses when calculating the sector count. Occasionally DOS sends the driver a sector count that causes the buffer's offset to overflow. For example, what if DOS called the input command with a buffer at 0324:FCD0 and asked for two 512-byte sectors? Hex addition shows FCD0+400=100D0—too large for an 8086 offset. The driver should ignore the excess bytes (known as the *wrap* or *wraparound*). The buffer's offset should never exceed FFFFH.

The *VERIFY OUTPUT* command should attempt to verify that the disk accepted the data correctly. Ideally, the driver would reread the sectors and compare them to the original data. The default DOS drivers only verify that the sectors written are readable and have a correct checksum, or CRC. Of course, the driver can simply treat *VERIFY OUTPUT* as *OUTPUT* if verification isn't possible or desired.

With DOS 4 and 5, one word may not be enough to specify the starting sector. For large disks, the word at *PACKET*+14H will equal FFFFH. This signals the driver that the actual starting sector is the 32-bit word at *PACKET*+16H.

Optional Commands

The *IOCTL INPUT*, *IOCTL OUTPUT*, *DEVICE OPEN*, and *DEVICE CLOSE* commands are identical for block and character drivers. When called for a block driver, *PACKET*+01H contains the unit number to which the command applies.

The *REMOVABLE MEDIA CHECK* command works with the *DEVICE OPEN* and *DEVICE CLOSE* commands. If a block driver supports any of these commands (indicated by bit 11 in the header), it must support them all. This command allows user programs to DOS IOCTL call (INT 21H, function 44H, subfunction 8) to determine whether the specified unit is removable. If it is, the driver should return with the BUSY bit (in the status return word) clear. If the bit is set, DOS reports that the unit is not removable.

DEVICE DRIVERS

Putting It All Together

Because device drivers must adhere to such a rigorous format, much of the drudgery associated with writing them is easy to automate. Listings 13-1 and 13-2 show DDASM, a driver development environment. The main file, DD.ASM (Listing 13-1), provides the device header and strategy, interrupt, and initialization routines. To write a device driver using DDASM, you must supply at least two files: a .CFG file telling DDASM about the device driver and a .DRV file containing the driver's main routines and data storage. If you wish, DDASM will call a user-defined subroutine while the *INIT* command is executing. If you enable this feature, the subroutine goes in a .CMD file. DDASM lets DOS reuse the space required by the code in that file.

Listing 13-1. DD.ASM.
```
;****************************************************************
;*                                                              *
;* File: dd.asm                                                 *
;*                                                              *
;* Main routine for DDASM. Assemble with DDASM.BAT.             *
;*                                                              *
;****************************************************************

IFDEF      PROGRAM
; macro to include files based on program name
XINCLUDE   MACRO  FNAM,EXT
INCLUDE           FNAM.&EXT
           ENDM

; Get configuration.
XINCLUDE   %PROGRAM,CFG

; macro to push/pop all--could be done better if we
; didn't have to run on 8088
PUSH_ALL   MACRO
           PUSH   AX
           PUSH   BX
```

DOS 5: A DEVELOPER'S GUIDE

```
                PUSH    CX
                PUSH    DX
                PUSH    SI
                PUSH    DI
                PUSH    BP
                PUSH    DS
                PUSH    ES
                ENDM

POP_ALL         MACRO
                POP     ES
                POP     DS
                POP     BP
                POP     DI
                POP     SI
                POP     DX
                POP     CX
                POP     BX
                POP     AX
                ENDM

; This macro generates a routine's offset if it exists or zero if
; it doesn't.
ADDOF           MACRO ROUTINE
IFDEF           ROUTINE
                DW      OFFSET ROUTINE
ELSE
                DW      0
ENDIF
                ENDM

; Define request packet.
DDPACKET        STRUC
LEN             DB      ?
UNIT            DB      ?
CMD             DB      ?
STATUS          DW      ?
DDPACKET        ENDS
```

DEVICE DRIVERS

```
_TEXT           SEGMENT  PARA PUBLIC
                ASSUME   CS:_TEXT,DS:_TEXT,SS:_TEXT
                ORG      0H

; Generate header.
DDSTART         EQU      $
                DW       -1,-1              ; pointer to next driver
                DW       DDATTRIB           ; attribute word
                DW       OFFSET DDSTR       ; pointer to strategy routine
                DW       OFFSET DDINT       ; pointer to int routine
DDNAME          DB       DD_NAME            ; driver name
NAMELEN         EQU      $-DDNAME           ; Calculate length of name.

; Blank-pad name, if required.
IF              NAMELEN LT 8
                REPT     8-(NAMELEN)
                DB       ' '
                ENDM
ENDIF

; slot to store pointer to packet
DD_REQ          EQUTHIS  DWORD
DD_REQO         DW       ?
DD_REQS         DW       ?

; slot to save stack
INISP           DW       ?
INTSS           DW       ?

; Strategy routine--save pointer to packet and return.
DDSTR           PROC     FAR
                MOV      CS:[DD_REQO],BX
                MOV      CS:[DD_REQS],ES
                RET
DDSTR           ENDP

; local stack (size defined in .CFG)

IFNDEF          STACKSIZE
STACKSIZE       EQU      128
```

DOS 5: A DEVELOPER'S GUIDE

```
ENDIF
            DB      STACKSIZE DUP (?)
DDSTACK     EQU     $

; Table of addresses for each command;
; unused commands generate zero.
CMDTBL      EQUTHIS WORD
            DW      OFFSET DDINIT
            ADDOF   MEDIA_PROC
            ADDOF   BBPB_PROC
            ADDOF   IIOCTL_PROC
            ADDOF   INPUT_PROC
            ADDOF   INPUTNW_PROC
            ADDOF   INSTAT_PROC
            ADDOF   INFLUSH_PROC
            ADDOF   OUTPUT_PROC
            ADDOF   OUTVER_PROC
            ADDOF   OUTSTAT_PROC
            ADDOF   OUTFLUSH_PROC
            ADDOF   OIOCTL_PROC
            ADDOF   OPEN_PROC
            ADDOF   CLOSE_PROC
            ADDOF   REMOVE_PROC
; reserved (used to be OTB--dropped from DOS 3.3)
            DW      0
            ADDOF   GIOCTL_PROC
            ADDOF   GETLOG_PROC
            ADDOF   SETLOG_PROC
DDLASTCMD   EQU     $

; interrupt routine
DDINT       PROC    FAR
            PUSH    AX
; Save stack.
            MOV     CS:[INTSS],SS
            MOV     CS:[INTSP],SP
; Switch stack.
            MOV     AX,CS
            MOV     SS,AX
            MOV     SP,OFFSET DDSTACK
```

DEVICE DRIVERS

```
; Save registers on new stack.
            PUSH_ALL
; Set DS=CS.
            PUSH       CS
            POP        DS
; Point es:di at packet.
            LES        DI,[DD_REQ]
; Get command in BX.
            MOV        BL,ES:[DI.CMD]
            XOR        BH,BH
; Multiply by 2 (2 bytes/entry in command table).
            SHL        BX,1
; See if command is too large--if so, unknown command.
            MOV        AX,8003H
            CMP        BX,OFFSET DDLASTCMD - OFFSET CMDTBL
            JAE        DDEXIT       ; unknown command if true
; Set cx to pointer to proper routine.
            MOV        CX,CMDTBL[BX]
            OR         CX,CX
; If pointer is zero, command is unimplemented.
            JZ         DDEXIT
            XOR        AX,AX        ; zero return status
            CALL       CMDTBL[BX]   ; Call routine.
DDEXIT:
; Point to packet in case user changed es:di.
            LES        DI,[DD_REQ]
            OR         AX,100H      ; Set done bit.
; Store ax in status word.
            MOV        ES:[DI].STATUS,AX
            POP_ALL                 ; Restore registers.
; Restore stack.
            MOV        SS,CS:[INTSS]
            MOV        SP,CS:[INISP]
            POP        AX
            RET
DDINT       ENDP

; Get user's driver code
            XINCLUDE %PROGRAM.DRV
DD_END      EQU        $
```

DOS 5: A DEVELOPER'S GUIDE

```
; Code below here is thrown away.
IFDEF       INIT_PROC
            XINCLUDE %PROGRAM,CMD
ENDIF

; default init code
DDINIT      PROC
IFDEF       INIT_PROC
            MOV    BX,ES:[DI+18]
; cx:bx points to command line.
            MOV    CX,ES:[DI+20]
            PUSH   ES
            PUSH   DI
            CALL   INIT_PROC   ; Must return number of units.
            POP    DI
            POP    ES
ELSE
            MOV    AL,1        ; default number of units
ENDIF
; User's routine must return.
; al= # of units
; si= ptr to BPBs if block device
; This implies you must have an INIT_PROC for block devices.
; Character drivers may omit INIT_PROC if no user processing
; is needed.

; Store # of units.
            MOV    ES:[DI+13],AL
; Store end address.
            MOV    ES:[DI+14],OFFSET DD_END
            OR     AL,AL       ; Are we aborting?
            JNZ    INITFIN     ; No...jump.
            XOR    AX,AX       ; Yes...zero end address.
; to abort installation
            MOV    ES:[DI+14],AX
INITFIN:
; Store BPB table pointer.
            MOV    ES:[DI+18],SI
; Fix up segment addresses.
            MOV    ES:[DI+20],DS
            MOV    ES:[DI+16],DS
```

DEVICE DRIVERS

```
; Status = OK (caller will set done).
            XOR    AX,AX
            RET
DDINIT      ENDP
_TEXT       ENDS
ELSE
IF2
            %OUT   YOU MUST SPECIFY A PROGRAM TITLE.
            %OUT   USE: MASM /DPROGRAM=NAME DD.ASM
ENDIF
            .ERR
ENDIF
            END
```

Listing 13-2. DDASM.BAT.

a. For use with MASM.
```
@echo off
if %1.==. goto :help
masm /DPROGRAM=%1 dd.asm,%1.obj;
if ERRORLEVEL 1 goto :end
link %1.obj;
if ERRORLEVEL 1 goto :end
exe2bin %1.exe %1.sys
erase %1.exe
goto :end
:help
echo DDASM by Al Williams
echo Usage: DDASM progname
echo DDASM looks for the following files and creates a driver:
echo      progname.DRV - main code
echo      progname.CFG - configuration
echo      progname.CMD - transient code
:end
```

b. For use with TASM.
```
@echo off
if %1.==. goto :help
tasm /m2 /DPROGRAM=%1 /w-PDC w-MCP dd.asm,%1.obj;
if ERRORLEVEL 1 goto :end
```

DOS 5: A DEVELOPER'S GUIDE

```
tlink %1.obj;
if ERRORLEVEL 1 goto :end
exe2bin %1.exe %1.sys
erase %1.exe
goto :end
:help
echo DDASM by Al Williams
echo Usage: DDASM progname
echo DDASM looks for the following files and creates a driver:
echo      progname.DRV   - main code
echo      progname.CFG   - configuration
echo      progname.CMD   - transient code
:end
```

The .CFG file allows you to set up various driver parameters. It also lets you specify which of your functions DDASM should call for each driver command. Table 13-11 shows the configuration variables allowed in the .CFG file.

DD_NAME	Name of character driver or number of block driver units.
MEDIA_PROC	Name of MEDIA CHECK subroutine.
BBPB_PROC	Name of BUILD BPB subroutine.
IIOCTL_PROC	Name of IOCTL INPUT subroutine.
INPUT_PROC	Name of INPUT subroutine.
INPUTNW_PROC	Name of INPUT (NO WAIT) subroutine.
INSTAT_PROC	Name of INPUT STATUS subroutine.
INFLUSH_PROC	Name of INPUT FLUSH subroutine.
OUTPUT_PROC	Name of OUTPUT subroutine.
OUTVER_PROC	Name of VERIFY OUTPUT subroutine.
OUTSTAT_PROC	Name of OUTPUT STATUS subroutine.
OUTFLUSH_PROC	Name of OUTPUT FLUSH subroutine.
OIOCTL_PROC	Name of IOCTL OUTPUT subroutine.
OPEN_PROC	Name of DEVICE OPEN subroutine.
CLOSE_PROC	Name of DEVICE CLOSE subroutine.
REMOVE_PROC	Name of REMOVABLE MEDIA CHECK subroutine.
GIOCTL_PROC	Name of GENERIC IOCTL subroutine.
GETLOG_PROC	Name of GET LOGICAL subroutine.
SETLOG_PROC	Name of SET LOGICAL subroutine.
INIT_PROC	Name of user's INIT handler subroutine.
STACKSIZE	Size of stack.

Table 13-11. DDASM configuration variables.

DEVICE DRIVERS

Sample Drivers

The best way to see how DDASM works is to study some examples. Listings 13-3 and 13-4 show a character driver named _PIPE. This driver allows a program to write characters into a first-in, first-out buffer (often called a *pipe*). Later, a program (possibly a different program) can read the characters back. This is especially useful in multitasking operating environments like DESQview and Windows. When multitasking, two windows can talk to each other via the pipe. However, even standard DOS lets you see how this driver works.

Listing 13-3. PIPE.CFG.

```
;**************************************************************
;*                                                             *
;* File: pipe.cfg                                              *
;*                                                             *
;* Configuration setup for PIPE driver.                        *
;*                                                             *
;**************************************************************

DD_NAME          EQU     '_PIPE'
DDATTRIB         EQU     8000H
STACKSIZE        EQU     1024
INPUT_PROC       EQU     UINPUT
INPUTNW_PROC     EQU     UINPUTCK
INSTAT_PROC      EQU     UINPUTST
INFLUSH_PROC     EQU     UFLUSH
OUTPUT_PROC      EQU     UOUTPUT
OUTVER_PROC      EQU     UOUTPUT
OUTSTAT_PROC     EQU     UOUTST
OUTFLUSH_PROC    EQU     UFLUSH
```

Listing 13-4. PIPE.DRV.

```
;****************************************************************
;*                                                              *
;* File: PIPE.DRV                                               *
;*                                                              *
;* Main code for the _PIPE device driver.                       *
;*                                                              *
;****************************************************************

; buffer to hold characters
PIPEBUF         DB      256 DUP ('?')
BUFEND          EQU     $

; head and tail of buffer
HEAD            DW      0
TAIL            DW      0

; circular increment routine
CIRCINC         PROC
                INC     BX
                CMP     BX,OFFSET BUFEND - OFFSET PIPEBUF
                JNZ     CINC1
                XOR     BX,BX
CINC1:
                CMP     BX,DX
                RET

CIRCINC         ENDP

; Get "input."
UINPUT          PROC
                XOR     CX,CX
; Get count.
                XCHG    CX,ES:[DI+18]
                PUSH    CX
                PUSH    ES
                PUSH    DI
```

DEVICE DRIVERS

```
; Get xfer address.
            LES     DI,ES:[DI+14]
            MOV     BX,HEAD
            MOV     DX,TAIL
            CMP     BX,DX
            JNZ     INLOOP
; No data to send.
INERR:
            MOV     AX,200H         ; Mark busy.
            JMP     SHORT INDONE
INFIN:      XOR     AX,AX
INDONE:
            MOV     HEAD,BX         ; Update queue pointer.
            POP     DI
            POP     ES
            POP     BX
            SUB     BX,CX
; Update count.
            MOV     ES:[DI+18],BX
            RET

; Get characters.
INLOOP:
            MOV     AL,PIPEBUF[BX]
; Move next character to DOS buffer.
            MOV     ES:[DI],AL
; Bump pointers.
            INC     DI
            DEC     CX
            CALL    CIRCINC
; Check for end of transfer or buffer full.
            JZ      INFIN
            JCXZ    INFIN
            JMP     INLOOP
UINPUT      ENDP
```

DOS 5: A DEVELOPER'S GUIDE

```asm
; Get input status.
UINPUTST    PROC
            MOV     AX,HEAD
            SUB     AX,TAIL
            MOV     AX,200H         ; busy
            JZ      ITESTFAIL
            XOR     AX,AX
ITESTFAIL:
            RET
UINPUTST    ENDP

; Get input with no wait...
UINPUTCK    PROC
            MOV     BX,HEAD
            CMP     BX,TAIL
            MOV     AX,200H         ; busy
            JZ      CKBUSY
            MOV     BL,[BX]
; or return character.
            MOV     ES:[DI+13],BL
            XOR     AX,AX
CKBUSY:
            RET
UINPUTCK    ENDP

; Output to our buffer.
UOUTPUT     PROC
            XOR     CX,CX
; Get count.
            XCHG    CX,ES:[DI+18]
            PUSH    CX
            PUSH    ES
            PUSH    DI
; Get xfer address.
            LES     DI,ES:[DI+14]
            MOV     BX,TAIL
            MOV     DX,HEAD
OUTLP:      PUSH    BX
            CALL    CIRCINC
            CMP     BX,DX
```

DEVICE DRIVERS

```
                POP     BX
                JNZ     OUTLOOP
; overflow
OUTERR:
                MOV     AX,8002H
                JMP     SHORT OUTDONE
OUTFIN:         XOR     AX,AX
OUTDONE:
                MOV     TAIL,BX
                POP     DI
                POP     ES
                POP     BX
                SUB     BX,CX
; Update count.
                MOV     ES:[DI+18],BX
                RET

; Move characters to buffer.
OUTLOOP:
                MOV     AL,ES:[DI]
                MOV     PIPEBUF[BX],AL
                INC     DI
                CALL    CIRCINC
                DEC     CX
                JZ      OUTFIN
                JMP     OUTLP
UOUTPUT         ENDP

; Flush input or output (the same in this case).
UFLUSH          PROC
                MOV     BX,HEAD
                MOV     TAIL,BX
                RET
UFLUSH          ENDP

; Check output status.
UOUTST          PROC
                MOV     BX,TAIL
                MOV     DX,HEAD
                CALL    CIRCINC
```

```
                MOV     AX,200H
                JZ      OTESTFAIL
                XOR     AX,AX
OTESTFAIL:
                RET
UOUTST          ENDP
```

The .DRV file contains all the working code and data structures to manage a circular buffer of characters. The *OUTPUT* and *VERIFY OUTPUT* commands write data into the buffer (no verification is attempted), and the *INPUT* command fetches it back. The status and flush commands are very straightforward.

To compile _PIPE, type:

```
DDASM PIPE
```

If your assembler isn't on the PATH, you may want to add it or modify DDASM.BAT (Listing 13-2). To see _PIPE in action, add the following line to your CONFIG.SYS file:

```
DEVICE=c:\path\PIPE.SYS
```

(where *c:\path* is the drive and directory that contains PIPE.SYS). Reboot the computer and type:

```
ECHO HELLO >_PIPE
COPY _PIPE CON
```

Before you start up a new device driver—especially one you're debugging—always make certain you have a bootable floppy disk that will fit your A: drive. If the driver won't load, you'll have to boot the system from a floppy and remove the *DEVICE* line from your CONFIG.SYS file.

DEVICE DRIVERS

A Block Driver

Listings 13-5 through 13-7 show a complete floppy-disk driver, NUDISK. NUDISK makes your A: drive look like the next available drive on the system. You can then access a disk in your A: drive through the default device driver (via A:) or with NUDISK (if you have one or two floppies and a hard disk, NUDISK will be D:). To simplify matters, NUDISK doesn't decode errors completely and takes shortcuts when detecting disk changes. However, it will work just like any other disk driver and is a good place to start if you want to develop one yourself.

Listing 13-5. NUDISK.CFG.

```
;*****************************************************************
;*                                                               *
;* File: nudisk.cfg                                              *
;*                                                               *
;* Configuration for NUDISK device driver.                       *
;*                                                               *
;*****************************************************************
;

DD_NAME         EQU     1
DDATTRIB        EQU     0
STACKSIZE       EQU     1024
INPUT_PROC      EQU     DISK_IO
OUTPUT_PROC     EQU     DISK_IO
OUTVER_PROC     EQU     DISK_IO
MEDIA_PROC      EQU     DISK_CK
BBPB_PROC       EQU     DISK_BPB
INIT_PROC       EQU     DISK_INIT

; This equate is not part of DDASM--it is used in NUDISK.DRV.
; Set to zero for XT compatibility.
ATCLASS         EQU     1
```

Listing 13-6. NUDISK.DRV.

```
;*******************************************************************
;*                                                                 *
;* File: nudisk.drv                                                *
;*                                                                 *
;* Main code for the NUDISK disk driver.                           *
;*                                                                 *
;*******************************************************************

; buffer to store BPB in
BPBBUFFER       EQU     THIS BYTE
BYTESPERSECT    EQU     THIS WORD
                DW      512
                DB      2
                DW      1
                DB      1
                DW      112
                DW      720
                DB      0FDH
                DW      4
SECPERTRK       DW      9
NRHEADS         DW      2
HIDEN           DW      0
                DB      ?               ; padding--not used

; place to read sector
; This assumes max 512-byte buffer.
DISKBUF         DB      512 DUP (?)

; pointer to DOS buffer
DOSBUF          EQU     THIS DWORD
DOSOFF          DW      ?
DOSBSEG         DW      ?

; address of BPB "table"
BPBTABLE        DW      OFFSET BPBBUFFER
BPBSEG          DW      ?

; This routine calls INT 13H for us.
```

DEVICE DRIVERS

```
; Since floppies take time to spin up, we have to retry any
; call that fails a few times.
INT13           PROC
                PUSH    SI
                MOV     SI,3            ; Retry 3 times.
INT13AGN:
                PUSH    AX
                INT     13H
                PUSHF
                JNC     INT13OK         ; Exit on success.
                DEC     SI              ; Only retry 3 times.
                JZ      INT13OK
                POPF
                POP     AX
                JMP     INT13AGN        ; Retry.
; Come here if OK or retry count expires.
INT13OK:
                POPF
                POP     SI              ; Discard old AX.
                POP     SI
                RET
INT13           ENDP

; Compute modulo (AX mod CX) answer in CX.
MODU            PROC
                PUSH    DX
                PUSH    AX
                PUSH    AX
                XOR     DX,DX
                DIV     CX              ; AX=AX/CX (integer truncate)
                MUL     CX              ; AX=INT(AX/CX)*CX
                POP     CX              ; CX=original number
; CX=CX-AX (this leaves modulo)
                SUB     CX,AX
                POP     AX
                POP     DX
                RET
MODU            ENDP
```

DOS 5: A DEVELOPER'S GUIDE

```
; Read boot sector of disk.
READBOOT        PROC
; Use int13 to read first sector.
                PUSH    DI
                MOV     AX,0201H
                MOV     CX,1
                XOR     DX,DX
                MOV     BX,OFFSET DISKBUF
                PUSH    ES
                PUSH    CS
                POP     ES
                CALL    INT13
; Copy BPB to bpbbuffer.
                MOV     SI,OFFSET DISKBUF+11
                MOV     DI,OFFSET BPBBUFFER
                MOV     CX,10
                REP     MOVSW
                POP     ES
                POP     DI
                RET
READBOOT        ENDP

; Convert DOS sector # to BIOS sector.
CVTSECT         PROC
                ADD     AX,HIDEN        ; Add hidden sectors.
                PUSH    AX
                MOV     AX,SECPERTRK
                MUL     NRHEADS
                MOV     CX,AX
                POP     AX
                PUSH    AX
                XOR     DX,DX
; dos_sector/(sect/trk * num_of_heads)
                DIV     CX
                MOV     BX,AX
                POP     AX
                MOV     CX,SECPERTRK
                CALL    MODU
                INC     CL
                MOV     CH,BL
                PUSH    CX
```

DEVICE DRIVERS

```
                XOR     DX,DX
                DIV     SECPERTRK
                MOV     CX,NRHEADS
                CALL    MODU
                MOV     DH,CL
                POP     CX
                XOR     DL,DL           ; Use drive A:.
                RET
CVTSECT         ENDP

; Check for disk change.
DISK_CK         PROC
IF              ATCLASS                 ; If possible, use AT hardware.
; Ask BIOS if disk changed.
                MOV     AH,16H
                XOR     DL,DL
                INT     13H
                MOV     CX,1
                JNC     CKDONE
                MOV     CX,0FFFFH
ELSE
; XT--see if media descriptor changed.
; You could and should do more here for a
; practical XT driver.
                                        ; Read BPB.
                CALL    READBOOT
                                        ; Media descriptor changed?
                MOV     AL,[BPBBUFFER+10]
                CMP     AL,ES:[DI+13]
                MOV     CX,0FFFFH
                                        ; Yes: return changed.
                JNZ     CKDONE
; A bunch of other tests can be done here.
; For example, you could compare the volume labels if you
; had read and saved the volume label before.
                                        ; Return don't know.
                XOR     CX,CX
ENDIF
CKDONE:
                MOV     ES:[DI+14],CX
```

DOS 5: A DEVELOPER'S GUIDE

```
                RET
DISK_CK         ENDP

; Read BPB for DOS.
DISK_BPB        PROC
                CALL    READBOOT
                JNC     BPBOK
; One error fits all--a better driver would decode the error
; to something appropriate.
                MOV     AX,8002H
                RET

BPBOK:          MOV     ES:[DI+18],OFFSET BPBBUFFER
                MOV     ES:[DI+20],CS
                XOR     AX,AX
                RET
DISK_BPB        ENDP

; Move sector between buffers.
; On entry cx:si=source, es:di=destination.
; Resets DS to CS--destroys AX and CX.
; si & di = new offsets
MOVESECT        PROC
                PUSH    CX
                MOV     CX,BYTESPERSECT
                MOV     AX,DI
                ADD     AX,CX
                JNC     MOVEIT
                MOV     CX,DI
                XOR     CX,0FFFFH
MOVEIT:
                SHR     CX,1
                POP     DS
                REP     MOVSW
                PUSH    CS
                POP     DS
                RET
MOVESECT        ENDP

; Move data from ES:BX -> DOS buffer.
MOVE2DOS        PROC
```

DEVICE DRIVERS

```
                PUSH    AX
                PUSH    CX
                PUSH    SI
                PUSH    DI
                PUSH    ES
                MOV     CX,ES
                MOV     SI,BX
                MOV     ES,DOSBSEG
                MOV     DI,DOSOFF
                CALL    MOVESECT
                MOV     DOSOFF,DI       ; Update DOS offset.
                POP     ES
                POP     DI
                POP     SI
                POP     CX
                POP     AX
                RET
MOVE2DOS        ENDP

; Move data from DOS buffer -> ES:BX.
MOVEFMDOS       PROC
                PUSH    AX
                PUSH    CX
                PUSH    SI
                PUSH    DI
                PUSH    ES
                MOV     CX,DOSBSEG
                MOV     SI,DOSOFF
                MOV     DI,BX
                CALL    MOVESECT
                MOV     DOSOFF,SI       ; Update DOS offset.
                POP     ES
                POP     DI
                POP     SI
                POP     CX
                POP     AX
                RET
MOVEFMDOS       ENDP

; This routine handles all input and output to disk.
```

```
DISK_IO         PROC
                                ; Get sector from es:[di+20].
                MOV     AX,ES:[DI+20]
                                ; Convert to BIOS fmt.
                CALL    CVTSECT
                XOR     SI,SI
                                ; doit
                MOV     BX,OFFSET DISKBUF
                MOV     AX,ES:[DI+14]
                MOV     DOSOFF,AX
                MOV     AX,ES:[DI+16]
                MOV     DOSBSEG,AX

IOLOOP:
; See if we are done.
                CMP     SI,ES:[DI+18]
                JZ      IO_DONE
                MOV     AL,ES:[DI+2]    ; Get command.
                PUSH    ES
                PUSH    DS
                POP     ES              ; Point ES at DS.
                CMP     AL,4            ; See if get or put.
                MOV     AX,201H         ; Get one sector.
                JZ      IOGET
                MOV     AX,301H         ; Put one sector.
                CALL    MOVEFMDOS       ; If put, load buffer.
                CALL    INT13           ; Call BIOS.
                JMP     XFERDONE        ; Keep going.
; Come here on get.
IOGET:          CALL    INT13           ; Call BIOS.
                PUSHF
                CALL    MOVE2DOS        ; Store buffer to DOS.
                POPF

; Get and put rejoin here.
XFERDONE:
                POP     ES
                JC      DISK_ERR        ; Handle errors.
                INC     SI              ; Mark sector read.
```

DEVICE DRIVERS

```
; Find next sector.
            INC     CL
            XOR     AX,AX
            MOV     AL,CL
            CMP     AX,SECPERTRK
            JBE     NEXTSEC
            MOV     CL,1
            INC     DH
            MOV     AL,DH
            CMP     AX,NRHEADS
            JB      NEXTSEC
            XOR     DH,DH
            INC     CH
NEXTSEC:
            JMP     IOLOOP          ; Do it again.

; Come here when transaction complete.
IO_DONE:
; Update count.
            MOV     ES:[DI+18],SI   ; Return OK.
            XOR     AX,AX
            RET

; Come here when transaction errors occur.
DISK_ERR:
; Update count.
            MOV     ES:[DI+18],SI
; general error only to simplify error code
            MOV     AX,800CH
            RET
DISK_IO     ENDP
```

Listing 13-7. NUDISK.CMD.

```
;****************************************************************
;*                                                              *
;* File: nudisk.cmd                                             *
;*                                                              *
;* Transient portion of NUDISK driver.                          *
;*                                                              *
;****************************************************************
```

```
SOMSG           DB      'NUDISK installed (drive '
NUDRV           DB      'A:).',13,10,'$'

DISK_INIT       PROC
                MOV     AL,ES:[DI+22]   ; Get device number.
                ADD     NUDRV,AL        ; Update message.
                MOV     AH,9            ; Print message.
                MOV     DX,OFFSET SOMSG
                INT     21H
                MOV     BPBSEG,DS       ; Point to BPB table.
                MOV     SI,OFFSET BPBTABLE
                MOV     AL,1            ; one unit
                RET
DISK_INIT       ENDP
```

NUDISK uses the BIOS INT 13H functions to access the floppy disk. The biggest challenge is to convert DOS sector numbers to the BIOS head/track/sector format. The CVTSECT routine handles this conversion using the data found in the boot record (see Table 13-7). Figure 13-3 shows the calculations NUDISK uses to convert to the BIOS format.

NUDISK uses one routine (DISKIO) for the *INPUT*, *OUTPUT*, and *VERIFY OUTPUT* commands. This routine converts the starting sector to the BIOS format via a call to CVTSECT. The driver transfers data one sector at a time to (or from) an internal buffer. There are two reasons for this:

- Moving one sector at a time helps NUDISK handle the buffer-wrapping problem. If NUDISK made the BIOS transfer directly into the DOS buffer, it could not prevent buffer wrapping.

- The BIOS can only transfer groups of sectors from one track at a time. If DOS requested 20 sectors from a nine-sector-per-track disk, the BIOS wouldn't understand how to find all 20 sectors. A better algorithm would transfer as many sectors as possible with each BIOS call. Of course, the last sector would be a special case because it might wrap the buffer.

DEVICE DRIVERS

```
REAL_SECTOR + DRV_SECTOR + HIDDEN SECTORS
TRACK = REAL_SECTOR / (SECT_PER_TRACK * HEADS)
SECTOR = REAL_SECTOR % SECT_PER_TRACK + 1
HEAD = (REAL_SECTOR / SECT_PER_TRACK) % HEADS

Where:

DRV_SECTOR = Sector number passed to driver
HIDDEN_SECTORS = Number of hidden sectors (from boot record)
SECT_PER_TRACK = Number of sectors per track (from boot record)
HEADS = Number of heads (from boot record)
TRACK = BIOS track number
SECTOR = BIOS sector number
HEAD = BIOS head number
```

Figure 13-3. Converting a DOS sector to a BIOS sector.

The *MOVEFMDOS* and *MOVE2DOS* subroutines transfer data between the disk buffer and the DOS buffer. They don't allow buffer wrapping. NUDISK examines the command byte in the request packet to determine which routine to call and which function the BIOS should perform.

If a disk error occurs, NUDISK returns a general error. A real-world device driver should examine the BIOS error code and return a more appropriate error. If no errors occurred and additional sectors remain to be processed, NUDISK computes the next sector number and loops around until it has completed the request.

The other driver commands are trivial. *MEDIA CHECK* examines the disk latches on AT and PS/2 computers. If the driver will only run on these machines, set *ATCLASS* in NUDISK.CFG to a nonzero value. If *ATCLASS* is zero, NUDISK makes a halfhearted attempt to discover disk changes using the media descriptor byte.

503

Debugging

Trying to debug a DOS device driver can bring anyone to the brink of despair. Drivers that refuse to load are the worst. With DDASM, however, you should have this problem infrequently. Of course, the *INIT* command can use the simple DOS I/O calls, so it's easy to pepper its code with debugging messages to the screen or printer.

If the driver loads, you can at least work at the DOS prompt. However, your debugging code must not use any DOS calls, though you can use BIOS calls to print messages to the screen or printer. Often, simply writing single characters directly to screen memory can be enough to find the problem. If your programs don't use the BIOS communications area (0040:00F0 through 0040:00FF), you can store words there and examine them with DEBUG.

At times it's useful to examine the internal data structures of a device driver with DEBUG. However, finding the driver in memory can be complicated. One solution is to make the *INIT* command print out its CS address. Another way to locate a driver is using the DDLIST program (see Listing 13-8). INT 21H, function 52H, returns the address of an internal DOS data structure. For DOS 2.X, the NUL device driver (always the first driver) starts 17H bytes from this address. In DOS 3.0 and above, the NUL driver is 22H bytes away. By examining the device header, DDLIST can determine the type and name of the device. After displaying that information, it uses the pointer in the header to find the next device.

Listing 13-8. DDLIST.C.

```
/***************************************************************
 *                                                              *
 * File: ddlist.c                                               *
 *                                                              *
 * Description:                                                 *
 * List device drivers currently loaded.                        *
 *                                                              *
 ***************************************************************/
```

DEVICE DRIVERS

```c
#include <stdio.h>
#include <stdlib.h>
#include <dos.h>

main()
   {
/* registers for general use */
   union REGS r;
   struct SREGS segs;
/* pointer to peek into memory */
   char far *peek;
   int flags,i;
   char name[9];
/* Get MSDOS internal address. */
   r.h.ah=0x52;
   int86x(0x21,&r,&r,&segs);
/* Location of nul driver depends on OS version. */
   if (_osmajor==2) r.x.bx+=0x17;
   else r.x.bx+=0x22;
/* Print header. */
   printf("Address   Name     Flags\n");
   do {
/* Point PEEK at the device driver. */
      FP_SEG(peek)=segs.es;
      FP_OFF(peek)=r.x.bx;
/* Read flags. */
      flags=*(int far *)(peek+4);
/* Get name. */
      for (i=0;i<8;i++) name[i]=*(peek+10+i);
      name[8]='\0';
/* Print data. */
      printf("%Fp   %-8s %04X\n",peek,flags&0x8000?name:
         "<BLOCK>",flags);
/* Get pointer to next driver. */
      segs.es=*(int far *)(peek+2);
      r.x.bx=*(int far *) peek;
      } while (r.x.bx!=0xFFFF);   /* Keep going until no more. */
   }
```

Where driver debugging is concerned, it's usually a good idea to start small. Get the required functions working first, then proceed to the IOCTL and other optional commands. Add one piece at a time. When an error occurs, you can be reasonably certain it occurred in the new code.

More Fun with Drivers

If you want to try your hand at writing device drivers, think about one of the following:

- A printer driver that prints to multiple printers at the same time.

- A printer driver that makes one brand of printer emulate another.

- A speaker driver that accepts musical notes from a program and plays them on the PC speaker.

- A RAM disk/cache driver. Any memory not used by the RAM disk would automatically be used to cache other disk drives. When the RAM disk needs more memory, it discards the least recently used sectors in the cache.

CHAPTER 14

TSR Programming

Terminate-and-stay-resident programs offer a limited form of multitasking for DOS programs. TSRs (Borland's SideKick is a commercial example) work even while other programs are running. There is a price to pay, however: These programs consume valuable memory from the 640 Kbytes DOS allots for user programs. For this reason, they should be written in assembly language. Many techniques exist for writing TSRs in high-level languages, but they will always consume more memory than is necessary.

TSR Architecture

TSR programs fall into two categories: pop-ups and interceptors. Programs like SideKick are pop-up programs—when activated, they take control of the computer. Many useful tasks don't require a full pop-up program, however. For example, we may wish to set the cursor to a large block and then prevent other programs from changing the cursor's size. A simple interceptor TSR that affects INT 10H could prevent another program from changing the cursor (unless the program directly manipulated the video chip). It would also be simple to leave a back door, a new INT 10H function, that could still change the cursor. We will write this program, and others, later in this chapter.

All TSRs have a transient section and a resident section. The transient part usually does the following:

- Checks to see if the TSR is already active
- Initializes values the resident portion will require
- Hooks the required interrupt vectors

- Frees any memory not required
- Exits to DOS with a TSR call.

In addition, many TSR transients can send commands to a resident part that is already active. The resident portion, of course, handles any interrupts hooked by the transient portion and any commands it receives.

A TSR normally receives control via an interrupt. For example, by hooking the timer interrupt, a TSR can wake up 18 times per second. The keyboard interrupt can trigger a TSR every time a key is pressed.

Since TSRs take up valuable memory space, it is important that they be kept small and not waste space. That's why the transient portion of the TSR doesn't remain in memory. Most TSRs don't require environment variables after they go resident (any pertinent variables can be copied into the TSR by the transient portion). Freeing these variables can reduce TSR memory usage considerably.

A TSR may be able to reuse a portion of the PSP if it doesn't do any disk I/O. Some TSRs use this area for data storage; others copy their code into it before going resident. Sophisticated TSR programs run some of their code in expanded memory or swap overlays in from disk to minimize RAM usage.

Live and Let Live

Microsoft didn't fully document the techniques used to write TSR programs in early versions of DOS, leading to the evolution of several different techniques. Unfortunately, many of these methods are incompatible with each other. While well-behaved TSRs coexist with other programs, others have problems sharing the PC with other TSRs or interfere with certain regular programs.

TSR PROGRAMMING

With later versions of DOS, Microsoft established guidelines for writing well-behaved TSRs. One of these new guidelines concerns the multiplex interrupt (INT 2FH). DOS reserves this interrupt for communications between programs and TSRs (including the TSRs supplied with the system, like PRINT.COM). TSRs can hook this interrupt to provide a command interface for other programs.

Each TSR selects a special one-byte signature (Microsoft reserves the signatures less than 0C0H). Programs place this signature in the AH register before calling INT 2FH. If a TSR receives an INT 2FH, it checks the AH register. If the register doesn't contain the TSR's signature, it must pass control to the original interrupt handler (the one that was active prior to the TSR's activation).

The TSR can provide any number of commands via the INT 2FH call. The AL register usually contains a function code, although other registers can be used. Each TSR must provide a command to check its installation status when AL is zero. Other TSRs will ignore the call (the signature will be wrong), and the AL register will still be zero when the interrupt returns if the TSR is inactive. If the TSR is active, it should return FFH in the AL register. Some TSRs return 1 if they are present but inactive.

A Simple Interceptor

We'll start with a simple interceptor TSR to slow down the computer. This can be handy with certain games, especially on fast 386 or 486 machines. To slow down processing, we'll capture the timer interrupt at 1CH and waste time during each tick. Listing 14-1 shows the code for WASTE0.ASM. Note that the program generates a .COM file. You should always try to use the .COM model for TSRs—it's smaller and simplifies some operations required to go resident.

When WASTE0 executes from the DOS prompt, the first instruction transfers control to the transient portion. This jump instruction becomes part of the resident code, but it never executes again. The resident portion could even use the location for temporary storage. In this case, saving a few bytes isn't important, so the bytes will go to waste.

DOS 5: A DEVELOPER'S GUIDE

Listing 14-1. WASTE0.ASM.
```
;****************************************************************
;*                                                              *
;* File: waste0.asm                                             *
;*                                                              *
;* Interceptor to waste CPU time  (crude version).              *
;*                                                              *
;* Use EXE2BIN to convert to .COM file or use TLINK's /t        *
;* option when linking.                                         *
;*                                                              *
;****************************************************************
; Create .COM file.
_TEXT           SEGMENT PARA PUBLIC
                ASSUME CS:_TEXT,DS:_TEXT,SS:_TEXT

; amount of time to waste
DELAYCT         EQU     2000H

; .COM files start at 100H.
                ORG     100H

; resident part
TSR             PROC
; Program jumps to transient part when executed.
                JMP     INIT

; Store address of old int 1CH vector.
OLD1CO          DW      ?
OLD1CS          DW      ?

; Control comes here when int 1CH occurs.
; The DS register isn't initialized, so either
; set it up (push CS/pop DS) or override with
; CS.
INT1CH:
                PUSH    CX              ; Save CX.
                MOV     CX,DELAYCT      ; Load count.
WASTE:
                DEC     CX              ; Loop til zero.
                JNZ     WASTE
                POP     CX              ; Restore CX.
```

TSR PROGRAMMING

```
; Continue with old int 1CH handler.
            JMP     DWORD PTR CS:[OLD1CO]


;****************************
; transient part

INIT:
; Address DS.
            PUSH    CS
            POP     DS
; Get old interrupt vector.
            MOV     AX,351CH
            INT     21H
; Save it for resident part.
            MOV     [OLD1CS],ES
            MOV     [OLD1CO],BX
; Free environment block.
; Get segment address of environment.
            MOV     ES,DS:[2CH]
            MOV     AH,49H
            INT     21H

; Take over int 1CH vector.
            MOV     DX,OFFSET INT1CH
            MOV     AX,251CH
            INT     21H
; Compute number of paragraphs to go resident.
; We want everything up to the transient code to
; be saved, so the offset of INIT - the offset of TSR
; plus the PSP size is the number of bytes to save.

; See if size is divisible by 16.
IF          (INIT-TSR) MOD 16
ROUNDUP     =       1
ELSE
ROUNDUP     =       0
ENDIF
            MOV     DX,((INIT-TSR)+100H)/16+ROUNDUP

; Tell DOS to exit TSR.
            MOV     AX,3100H
```

```
                    INT     21H
TSR         ENDP
_TEXT       ENDS
                    END     TSR
```

Jumping ahead to the transient part (INIT), we see that the basic operations aren't that difficult. The transient code stores the vector for INT 1CH where the resident code can find it, then frees the environment block. WASTE0 then revectors INT 1CH to the resident code (INT1CH).

All that remains is to exit to DOS. TSRs use INT 21H, function 31H, to leave a portion of the program resident. The amount to leave, specified in paragraphs, is in the DX register. WASTE0 needs to save everything from its PSP (at CS:0) to the *INIT* label. Therefore, the offset of INIT is the number of bytes to save. Dividing the number of bytes by 16 and rounding up for any remainder yields the number of paragraphs.

When the timer interrupt occurs, the code at INT 1CH executes. This simple code wastes a little time and continues with the old interrupt routine. Notice that all registers must be preserved; that's because the timer uses a hardware interrupt (the processor automatically preserves the flags before servicing interrupts). This program doesn't use the stack, but if it did we might have to switch to a private stack—you can't depend on the interrupted program to have more than a few bytes free on its stack.

As a rule, the host interrupt limits what an interceptor can do. You can't call DOS or the BIOS from inside the timer interrupt, so you can't from the interceptor, either.

If you experiment with WASTE0, be warned: High *DELAYCT* values can cause your system's time-of-day clock to lose time and may cause other erratic behavior. Oddly, zero is the highest possible value because WASTE0 decrements the value before testing it.

TSR PROGRAMMING

WASTE0 can be installed more than once—each copy makes the machine run slower. Once you install WASTE0, you can't uninstall it without rebooting the machine. If you have access to commercial or shareware TSR utilities like MARK or RESPRO, you can use them to remove WASTE0.

WASTE1: The Next Step

Listing 14-2 contains WASTE1, a modified version of WASTE0. While WASTE1.COM is larger than WASTE0.COM, WASTE1 doesn't take as much memory when it loads. The transient portion overlays part of the PSP before exiting.

Listing 14-2. WASTE1.ASM.

```
;****************************************************************
;*                                                              *
;* File: waste1.asm                                             *
;*                                                              *
;* Interceptor to waste CPU time (improved).                    *
;*                                                              *
;* Use EXE2BIN to convert to .COM file or use TLINK's /t        *
;* option when linking.                                         *
;*                                                              *
;****************************************************************
; Create .COM file.
_TEXT           SEGMENT PARA PUBLIC
                ASSUME CS:_TEXT,DS:_TEXT,SS:_TEXT

; amount of time to waste
DELAYCT         EQU     2000H

; .COM files start at 100H.
                ORG     100H

; resident part
TSR             PROC
; Program jumps to transient part when executed.
                JMP     INIT
```

513

DOS 5: A DEVELOPER'S GUIDE

```
; Store address of old int 1CH vector.
OLD1CO          DW      ?
OLD1CS          DW      ?

; Control comes here when int 1CH occurs.
; The DS register isn't initialized, so either
; set it up (push CS/pop DS) or override with
; CS.
INT1CH:
                PUSH    CX              ; Save CX.
                MOV     CX,DELAYCT      ; Load count.
WASTE:
                DEC     CX              ; Loop til zero.
                JNZ     WASTE
                POP     CX              ; Restore CX.

; Continue with old int 1CH handler.
                JMP     DWORD PTR CS:[OLD1CO]


;*****************************
; transient part

INIT:
; Address DS.
                PUSH    CS
                POP     DS
; Get old interrupt vector.
                MOV     AX,351CH
                INT     21H
; Save it for resident part.
                MOV     [OLD1CS],ES
                MOV     [OLD1CO],BX
; Free environment block.
; Get segment address of environment.
                MOV     ES,DS:[2CH]
                MOV     AH,49H
                INT     21H

; Overlay PSP.
                CLD
```

TSR PROGRAMMING

```
            MOV     SI,100H      ; Move code from 100H to 60H.
            MOV     DI,60H
            PUSH    DS
            POP     ES
            MOV     CX,INIT-TSR
            REP     MOVSB
; Calculate segment after relocation.
            MOV     AX,DS
            SUB     AX,0AH
            MOV     DS,AX

; Take over int 1CH vector.
            MOV     DX,OFFSET INT1CH
            MOV     AX,251CH
            INT     21H
; Compute number of paragraphs to go resident.
; We want everything up to the transient code to
; be saved, so the offset of INIT - the offset of TSR
; plus the PSP size is the number of bytes to save.

; See if size is divisible by 16.
IF              (INIT-TSR) MOD 16
ROUNDUP         =       1
ELSE
ROUNDUP         =       0
ENDIF
            MOV     DX,((INIT-TSR)+60H)/16+ROUNDUP

; Tell DOS to exit TSR.
            MOV     AX,3100H
            INT     21H
TSR         ENDP
_TEXT       ENDS
            END     TSR
```

TSRs should not overlay the first part of the PSP. WASTE1 moves the code down to offset 60H in the PSP. It's easiest to relocate the resident code starting at 100H to an even paragraph boundary. Then, when the segment value is recalculated, all the offsets remain the same. A little math reveals the following:

515

DOS 5: A DEVELOPER'S GUIDE

100H-60H=0A0H bytes = 0AH paragraphs

Relocated_segment = CS - 0AH

This becomes the program's new segment address. Of course, the size passed to function 31H must account for this; otherwise, DOS would still reserve the full space for the program.

WASTE: The Final Version

WASTE (see Listing 14-3) is a full-blown version of the time-wasting program. There are several major changes:

- WASTE now includes an interface, via the multiplex interrupt, that other programs can use to send it commands. Using this interface, a program can determine whether the TSR is active, remove it, or read and write the delay count.

- A variable stores the delay count (so it can be changed).

- Code to remove the TSR is present.

- The transient portion presents a menu of choices when it finds that the TSR is already active.

Listing 14-3. WASTE.ASM.
```
;****************************************************************
;*                                                              *
;* File: waste.asm                                              *
;*                                                              *
;* Interceptor to waste CPU time.                               *
;*                                                              *
;* Use EXE2BIN to convert to .COM file or use TLINK's /t        *
;* option when linking.                                         *
;*                                                              *
;****************************************************************
```

TSR PROGRAMMING

```
; Create .COM file.
_TEXT           SEGMENT PARA PUBLIC
                ASSUME CS:_TEXT,DS:_TEXT,SS:_TEXT
; amount of time to waste
DELAYCT         EQU     2000H
SIG             EQU     0C9H


; .COM files start at 100H.
                ORG     100H


; resident part
TSR             PROC
; Program jumps to transient part when executed.
                JMP     INIT


; Store address of old int 1CH vector.
OLD1CO          DW      ?
OLD1CS          DW      ?


; Store address of old mux vector.
OLD2FO          DW      ?
OLD2FS          DW      ?


DELAYTM         DW      DELAYCT
INACTIVE        DB      0

NEWMUX:
                XCHG    AL,CS:[INACTIVE]
                OR      AL,AL
                XCHG    AL,CS:[INACTIVE]
                JNZ     NOTME
                CMP     AH,SIG
                JNZ     NOTME
                OR      AL,AL
                JNZ     NEWCMD
; Return installed status.
                MOV     AL,0FFH
NOTME:
                JMP     DWORD PTR CS:[OLD2FO]
NEWCMD:
```

DOS 5: A DEVELOPER'S GUIDE

```
                DEC     AL
                JNZ     ISREMOVE
; here for command 1, cx=new delaytm
                OR      CX,CX
                JNZ     SETD
; Return value instead.
                MOV     CX,CS:[DELAYTM]
SETD:
                MOV     CS:DELAYTM,CX
ENDCMD:
                IRET
ISREMOVE:
                DEC     AL
                JNZ     ENDCMD          ; unknown command
; REMOVE TSR
                PUSH    DS
                PUSH    CS
                POP     DS              ; Initialize DS.
                PUSH    ES              ; Save ES.
                MOV     AX,351CH
                INT     21H
                CMP     BX,OFFSET INT1CH
                JNZ     NOREM
                MOV     BX,ES
                MOV     DX,CS
                CMP     DX,BX
                JNZ     NOREM
                MOV     AX,352FH
                INT     21H
                CMP     BX,OFFSET NEWMUX
                JNZ     NOREM
                MOV     BX,ES
                CMP     DX,BX
                JNZ     NOREM
; OK to remove--we are first on the list.
                CLI
                LDS     DX,DWORD PTR OLD2F0
                MOV     AX,252FH
                INT     21H             ; Unhook mux int.
                PUSH    CS
```

TSR PROGRAMMING

```
                POP     DS
                LDS     DX,DWORD PTR OLD1C0
                MOV     AX,251CH
                INT     21H
                STI
                MOV     AX,CS
                ADD     AX,0AH          ; Calculate PSP.
                MOV     ES,AX
                MOV     AH,49H          ; Free memory.
                INT     21H
                JMP     SHORT REMOUT
; Can't remove--other programs are in the way.
NOREM:
                MOV     AL,1
                MOV     INACTIVE,AL
REMOUT:
                POP     ES
                POP     DS
                IRET

; Control comes here when int 1CH occurs.
; The DS register isn't initialized, so either save DS and
; set it up (push DS/push CS/pop DS) or override with
; CS.
INT1CH:
                XCHG    AL,CS:[INACTIVE]
                OR      AL,AL
                XCHG    AL,CS:[INACTIVE]
                JNZ     DONE
                PUSH    CX              ; Save CX.
; Load count..
                MOV     CX,CS:DELAYTM
WASTE:
                DEC     CX              ; Loop til zero.
                JNZ     WASTE
                POP     CX              ; Restore CX.
DONE:
; Continue with old int 1CH handler.
                JMP     DWORD PTR CS:[OLD1C0]
```

DOS 5: A DEVELOPER'S GUIDE

```
;*****************************
; transient part

INIT:
; Check to see if already installed.
            MOV     AX,(SIG SHL 8)
            INT     2FH
            CMP     AL,0FFH
            JZ      COMMAND
            JMP     STARTIT
COMMAND:
; already installed
; Write prompt.
            MOV     DX,OFFSET PROMPT
            MOV     AH,9
            INT     21H
; Read key.
            MOV     AH,1
            INT     21H
; auto - CRLF
            PUSH    AX
            MOV     AH,2
            MOV     DL,13
            INT     21H
            MOV     AH,2
            MOV     DL,10
            INT     21H
            POP     AX
; Check key.
            OR      AL,AL
            JNZ     KEYPROC
            MOV     AH,1
            INT     21H
            JMP     XIT         ; Ignore function keys.
KEYPROC:
            AND     AL,0DFH     ; Make uppercase.
            MOV     DX,-100H
            CMP     AL,'F'
            JZ      SPEED
```

TSR PROGRAMMING

```
                MOV     DX,100H
                CMP     AL,'S'
                JZ      SPEED
                CMP     AL,'R'
                JNZ     XIT
; Remove TSR.
                MOV     AX,(SIG SHL 8) OR 2
                INT     2FH
                JMP     XIT
SPEED:
                MOV     AX,(SIG SHL 8) OR 1
                XOR     CX,CX
                INT     2FH             ; Read speed.
                ADD     CX,DX
                MOV     AX,(SIG SHL 8) OR 1
                INT     2FH
XIT:
                MOV     AX,4C00H
                INT     21H

PROMPT          DB      'WASTE is already installed.',13,10
                DB      'Press <F>aster, <S>lower, <R>emove,'
                DB      ' or any other key to continue: $'

STARTIT:
; Get old interrupt vectors.
                MOV     AX,351CH
                INT     21H
; Save it for resident part.
                MOV     [OLD1CS],ES
                MOV     [OLD1CO],BX
                MOV     AX,352FH
                INT     21H
                MOV     [OLD2FS],ES
                MOV     [OLD2FO],BX
; Free environment block.
; Get segment address of environment.
                MOV     ES,DS:[2CH]
                MOV     AH,49H
                INT     21H
```

521

```
; Overlay PSP.
            CLD
            MOV     SI,100H         ; Move code from 100H to 60H.
            MOV     DI,60H
            PUSH    DS
            POP     ES
            MOV     CX,INIT-TSR
            REP     MOVSB
; Calculate segment after relocation.
            MOV     AX,DS
            SUB     AX,0AH
            MOV     DS,AX

; Take over int 1CH vector.
            MOV     DX,OFFSET INT1CH
            MOV     AX,251CH
            INT     21H

; Take over int 2FH vector.
            MOV     DX,OFFSET NEWMUX
            MOV     AX,252FH
            INT     21H

; Compute number of paragraphs to go resident.
; We want everything up to the transient code to
; be saved, so the offset of INIT - the offset of TSR
; plus the PSP size is the number of bytes to save.

; See if size is divisible by 16.
IF              (INIT-TSR) MOD 16
ROUNDUP         =       1
ELSE
ROUNDUP         =       0
ENDIF
            MOV     DX,((INIT-TSR)+60H)/16+ROUNDUP

; Tell DOS to exit TSR.
            MOV     AX,3100H
            INT     21H
TSR         ENDP
_TEXT       ENDS
            END     TSR
```

TSR PROGRAMMING

The code to catch the multiplex interrupt (INT 2FH) is similar to the code used for the timer interrupt. You can handle commands for TSRs in two ways. First, you can provide commands that programs send to the TSR via INT 2FH (or add subfunctions to another interrupt). Called the *API approach*, it allows other programs to command the TSR without knowing its internal structure. If the TSR changes, other programs still function as long as the API doesn't change. One disadvantage is that the code to process these commands may take up a large amount of space.

Second, if the multiplex interrupt contains a command that returns the segment address of the TSR, other programs can directly manipulate the TSR's data structures and code. This technique saves space but can be difficult to maintain if many programs interact with the TSR. For programs in which only the resident portion sends commands to the TSR, this technique works very well.

WASTE uses the first method, but our next program will use a combination of methods.

Much of WASTE's new code handles its removal from memory (a TSR can't always be removed). WASTE first checks the system's interrupt vectors. If they no longer point to WASTE's interrupt handlers, another TSR has loaded and WASTE can't be removed. In this case, WASTE sets a flag so it doesn't do any further processing. This turns off WASTE but doesn't free its memory.

If the vectors do point to WASTE, the TSR restores the original interrupt vectors, removing it from the interrupt chain. WASTE then frees its memory using INT 21H, function 49H.

The transient portion of WASTE allows the user to adjust the speed in fixed increments. Listing 14-4 is a small C program that lets you adjust the speed to any value. This is a good example of the API at work. Often you can write a small TSR "server" to perform certain functions, then interface it with a C (or other high-level language) program.

DOS 5: A DEVELOPER'S GUIDE

Listing 14-4. SETSPEED.C.

```c
/****************************************************************
 *                                                              *
 * File: setspeed.c                                             *
 *                                                              *
 * Description:                                                 *
 * C utility to control WASTE interceptor TSR.                  *
 *                                                              *
 ****************************************************************/
#include <stdio.h>
#include <dos.h>
main(int argc,char *argv[])
   {
   union REGS r;
/* Make sure WASTE is loaded. */
   r.x.ax=0xC900;
   int86(0x2f,&r,&r);
   if (r.h.al!=0xFF)
      {
      printf("ERROR: Resident portion not loaded!\n");
      exit(1);
      }

/* Get speed from command line or prompt for it. */
   if (argc>1)
      {
      sscanf(argv[1],"%x",&r.x.cx);
      }
   else
      {
      printf("Speed (0000-FFFF)? ");
      scanf("%x",&r.x.cx);
      }

/* Use the WASTE API to change the delay. */
   r.x.ax=0xC901;
   int86(0x2f,&r,&r);
   exit(0);
   }
```

INTASM: A Development Environment for Interceptors

Notice that when WASTE1 became WASTE much of the code was repetitive. The INT 2FH intercept looked a lot like the existing INT 1CH intercept. As you might expect, this can be handled by some clever macros. Look at Listing 14-5, WASTEX.INT. This program is similar to WASTE, but the only code present is the actual INT 1CH routine, part of the INT 2FH routine, and a line listing the interrupts to be hooked. As many interrupts as you like can be hooked in this fashion.

Listing 14-5. WASTEX.INT.

```
;****************************************************************
;*                                                              *
;* File: wastex.int                                             *
;*                                                              *
;* Interceptor to waste CPU time. Uses INTASM environment.      *
;*                                                              *
;****************************************************************
; Set up for INTASM.
SIG             EQU     0C9H
MUXCMD          EQU     ONMUX

; default delay time
DELAYW          DW      2000H

; timer interrupt routine
INT1C           PROC
                PUSH    CX
; Get delay count and waste time.
                MOV     CX,CS:DELAYW
LP:
                DEC     CX
                JNZ     LP
                POP     CX
                RESUME  INT1C
INT1C           ENDP
```

```
; Handle commands--INTASM only calls this
; routine when INT 2F fires with AH==SIG and AL!=0.
ONMUX           PROC
; Check for command #1.
                CMP     AL,1
                JNZ     NOTSP
; Command 1--load delay count from CX unless CX=0.
; If CX=0, store delay count into CX for caller to read.
                OR      CX,CX
                JNZ     SETSP
                MOV     CX,CS:DELAYW    ; Read speed if cx==0.
SETSP:
                MOV     CS:DELAYW,CX    ; If cx==0, this is a nop.
NOTSP:
; Return--intercept takes care of IRET.
                RET
ONMUX           ENDP

; Tell INTASM what to do.
                INTS    <1CH,INT1C>
```

The INTASM environment consists of two files: INTERCPT.ASM (Listing 14-6) and INTASM.BAT (Listing 14-7). INTERCPT.ASM places all the code required for an interceptor in the macro *INTS*. Your program (placed in an .INT file) starts with configuration variables and resident code. Following the resident code, the *INTS* macro appears with the interrupt vector information. For example,

```
INTS <1CH,INT1C,21H,DOSINT,9,KBINT>
```

will vector INT 1CH to the *INT1C* routine, INT 21H to *DOSINT*, and INT 9 to *KBINT*. If you specify a routine for INT 2FH, you must write the entire handler yourself. INTASM provides a handler automatically if none is specified. If you define the *MUXCMD* symbol, that routine will be called when the default handler doesn't recognize a command directed at the TSR. You can see an example of this in the WASTEX program.

TSR PROGRAMMING

Listing 14-6. INTERCPT.ASM.

```
;****************************************************************
;*                                                              *
;* File: intercpt.asm                                           *
;*                                                              *
;* Main program for INTASM. Use INTASM.BAT to compile this      *
;* with your interceptor code.                                  *
;*                                                              *
;****************************************************************
.lall
IFDEF           PROGRAM

; temp macro to title program
VTITLE          MACRO   PNAME
                TITLE   PNAME
                ENDM
                VTITLE  %PROGRAM
                PURGE   VTITLE

; macro to include files based on program name
XINCLUDE        MACRO   FN,SUFFIX
                INCLUDE &FN&.&SUFFIX
                ENDM

ABORT           MACRO
; End TSR: return to interrupted program, not
; the original interrupt vector.
                IRET
                ENDM

RESUME          MACRO   PROCNAME
; End TSR: continue with original interrupt.
                JMP     DWORD PTR CS:0&PROCNAME&0
                ENDM

OLDINT          MACRO   PROCNAME
; Perform old interrupt hooked to procname,
; then continue processing.
                PUSHF
                CALL    DWORD PTR CS:0&PROCNAME&0
                ENDM
```

```
; Main macro...user puts this between resident and transient
; portions of code. INTLIST looks like this:
; <int #, procedure, int #, procedure, int #, procedure ......>
INTS            MACRO   INTLIST
                LOCAL   CTR
                LOCAL   K1,K2

; Set default for FREE_ENV if user didn't set it.
IFNDEF          FREE_ENV
FREE_ENV        =       1
ENDIF

CTR             =       0
; Set up storage for old interrupt vectors.
                IRP     NAME,<&INTLIST>
IF              CTR     AND 1
O&&NAME&&O      DW      ?
O&&NAME&&S      DW      ?
ELSE
; If user defines MUX interrupt, set USERMUX so we won't.
IF              &&NAME EQ 2FH
USERMUX         EQU     1
ENDIF
ENDIF
CTR             =       CTR+1
                ENDM

; If we are supplying the MUX interrupt, make space for it too.
IFNDEF          USERMUX
OMUXO           DW      ?
OMUXS           DW      ?

; Make code too.
DEFAULTMUX      PROC
                CMP     AH,SIG          ; addressed to us?
                JNZ     NOTME           ; nope
                OR      AL,AL           ; installed command?
                JNZ     MUXOUT          ; nope
                MOV     AL,0FFH         ; Return installed
                MOV     BX,CS           ; and segment.
                IRET
```

TSR PROGRAMMING

```
MUXOUT:
; If user wants to process MUX commands, let him.
IFDEF           MUXCMD
                CALL    MUXCMD
ENDIF
                IRET
NOTME:          JMP     DWORD PTR CS:[OMUXO]
DEFAULTMUX      ENDP

ENDIF

; default signature
IFNDEF          SIG
SIG             EQU     0C1H
ENDIF

; ******** Everything from here on is discarded.

INIT:
; Check to see if already installed.
IFDEF           PRETSR
                MOV     BX,CS
ENDIF
                MOV     AX,(SIG SHL 8)
                INT     2FH
; If user asked, call PRETSR first. AL=installed state,
; BX=segment address. If AL=0, then BX=our CS.
IFDEF           PRETSR
                PUSH    AX
                PUSH    BX
                CALL    PRETSR
                POP     BX
                POP     AX
ENDIF
                CMP     AL,0FFH
; Installed--go to command.
                JZ      COMMAND
; Not installed--start it up.
                JMP     STARTIT
```

DOS 5: A DEVELOPER'S GUIDE

```
COMMAND:
; already installed
; If user asked, call POSTTSR to process commands.
IFDEF           POSTTSR
                PUSH    BX
                CALL    POSTTSR
                POP     BX
ENDIF
; If no user routine or it returns, kill TSR.
                CALL    TSRREMOVE
; Return to DOS.
                MOV     AX,4C00H
                INT     21H


;*****************************************

; Make TSR resident.
STARTIT:
; Get and save old interrupt vectors.
VECTOR          =       100H
                IRP     NAME,<&INTLIST>
IF              VECTOR EQ 100H
VECTOR          =       &&NAME
ELSE
                MOV     AX,3500H OR VECTOR
                INT     21H
                MOV     [O&&NAME&&O],BX
                MOV     [O&&NAME&&S],ES
VECTOR          =       100H
ENDIF
                ENDM

; Handle 2f if we are using default.
IFNDEF          USERMUX
                MOV     AX,352FH
                INT     21H
                MOV     [OMUXO],BX
                MOV     [OMUXS],ES
ENDIF
```

TSR PROGRAMMING

```
            IF              FREE_ENV
; Free environment block.
; Get segment address of environment.
                MOV     ES,DS:[2CH]
                MOV     AH,49H
                INT     21H
            ENDIF

; Overlay PSP.
                CLD
                MOV     SI,100H         ; Move code from 100H to 60H.
                MOV     DI,60H
                PUSH    DS
                POP     ES
                MOV     CX,INIT-TSR
                REP     MOVSB
; Calculate segment after relocation.
                MOV     AX,DS
                SUB     AX,0AH
                MOV     DS,AX

; Set up new interrupt vectors.
VECTOR          =       100H
                IRP     NAME,<&INTLIST>
            IF          VECTOR EQ 100H
VECTOR          =       &&NAME
            ELSE
                MOV     DX,OFFSET &&NAME
                MOV     AX,2500H OR VECTOR
                INT     21H
VECTOR          =       100H
            ENDIF
                ENDM

; Set up default 2f if asked.
            IFNDEF      USERMUX
                MOV     DX,OFFSET DEFAULTMUX
                MOV     AX,252FH
                INT     21H
            ENDIF
```

531

DOS 5: A DEVELOPER'S GUIDE

```
; If user asked, call POSTTSR. AL=0 (just installed),
; BX=segment of resident code.
IFDEF           POSTTSR
                XOR     AL,AL
                MOV     BX,DS
                CALL    POSTTSR
ENDIF

; Print install message.
                PUSH    CS
                POP     DS
                MOV     DX,OFFSET MSG_INS
                MOV     AH,9
                INT     21H

; Compute number of paragraphs to go resident.
; We want everything up to the transient code to
; be saved, so the offset of INIT - the offset of TSR
; plus the PSP size is the number of bytes to save.

; See if size is divisible by 16.
IF              (INIT-TSR) MOD 16
ROUNDUP         =       1
ELSE
ROUNDUP         =       0
ENDIF
                MOV     DX,((INIT-TSR)+60H)/16+ROUNDUP

; Tell DOS to exit TSR.
                MOV     AX,3100H
                INT     21H

; Routine to kill TSR program from memory.
; Assumes BX=segment of resident program.
TSRREMOVE       PROC
                PUSH    DS
                MOV     DS,BX
```

TSR PROGRAMMING

```
; If environment wasn't freed, free it now.
IFE             FREE_ENV
                MOV     ES,DS:[2CH]
                MOV     AH,49H
                INT     21H
ENDIF

; Check to make sure we are last program to hook each vector.
VECTOR          =       100H
                IRP     NAME,<&INTLIST>
IF              VECTOR EQ 100H
VECTOR          =       &&NAME
ELSE
; Get vector.
                MOV     AX,3500H OR &&VECTOR
                INT     21H
; Compare offset.
                CMP     BX,OFFSET &&NAME
                JZ      K1
                JMP     NOREM
K1:
                MOV     BX,ES       ; Compare segment.
                MOV     DX,DS
                CMP     BX,DX
                JZ      K2
                JMP     NOREM
K2:
VECTOR          =       100H
ENDIF
                ENDM
; Check default MUX int if used.
IFNDEF          USERMUX
                MOV     AX,352FH
                INT     21H
                CMP     BX,OFFSET DEFAULTMUX
                JZ      _K1
                JMP     NOREM
```

DOS 5: A DEVELOPER'S GUIDE

```
_K1:
            MOV     BX,ES
            MOV     DX,DS
            CMP     BX,DX
            JZ      _K2
            JMP     NOREM
_K2:
ENDIF

; OK to remove.
            PUSH    DS

            CLI

; Restore each vector.
VECTOR      =       100H
            IRP     NAME,<&INTLIST>
IF          VECTOR EQ 100H
VECTOR      =       &&NAME
ELSE
            LDS     DX,DWORD PTR O&&NAME&&O
            MOV     AX,2500H OR VECTOR
            INT     21H
VECTOR      =       100H
ENDIF
            ENDM

; default 2f handler too!
IFNDEF      USERMUX
            POP     DS
            PUSH    DS
            LDS     DX,DWORD PTR OMUXO
            MOV     AX,252FH
            INT     21H
ENDIF

; Calculate PSP of TSR.
            POP     DS
            MOV     AX,DS
            ADD     AX,0AH
            MOV     ES,AX
```

TSR PROGRAMMING

```
; Free it.
                MOV     AH,49H
                INT     21H
                POP     DS
; Print removed message.
                MOV     DX,OFFSET MSG_REM
                MOV     AH,9
                INT     21H
                RET

; Can't remove--deactivate.
NOREM:
; Make sure interrupt disabled--IRET will restore original.
                CLI
; For each interrupt vector, short-circuit it.
; That is, make first instruction of each routine:
;   RESUME routine
VECTOR          =       100H
                IRP     NAME,<&INTLIST>
IF              VECTOR EQ 100H
VECTOR          =       &&NAME
ELSE
VECTOR          =       100H
                MOV     BYTE PTR DS:[&&NAME],2EH
                MOV     WORD PTR DS:[&&NAME+1],2EFFH
                MOV     AX,OFFSET 0&&NAME&&0
                MOV     WORD PTR DS:[&&NAME+3],AX
ENDIF
                ENDM
                POP     DS
; Tell user TSR not removed.
                MOV     DX,OFFSET MSG_NOREM
                MOV     AH,9
                INT     21H
                RET
TSRREMOVE       ENDP

; Messages--default can be overriden from user's program.
IFNDEF          INSTALL_MESSAGE
MSG_INS         DB      'Installed.',13,10,'$'
ELSE
```

```
MSG_INS         DB      INSTALL_MESSAGE
                DB      13,10,'$'
ENDIF

IFNDEF          REMOVE_MESSAGE
MSG_REM         DB      'Removed.',13,10,'$'
ELSE
MSG_REM         DB      REMOVE_MESSAGE
                DB      13,10,'$'
ENDIF

IFNDEF          REMERR_MESSAGE
MSG_NOREM       DB      'Can''t remove. Deactivating.',13,10,'$'
ELSE
MSG_NOREM       DB      REMERR_MESSAGE
                DB      13,10,'$'
ENDIF

                ENDM

;*****************
; start of program

_TEXT           SEGMENT PARA PUBLIC
                ASSUME CS:_TEXT, DS:_TEXT, SS:_TEXT
                ORG     100H
TSR             PROC
                JMP     INIT            ; Jump to first transient code.
TSR             ENDP

; Get user's program.
XINCLUDE        %PROGRAM,INT
ELSE
IF2
                %OUT    YOU MUST SPECIFY A PROGRAM TITLE.
                %OUT    USE: MASM /DPROGRAM=NAME TSR.ASM
ENDIF
                .ERR
ENDIF
_TEXT           ENDS
                END     TSR
```

Listing 14-7. INTASM.
a. INTASM batch file for MASM.
```
@echo off
REM You should change the path names for your system.
REM If the directories are on the path, they can be omitted.
if %1.==. goto err
masm /DPROGRAM=%1 intercpt.asm,%1.obj,%1.LST;
if ERRORLEVEL 1 goto end
link %1.obj;
if ERRORLEVEL 1 goto end
exe2bin %1.exe %1.com
erase %1.exe
goto end
:err
echo INTASM by Al Williams
echo usage: INTASM program_name
echo Converts .INT file into an interceptor
:end
```

b. INTASM batch file for TASM.
```
@echo off
REM You should change the path names for your system.
REM If the directories are on the path, they can be omitted.
if %1.==. goto err
tasm /m2 /DPROGRAM=%1 /w-PDC w-MCP intercpt.asm,%1.obj
if ERRORLEVEL 1 goto end
tlink /t %1.obj;
goto end
:err
echo INTASM by Al Williams
echo usage: INTASM program_name
echo Converts .INT file into an interceptor
:end
```

Any code and data occurring after the *INTS* macro call won't remain resident. Two configuration variables, *PRETSR* and *POSTTSR*, may be set to procedure names that occur in this section. The main program checks to see if the TSR is resident, then calls the *PRETSR* routine. Just before the main program exits, it calls the *POSTTSR* routine. When these routines start, the AL register contains zero if the TSR wasn't active when the program started and FFH if it was. The BX register contains the segment address of the resident copy.

By default, the main routine uninstalls the TSR if it's already active. However, the *POSTTSR* routine can override this behavior by exiting to DOS instead of returning. Unlike WASTE, the INTASM code handles TSR removal in the transient portion of the program. By learning the segment address of the TSR, the transient portion can unload the TSR. Because the transient and resident portions compile together, this isn't usually a problem. If you load the TSR, change the code, and recompile, however, attempting to unload the TSR with the new copy will probably cause the system to crash. For TSRs distributed in executable form, this isn't a problem.

Figure 14-1 shows the configuration variables available and their default values. These should appear at the top of the .INT file and must come before the *INTS* macro call. INTASM provides three useful macros. *ABORT* is a synonym for *IRET*; use it when processing is complete and you don't want the old interrupt handler to get control. *RESUME* ends the TSR and passes control to the old interrupt handler. WASTEX uses *RESUME*—look at the listing for an example. The *OLDINT* macro is somewhat like *RESUME* except that your program regains control after the old interrupt handler finishes. The stack must be clean before *ABORT* or *RESUME* is used. Don't use them from inside subroutines or while you still have data pushed on the stack.

INTASM.BAT (Listing 14-7) calls the assembler and linker to build an interceptor. Before using this batch file, you should have the assembler and linker directories in your DOS PATH. You could put the full path name for the programs in the batch file, if you prefer.

TSR PROGRAMMING

SIG	The signature used for the default INT 2FH handler.
FREE_ENV	A zero in this variable prevents the environment block from being freed.
INSTALL_MESSAGE	Message to print when successfully installed. Must not contain the '$' character.
REMOVE_MESSAGE	Message to print when removed Must not contain the '$' character.
REMERR_MESSAGE	Message to print when unable to remove. Must not contain the '$' character.
PRETSR	If defined, the main program will call the named routine prior to doing anything. On entry, AL=0 if the TSR will be installed or FFH if it is already installed. BX=the segment address of the TSR. The named routine should occur after the INTS macro call.
POSTTSR	The same as PRETSR, except the named routine runs after most processing. If AL=FFH, the TSR will be removed if the routine returns. The named routine should occur after the INTS macro.
MUXCMD	If defined, the named routine will be called when the default INT 2FH handler can't interpret a command. The entry is exactly like the entry from INT 2FH. The signature is certain to match the TSR's signature. The routine must return with a RET instruction and must be placed before the INTS macro call.

Defaults:

SIG EQU 0C1H
FREE_ENV EQU 1
INSTALL_MESSAGE EQU 'Installed.'
REMOVE_MESSAGE EQU 'Removed.'
REMERR_MESSAGE EQU 'Can't remove. Deactivating.'

Figure 14-1. INTASM configuration variables.

Controlling Cursor Size

CURLOCK (see Listing 14-8) is a resident utility that is most useful for laptop computers with LCD screens. It changes the cursor to a large block and prevents other programs from changing it via the BIOS. A new INT 10H subfunction provides a back door to allow you to change the cursor's size. The CURSIZE program (Listing 14-9) uses this back door to modify the cursor's size.

CURLOCK uses the INTASM environment. A *PRETSR* routine (*CUR_SETUP*) sets the initial cursor shape. If CURLOCK is already active, the *POSTTSR* function (*CUR_DONE*) allows you to remove it or exit to DOS.

Listing 14-8. CURLOCK.INT.

```
;****************************************************************
;*                                                              *
;* File: curlock.int                                            *
;*                                                              *
;* Interceptor to "lock" cursor to a large size.                *
;*                                                              *
;****************************************************************
; INTASM program to lock cursor size

; configuration info for INTASM
PRETSR          EQU     CUR_SETUP       ; Pre-TSR routine
POSTTSR         EQU     CUR_DONE        ; Post-TSR routine
SIG             EQU     0F7H            ; INT 2FH signature

; Replacement for INT 10H. If function 1, ignore it;
; otherwise continue with the old interrupt.
; New function C0 sets cursor when locked.
NEW10           PROC
                CMP     AH,1            ; Is it a set cursor operation?
                JZ      KILLIT
                CMP     AH,0C0H         ; Back door?
                JNZ     DOIT
                MOV     AH,1            ; Set ah=1 and make call.
```

TSR PROGRAMMING

```
DOIT:
                RESUME  NEW10           ; Call old interrupt.
KILLIT:
                ABORT                   ; Return to caller.
NEW10           ENDP

; ******* END of resident code
; Ask INTASM to set us up--use default INT 2F handler.
                INTS    <10H,NEW10>
; ******* BEGIN transient code

; This routine is called before CURLOCK goes resident.
CUR_SETUP       PROC
; Set up large cursor. (This assumes you have a color card. If you
; don't, it will look a little funny.)
                MOV     AH,1
                MOV     CX,7
                INT     10H
                RET
CUR_SETUP       ENDP

CKMSG           DB      'Uninstall CURLOCK? (Y/N) $'

; This routine is called after CURLOCK goes resident.
CUR_DONE        PROC
                CMP     AL,0FFH         ; Already installed?
                JNZ     CUR_OUT
; Ask user if he wants to remove TSR.
                MOV     DX,OFFSET CKMSG
                MOV     AH,9
                INT     21H
GETKEY:
                XOR     AH,AH
                INT     16H             ; Read keyboard.
                OR      AL,20H          ; Convert to lowercase.
                CMP     AL,'y'
                JZ      CUR_OUT
                CMP     AL,'n'
                JNZ     GETKEY
```

DOS 5: A DEVELOPER'S GUIDE

```
; Don't return or TSR will uninstall.
             MOV     AX,4C00H
             INT     21H
CUR_OUT:     MOV     DL,13       ; CRLF
             MOV     AH,2
             INT     21H
             MOV     DL,10
             MOV     AH,2
             INT     21H
             RET
CUR_DONE     ENDP
```

Listing 14-9. CURSIZE.C.

```c
/******************************************************************
 *                                                                *
 * File: cursize.c                                                *
 *                                                                *
 * Description:                                                   *
 * C utility to change cursor size when cursor is locked          *
 * with the CURLOCK TSR.                                          *
 *                                                                *
 ******************************************************************/

#include <stdio.h>
#include <dos.h>

/* Must match the signature in CURLOCK.INT */
#define SIG 0xF7

main()
   {
   int s,e;
   union REGS r;
/* Check to make sure CURLOCK installed. */
   r.x.ax=SIG<<8;
   int86(0x2f,&r,&r);
   if (r.h.al!=0xFF)
      {
```

TSR PROGRAMMING

```
      printf("CURLOCK not active\n");
      exit(1);
      }
/* Prompt for cursor size. */
   printf("New start and end lines? ");
   scanf("%d %d",&s,&e);
/* Use CURLOCK's API to change cursor size. */
   r.h.ch=s;
   r.h.cl=e;
   r.h.ah=0xC0;
   int86(0x10,&r,&r);
   exit(0);
   }
```

More Fun with Interceptors

Once you begin experimenting with interceptors, you'll be surprised how useful they are. Here are some ideas to get you started:

- Press a key combination to clear the type-ahead buffer.

- Intercept INT 10H and change the color of all screen writes.

- Intercept INT 16H and translate certain keys into strings.

- Intercept the timer interrupt and display a clock at the top of the screen. Perhaps you could press a key to turn it on or off.

As you write your own interceptors, keep the following in mind:

- Don't depend on the interrupted program to provide a large stack. If you need more than a few bytes, switch to a private stack.

- If you do division (using *DIV* or *IDIV*) in your program, make sure the program doesn't divide by zero. Doing so will cause DOS to abort the current program, a nasty surprise to the interrupted program.

- Don't call other interrupts from inside an interceptor unless you're sure it's safe. For example, calling INT 10H from an INT 21H intercept is acceptable; calling INT 21H from an INT 10H intercept is a bad idea. (The rest of this chapter will help clarify which interrupts can be called and when.)

- Any code or data referenced by code above the *INTS* macro must occur before that macro. Everything following *INTS* disappears when the program goes resident.

Pop-Up Fundamentals

Unlike interceptors, pop-up programs usually interact with the user. Most pop-up programs become active when they sense a particular key combination. This combination, known as the *hot key*, is usually something unusual (pressing both shift keys, for example).

Pop-up programs differ from interceptors in that they call DOS and BIOS functions. Actually, they can't call every DOS function—the techniques we'll use only allow INT 21H calls from subfunction 0DH and above. Interrupt routines usually can't call DOS because it isn't reentrant. In particular, DOS uses two fixed stacks to service interrupt routines. If a call is in progress when another call occurs, the new call will overwrite the old call's stack. DOS uses one stack for functions 00 through 0CH and another for most of the remaining functions.

DOS provides an undocumented flag, called the *INDOS flag*, that is zero when it's safe to call DOS. In addition, DOS periodically issues an INT 28H when using the first stack. Therefore, a program may call subfunction 0DH and above from inside an INT 28H routine or when INDOS is zero.

Pop-ups shouldn't interrupt certain other operations. In particular, video and disk calls (INT 10H and INT 13H) should always run to completion. Our TSR can hook these interrupts and keep a count of the calls made. When the interrupt occurs, the counter increases; when it returns, the counter decreases. When the counter is zero, it's safe to pop up.

TSR PROGRAMMING

Safely calling DOS is only half the story; conflicts with other programs must be resolved (this is known as *context management*). For example, say a user runs a program that opens all available files. What if he then pops up our TSR? If the TSR tries to open a file, things won't go well. Also, the TSR will need to set up parameters (like the INT 23H and 24H vectors) that must be restored before returning to the interrupted programs.

DOS Access

Microsoft doesn't document the INDOS flag, and its location might not be the same on every machine. However, INT 21H, function 34H (DOS doesn't document this function; see Chapter 6), returns the address of this flag in ES:BX.

The TSRs in this chapter will look for normal hot keys when the keyboard interrupt occurs. (If the hot key comprises only shift keys, the TSR checks for it during the timer interrupt.) If the hot key is found, a flag is set. The TSR checks this flag during the timer interrupt. If the flag is set and INDOS is clear, the TSR pops up. The TSR also checks the flag during INT 28H. If the flag and INDOS are set during an INT 28H call, the TSR pops up.

If your TSR code stays active while not calling DOS (perhaps while polling the keyboard via the BIOS), it should issue INT 28H to allow other TSRs to pop up.

Critical Sections

Protecting the video and disk BIOS calls is straightforward. The following code does the job:

```
ONVIDEO PROC FAR
    INC CS:[VIDEOBUSY]
    PUSHF
    CALL DWORD PTR CS:[OLD10O]      ; Call original INT 10H.
    DEC CS:[VIDEOBUSY]
    IRET
ONVIDEO ENDP
```

The flag, VIDEOBUSY, counts the number of calls. Since the BIOS can call itself, a simple on/off flag won't do. A similar flag, DISKBUSY, tracks the status of the disk BIOS routines. If either flag is nonzero, the TSR won't pop up.

Since the disk routine returns information in the carry flag, the *ONDISK* routine ends with a *RET 0002* instruction instead of an *IRET*. This way, the calling program will receive the correct carry bit.

Context Management

Certain items must be preserved at the start of the TSR, changed, and then restored before the TSR returns control to the interrupted (or host) program:

- The CPU registers
- The PSP
- The DTA
- The stack
- The Control-Break setting (ON or OFF)
- Control-Break interrupts
- Critical error interrupts
- Extended error information.

Other items will need to be preserved only if your TSR changes them. These include the current disk, current directory, video mode and page, cursor shape and location, contents of the screen, and divide-by-zero interrupts.

Changing the PSP necessitates an undocumented DOS call (INT 21H, function 50H). Sadly, in DOS versions prior to DOS 3.0, this call operated on the first stack and TSRs couldn't call it. While a few awkward methods can work around this, we will simply require our TSRs to run under DOS 3.0 or higher. (If you need to support older versions of DOS, see the section on INT 21H, function 5D06H, in Chapter 6.) Our pop-up programs will check the DOS version. If it isn't at least 3.0, the TSR will refuse to load.

The undocumented INT 21H, function 5D0AH, saves the extended error information in DOS 3.1 and above. In DOS 3.0, you risk destroying the extended error information. In versions below 3.0, there is no extended error information to destroy. In practice, few TSRs pop up when this information is important.

The remaining context items are easy to switch. Most TSRs ignore Control-Breaks and critical errors. However, they must catch these conditions—it would be disastrous if the interrupted program's handlers regained control.

The TSR must not generate divide-by-zero interrupts. If that possibility exists, you must replace the default INT 00H handler with your own routine. Don't forget to restore the old handler before the TSR exits. Few pop-ups use the divide instructions; those that do can check for illegal operands before executing the divide instruction.

After a pop-up TSR obtains free access to DOS and switches its context, it is much like an interceptor. However, a pop-up can call most DOS and BIOS functions freely.

TSRASM: A Pop-up Development Environment

Listings 14-10 through 14-17 show TSRASM, a pop-up development environment. Every TSRASM program consists of three files: a .TSR, a .CMD, and a .CFG. The .TSR file contains the resident portion of the code. The transient portion is in the .CMD file. The .CFG file sets certain configuration parameters for the pop-up program.

DOS 5: A DEVELOPER'S GUIDE

Listing 14-10. TSR.ASM.

```
;****************************************************************
;*                                                              *
;* File: tsr.asm                                                *
;*                                                              *
;* This is the main program for TSRASM. Use TSRASM.BAT to       *
;* compile this file with your application.                     *
;*                                                              *
;****************************************************************

; temp macro to title program
IFDEF           PROGRAM
VTITLE          MACRO   PNAME
                TITLE   PNAME
                ENDM
                VTITLE  %PROGRAM
                PURGE   VTITLE

; Begin code.
_TEXT           SEGMENT PARA PUBLIC
                ASSUME CS:_TEXT,DS:_TEXT,SS:_TEXT

                ORG     100H
START           PROC    NEAR
; Jump to transient start-up code.
                JMP     TSRSTART
START           ENDP

; Load macros.
INCLUDE         TSRMAC.INC

; Include user's configuration file.
XINCLUDE        %PROGRAM.CFG

; Include default configurations.
INCLUDE         TSRCFG.INC

; Include variables.
INCLUDE         TSRVARS.INC
```

TSR PROGRAMMING

```
; If user asked for video context save, include it.
IF              VIDEO
INCLUDE         TSRVIDEO.INC
ENDIF

; Include interrupt routines.
INCLUDE         TSRINTS.INC

; Assumes DS is set up.
GO_POPUP        PROC    NEAR
                INC     POPED           ; Mark popped-up status.
                CLI
                MOV     HOSTSS,SS       ; Save and switch stack.
                MOV     HOSTSP,SP
                MOV     SS,TSRSS
                MOV     SP,TSRSP
                STI
; Save all registers (80286/386 could use fewer instructions).
                PUSH_ALL
; Make sure CLD is done or MOVSW in video might bomb.
                CLD
; See if we are in a text mode--only pop up in a text mode.
                MOV     AH,0FH
                INT     10H
; Save video parameters.
                MOV     HOSTVMODE,AL
                MOV     HOSTVWIDTH,AH
                CMP     AL,7
                JNZ     NOMONO
; Mono -- OK to pop up.
                MOV     AX,0B000H       ; mono segment address
                JMP     SHORT DOIT
; Check for modes 0-3.
NOMONO:         CMP     AL,4
                JL      COLOR
; Can't pop up--beep three times and quit.
                MOV     AX,0E07H
                INT     10H
                MOV     AX,0E07H
                INT     10H
                MOV     AX,0E07H
```

549

DOS 5: A DEVELOPER'S GUIDE

```
                INT     10H
                JMP     CANT

; OK to pop up in color mode.
COLOR:
                MOV     AX,0B800H
; Color and mono pop-up come here.
DOIT:
                MOV     TSRVIDSEG,AX
                MOV     HOSTVPAGE,BH
; If we are switching video context, do it now.
IF              VIDEO
                CALL    TSR_VIDUP
ENDIF
; Get host crit err, break, and ^C vectors + BREAK SETTING.
                STOVECT 1BH,HOST1B0
                STOVECT 23H,HOST230
                STOVECT 24H,HOSTCRIT0
                MOV     AX,3300H
                INT     21H
                MOV     HOSTBREAKF,DL
; Set same.
                SETVECT 1BH,ONBREAK
                SETVECT 23H,ONBREAK
                SETVECT 24H,ONINT24
                MOV     AX,3301H
                XOR     DL,DL
                INT     21H
; Get HOSTPSP.
                MOV     AH,62H
                INT     21H
                MOV     HOSTPSP,BX
; Set TSRPSP.
                MOV     BX,TSRPSP
                MOV     AH,50H
                INT     21H
; Get DTA and save.
                MOV     AH,2FH
                INT     21H
                MOV     HOSTDTA0,BX
                MOV     HOSTDTAS,ES
```

TSR PROGRAMMING

```
; Set our DTA.
                PUSH    DS
                LDS     DX,TSRDTA
                MOV     AH,1AH
                INT     21H
                POP     DS
; Save extended error information.
                PUSH    DS
                MOV     AH,59H
                XOR     BX,BX
                INT     21H
                MOV     CS:EXTSAVE[12],DS
                POP     DS
                MOV     EXTSAVE,AX
                MOV     EXTSAVE[2],BX
                MOV     EXTSAVE[4],CX
                MOV     EXTSAVE[6],DX
                MOV     EXTSAVE[8],SI
                MOV     EXTSAVE[10],DI
                MOV     EXTSAVE[14],ES
; Check to see if a transient program has set our kill
; word. If so, don't pop up; we just need to remove TSR.
                MOV     AL,KILL
                OR      AL,AL
                JNZ     SKIPPOP
; Real pop-up command.
; Call pop-up program (must return with SP:SS unchanged).
                CALL    MAIN_PROC
; Assume DS was destroyed.
                PUSH    CS
                POP     DS
SKIPPOP:
; Handle kill command if present.
                MOV     AL,KILL
                OR      AL,AL
                JNZ     NOTALIVE
                JMP     ALIVE
; Here's the killer.
NOTALIVE:
```

DOS 5: A DEVELOPER'S GUIDE

```
; See if we are on top; if not go to softkill.
            CMPVECT  10H,ONVIDEO,SOFTKILL
            CMPVECT  13H,ONDISK,SOFTKILL
            CMPVECT  9,ONKEYBD,SOFTKILL
            CMPVECT  28H,ONINT28,SOFTKILL
            CMPVECT  1CH,ONTIMER,SOFTKILL
            CMPVECT  2FH,ONMUX,SOFTKILL
; We are on top; OK to hard kill.
; Call user's exit routine.
IFDEF       EXIT_PROC
            CALL     EXIT_PROC
ENDIF
; Reset all vectors.
            RESETVECT 9,OLD90
            RESETVECT 10H,OLD100
            RESETVECT 13H,OLD130
            RESETVECT 1CH,OLD1C0
            RESETVECT 28H,OLD280
            RESETVECT 2FH,OLD2F0
            MOV      ES,TSRPSP
; If the environment wasn't freed, do it now.
IFE         FREE_ENV
            PUSH     ES
            MOV      ES,ES:[2CH] ; Get environment segment.
            MOV      AH,49H
            INT      21H         ; Free it.
            POP      ES          ; Free us too.
ENDIF
; Free TSR's memory block.
            MOV      AH,49H
            INT      21H
            JMP      SHORT ALIVE
; Soft kill. Just set inactive--TSR can be reactivated
; later. Ring bell to inform user.
SOFTKILL:   MOV      AX,1
            MOV      KILL,AH
            MOV      STOPPED,AL
            MOV      AH,0FH
            INT      10H         ; Get page.
            MOV      AX,0E07H    ; Ring bell.
            INT      10H
```

TSR PROGRAMMING

```
ALIVE:
; Reset extended error info.
            MOV     AH,EXTSAVF
            OR      AH,AH
            JZ      RDTA
            MOV     DX,OFFSET EXTSAVE
            MOV     AX,5D0AH
            INT     21H
; Reset DTA.
RDTA:
            PUSH    DS
            LDS     DX,HOSTDTA
            MOV     AH,1AH
            INT     21H
            POP     DS
; Reset PSP.
            MOV     AH,50H
            MOV     BX,HOSTPSP
            INT     21H
; Reset break setting.
            MOV     AX,3301H
            MOV     DL,HOSTBREAKF
            INT     21H
; Reset vectors.
            RESETVECT 1BH,HOST1B0
            RESETVECT 23H,HOST230
            RESETVECT 24H,HOSTCRIT0
; Pop down video if user asked us to do video.
IF          VIDEO
            CALL    TSR_VIDDN
ENDIF
; Either we are done or we couldn't pop up.
CANT:
            POP_ALL             ; Restore all registers.
            CLI
            MOV     SS,HOSTSS   ; Switch stack back.
            MOV     SP,HOSTSP
            STI
            DEC     POPED       ; Mark done.
            RET
GO_POPUP    ENDP
```

DOS 5: A DEVELOPER'S GUIDE

```
; Local stack
; The following line works with TASM but doesn't
; work with MASM for some unknown reason.
;               DB      STKSIZE DUP (0)
; This works with both.....
                REPT    STKSIZE
                DB      ?
                ENDM
TSTACK          EQU     $

; This should include tsr_main and tsr_exit.
XINCLUDE        %PROGRAM,TSR

IFNDEF          LAST
LAST            EQU     $
ENDIF

;***********************************************************
; Everything from here down gets thrown away, so we can
; waste as much space as we need to.

TSRSTART        PROC    NEAR
                MOV     AX,CS
                MOV     DS,AX
; MOV SS will auto disable interrupt for next inst.
                MOV     SS,AX
                MOV     SP,OFFSET TSTACK
; Check DOS version.
                MOV     AH,30H
                INT     21H
                CMP     AL,3
                JGE     DOSOK
                MOV     DX,OFFSET LOWDOS
                MOV     AH,9
                INT     21H
; Use old style exit -- might even be DOS 1.
; (No support for INT 21/4C.)
                XOR     AH,AH
                INT     21H
```

TSR PROGRAMMING

```
DOSOK:
; Check for DOS 3.0 (if 3.0, we can't restore extended error
info).
            CMP     AX,0030H
            JNZ     DOSOK1
            MOV     EXTSAVF,AH
DOSOK1:
; Prevent break/critical errors from interfering.
            SETVECT 23H,ONBREAK
            SETVECT 24H,ONINT24
; Save PSP.
            MOV     TSRPSP,ES
; Check for TSR.
            MOV     AX,(SIG SHL 8)
            INT     2FH
            OR      AL,AL
            JZ      TSRINST
; It was already installed; call userinstall and quit.
            CALL    USERINSTALL
QUIT:
            MOV     AX,4C01H
            INT     21H


; Install TSR.
TSRINST:

; Preserve stack for later.
            MOV     TSRSS,SS
            MOV     TSRSP,SP
; Get DTA.
            MOV     AH,2FH
            INT     21H
; Save DTA.
            MOV     TSRDTAO,BX
            MOV     TSRDTAS,ES
; Find DOS busy flag.
            MOV     AH,34H
            INT     21H
            MOV     DOSBUSYS,ES
            MOV     DOSBUSYO,BX
```

555

DOS 5: A DEVELOPER'S GUIDE

```
; Get timer, kb, disk, video, MUX, INT 28 vectors.
            STOVECT  1CH,OLD1C0
            STOVECT  10H,OLD100
            STOVECT  13H,OLD130
            STOVECT  09H,OLD90
            STOVECT  28H,OLD280
            STOVECT  2FH,OLD2F0

; Attach timer, kb, disk, video, MUX, INT 28 vectors.
            SETVECT  1CH,ONTIMER
            SETVECT  10H,ONVIDEO
            SETVECT  13H,ONDISK
            SETVECT  9H,ONKEYBD
            SETVECT  28H,ONINT28
            SETVECT  2FH,ONMUX
            XOR      AL,AL          ; Signal fresh load.
            MOV      BX,CS
; Call user install.
            CALL     USERINSTALL
; Free the environment if user asked.
IF          FREE_ENV
            MOV      ES,TSRPSP
            MOV      ES,ES:[2CH]    ; Get environment segment.
            MOV      AH,49H
            INT      21H            ; Free it.
ENDIF

; Get size.
            MOV      DX,TSRSIZE
            OR       DX,DX
            JNZ      GO_TSR
; If size is 0, calculate size.
            MOV      DX,OFFSET LAST
            SHR      DX,1
            SHR      DX,1
            SHR      DX,1
            SHR      DX,1
            INC      DX
GO_TSR:
            MOV      AX,3100H
            INT      21H            ; TSR
```

TSR PROGRAMMING

```
; TSR
TSRSTART        ENDP

; Process options, etc.
USERINSTALL     PROC    NEAR
; Find command line.
                MOV     ES,TSRPSP
                XOR     CX,CX
                MOV     SI,80H
                MOV     CL,ES:[SI]
                INC     CL
; Skip leading white space in command line.
SKIPB:
                DEC     CL
                JZ      NOTAIL
                INC     SI
                MOV     DL,ES:[SI]
                CMP     DL,' '
                JZ      SKIPB
                CMP     DL,9
                JZ      SKIPB
                CMP     DL,13
                JZ      SKIPB
                CMP     DL,10
                JZ      SKIPB
NOTAIL:
                XOR     DX,DX           ; zero commands processed
; If user enabled default commands, do them.
IF              DEF_CMDS
                CALL    COMMANDS
ENDIF
; If user wants a chance at the command line, do it.
IFDEF           INIT_PROC
                CALL    INIT_PROC
ENDIF
                RET
USERINSTALL     ENDP
```

DOS 5: A DEVELOPER'S GUIDE

```
; Low MS-DOS version message.
LOWDOS          DB      'Error: Requires MSDOS/PCDOS 3.0 or above)'
                DB      7,13,10,'$'

; If default commands are used, include the code here.
IF              DEF_CMDS
INCLUDE         TSRCMDS.INC
ENDIF

; Should include tsr_init, tsr_help.

XINCLUDE        %PROGRAM,CMD
_TEXT           ENDS

ELSE
IF2
                %OUT    YOU MUST SPECIFY A PROGRAM TITLE.
                %OUT    USE: MASM /DPROGRAM=NAME TSR.ASM
ENDIF
                .ERR
ENDIF
                END     START
```

Listing 14-11. TSRMAC.INC.

```
;****************************************************************
;*                                                              *
;* File: tsrmac.inc                                             *
;*                                                              *
;* Macros for TSRASM programs.                                  *
;*                                                              *
;****************************************************************
; Push all registers (could be better written on 286/386).
PUSH_ALL        MACRO
                PUSH    AX
                PUSH    BX
                PUSH    CX
                PUSH    DX
                PUSH    SI
                PUSH    DI
```

TSR PROGRAMMING

```
                PUSH    BP
                PUSH    DS
                PUSH    ES
                ENDM

; Pop all registers.
POP_ALL         MACRO
                POP     ES
                POP     DS
                POP     BP
                POP     DI
                POP     SI
                POP     DX
                POP     CX
                POP     BX
                POP     AX
                ENDM

; Store interrupt vector.
STOVECT         MACRO   INTNO,WHERE
                MOV     AX,3500H OR INTNO
                INT     21H
                MOV     WHERE,BX
                MOV     [WHERE+2],ES
                ENDM

; Set interrupt vector.
SETVECT         MACRO   INTNO,SUBR
                MOV     AX,2500H OR INTNO
                MOV     DX,OFFSET SUBR
                INT     21H
                ENDM

; Reset interrupt vector.
RESETVECT       MACRO   INTNO,FROM
                PUSH    DS
                MOV     AX,2500H OR INTNO
                LDS     DX,DWORD PTR [FROM]
                INT     21H
                POP     DS
                ENDM
```

```
; Compare interrupt vector.
CMPVECT         MACRO   INTNO, WHERE, FAIL
                LOCAL   C1,C2
                MOV     AX,3500H OR INTNO
                INT     21H
                CMP     BX,OFFSET WHERE
                JZ      C2
C1:
                JMP     FAIL
C2:
                MOV     BX,CS
                MOV     AX,ES
                CMP     AX,BX
                JNZ     C1
                ENDM

; macro to include .TSR, .CMD, and .CFG files
XINCLUDE        MACRO   FN,SUFFIX
                INCLUDE &FN&.&SUFFIX
                ENDM
```

Listing 14-12. TSRVARS.INC.

```
;***************************************************************
;*                                                             *
;* File: tsrvars.inc                                           *
;*                                                             *
;* Variables used in TSRASM.                                   *
;*                                                             *
;***************************************************************
; pointer to TSR's stack
TSRSTK          EQU     THIS DWORD
TSRSP           DW      ?
TSRSS           DW      ?

; pointer to TSR's DTA
TSRDTA          EQU     THIS DWORD
TSRDTAO         DW      ?
TSRDTAS         DW      ?
```

TSR PROGRAMMING

```
; TSR's PSP segment
TSRPSP          DW      ?

; TSR's video segment
TSRVIDSEG       DW      ?
; If not zero, size of TSR (used to override default).
TSRSIZE         DW      0

; video width, mode, and page of host program
HOSTVWIDTH      DB      ?
HOSTVMODE       DB      ?
HOSTVPAGE       DB      ?

; host's SS:SP
HOSTSTK         EQU     THIS DWORD
HOSTSP          DW      ?
HOSTSS          DW      ?

; host's DTA
HOSTDTA         EQU     THIS DWORD
HOSTDTAO        DW      ?
HOSTDTAS        DW      ?

; host's PSP segment
HOSTPSP         DW      ?

; host's break flag
HOSTBREAKF      DB      ?

; host's critical error handler
HOSTCRITO       DW      ?
HOSTCRITS       DW      ?

; host's break handlers
HOST230         DW      ?
HOST23S         DW      ?
HOST1BO         DW      ?
HOST1BS         DW      ?
```

DOS 5: A DEVELOPER'S GUIDE

```
; pointer to INDOS flag
DOSBUSY         EQU     THIS DWORD
DOSBUSYO        DW      ?
DOSBUSYS        DW      ?

; control variables
POPED           DB      0               ; Already popped up.
POPUP           DB      0               ; Do it!
STOPPED         DB      0               ; Don't execute.
KILL            DB      0               ; Set to 1 to kill TSR.

; critical section flags
DISKBUSY        DB      0
VIDEOBUSY       DB      0

; old interrupt vectors (o=offset, s=segment)
OLD9O           DW      ?
OLD9S           DW      ?
OLD10O          DW      ?
OLD10S          DW      ?
OLD13O          DW      ?
OLD13S          DW      ?
OLD1CO          DW      ?
OLD1CS          DW      ?
OLD28O          DW      ?
OLD28S          DW      ?
OLD2FO          DW      ?
OLD2FS          DW      ?

; keyboard definitions
SCAN_CODE       DB      DEF_SCAN        ; Escape
SHIFT_MASK      DB      DEF_MASK        ; both shift keys

; save area for extended error info
EXTSAVE         DW      11 DUP (0)
; Flag is clear if not OK to restore error info (DOS 3.0).
EXTSAVF         DB      1
```

TSR PROGRAMMING

Listing 14-13. TSRCFG.INC.

```
;****************************************************************
;*                                                               *
;* File: tsrcfg.inc                                              *
;*                                                               *
;* Default configuration set up for TSRASM. These values can     *
;* be overriden in the .CFG file.                                *
;*                                                               *
;****************************************************************
; TSR signature (00-FF); PRINT.COM uses 01, APPEND uses 2.
; SHARE uses 10H, APPEND uses B7H.
; C0-FF is reserved for user TSRs.
IFNDEF          SIG
SIG             EQU     0C2H
ENDIF

; size of local stack
IFNDEF          STKSIZE
STKSIZE         EQU     256
ENDIF

; default scan code
IFNDEF          DEF_SCAN
DEF_SCAN        EQU     1
ENDIF

; default shift mask
IFNDEF          DEF_MASK
DEF_MASK        EQU     3
ENDIF

; If 1, free environment. tsr_init has access to it in any event.
IFNDEF          FREE_ENV
FREE_ENV        EQU     1
ENDIF

; If 1, process default commands ( -U, -S, -G, -H, -?).
IFNDEF          DEF_CMDS
DEF_CMDS        EQU     1
ENDIF
```

DOS 5: A DEVELOPER'S GUIDE

```
; Define option character (usually / or -).
IFNDEF          OPT_CHAR
OPT_CHAR        EQU     '-'
ENDIF


; If 1, save entire video state.
IFNDEF          VIDEO
VIDEO           EQU     1
ENDIF

; If 1 and video==1 then always force to page 0.
IFNDEF          VIDP0
VIDP0           EQU     0
ENDIF
```

Listing 14-14. TSRINTS.INC.
```
;****************************************************************
;*                                                              *
;* File: tsrints.inc                                            *
;*                                                              *
;* Interrupt handlers for TSRASM programs.                      *
;*                                                              *
;****************************************************************
; INT 2F handler
ONMUX           PROC    FAR
                CMP     AH,SIG
                JNZ     OUTMUX
                OR      AL,AL
                JNZ     MUXC1
                MOV     AL,CS:STOPPED
                OR      AL,AL
; AL=1 inactive + segment in BX
                MOV     AL,1
                JNZ     MUXGO
; AL=0 installed + segment in BX
                MOV     AL,0FFH
MUXGO:
                MOV     BX,CS
                IRET
```

TSR PROGRAMMING

```
MUXC1:          DEC     AL              ; AL=1 reset stopped flag
                JNZ     MUXC2
                MOV     CS:STOPPED,AL
                IRET
MUXC2:          DEC     AL              ; AL=2 set stopped flag
                JNZ     MUXC3
                INC     AL
                MOV     CS:STOPPED,AL
                IRET
MUXC3:          DEC     AL              ; AL=3 set key codes
                JNZ     MUXERR
                MOV     CS:SCAN_CODE,BL
                MOV     CS:SHIFT_MASK,BH
MUXERR:
; Don't chain to next handler--return to caller.
                IRET

; Chain to next MUX interrupt handler.
OUTMUX:
                JMP     DWORD PTR CS:[OLD2F0]
ONMUX           ENDP


; INT 1BH/23H handler (ignore breaks)
ONBREAK         PROC    FAR
                IRET
ONBREAK         ENDP


; INT 24H handler (ignore all errors)
ONINT24         PROC    FAR
                XOR     AL,AL
                IRET
ONINT24         ENDP


; INT 9 handler (search for hot key)
ONKEYBD         PROC    FAR
                PUSH    AX
                PUSH    DS
                PUSH    ES
                PUSH    CS
                POP     DS
```

565

```
; Don't do anything if stopped.
            MOV     AL,STOPPED
            OR      AL,AL
            JNZ     NOTKEY
; Don't check hot key if already popped up.
            MOV     AL,POPED
            OR      AL,AL
            JNZ     NOTKEY
; Get scan code.
            IN      AL,60H
            CMP     AL,SCAN_CODE
            JNZ     NOTKEY
; If it matches, look at shift keys.
            XOR     AX,AX
            MOV     ES,AX
            MOV     AL,ES:[417H] ; Shift status.
            AND     AL,SHIFT_MASK
            CMP     AL,SHIFT_MASK
            JNZ     NOTKEY
; If both matched, eat keystroke and set flag.
            IN      AL,61H
            MOV     AH,AL
            OR      AL,80H
            OUT     61H,AL
            MOV     AL,AH
            OUT     61H,AL
; Acknowledge hardware interrupt.
            MOV     AL,20H
            OUT     20H,AL
            MOV     AL,1
            MOV     POPUP,AL
            JMP     SHORT KEYOUT
; Wasn't for us--call old handler.
NOTKEY:     PUSHF
            CALL    DWORD PTR [OLD90]
KEYOUT:     POP     ES
            POP     DS
            POP     AX
            IRET
ONKEYBD     ENDP
```

TSR PROGRAMMING

```
; timer tick interrupt (check for pop-up and shift-only hot key)
ONTIMER         PROC    FAR
                PUSHF
; Call old timer routine.
                CALL    DWORD PTR CS:[OLD1C0]
                PUSH    DS
                PUSH    ES
                PUSH    BX
                PUSH    AX
                PUSH    CS
                POP     DS
; If stopped, forget it.
                MOV     AL,STOPPED
                OR      AL,AL
                JNZ     TIMER0
; If no scan_code in hot key, check for shift-only hot key.
                MOV     AL,SCAN_CODE
                OR      AL,AL
                JNZ     TIMER0
; If popped up, forget it.
                MOV     AL,POPED
                OR      AL,AL
                JNZ     TIMER0
; Check shift keys.
                XOR     AX,AX
                MOV     ES,AX
                MOV     AL,ES:[417H]
                AND     AL,SHIFT_MASK
                CMP     AL,SHIFT_MASK
                JNZ     TIMER0
; If hot key, set flag.
                MOV     AL,1
                MOV     POPUP,AL

TIMER0:
; Is DOS busy?
                LES     BX,DOSBUSY
                MOV     AL,ES:[BX]
                OR      AL,AL
                JNZ     TIMEROUT
```

567

DOS 5: A DEVELOPER'S GUIDE

```
; If not, is TSR ready to pop up?
                MOV     AL,POPUP
                OR      AL,AL
                JZ      TIMEOUT
; If TSR ready, ARE disk and video free?
                MOV     AL,DISKBUSY
                OR      AL,VIDEOBUSY
                JNZ     TIMEOUT

; Clear pop-up flag.
                MOV     POPUP,AL
; Acknowledge hardware interrupt.
                MOV     AL,20H
                OUT     20H,AL
; Do it!
                CALL    GO_POPUP

TIMEOUT:        POP     AX
                POP     BX
                POP     ES
                POP     DS
                IRET
ONTIMER         ENDP

; INT 28 service
ONINT28         PROC    FAR
; Call old int28 routine.
                PUSHF                   ; Look like an INT.
                CALL    DWORD PTR CS:[OLD280]
                PUSH    DS
                PUSH    ES
                PUSH    BX
                PUSH    AX
                PUSH    CS
                POP     DS
; Is DOS busy?
                LES     BX,DOSBUSY
                MOV     AL,ES:[BX]
                OR      AL,AL
                JZ      INT28OUT
```

TSR PROGRAMMING

```
; If it is, is program ready?
            MOV     AL,POPUP
            OR      AL,AL
            JZ      INT28OUT
; If it is, clear pop-up flag and do it.
            XOR     AL,AL
            MOV     POPUP,AL
            CALL    GO_POPUP
INT28OUT:
            POP     AX
            POP     BX
            POP     ES
            POP     DS
            IRET
ONINT28     ENDP

; INT 13 routine (count disk access calls )
ONDISK      PROC    FAR
            INC     CS:[DISKBUSY]
            PUSHF
            CALL    DWORD PTR CS:[OLD130]
            PUSHF
            DEC     CS:[DISKBUSY]
            POPF
            RET     2
ONDISK      ENDP

; INT 10 routine (count video access calls)
ONVIDEO     PROC    FAR
            INC     CS:[VIDEOBUSY]
            PUSHF
            CALL    DWORD PTR CS:[OLD100]
            DEC     CS:[VIDEOBUSY]
            IRET
ONVIDEO     ENDP
```

DOS 5: A DEVELOPER'S GUIDE

Listing 14-15. TSRCMDS.INC.

```
;****************************************************************
;*                                                               *
;* File: tsrcmds.inc                                             *
;*                                                               *
;* Process default commands for TSRASM programs.                 *
;*                                                               *
;****************************************************************
; default command processor
IFNDEF          NUMKEYS
NRKEYS          =       3
DEFKEYTAB       DW      0301H           ; double shift-Escape
                DW      0300H           ; double shift
                DW      0839H           ; alt-spacebar
                DW      0A00H           ; alt-left shift
ELSE
NRKEYS          EQU     NUMKEYS-1
ENDIF

COMERRM         DB      'Invalid option.',7,13,10,'$'
CANTUN          DB      'U option invalid: TSR was just'
                DB      ' loaded.',7,13,10,'$'

COMMANDS        PROC    NEAR
                PUSH    SI
                PUSH    CX
                PUSH    AX
                MOV     AH,AL
                JMP     SHORT COMFIRST
COMTOP:
                INC     SI
                DEC     CX
COMFIRST:
                JCXZ    NOCOM
                CMP     BYTE PTR ES:[SI],OPT_CHAR
                JNZ     COMTOP
                INC     SI
                DEC     CX
                MOV     AL,ES:[SI]
```

570

TSR PROGRAMMING

```
        IFDEF           HELP_PROC
                CMP     AL,'?'
                JNZ     COMU
                CALL    HELP_PROC
                INC     DX
                JMP     COMTOP
        ENDIF

COMU:           OR      AL,20H          ; Convert to lowercase.
                CMP     AL,'u'
                JNZ     COMST
; Uninstall.
                CMP     AH,0FFH         ; If fresh load, U is illegal.
                JZ      OKUNINS
                MOV     DX,OFFSET CANTUN
                MOV     AH,9
                INT     21H
                INC     DX
                JMP     COMTOP
OKUNINS:
; OK to try to uninstall--set kill and pop-up flags.
; TSR will kill itself.
                PUSH    ES
                MOV     ES,BX
                MOV     AL,1
                MOV     ES:KILL,AL
                MOV     ES:POPUP,AL
                POP     ES
                INC     DX
                JMP     COMTOP
COMST:          CMP     AL,'s'
                JNZ     COMGO
; Set stop flag.
                MOV     AL,2
COMSVC:
                MOV     AH,SIG
                INT     2FH
                INC     DX
                JMP     COMTOP
```

DOS 5: A DEVELOPER'S GUIDE

```
COMGO:          CMP     AL,'g'
                JNZ     COMH
; Set go flag.
                MOV     AL,1
                JMP     COMSVC
COMH:           CMP     AL,'h'          ; Set hot key.
                JNZ     NOCOM
; Set up hot key.
; Find number and look up in defkeytab.
                INC     SI
                DEC     CX
                MOV     AL,ES:[SI]
                SUB     AL,'1'
                CMP     AL,NRKEYS
                JBE     COMHGO
; bad number
                MOV     DX,OFFSET COMERRM
                MOV     AH,9
                INT     21H
                JMP     COMTOP
COMHGO:
                CBW
                MOV     DI,AX
                SHL     DI,1
                PUSH    BX
                MOV     BX,[DEFKEYTAB+DI]
; Tell TSR.
                MOV     AL,3
                MOV     AH,SIG
                INT     2FH
                POP     BX
                INC     DX
                JMP     COMTOP

NOCOM:
                POP     AX
                POP     CX
                POP     SI
                RET
COMMANDS        ENDP
```

TSR PROGRAMMING

Listing 14-16. TSRVIDEO.INC.
```
;****************************************************************
;*                                                              *
;* File: tsrvideo.inc                                           *
;*                                                              *
;* Video context management for TSRASM.                         *
;*                                                              *
;****************************************************************
; video state package

; variables
; TSR's video page
TSRVPAGE        DB      ?

; host's cursor type and position
HOSTCTYPE       DW      ?
HOSTCURSOR      DW      ?

; storage for host's screen
HOSTVID         DB      4096 DUP (?)
; Save video state.
; Assume BH=page.
TSR_VIDUP       PROC    NEAR
; Set to page 0 if asked.
IF              VIDP0
                MOV     AX,0500H
                INT     10H
                XOR     BH,BH
ENDIF
                MOV     TSRVPAGE,BH
; Save cursor info.
                MOV     AH,03H
                INT     10H
                MOV     HOSTCTYPE,CX
                MOV     HOSTCURSOR,DX
; Set cursor to default (different for mono/color).
                MOV     CX,0B0CH
                CMP     HOSTVMODE,7
                JZ      MONOCUR
                MOV     CX,0607H
MONOCUR:        MOV     AH,1
```

573

```
                INT     10H
; Save host's screen.
                MOV     AL,HOSTVWIDTH
                MOV     CX,4096         ; 80X25 or...
                CMP     AL,40
                JNZ     COL80
                MOV     CX,2048         ; 40X25
COL80:          MOV     AL,BH
                CBW
                MUL     CX
                MOV     SI,AX
                PUSH    DS
                POP     ES
                MOV     DI,OFFSET HOSTVID
                SHR     CX,1
                PUSH    DS
                MOV     DS,TSRVIDSEG
                REP     MOVSW
                POP     DS
                RET
TSR_VIDUP       ENDP

; Restore video state.
TSR_VIDDN       PROC    NEAR
; Get page, etc.
                MOV     AH,0FH
                INT     10H
; Restore 4,096 or 2,048 bytes.
                MOV     AL,HOSTVWIDTH
                MOV     CX,4096
                CMP     AL,40
                JNZ     COL801
                MOV     CX,2048
COL801:         MOV     AL,BH
                CBW
                MUL     CX
                MOV     DI,AX
                MOV     ES,TSRVIDSEG
                MOV     SI,OFFSET HOSTVID
                SHR     CX,1
                REP     MOVSW
```

TSR PROGRAMMING

```
; Reset cursor.
            MOV      CX,HOSTCTYPE
            MOV      AH,1
            INT      10H
            MOV      DX,HOSTCURSOR
            MOV      AH,2
            INT      10H
; Reset page.
            MOV      AH,5
            MOV      AL,HOSTVPAGE
            INT      10H
            RET
TSR_VIDDN   ENDP

; Clear screen helper routine for user.
TSR_CLS     PROC     NEAR
; Use scroll to clear screen.
            MOV      AX,0600H
            XOR      CX,CX
            MOV      BH,7
            MOV      DX,184FH
            INT      10H
; home cursor
            MOV      DX,CX
            MOV      AH,2
            MOV      BH,TSRVPAGE
            INT      10H
            RET
TSR_CLS     ENDP
```

Listing 14-17. TSRASM.BAT.
a. TSRASM batch file for MASM.

```
@echo off
REM if the assembler or linker isn't on your path
REM either add them or edit this file to call
REM them directly
if %1.==. goto err
masm /DPROGRAM=%1 tsr.asm,%1.obj,%1.lst;
if ERRORLEVEL 1 goto end
```

DOS 5: A DEVELOPER'S GUIDE

```
link %1.obj;
if ERRORLEVEL 1 goto end
exe2bin %1.exe %1.com
erase %1.exe
goto end
:err
echo TSRASM by Al Williams
echo usage: TSRASM program_name
echo Converts .TSR, .CMD, and .CFG files into a pop-up program
:end
```

b. TSRASM batch file for TASM.
```
@echo off
REM if the assembler or linker isn't on your path
REM either add them or edit this file to call
REM them directly
if %1.==. goto err
tasm /m2 /DPROGRAM=%1 /w-PDC /w-MCP tsr.asm,%1.obj
if ERRORLEVEL 1 goto end
tlink /t %1.obj
goto end
:err
echo TSRASM by Al Williams
echo usage: TSRASM program_name
echo Converts .TSR, .CMD, and .CFG files into a pop-up program
:end
```

TSRASM provides most of the services you need to write full pop-up programs. You declare a routine to pop up (using the *MAIN_PROC* equate). This routine will run when the hot key occurs and DOS is available. TSRASM also protects the disk and video routines. The *MAIN_PROC* routine need not do the mandatory context switches—TSRASM does them automatically. Because most pop-ups use the video screen, TSRASM can save the screen context if you request it. In addition, TSRASM can switch the TSR to video page 0. This makes it easier to access the screen directly.

TSRASM programs can only pop up in text modes. If a pop-up finds the screen in a graphics mode, it beeps and returns to the interrupted program. TSRASM doesn't save the current working directory and current drive—you must save and restore them if you use them.

TSR PROGRAMMING

Unless you ask it not to, TSRASM processes several default commands from the command line (see Figure 14-2). You also can process the command line by setting *INIT_PROC* (discussed below).

-?	Call user's HELP_PROC routine (only if HELP_PROC defined)
-S	Stops TSR temporarily.
-G	Resume TSR after an -S operation.
-U	Uninstall TSR if possible. If not possible, TSR beeps and stops as if it received an -S option. This option is not valid when the TSR first loads.
-Hn	Change hot key from hot-key table. n must be at least 1 and can't be greater than the number of keys defined (see NUMKEYS in Figure 14-3).

Notes: Default commands must be enabled (see DEF_CMDS in Figure 14-3).

The option character defaults to a '-'. This may be changed with the OPT_CHAR configuration variable (see Figure 14-3).

Options are not case-sensitive.

Figure 14-2. TSRASM default commands.

The .CFG file controls all the options for the pop-up (Figure 14-3 shows the permissible options). All have a default value. This file also defines the pop-up's routines (*MAIN_PROC, INIT_PROC, EXIT_PROC*, and *HELP_PROC*). Only *MAIN_PROC*, the pop-up routine, is mandatory. *HELP_PROC* is called when the default command handler finds a -? option. TSRASM calls *INIT_PROC* and *EXIT_PROC* when the TSR is installed and unloaded, respectively (see Figure 14-4 for more details).

It's convenient to put DEFKEYTAB, the hot-key table, in the .CFG file. However, this causes the table to remain resident and therefore waste space. If space is at a premium, define DEFKEYTAB in the .CMD file.

DOS 5: A DEVELOPER'S GUIDE

SIG	The signature used for the default INT 2FH handler.
FREE_ENV	A zero in this variable prevents the environment block from being freed.
STKSIZE	Size of TSR's local stack in bytes.
DEF_SCAN	Default hot-key scan code. If 0, then only use shift status mask for pop-up. (See Appendix D for a table of scan codes.)
DEF_MASK	Default shift status mask. The indicated shift keys must be pressed with the hot-key scan code (DEF_SCAN) to cause the TSR to pop up. The format of the shift status byte is the same as the BIOS uses for INT 16H, function 02H.
DEF_CMDS	Process default commands if not zero (see Figure 14-2).
OPT_CHAR	Sets option character for the default command handler.
NUMKEYS	Number of hot keys defined for -H option.
DEFKEYTAB	Table of hot keys for the -H option. You must specify NUMKEYS if you set this table up yourself. DEFKEYTAB isn't a variable, but an address. For example, the default setup is:

```
NUMKEYS    EQU    4
DEFKEYTAB  DW     0301H  ; Both shift keys+Escape
           DW     0300H  ; Both shift keys
           DW     0834H  ; Alt+Space
           DW     0A00H  ; Alt+Left shift
```

VIDEO	If not zero, TSRASM performs video context-switching for the TSR.
VIDP0	If video context-switching is enabled (see VIDEO) and this flag is not zero, TSRASM uses page 0 of the display for the TSR.

Defaults:

```
SIG         EQU   0C2H
FREE_ENV    EQU   1
STK_SIZE    EQU   256
DEF_SCAN    EQU   1
DEF_MASK    EQU   3
DEF_CMDS    EQU   1
OPT_CHAR    EQU   '-'
NUMKEYS     EQU   4
DEFKEYTAB   (see above)
VIDEO       EQU   1
VIDP0       EQU   0
```

Figure 14-3. TSRASM configuration variables.

TSR PROGRAMMING

Some options don't apply in every situation. *VIDP0*, for instance, has no effect if *VIDEO* is zero. *OPTCHAR* only works when *DEF_CMDS* is nonzero. Also, if you set up a *DEFKEYTAB* and if *DEF_CMDS* isn't zero, you must set *NUMKEYS* as well. If *VIDEO* isn't zero, you can call *TSR_CLS* to clear the screen. TSRASM doesn't automatically clear the screen; your pop-up might want to examine or modify the existing screen.

TSRASM also maintains two variables you may want to use. The STOPPED variable disables the TSR until a *-G* option restarts it. If you use the STOPPED flag rather than the default commands, you should provide a similar option. Your program can also set the KILL flag, which causes the TSR to unload. If the TSR can't uninstall, TSRASM beeps and sets the STOPPED flag. Figure 14-5 shows the variables you might need in your program. When the STOPPED flag is set, the INT 2FH handler returns AL=1. This indicates that the TSR is present but inactive.

Before you use TSRASM.BAT, you should have the assembler and linker in your DOS PATH. You can put the full path name for the programs in the batch file, if you prefer.

Some Sample Pop-ups

The POPDIR program (Listings 14-18 through 14-20) uses TSRASM to provide a directory on the screen when the hot key is detected. The program is simple but does use DOS for file operations. It's handy with old programs, such as DEBUG, that don't let you display a directory. POPDIR only shows the current working directory.

Notice that the *INIT_PROC* routine (*TSR_INIT*) prints a message when the TSR loads or if the TSR is active but can process no commands. Of course, *TSR_INIT* could process additional commands if desired.

Listings 14-21 through 14-23 show another pop-up program, SDUMP. SDUMP copies the current screen to a file when you press both shift keys (this is the default hot key POPDIR uses; if you want to run both programs at the same time, you'll have to change one of their hot keys). This pop-up's RAM usage is much smaller because it doesn't switch the video context.

DOS 5: A DEVELOPER'S GUIDE

INIT_PROC		Called after TSR is loaded, but before return to DOS. The procedure should be in the .CMD file. Entry conditions:
	AL =	0 if TSR was just loaded, 1 if TSR is loaded but inactive, 0FFH if TSR was active when program started
	BX =	Segment address of TSR
	DX =	Number of commands already processed
	ES:SI =	Pointer to command line after any leading blanks
MAIN_PROC		Main TSR routine. This procedure belongs in the .TSR file. On entry:
		DS=CS
END_PROC		Called before the TSR unloads. Place in .TSR file.
HELP_PROC		Called if -? found on command line.

Figure 14-4. TSRASM user-defined procedures.

TSRPSP	PSP of TSR program
TSRVIDSEG	Current video segment
HOSTVWIDTH	Width of host's video screen
HOSTVMODE	Host's video mode
HOSTPSP	Host's PSP
STOPPED	Set to nonzero if TSR has been stopped with -S
KILL	Request that TSR remove itself
SCAN_CODE	Scan code for hot key (if zero, shift only)
SHIFT_MASK	Shift mask for hot key

The following variables are only available when VIDEO=1:

TSRVPAGE	TSR's video page
HOSTCURSOR	Cursor location on host screen (high byte is row, low byte is column)
HOSTVID	4K array corresponding to host's video screen. If VIDP0=1, this is the host's page 0, not necessarily the page that was displayed when the TSR was called.

Figure 14-5. TSRASM variables.

TSR PROGRAMMING

Listing 14-18. POPDIR.TSR.

```
;****************************************************************
;*                                                               *
;* File: popdir.tsr                                              *
;*                                                               *
;* Main file for POPDIR TSR.                                     *
;* This TSR displays the current directory when activated.       *
;*                                                               *
;****************************************************************

; directory mask
WILDCARD        DB      '*.*',0

; various messages
DMSG            DB      'Directory of ',0
WMSG            DB      13,10,'Press any key to continue',0

; storage for directory name
PATHBUF         DB      64 DUP (0)

; pop-up routine
TSR_MAIN        PROC    NEAR
                CALL    TSR_CLS         ; Clear the screen.
                PUSH    DS
                POP     ES
                MOV     BX,OFFSET DMSG
; Write "Directory of ".
                CALL    WRITE_S
; Get current disk drive.
                MOV     AH,19H
                INT     21H
; Convert to A,B,C, etc.
                ADD     AL,'A'
                CALL    OUCH
                MOV     AL,':'
                CALL    OUCH
                MOV     AL,'\'
                CALL    OUCH
```

```
; Get and print current directory.
            MOV     SI,OFFSET PATHBUF
            XOR     DL,DL
            MOV     AH,47H
            INT     21H
            MOV     BX,SI
            CALL    WRITE_S
            MOV     AL,13
            CALL    OUCH
            MOV     AL,10
            CALL    OUCH
; Get DTA address.
            MOV     AH,2FH
            INT     21H
            ADD     BX,30
; Find first file.
            MOV     AH,4EH
            XOR     CX,CX
            MOV     DX,OFFSET WILDCARD
            INT     21H
DIRLOOP:
            JC      TSR_OUT         ; no more files
; Write file name.
            CALL    WRITE_S
; Tab over.
            CALL    BUMP16
; Check for key.
            MOV     AH,1
            INT     16H
            JZ      DIRMORE
; If key pressed, read it and wait for another one (pause).
            XOR     AH,AH
            INT     16H
            XOR     AH,AH
            INT     16H
DIRMORE:
; Find next file.
            MOV     AH,4FH
            INT     21H
```

TSR PROGRAMMING

```
; Do it again.
            JMP     DIRLOOP

; Done --prompt and wait for key.

TSR_OUT:
            PUSH    DS
            POP     ES
            MOV     BX,OFFSET WMSG
            CALL    WRITE_S
            XOR     AX,AX
            INT     16H
            RET
TSR_MAIN    ENDP

; Write string in ES:[BX].
WRITE_S     PROC    NEAR
            PUSH    BX              ; Ouch destroys BX.
            MOV     SI,BX
WFLOOP:
            MOV     AL,ES:[SI]
            OR      AL,AL
            JZ      WFNOUT
            CALL    OUCH
            INC     SI
            JMP     WFLOOP
WFNOUT:
            POP     BX
            RET
WRITE_S     ENDP

; Output character in AL.
OUCH        PROC    NEAR
            MOV     AH,0EH
            MOV     BH,TSRVPAGE
            INT     10H
            RET
OUCH        ENDP
```

```
; Tab over to next column.
BUMP16          PROC    NEAR
                PUSH    BX
; Read cursor position.
                MOV     AH,3
                MOV     BH,TSRVPAGE
                INT     10H
; Move it to or past next column.
                ADD     DL,16
; Round it back to start of column.
                AND     DL,0F0H
; Did we go over the screen?
                CMP     DL,HOSTVWIDTH
                JL      BUMP
; yes...CRLF
                MOV     AL,13
                CALL    OUCH
                MOV     AL,10
                CALL    OUCH
                POP     BX
                RET
; no... move cursor
BUMP:
                MOV     AH,2
                INT     10H
                POP     BX
                RET
BUMP16          ENDP
```

Listing 14-19. POPDIR.CFG.

```
;****************************************************************
;*                                                              *
;* File: popdir.cfg                                             *
;*                                                              *
;* TSR configuration for POPDIR TSR.                            *
;*                                                              *
;****************************************************************
; TSR configuration options
; Legal variables are (values shown are defaults):
```

TSR PROGRAMMING

```
; SIG=C2         Byte to identify the TSR. Values of C0-FF are
;                recommended.
;
; STKSIZE=256    Number of bytes to reserve for local stack.
;
; DEF_SCAN=1     Scan code of default hot key--if 0, TSR will
;                pop up on shift-key status only (see below).
;
; DEF_MASK=3     Mask for shift-key status.
;                INS=80H
;                CAPS-LOCK=40H
;                NUM-LOCK=20H
;                SCROLL-LOCK=10H
;                ALT=8
;                CTRL=4
;                LEFT-SHIFT=2
;                RIGHT-SHIFT=1
;                Example: Use 3 for both shift keys.
;
; FREE_ENV=1     If 1, the environment is freed before the TSR
;                goes resident.
;
; VIDEO=1        If 1, the TSR saves the entire screen before the
;                user TSR code is called. This adds over 4K to the
;                size of the TSR.
;
; VIDP0=1        If 1, the TSR forces the video page to page 0
;                before the user TSR code is called. This is only
;                effective if VIDEO=1 (see above).
;
; DEF_CMDS=1     If 1, the TSR processes default commands (-U, -S,
;                -G, -?, -Hn). If 0, no default commands are
;                processed.
;
; OPT_CHAR='-'   Set to character used for options when DEF_CMDS=1.
;
; NUMKEYS=4      Number of preset hot keys for -H option. Used only
;                when DEF_CMDS=1.
;
; DEFKEYTAB      Table of shift masks and scan codes for the -H
```

DOS 5: A DEVELOPER'S GUIDE

```
;                       option. Used only when DEF_CMDS=1. This isn't
;                       an equate, but a data table. The default table is:
;                       DEFKEYTAB   dw    0301H    ; double shift-Escape
;                                   dw    0300H    ; double shift
;                                   dw    0839H    ; alt-space bar
;                                   dw    0A00H    ; alt-left shift
;
; These variables specify a PROC.
; There are no default values. You must use EQU, not =, for MASM.
;
; MAIN_PROC             Name of pop-up routine. This value is mandatory.
;                       This routine should appear in the .TSR file.
;
; INIT_PROC             Called before TSR is resident or if TSR is already
;                       resident. AL=0 if installed, FF if already
;                       installed. BX=segment of TSR, DX=number of commands
;                       processed by default command handler. Should appear
;                       in the .CMD file.
;
; EXIT_PROC             Called before TSR uninstalls. Should appear in .TSR
;                       file.
;
; HELP_PROC             If default commands are used, this routine is
;                       called when -? is found on the command line. Should
;                       appear in .CMD file.

SIG=0C2H
DEF_SCAN=0
DEF_MASK=3
 NUMKEYS           EQU     4
; Putting the table here instead of in the .CMD file wastes some
; space but is convenient.
DEFKEYTAB         DW      0300H           ; double shift
                  DW      0301H           ; double shift-escape
                  DW      0C00H           ; alt-ctrl
                  DW      0A00H           ; alt-left shift

INIT_PROC         EQU     TSR_INIT
MAIN_PROC         EQU     TSR_MAIN
HELP_PROC         EQU     TSR_HELP
```

TSR PROGRAMMING

Listing 14-20. POPDIR.CMD.
```
;****************************************************************
;*                                                               *
;*                                                               *
;* File: popdir.cmd                                              *
;*                                                               *
;* Transient portion of POPDIR TSR.                              *
;*                                                               *
;****************************************************************

; transient portion of POPDIR

; messages
LMSG            DB      'TSR already loaded.',13,10,'$'
FMSG            DB      'TSR loaded.',13,10,'$'

; This routine is called once at TSR load time.
; If AL==0 then:
; The program is already hooked into the system, but the TSR
; call to DOS hasn't happened yet.
; If AL==FF then:
; Called with BX=segment of resident copy.
; DX=# of commands processed by default command handler.

TSR_INIT        PROC    NEAR
; fresh load
                PUSH    DX
                MOV     DX,OFFSET FMSG
                OR      AL,AL
                JZ      FRESH
                POP     DX
; If default commands processed, exit...
                OR      DX,DX
                JNZ     NOPROC
; else print message.
                PUSH    DX
                MOV     DX,OFFSET LMSG
; Print one message or the other.
FRESH:
                MOV     AH,9
                INT     21H
                POP     DX
```

587

DOS 5: A DEVELOPER'S GUIDE

```
NOPROC:
                RET
TSR_INIT        ENDP


; help stuff

HELPTEXT        DB      'POPDIR - A simple TSR program by'
                DB      ' Al Williams.',13,10
                DB      'Press both shift keys to activate.'
                DB      13,10,'$'

TSR_HELP        PROC    NEAR
; Print message.
                MOV     DX,OFFSET HELPTEXT
                MOV     AH,9
                INT     21H
                RET
TSR_HELP        ENDP
```

Listing 14-21. SDUMP.TSR.

```
;****************************************************************
;*                                                              *
;* File: sdump.tsr                                              *
;*                                                              *
;* Main file for SDUMP TSR.                                     *
;* This TSR dumps the screen to a file when activated.          *
;*                                                              *
;****************************************************************
; default file name
FNAME           DB      'SDUMP.'
FEXT            DB      'A'-1,0         ; part to change

; space for file handle
FHANDLE         DW      ?

; main pop-up routine

TSR_MAIN        PROC    NEAR
```

588

TSR PROGRAMMING

```
; Look for SDUMP.A, SDUMP.B, etc. until one is not found.
            MOV     AH,'A'-1
            MOV     FEXT,AH
FINDFILE:
            INC     FEXT
            MOV     AH,4EH
            MOV     CX,037H
            MOV     DX,OFFSET FNAME
            INT     21H
; File exists; try again.
            JNC     FINDFILE
; Create file.
            MOV     AH,3CH
            XOR     CX,CX
            MOV     DX,OFFSET FNAME
            INT     21H
; If you can't create, beep once and quit.
            JC      ERROR1
; Save handle.
            MOV     FHANDLE,AX
; Get video page and calculate start of screen.
; Assumes 80X25 text mode.
            MOV     AH,0FH
            INT     10H
            MOV     DL,BH
            XOR     DH,DH
            MOV     CL,13
            SHL     DX,CL
; Set up for dump.
            MOV     BX,FHANDLE
            MOV     DS,TSRVIDSEG
            MOV     SI,2000     ; Dump 2,000 characters,
            MOV     CX,1        ; one at a time.
WLOOP:      MOV     AH,40H      ; Write character.
            INT     21H
            JC      ERROR2      ; If error, beep twice.
            INC     DX
            INC     DX
            DEC     SI
            JNZ     WLOOP       ; next character
```

DOS 5: A DEVELOPER'S GUIDE

```
FCLOSE:         MOV     AH,3EH
                INT     21H
                JC      ERROR3      ; Beep twice and exit if error.
                RET

ERROR2:         CALL    FCLOSE      ; If write error, close file.
ERROR3:                             ; two beeps on write/close
                                    ; error
                MOV     AX,0E07H
                INT     10H
ERROR1:         MOV     AX,0E07H    ; Beep once for open error.
                INT     10H
                RET
TSR_MAIN        ENDP
```

Listing 14-22. SDUMP.CFG.
```
;***************************************************************
;*                                                             *
;* File: sdump.cfg                                             *
;*                                                             *
;* Configuration file for SDUMP TSR.                           *
;*                                                             *
;***************************************************************
; TSR configuration options
; Legal variables are (values shown are defaults):
;
; SIG=C2        Byte to identify the TSR. Values of C0-FF are
;               recommended.
;
; STKSIZE=256   Number of bytes to reserve for local stack.
;
; DEF_SCAN=1    Scan code of default hot key--if 0, TSR will
;               pop up on shift-key status only (see below).
;
```

TSR PROGRAMMING

```
; DEF_MASK=3    Mask for shift-key status.
;               INS=80H
;               CAPS-LOCK=40H
;               NUM-LOCK=20H
;               SCROLL-LOCK=10H
;               ALT=8
;               CTRL=4
;               LEFT-SHIFT=2
;               RIGHT-SHIFT=1
;               Example: Use 3 for both shift keys.
;
; FREE_ENV=1    If 1, the environment is freed before the TSR
;               goes resident.
;
; VIDEO=1       If 1, the TSR saves the entire screen before the
;               user TSR code is called. This adds over 4K to the
;               size of the TSR.
;
; VIDP0=1       If 1, the TSR forces the video page to page 0
;               before the user TSR code is called. This is only
;               effective if VIDEO=1 (see above).
;
; DEF_CMDS=1    If 1, the TSR processes default commands (-U, -S,
;               -G, -?, -Hn). If 0, no default commands are
;               processed.
;
; OPT_CHAR='-'  Set to character used for options when DEF_CMDS=1.
;
; NUMKEYS=4     Number of preset hot keys for -H option. Used only
;               when DEF_CMDS=1.
;
; DEFKEYTAB     Table of shift masks and scan codes for the -H
;               option. Used only when DEF_CMDS=1. This isn't
;               an equate, but a data table. The default table is:
;                   DEFKEYTAB  dw    0301H    ; double shift-Escape
;                              dw    0300H    ; double shift
;                              dw    0839H    ; alt-space bar
;                              dw    0A00H    ; alt-left shift
;
```

DOS 5: A DEVELOPER'S GUIDE

```
; These variables specify a PROC.
; There are no default values. You must use EQU, not =, for MASM.
;
; MAIN_PROC     Name of pop-up routine. This value is mandatory.
;               This routine should appear in the .TSR file.
;
; INIT_PROC     Called before TSR is resident or if TSR is already
;               resident. AL=0 if installed, FF if already
;               installed.
;               BX=segment of TSR, DX=number of commands processed
;               by default command handler. Should appear in the
;               .CMD file.
;
; EXIT_PROC     Called before TSR uninstalls. Should appear in .TSR
;               file.
;
; HELP_PROC     If default commands are used, this routine is
;               called when -? is found on the command line. Should
;               appear in .CMD file.

SIG=0D9H
DEF_SCAN=0
DEF_MASK=3
VIDEO=0
INIT_PROC EQU TSR_INIT
MAIN_PROC EQU TSR_MAIN
HELP_PROC EQU TSR_HELP
NUMKEYS=4
; Putting the table here instead of in the .CMD file wastes space
; but is convenient.
DEFKEYTAB       DW      0300H           ; double shift
                DW      0301H           ; double shift-escape
                DW      0C00H           ; alt-ctrl
                DW      0A00H           ; alt-left shift
```

TSR PROGRAMMING

Listing 14-23. SDUMP.CMD.

```
;******************************************************************
;*                                                                *
;* File: sdump.cmd                                                *
;*                                                                *
;* Transient portion of SDUMP TSR.                                *
;*                                                                *
;******************************************************************

; messages
LMSG            DB      'TSR already loaded.',13,10,'$'
FMSG            DB      'TSR loaded.',13,10,'$'

; Start.
TSR_INIT        PROC    NEAR
                PUSH    DX
                MOV     DX,OFFSET FMSG
                OR      AL,AL
; If fresh load, print message...
                JZ      FRESH
; else see if default commands were processed.
                POP     DX
                OR      DX,DX
; If so, take no action...
                JNZ     NOPROC
; else print error message.
                PUSH    DX
                MOV     DX,OFFSET LMSG
FRESH:
                MOV     AH,9
                INT     21H
                POP     DX
NOPROC:
                RET
TSR_INIT        ENDP

; help stuff
```

593

```
HELPTEXT        DB      'SDUMP: Press both shift keys to save the '
                DB      'screen to a file.',13,10
                DB      'The file will be placed in the current'
                DB      ' directory and will',13,10
                DB      'have the name SDUMP.x,'
                DB      ' where x is A, B, C,....',13,10,'$'

; Print help message.
TSR_HELP        PROC    NEAR
                MOV     DX,OFFSET HELPTEXT
                MOV     AH,9
                INT     21H
                RET
TSR_HELP        ENDP
```

SDUMP looks in the current directory for files named SDUMP.A, SDUMP.B, and so on. If it finds a file with that name, it keeps looking. If the file doesn't exist, SDUMP creates it and copies the screen to the file. For simplicity, SDUMP assumes the screen is in an 80-by-25 text mode.

If Your TSR Doesn't Work

Debugging TSR programs can be a frustrating task. If you rewrite any of the TSRASM or INTASM kernel code, try compiling one small TSR program that doesn't do anything.

Getting the program to go resident is the first step. One of two things is then likely to happen: The program will hang when activated (for a hardware interrupt, it might seem to hang immediately), or everything will seem fine but the TSR won't work as expected.

If you have the second problem, you're in luck. You can simply use INT 2FH to learn the address of the TSR and then use DEBUG or another debugger to study your code. You probably can't single-step it, but you can look at the variables.

TSR PROGRAMMING

The first problem is somewhat more difficult. Start with one interrupt handler and add them until the program hangs. Study the handler carefully, and eventually you'll see a minor mistake that is causing the TSR to crash.

You may find the following tips helpful when debugging TSRs:

- Put a debugging variable in your program. By setting different bits in the word at various points in your program, you can verify program operation. When the program works, remove the variable and the related code.

- If possible, have your main program running as a regular program before you make it resident. When this isn't possible, you may still be able to test portions of your code as a regular program.

- If an interrupt routine causes the system to hang, relocate it to INT 60H through 67H (the user interrupts). Examine the interrupt vector first—if it's 0000:0000, the interrupt is free to use. Don't use an interrupt that's already in use. When the routine hooks the new interrupt, the system won't hang; of course, your TSR won't work either. However, you can easily set up a call to it from DEBUG and single-step it to find the problem. If you use this method, you may have to simulate the calls to other interrupts.

Some common errors to watch for are:

- Illegal interrupt calls (don't use INT 21H, functions 00 through 0CH)

- Division by zero

- Using memory returned to DOS when the program went resident

- Using code or data in the transient portion from the resident portion

595

- Depending on a large stack from the host (primarily with INTASM)

- Using a private stack that's too small or outside the reserved memory

- Using a signature that another TSR already uses (the TSR will refuse to install, reporting that it is already installed). There's no way to ensure that your TSR's signature is unique, a major problem for the TSRs you distribute commercially.

PART III

Protected-Mode Techniques

CHAPTER 15

80386 Protected Mode

The 80386 and 80486 give PCs the power to support modern applications and operating systems. The 386 rectifies the deficiencies of the 8086—little or no support for memory protection, virtual memory, multitasking, or memory above 640 Kbytes—while remaining compatible with the 8086 (and with the 286). For our purposes, the 386 and 486 chips are identical. The discussion of 386 features in this chapter applies to the 486 as well.

The 8086 only runs in one mode. When Intel engineers designed the 286, they wanted to support extra features that would be incompatible with the 8086. They also wanted to maintain 8086 compatibility. To satisfy these requirements, the 286 uses two modes. Real mode, the default, makes the chip act like an 8086 with only minor enhancements. The differences appear in protected mode. Most programs designed to run on an 8086 won't run under protected mode without changes. DOS is one of these programs.

The 386 supports even more modes because it has more functions. Once again, the default is real mode. Like the 286, the 386 can operate in protected mode. Most 286 protected-mode programs can run under the 386's protected mode. However, the latter is vastly different internally. Protected mode on the 386 offers the programmer better protection and more memory than on the 286.

The 386 also supports a third mode, virtual 8086 (V86). In V86 mode, the 386 operates in protected mode but allows some of the programs it is running to use a simulated real-mode environment. That means programs like DOS can coexist with protected-mode programs.

The Benefits

All the 386's special features become available in the processor's protected mode. Let's take a brief look at the extra power this mode provides.

Access to 4 gigabytes of memory—This is the most obvious difference between protected mode and real mode. Protected-mode programs can use up to 4 Gbytes of memory for data, code, or stack space. If you're willing to gamble on undocumented features, real-mode programs can access the memory above 1 Mbyte for data storage (see Chapter 18). However, using these techniques for code and stack space is generally impractical. Of course, you probably don't have 4 Gbytes of memory in your PC. That brings us to the next feature.

Virtual memory—The memory management unit (MMU) on the 386 supports virtual memory, which makes a program think it has 4 Gbytes of memory when it has less (usually much less). The 386 and special operating system software simulate the extra memory using a mass storage device (like a hard disk drive). Of course, to have 4 Gbytes of virtual memory you need about 4 Gbytes of disk storage, but that's another problem.

Address translation—The MMU also allows addresses to be translated, or mapped, before use. For example, you might want to translate all references to a 4-Kbyte block at segment B800H (the CGA text buffer) to a data buffer in your program. Later, your program could copy the buffer to the screen. This is useful when redirecting the output of a program that writes directly to the screen. Translation can also simulate expanded memory without an expanded memory board.

Programs work with logical addresses. The 386 converts these addresses into 32-bit linear (nonsegmented) addresses. The MMU then converts linear addresses to physical addresses. If the MMU isn't active, linear and physical addresses are equivalent. Applying this terminology to real mode, the address B800:0010 is a logical address. Its equivalent linear address is B8010H. Since real mode doesn't use the MMU, the physical address is the same as the linear address.

80386 PROTECTED MODE

Improved segmentation—In real mode, all segments are 64 Kbytes long and are in fixed locations. In protected mode, segments can be as short as one byte or as long as 4 Gbytes. Attempting to access memory past the end of a segment will cause an error. Segments may start at any location. In addition, the programmer determines each segment's intended use, which the 386 enforces. That is, if a program attempts to write data into a segment meant for code, the 386 will force an error. You also can define a segment that covers the entire address range (4 Gbytes) and effectively dispense with segments altogether. All memory references are then via 32-bit nonsegmented pointers. These flat pointers correspond directly to linear addresses.

Memory protection—The 386 allows memory to be protected. For example, a user's program may not be able to write over operating system data. This, combined with the checks on segments (described above), protects programs against bugs that would crash the computer.

Process protection—In a similar fashion to memory protection, different programs (or parts of a program) can be protected from each other. One program might not have access to another's data, while the operating system might have access to everyone's data. Conversely, user programs may have only limited access to the operating system's data.

32-bit registers—All general-purpose registers on the 386 are 32 bits wide. Except for the *E* prefix (for example, EAX instead of AX), these registers have the same names as in the 8086. Two new segment registers (FS and GS) are also available; they are accessible from all modes but are most useful in protected-mode programs.

Improved addressing modes—In real mode, programmers can only form addresses with constant values, the BX or BP register, and the SI or DI register. In protected mode programs, any register can form addresses. An index can include a scale factor of two, four, or eight. This allows you to write instructions like

```
MOV EBX, [EDI][EAX*8]+2
```

601

Multitasking support—The 386 has special provisions to save the current processor state and switch to a new task (known as a *context switch*). A single instruction can switch contexts rapidly. This has important ramifications for operating systems and real-time processing.

Hardware debugging—The 386 has special hardware for implementing single-step code and data breakpoints. This hardware is available in real mode with some special techniques.

Don't worry if some of these features don't make sense yet. The following sections will cover 386 protected-mode operation in greater detail.

Privileged Segments

Segment Selectors. Understanding segments is the key to understanding protected mode. Protected-mode segments have little in common with real-mode segments. A protected-mode segment register holds a 16-bit segment selector (see Figure 15-1). Unlike real mode, the selector has nothing to do with the segment's location in memory; it is an index into a table of segment descriptors. Each descriptor defines one segment and determines where the segment resides, the segment type, and other important parameters.

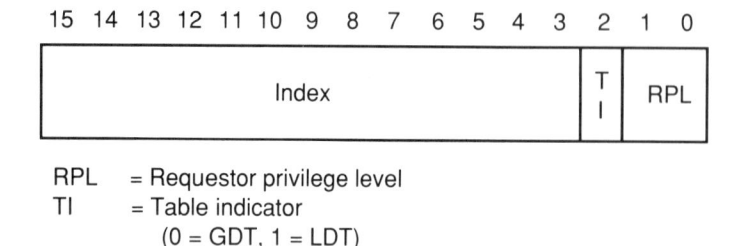

```
15 14 13 12 11 10 9  8  7  6  5  4  3   2   1  0
┌─────────────────────────────────────┬───┬──────┐
│              Index                  │ T │ RPL  │
│                                     │ I │      │
└─────────────────────────────────────┴───┴──────┘
```

RPL   = Requestor privilege level
TI   = Table indicator
        (0 = GDT, 1 = LDT)
Index = Index into table

Figure 15-1. Protected-mode segment selector.

Notice in Figure 15-1 that the selector contains three fields. The two lowest bits (RPL, for requestor privilege level, in the figure) pertain to the 386's protection mechanism, which we will cover shortly. The next bit, TI, determines which table

80386 PROTECTED MODE

of descriptors defines the segment. There are three segment descriptor tables: the global descriptor table (GDT), the local descriptor table (LDT), and the interrupt descriptor table (IDT). Segment selectors never refer to the IDT. If TI is zero, the segment's definition is in the GDT. If it is one, the LDT contains the definition.

The Tables. Each descriptor table can hold up to 8,192 descriptors. The INDEX bits (bits 15 through 3) in the selector determine which descriptor to use.

The GDTR and IDTR registers determine the location of the GDT and IDT, respectively. Each contains a 32-bit address and a 16-bit limit (for a total of 48 bits). The limit is one less than the length of the table in bytes. The address is linear rather than a segment-offset pair. Each table can contain up to 64 Kbytes, or 8,192 descriptors.

The GDT, as its name implies, is global; even when the 386 is multitasking, all tasks share the GDT. This is also true of the IDT—each task uses the same one. If one task changes the GDT or IDT, all tasks are affected.

The LDTR determines the location of the LDT. Unlike the GDT, each task usually has its own LDT. Unlike the GDTR, the LDTR does not contain a 48-bit address and limit. Instead, it holds a segment selector that must point to a special entry in the GDT. This GDT entry points to the LDT. Of course, the GDT can contain pointers to many LDTs.

The IDT is analogous to the real-mode interrupt vector table. Each descriptor defines the response to one of the 256 possible interrupts. Even though the IDT can contain up to 8,192 descriptors, any more than 256 is a waste.

Figure 15-2 shows the logical format of a basic descriptor table entry. Figures 15-3 through 15-8 show the layout of the possible 386 descriptors. Many special descriptors don't define segments; for example, Figure 15-4 shows the descriptor that defines LDTs. We will cover other special descriptors as we need them.

DOS 5: A DEVELOPER'S GUIDE

```
Present flag              - Indicates if segment is present or absent
Base address              - Beginning of segment (32-bit linear address)
Limit                     - Maximum (or minimum) legal offset
Type                      - Type of segment (code, data, etc.)
Descriptor privilege level - Segment's protection level
Miscellaneous             - Varies depending on descriptor type
```

Figure 15-2. Basic descriptor fields.

63 62 61 60 59 58 57 56	55 54 53 52 51 50 49 48	47 46 45 44	43 42 41 40	39 38 37 36 35 34 33 32
Base Address (Bits 31-24)	G D X U / Limit (Bits 19-16)	P / DPL	Type / A	Base Address (Bits 23-16)

31 30 29 28 27 26 25 24 23 22 21 20 19 18 17 16	15 14 13 12 11 10 9 8 7 6 5 4 3 2 1 0
Base Address (Bits 15-0)	Limit (Bits 15-0)

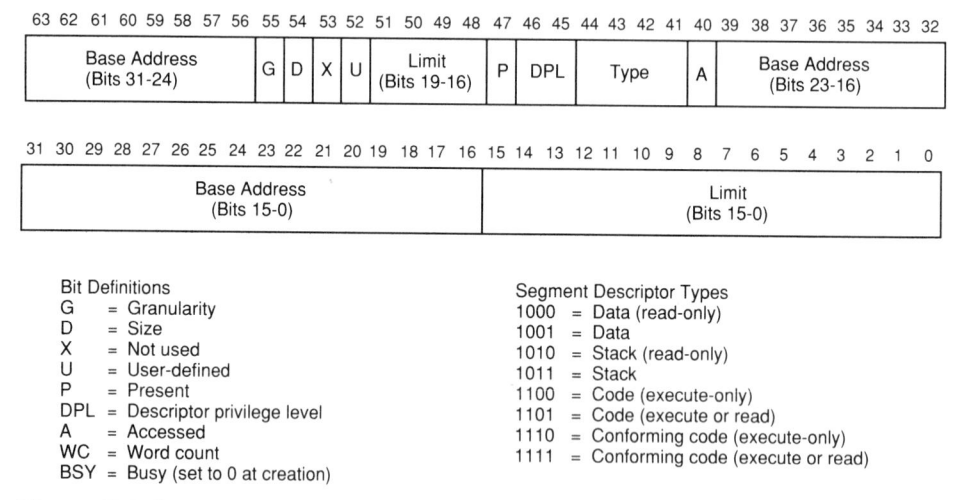

```
Bit Definitions                          Segment Descriptor Types
G   = Granularity                        1000 = Data (read-only)
D   = Size                               1001 = Data
X   = Not used                           1010 = Stack (read-only)
U   = User-defined                       1011 = Stack
P   = Present                            1100 = Code (execute-only)
DPL = Descriptor privilege level         1101 = Code (execute or read)
A   = Accessed                           1110 = Conforming code (execute-only)
WC  = Word count                         1111 = Conforming code (execute or read)
BSY = Busy (set to 0 at creation)
```

Figure 15-3. Code and data descriptors.

63 62 61 60 59 58 57 56	55 54 53 52 51 50 49 48	47 46 45 44 43 42 41 40	39 38 37 36 35 34 33 32
Base Address (Bits 31-24)	0 0 0 0 / Limit* (Bits 19-16)	P / 0 0 0 0 0 1 0	Base Address (Bits 23-16)

31 30 29 28 27 26 25 24 23 22 21 20 19 18 17 16	15 14 13 12 11 10 9 8 7 6 5 4 3 2 1 0
Base Address (Bits 15-0)	Limit (Bits 15-0)

* Not used; LDT can't be >64 Kbytes

Figure 15-4. LDT descriptor.

80386 PROTECTED MODE

63 62 61 60 59 58 57 56	55	54	53	52	51 50 49 48	47	46 45 44	43 42 41 40	39 38 37 36 35 34 33 32
Base Address (Bits 31-24)	G	D	X	U	Limit (Bits 19-16)	P	DPL	0 1 0 BSY 1	Base Address (Bits 23-16)

31 30 29 28 27 26 25 24 23 22 21 20 19 18 17 16	15 14 13 12 11 10 9 8 7 6 5 4 3 2 1 0
Base Address (Bits 15-0)	Limit (Bits 15-0)

Figure 15-5. TSS descriptor.

63 62 61 60 59 58 57 56 55 54 53 52 51 50 49 48	47	46 45 44	43 42 41 40 39 38 37 36 35 34 33 32
User-Defined	P	DPL	0 0 1 0 1 User-Defined

31 30 29 28 27 26 25 24 23 22 21 20 19 18 17 16	15 14 13 12 11 10 9 8 7 6 5 4 3 2 1 0
TSS Selector	User-Defined

Figure 15-6. Task gate.

63 62 61 60 59 58 57 56 55 54 53 52 51 50 49 48	47	46 45 44	43 42 41 40 39 38 37 36 35 34 33 32
Destination Offset (Bits 31-16)	P	DPL	0 1 1 0 0 0 0 0 WC

31 30 29 28 27 26 25 24 23 22 21 20 19 18 17 16	15 14 13 12 11 10 9 8 7 6 5 4 3 2 1 0
Destination Selector	Destination Offset (Bits 15-0)

Figure 15-7. Call gate.

63 62 61 60 59 58 57 56 55 54 53 52 51 50 49 48	47	46 45 44	43 42 41 40 39 38 37 36 35 34 33 32
Destination Offset (Bits 31-16)	P	DPL	0 1 1 1 ** Reserved

31 30 29 28 27 26 25 24 23 22 21 20 19 18 17 16	15 14 13 12 11 10 9 8 7 6 5 4 3 2 1 0
Destination Selector	Destination Offset (Bits 15-0)

**0 = Interrupt gate
1 = Trap gate

Figure 15-8. Trap and interrupt gates.

Two fields in the descriptor are particularly interesting. The P bit (bit 47) determines whether the segment is present. An operating system can clear this bit to create a virtual segment. When a program tries to use a virtual segment, the 386 generates an error. The operating system can then load the segment from disk and try again. When P is clear, bits 0 through 39 and 48 through 63 can contain any values. The operating system could store a disk address here, for example. With any luck, you won't need to swap 1-Gbyte segments in and out too often. Fortunately, the 386 provides a better way to create virtual memory.

The other interesting field is the A bit (bit 40). The 386 sets this bit when any program writes to the segment. Our crude virtual memory system might use this bit to decide whether it should write a segment to disk before marking it absent and reusing its space.

You may wonder how a descriptor can specify a segment from one byte to 4 Gbytes long. After all, the limit field length is only 20 bits. This is where the G bit (bit 55) comes into play. If G is zero, the limit field corresponds to the segment's maximum legal offset (one less than its length). If G is one, however, the 386 shifts the limit field left 13 places to make a 32-bit limit. The 386 fills the bottom 12 bits with ones. If a descriptor has a limit field of one and G is one, the actual limit is 1FFFH. Curiously, when G is one and the limit field is zero, the limit is FFFH.

This scheme allows us to specify a segment with a length of less than 1 Mbyte or a multiple of 4 Kbytes. When G is zero, the segment can range from one byte to 1 Mbyte long. When G is one, the segment can range from 4 Kbytes to 4 Gbytes in length (in 4-Kbyte steps).

Nothing prevents the creation of two descriptors that point to the same area of memory. An operating system, for example, might load a file into a data segment and jump to a code segment that starts in the same place. As mentioned earlier, this process is known as *aliasing*. The operating system must have some way of creating

80386 PROTECTED MODE

the GDT and other tables. Therefore, it will usually have a data-segment alias to the GDT. Some systems set up a data segment that covers all 4 Gbytes of memory. Tables can then be written directly with that data segment. Operating systems rarely allow user programs to access the GDT, IDT, and other system tables directly.

The processor reserves the first slot of the GDT. The selector for this slot is the null selector, and using it always causes an error. The null selector's descriptor should be all zeros.

Don't worry if you don't understand all the bits in the descriptor yet; things will clear up as we learn more about protected mode's privilege mechanisms.

Protected-Mode Privilege. Protected mode gets its name from the 386's privilege protection. Each program has a privilege level, or PL, from zero to three. Programs at PL 0 can execute any instruction and access any data. Programs at PL 3 can't execute certain instructions; they also can't access data that belongs to more privileged programs. Each segment descriptor has a descriptor privilege level (DPL) that the 386 uses for protection. The 386 also controls which programs can execute I/O instructions.

A privilege hierarchy is important for supporting modern operating systems. In a typical operating system, the main kernel runs at PL 0. Other parts of the operating system might run at PL 1. Device drivers can run at PL 2; they need to do direct device I/O. User programs in this system would run at PL 3. This scheme has many advantages. In particular, a wild (or malicious) program can't damage the operating system or other user programs.

The hierarchy is often represented as concentric rings (the so-called onion model; see Figure 15-9). It's not uncommon to hear privilege levels called *rings* (as in *ring 3*).

DOS 5: A DEVELOPER'S GUIDE

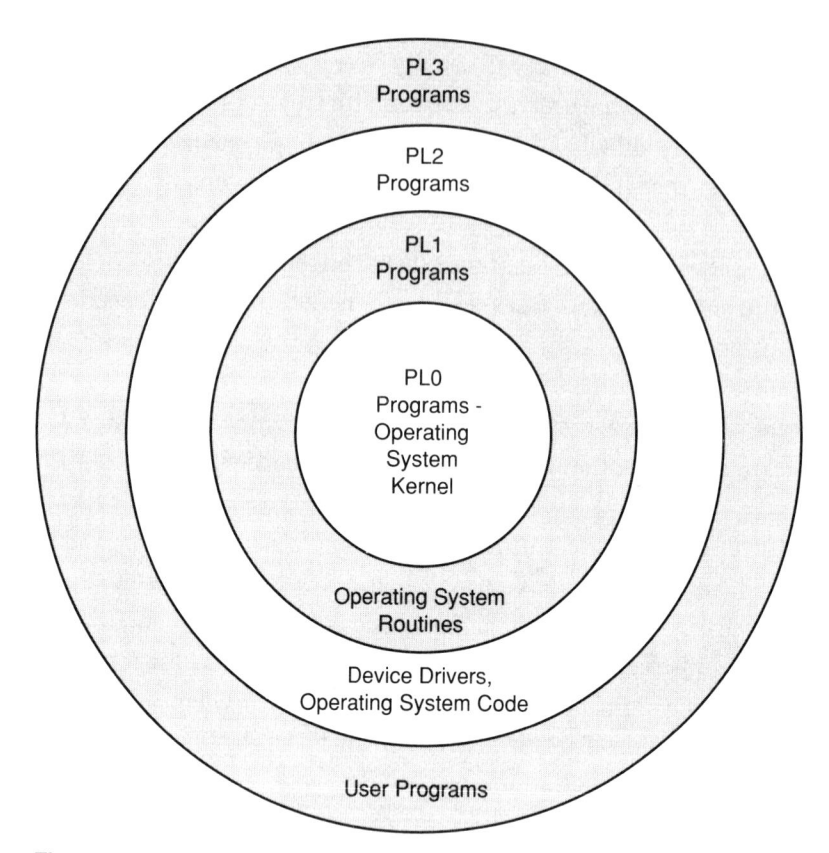

Figure 15-9. The onion model.

PL 0 programs can only execute the following instructions:

- *HLT*
- *CLTS*
- *LGDT*
- *LIDT*
- *LLDT*
- *LTR*
- *LMSW*
- *MOV* (to/from control/debug/test registers).

80386 PROTECTED MODE

If a PL 3 program could, for example, reload *LDTR*, privilege protection would be meaningless. By allowing only PL 0 programs to do this, the operating system designer has complete control over the lower-privilege programs.

In some computer systems, you may not want all programs doing I/O directly. Multitasking systems are a good example. In our hypothetical operating system, only device drivers and the kernel should perform I/O. All user programs request I/O from the kernel.

The IOPL field in the EFLAGS register allows the operating system to control who can do I/O. These two bits determine the minimum privilege level a program must have to execute I/O instructions (*CLI*, *STI*, *IN*, *INS*, *OUT*, and *OUTS*). If IOPL is zero, only PL 0 programs can do I/O. If IOPL is 3, all programs can execute I/O instructions. Only a PL 0 program can modify the IOPL bits. When other programs modify the flags, IOPL doesn't change.

Incidentally, a program's privilege level is equal to the RPL field of the selector in the CS register. This is the current privilege level, or CPL. While you can't directly modify the CS register so that it has a different RPL, you can call higher- or lower-privileged code.

Data Access. Programs can't load a segment register with just any selector. When a data segment register (DS, ES, FS, or GS) is loaded, the 386 checks the DPL against the program's CPL and the selector's RPL. The 386 first compares the CPL to the RPL. The largest one becomes the effective privilege level (EPL). If the DPL is greater than or equal to the EPL, the 386 loads the segment register; otherwise, an error occurs.

The stack segment is a little different. The SS register must be loaded with a segment whose DPL is equal to the program's CPL. The 386 also checks to make sure a stack segment is readable, writable, and present.

The 386 provides a special stack segment type. You can also use a plain data segment for a stack, if you wish. The advantage of stack segments is that they start at the top and work down. A stack segment's limit field indicates the lowest legal offset in the segment. In a 16-bit stack segment, G must be set to zero; a 32-bit stack segment must have G set to one. Therefore, a 16-bit stack segment starts at FFFFH, and a 32-bit stack starts at FFFFFFFFH and continues down to its limit. This is useful when you need to expand a stack segment. By changing the limit, you can make the segment grow down.

It's always legal to load a null selector (00H through 03H) into a segment register. However, any attempt to access memory via this selector will cause an error.

Privilege Level for Code Segments. Most often, the CS register changes when a jump, call, or return instruction executes. Like the other segment registers, CS can only contain certain selectors. A code segment must be present and executable. In addition, the DPL of the segment must equal the CPL.

One type of code segment relaxes this restriction somewhat. A conforming code segment executes with the CPL of the program that called it (or jumped to it). Such a segment still has a DPL—it just doesn't become the CPL. However, the DPL of a conforming code segment must be less than or equal to the CPL of the calling program. You can't transfer control to a less privileged conforming code segment. If you did, it would cause a dilemma when the less privileged code tried to return.

If you can't jump to or call a code segment with a different privilege, how does privilege change? Several mechanisms are available: The CPL can change involuntarily when an internal or external interrupt occurs (interrupt handling is discussed later in this chapter); switching to a new task can also change the CPL, as can a special segment descriptor known as a *call gate*. Since tasking plays a big part in CPL changes, we'll return to the subject of code privilege after we learn more about multitasking.

80386 PROTECTED MODE

Multitasking

The 386 uses task state segments (TSSs) to assist multitasking, handle interrupts, and implement coroutines. A TSS descriptor (Figure 15-5) points to a buffer in memory (Figure 15-10). This buffer must be at least 104 bytes long. User programs cannot access this buffer with the TSS selector; the 386 uses the TSS selector internally. When the operating system fills in a TSS, it must use a data segment (either an alias or one that allows it to access all memory). TSS selectors always appear in the GDT, never in the LDT or IDT.

Most of the fields in the TSS contain a task's registers. Of course, the registers are only valid when the task isn't running. Before a new task takes over, the 386 updates many of the fields in the TSS (the shaded fields in Figure 15-10). The operating system is responsible for filling in the other fields. The 386 then reads the entire new TSS.

Notice the slots for stack segments and pointers for PL 0, PL 1, and PL 2 near the top of the TSS. A program must maintain separate stacks for each privilege ring it may use. The processor uses these stacks when the CPL changes, as we will see shortly.

Far call and jump instructions can reference TSSs. The processor will save the current task (whose TSS selector is in the TR register) and load the new one. The offset of the call or jump is unimportant. As always, the EPL must be less than or equal to the TSS's DPL.

You also can start a task with a task gate (Figure 15-6). The gate's DPL must be greater than or equal to the EPL. Jumping to or calling a task gate is the same as jumping to or calling the TSS. Task gates are useful because, unlike the TSS, they can appear in the LDT or the IDT.

DOS 5: A DEVELOPER'S GUIDE

Offset	31 15	0
0	X	Back Link
4	PL 0 ESP	
8	X	PL 0 SS
12	PL 1 ESP	
16	X	PL 1 SS
20	PL 2 ESP	
24	X	PL 2 SS
28	CR3	
32	EIP	
36	EFLAGS	
40	EAX	
44	ECX	
48	EDX	
52	EBX	
56	ESP	
60	EBP	
64	ESI	
68	EDI	
72	X	ES
76	X	CS
80	X	SS
84	X	DS
88	X	FS
92	X	GS
96	X	LDT
100	Pointer to I/O Bit Map	X	T Flag

Figure 15-10. Task state segments.

80386 PROTECTED MODE

A new task can return to an old task with an *IRET* instruction. When calling a task, the 386 stores the old task's TSS selector in the new TSS's back-link field. Also, the NT bit in EFLAGS is set. When an *IRET* detects NT, it does a task switch to the TSS in the current task's back-link field. The same steps occur when a task executes as a result of an exception or interrupt.

Note that TSSs aren't reentrant. If a task called itself or a task that called it, the results would be disastrous. To prevent this, the 386 sets bit 41 (the BUSY bit) in the TSS descriptor whenever the task is executing. If a jump to a new task occurs, it clears that bit. Calling a task doesn't reset the old task's BUSY bit. Of course, it does set that bit in the new TSS. When the called task returns, its BUSY bit will clear. The 386 will refuse to execute a TSS with its BUSY bit set.

Another important point: If a task returns via an *IRET*, it resumes execution immediately following that instruction. Tasks often look like this:

```
TASK1:     ; whatever operation the task does
   .
   .
   .
   IRET
   JMP TASK1
```

It's not uncommon to find TSSs larger than 104 bytes. The extra space can hold information specific to the operating system. The working directory might go in the TSS. Coprocessor state information is also important if multiple tasks use the coprocessor.

Another common use for extra space in the TSS is the I/O bit map. The field at offset 66H in the TSS contains a pointer to the optional I/O bit map. Since the 16-bit field is relative to the start of the TSS, the bit map must be nearby. Multiple TSSs can share a bit map if they are close enough.

Each bit in the I/O bit map corresponds to an I/O port. If a task tries to do I/O, the processor checks the task's CPL against the IOPL. If the CPL is less than or equal to the IOPL, all is well; if not, the 386 checks the I/O bit map. If the bit corresponding to the port used by the I/O instruction is zero, the 386 allows the access. If it is set or the I/O bit map is not present, the processor denies access.

A full bit map is 8 Kbytes long, but it can be shorter. The processor considers any entries past the end to be ones. The bit map should always end with FFH.

Code Segments Revisited

Now that we know about the TSS, we can return to the subject of CPL changes. When a TSS loads, the CPL can change to any value. A TSS (or task gate) is usable as long as its DPL is greater than or equal to the calling program's EPL.

If a TSS has a DPL of three, any task—including a PL 3 task—can jump to it (even if it points to a PL 0 task). This isn't a protection problem because the old task can't affect the new task; the old task resumes exactly where it left off and with the same registers as when it stopped.

Switching to a new task is a drastic way of changing the CPL. Suppose we need to call an operating system function from a PL 3 program. Because the operating system runs at PL 0, the CPL will change. Switching tasks isn't suitable here; it makes it difficult for the user program to send the operating system function parameters or receive return values.

Call gates (Figure 15-7) are the best way to handle function calls to a different CPL. Each call gate, which is a special segment descriptor, defines an entry point to a function. A far call instruction activates a call gate. When the 386 detects a call to a call gate, it verifies that the gate is accessible. It does that by computing the EPL (the larger of the RPL and the CPL). If the EPL is less than or equal to the gate's DPL, the gate is accessible. In all cases, the new segment's DPL must be less than or equal to the current CPL value.

If the gate is accessible, the 386 discards the offset supplied with the call. Instead, execution transfers to the location specified by the segment and offset in the call gate. This way, the call gate, not the user program, decides what code to execute.

Of course, if a call gate doesn't change the CPL, it works like a far call. If the CPL does change, the 386 consults the TSS. Recall that the TSS has three fields for PL 0, PL 1, and PL 2 stacks. The 386 loads the stack pointer and segment from the appropriate fields, then pushes the old pointer and segment on the new stack.

Some functions require arguments on the stack. This is when the call gate's WC field comes into play. The 386 copies the indicated number of parameters from the old stack to the new stack. A 16-bit call gate copies 16-bit words, and a 32-bit call gate copies 32-bit words. The parameters appear after the old stack pointer but before the return address on the stack.

When a program calls a subroutine via a call gate, the routine eventually returns. If the CPL changed, the 386 reverses the above steps to restore it. If WC is not zero, the subroutine must use a return that removes the parameters (such as *RETF 8*). The 386 removes the parameters from both stacks. As a security measure, it also clears any segment registers containing selectors that the subroutine used but that the calling program can't use.

Exceptions

The IDT can contain up to 256 trap, interrupt, or task gates. Each gate specifies how to handle exceptions (interrupts). External events can cause interrupts; so can internal events. External interrupts in a 386-based PC are similar to those of any PC. However, the 386 can generate many internal interrupts based on a variety of error conditions.

The 386 divides internal interrupts into three classes: faults, traps, and aborts. A fault occurs when the 386 detects a correctable error. For instance, an attempt to load a nonexistent segment is a fault. The operating system can load the segment, mark it as present, and restart the operation.

Traps occur for software interrupts (the *INT* and *INTO* instructions) and some debugging interrupts. The system cannot restart traps.

Aborts are serious errors that are likely to result in program termination. An abort indicates that something is very wrong with a program or perhaps with the operating system itself.

Table 15-1 lists the internal exceptions for the 386. The debug interrupt (INT 1) is sometimes a trap and sometimes a fault. (Chapter 17 covers hardware debugging in more detail.) Some exceptions push an error code on the stack. Except for exception 0EH (which occurs for page faults), the error code is the selector that caused the error. If the code is zero, the null selector caused the error or the 386 could not determine which selector caused the error. Exception 0EH has a special error code.

Name	INT#	Type	Error Code	Possible Causes
Divide error	0	FAULT	No	DIV or IDIV
Debug	1	N/A	No	Debug condition
Breakpoint	3	TRAP	No	INT 3
Overflow	4	TRAP	No	INTO
Bounds check	5	FAULT	No	BOUND
Bad opcode	6	FAULT	No	Illegal instruction
No 80X87	7	FAULT	No	ESC, WAIT with no coprocessor, or when coprocessor was last used by another task
Double fault	8	ABORT	Yes (always 0)	Any instruction that can generate an exception
NPX overrun	9	ABORT	No	Any operand of an ESC that wraps around the end of a segment
Invalid TSS	10	FAULT	Yes	JMP, CALL, IRET, or interrupt
No segment	11	FAULT	Yes	Any reference to a not-present segment
Stack error	12	FAULT	Yes	Any reference with SS register
Gen'l protect	13	FAULT	Yes	Any memory references including code fetches
Page fault	14	FAULT	Yes	Any memory references including code fetches
NPX error	16	FAULT	No	ESC WAIT

Table 15-1. Protected-mode exceptions.

80386 PROTECTED MODE

Trap and interrupt gates (Figure 15-8) are conceptually similar to call gates. Of course, they don't have a WC field. Although trap and interrupt gates have a DPL, you should almost always set them to three, especially if the gate handles hardware interrupts or internal errors. If an interrupt occurs while the CPU is executing PL 3 code and the gate has a different DPL, the processor will be unable to handle the interrupt.

These gates are identical except for their handling of the IF flag. When control passes through an interrupt gate, the 386 clears the IF flag. This disables hardware interrupts (except for NMI), just as the 8086 does when it processes an interrupt. Trap gates don't modify IF. The type of gate you need depends on the type of interrupt you're handling.

Interrupts can also initiate a task switch via a task gate. This is especially useful for hardware interrupts. On the 8086, for example, a clock interrupt handler has to save all the registers it will use and restore them when done. With a task gate, the 386 saves everything before starting the interrupt handler. When you handle interrupts with task gates, remember that tasks are not reentrant. If a second interrupt of the same type occurs while the task is still running, a general protection fault will occur.

Exception 0DH is the general protection fault. The 386 generates it as a catchall exception. This fault is probably the most common one 386 programmers encounter. While the other exceptions result from a well-defined class of errors, this fault can mean most anything. Some of the possible causes are:

- Trying to access a segment with an offset greater than the segment's limit
- Loading CS with a nonexecutable segment
- Loading a segment register (except CS) with an execute-only segment
- Writing to a read-only segment
- Using the null selector
- Switching to a busy task.

617

Memory Management

The 386 MMU supports at least three programming techniques: virtual memory, page protection, and address translation.

Some of the MMU functions partially duplicate the functions segmentation provides. To activate the MMU, a PL 0 program must set bit 31 of CR0. Only PL 0 programs can activate and set up the MMU. Allowing other programs to manipulate the MMU would undermine the privilege protection scheme. Ordinary programs never know the MMU exists.

The MMU deals with memory in 4-Kbyte pages. For each page, the MMU tracks three basic pieces of information: whether or not the page is present, its access level, and its physical address.

Virtual memory systems can use the MMU's present bit much like a segment's present bit. If a page isn't present, the 386 generates an error. The operating system can load the page from disk. This is much more efficient than using the segment's present bit. After all, a page is 4 Kbytes long; a segment might be 4 Gbytes long.

Page Access. The access level protects each page from unauthorized access. A page can be marked as a system or user page. Any program can access a user page, but PL 3 programs can't access a system page. Even if a page is marked as user, the MMU can prevent PL 3 programs from writing to it.

It's important to understand that this protection is over and above that provided by segmentation. Programs form linear addresses by specifying a segment and an offset. The 386 adds the base address of the segment to the offset to generate a linear address. Programs can only generate linear addresses in certain ranges based on their access to segments.

The MMU can also designate 4-Mbyte blocks as user or system blocks or make them read-only to PL 3 programs, for reasons that will soon become obvious.

80386 PROTECTED MODE

Address Translation. The MMU uses two types of tables to translate addresses. The page directory contains pointers to page tables (see Figures 15-11 and 15-12). Each table has exactly 1,024 entries (4 Kbytes). Each page directory entry (PDE) corresponds to 4 Mbytes of contiguous memory; each page table entry (PTE) corresponds to a 4-Kbyte page. To translate a linear address, the 386 splits it into three fields. The first field (bits 31 through 22) selects one of the 1,024 PDEs. The PDE points to a page table (via a physical address). The second field (bits 21 through 12) selects one of the 1,024 PTEs in the selected page table. The physical address's lower 12 bits are from the third field (bits 11 through 0 of the linear address). The top bits come from the selected PTE.

```
31 30 29 28 27 26 25 24 23 22 21 20 19 18 17 16 15 14 13 12 11 10 9  8  7  6  5  4  3  2  1  0
```

| Page Table's Physical Address | User-Defined | X | A | X | U/S | R/W | P* |

Bit Definitions
X   = Not used
A   = Accessed
U/S = User (1) or system (0)
R/W = 1 if page is writable
P   = Present

* If P = 0 then all other bits are user-defined.

Figure 15-11. Page directory entry.

```
31 30 29 28 27 26 25 24 23 22 21 20 19 18 17 16 15 14 13 12 11 10 9  8  7  6  5  4  3  2  1  0
```

| Top 20 Bits of 4K Page's Physical Address | User-Defined | X | D | A | X | U/S | R/W | P* |

Bit Definitions
X   = Not used
A   = Accessed
U/S = User (1) or system (0)
R/W = 1 if page is writable
P   = Present
D   = Dirty

* If P = 0 then all other bits are user-defined.

Figure 15-12. Page table entry.

The CR3 register, the page directory base register (PDBR), selects the page directory in use. Since the directory holds 1,024 entries and each entry corresponds to 4 Mbytes, the directory covers the entire 4-Gbyte address range. Notice that each task has its own CR3 register in its TSS (see Figure 15-10). CR3 contains a physical address.

Each PDE has a set of protection bits. If its system bit is zero, the entire 4-Mbyte range is inaccessible to PL 3 programs. The PDE's R/W bit also affects the 4-Mbyte range. The MMU ignores the PTE bits if the PDE protects the pages. Similarly, if a PDE's present bit is zero, the 386 generates a fault and doesn't attempt to read the page table.

For performance reasons, the 386 can't read tables each time it references an address. It caches PDEs and PTEs as it uses them. If you change the PDE or PTE, you must change CR3. When CR3 changes, the 386 invalidates its cache. Of course, the 386 won't know if you write to CR3 with the same value. You can use the following code:

```
MOV EAX,CR3
MOV CR3,EAX
```

One other caution: Never change the mapping tables that affect the page containing the currently executing code. The 386 prefetches instructions, so the results might surprise you.

Page Faults. The MMU generates exception 0EH when a page fault occurs. Any of the following conditions can cause a page fault:

- The PTE's present bit is clear.
- The PDE's present bit is clear.
- A PL 3 task tried to write to a read-only page.
- A PL 3 task tried to access a system page.

The error code on the stack (Figure 15-13) can differentiate between these cases. In addition, the CR2 register will contain the linear address that caused the fault.

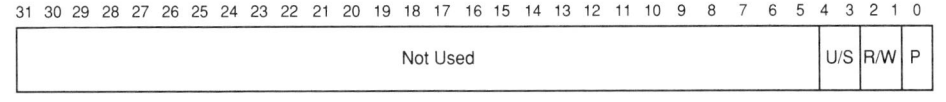

80386 PROTECTED MODE

```
31 30 29 28 27 26 25 24 23 22 21 20 19 18 17 16 15 14 13 12 11 10 9 8 7 6 5 4 3 2 1 0
```

Not Used	U/S	R/W	P

Bit Definitions
U/S = Set if fault occurred in PL 3 code
R/W = Set if fault occurred on write
P   = Set if fault was due to missing PTE or page

Figure 15-13. Page fault error code.

Protection violations are easy to handle—most operating systems simply terminate the offender. An absent PTE is also simple—just swap the page in from disk and update the PTE.

At first glance, an absent PDE may not seem useful. Consider an operating system that allows each task a virtual memory space of 4 Gbytes. The MMU tables for each task will require more than 4 Mbytes of storage, making MMU operations prohibitive for most computers. However, tasks don't normally use the entire 4 Gbytes of space, and certainly none use it all at once.

A task can start out with a 4-Kbyte page directory. When it accesses a page, the operating system can create the corresponding page table. If the task uses many page tables, they can be swapped to and from disk by manipulating the present bits in the page directory. When the present bit is zero, all other bits in the PTE or PDE are user-defined. This allows the operating system to store data about the absent page table or page (for example, a disk address).

Living in the Past: Real and V86 Modes

In real mode (the default) and V86 mode, the 386 operates like an 8086. Real-mode programs have access to almost all the 386's instructions. (The exceptions are *ARPL*, *LAR*, *LLDT*, *LSL*, *LTR*, *SLDT*, *STR*, *VERR*, and *VERW*.) The MMU doesn't work in real mode, and the processor acts like a very fast 8086 with extra (and larger) registers.

V86 mode applies to individual tasks. A protected-mode task is a V86 task if the VM bit in the EFLAGS register is set. Usually, an operating system sets this bit in the task's TSS before starting it. V86 tasks can peacefully coexist with normal protected-mode tasks.

A V86 task acts like an 8086 in most respects. It can access 1 Mbyte of memory, and the segmentation scheme is exactly like the 8086's. V86 tasks don't use the GDT or LDT. However, to protect other tasks, the processor won't allow a V86 task to execute certain instructions. That task can't execute the following instructions:

- *ARPL*
- *CLTS*
- *HLT*
- *LAR*
- *LGDT*
- *LIDT*
- *LLDT*
- *LMSW*
- *LSL*
- *LTR*
- *MOV* (to/from control/debug/test registers)
- *SLDT*
- *STR*
- *VERR*
- *VERW*

V86 tasks always run at PL 3. They can only access I/O ports if the I/O bit map in their TSS allows it. IOPL is irrelevant. Instead, the IOPL bits in EFLAGS protect certain potentially critical instructions: *CLI*, *INT* (not including *INT 3* and *INTO*), *IRET*, *LOCK*, *POPF*, *PUSHF*, and *STI*. If IOPL is 3, the V86 task can execute these instructions; if not, the instructions cause a general protect fault (exception 0DH).

A V86 task completely subverts the normal privilege mechanism. It can write to the first megabyte of memory with no restrictions from the protected-mode segmentation hardware. Fortunately, the MMU is still operative for a V86 task. This allows the operating system to protect pages by making them system or read-only. Better still, what the task thinks is the first megabyte of memory can be remapped by the MMU. Without the MMU, only one V86 task could run at a time—multiple tasks would vie for the first megabyte of memory. With the MMU, each V86 task can generate linear addresses that translate to different physical addresses.

80386 PROTECTED MODE

Handling Interrupts in V86 Mode

Once the CPU enters protected mode, all interrupt processing occurs in protected mode, even if the current task is in V86 mode. The CPU will switch to protected mode and to the PL 0 stack in the task's TSS. Trap and interrupt gates that might activate while a V86 task is running must have a DPL of three and must point to a code segment with DPL 0. In addition, the 286-compatible 16-bit trap and interrupt gates won't work with V86-mode programs.

The 386 pushes all the segment registers on the PL 0 stack when it interrupts a V86 task (see Figure 15-14). The segment registers will contain values that are probably illegal in protected mode. Since this is true, the 386 zeros the segment registers before servicing the interrupt.

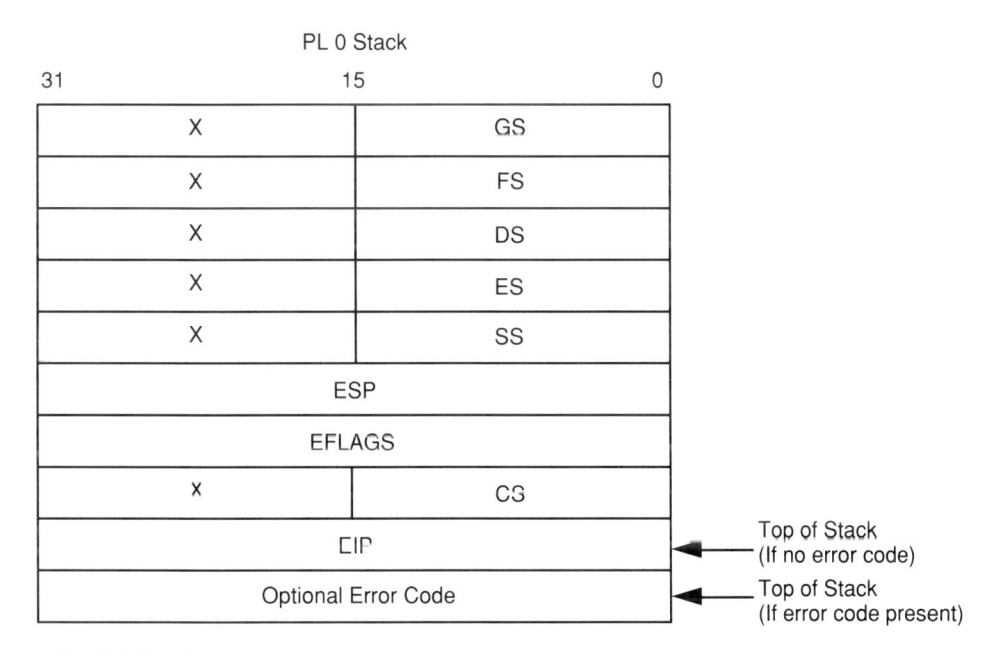

```
                    PL 0 Stack
31                      15                      0
┌───────────────────────┬───────────────────────┐
│           X           │          GS           │
├───────────────────────┼───────────────────────┤
│           X           │          FS           │
├───────────────────────┼───────────────────────┤
│           X           │          DS           │
├───────────────────────┼───────────────────────┤
│           X           │          ES           │
├───────────────────────┼───────────────────────┤
│           X           │          SS           │
├───────────────────────┴───────────────────────┤
│                     ESP                       │
├───────────────────────────────────────────────┤
│                    EFLAGS                     │
├───────────────────────┬───────────────────────┤
│           X           │          CS           │
├───────────────────────┴───────────────────────┤  ◄── Top of Stack
│                     EIP                       │      (If no error code)
├───────────────────────────────────────────────┤  ◄── Top of Stack
│              Optional Error Code              │      (If error code present)
└───────────────────────────────────────────────┘
```

X − Not Used

Figure 15-14. VM86 interrupt stack frame.

When a general protection exception occurs, the handler must see if a V86 task caused it by executing an illegal instruction (like *INT*). If so, the handler must decide whether it wants to emulate the instruction or raise an error. In the case of the *INT* instruction, the handler might call the original DOS interrupt handler (in V86 mode) for the task that caused the general protection exception.

Switching to Protected Mode

When a 386 microprocessor resets, it starts in real mode. This gives the operating system a chance to set up the necessary tables for protected mode. Of course, many PCs just boot up and stay in real mode to run DOS.

In Part I we saw that AT motherboards disable A20 to enhance their compatibility with the 8086. Strictly speaking, enabling A20 isn't part of switching to protected mode. However, 1 Mbyte is an artificial limit in protected mode—all memory is the same. Most of the time, you'll need to enable A20 before entering protected mode.

When the original PC was designed, IBM assigned hardware interrupts to vectors that Intel reserved but that the 8086 did not use. The 386 uses these reserved interrupt vectors extensively in protected mode. Some protected-mode programs don't have to reprogram the PICs to relocate the hardware interrupts, but most do.

Required Tables. As a bare minimum, the GDT must be set up before the system enters protected mode. As a practical matter, you should have the IDT set up before (or soon after) entering protected mode. Setting up the GDT is easy; the IDT requires some work.

In real mode, the IDTR points to the 8086 interrupt vector table. Because real mode is compatible with the 8086, the IDTR is initially zero and the limit is 3FFH. When you load the IDTR, you must disable interrupts (including NMI). You can reload the IDTR just before or just after you switch to protected mode. No matter when you do it, the IDTR will always point to an invalid IDT (or interrupt vector table) at some point. Any interrupts, internal or external, during this time will cause unpredictable results.

80386 PROTECTED MODE

The 386 can't disable NMI, but the motherboard can. In practice, the motherboard only generates a true NMI when a catastrophic error occurs, so you can usually get away with not disabling it.

Very short protected-mode routines that don't use interrupts and can run with interrupts disabled might consider not loading the IDTR. However, any fault that occurs will cause complete disaster, so be careful. If you set the IDTR to all zeros and an interrupt occurs, the processor will shut down.

Of course, you may construct the other tables (LDT, page directories, and so on) in real or protected mode. It's usually easiest to set them in protected mode.

Switching Modes. Once you have set up the GDT (and perhaps the IDT), you're ready to go. Bit 0 of CR0 enables protected mode. Since the 386 prefetches instructions, you should clear the prefetch queue at once. You can do this by executing a jump immediately after the mode switch. Even a jump to the next instruction will work.

When the 386 is reset, it loads the segment descriptor cache with pseudo-descriptors. These descriptors look like 8086 segments and mirror them during execution. When you switch to protected mode, the segments point to the same place as before the switch. A very short protected-mode routine that doesn't enable interrupts might get away with using these pseudosegments. However, you must load protected-mode segments before enabling interrupts. If you generate an exception before the CS register contains a protected-mode segment selector, you won't be able to handle it properly.

Loading the DS, ES, FS, GS, and SS registers is easy. The CS register is set with a far jump, which may very well be to the next instruction.

Setting TR. If you'll be using multitasking or V86 mode, you must set up at least two TSSs. The first can be empty; the second should contain the state you want for your first task. Load TR (using the *LTR* instruction) with the selector for the first TSS, then jump to the second TSS. The 386 saves the current state in the first TSS. You usually don't need this state information; you can reuse the selector and memory area later.

By setting up the new TSS, you can jump to new code, change privilege levels, enable paging, and so on. You can also do all these things later if that's easier.

Enabling Paging. You can enable paging at the same time you switch to protected mode, but it's usually easier to wait. The following steps will enable paging:

1. Create the page directory and as many page tables as you need.
2. Load CR3 with the physical address of the page directory.
3. Set bit 31 in CR0.
4. Clear the prefetch queue with a jump instruction.

The code that turns on paging must not remap its own page. The page that contains the initialization code should map to its own physical address.

Returning to Real Mode. To return to real mode, simply reverse the above steps. Disable paging by clearing bit 31 of CR0, then store a zero in CR3. You must load the segment registers with descriptors that closely approximate real-mode segments. The data segment registers (including SS) should receive selectors for segments with the following characteristics:

Limit=FFFFH
Granularity=0
Type=R/W data
Present=1

80386 PROTECTED MODE

The CS register is then loaded with a similar code segment. In some cases, you'll want to ignore segment register reloading. For instance, the programs in Chapter 18 violate this rule to provide extended addressing for DOS programs.

Be prepared to handle interrupts when you return to real mode. If you used the memory at 0000:0000, you'll have to rebuild the real-mode interrupt vector table. Disable interrupts and reset bit 0 of CR0, and you'll be back in real mode. Once you reset the IDTR (base=00000000, limit=3FFH), you can reenable interrupts.

Protected Mode on a PC

If protected mode is so great, why don't more 386 PCs use it? Actually, it's hard to get a DOS-based PC to do anything useful in protected mode. The primary difficulty is DOS itself; it expects to run in real mode.

As we have seen, the three main problems and their solutions are:

- DOS wants to run in real mode. (Solution: Run DOS in V86 mode.)
- The motherboard disables A20. (Solution: Enable it.)
- DOS and the BIOS use 386 internal interrupts. (Solution: Relocate or emulate them.)

Software that allows programs to run in protected mode and access DOS and BIOS functions is a DOS extender. As we'll discuss later, not all DOS extenders use the same solutions to these problems.

According to the Intel documentation, running 8086 code in V86 mode is straightforward. However, attempts to implement Intel's strategy fail when it comes to the PC's BIOS and DOS. Intel assumes that your 8086 code will always call interrupts with an *INT* instruction, and the interrupt routine will end with an *IRET*. However, this is the exception rather than the rule with the PC's system software.

To run the BIOS and DOS in V86 mode, a DOS extender must provide the 386 with a V86 task. It has to emulate certain instructions, most notably interrupts for the V86 task. It also has to reprogram the hardware interrupt controllers and redirect their interrupts to the proper routines.

A V86 task requires emulation for the *CLI*, *STI*, *LOCK*, *PUSHF*, *POPF*, *INT*, and *IRET* instructions. This is to prevent the V86 task from disrupting other tasks that might be running under protected mode. A DOS extender must provide emulation for any of these instructions that might occur in the BIOS or DOS code programs will use.

In theory, emulating *INT* and *IRET* is straightforward. The execution of one of these instructions in V86 mode will cause a general protection exception (INT 0DH). When you detect an *INT* instruction, simply determine the required interrupt vector address, simulate the interrupt, catch the corresponding *IRET* (which also causes an INT 0DH), and return to the calling program. In practice, the PC BIOS and DOS do not always have a one-to-one correspondence between *INT*s and *IRET*s (a problem we will explore in detail in Chapter 19). Only the normal *INT/IRET* sequence provides the INT 0DH required to emulate these instructions.

Most DOS extenders switch the processor back to real mode for each call to DOS or the BIOS. Other V86 programs (such as EMS memory simulators) let real-mode calls run unprotected, shutting you off from many of the 386's special features and only allowing DOS calls from V86 mode. While these methods are easy to implement, they cause problems for programs that take advantage of the 386's special capabilities (like paging, multitasking, and protection).

While a DOS extender that operates entirely in protected mode is more difficult to create, the benefits are worth the effort. Chapter 19 contains a 386 DOS extender that runs entirely in protected mode.

CHAPTER 16

Using Extended Memory

DOS programs can access extended memory on 286, 386, and 486 PCs. Perhaps the most common example of a program that accesses extended memory is VDISK, IBM's RAM disk driver. A program might use extended memory in two ways. If the program uses it as conventional memory—that is, for program, stack, and data storage—the program must run with a DOS extender. We'll look at DOS extenders in Chapter 19.

Many programs only use extended memory for data storage. VDISK, for example, doesn't require much code. The RAM disk's data is what takes up so much space. Programs that need large data areas can easily access extended memory with a BIOS call. The BIOS call works equally well on 286-based ATs and 386/486 computers; however, it only works with the first 16 Mbytes of memory.

BIOS Calls

Programs use INT 15H, function 88H, to determine the amount of extended memory present. This function returns, in the AX register, the number of 1-Kbyte extended memory blocks available. If AX is zero, either no extended memory exists or it is all being used. A 286 computer will always have 15 Mbytes or less of extended memory. On 386 machines, the maximum reported will be 15 or 64 Mbytes, depending on the BIOS. If you think more memory may be available, you have to write your own code to test for it.

One BIOS function copies blocks of data that lie within the first 16 Mbytes of memory. Most often, programs use the function to copy blocks of conventional memory to extended memory or vice versa. However, it can copy between any two locations. The blocks can be in conventional or extended memory.

INT 15H, function 87H, moves 16-bit words. It receives the number of words in the CX register. ES:SI points to a 16-bit GDT that the BIOS uses in protected mode. When the BIOS function returns, the AH register contains a zero if all went well. Any other number indicates an error (see Table 16-1).

Condition	Status
AH = 0 (Carry clear)	Success
AH = 1	Parity error
AH = 2	Exception occurred
AH = 3	A20 error

Note: Carry is set for all errors.

Table 16-1. Interrupt 15H, function 87H, error codes.

Table 16-2 shows the GDT's format. The GDT specifies the source and destination addresses as 24-bit linear addresses. The limit fields in the GDT must be at least as big as the transfer size (2*CX-1).

Offset	Contents
00H - 07H	Null descriptor (all zeros)
08H - 0FH	Reserved descriptor (all zeros)
10H - 11H	Segment limit (at least 2*CX-1)
12H - 14H	24-bit source address
15H	93H
16H - 17H	Zero
18H - 19H	Segment limit (at least 2*CX-1)
1AH - 1CH	24-bit destination address
1DH	93H
1EH - 1FH	Zero
20H - 27H	Reserved descriptor (all zeros)
28H - 2FH	Reserved descriptor (all zeros)

Table 16-2. GDT for interrupt 15H, function 87H.

USING EXTENDED MEMORY

Be careful when moving large blocks of data with this function: The BIOS disables interrupts during the move. If you depend on hardware interrupts (to read the COM ports, perhaps), you won't want to move large blocks.

Interrupt latency is even worse on 286 machines or those with 286 BIOS ROMs. The 286 can't switch from protected mode to real mode directly; the BIOS must ask the keyboard controller to reset the CPU. Special code in the BIOS detects a flag in the CMOS RAM. The flag tells the BIOS not to reboot but to restart the program that asked to switch modes. This is a more time-consuming task than you might think.

Allocating Extended Memory

Moving blocks around in memory could quickly destroy other programs' code and data if you're not careful. Under 640 Kbytes, you should only move to and from blocks that DOS allocates to you. Above 1 Mbyte, no standard exists for allocating memory. Three methods are commonly used to allocate extended memory directly:

- The laissez-faire method. Some programs assume they can use any extended memory they find. Some even go so far as to search for memory without using the BIOS. These programs are impolite and won't work with other programs that use extended memory. You should never write such programs. Amazingly, several commercial products work this way.

- The VDISK method. VDISK uses memory from the beginning of extended memory (100000H). It places a special header at its start that contains the amount of memory it is reserving. Because the format of this header varies from version to version of VDISK, however, it's not a good idea to depend on VDISK headers for allocating memory.

- The top-down method. Most programs allocate extended memory this way. With this method, your program captures INT 15H. If another program asks for the extended memory size, your program lies—it reports less memory than is actually present. The memory it doesn't report is the amount it is using. Of course, if another program tries to allocate memory, it starts with the phony memory size. This works out just right: The new program uses the block just below the first program's block, and any remaining memory is available to other programs.

As an example, consider a machine with 1 Mbyte of extended memory. A program wishes to allocate 256 Kbytes of memory. Here is the play-by-play:

1. Use INT 15H, function 88H, to determine the amount of extended memory present (1,024 Kbytes). Many programs allow a command-line switch to indicate how much space VDISK is using. If the program does this, make sure enough space remains after VDISK's allocation is deducted.

2. Compute the start of the allocated block. Extended memory starts at linear address 100000H. The top of memory is one byte below address 200000H; the block's length is 40000H. Therefore:

   Start = 200000H-40000H = 1FC0000H

3. Hook INT 15H. The new handler examines the AH register. If AH doesn't equal 88H, control passes to the old interrupt handler. If AH does equal 88H, the new handler returns 768 (1,024 - 256).

Freeing extended memory can be complicated, depending on where the INT 15H vector points. If it points to your interrupt handler, you simply restore the interrupt vector and the memory is free. If it points somewhere else, you have trouble. Another program might have hooked INT 15H for the same reasons you did. Worse, you may have no idea why another program hooked that interrupt. Restoring the vector is probably not a good idea. However, if you don't restore the vector you can't exit—if you do, an INT 15H might jump to your nonexistent interrupt handler.

No perfect solution exists for this dilemma. If the program is a TSR, it can simply refuse to unload. A regular program almost has to restore INT 15H and hope for the best.

USING EXTENDED MEMORY

The CEXT Library

Listings 16-1 and 16-2 contain the CEXT library, C functions that detect and allocate extended memory. CEXT.H (Listing 16-1) defines a new type, the LPTR, that can hold linear addresses up to 32 bits long. CEXT only uses 24 bits of the LPTR. A later chapter will use the entire LPTR.

Listing 16-1. CEXT.H.
```
/****************************************************************
 *                                                              *
 * File: cext.h                                                 *
 *                                                              *
 * Description:                                                 *
 *                                                              *
 * Header file for CEXT library. CEXT manages allocation and    *
 * access of extended memory.                                   *
 *                                                              *
 ****************************************************************/

#ifndef CEXTHEADER
#define CEXTHEADER
#include <dos.h>

typedef unsigned long LPTR;

/* Convert segmented address to linear address. */
#define seg_to_linear(fp)(((LPTR) FP_SEG(fp)<<4)+FP_OFF(fp))

unsigned int ext_size(void);
LPTR ext_alloc(unsigned size);
LPTR ext_realloc(unsigned size);
int ext_free(int exitflag);
int extmemcpy(LPTR dst,LPTR src,unsigned int wc);
#endif
```

DOS 5: A DEVELOPER'S GUIDE

Listing 16-2. CEXT.C.

```c
/****************************************************************
 *                                                              *
 * File: cext.c                                                 *
 *                                                              *
 * Description:                                                 *
 * Manage allocation and access of extended memory.             *
 *                                                              *
 ****************************************************************/
#include <dos.h>
#define NOCLSFUNC 1           /* Don't include msc_cls(). */

#include "compat.h"
#include "cext.h"

/* GDT structure for INT 15H */
struct _gdte
   {
   unsigned int limit;
   unsigned int adrbot;
   unsigned char adrtop;
   char arb;
   int zero;
   };

static struct _gdte gdt[6];

#ifdef __POWERC

static void far *old15;

#else

static void(far interrupt *old15)();

#endif

static int installed=0;
```

634

USING EXTENDED MEMORY

```c
/* amount of memory/amount allocated */
static unsigned e_size,e_alloc;

/* definitions for Power C and Turbo C */
#if defined(__POWERC)||defined(__TURBOC__)

/* This is a kludge to emulate Microsoft's _chain_intr().
   The strategy is to change the return address to the code in
   __chain[] and then return. The code in __chain[] sets up
   the stack and simulates an interrupt to the old handler. */

unsigned __chain[14]=
   {
   0x559c,0xe589,0xb850,0,0x4687,0x87fe,0x46,0xb850,0,0x4687,
     0x5d00,0xeafa,0,0
   };

void far *__cptr;

#define _chain_intr(ptr) { __cptr=(void far *)  chain; \
                          __chain[12]=FP_OFF(ptr); \
                          __chain[13]=FP_SEG(ptr);\
                          __chain[3]=Rip;\
                          __chain[8]=Rcs; Rcs=FP_SEG(__cptr);\
                          Rip=FP_OFF(__cptr);\
                          return; }

#endif

/* private routine to capture requests for extended memory size */
static void interrupt __FAR trap15(INTREGS)
   {
   if ((Rax&0xFF00)!=0x8800) _chain_intr(old15);
   Rax=e_size;
   return;
   }

/****************************************************************
 * Get extended memory size (in K) from BIOS.                   *
 ****************************************************************/
unsigned int ext_size()
```

DOS 5: A DEVELOPER'S GUIDE

```c
   {
   union REGS r;
   r.h.ah=0x88;
   int86(0x15,&r,&r);
   return r.x.ax;
   }

/******************************************************************
 * Allocate memory in 1K blocks; return start address of block    *
 * or (LPTR) -1 if unable to allocate memory.                     *
 ******************************************************************/
LPTR ext_alloc(unsigned size)
   {
   if (installed) return ext_realloc(size+e_alloc);
   e_alloc=size;
   e_size=ext_size();
   if (e_size<size) return(LPTR)-1L;
   e_size-=size;
   old15=getvect(0x15);
   setvect(0x15,trap15);
   installed=1;
   return 0x100000+e_size*1024;
   }

/******************************************************************
 * Attempt to change the size of an allocated block (size in K).  *
 * Returns start address or (LPTR) -1 if unsuccessful.            *
 ******************************************************************/
LPTR ext_realloc(unsigned size)
   {
   if (!installed) return ext_alloc(size);
   if (size>e_alloc+e_size) return(LPTR)-1L;
   if (size<e_alloc)
      {
      e_size+=e_alloc-size;
      e_alloc=size;
      }
   else if (size>e_alloc)
      {
      if (getvect(0x15)!=trap15) return(LPTR)-1L;
      e_size-=size-e_alloc;
```

USING EXTENDED MEMORY

```
      e_alloc=size;
      }
   return 0x100000+e_size*1024;
   }

/******************************************************************
 * Free the extended block. Always call before exiting.           *
 * If exitflag is set, the INT 15 trap will be reset. If another *
 * program has captured INT 15, ext_free will return a -1. If    *
 * you call with exitflag == 0 and another program has captured  *
 * INT 15, the vector is not reset and ext_free returns a 1.     *
 * Otherwise, ext_free returns 0 and releases INT 15.            *
 ******************************************************************/
int ext_free(int exitflag)
   {
   int rc=0;
   if (!installed) return rc;
   if (getvect(0x15)==trap15||exitflag)
      {
      if (getvect(0x15)!=trap15) rc=-1;
      installed=0;
      setvect(0x15,old15);
      }
   else
      {
      e_size+=e_alloc;
      e_alloc=0;
      rc=1;
      }
   return rc;
   }

/******************************************************************
 * Move a block of memory using BIOS calls. Works with up to 16  *
 * Mbytes.                                                        *
 ******************************************************************/
int extmemcpy(LPTR dst,LPTR src,unsigned wc)
   {
   union REGS r;
   struct SREGS s;
```

```c
    void far *gdtptr;
    gdtptr=(void far *) gdt;
/* Clear GDT. */
    memset(gdt,0,sizeof(gdt));
/* Set up GDT. */
    gdt[3].limit=gdt[2].limit=wc*2-1;
    gdt[2].adrbot=src&0xffff;
    gdt[2].adrtop=(src&0xff0000L)>>16;
    gdt[3].adrbot=dst&0xffff;
    gdt[3].adrtop=(dst&0xff0000L)>>16;
    gdt[2].arb=gdt[3].arb=0x93;
    s.es=FP_SEG(gdtptr);
    r.h.ah=0x87;
    r.x.cx=wc;
    r.x.si=FP_OFF(gdtptr);
    int86x(0x15,&r,&r,&s);
    return r.h.ah;
    }
```

To check the amount of extended memory available, call *ext_size()*; it returns the number of free 1-Kbyte pages. If you need to allocate extended memory, use *ext_alloc()* and *ext_realloc()*. These functions take the number of 1-Kbyte pages desired and return an LPTR to the start of the memory block. If the request cannot be honored, the routines return (LPTR)-1L.

Note that these functions are not like the traditional *malloc()* functions found in the standard C library. Rather than calling them repeatedly to allocate small chunks of memory, you should allocate all the extended memory you need in one call. This is especially true of resident programs. If another program has allocated extended memory after your first call to *ext_alloc()*, you'll be unable to expand your memory allocation.

When you finish using the allocated extended memory, free it with *ext_free()*. Exercise caution when using this function with other programs that use extended memory. *ext_free(1)* forcibly frees all extended memory allocated since the first call

USING EXTENDED MEMORY

to *ext_alloc()*. If you have allocated extended memory, you must call *ext_free(1)* before you exit your program. Failure to do so will lock up the computer. Calling *ext_free(0)* frees up the memory but won't forcibly replace INT 15H if another program has also hooked it. If *extfree(0)* restores INT 15H, it returns a zero.

The *extmemcpy()* function calls INT 15H, function 87H. This call mimics the standard library's *memcpy()* function and returns the error code, if any.

Listing 16-3 shows VM_EXT.C, a virtual memory driver for DUP.C (see Chapter 12). This driver allows DUP to copy a disk into extended memory, then make copies of the disk from the extended memory image.

Listing 16-3. VM_EXT.C.
```
/****************************************************************
 *                                                              *
 * File: vm_ext.c                                               *
 *                                                              *
 * Description:                                                 *
 * Manages virtual memory for DUP.C using extended memory.      *
 * Requires CEXT.C.                                             *
 *                                                              *
 ****************************************************************/

#include <dos.h>
#include "cext.h"
#define PAGESIZE 16384
static int vmpage=-1;
static LPTR vmstart=0L;
static char vmbuffer[PAGESIZE];

/* Allocate VM swap space. */
int vm_alloc(unsigned long size)
   {
/* Free any already allocated. */
   if (vmstart) ext_free(1);
```

639

```c
/* Compute number of 1K pages required. */
   if (size%PAGESIZE) size=(size/PAGESIZE+1)*PAGESIZE;
   size/=1024;
   if (ext_size()<size) return 1;
/* Allocate from CEXT. */
   vmstart=ext_alloc((unsigned) size);
   if (!vmstart) return 1;                /* should never happen */
   return 0;
   }

/* Free VM. */
void vm_free()
   {
   ext_free(1);
   }

/* Map a VM address. */
char far *vm_map(unsigned long offset)
   {
   int page;
   char far *rval=(char far *)0;
   char far *mixbug=(char far *) vmbuffer;
/* Compute page. */
   page=offset/PAGESIZE;
/* If page isn't the current page... */
   if (page!=vmpage)
      {
/* Commit current page. */
      if (vm_commit()) return rval;
      vmpage=page;
/* Copy in new page. */
      if (extmemcpy(seg_to_linear(mixbug),vmstart+(unsigned long)
         vmpage*PAGESIZE,PAGESIZE/2)) return rval;
      }
/* Compute offset in page buffer. */
   FP_SEG(rval)=FP_SEG(mixbug);
   FP_OFF(rval)=offset-(unsigned long)
      page*PAGESIZE+FP_OFF(mixbug);
   return rval;
   }
```

USING EXTENDED MEMORY

```
/* Commit VM page to extended memory. */
int vm_commit()
  {
  void far *mixbug=(void far *) vmbuffer;
/* Don't do initial page. */
  if (vmpage==-1) return 0;
/* Copy it out. */
  if (extmemcpy(vmstart+(unsigned long) vmpage*PAGESIZE,
    seg_to_linear(mixbug),PAGESIZE/2)) return 1;
  return 0;
  }
```

If you use DUP with VM_EXT.C, make sure VDISK or RAMDRIVE will leave enough memory to copy the disk. Alternatively, you can remove VDISK before using VM_EXT.

Other Ways to Access Extended Memory

Chapter 18 shows an unusual method of accessing extended memory that only works on a 386. There are, however, more standard methods.

The Extended Memory Specification (XMS), developed by Microsoft, Intel, Lotus, and AST, allows programs to use extended memory in several ways. While XMS is a good idea, it requires a software driver. Users who have an EMS board must have an EMS driver. Users who have extended memory may not have an XMS driver (although the driver is standard with DOS 5). For this reason, many developers don't support XMS. Others may use XMS if it is present and work directly if it's not. If you need more information on XMS, you can request the specification from Microsoft or Intel. (See Appendix E, the bibliography.)

Most DOS extenders provide services for programs to allocate extended memory. We'll take up the subject of DOS extenders in Chapter 19.

CHAPTER 17

80386 Debugging

It's disappointing to learn how powerful the 80386 is and then realize that DOS won't let you take advantage of the protected-mode benefits. However, the hardware debugging features are usable no matter what mode the 386 is using.

Hardware Debugging

Most PC developers are familiar with some type of hardware debug assistance. Even the 8088 has a breakpoint interrupt and a single-step flag. (The latter allows debuggers to trace code one instruction at a time.) The 386 shares these features with the earlier processors but adds eight debug registers, two of which Intel reserves. These debug registers control the hardware breakpoint features.

Hardware breakpoints are much more powerful than ordinary breakpoints (such as those in DEBUG) for two reasons. First, they don't modify your program. This means you can set breakpoints anywhere, even in ROM. Also, a program can't overwrite a breakpoint when it modifies itself or loads an overlay. Hardware breakpoints can be set on data. A data breakpoint triggers when your program accesses a certain memory location.

Most commercial debuggers implement similar data breakpoints, called *tracepoints*. To maintain compatibility with non-386 PCs, however, many of these debuggers don't use 386 features. As a result, they check tracepoints after the execution of each instruction. This is, of course, terribly slow. If you move the tracepoints to 386 hardware, execution doesn't slow down at all. (In practice, you'll usually want to slow down execution slightly.)

Because the 386 has four debug address registers, four breakpoints can be active at once. Each address register (DR0 through DR3) represents a linear address at which a different breakpoint will occur. In protected mode, the concept of a linear address is not straightforward. In real-mode programs, however, you can easily calculate a linear address from a segment/offset pair: Simply multiply the segment value by 10H (shift left four bits) and add the offset. For example, to set a data breakpoint at B800:0020 (somewhere in the CGA video buffer), you would need a linear address of

```
B800 * 10 + 20 = B8020
```

Once you have loaded the address registers, you must use special bits to enable the breakpoints you wish to use and tell the processor what type of breakpoints they are. The debug control register (DR7) contains bits to enable each breakpoint and to set its type individually (see Figure 17-1). You'll notice that DR7 has global and local enable bits and global and local exact bits (these will be explained shortly). The difference between the various global and local bits is only important when the 386 is multitasking in protected mode. When it switches to a new task, it resets the local bits; the global bits don't change. In real mode, these bits function identically.

31 30	29 28	27 26	25 24	23 22	21 20	19 18	17 16	15	14	13	12	11 10	9	8	7	6	5	4	3	2	1	0
Len 3	R/W 3	Len 2	R/W 2	Len 1	R/W 1	Len 0	R/W 0	X	X	GD	X	X	GE	LE	G3	L3	G2	L2	G1	L1	G0	L0

Bit Definitions

```
X     = Not used
Len   = Breakpoint length
R/W   = Breakpoint read/write status
GE    = Global exact
LE    = Local exact
G0-G3 = Global breakpoint enable (breakpoints 0 - 3)
L0-L3 = Local breakpoint enable (breakpoints 0 - 3)
GD    = General detect
```

Figure 17-1. DR7 register.

The Exact Bits and Other Flags

The exact bits are flags that tell the 386 to slow down. This may not seem helpful at first glance, but a detailed look at the 386 architecture reveals their purpose.

The 386 gains some of its speed by overlapping instruction fetches and data fetches. This is an excellent idea during execution, but it causes problems during debugging. Without the exact bit set, a data breakpoint won't occur at the instruction that caused the data access. Because this is somewhat inconvenient, Intel included the global exact (GE) and local exact (LE) bits. With either (or both) of them set, data breakpoints occur immediately after the instruction that caused them, although the processor will lose speed slightly.

All debug breakpoints generate an INT 1. To distinguish between the various breakpoints, you must read the debug status register (DR6). DR6 has bits corresponding to the various breakpoint conditions (including single-step; see Figure 17-2). Note the BT flag at bit 15. As with the local bits in DR7, only multitasking systems use the BT flag (the 386 sets it when a task-switch breakpoint occurs, as discussed below). The 386 never clears the bits in DR6, so you should do so after determining the cause of the interrupt.

31 30 29 28 27 26 25 24 23 22 21 20 19 18 17 16	15	14	13	12 11 10 9 8 7 6 5 4	3	2	1	0
Not Used	BT	BS	BD	Not Used	B3	B2	B1	B0

Bit Definitions
B0-3 = Breakpoint occurred (breakpoint 0 - 3)
BD   = Illegal access to breakpoint registers
BS   = Single-step interrupt occurred
BT   = Task switch occurred

Figure 17-2. DR6 register.

With the general detect (GD) bit set in DR7, the 386 prohibits access to the debug registers. Any attempt to access them will cause an INT 1 with the BD flag set in DR6. Intel's in-circuit emulator uses this feature, although you can use it if you have any reason to disable or control access to the debug registers. When a GD interrupt occurs, the 386 clears the GD bit and invokes the interrupt handler. If the 386 didn't clear the GD bit, the handler would fault when it read DR6 and cause an endless loop.

You can decide in the interrupt routine whether to terminate the user program or allow access to the registers. This bit is most useful to in-circuit emulators and advanced operating systems; under DOS there is little reason to use it.

Task-Switch Breakpoints

When the 386 switches to a new task, it examines the T bit in the TSS. If this bit is on, it triggers a debug interrupt. The BT flag in DR6 indicates this condition.

A task-switch breakpoint can be useful for debugging. For example, the local bits must be set for a task being debugged every time it becomes active. Task-switch breakpoints are also useful for nondebugging purposes. Imagine a multitasking operating system that saves each task's coprocessor state in the TSS. A task-switch breakpoint will allow it to restore the coprocessor's state from the TSS before starting the task.

The last consideration with breakpoint interrupts is how to resume the interrupted program. If we simply return (using an *IRET*), there is nothing to stop a code breakpoint from recurring immediately. The resume flag (found in the FLAGS register) prevents this. It inhibits further debug exceptions while set and resets automatically as soon as one instruction successfully executes. Control of the resume flag is automatic in protected mode. Controlling it from real mode, however, is somewhat more difficult.

BREAK386

BREAK386 (Listing 17-1) isn't a traditional debugger like DEBUG, Microsoft's CodeView, or Borland's Turbo Debugger. By adding BREAK386 to your assembly-language code, you can study it with code, data, and single-step breakpoints. You also can examine DOS or BIOS interrupts that your program calls. In addition, BREAK386 can add the same 386 hardware debugging to your C programs.

Listing 17-1. BREAK386.ASM.

```
;***************************************************************
;*                                                              *
;* File: BREAK386.ASM                                            *
;*                                                              *
;* Description:                                                  *
;* BREAK386 "main programs". Contains setup386, clear386,        *
;* break386 and int1 386.                                        *
;*                                                              *
;* Compile with: MASM /Ml BREAK386                               *
;*           or TASM /Ml BREAK386                                *
;*                                                              *
;***************************************************************

        .MODEL          SMALL
        .386P

                PUBLIC _break386,_clear386,_setup386,_int1_386

; Set up stack offsets for word size arguments based on the
; code size. Be careful: regardless of what Microsoft's
; documentation says, you must use @CodeSize (not @codesize, etc.)
; when compiling with /Ml.
IF              @CodeSize               ; true for models with far code
ARG1            EQU     <[BP+6]>
ARG2            EQU     <[BP+8]>
ARG3            EQU     <[BP+10]>
ARG4            EQU     <[BP+12]>
ELSE
ARG1            EQU     <[BP+4]>
ARG2            EQU     <[BP+6]>
ARG3            EQU     <[BP+8]>
ARG4            EQU     <[BP+10]>
ENDIF

        .DATA

; things you may want to change
; If 0 use BIOS; if 1 use direct video access.
DIRECT          EQU     0
```

DOS 5: A DEVELOPER'S GUIDE

```
; # of words to dump off the stack
STKWRD          EQU     32

; When 0, don't display interrupt stack words.
INTSTACK        EQU     1

; Set to 0 to disable int1_386().
USE_INT1        EQU     1

; old int 1 vector
OLDOFFSET       DW      0
OLDSEGMENT      DW      0

        IF              USE_INT1
; segment of video adapter (changed by vinit)
VIDEO           DW      0B000H
CSIP            DB      'CODE=',0
DONE            DB      'Program terminated normally.',0
NOTDONE         DB      'Program breakpoint:',0
STKMESS         DB      'Stack dump:',0

VPAGE           DB      0
VCOLS           DB      80

        IFE             DIRECT
PROMPT          DB      '<V>iew output, <T>race toggle, '
                DB      '<C>ontinue or <A>bort? ',0
SAVCURSOR       DW      0               ; inactive video cursor
VBUFF           DD      1000 DUP (07200720H)
        ELSE
CURSOR          DW      0
COLOR           DB      7
        ENDIF
        ENDIF

        .CODE

; This is the start-up code. The old interrupt one vector is
; saved in oldsegment, oldoffset. int1_386 does not chain to
; the old vector; it simply replaces it.
```

80386 DEBUGGING

```
_setup386       PROC
                PUSH    BP
                MOV     BP,SP
                PUSH    ES
                MOV     AX,3501H        ; Get old int1 vector.
                INT     21H
                MOV     OLDSEGMENT,ES
                MOV     OLDOFFSET,BX
                POP     ES
; Get new interrupt handler address.
                MOV     AX,ARG2
                PUSH    DS
                MOV     DX,ARG1
; If int1_386 is being assembled, setup386 will check to see if
; you are installing int1386. If so, it will call vinit to set
; up the video parameters that int1_386 requires.
IF              USE_INT1
                CMP     AX,SEG _int1_386
                JNZ     NOTUS
                CMP     DX,OFFSET _int1_386
                JNZ     NOTUS
                PUSH    DX
                PUSH    AX
; int'l video if it is our handler
                CALL    VINIT
                POP     DS
                POP     DX
ENDIF
; Store interrupt address in vector table.
NOTUS:          MOV     AX,2501H
                INT     21H
                POP     DS
                XOR     EAX,EAX         ; Clear DR7/DR6 (just in case).
                MOV     DR7,EAX
                MOV     DR6,EAX
                POP     BP
                RET
_setup386       ENDP
```

DOS 5: A DEVELOPER'S GUIDE

```
; This routine sets/clears breakpoints.
; Inputs:
;     breakpoint # (1-4)
;     breakpoint type (see BREAK386.INC)
;     segment/offset of break address (or null to clear
;           breakpoint)
; Outputs:
;     AX=0 if successful
;     AX=-1 if not successful

_break386       PROC
                PUSH    BP
                MOV     BP,SP
                MOV     BX,ARG1         ; breakpoint # (1-4)
                CMP     BX,1
                JB      OUTRANGE
                CMP     BX,4
                JNA     NOTHIGH
OUTRANGE:
; error: breakpoint # out of range
                MOV     AX,0FFFFH
                POP     BP
                RET
NOTHIGH:
; Get breakpoint address.
                MOVZX   EAX,WORD PTR ARG4
                SHL     EAX,4
; Calculate linear address.
                MOVZX   EDX,WORD PTR ARG3
                ADD     EAX,EDX         ; If address = 0 then
                JZ      RESETBP         ; turn breakpoint off!
                DEC     BX              ; Set correct address reg.
                JZ      BP0
                DEC     BX
                JZ      BP1
                DEC     BX
                JZ      BP2
                MOV     DR3,EAX
                JMP     SHORT BRCONT
BP0:            MOV     DR0,EAX
```

80386 DEBUGGING

```
                JMP     SHORT BRCONT
BP1:            MOV     DR1,EAX
                JMP     SHORT BRCONT
BP2:            MOV     DR2,EAX
BRCONT:
; Get type.
                MOVZX   EAX,WORD PTR ARG2
                MOV     CX,ARG1         ; Calculate proper position.
                PUSH    CX
                DEC     CX
                SHL     CX,2
                ADD     CX,16
                SHL     EAX,CL          ; Rotate type.
                MOV     EDX,0FH
                SHL     EDX,CL          ; Calculate type mask.
                NOT     EDX
                POP     CX
                SHL     CX,1            ; Calculate pos of enable bit.
                DEC     CX
                MOV     EBX,1
                SHL     EBX,CL
                OR      EAX,EBX         ; Enable bp.
                MOV     EBX,DR7         ; Get old DR7.
                AND     EBX,EDX         ; Mask out old type.
                OR      EBX,EAX         ; Set new type/enable bits.
; Adjust enable bit (set on for data bp's, off if no data bp's).
ADJGE:
                MOV     EAX,200H
; Reset GE bit.
                AND     EBX,0FFFFFDFFH
; Test for data bp's.
                TEST    EBX,033330000H
                JZ      NODATABP
                OR      EBX,512
NODATABP:
                MOV     DR7,EBX
                POP     BP
                XOR     AX,AX
                RET
```

```
; Here we reset a breakpoint by turning off its enable bit
; and setting type to 0.
; Clearing the type is required so that disabling all data
; breakpoints will clear the GE bit also.
RESETBP:
; Calculate type/len bit positions.
                MOV     CX,BX
                MOV     EDX,0FH
                DEC     CX
                SHL     CX,2
                ADD     CX,16
                SHL     EDX,CL
                NOT     EDX
; Calculate enable bit position.
                MOV     CX,BX
                SHL     CX,1
                DEC     CX
                MOV     EAX,1
                SHL     EAX,CL
                NOT     AX              ; Flip bits.
                MOV     EBX,DR7
                AND     EBX,EAX         ; Clear enable.
                AND     EBX,EDX         ; Clear type.
                JMP     ADJGE
_break386       ENDP

; Reset the debug registers, disabling all breakpoints. Also
; restore the old interrupt 1 vector.
_clear386       PROC
                PUSHF
                POP     AX
                AND     AX,0FEFFH       ; Turn off trace flag.
                PUSH    AX
                POPF
; Turn off all other breakpoints.
                XOR     EAX,EAX
                MOV     DR7,EAX
                MOV     DR0,EAX
                MOV     DR1,EAX
                MOV     DR2,EAX
```

80386 DEBUGGING

```
                MOV     DR3,EAX
                MOV     DR6,EAX
                MOV     AX,2501H        ; Restore old int 1 vector.
                PUSH    DS
                MOV     DX,OLDOFFSET
                MOV     DS,OLDSEGMENT
                INT     21H
                POP     DS
                RET
_clear386       ENDP

IF              USE_INT1
; This is all code relating to the optional INT 1 handler.

; This macro is used to get a register value off the stack
; and display it.
; R is the register name and n is the position of the register
; on the stack; i.e., outreg 'AX',10.

OUTREG          MACRO   R,N
                MOV     AX,&R
                MOV     DX,[EBP+&N SHL 1]
                CALL    REGOUT
                ENDM

; This is the interrupt 1 handler.
_int1_386       PROC    FAR
                STI                     ; Enable interrupts (see text).
                PUSHA                   ; Save all registers.
                PUSH    DS
                PUSH    ES
                PUSH    SS
                PUSH    @data
                POP     DS              ; Reload DS.
                MOV     BP,SP           ; Point EBP to top of stack.
IFE             DIRECT
                CALL    SAVEVIDEO
ENDIF

                MOV     ES,VIDEO        ; Get video addressability.
                ASSUME  CS:@code,DS:@data
```

DOS 5: A DEVELOPER'S GUIDE

```
; Display breakpoint message.
            MOV     BX,OFFSET NOTDONE
            CALL    OUTSTR
            MOV     EDX,DR6
            CALL    HEXOUT
            XOR     EDX,EDX
            MOV     DR6,EDX
            CALL    CRLF
; Do register dump.
            OUTREG  'AX',10
            OUTREG  'FL',13
            OUTREG  'BX',7
            OUTREG  'CX',9
            OUTREG  'DX',8
            CALL    CRLF
            OUTREG  'SI',4
            OUTREG  'DI',3
            OUTREG  'SP',6
            OUTREG  'BP',5
            CALL    CRLF
            OUTREG  'CS',12
            OUTREG  'IP',11
            OUTREG  'DS',2
            OUTREG  'ES',1
            OUTREG  'SS',0
            CALL    CRLF
                                    ; Do stack dump.
IF          STKWRD
            MOV     BX,OFFSET STKMESS
            CALL    OUTSTR          ; Print stack dump title.
            PUSH    FS
; Get program's ss.
; (Technically, WORD PTR isn't needed here. However,
; some early turbo assemblers couldn't infer the size
; going into FS and would produce a warning without it.)
            MOV     FS,WORD PTR [EBP]
            MOV     AL,'('
            CALL    OUCH
            MOV     AL,' '
            CALL    OUCH
```

80386 DEBUGGING

```
                CALL    HEXOUT
                MOV     AL,':'
                CALL    OUCH
                MOV     AL,' '
                CALL    OUCH
; Get stack pointer (before pusha).
                MOV     BX,[EBP+12]
IFE             INTSTACK
                ADD     BX,6            ; Skip interrupt info.
ENDIF
                MOV     DX,BX
                PUSH    BX
                CALL    HEXOUT
                MOV     AL,')'
                CALL    OUCH
                CALL    CRLF
                POP     BX
                MOV     CX,STKWRD
SLOOP:
                MOV     DX,FS:[BX]      ; Get word at stack.
                PUSH    BX
                PUSH    CX
                CALL    HEXOUT          ; Display it.
                POP     CX
                POP     BX
                INC     BX
                INC     BX
                LOOP    SLOOP
                POP     FS
ENDIF
NOSTACK:
; Here we will dump 16 bytes starting 8 bytes prior to the
; instruction that caused the break.
                PUSH    FS
                CALL    CRLF
                MOV     BX, OFFSET CSIP
                CALL    OUTSTR
                MOV     CX,8
```

```
; Get cs
                MOV     FS,WORD PTR [EBP+24]
; and ip.
                MOV     BX,WORD PTR [EBP+22]
                CMP     BX,8            ; Make sure 8 bytes before
                JNB     IPBEGIN         ; the beginning of the segment.
                MOV     CX,BX           ; If not, only dump from start
IPBEGIN:        SUB     BX,CX           ; of the segment.
                PUSH    BX
                PUSH    CX
                MOV     DX,FS           ; Display address.
                CALL    HEXOUT
                MOV     AL,':'
                CALL    OUCH
                MOV     AL,' '
                CALL    OUCH
                MOV     DX,BX
                CALL    HEXOUT
                MOV     AL,'='
                CALL    OUCH
                POP     CX
                POP     BX
; If starting at 0, don't display any before IP.
                OR      BX,BX
                JZ      IPSKIP
IPLOOP:
                MOV     DL,FS:[BX]      ; Get byte.
                PUSH    BX
                PUSH    CX
                CALL    HEX1OUT         ; Output it.
                POP     CX
                POP     BX
                INC     BX
                LOOP    IPLOOP
IPSKIP:
                PUSH    BX
                MOV     AL,'*'          ; Put '*' before IP location.
                CALL    OUCH
                MOV     AL,' '
```

80386 DEBUGGING

```
                CALL    OUCH
                POP     BX
; This is basically a repeat of the above loop except it dumps
; the 8 bytes starting at IP.
                MOV     CX,8
XIPLOOP:
                MOV     DL,FS:[BX]
                PUSH    BX
                PUSH    CX
                CALL    HEX1OUT
                POP     CX
                POP     BX
                INC     BX
                LOOP    XIPLOOP
                CALL    CRLF
                CALL    CRLF
                POP     FS
IFE             DIRECT
; Here we will ask if we should continue or abort.
                MOV     BX,OFFSET PROMPT
                CALL    OUTSTR
KEYLOOP:
                XOR     AH,AH           ; Get keyboard input.
                INT     16H
                AND     AL,0DFH         ; Make uppercase.
                CMP     AL,'T'
                JZ      TTOGGLE
                CMP     AL,'A'
                JZ      Q1
                CMP     AL,'C'
                JZ      C1
                CMP     AL,'V'
                JNZ     KEYLOOP
; Display program's screen until any key is pressed.
                CALL    SAVEVIDEO
                XOR     AH,AH
                INT     16H
                CALL    SAVEVIDEO
                JMP     KEYLOOP
```

DOS 5: A DEVELOPER'S GUIDE

```
; Execution comes here to toggle trace flag and continue.
TTOGGLE:
            XOR     WORD PTR [BP+26],256

; Execution comes here to continue running the target program.
C1:
            CALL    CRLF
IFE         DIRECT
            CALL    SAVEVIDEO
ELSE
            XOR     AX,AX
            MOV     CURSOR,AX
ENDIF
            POP     SS
            POP     ES
            POP     DS
            POPA
; This seems complicated at first.
; You MUST ensure that RF is set before continuing. If RF is not
; set, you will just cause a breakpoint immediately!
; In protected mode, this is handled automatically. In real mode
; it isn't since RF is in the high 16 bits of the flags register.
; Essentially we have to convert the stack from:
;
;   16-bit flags            32-bit flags  (top word = 1 to set RF)
;   16-bit CS     to  —>    32-bit CS     (garbage in top 16 bits)
;   16-bit IP               32-bit IP     (top word = 0)
;
; All this so we can execute an IRETD that will change RF.

            SUB     ESP,6         ; Make a double stack frame.
            XCHG    AX,[ESP+6]    ; Get IP in AX.
            MOV     [ESP],AX      ; Store it.
            XOR     AX,AX
            MOV     [ESP+2],AX    ; eip = 0000:ip
            MOV     AX,[ESP+6]
            XCHG    AX,[ESP+8]    ; Get CS.
            MOV     [ESP+4],AX
; Zero that stack word and restore AX.
```

80386 DEBUGGING

```
                XOR     AX,AX
                MOV     [ESP+6],AX
                MOV     AX,[ESP+8]
                XCHG    AX,[ESP+10]     ; Get flags.
                MOV     [ESP+8],AX
                MOV     AX,1            ; Set RF.
                XCHG    AX,[ESP+10]
                IRETD                   ; DOUBLE IRET (32 bits!)

ENDIF

; Execution resumes here to abort the target program.
Q1:
IFE             DIRECT
                CALL    SAVEVIDEO
ENDIF
                CALL    QUIT
_int1_386       ENDP


IFE             DIRECT
; Save video screen and restore ours (only with BIOS, please!).
; (Assumes 25 lines/page.)
SAVEVIDEO       PROC
                PUSHA
                PUSH    ES
                MOV     AH,0FH
                INT     10H             ; Reread video page/size
                MOV     VPAGE,BH        ; in case program changed it.
                MOV     VCOLS,AH

                PUSH    SAVCURSOR
                MOV     AH,3            ; Get old cursor.
                MOV     BH,VPAGE
                INT     10H
                MOV     SAVCURSOR,DX
                POP     DX
                MOV     AH,2            ; Set new cursor.
                INT     10H
                MOVZX   AX,VPAGE
                MOV     CL,VCOLS        ; Compute # bytes/page.
```

DOS 5: A DEVELOPER'S GUIDE

```
                XOR     CH,CH
                MOV     DX,CX           ; vcols * 25 * 2
                SHL     CX,3
                SHL     DX,1
                ADD     CX,DX
                MOV     DX,CX
                SHL     CX,2
                ADD     CX,DX
                PUSH    CX
                MUL     CX
                MOV     DI,AX           ; Start at beginning of page.
                POP     CX
                SHR     CX,2
; CX now = # of double words to transfer.
                MOV     ES,VIDEO
; Store inactive screen in vbuff.
                MOV     SI,OFFSET VBUFF
XLOOP:          MOV     EAX,ES:[DI]     ; Swap screens.
                XCHG    EAX,[SI]
                MOV     ES:[DI],EAX
                ADD     SI,4
                ADD     DI,4
                LOOP    XLOOP
                POP     ES
                POPA
                RET
SAVEVIDEO       ENDP
ENDIF

; This routine prints a register value complete with label.
; The register name is in AX and the value is in DX (see the
; outreg macro).
REGOUT          PROC
                PUSH    DX
                PUSH    AX
                MOV     AL,AH
                CALL    OUCH
                POP     AX
                CALL    OUCH
                MOV     AL,'='
```

80386 DEBUGGING

```
                CALL    OUCH
                POP     DX
                CALL    HEXOUT
                RET
REGOUT          ENDP

; plain vanilla hexadecimal digit output routine
HEXDOUT         PROC
                AND     DL,0FH
                ADD     DL,'0'
                CMP     DL,3AH
                JB      DDIGIT
                ADD     DL,'A'-3AH
DDIGIT:
                MOV     AL,DL
                CALL    OUCH
                RET
HEXDOUT         ENDP

; plain vanilla hexadecimal word output routine
HEXOUT          PROC
                PUSH    DX
                SHR     DX,12
                CALL    HEXDOUT
                POP     DX
                PUSH    DX
                SHR     DX,8
                CALL    HEXDOUT
                POP     DX
; Call with this entry point to output just a byte.
HEX1OUT:
                PUSH    DX
                SHR     DX,4
                CALL    HEXDOUT
                POP     DX
                CALL    HEXDOUT
                MOV     AL,' '
                CALL    OUCH
                RET
HEXOUT          ENDP
```

DOS 5: A DEVELOPER'S GUIDE

```
; These routines are for direct video output. Using them allows
; you to debug video BIOS calls but prevents you from single-
; stepping.
IF              DIRECT
; Output a character in AL; assumes ds=dat, es=video.
; Destroys bx,ah.
OUCH            PROC
                MOV     BX,CURSOR
                MOV     AH,COLOR
                MOV     ES:[BX],AX
                INC     BX
                INC     BX
                MOV     CURSOR,BX
                RET
OUCH            ENDP

; <CR> <LF> output. Assumes ds=dat, es=video.
; Destroys ax, cx, dx, di. Clears df.
CRLF            PROC
                MOV     AX,CURSOR
                MOV     CX,160
                XOR     DX,DX
                DIV     CX
                INC     AX
                MUL     CX
                MOV     CURSOR,AX
                MOV     CX,80
                MOV     AH,COLOR
                MOV     AL,' '
                MOV     DI,CURSOR
                CLD
                REP     STOSW
                RET
CRLF            ENDP

ELSE
; These are the BIOS output routines.
; Output a character.
OUCH            PROC
```

80386 DEBUGGING

```
                MOV     AH,0EH
                MOV     BH,VPAGE
                INT     10H
                RET
OUCH            ENDP

; <CR> <LF> output
CRLF            PROC
                MOV     AL,0DH
                CALL    OUCH
                MOV     AL,0AH
                CALL    OUCH
                RET
CRLF            ENDP

ENDIF

; Initialize the video routines.
VINIT           PROC
                MOV     AH,0FH
                INT     10H
                MOV     VCOLS,AH
                MOV     VPAGE,BH
                CMP     AL,7            ; monochrome
                MOV     AX,0B000H
                JZ      VEXIT
                MOV     AX,0B800H
VEXIT:          MOV     VIDEO,AX
                RET
VINIT           ENDP

; Outputs string pointed to by ds:bx (ds must be dat).
; es=video when DIRECT=1.
OUTSTR          PROC
OUTAGN:
                MOV     AL,[BX]
                OR      AL,AL
                JZ      OUTOUT
                PUSH    BX
                CALL    OUCH
                POP     BX
```

663

```
                INC     BX
                JMP     OUTAGN
OUTOUT:         RET
OUTSTR          ENDP

; This routine is called to return to DOS.
QUIT            PROC
                CALL    _clear386
                MOV     AX,4C00H    ; Return to DOS.
                INT     21H
QUIT            ENDP

ENDIF

                END
```

This debugger works with Microsoft C and Turbo C. Unfortunately, the utility Mix's Power C provides to convert .OBJ files can't handle the 386 code used by BREAK386. BREAK386 would work with Power C if it could link with the .MIX files Power C uses. You could, with some difficulty, convert BREAK386 to work with Mix's *asm( )* function, but for now BREAK386 cannot be used with Power C.

BREAK386 provides functions to set up 386 debugging (*setup386()*), set breakpoints (*break386()*), and reset 386 debugging (*clear386()*). In addition, BREAK386 provides an optional interrupt handler (*int1_386()*) that supports register, stack, and code dumps along with single-stepping. You can use any of these functions from either C or assembly language.

In some cases you may wish to modify *int1_386()* or write your own interrupt handler. For example, you may want to send the register dumps to a printer and automatically restart your program. With C, you'll often want the interrupt handler to print out variables instead of registers.

80386 DEBUGGING

You must assemble BREAK386 before you can use it. Be sure to change the *.MODEL* statement to reflect the model you're using. If you're using explicit segment definitions in assembly, you must decide how to integrate BREAK386's code and data segments with your own. If you're using BREAK386 with C, assemble with the */Ml* option to prevent the assembler from converting all labels to uppercase. The resulting .OBJ file can be linked with your programs just as with any other object module.

If you're using programs (such as memory managers and multitaskers) that also use 386-specific functions, you may have to remove these programs before BREAK386 will function. The other program will usually report a "privilege exception" or something similar. Simply remove the other 386 programs and try again.

To add 386 breakpoints to your program, follow these steps:

- Call *setup386()* to set the debug interrupt handler address.
- Set up breakpoints with the *break386()* call.
- Call *clear386()* before your program returns to DOS.

Note that when these routines are called from assembly, their names contain leading underscores. For convenience, Listing 17-2 (BREAK386.INC) contains the assembly-language definitions for using BREAK386. Listing 17-3 (BREAK386.H) contains the same definitions for C. BREAK386.INC also includes two macros, *TRACEON* and *TRACEOFF*, that turn single-stepping on and off from within the program.

Listing 17-2. BREAK386.INC.

```
;******************************************************************
;*                                                                *
;* File: BREAK386.INC                                             *
;*                                                                *
;* Description:                                                   *
;* Header file to include with assembly-language programs         *
;* using BREAK386.                                                *
;*                                                                *
;******************************************************************

        IF          @CodeSize         ; If large style models
                    EXTRN   _break386:FAR,_clear386:FAR
                    EXTRN   _setup386:FAR,_int1_386:FAR
        ELSE
                    EXTRN   _break386:NEAR,_clear386:NEAR
                    EXTRN   _setup386:NEAR,_int1_386:FAR
        ENDIF

; breakpoint equates
BP_CODE         EQU     0           ; code breakpoint
BP_DATAW1       EQU     1           ; one-byte data write breakpoint
BP_DATARW1      EQU     3           ; one-byte data R/W breakpoint
BP_DATAW2       EQU     5           ; two-byte data write breakpoint
BP_DATARW2      EQU     7           ; two-byte data R/W breakpoint
BP_DATAW4       EQU     13          ; four-byte data write breakpoint
BP_DATARW4      EQU     15          ; four-byte data R/W breakpoint

; macros to turn tracing on and off
; Note: When tracing, you will actually "see" traceoff before it
;       turns tracing off.

TRACEON         MACRO
                PUSH    BP
                PUSHF
                MOV     BP,SP
                XCHG    AX,[BP]
                OR      AX,100H
                XCHG    AX,[BP]
                POPF
```

80386 DEBUGGING

```
                POP     BP
                ENDM

TRACEOFF        MACRO
                PUSH    BP
                PUSHF
                MOV     BP,SP
                XCHG    AX,[BP]
                AND     AX,0FEFFH
                XCHG    AX,[BP]
                POPF
                POP     BP
                ENDM
```

Listing 17-3. BREAK386.H.

```
/***************************************************************
 *                                                              *
 * File: BREAK386.H                                             *
 *                                                              *
 * Description:                                                 *
 * C header for C programs using BREAK386 or CBRK386.           *
 *                                                              *
 ***************************************************************/

#ifndef DBG386HEADER
#define DBG386HEADER

#ifndef NO_EXT_KEYS
#define _CDECL cdecl
#else
#define _CDECL
#endif

#ifndef BR386_HEADER
#define BR386_HEADER

/* Declare functions. */
void _CDECL setup386(void(interrupt far *)());
void _CDECL csetup386(void(_CDECL far *)());
```

DOS 5: A DEVELOPER'S GUIDE

```c
void _CDECL clear386(void);
int _CDECL break386(int,int,void far *);
void far interrupt int1_386();

/* breakpoint types */

/* CODE BREAKPOINT*/
#define BP_CODE 0

/* ONE-BYTE DATA WRITE BREAKPOINT*/
#define BP_DATAW1 1

/* ONE-BYTE DATA R/W BREAKPOINT*/
#define BP_DATARW1 3

/* TWO-BYTE DATA WRITE BREAKPOINT*/
#define BP_DATAW2 5

/* TWO-BYTE DATA R/W BREAKPOINT*/
#define BP_DATARW2 7

/* FOUR-BYTE DATA WRITE BREAKPOINT*/
#define BP_DATAW4 13

/* FOUR-BYTE DATA R/W BREAKPOINT*/
#define BP_DATARW4 15

#endif
#endif
```

Figure 17-3 shows the output from a breakpoint dump when using *int1_386()*. The hexadecimal number on the first line reflects the contents of the lower half of the DR6 register when the breakpoint occurred. The display shows all 16-bit and segment registers (except FS and GS). Following that is a dump of 32 words of memory starting at the bottom of the stack (1CB1:09FA, in the example). The first three words of the stack are from the debug interrupt. The first word is the IP register, followed by the CS register and the flags. A simple change in the interrupt handler can remove this extra data from the display (as explained in the following section).

80386 DEBUGGING

```
Program breakpoint:0FF1
AX=0000 FL=7216 BX=0080 CX=0007 DX=06AA
SI=0000 DI=0A00 SP=09FA BP=0882
CS=1B66 IP=0051 DS=1BAD ES=1B56 SS=1CB1
Stack dump:(1CB1 : 09FA)
0051 1B66 7216 0000 0000 0000 0000 0000 0000 0000 0000 0000 0000 0000 0000 0000
0000 0000 0000 0000 0000 0000 0000 0000 0000 0000 0000 0000 0000 0000 0000 0000

CODE=1B66 : 0049 =6A 04 E8 3F 00 83 C4 08 * B9 14 00 8A D1 80 C2 41

<V>iew output, <T>race toggle, <C>ontinue or <A>bort?_
```

Figure 17-3. Sample output from a breakpoint dump.

Below the stack dump is a dump of program code, which usually consists of 16 bytes: eight bytes before the current instruction and eight at the instruction pointer. This is convenient for data breakpoints because they occur after the offending instruction executes. The dump shows the starting memory address (1B66:0049) followed by the bytes at that address. An asterisk marks the current CS:IP location, followed by the remaining eight bytes. If IP is less than eight, the code dump starts at CS:0, resulting in fewer than eight bytes before the asterisk.

The last line of the dump prompts you for further action. You can:

- View your program's output screen. When you select this option, BREAK386 replaces the current screen with your program's original output. To restore the debugging screen, press any key.

- Toggle the trace flag. This will switch the state of the trace or single-step flag and continue the program in the same manner as the *C* command (see the following option). To determine whether tracing is on, examine the value of DR6. If bit 14 is set (4000H), tracing is on.

- Continue execution of the program. This option causes the program to resume where it left off and execute until the next breakpoint (if the trace flag is clear) or to the next instruction (if the trace flag is set).

669

DOS 5: A DEVELOPER'S GUIDE

- Abort the program. This will cause the program to exit. Be careful when using this option: If you have interrupt vectors intercepted, expanded memory allocated, or anything else that need to be fixed before you quit, the *A* command won't resolve these things unless you rewrite the interrupt handler or *clear386()*. (Also, if your program spawns child processes and the breakpoint occurred in the child, the abort command will terminate the child; the parent program will continue without breakpoints.)

Listings 17-4 and 17-5 show examples of how BREAK386 is used in assembly and C. BREAK386.H and BREAK386.INC define the identifiers beginning with *BP_*.

Listing 17-4. DEBUG386.ASM.

```
;****************************************************************
;*                                                              *
;* File: DEBUG386.ASM                                            *
;*                                                              *
;* Description:                                                 *
;* Sample assembly-language program for use with BREAK386.       *
;*                                                              *
;* Compile with MASM /Ml DEBUG386.ASM                            *
;*          or TASM /Ml DEBUG386.ASM                             *
;*                                                              *
;****************************************************************

        .MODEL      SMALL

        INCLUDE     BREAK386.INC
        .STACK      0A00H
        .386
        .DATA
        ALIGN       2                   ; Make sure word is aligned.
        MEMCELL     DW      0           ; cell to write to
```

80386 DEBUGGING

```
.CODE

MAIN            PROC
;Set up data segment.
            MOV     AX,@data
            MOV     DS,AX
            ASSUME  CS:@code,DS:@data

; Start debugging.
; Push segment of int handler and...
            PUSH    SEG _int1_386
; offset of int handler.
            PUSH    OFFSET _int1_386
            CALL    _setup386
            ADD     SP,4            ; Balance stack.
; Set up a starting breakpoint.
            PUSH    SEG BP1         ; segment of breakpoint
            PUSH    OFFSET BP1      ; offset of breakpoint
            PUSH    BP_CODE         ; breakpoint type
            PUSH    1               ; breakpoint # (1-4)
            CALL    _break386
            ADD     SP,8            ; Balance the stack.

            PUSH    SEG BP2         ; Set up breakpoint #2.
            PUSH    OFFSET BP2
            PUSH    BP_CODE
            PUSH    2
            CALL    _break386
            ADD     SP,8

            PUSH    SEG BP3         ; Set up breakpoint #3.
            PUSH    OFFSET BP3
            PUSH    BP_CODE
            PUSH    3
            CALL    _break386
            ADD     SP,8

            PUSH    @data           ; Set up breakpoint #4 (DATA).
            PUSH    OFFSET MEMCELL
            PUSH    BP_DATAW2
            PUSH    4
```

DOS 5: A DEVELOPER'S GUIDE

```
                CALL    _break386
                ADD     SP,8

BP1:
                MOV     CX,20           ; Loop 20 times.
LOOP1:
                MOV     DL,CL           ; Print some letters.
                ADD     DL,'@'
                MOV     AH,2
BP2:
                INT     21H
BP3:
                LOOP    LOOP1           ; Repeat.
; Point BX at memory cell.
                MOV     BX,OFFSET MEMCELL
                MOV     AX,[BX]         ; Read cell (no breakpoint).
                MOV     [BX],AH         ; This should be fire # 4.
                CALL    _clear386       ; Shut off debugging.
                MOV     AH,4CH
                INT     21H             ; back to DOS
MAIN            ENDP
                END     MAIN
```

Listing 17-5. DBG386.C.

```c
/*****************************************************************
 *                                                               *
 * File: DBG386.C                                                *
 *                                                               *
 * Sample C program using BREAK386 with the built-in interrupt   *
 * handler.                                                      *
 *                                                               *
 *****************************************************************/

#include <stdio.h>
#include <dos.h>
#include "break386.h"

int here[10];
void far *bp;
int i;
```

80386 DEBUGGING

```
main()
   {
   int j;
   setup386(int1_386);                    /* Set up debugging. */
/* Make long pointer to data word. */
   bp=(void far *)&here[2];
   break386(1,BP_DATAW2,bp);              /* Set breakpoint. */
   for (j=0;j<2;j++)                      /* Loop twice. */
      {
/* for each element in here[] */
      for (i=0;i<10;i++)
         {
         char x;
         putchar(i+'0');                  /* Print index digit. */
/* Assign # to array element. */
         here[i]=i;
         }
/* Turn off breakpoint on 2nd pass. */
      break386(1,0,NULL);
      }
   clear386();                            /* Turn off debugging. */
   }
```

Your program must call *setup386()* before any other BREAK386 calls. You should pass it a segment and an offset pointing to the interrupt handler. After calling *setup386()*, you may use *break386()* to set and clear breakpoints. Figure 17-4 shows the parameters *break386()* requires.

Keep in mind a few facts about the 386 when setting breakpoints or tracing. First, two- and four-byte data breakpoints must be aligned according to their size. For example, it is incorrect to set a two-byte breakpoint at location 1000:0015 because that location is on an odd byte. Similarly, a four-byte breakpoint can monitor address 1000:0010 or 1000:0014 but not address 1000:0013. If you must watch an unaligned data item, you'll have to set multiple breakpoints. For example, to monitor two bytes at 1000:0015, set a one-byte breakpoint at 1000:0015 and another at 1000:0016.

673

DOS 5: A DEVELOPER'S GUIDE

---

retcode=break386(n,type,address);
where:
    n is the breakpoint number (from 1 to 4).
    type is the type of breakpoint. This should be one of the manifest constants defined in BREAK386.H (or BREAK386.INC0. If you are clearing the breakpoint, the type is not meaningful.
    address is the breakpoint address. This must be a far address (that is, one with both segment and offset). If you are using a small model C, you should cast the pointer to be a far type (see the example). To clear a breakpoint, set address to 0000:0000 (or a far NULL in C).
    retcode is returned by the function. A zero indicates success. A nonzero value means that you tried to set a breakpoint less than 1 or greater than 4. Note that the type parameter is not checked for validity.

The types available are:
- BP_CODE   • Code breakpoint
- BP_DATAW1   • One-byte data write breakpoint
- BP_DATARW1   • One-byte data read/write breakpoint
- BP_DATAW2   • Two-byte data write breakpoint
- BP_DATARW2   • Two-byte data read/write breakpoint
- BP_DATAW4   • Four-byte data write breakpoint
- BP_DATARW4   • Four-byte data read/write breakpoint

Figure 17-4. The parameters required by breakpoint386().

Also keep in mind that a data breakpoint will occur even if you access only a portion of its range. For instance, if you're monitoring a word at 2200:00F0 and a program writes a byte to 2200:00F1, a breakpoint will occur. Since the breakpoint addresses are linear, a write to address 220F:0000 will also trigger the breakpoint.

Setting a data breakpoint with *break386()* will also set the GE bit. When the program reassigns or deactivates all data breakpoints, *break386()* will clear the exact bit.

Because *int1_386()* always sets the resume flag, you'll find that a code breakpoint immediately following a data breakpoint won't work. We'll see how to rectify this problem shortly.

80386 DEBUGGING

The *INT* and *INTO* instructions temporarily clear the trace flag, so BREAK386 won't single-step through interrupt handlers. If you wish to do so, you must set a breakpoint on the routine's first instruction. A replacement for *int1_386()* might emulate *INT* and *INTO* to solve this problem.

Because BREAK386 uses BIOS keyboard and video routines, you shouldn't place breakpoints in these routines. In addition, refrain from single-stepping BIOS keyboard and video routines. If you must debug in these areas, reassemble BREAK386 so that it doesn't use the BIOS (see the *DIRECT* equate in BREAK386.ASM). Note, however, that many of its features will no longer function. Finally, you should avoid setting breakpoints in BREAK386's code or data.

BREAK386.INC contains two macros, *TRACEON* and *TRACEOFF*, that you can insert anywhere in your code to enable or disable tracing. Remember, however, that you'll see the *TRACEOFF* macro along with your own code when single-stepping.

The function *clear386()*, which turns off the breakpoint handlers, must be called before the program exits. If you fail to call this function for any reason (for instance, a Control-Break or a critical error), the next program that uses a location for which you have set a breakpoint will cause the break to occur. Unfortunate consequences can result because your INT 1 handler is probably no longer in memory. If you find that you have exited a program without turning off debugging and have not encountered a breakpoint, cross your fingers and run DBGOFF (Listing 17-6) to turn off hardware debugging.

If care is taken, BREAK386 can be used with other debuggers. In CodeView, for example, BREAK386 works fine as long as you don't single-step. When you do, data breakpoints are ignored and BREAK386 code breakpoints "freeze" CodeView at that step. If you're using BREAK386 with CodeView, it's a good idea to leave the code breakpoints and single-stepping to CodeView.

Listing 17-6. DBGOFF.ASM.

```
;******************************************************************
;*                                                                *
;* File: DBGOFF.ASM                                               *
;*                                                                *
;* Description:                                                   *
;* Try this program if you leave a program abnormally (say,       *
;* with a stack overflow). It will reset the debug register.      *
;*                                                                *
;* Compile with MASM DBGOFF                                       *
;*         or TASM DBGOFF                                         *
;*                                                                *
;******************************************************************

        .MODEL      SMALL
        .STACK      32
        .386P
        .CODE

MAIN            PROC
                XOR     EAX,EAX         ; Clear DR7.
                MOV     DR7,EAX
                MOV     AH,4CH          ; Exit to DOS.
                INT     21H
MAIN            ENDP
                END     MAIN
```

Detailed Program Operation

BREAK386 begins with the *.386P* directive, which ensures that Turbo Assembler or Microsoft Assembler will generate references to the debug registers. Be careful to place the *.MODEL* directive before the *.386P*; otherwise, 32-bit segments will be generated (they don't work well with unmodified DOS!).

The parameters you may want to change are near the top of the source file. The equate to *DIRECT* controls the video mode. If *DIRECT* is zero, BREAK386 uses the BIOS for I/O. If, however, you want to poke around in the keyboard or video routines, you must set *DIRECT* to one. This will cause BREAK386 to use direct video output

80386 DEBUGGING

for the debug dump. It will share the screen with your program (no video swapping), and breakpoints will simply terminate the program in a similar manner to the *A* command mentioned earlier.

You can change the *STKWRD* equate to control the number of words *int1_386()* dumps from the stack. Setting this equate to zero will completely disable stack dumping. Similarly, if you set *INTSTACK* to zero, the display won't show the IP, CS, and FLAGS registers at the top of the stack. If you're writing your own interrupt handler and don't need *int1_386()*, you can assemble with *ENABLE_INT1* set to zero to reduce BREAK386's size.

While the operation of *start386()*, *clear386()*, and *break386()* is straightforward, the implementation of *int1_386()* deserves some comment. It's important to realize that *int1_386()* only debugs non-386-specific programs because it saves the 16-bit registers and 8086 segment registers (it doesn't destroy FS and GS). *int1_386()* only runs on a 386, so it does use the 32-bit registers. You can easily modify it to save all the 386 registers, but it will require more space on the interrupted program's stack.

The most difficult aspect of the interrupt handler is resume-flag management. The code below label *C1* converts the three words at the top of the stack into six words to allow the resume flag to be set. There are three things to remember about how BREAK386 manages the resume flag:

1. As mentioned earlier, *int1_386()* always sets the resume flag. As a result, a code breakpoint that occurs immediately after a data breakpoint won't cause an interrupt. This is because the resume flag is set even though the instruction that generated the data breakpoint has already executed. When the program restarts, the next instruction will execute with the resume flag set. You can rectify this problem by not setting the resume flag in the interrupt handler when processing data breakpoints.

2. An interrupt handler written entirely in C has no way to manipulate the resume flag properly. Listing 17-7, however, shows two assembly-language

677

DOS 5: A DEVELOPER'S GUIDE

functions that allow you to write your handler in C. (See the following section for more details on writing C interrupt handlers.)

3. In real mode, hardware interrupt handlers (for example, those in the BIOS) probably won't preserve the resume flag. This means that if your code runs with interrupts enabled, there is a slight chance that one code breakpoint will cause two interrupts. This chance increases greatly if interrupts remain disabled during the INT 1 processing. That's because if the 386 receives a hardware interrupt just before executing an instruction with the resume flag set, it will process that interrupt. When the interrupt returns, the resume flag is clear and the breakpoint occurs again. If the program disables interrupts for the duration of breakpoint processing, it is much more likely that an interrupt will be pending when the program restarts. If the debug interrupt enables interrupts, however, there is little chance of this happening. If it does, simply press C (when using *int1_386()*).

Listing 17-7. CBRK386.ASM.

```
;****************************************************************
;*                                                              *
;* File: CBRK386.ASM                                            *
;*                                                              *
;* Description:                                                 *
;* Functions to allow breakpoint handlers to be written in C.   *
;*                                                              *
;* Compile with MASM /Ml CBRK386.ASM                            *
;*         or TASM /Ml CBRK386.ASM                              *
;*                                                              *
;****************************************************************

; If using Microsoft C, set MSC to 1--this allows CBRK386 to
; fool Microsoft's stack-checking algorithm. (You could disable
; stack checking, but most of the library has stack checking.)
; For Turbo C, just disable stack checking and set MSC to 0.
MSC             EQU     0
.MODEL          SMALL
.386P
```

80386 DEBUGGING

```
                PUBLIC  _csetup386

; Set up stack offsets for word size arguments based on the code
; size.
; Be careful: regardless of what Microsoft's documentation says,
; you must use @CodeSize (not @codesize, etc.).

IF              @CodeSize
; true for models with far code
ARG1            EQU     <[BP+6]>
ARG2            EQU     <[BP+8]>
ARG3            EQU     <[BP+10]>
ARG4            EQU     <[BP+12]>
ELSE
; true for models with near code
ARG1            EQU     <[BP+4]>
ARG2            EQU     <[BP+6]>
ARG3            EQU     <[BP+8]>
ARG4            EQU     <[BP+10]>
ENDIF



        .DATA
; You may need to change the next line to expand the stack
; your breakpoint handler runs with.
STACKSIZE       EQU     2048

; old INT 1 vector
OLDOFFSET       DW      0
OLDSEGMENT      DW      0

; old stack
OLDSTACK        EQU     THIS DWORD
SP_SAVE         DW      0
SS_SAVE         DW      0

; old ds/es
DS_SAVE         DW      0
ES_SAVE         DW      0
```

```
; C routine's address is saved here.
CCALL           EQU     THIS DWORD
C_OFF           DW      0
C_SEG           DW      0
        IF      MSC
OLDSTKHQQ       DW      0               ; old start of stack
        ENDIF

; new stack address for C routine
NEWSP           EQU     THIS DWORD
                DW      OFFSET STACKTOP
                DW      SEG NEWSTACK

; Here is the new stack. DO NOT MOVE IT OUT OF DGROUP.
; That is, leave it in the DATA or DATA? segment.
NEWSTACK        DB      STACKSIZE DUP (0)
STACKTOP        EQU     $

        IF      MSC
; Microsoft heap/stack bound
                EXTRN   STKHQQ:WORD
        ENDIF

.CODE

; This routine is called in place of setup386(). You pass it the
; address of a void far function that you want invoked on a
; breakpoint.
; Its operation is identical to setup386() except:
;
;       1) The int 1 vector is set to cint1_386() (see below)
;       2) The address passed is stored in location CCALL
;       3) DS and ES are stored in ds_save and es_save

_csetup386      PROC
                PUSH    BP
                MOV     BP,SP
                PUSH    ES
                MOV     ES_SAVE,ES
                MOV     DS_SAVE,DS
                MOV     AX,3501H
```

80386 DEBUGGING

```
                INT     21H
                MOV     OLDSEGMENT,ES
                MOV     OLDOFFSET,BX
                POP     ES
                MOV     AX,ARG2
                PUSH    DS
                MOV     DX,ARG1
                MOV     C_SEG,AX
                MOV     C_OFF,DX
                MOV     AX,SEG _cint1_386
                MOV     DS,AX
                MOV     DX,OFFSET _cint1_386
                MOV     AX,2501H
                INT     21H
                POP     DS
                XOR     EAX,EAX
                MOV     DR6,EAX
                POP     BP
                RET
_csetup386      ENDP

;****************************************************************
;*                                                              *
;* Here is the interrupt handler!!!                             *
;* Two arguments are passed to C: a far pointer to the base of  *
;* the stack frame and the complete contents of dr6 as a long   *
;* unsigned int.                                                *
;*                                                              *
;* The stack frame is as follows:                               *
;*                                                              *
;*       .                                                      *
;*       .                                                      *
;*    (interrupted code's stack)                                *
;*    FLAGS                                                     *
;*    CS                                                        *
;*    IP  <─┐                                                   *
;*    AX    │                                                   *
;*    CX    │                                                   *
;*    DX    │                                                   *
;*    BX    │                                                   *
;*    SP  ──┘   (Stack pointer points to IP above.)             *
```

DOS 5: A DEVELOPER'S GUIDE

```
;*      BP                                                          *
;*      SI                                                          *
;*      DI                                                          *
;*      ES                                                          *
;*      DS                                                          *
;*      SS <─────  pointer passed to your routine points here.      *
;*                                                                  *
;* The pointer is two-way. That is, you can read the values or      *
;* set any of them except SS. You should, however, refrain from     *
;* changing CS, IP, or SP.                                          *
;*                                                                  *
;********************************************************************

_cint1_386      PROC
                PUSHA                   ; Save registers.
                PUSH    ES
                PUSH    DS
                PUSH    SS
                MOV     AX,@data        ; Point at our data segment.
                MOV     DS,AX
                MOV     SS_SAVE,SS      ; Remember old stack location.
                MOV     SP_SAVE,SP
                CLD
                LSS     SP,NEWSP        ; Switch stacks.

IF              MSC
                MOV     AX,STKHQQ       ; Save old end of stack.
                MOV     OLDSTKHQQ,AX
; Load new end of stack.
                MOV     AX,OFFSET NEWSTACK
                MOV     STKHQQ,AX
ENDIF
                STI
                MOV     EAX,DR6         ; Put DR6 on stack for C.
                PUSH    EAX
                PUSH    SS_SAVE         ; Put ptr to stack frame
                PUSH    SP_SAVE         ; on new stack for C.
                MOV     ES,ES_SAVE      ; Restore es/ds.
                MOV     DS,DS_SAVE
                CALL    CCALL           ; Call the C program.
                XOR     EAX,EAX         ; Clear DR6.
```

80386 DEBUGGING

```
                MOV     DR6,EAX
                MOV     AX,@data
                MOV     DS,AX           ; Regain access to data.
                LSS     SP,OLDSTACK     ; Restore old stack.
                ADD     SP,2            ; Don't pop off SS
                                        ; (in case user changed it).
IF      MSC
                MOV     AX,OLDSTKHQQ    ; Restore end of stack.
                MOV     STKHQQ,AX
ENDIF
                POP     DS
                POP     ES
                POPA
```

; This seems complicated at first.
; You MUST ensure that RF is set before continuing. If RF is not
; set, you will just cause a breakpoint immediately (for code)!
; In protected mode this is handled automatically. In real mode
; it isn't since RF is in the high 16 bits of the flags register.
; Essentially we have to convert the stack from:
;
; 16-bit flags   32-bit flags (top word = 1 to set RF)
; 16-bit CS   to —> 32-bit CS   (garbage in top 16 bits)
; 16-bit IP   32-bit IP   (top word = 0)
;
; All this so we can execute an IRETD, which will change RF.

```
                SUB     ESP,6           ; Make a double stack frame.
                XCHG    AX,[ESP+6]      ; Get IP in AX.
                MOV     [ESP],AX        ; Store it.
                XOR     AX,AX
                MOV     [ESP+2],AX      ; eip = 0000:ip
                MOV     AX,[ESP+6]
                XCHG    AX,[ESP+8]      ; Get CS.
                MOV     [ESP+4],AX
                XOR     AX,AX
                MOV     [ESP+6],AX
                MOV     AX,[ESP+8]      ; Zero stack word & restore AX.
                XCHG    AX,[ESP+10]     ; Get flags
                MOV     [ESP+8],AX
                MOV     AX,1            ; Set RF.
```

```
                XCHG    AX,[ESP+10]
                IRETD                   ; double IRET (32 bits!)
_cint1_386      ENDP
                END
```

Advanced Interrupt Handlers in C

An interrupt handler that monitors data breakpoints could be written entirely in C. The handler must be declared as a far interrupt function. For example, the following function could be linked with the example in Listing 17-5:

```
void interrupt far new1(INTREGS)
    {
    printf("\nBreakpoint reached.\n");
    }
```

By calling *setup386(new1)* instead of *setup386(int1_386)*, you cause *new1()* to be invoked for every breakpoint. Your function can read and write the interrupted program's registers using the supplied parameters (*Rax*, *Rbx*, and so on). Keep in mind that you cannot use this technique for code breakpoints. C's inability to manipulate the resume flag will cause an endless loop on a code breakpoint.

If you use Turbo C, don't enable stack checking for the interrupt function or any functions that the interrupt function calls. By default, Turbo C doesn't stack check; if you use the defaults, everything will work fine.

Listing 17-7 (CBRK386.ASM) provides the functions to write interrupt handlers in C. The procedure is much the same as described earlier except that you must call *csetup386()* instead of *setup386()*. The argument to *csetup386()* is always a pointer to an ordinary far function (even in the small model).

If you plan to use Microsoft C, you must set the *MSC* equate at the top of CBRK386.ASM to one. This will enable code that tricks Microsoft's stack-checking functions. Since most of the Microsoft library always checks the stack, BREAK386

80386 DEBUGGING

must use this code when it switches the stack. Otherwise, erroneous stack overflow messages will occur. With Turbo C, you should set *MSC* to zero.

The actual interrupt handler is *_cint1_386()*. This function will call your C code when an interrupt occurs and pass your routine two arguments. The first, a far void pointer, points to the beginning of the interrupted stack frame (see Figure 17-5 for the format of the stack frame). The second argument is an unsigned long integer that contains the contents of DR6.

Address	Contents	
PTR + 28	Code's stack	
PTR + 26	Flags	
PTR + 24	CS	
PTR + 22	IP	
PTR + 20	AX	
PTR + 18	CX	
PTR + 16	DX	
PTR + 14	BX	
PTR + 12	SP	← Points to IP (above)
PTR + 10	BP	
PTR + 8	SI	
PTR + 6	DI	
PTR + 4	ES	
PTR + 2	DS	
PTR + 0	SS	← Pointer passed to C routine (PTR)

Example:

To read AX use:

n=*((unsigned int far*)PTR+10);

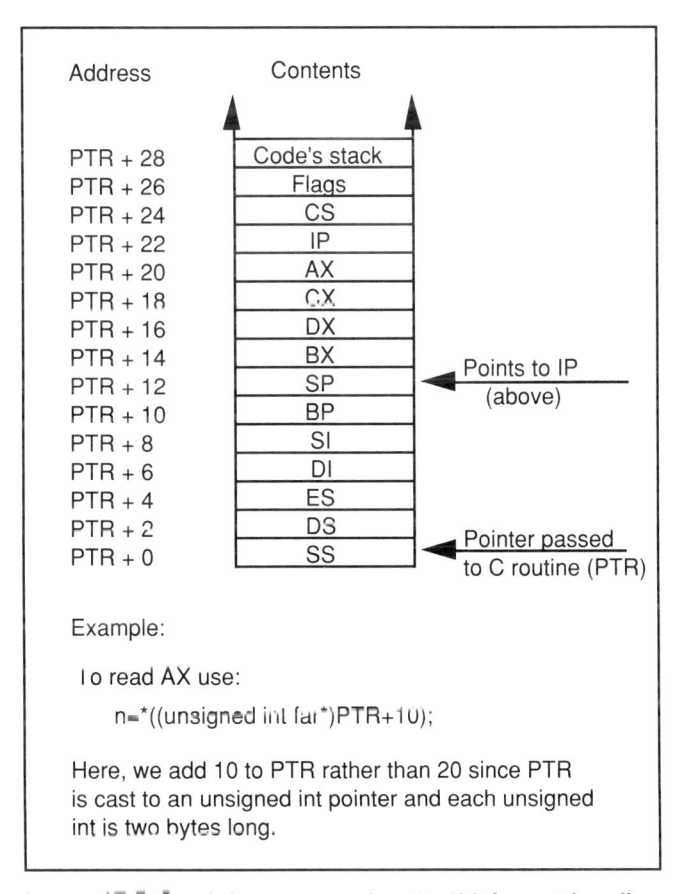

Here, we add 10 to PTR rather than 20 since PTR is cast to an unsigned int pointer and each unsigned int is two bytes long.

Figure 17-5. Stack frame passed to the C interrupt handler.

All registers and local variables on the stack can be read using the pointer to the stack frame (if you know where to look). In addition, all values (except SS) can be modified. It's usually wise not to modify SP, CS, or IP.

_cint1_386() switches to a local stack. The size of the stack can be controlled using *STACKSIZE* (near the top of Listing 17-7). Be sure to adjust the stack if you need more space.

Listing 17-8 shows an interrupt handler in C. This example displays a breakpoint message and allows you to continue with or without breakpoints, abort the program, or change the value of a local variable in the *loop()* function. The variable only changes in this function—the value of *i* in *main()* remains the same.

Listing 17-8. CBRKDEMO.C.
```
/***************************************************************
 *                                                              *
 * File: CBRKDEMO.C                                             *
 *                                                              *
 * Sample C interrupt handler for use with CBRK386.             *
 *                                                              *
 ***************************************************************/

#include <stdio.h>
#include <conio.h>
#include <ctype.h>
#include <dos.h>
#include "break386.h"

/* functions we will reference */
int loop();

void far broke();

main()
   {
   int i;
```

80386 DEBUGGING

```
/* Declare function broke as our interrupt handler. */
   csetup386(broke);
/* Set break at function loop. */
   break386(1,BP_CODE,(void far *) loop);
   for (i=0;i<10;i++) loop(i);
   printf("Returned to main.\n");
/* Turn off debugging. */
   clear386();
   }

/* This function has a breakpoint on its entry. */
loop(int i)
   {
   printf("Now in loop (%d)\n",i);
   }


/*****************************************************************
 *                                                                *
 * Here is the interrupt handler!!!                               *
 * Note it must be a far function (normal in large, huge, and    *
 * medium models). Two arguments are passed: a far pointer to    *
 * base of the stack frame and the complete contents of DR6 as   *
 * a long unsigned int.                                           *
 *                                                                *
 * The stack frame is as follows:                                 *
 *                                                                *
 *      .                                                         *
 *      .                                                         *
 *   (interrupted code's stack)                                   *
 *   FLAGS                                                        *
 *   CS                                                           *
 *   IP <──┐                                                      *
 *   AX    │                                                      *
 *   CX    │                                                      *
 *   DX    │                                                      *
 *   BX    │                                                      *
 *   SP ───┘(Stack pointer points to IP above.)                   *
 *   BP                                                           *
 *   SI                                                           *
 *   DI                                                           *
```

```
 *    ES                                                         *
 *    DS                                                         *
 *    SS <──────pointer passed to your routine points here.      *
 *                                                               *
 * The pointer is two-way. That is, you can read the values or   *
 * set any of them except SS. You should, however, refrain from  *
 * changing CS, IP, or SP.                                       *
 *                                                               *
 ****************************************************************/
void far broke(void far *p,long dr6)
    {
/* Don't do anything if breaking=0. */
   static int breaking=1;
   int c;
   if (breaking)
       {
       int n;
       int far *ip;
/****************************************************************
 *                                                               *
 * Here we will read the local variable off the interrupted      *
 * program's stack! Assuming small model, the stack above our    *
 * stack frame looks like this:                                  *
 *                                                               *
 *      i   -  variable sent to loop                             *
 *      add -  address to return to main with                    *
 *    <our stack frame starts here>                              *
 *                                                               *
 * This makes i the 15th word on the stack (16th on models with  *
 * far code).                                                    *
 *                                                               *
 ****************************************************************/

/* Use 16 for large, medium, or huge model. */
#define IOFFSET 15

     n=*((unsigned int far *) p+IOFFSET);
     printf("\nBreakpoint reached! (DR6=%lX i=%d)\n",dr6,n);
/* Ask user what to do. */
     do {
```

80386 DEBUGGING

```
        printf("<C>ontinue, <M>odify i,"
          " <A>bort, or <N>o breakpoint? ");
        c=getche();
        putch('\r');
        putch('\n');                     /* Start a new line. */
/* function key pressed */
        if (!c)
          {
          getch();
          continue;
          }
        c=toupper(c);
/* Modify loop's copy of i (doesn't change main's i). */
        if (c=='M')
          {
          int newi;
          printf("Enter new value for i: ");
          scanf("%d",&newi);
          *((unsigned int far *) p+IOFFSET)=newi;
          continue;
          }
        if (c=='A')                      /* exiting */
          {
/* ALWAYS turn off debugging!!! */
          clear386();
          exit(0);
          }
/* We could turn off breakpoints, but instead
   we'll set breaking to zero. */

        if (c=='N') breaking=0;
        } while (c!='A'&&c!='N'&&c!='C');
      }
   }
```

Many enhancements and modifications are possible with BREAK386. By altering the words on *int1_386()*'s stack, for example, you can modify registers. You can redirect output to the printer by replacing the OUCH routine. Perhaps the most

689

ambitious enhancement would be to use BREAK386 as the core of your own debugger. You could write a stand-alone or TSR debugger that would pop up over another debugger.

Keep in mind that 386 hardware breakpoints aren't just for debugging; the data breakpoint capability has many uses. For example, you might want to monitor the BIOS keyboard type-ahead buffer's head and tail pointers to see when a keystroke occurs (or is read). You could then capture the keyboard interrupt in such a way that other programs couldn't reprogram your interrupt vector. You also can use data breakpoints to detect interrupt vector changes or interrupt processing. Some assembly-language programs could use data breakpoints for automatic stack overflow detection. Programs that decrement the stack pointer without using a push instruction (C programs, for example) are not candidates for this type of stack protection.

CHAPTER 18

Accessing 4 Gigabytes in Real Mode

Ever since Intel introduced the 8088 and 8086, programmers have chafed at the 64-Kbyte limit imposed by the 8086's segmented architecture. Dealing with data structures greater than 64 Kbytes has required great feats of legerdemain and been all but impossible in some high-level languages. The 286 came along, but it still used 64-Kbyte segments. Though the 286 can address 16 Mbytes of memory, DOS only knows how to deal with the first megabyte. Finally, the 386 arrived on the scene. As we have seen, protected mode gives programmers unprecedented flexibility in dealing with segments and memory space.

Unfortunately, DOS still limits programmers to 1 Mbyte. In this chapter, we will look at a method for accessing the entire 386 address space (4 Gbytes) as one flat range of addresses. The sample programs in this chapter use CEXT.C from Chapter 16.

The Plan

We can access 4 Gbytes from DOS due to the undocumented behavior of the 386 in real mode. Intel recommends setting all the segment registers to selectors that have a 64-Kbyte limit before switching from protected mode to real mode. If, however, you disregard the documentation and set the segment registers to selectors with a different limit, the 386 retains that limit during real-mode operations. You can set up protected-mode segment registers with a 4-Gbyte limit before returning to real mode, and DOS will have access to the entire 386 address space.

To address the entire memory space from real mode, you must:

1. Disable interrupts, including NMI.
2. Switch to protected mode.
3. Load one or more segment registers with a "big" (4-Gbyte) segment.
4. Switch back to real mode.
5. Enable interrupts.

Once the program completes these steps, the segment registers remain modified until a processor is reset or another protected-mode program reloads them. Because real mode doesn't use segment descriptors, real-mode programs never reload the descriptor cache.

Listings 18-1 through 18-4 show the SEG4G library that performs these functions. Don't try to compile them, however, until you read the next section.

Listing 18-1. ASMFUNC.H.

```
/****************************************************************
*                                                                *
* File: asmfunc.h                                                *
*                                                                *
* Description:                                                   *
* Execute an assembly-language routine in an array. The          *
* function can return an int and should be called as a far       *
* function no matter what model the C program uses.              *
*                                                                *
* For example, to call an array named foo with arguments bar     *
* and bar1, use:                                                 *
*       (asmfunc foo)(bar,bar1);                                 *
*                                                                *
****************************************************************/

#define asmfunc *(int (far *)())
```

ACCESSING 4 GIGABYTES IN REAL MODE

Listing 18-2. SEG4G.H.
```
/****************************************************************
 *                                                              *
 * File: seg4g.h                                                *
 *                                                              *
 * Description:                                                 *
 * Header for programs using the SEG4G library.                 *
 *                                                              *
 ****************************************************************/

#ifndef SEG4GHEADER
#define SEG4GHEADER
#include "cext.h"

/* Set this variable to 0 for normal 386,
   1 for Intel Inboard 386/PC. */
extern int inboard;

/* function prototypes */
void far *linear_to_seg(LPTR lin);
void extend_seg(void);
void a20(int flag);
unsigned int big_read(LPTR address);
void big_write(LPTR address,unsigned int byte);
void big_xfer(LPTR src, LPTR dst, unsigned long count);

#endif
```

Listing 18-3. SEG4G.C.
```
/****************************************************************
 *                                                              *
 * File: seg4g.c                                                *
 *                                                              *
 * Description:                                                 *
 * Allow access to a flat memory space (up to 4GB) under real   *
 * mode.                                                        *
 *                                                              *
 ****************************************************************/
```

DOS 5: A DEVELOPER'S GUIDE

```c
/*
    You may select one of three methods for incorporating
    assembly-language subroutines into SEG4G.
    The three methods are:
    ASM    - Use Microsoft's MASM 5.1 (Microsoft & Turbo only)
    DATA   - Use the asmfunc macro defined in ASMFUNC.H (all)
    ASMARY - Use the asm function in Power C (Power C only)

    The DATA method works with all of the supported compilers, but
    the other methods are included as points of interest.

    You must select one of the three methods below:
*/

#define ASM 1
#define DATA 2
#define ASMARY 3

/* Make your selection here: */
#define METHOD DATA

/* If using an Intel Inboard 386/PC, set this variable to 1. */
int inboard=0;
/* If using a PS/2, set this variable to 1. */
int ps2=0;

#include <dos.h>
/* Don't get CLS function in COMPAT.H. */
#define NOCLSFUNC 1
#include "compat.h"
#include "seg4g.h"

/* Only include asmfunc.h if required. */
#if METHOD==DATA
#include "asmfunc.h"
#endif

/* keyboard controller defines */
#define RAMPORT 0x70
#define KB_PORT 0x64
```

ACCESSING 4 GIGABYTES IN REAL MODE

```c
#define PCNMIPORT 0xA0
#define INBA20 0x60
#define INBA20ON 0xDF
#define INBA20OFF 0xDD
#define PS2PORT 0x92

/******************************************************************
 * Convert a linear address to a far pointer.                     *
 ******************************************************************/

void far *linear_to_seg(LPTR lin)
   {
   void far *p;
   FP_SEG(p)=(unsigned int)(lin>>4);
   FP_OFF(p)=(unsigned int)(lin&0xF);
   return p;
   }

/* global descriptor table */
struct _GDT
   {
   unsigned int limit;
   unsigned int base;
   unsigned int access;
   unsigned int hi_limit;
   };

static struct _GDT GDT[2]=
   {
      {0,0,0,0},                     /* null selector slot */
      {0xFFFF,0,0x9200,0x8F}         /* 4-gig data segment */
   };

/* FWORD pointer to GDT */
   struct fword
      {
      unsigned int limit;
      unsigned long linear_add;
      };
```

695

DOS 5: A DEVELOPER'S GUIDE

```c
static struct fword gdtptr;              /* fword ptr to GDT */
#if METHOD==ASMARY||METHOD==DATA

/* protected-mode assembly-language routine */
static unsigned char code[]={
#if METHOD==DATA
        0x55,                   /* PUSH BP               */
        0x89, 0xe5,             /* MOV BP,SP             */
        0x1e,                   /* PUSH DS               */
        0xc5, 0x5e, 0x06,       /* LDS BX,[BP+6]         */
        0x0F, 0x01, 0x17,       /* LGDT FWORD PTR [BX]   */
        0x1f,                   /* POP DS                */
        0x0f, 0x20, 0xc0,       /* MOV EAX,CR0           */
        0x0c, 0x01,             /* OR AL,1               */
        0x0f, 0x22, 0xc0,       /* MOV CR0, EAX          */
        0xeb, 0x00,             /* JMP SHORT 00          */
        0xbb, 0x08, 0x00,       /* MOV BX,8              */
        0x8e, 0xeb,             /* MOV GS,BX             */
        0x8e, 0xc3,             /* MOV ES,BX             */
        0x24, 0xfe,             /* AND AL,0FEH           */
        0x0f, 0x22, 0xc0,       /* MOV CR0,EAX           */
        0x5d,                   /* POP BP                */
        0xcb};                  /* RETF                  */
#else
        0x0f, 0x01, 0x17,       /* LGDT [BX]             */
        0x0f, 0x20, 0xc0,       /* MOV EAX,CR0           */
        0x0c, 0x01,             /* OR AL,1               */
        0x0f, 0x22, 0xc0,       /* MOV CR0,EAX           */
        0xEB, 0x00,             /* JMP SHORT 0           */
        0xbb, 0x08, 0x00,       /* MOV BX,8              */
        0x8e, 0xeb,             /* MOV GS,BX             */
        0X8e, 0xc3,             /* MOV ES,BX             */
        0x24, 0xfe,             /* AND AL,0FEH           */
        0x0f, 0x22, 0xc0,       /* MOV CR0,EAX           */
        0xC3 };                 /* RETN                  */
#endif
#endif
```

ACCESSING 4 GIGABYTES IN REAL MODE

```c
/******************************************************************
 * Adjust the GS register's limit to 4 Gbytes.                    *
 * Note: Interrupts are enabled by this call.                     *
 ******************************************************************/
void extend_seg()
   {
   void far *mixbug=(void far *) GDT;
/* Compute linear address and limit of GDT. */
   gdtptr.linear_add=seg_to_linear(mixbug);
   gdtptr.limit=15;
/* Disable regular interrupts. */
   disable();
/* Disable NMI. */
   if (inboard) outp(PCNMIPORT,0);
   else outp(RAMPORT,inp(RAMPORT)|0x80);
/* Call protected-mode code. */

#if METHOD==ASM
   protsetup(&gdtptr);
#elif METHOD==DATA
   (asmfunc code)((void far *)&gdtptr);
#else
   asm(code,&gdtptr);
#endif

/* Turn interrupts back on. */
   enable();
/* Turn NMI back on. */
   if (inboard) outp(PCNMIPORT,0x80);
   else outp(RAMPORT,inp(RAMPORT)&0x7F);
   }

/* macro to clear keyboard port */
#define keywait(){while (inp(KB_PORT)&2);}

/******************************************************************
 * general-purpose routine to allow A20 (flag=1) or disable A20   *
 * (flag=0)                                                       *
 ******************************************************************/
void a20(int flag)
```

697

DOS 5: A DEVELOPER'S GUIDE

```c
    {
    if (inboard)
        {
        outp(INBA20,flag?INBA20ON:INBA20OFF);
        }
    else if (ps2)
        {
        outp(PS2PORT,flag?(inp(PS2PORT)|2):(inp(PS2PORT)&~2));
        while (((inp(PS2PORT)&2)>>1)!=flag);
        }
    else
        {
        keywait();
        outp(KB_PORT,0xD1);
        keywait();
        outp(INBA20,flag?INBA20ON:INBA20OFF);
        keywait();
        outp(KB_PORT,0xFF);
        keywait();
        }
    }

#if METHOD==DATA||METHOD==ASMARY

/* assembly code to read a byte */
static unsigned char rcode[]={
#if METHOD==DATA
        0x55,                           /* PUSH BP              */
        0x89, 0xe5,                     /* MOV BP,SP            */
        0x33, 0xc0,                     /* XOR AX,AX            */
        0x8e, 0xe8,                     /* MOV GS,AX            */
        0x66, 0x8b, 0x46, 0x06,         /* MOV EAX,[BP+6]       */
        0x65, 0x67, 0x8a, 0x00,         /* MOV AL,GS:[EAX]      */
        0x32, 0xe4,                     /* XOR AH,AH            */
        0x5d,                           /* POP BP               */
        0xcb};                          /* RETF                 */

#else
        0x31, 0xC0,                     /* XOR AX,AX            */
        0x65, 0x8e, 0xC0,               /* MOV GS,AX            */
```

ACCESSING 4 GIGABYTES IN REAL MODE

```
        0x66, 0x8b, 0x07,              /* MOV EAX,[BX]      */
        0x65, 0x67, 0x8a, 0x00,        /* MOV AL,GS:[EAX]   */
        0xC3 };                        /* RETN              */

#endif

/* assembly code to write a byte */
static unsigned char wcode[]=
    {
#if METHOD==DATA
        0x55,                          /* PUSH BP           */
        0x89, 0xe5,                    /* MOV BP,SP         */
        0x33, 0xc0,                    /* XOR AX,AX         */
        0x8e, 0xe8,                    /* MOV GS,AX         */
        0x66, 0x8b, 0x46, 0x06,        /* MOV EAX,[BP+6]    */
        0x8b, 0x5e, 0x0a,              /* MOV BX,[BP+10]    */
        0x65, 0x67, 0x88, 0x18,        /* MOV GS:[EAX],BL   */
        0x5d,                          /* POP BP            */
        0xcb};                         /* RETF              */
#else
        0x31, 0xC0,                    /* XOR AX,AX         */
        0x65, 0x8e, 0xC0,              /* MOV GS,AX         */
        0x66, 0x8b, 0x07,              /* MOV EAX,[BX]      */
        0x65, 0x67, 0xc6, 0x00, 0x00,  /* MOV GS:[EAX],??   */
        0xC3 };                        /* RETN              */
#endif

/* assembly code to block move bytes */
static unsigned char xcode[]=
    {
#if METHOD==DATA
        0x55,                          /* PUSH BP           */
        0x89, 0xe5,                    /* MOV BP,SP         */
        0x06,                          /* PUSH ES           */
        0x56,                          /* PUSH SI           */
        0X57,                          /* PUSH DI           */
        0x33, 0xc0,                    /* XOR AX,AX         */
        0x8e, 0xC0,                    /* MOV ES,AX         */
        0X66, 0X8B, 0X76, 0x06,        /* MOV ESI,[BP+6]    */
        0X66, 0X8B, 0X7E, 0X0A,        /* MOV EDI,[BP+0A]   */
```

```
                0X66, 0X8B, 0X4E, 0X0E,        /* MOV ECX,[BP+0E]   */
                0XFC,                          /* CLD               */
                0X67, 0XE3, 0X29,              /* JECX XEXIT        */
                0XF7, 0XC6, 0X03, 0X00,        /* TEST SI,3         */
                0x74, 0x0D,                    /* JZ XMAIN          */
                0XF7, 0XC7, 0X03, 0X00,        /* TEST DI,3         */
                0x74, 0x07,                    /* JZ XMAIN          */
                0X67, 0X26, 0XA4,              /* MOVSB ES:         */
                0x66, 0X49,                    /* DEC ECX           */
                0XEB, 0XEA,                    /* JMP XTEST         */
                0X51,                          /* PUSH CX           */
                0X66, 0XC1, 0XE9, 0X02,        /* SHR ECX,2         */
                0XF3, 0X67, 0X66, 0X26, 0XA5,  /* REP MOVSD ES:     */
                0X59,                          /* POP CX            */
                0X80, 0XE1, 0X03,              /* AND CX,3          */
                0XE3, 0X06,                    /* JCXZ XEXIT        */
                0X67, 0X26, 0XA4,              /* MOVSB ES:         */
                0X49,                          /* DEC CX            */
                0XEB, 0XF8,                    /* JMP XBYTE         */
                0X5F,                          /* POP DI            */
                0X5E,                          /* POP SI            */
                0x07,                          /* POP ES            */
                0X5D,                          /* POP BP            */
                0XCB};                         /* RETF              */

#else
                0x55,                          /* PUSH BP           */
                0x89, 0xe5,                    /* MOV BP,SP         */
                0x06,                          /* PUSH ES           */
                0x33, 0xc0,                    /* XOR AX,AX         */
                0x8E, 0xC0,                    /* MOV ES,AX         */
                0X66, 0XBE,                    /* MOV ESI,          */
                  0X00, 0X00, 0x00, 0x00,      /* SRC ADDRESS       */
                0x66, 0xBF,                    /* MOV EDI,          */
                  0x00, 0x00, 0x00, 0x00,      /* DST ADDRESS       */
                0x66, 0xB9,                    /* MOV ECX,          */
                  0x00, 0x00, 0x00, 0x00,      /* COUNT             */
                0XFC,                          /* CLD               */
                0X67, 0XE3, 0X29,              /* JECX XEXIT        */
                0XF7, 0XC6, 0X03, 0X00,        /* TEST SI,3         */
```

ACCESSING 4 GIGABYTES IN REAL MODE

```
    0x74, 0x0D,                      /* JZ XMAIN            */
    0XF7, 0XC7, 0X03, 0X00,          /* TEST DI,3           */
    0x74, 0x07,                      /* JZ XMAIN            */
    0X67, 0X26, 0XA4,                /* MOVSB ES:           */
    0x66, 0X49,                      /* DEC ECX             */
    0XEB, 0XEA,                      /* JMP XTEST           */
    0X51,                            /* PUSH CX             */
    0X66, 0XC1, 0XE9, 0X02,          /* SHR ECX,2           */
    0XF3, 0X67, 0X66, 0X26, 0XA5,    /* REP MOVSD ES:       */
    0X59,                            /* POP CX              */
    0X80, 0XE1, 0X03,                /* AND CX,3            */
    0XE3, 0X06,                      /* JCXZ XEXIT          */
    0X67, 0X26, 0XA4,                /* MOVSB ES:           */
    0X49,                            /* DEC CX              */
    0XEB, 0XF8,                      /* JMP XBYTE           */
    0x07,                            /* POP ES              */
    0X5D,                            /* POP BP              */
    0xC3};                           /* RETN                */

#endif

/***************************************************************
 * Read a single byte from memory given a linear address.      *
 ***************************************************************/
unsigned int big_read(LPTR address)
    {
#if METHOD==DATA
    return(asmfunc rcode)(address);
#else
    return asm(rcode,&address)&0xFF;
#endif
    }

/***************************************************************
 * Write a single byte to memory given a linear address.       *
 ***************************************************************/
void big_write(LPTR address,unsigned int byte)
    {
#if METHOD==DATA
    (asmfunc wcode)(address,byte);
```

DOS 5: A DEVELOPER'S GUIDE

```c
#else
   wcode[12]=byte;
   asm(wcode,&address);
#endif
   }

/******************************************************************
 * Block-move a number of bytes from one area to another.         *
 ******************************************************************/
void big_xfer(LPTR src,LPTR dst,unsigned long count)
   {
#if METHOD==DATA
   (asmfunc xcode)(src,dst,count);
#else
   *(LPTR *)&xcode[10]=src;
   *(LPTR *)&xcode[16]=dst;
   *(unsigned long *)&xcode[22]=count;
   asm(xcode,(void *)0);
#endif
   }

#endif
```

Listing 18-4. SEG4GB.ASM.

```
;******************************************************************
;*                                                                *
;* File: seg4gb.asm                                               *
;*                                                                *
;* Description:                                                   *
;* Enters protected mode and sets ES and GS to 4-Gbyte limit.     *
;* Also supplies read and write routines for LPTRs.               *
;*                                                                *
;******************************************************************

        .MODEL      SMALL,C
                    PUBLIC protsetup,big_read,big_write,big_xfer
        .386P

        .CODE
```

ACCESSING 4 GIGABYTES IN REAL MODE

```
IF              @DataSize
protsetup       PROC    FPOINTER:DWORD,C
                PUSH    DS
                LDS     BX,FPOINTER
ELSE
protsetup       PROC    FPOINTER:WORD,C
                MOV     BX,FPOINTER
ENDIF
; Load GDT.
                LGDT    FWORD PTR [BX]
IF              @DataSize
                POP     DS
ENDIF
                MOV     EAX,CR0         ; Goto prot mode.
                OR      AL,1
                MOV     CR0,EAX
                JMP     SHORT NXTLBL    ; Purge instruction.
NXTLBL:         MOV     BX,8            ; prefetch
                MOV     GS,BX           ; Load GS/ES.
                MOV     ES,BX
                AND     AL,0FEH         ; Go back to real mode.
                MOV     CR0,EAX
                RET
protsetup       ENDP

; Read a byte from an LPTR.
big_read        PROC    ADDRESS:DWORD,C
                XOR     AX,AX           ; Zero GS.
                MOV     GS,AX
                MOV     EAX,ADDRESS     ; Load LPTR
                MOV     AL,GS:[EAX]     ; Load byte.
                XOR     AH,AH           ; Zero AH.
                RET
big_read        ENDP

; Write a byte to an LPTR address.
big_write       PROC    ADDRESS:DWORD, BYT:WORD,C
                XOR     AX,AX           ; Zero GS.
                MOV     GS,AX
                MOV     EAX,ADDRESS     ; Load LPTR.
                MOV     BX,BYT          ; Load byte.
```

DOS 5: A DEVELOPER'S GUIDE

```
; Store byte -> LPTR.
                MOV     BYTE PTR GS:[EAX],BL
                RET
big_write       ENDP

; Block-move bytes between LPTRs.
big_xfer        PROC    SOURCE:DWORD, DEST:DWORD, COUNT:DWORD,C
                PUSH    ES
                PUSH    SI
                PUSH    DI
                XOR     AX,AX           ; Zero ES
                MOV     ES,AX
                MOV     ESI,SOURCE      ; Load source buffer.
                MOV     EDI,DEST        ; Load dest buffer.
                MOV     ECX,COUNT       ; Load count.
                CLD
; The following code tries its best to make efficient moves
; by moving bytes until word alignment is achieved.
XTEST:
                JECXZ   XEXIT           ; done?
                TEST    SI,3            ; SI word aligned?
                JZ      SHORT XMAIN
                TEST    DI,3            ; DI word aligned?
                JZ      SHORT XMAIN
; Move a byte.
                MOVS    ES:[ESI],BYTE PTR ES:[EDI]
                DEC     ECX             ; Update count.
                JMP     SHORT XTEST     ; Recheck alignments.
XMAIN:
                PUSH    CX
                SHR     ECX,2           ; Calculate number of dwords
                                        ; and move all of them.
                REP     MOVS DWORD PTR ES:[ESI],DWORD PTR ES:[EDI]
                POP     CX
                AND     CL,3            ; Move left-over bytes,
XBYTE:          JCXZ    XEXIT           ; if any.
                MOVS    ES:[ESI],BYTE PTR ES:[EDI]
                DEC     CX
                JMP     SHORT XBYTE
XEXIT:
                POP     DI
```

ACCESSING 4 GIGABYTES IN REAL MODE

```
                POP     SI
                POP     ES
                RET
big_xfer        ENDP

                END
```

Some Assembly Required

To switch modes and perform other 386 magic, we need some assembly-language routines. However, not everyone has access to an assembler that generates 80386 protected-mode code. That's why SEG4G offers three ways to incorporate the assembly-language code. The first uses Microsoft or Turbo Assembler; the second works with Microsoft C, Turbo C, and Power C; and the third doesn't work with Microsoft C.

The second and third methods don't require an assembler. While Power C provides an *asm()* function, Microsoft and Turbo C do not. The macro in ASMFUNC.H (Listing 18-1) remedies this absence by allowing you to create a character array containing the machine code you want to execute. You then call it as a function, complete with arguments and an integer return value.

Before compiling, you must select one of the assembly methods (ASM, DATA, or ASMARY) at the top of SEG4G.C (Listing 18-3). If you pick ASM, you must assemble SEG4GB.ASM (Listing 18-4) separately and link it with SEG4G. Be sure to change the *.MODEL* directive at the top of SEG51 to match the model you're using for your C programs.

In addition, if you use an Intel Inboard 386/PC, set the variable *inboard* (defined near the top of SEG4G.C) to one. The Inboard is an accelerator card that adds a 386 to an XT-style computer and is representative of many similar products. While an accelerator provides a 386 processor, it doesn't usually supply an AT BIOS. In addition, the XT has only one PIC, fewer DMA channels, and a less sophisticated keyboard controller. Most accelerator cards don't supply this hardware.

Using the SEG4G Library

To force the GS and ES registers' limit to 4 Gbytes, call the *extend_seg()* routine. This call modifies the segment registers, which retain their modified values until the computer reboots. If you plan to access extended memory, you must also enable the A20 line by calling the *a20()* function. Use *a20(1)* to turn on A20 and *a20(0)* to turn it off.

SEG4G uses all 32 bits of the LPTR type defined in CEXT.H (Listing 16-1). Programs that access extended memory via SEG4G may want to use the extended memory allocation services in CEXT.C (Listing 16-2). Of course, the allocation services don't work for the entire 4-Gbyte range. Be careful when writing to any location with SEG4G; you can easily overwrite other programs (including DOS).

Once you have done the required setup, you're ready to access memory. The functions *big_read()*, *big_write()*, and *big_xfer()* read, write, and move blocks of memory. These functions need not operate on extended memory—they work on any linear address.

The functions *big_read()* and *big_write()* are straightforward. The *big_xfer()* function, however, becomes more efficient when you obey certain rules. In particular, performance is best when you move 32-bit words that lie on 32-bit boundaries. For example, moving 128 bytes from location 0x42050 to location 0xB8000 is very fast; moving 127 bytes is somewhat less efficient, and moving 128 bytes from location 0x42051 to location 0xB8000 is also somewhat slower. The *big_xfer()* function tries to optimize transfers by making as many full-word moves as possible. It also attempts to move as much on 32-bit word boundaries as possible.

Some Examples

SEGTEST.C (Listing 18-5) is a sample program that uses the SEG4G library. (If you're using VDISK, HIMEM, or RAMDRIVE, be sure you have at least 2 Kbytes of extended memory that the RAM disk isn't using before running this program.)

ACCESSING 4 GIGABYTES IN REAL MODE

SEGTEST allocates 1 Kbyte of extended memory, then calls *extend_seg()* to set up the 4-Gbyte segments and enables A20. If successful, it writes a data byte to the entire block and tries to read it back. Next, the program expands the block to 2 Kbytes and frees the block. At this point, a loop executes so you can examine memory anywhere in the computer's address range.

Figure 18-1 shows a session with the test program and the RAMDRIVE driver installed. Notice the RAMDRIVE message at the start of extended memory. When you're ready to leave the program, enter a Ctrl-Z.

```
C:\SEG4G>SEGTEST

1280K of extended memory available
1K of extended memory allocated at    10FC00. 1279K remains.
Data written to extended memory

Data read back OK.
Expanding allocation to 2K
2K of extended memory allocated at    10F800. 1278K remains.
Extended memory freed. 1280K Available.
Enter ^Z to quit.
Address and count? 0x100000 256
MICROSOFT.EMM.CTRL.VERSION.1.00.CONTROL BLOCK . . . @ . . .
. . . . . . . . . . . . . . . . . . . . . . . . . . . . .
. . . . . . . . . . . . . . . . . . . . . . . . . . . . .
Enter ^Z to quit.
Address and count? ^Z

C:SEG4G>
```

Figure 18-1. Typical session using SEGTEST C with the RAMDRIVE driver installed.

707

DOS 5: A DEVELOPER'S GUIDE

Listing 18-5. SEGTEST.C.

```c
/****************************************************************
 *                                                                *
 * File: segtest.c                                                *
 *                                                                *
 * Description:                                                   *
 * Test the SEG4G library.                                        *
 *                                                                *
 ****************************************************************/
#include <stdio.h>
#include <ctype.h>
#include <dos.h>
#include "compat.h"
#include "seg4g.h"

void far interrupt onbreak()
   {
   }

main()
   {
   LPTR ad,aptr;
   int ct=1024,i;
   int data=0xAA;
/* Ignore breaks. */
   setvect(0x23,onbreak);
   printf("%dK of extended memory available\n",ext_size());
/* Allocate 1K of extended. */
   ad=ext_alloc(1);
   if (ad==-1L)
      {
      printf("Not enough extended memory. Only %dK available.\n",
         ext_size());
      exit(1);
      }
   printf("1K of extended mem allocated at %8lX. %dK remains.\n",
      ad,ext_size());

/* Make 4-Gbyte segments. */
   extend_seg();
```

ACCESSING 4 GIGABYTES IN REAL MODE

```c
/* Turn on A20. */
   a20(1);

/* Write data to block. */
   aptr=ad;
   for (i=0;i<ct;i++)
       {
       big_write(aptr++,data);
       }
   printf("Data written to extended memory\n\n");

/* Read it back. */
   aptr=ad;
   for (i=0;i<ct;i++)
       {
       if (big_read(aptr++)!=data)
           {
           printf("Error reading extended memory\n\n");
           ext_free(1);
           a20(0);
           exit(1);
           }
       }
   printf("Data read back OK.\nExpanding allocation to 2K\n");

/* Expand memory allocation for no good reason. */
   ad=ext_realloc(2);
   if (ad==-1L)
       {
       printf("Not enough extended memory. Only %dK is
           available.\n",ext_size());
       exit(1);
       }
   printf("2K of extended mem allocated at %8lX. %dK remains.\n",
       ad,ext_size());

/* Free memory. */
   ext_free(1);
   printf("Extended memory freed. %dK Available.\n",ext_size());
```

```
/* Enter memory examine loop. */
   while (1)
      {
      printf("Enter ^Z to quit.\nAddress and count? ");
      if (scanf("%li %i",&ad,&ct)!=2)
         {
         a20(0);
         exit(0);
         }
      while (ct--)
         {
         data=big_read(ad++);
         printf("%c",isgraph(data)?data:'.');
         }
      printf("\n\n");
      }
}
```

Listing 18-6 shows BLKTEST.C, an example of *big_xfer()* in action. Because the program writes directly to the screen, you must change the *COLOR* definition to match your computer's display.

Listing 18-6. BLKTEST.C.
```
/****************************************************************
 *                                                              *
 * File: blktest.c                                              *
 *                                                              *
 * Description:                                                 *
 * Try out the SEG4G block routines.                            *
 *                                                              *
 ****************************************************************/

#include <stdio.h>
#include <dos.h>
#include "seg4g.h"

/* Set COLOR to 0 if you have a monochrome monitor. */
```

ACCESSING 4 GIGABYTES IN REAL MODE

```
#define COLOR 1

#define SCREEN_SIZE 4000
#define ALIGN_SIZE 3

unsigned char pattern[SCREEN_SIZE+ALIGN_SIZE];

main()
   {
   LPTR data,screen;
   unsigned char far *p;
   int i;
   extend_seg();
#if COLOR
   screen=0xb8000;
#else
   screen=0xb0000;
#endif

   p=pattern;
/* Align to nearest 4-byte boundary. */
/* This isn't required but does make big_xfer() more efficient. */
   while (FP_OFF(p)&3) p++;
   data=seg_to_linear(p);
   for (i=0;i<SCREEN_SIZE;i+=4)
      {
      p[i]='A';
      p[i+3]=p[i+1]=0x70;
      p[i+2]='B';
      }
   big_xfer(data,screen,(unsigned long) SCREEN_SIZE);
   }
```

SEG4G can simplify such memory-intensive applications as expanded memory drivers, RAM caches, speech/video buffers, and databases. Of course, SEG4G may not be compatible with some programs. Programs that assume they own all extended memory won't work well with any program that accesses extended memory (with or without SEG4G). Of course, DOS extenders, multitaskers, and memory managers that use PM or V86 may not coexist with SEG4G, either.

As with any undocumented feature, this one could vanish at any time. However, it is unlikely that the segment cache scheme used in the 386 will change anytime soon. While SEG4G may not be the answer to all your memory problems, it can give you more usable space under DOS, along with some working experience with the 386's protected mode.

CHAPTER 19

DOS Extenders

The 80386 has many advanced features that support modern applications and make programming easier. Unfortunately, DOS programmers can't take advantage of many of these features because their operating system is unable to use the 386's special protected mode. So what can you do when you need to write PC programs that require large amounts of memory, multitasking, or other sophisticated features?

One solution is to move to a protected-mode operating system such as a Unix 386 or OS/2. Another approach is to use a DOS extender that provides some mechanism for interrupt-driven I/O and for making DOS and BIOS calls in a protected-mode program. Some DOS extenders switch between real and protected modes to handle interrupts and make DOS calls, but the preferred method is to run DOS in V86 mode, causing the 386 to emulate an 8086.

In this chapter we will use and dissect a 386 protected-mode DOS extender, PROT. To use PROT, you'll need Microsoft's MASM 5.1 or above or Borland's TASM and an AT-style computer with a 386, 486, or 386SX CPU or an Intel Inboard 386/PC. You should also understand the 386's protected mode (see Chapter 15).

About PROT

PROT (see Listings 19-1 through 19-18 at the end of this chapter) is a true 32-bit DOS extender. It allows you to write assembly-language programs that use 32-bit addressing and access all the 386's special features. In addition, PROT allows you to do I/O using the ROM BIOS or DOS. This extender also has provisions for direct access to the PC hardware (for instance, to write directly to the screen).

PROT cannot spawn DOS subprocesses using INT 21H, function 4BH, nor does it allow the undocumented DOS command processor "back-door" interrupt (INT 2EH). Of course, if you must spawn a subprocess, you can always return to real mode temporarily. BIOS INT 15H, function 89H (switch to protected mode), is superfluous and unsupported by PROT. INT 15H, function 87H, is not needed for protected-mode programs. However, because many disk caches and RAM disks use this function, PROT emulates it for V86 programs only.

Because the linker that comes with some versions of MASM doesn't handle certain 32-bit references properly, PROT does include macros to assemble some 32-bit instructions. These macros are particularly useful when the assembler generates a negative 32-bit relative number. In that case, the linker only fills in the bottom 16 bits of the number, changing the negative relative jump into a positive jump. The supplied macros overcome this difficulty.

A V86 task requires emulation for the *CLI*, *STI*, *LOCK*, *PUSHF*, *POPF*, *INT*, and *IRET* instructions. This is to prevent the V86 task from disrupting other tasks that might be running under protected mode. PROT emulates all of these instructions except *LOCK*, which is really a prefix rather than an instruction. Only multiprocessor systems use *LOCK*, so PC software runs fine without it.

Most DOS extenders use a different approach from PROT's. Some actually switch the processor back to real mode for each call to DOS or the BIOS. Other V86 programs (such as EMS memory simulators) let real-mode calls run unprotected, which shuts you off from many of the 386's special features and only allows DOS calls from V86 mode. PROT actually runs DOS and the BIOS as a V86 task.

Note that some of the protected-mode features available in real mode are unavailable in V86 mode. For example, a V86 task can't switch the processor into protected mode the way a real-mode program can. This means some 386-specific software may not run with PROT. Also, some very specific BIOS routines that deal with extended memory and protected mode may not work. However, with protected-mode programming, you won't need BIOS services to manage extended memory or switch modes.

DOS EXTENDERS

PROT provides facilities to handle Control-C interrupts and critical device errors in protected mode. By default, it ignores Control-C interrupts and has a critical error handler similar to the one provided by DOS. PROT also catches and ignores the Ctrl-Alt-Del keystroke that normally resets the computer because the PC's BIOS won't reboot in protected mode.

PROT reprograms the interrupt controllers so that hardware interrupts can coexist with 386 exceptions. When PROT detects a hardware interrupt, PROT automatically redirects it to the proper BIOS or DOS interrupt handler.

You can use PROT in two modes. In stand-alone mode, PROT produces object files that you link with your protected-mode code. In dynamic link mode, your program uses an interrupt to enter protected mode.

Dynamic linking makes it possible to write protected-mode code in any language that can generate an interrupt. Of course, some restrictions apply—you probably won't be able to use 32-bit pointers in most languages, and any operations that cause a DOS or BIOS interrupt must be rewritten. Dynamic link programs require a special loader, X386, to execute. To avoid confusion, *PROT* refers to the stand-alone DOS extender and *X386* refers to the dynamic link version.

When assembling the PROT files, you must specify the *DLL* equate on the assembler command line. A zero value generates PROT; a nonzero value creates X386. The MAKE files in this chapter automatically set *DLL*.

Using PROT

Before we can understand how PROT works, we need to know what it does. Though X386 is similar to PROT, we will defer most of the discussion of it until later in the chapter.

The Segments. Any program written with PROT starts with 23 segments (26 for X386) that are defined in the GDT, although you can define more in your program. PROT doesn't set up an LDT, but your code can easily do that if you require it. The segments your programs will use are shown in Table 19-1.

Segment	Function
SEL_DATA0	4-Gbyte data segment starting at location 0. With this segment, you can address any memory location you please. Be careful.
SEL_GDT	Alias for the GDT. You may need this to add more segments or find information about the predefined segments.
SEL_VIDEO	4-Kbyte data segments at video page 0. PROT determines your video adapter type, sets the page to 0, and sets SEL_VIDEO to the proper address.
SEL_DATA	Contains PROT's system data area. Several useful variables reside in this segment.
SEL_IDT	Alias for the protected-mode interrupt descriptor table. You may wish to modify this segment so you can add interrupts to the system.
SEL_UCODE*	Your program's default code segment (unless using X386).
SEL_UDATA*	Your program's default data segment (unless using X386).
SEL_PSP	256-byte long data segment that contains PROT's DOS PSP. You can use this segment to access the command line and other MS-DOS specific data.
SEL_ENV	Contains PROT's DOS environment block.
SEL_FREE*	Starts at the first free location of DOS memory and goes to the end of DOS RAM (640K or less).
SEL_EXT	Similar to SEL_FREE, but begins at the start of extended memory and continues to the end of extended memory as reported by INT 15H, function 88H. If no extended memory exists, SEL_EXT will have a limit of 0.
SEL_STACK	32-bit stack segment.
SEL_CCS**	X386's client code segment.
SEL_CDS**	X386's client data segment.
SEL_86INT**	Call gate for X386 functions.
SEL_TSS0	Data-alias for dummy TSS.
TSS0	Dummy TSS. PROT requires TSS selectors to be immediately preceded by their data-alias.
SPARE0–SPARE 31	32 empty selectors for your own use.

* Not very useful for X386 programs.
** X386 only.

Table 19-1. Segments used by a PROT program.

DOS EXTENDERS

When your program runs, the segment registers are initialized to the following values:

```
DS=SEL_UDATA
ES=SEL_DATA
FS=SEL_DATA0
GS=SEL_VIDEO
CS=SEL_UCODE
SS=SEL_STACK
PL=0
TR=TSS1
```

GDT.ASM (Listing 19-4) contains the names of all the predefined segment descriptors. Your program will begin as a privilege level 0 task with interrupts enabled.

The *SEL_EXT* segment points to DOS extended memory. It always starts at linear address 100000H. If no extended memory is present, *SEL_EXT* has a limit of zero. This implies that one byte of extended memory is available. Of course, you can never have only one byte of extended memory, so this is a convenient way to determine whether extended memory is present. PROT uses INT 15H, function 88H, to find how much extended memory is present; therefore, the limit will always be less than 64 Mbytes (or 15 Mbytes, depending on the BIOS) even if more memory is available. If you anticipate using more than 15 Mbytes of extended memory, you'll have to find the top of memory yourself.

Writing a Program. Your program should consist of the user segments *SEL_UDATA* and *SEL_UCODE*. Execution begins with the USER procedure. Listing 19-19 (given at the end of this chapter) shows the simplest possible PROT program (SIMPLE.ASM); it switches to protected mode, then returns to real mode and exits to DOS. The *NODATA* macro declares an empty data segment because the program uses no data. The line *BACK2DOS* is equivalent to *JMPABS32 SEL_CODE16,BACK16*, which returns to DOS. If you load a value in the AL register before making this jump, DOS receives that value as the return code. The *BACK2DOS* macro accepts an optional argument, which the macro loads into AL for you. PROT

717

will also return to DOS if a breakpoint or an unexpected interrupt occurs. In this case, DOS receives a return code of 7FH.

The normal way to terminate PROT is by calling INT 21H, function 4CH. The user program can also call INT 20H or INT 21H, function 0. These calls are functionally equivalent. For PROT, use *BACK2DOS*. With X386, you must use the DOS interrupts—the offset generated by *BACK2DOS* could change from version to version of X386.

The *PROT_CODE* and *PROT_CODE_END* statements are actually macros defined in EQUMAC.INC (Listing 19-9). Use these macros to define your main code segment. The corresponding *PROT_DATA* and P*ROT_DATA_END* macros allow you to define your main data segment if needed.

Most programs make calls to DOS or the BIOS. In PROT, *CALL86* makes this possible. This routine takes a pointer in ES:EBX to a parameter block (see Figure 19-1). A macro, *VM86CALL*, performs the far call to *CALL86*.

Address		Member name
BLOCK+0	Segment register flag (see text)	VMSEGFLAG
BLOCK+4	Interrupt number	VMINT
BLOCK+8	EFLAGS	VMFLAGS
BLOCK+12	ESP	VMESP
BLOCK+16	SS	VMSS
BLOCK+20	ES	VMES
BLOCK+24	DS	VMDS
BLOCK+28	FS	VMFS
BLOCK+32	GS	VMGS
BLOCK+36	EBP	VMEBP
BLOCK+40	EBX	VMEBX

Figure 19-1. Parameter block for CALL86 routine.

Listing 19-20 shows a short DOS program that prints a message using DOS function 9 and the corresponding program written with PROT (PMDEMO.DOS and

DOS EXTENDERS

PMDEMO.ASM, respectively). The statement *PROT_STARTUP* (again, a macro in EQUMAC.INC) sets the default parameter block's data segment and stack. You can override these defaults when you call *PROT_STARTUP*.

When you call *CALL86*, all registers except the segment registers, EFLAGS, EBX, and EBP are passed to the V86 interrupt unchanged; the remaining registers receive their values from the parameter block. If you want the segment registers returned in the parameter block, set the first word in the block to a nonzero value. Otherwise, the parameter block remains unchanged. Upon return, all nonsegment registers will contain the values returned by the V86 call.

The *SEL_DATA* segment defines a default parameter block (*PINTFRAME*). You may use this for all your DOS calls or, for better performance, define multiple blocks using the *VM86BLK* structure in EQUMAC.INC. For instance, you might define three blocks: one for disk reads, one for BIOS screen writes, and one for other BIOS calls. Don't use the other parameter blocks defined in *SEL_DATA* (*HINTFRAME* and *CINTFRAME*) in your programs; they handle hardware interrupts and critical errors exclusively.

Your program may change privilege levels, if desired. However, every task must define a PL 0 stack in its TSS. The real-mode interrupt emulation uses the PL 0 stack. Even if a task never makes real-mode calls, hardware interrupts may occur.

Whenever you pass addresses to DOS and BIOS routines, you must ensure that they point somewhere in the first megabyte of memory. If you're using many extended memory areas for storage, it might be wise to allocate one or two temporary storage areas in low memory just for DOS calls.

By default, PROT ignores Control-C interrupts. Your program can test the flag BREAKKEY in the *SEL_DATA* segment to see if a break event occurred. If you wish, you can set the locations *BREAK_SEG* and *BREAK_OFF* to the address of your own protected-mode break handler. If a break occurs, the routine pointed to will execute after a DOS or BIOS routine is called with *CALL86*. PROT also ignores the Ctrl-Alt-Del keystroke that normally reboots the computer; rebooting in protected mode will cause the system to crash.

PROT provides a default critical error handler similar to the one found in DOS. By setting *CRIT_SEG* to zero, you can completely disable critical error handling and cause PROT to ignore critical errors. You can set *CRIT_SEG* and *CRIT_OFF* to the segment and offset of your own critical error handler.

A protected-mode critical error handler is similar to a normal real-mode error handler, which gets status information from the AX, DI, BP, and SI registers. For protected-mode handlers, the AX value is in *CRITAX*; the DI, BP, and SI values are in *CRITDI*, *CRITBP*, and *CRITSI*, respectively. Your error handler must return a value in AL that determines the action to take. If AL is zero, PROT fails the error; if it's one, PROT retries the error; and if it's two, PROT aborts to DOS. If you choose to abort the program due to a critical error, PROT returns a 7FH to DOS.

Two DOS interrupts, INT 25H and 26H, don't return to their callers properly. They normally leave the callers' flags on the stack when returning. When you program with PROT in protected mode, remember that these flags don't remain on the stack. The same effect can be obtained with the code shown in the following code fragment.

```
MOV PINTFRAME.VMINT,25H
PUSHF       ; (or PUSHFD)
VM86CALL    ; Call INT 25 or 26.
    .
    .
    .
```

This is only a problem in protected mode, however—not when you're running programs in V86 mode. Of course, if you don't need the old flags, and you usually won't, you need not take any special action.

PROT uses several routines and variables that may also be useful to the applications programmer, as shown in Table 19-2. Your programs can call the routines via a far call (the *CALL32F* macro).

DOS EXTENDERS

Routine	Purpose
CLS	Clears page 0 of the video display directly.
OUCH	Prints the character in AL to page 0 of the video display using direct video access.
CRLF	Performs a carriage return/line feed using the OUCH routine.
MESSOUT	Prints the zero-terminated string pointed to by DS:EDX using OUCH. Modifies EBX.
HEXOUT	Outputs the byte in AL in hex using OUCH.
HEXOUT2	Outputs the word in AX in hex using OUCH.
HEXOUT4	Outputs the double word in EAX in hex using OUCH.
MAKE_GATE	Creates a task gate, trap gate, interrupt gate, or call gate. Call this routine with ES:EDX pointing to the table's (GDT, LDT, or IDT) base address (as a read/write segment). Set CX to the target descriptor, EBX to the target offset (if applicable), SI to the selector for the gate, AH to one of the access right bytes (ARB) defined in EQUMAC.INC (Listing 19-9), and AL to the word count (for call gates only).
MAKE_SEG	Makes a segment descriptor. Call this routine with ES:EDX pointing to the GDT or LDT table base address (as a read/write data segment). EBX is the base address of the segment, ECX is the limit (in bytes), AL is 0 for a 16-bit segment or 1 for a 32-bit segment, and AH is one of the ARBs defined in EQUMAC.INC.

Table 19-2. Important PROT functions and variables.

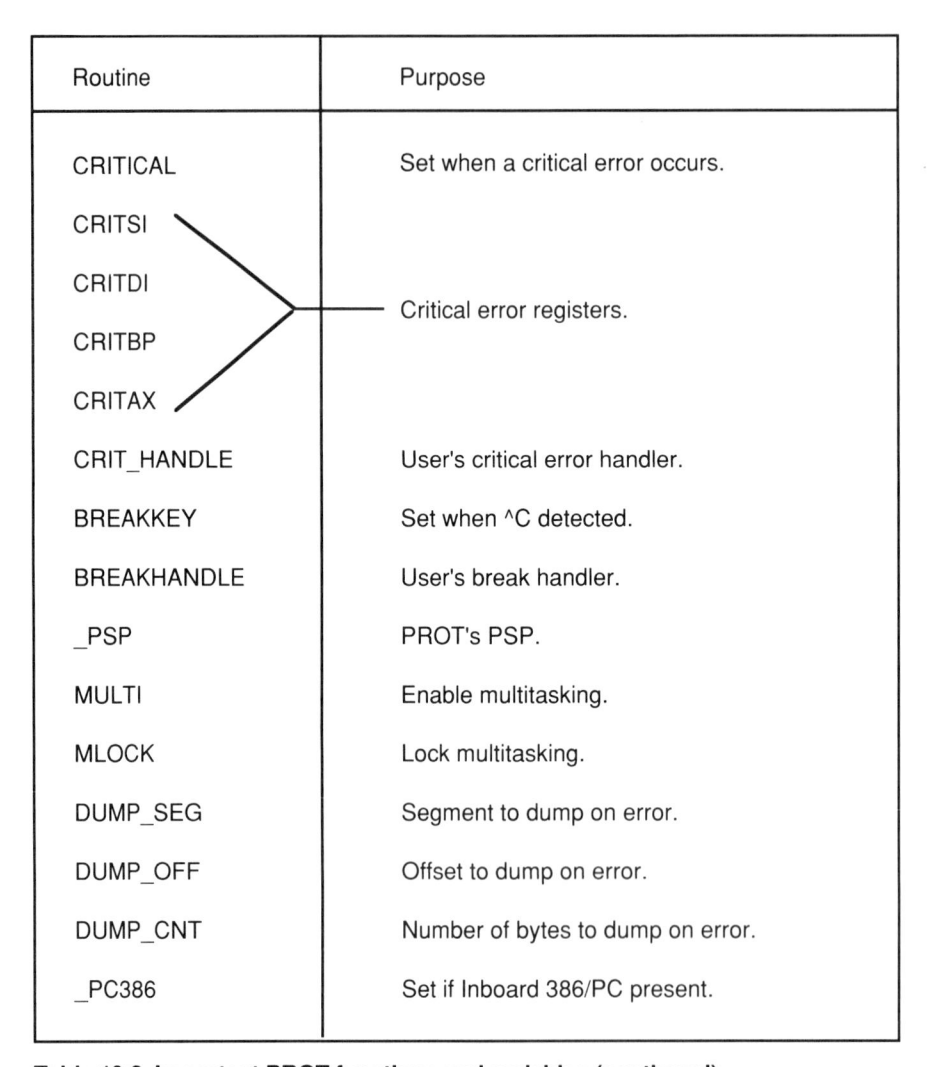

Routine	Purpose
CRITICAL	Set when a critical error occurs.
CRITSI	
CRITDI	
CRITBP	Critical error registers.
CRITAX	
CRIT_HANDLE	User's critical error handler.
BREAKKEY	Set when ^C detected.
BREAKHANDLE	User's break handler.
_PSP	PROT's PSP.
MULTI	Enable multitasking.
MLOCK	Lock multitasking.
DUMP_SEG	Segment to dump on error.
DUMP_OFF	Offset to dump on error.
DUMP_CNT	Number of bytes to dump on error.
_PC386	Set if Inboard 386/PC present.

Table 19-2. Important PROT functions and variables (continued).

Putting It Together

After setting any equates that you want to change at the top of EQUMAC.INC, assemble each .ASM file (Listings 19-1 through 19-6) or use PROT.MAK (Listing 19-15) to create the .OBJ files. The following are some useful equates in EQUMAC.INC:

DOS EXTENDERS

- *CRITSTACK* - Size of critical error stack
- *DOSSTACK* - Size of real-mode stack
- *PMSTACK* - Size protected-mode stack
- *PVSTACK* - Size of pseudostack (used for emulation)
- *SPEEDUP* - Speeds up system clock by four
- *VM86STACK* - Size of VM86 interrupt stack.

PROT depends on its interrupt routines' being the same length. That's why you should avoid the multiple-pass option when using TASM. If TASM compresses the interrupt handlers, the IDT will be incorrect and the system will crash.

Assemble your protected-mode program in the usual way, then link it to the PROT files. The PROTEXT.INC file (Listing 19-11) defines the external references. You can use the PROTASM.BAT batch file (Listing 19-16) to simplify compilation; just supply the names of each source file (without the .ASM extension) in your program. PROTASM will assemble each file, run MAKE to ensure the PROT files are up to date, and link the program. You'll need to change PROT.MAK, PROTASM.BAT, and _PROTASM.BAT (Listings 19-15 through 19-17) to reflect the assembler, linker, and MAKE you're using.

The resulting .EXE file will execute from the DOS prompt. If PROT doesn't find a 386 or 486, it will exit with an error message and return 80H to DOS. PROT will also exit with an 80H to DOS if another program already has the computer in protected mode.

If you have a librarian that can handle the 32-bit records in PROT's .OBJ file, you might want to create a PROT library. However, many librarians and other utilities don't recognize those records.

Dynamic Link Mode

X386 works much like PROT. To create it, set the *DLL* equate to one, reassemble the .ASM files, and link all the .OBJ files together into X386.EXE. You can use the X386.MAK file (Listing 19-18) to automate these steps. You'll need to modify the MAKE file to reflect the assembler and linker you're using. X386 takes a single argument, the name of the file to execute. It passes any other arguments to the target program.

The X386 loader will append .EXE to the file name, if necessary. If you want to run .COM files, you must specify the .COM extension explicitly.

X386 starts your program in real mode. It sets up one of the user-defined interrupts to switch the program to protected mode. Your program runs in real mode until it calls this interrupt. The DLLEQU.INC file (Listing 19-13) supplies many useful equates and macros for an X386 client program. Before including the file, however, you must set the *BITS* equate to 16 or 32, depending on the mode you intend to use.

When the user program wishes to switch modes, it examines the BIOS scratch area (starting at 0040:00F0) for a three-byte signature. If it finds the string *"XP="*, X386 is present. (The fourth byte contains the interrupt vector for the X386 entry point.) X386 saves the scratch area and restores it when the client program ends. This should minimize incompatibility with other programs that use the scratch area.

The program must set up certain registers (see Figure 19-2) and generate the required interrupt. Upon its return, the processor will be in protected mode and the GDT will contain the PROT segments. The current code segment will be *SEL_CCS*, and DS will contain *C_DS*. The ES, FS, GS, and SS registers will also contain *SEL_CDS*. X386 expects the stack to reside in the data segment.

Interrupts are active when your program begins in protected mode. Listing 19-14 shows GOPROT.INC, which contains typical routines for switching modes.

DOS EXTENDERS

```
Before using GOPROT macro:
    DS=SS  = Data segment
    CS     = Code segment
    AX     = 0 for 16-bit code or
             1 for 32-bit code
Call GOPROT macro
Then:
ES=FS=GS=DS=SS=Data segment (SEL_CDS)
    CS     = Code segment   (SEL_CCS)
    PL     = 0
    TR     - TSS1
    Interrupts enabled
```

Figure 19-2. Entering protected mode with X386.

The switching routine must be in the same segment as the DOS code and the protected-mode code. When using 32-bit segments, you need to use two segments. One, a 16-bit segment, will contain the initial DOS code and the mode-switching routine; the 32-bit segment will contain the protected-mode code. The sample program at the end of this chapter (Listing 19-22) shows how segments of different sizes can be used together.

Because the program was assembled separately from X386, it may not be wise to call PROT routines directly. Instead, a call gate (*SEL_86INT*) provides an interface to the most important functions via the *DISPATCH* routine. The call gate functions, seen in Table 19-3, either duplicate PROT functions or manipulate PROT variables. The last four call-gate commands, which concern multitasking, are examined in more detail later in this chapter.

Each call-gate command takes a variable-length command packet (see Figures 19-3 through 19-11). ES:EBX must point to the command packet. Some packets contain only the command word; others require additional data. Many also return data in the packet. Packet types 0 and 1 are identical to those used by PROT for V86 calls.

Function	Description
0	Call VM86 interrupt (segment registers not returned)
1	Call VM86 interrupt (return segment registers)
2	Make descriptor
3	Make gate
4	Read and clear break flag
5	Set break address
6	Read critical error information
7	Set critical error handler
8	Multitasking off
9	Multitasking on
10	Increment multitasking lock
11	Decrement multitasking lock

Table 19-3. Call gate functions.

INPUT:

ES:EBX=Pointer to parameter block
Parameter block:

0
Interrupt number
EFLAGS
ESP
SS
ES
DS
FS
GS
EBP
EBX

OUTPUT:

As defined by interrupt
No segment register returned

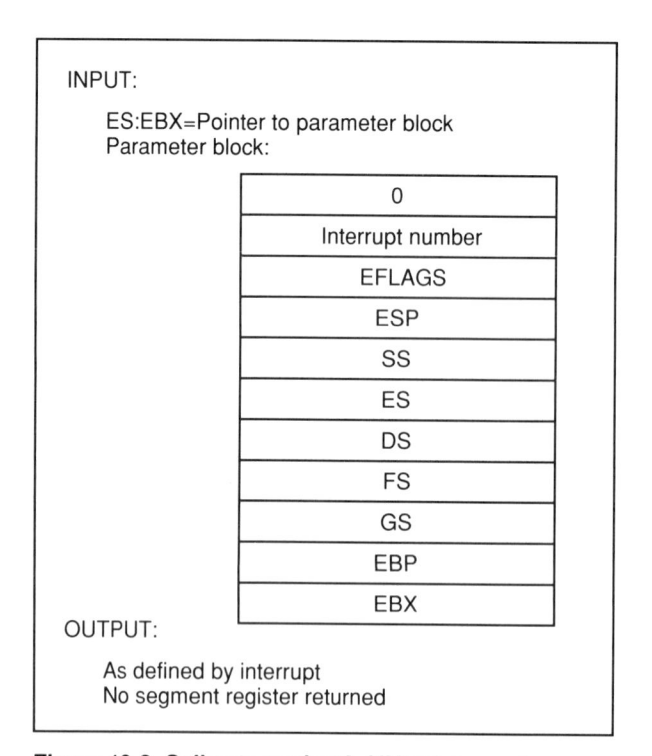

Figure 19-3. Call gate packet 0: VM86 interrupt.

DOS EXTENDERS

```
INPUT:
    ES:EBX=Pointer to parameter block
    Parameter block:
```

1
Interrupt number
EFLAGS
ESP
SS
ES
DS
FS
GS
EBP
EBX

```
OUTPUT:
    As defined by interrupt
    Segment registers returned in parameter block
```

Figure 19-4. Call gate packet 1: VM86 interrupt.

```
INPUT:
    ES:EBX= Pointer to parameter block
    EDX   = Base address of segment
    ECX   = Limit
    AH    = Access rights byte
    AL    = Size (0 for 16-bit, 1 for 32-bit)
    SI    = Selector
    Parameter block:
```

2
Offset of table's base
Segment of table's base

```
OUTPUT:
    None
```

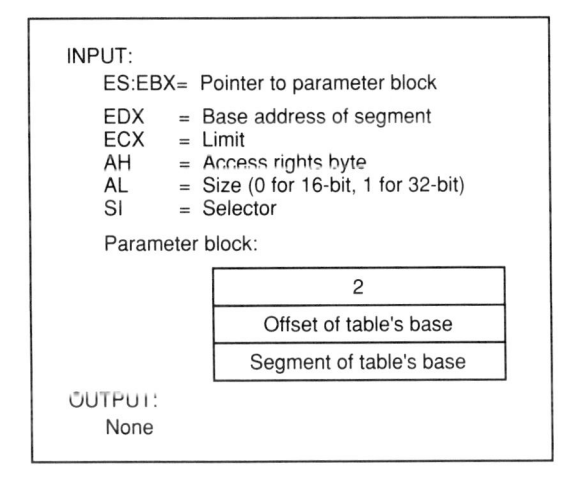

Figure 19-5. Call gate packet 2: Make descriptor.

DOS 5: A DEVELOPER'S GUIDE

```
INPUT:

    ES:EBX = Pointer to parameter block

    EDX = Gate offset
    CX  = Gate selector
    AH  = Access rights byte
    SI  = Selector
    AL  = WC (call gates only)

    Parameter block:

        +---------------------------+
        |             3             |
        +---------------------------+
        |   Offset of table's base  |
        +---------------------------+
        |  Segment of table's base  |
        +---------------------------+

OUTPUT:

    None
```

Figure 19-6. Call gate packet 3: Make gate.

```
INPUT:

    ES:EBX = Pointer to parameter block
    Parameter block:

        +---------------------------+
        |             4             |
        +---------------------------+

OUTPUT:

    AX = Break flag status
    Break flag is reset
```

Figure 19-7. Call gate packet 4: Read/clear break flag.

DOS EXTENDERS

```
INPUT:
    ES:EBX=Pointer to parameter block
    Parameter block:
        +-----------------------+
        |          5            |
        +-----------------------+
        |   Offset of handler   |
        +-----------------------+
        |  Segment of handler   |
        +-----------------------+

OUTPUT:
    Returns old handler address in parameter block
```

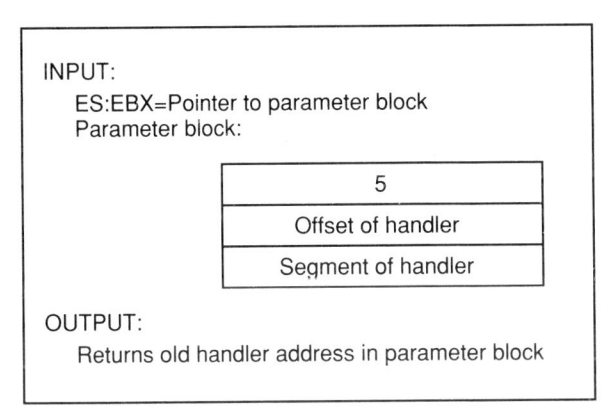

Figure 19-8. Call gate packet 5: Set/read packet address.

```
INPUT:
    ES:EBX=Pointer to parameter block
    Parameter block:
        +-----------------------+
        |          6            |
        +-----------------------+
        |       Reserved        |
        +-----------------------+
        |       Reserved        |
        +-----------------------+
        |       Reserved        |
        +-----------------------+
        |       Reserved        |
        +-----------------------+
        |       Reserved        |
        +-----------------------+

OUTPUT:
    Parameter block:
        +-----------------------+
        |          6            |
        +-----------------------+
        |  Critical error flag  |
        +-----------------------+
        |          AX           |
        +-----------------------+
        |          DI           |
        +-----------------------+
        |          BP           |
        +-----------------------+
        |          SI           |
        +-----------------------+
    Critical error flag is reset
```

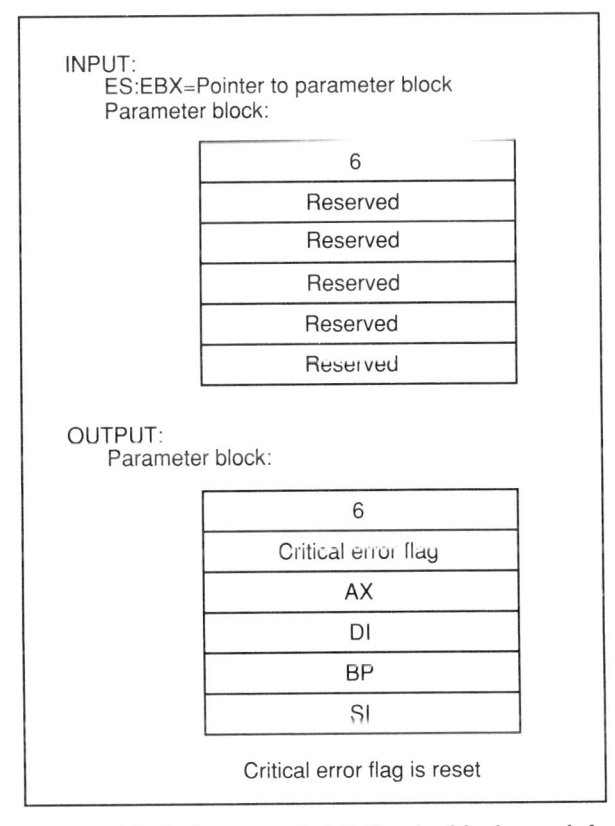

Figure 19-9. Call gate packet 6: Read critical error information.

```
INPUT:

    ES:EBX=Pointer to parameter block
    Parameter block:

            ┌─────────────────────────────────────┐
            │                  7                  │
            ├─────────────────────────────────────┤
            │   Offset of critical error handler  │
            ├─────────────────────────────────────┤
            │  Segment of critical error handler  │
            └─────────────────────────────────────┘

OUTPUT:

    Returns old handler address in parameter block
```

Figure 19-10. Call gate packet 7: Set/read critical error handler.

```
INPUT:

    ES:EBX=Pointer to parameter block
    Parameter block:

            ┌─────────────────────────────────────┐
            │                CODE                 │
            └─────────────────────────────────────┘

            Where CODE is

                 8 = Multitasking off
                 9 = Multitasking on
                10 = Increment multitasking lock
                11 = Decrement multitasking lock

OUTPUT:

    None
```

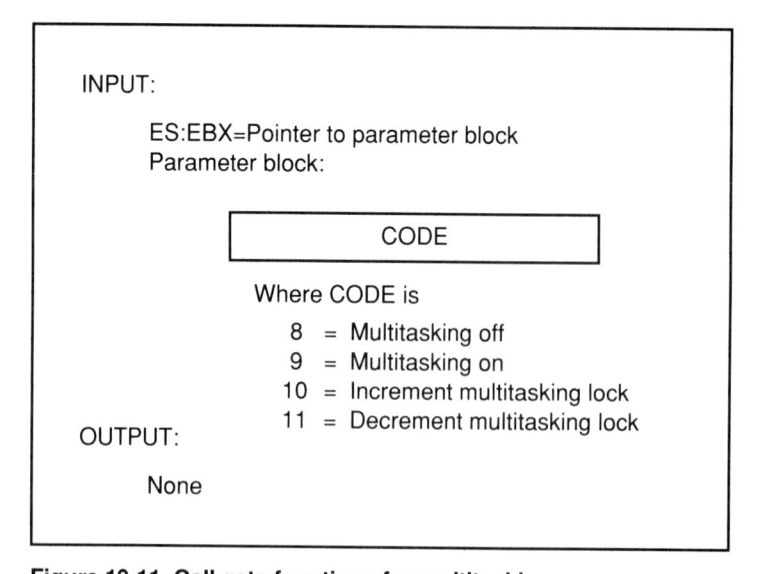

Figure 19-11. Call gate functions for multitasking.

DOS EXTENDERS

Debugging

Because most programs don't work correctly the first few hundred times you try them, PROT contains full debugging support. Of course, the 386 has many hardware debugging features built in. Except for the single-step capability, all are available with PROT. In addition, EQUMAC.INC (Listing 19-9) contains macros to set normal, conditional, and counterbreakpoints. When a breakpoint or unexpected interrupt occurs, PROT displays a register and stack dump. You can instruct PROT to dump a memory region along with the register.

Figure 19-12 shows the screen PROT displays when an unexpected interrupt occurs. This interrupt may be a breakpoint (INT 3) or a 386 exception. Most likely it will be INT 0DH, the dreaded general protection interrupt. PROT prints the display on the screen using OUCH and its related routines. This means that if you have changed the video mode or the page in your program, you may have to modify the OUCH routine to accommodate those changes. You could, for instance, modify OUCH to output to a printer. Be careful, however, not to use any DOS or BIOS routines in OUCH; you can't be sure what state the system will be in when OUCH is called.

```
ES=0040           DS=0090           FS=0010           GS=0038
EDI=00000000      ESI=00000000      EBP=00000000      ESP=00000FF0 EBX=00000000
EDX=00000000      ECX=00000000      EAX=00000000      INT=03 TR=0070
Stack Dump:
0000002B 00000088 00000202
```

Figure 19-12. PROT interrupt/breakpoint display.

The display is largely self-explanatory. PROT displays the registers and interrupt number at the top of the screen. Below the registers is a stack dump, starting with the location at ESP and continuing to the end of the stack segment. If the location *DUMP_SEL* is nonzero, PROT also prints *DUMP_CNT* bytes starting at *DUMP_SEL:DUMP_OFF*. Note that the *BREAKDUMP* and *NBREAKDUMP* macros automatically set these values for you. After printing this screen, PROT returns to DOS with an error code of 7FH.

The following are the macros for setting breakpoints:

- *BREAKPOINT* - Cause immediate, unconditional breakpoint
- *NBREAKPOINT* - Conditional breakpoint
- *BREAKON* - Enable *NBREAKPOINT*s
- *BREAKON n* - Cause a break after *n* *BREAKPOINT*s
- *BREAKOFF* - Disable *NBREAKPOINT*s
- *BREAKDUMP sel,off,nr* - Breakpoint and dump *nr* words from *sel:off*
- *NBREAKDUMP sel,off,nr* - *NBREAKPOINT* with dump.

Some 386 exceptions push an error code on the stack. For these exceptions, that will be the first word on the stack. The next two words will be the value of CS:EIP at the time of the interrupt. In Figure 19-12, for example, the value of CS:EIP is 88H:2BH. The next word will be the flags (202H in the figure).

The stack dump displays the protected-mode stack, even if a V86-mode program was interrupted. If you need to look at your V86 stack, you can use the memory-dump feature. When an interrupt occurs during a V86 program, the words following the flags on the stack are the SS, ES, DS, FS, and GS registers, in that order. Segment registers appear as 32 bits on the stack even though they contain only 16 significant bits. If any segment register values are on the stack, the 386 will set their top 16 bits to unpredictable values.

X386 uses the same debugging support as PROT. Because the counter and conditional breakpoints rely on local variables, they aren't available with X386. However, ordinary breakpoints and hardware breakpoints can be used. The call gate allows X386 programs to set the dump addresses with a special packet.

What Went Wrong?

Real-mode debuggers, such as CodeView, Turbo Debugger, and DEBUG, won't help you troubleshoot PROT programs. When an exception display screen appears, you should note the CS:EIP (from the stack dump). By referring to the listing file generated by the assembler, you should be able to pinpoint the instruction that caused the exception.

Referencing segment registers that contain zero (the null selector), addressing outside of a segment, and attempting to write into a code segment are common causes of exceptions. Another common error stems from the linker's inability to generate 16-bit relative offsets. For instance, consider the following code fragment:

```
.386P
SEGMENT   EXAMPLE PARA 'CODE32' USE 32
    .
BACKWARD:
    .
    .
    .
    CMP EBX,EAX
    JA FORWARD      ; This jump is OK.
    JB BACKWARD     ; This jump is improperly assembled.
    .
    .
    .
FORWARD:
```

This code makes two conditional jumps: one if the value in EBX is above EAX and the other if it is below. Because the code contains the *.386P* (or *.386*) directive, all conditional jumps default to 32-bit relative jumps in a 32-bit segment. The first jump will be correct because it requires a positive offset less than 64 Kbytes away. The second jump will probably cause a general protection fault because the linker only generates two bytes of the four-byte offset.

For example, if the jump's offset is -10 (FFFFFFF6H), the linker will generate 0000FFF6H, a 32-bit offset of 65,526. This is sure to cause an unexpected result. If you're lucky, the segment isn't that large and a general protection fault will occur. Otherwise, the 386 will just jump to a new location. This location may not contain a valid instruction, causing an exception 6. Other times, your program will start behaving unpredictably. To prevent this, and for efficiency, you should specify all jumps to be short, if possible. If not, you can use the *JCC32* macro provided in Listing 19-9 to generate proper 32-bit conditional jumps.

Multitasking

PROT contains hooks to help you multitask. When it starts, it runs your code in the first TSS (TSS1), which is always the root task. Each time PROT finishes servicing the timer-tick interrupt, it examines *MULTI*, the multitasking flag. If this flag is zero (the default value), PROT takes no action; otherwise, it examines *MLOCK*. This counter protects critical sections of code. While *MLOCK* is nonzero, PROT won't switch tasks. If *MULTI* is set and *MLOCK* is zero, PROT looks at the current TSS. If it is TSS1, PROT returns from the interrupt with no further action. If the current task is not TSS1, however, PROT switches to TSS1. It locks multitasking (with *MLOCK*) while servicing hardware interrupts.

To multitask effectively, the root task must contain a scheduler to set up other tasks and start them when they're ready to run. On each timer tick, the scheduler gets control and decides whether it should resume the old task or let a new task run. A scheduler can be very simple or quite complex.

When multitasking, be careful to protect nonreentrant resources. For example, when a DOS call occurs, other processes must not call DOS until the call completes. A simple way to ensure this is to lock a task (using *MLOCK*) before calling DOS. A more efficient method, however, would be to use a semaphore flag to determine whether DOS is in use. Tasks must set *MLOCK*, test the flag, set the flag if DOS is free, and clear *MLOCK*. This way, other tasks can proceed as long as they don't need DOS.

With X386, multitasking works in a similar fashion. Of course, *MLOCK* and *MULTI* are set with call gate packets 08H through 0BH (see Table 19-3).

The PC clock ticks about 18.2 times per second. For multitasking systems, this isn't very fast. If you set the *SPEEDUP* equate in EQUMAC.INC (Listing 19-9), PROT will speed up the system clock by a factor of four (72.8 times per second). On every fourth clock tick, it will call the BIOS timer routines to ensure the accuracy of the time-of-day count.

Because the scheduler is in TSS1, a jump to this segment will switch to the scheduler. You can use a global variable to pass commands to the scheduler, if necessary.

Under the Hood

PROT's implementation is essentially straight out of the Intel documentation. The program sets up the GDT, disables interrupts, and switches the machine to protected mode. In protected mode, PROT sets up the IDT, reprograms the interrupt controllers, and reenables interrupts before calling the user's code. While running DOS or BIOS code, PROT emulates the *PUSHF*, *POPF*, *STI*, *CLI*, *INT*, and *IRET* instructions.

As mentioned earlier, interrupts pose the single biggest problem for a DOS extender. The simplest situation is when a program calls an interrupt routine with *INT* and the interrupt routine ends with *IRET*. Most of the DOS/BIOS calls, however, return information in the flags register. Because IRET restores the flags, these calls need some way of overriding the old flags. From a DOS extender's point of view, the best approach is to modify the flags on the stack. This causes *IRET* to restore the flags we want instead of the original ones.

Unfortunately, few system calls do this. One common method of sending flags back to the caller is to return using an *RETF 2* instruction instead of *IRET*. In real mode, this has the same effect as *IRET* except that it destroys the saved flags. Of course, a V86 *RETF* instruction can't return to a protected-mode task, so a DOS extender has to find a way around this.

DOS handles flags in yet another way: The absolute disk read and write interrupts (INT 25H and 26H) leave the original flags at the top of the stack by executing *RETF*.

Another problem lies in the DOS and BIOS methods of calling interrupts. Most often, these routines use an *INT* instruction to start an interrupt routine. However, system routines sometimes push flags on the stack and then do a far call. In real mode, this is exactly equivalent to an *INT*. In protected mode, however, it will wreak havoc on our attempts to emulate the *IRET*. Fortunately, the method we will use to handle the *RETF 2* return also suggests a solution to this problem.

Finally, the system routines sometimes pass control by pushing the flags and an address on the stack and executing an *IRET* instruction. This resembles the far call/ *IRET* case, and PROT handles it the same way. These problem cases are detailed in Figure 19-13.

```
Case 1
     Normal INT/RET
                    INT 10H              ; Perform interrupt
                      •
                      •
                      •
     ISR:                                ; Interrupt 10H service routine
                      •
                      •
                      •
                    IRET
Case 2
     INT/RETF 2
                    INT 10H              ; Perform interrupt
                      •
                      •
                      •
     ISR:                                ; Interrupt 10H service routine
                      •
                      •
                      •
                    RETF 2
```

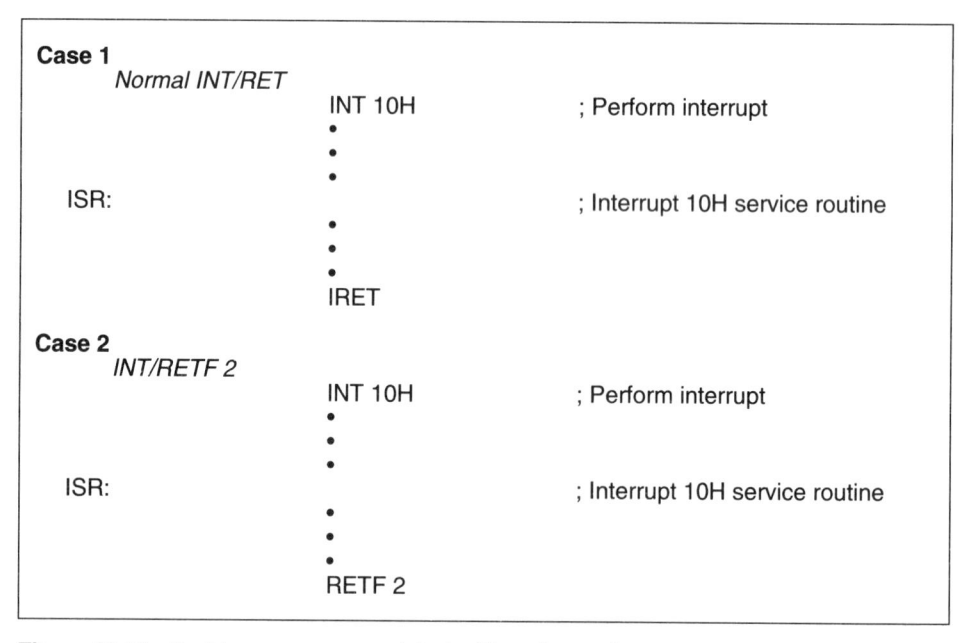

Figure 19-13. Problem cases associated with software interrupts.

DOS EXTENDERS

```
Case 3
    INT/RETF (Only used by INT 25H and 26H)
                    INT 10H           ; Perform interrupt
                      •
                      •
    ISR:                               ; Interrupt 10H service routine
                      •
                      •
                      •
                    RETF

Case 4
    PUSH/FAR CALL
                    PUSHF             ; Simulate interrupt
                    CALL FAR ISR
                      •
                      •
                      •
    ISR:                               ; Interrupt 10H service routine
                      •
                      •
                      •
                    IRET

Case 5
    PUSHF/PUSH ADDRESS/IRET
                    PUSHF             ; Jump to address TARGET
                    PUSH SEG TARGET
                    PUSH OFFSET TARGET
                    IRET
                      •
                      •
                      •
    TARGET:                            ; Destination of IRET
                      •
                      •
                      •
    -or-
                      •
                      •
                      •
                    PUSHF             ; Simulate interrupt
                    PUSH SEG RETAD
                    PUSH OFFSET RETAD
                    JMP FAR ISR
    RETAD:
                      •
                      •
    ISR:                               ; Interrupt routine
                      •
                      •
                    IRET
```

Figure 19-13. Problem cases associated with software interrupts (continued).

The Seven-Percent Solution

Our DOS extender must have a V86 mode segment (called *QISR*) that contains the following code:

```
QISR SEGMENT PARA 'CODE16' USE16
ASSUME CS:QISR
   QIRET:
      PUSH 0
      PUSH 0
      PUSH 0
      IRET
QISR ENDS
```

When the DOS extender detects an *INT* being executed from real mode, it emulates the instruction as outlined in the Intel documentation. The 386 places the actual flags and a return address on the PL 0 stack via the general protection fault caused by the INT. The secret to managing DOS's odd interrupt handling lies in manipulating the V86 stack. You can push a 16-bit copy of the flags on the V86 stack, followed by the address of *QIRET*. The DOS extender then transfers control (in V86 mode) to the real-mode interrupt handler.

When an *IRET* executes, another general protection fault occurs. We can determine the case by examining the top of the V86 stack. If the top three words of the stack are zeros, we have found case 2 or 3 in Figure 19-13. If the address on the top of the stack is *QIRET*'s, the normal case (case 1) occurred. Any other address at the top of the stack indicates case 4 or 5.

Now that we know what case caused the *IRET*, what action does the DOS extender take? PROT uses the following logic:

- In case 1, merge the 16-bit flags on the V86 stack with the top 16 bits of the flags pushed on the PL 0 stack during the *INT* handling. This may seem redundant, but the system routines may modify these flags, and the caller will expect the modified flags.

- Balance the V86 stack and restore the return address from the PL 0 stack; cases 2 and 3 are much the same as case 1 except that PROT restores the current flags (which are on the PL 0 stack) instead of those on the V86 stack.

- Cases 4 and 5 don't go through the *INT* logic just described. Therefore, the DOS extender must build an artificial PL 0 stack frame that looks as though the *INT* logic executed earlier. The execution then continues as in case 1.

When a protected-mode program needs to call a DOS or BIOS service, it calls *CALL86*. This routine uses PROT's INT 30H function to build a stack frame much like the one used in cases 4 and 5 and simulates the DOS (or BIOS) interrupt.

Hardware Interrupts

INT 30H handles hardware interrupts directly. Because these interrupts can occur at any time, PROT examines the flags of the interrupted program. If this is a V86 program, PROT uses the current V86 stack to handle the interrupt; if it is a protected-mode program, PROT switches to a special stack for hardware interrupt processing.

The PC's first interrupt controller is reprogrammed to generate different interrupts from the normal ones. PROT translates these interrupts to the correct service routines, preventing hardware interrupts from being confused with 386 exceptions. Also, the interrupts from the second controller (on AT-type machines only) are reprogrammed to simplify construction of the interrupt table.

Sixteen-Bit Tools in a 32-Bit World

PROT contains some confusing code to cope with DOS assemblers and linkers. The macro that generates conditional jumps, for example, would be unnecessary if the MASM linker worked correctly. Another oddity appears in TSS.ASM (Listing 19-5). Some versions of TASM have trouble initializing structure members with external references, so PROT doesn't use the *TSSBLK* structure (defined in Listing 19-11) to declare TSSs. The correct code and the work-around code appear in Listing

19-5; if you're using MASM or a later version of TASM, you may want to restore the correct code and delete the work-around patch.

Many DOS products aren't meant to work with 32-bit programs. You may find that your object librarians and other utilities refuse to work with PROT object files. If you have a program that doesn't run and you can't figure out why, you may have found some code that your assembler or linker can't handle. Careful (and tedious) examination of the listings, map files, and executable can help pinpoint these problems.

Sample Programs

We will look at a file-browsing program, FBROWSE, to see how PROT is used. FBROWSE uses extended memory to store the file's data. Listing 19-21 shows this program for use with PROT; Listing 19-22 shows the same program for use with X386 (FB.ASM).

FBROWSE is not complex. It maintains two pointers to memory—one to the top of memory and another to the bottom—and stores lines backwards, starting at the top of memory and going down. A table of pointers to each line starts at the bottom and works its way up. If the two pointers cross, FBROWSE is out of memory.

Each line ends with a carriage return or line feed. A carriage return indicates that FBROWSE should start a new line. Lines that are exactly 80 characters long leave the cursor at the start of a new line and end with line feeds, indicating that FBROWSE need not take action before starting the new line. FBROWSE breaks long lines into 80-character lines as it reads them.

If the *DIRECT* equate is zero, FBROWSE uses DOS calls for output. This is slow but demonstrates PROT's ability to handle a variety of DOS calls. If *DIRECT* isn't zero, FBROWSE writes directly to the screen.

FB.ASM (Listing 19-22) illustrates several important techniques. Execution begins in a 16-bit code segment (*_START*). When initialization is complete, FB jumps to the *MAIN32* label in the 32-bit segment, *_COD*. The first instruction in

_COD switches to protected mode. You must not execute any other instructions first in a USE32 segment because the processor will be in 16-bit mode until this call is made.

X386 requires that FB's data segment contain its stack. Rather than bother with groups, FB simply uses a private stack in its data segment. That's why the linker generates a warning that no stack segment is present. You can safely ignore this warning.

Listing 19-23 shows a simple multitasking example. The main task creates another task and runs it. When the second task is interrupted, the main task does some work, then restarts the second task. In this example, the fact that only one task uses DOS simplifies resource management.

The Future

While PROT is a complete protected-mode environment, you may nevertheless want to try some interesting enhancements. For completeness, PROT should emulate *IRETD*, *PUSHFD*, and *POPFD* in V86 mode. Additional support for memory paging would also be helpful.

PROT's most noticeable shortcoming is its inability to work with other 386-specific programs. Standards such as the Virtual Control Program Interface and DOS Protected Mode Interface allow programs like PROT to share the 386 with other programs that use the processor's special features. Adding VCPI or DPMI support to PROT shouldn't be very difficult. The specification for VCPI is available, free of charge, from Phar Lap Software Inc., 60 Aberdeen Ave., Cambridge, Mass. 02138, (617) 661-1510. You can order the DPMI specification, also free of charge, from Intel Literature Sales, P.O. Box 58130, Santa Clara, Calif. 95052, (800) 548-4725 (Intel part #240763-001).

With X386, you can use PROT with a C compiler. If the generated code doesn't try to reload the segment registers in a small model, the code will run with 16-bit segments. Of course, any library routines that call DOS must be rewritten. If you rewrite the library, you can change the start-up code to call *GOPROT* directly. You can also write moderately sophisticated multitasking schedulers in C fairly easily.

Commercial DOS Extenders

Almost all commercial DOS extenders support DPMI (or VCPI) and a C compiler. This, combined with good debuggers, makes them much easier to develop with than PROT. On the other hand, PROT isn't nearly as expensive as a commercial package. It also runs entirely in protected mode; it doesn't switch into real mode to execute DOS or BIOS calls. Besides, PROT has no secrets—the source code is here for you to experiment with or change. The things you learn about the 386's protected mode with PROT will serve you well if you move on to a commercial DOS extender.

DOS extenders allow developers to launch sophisticated applications quickly. By using PROT, you can learn more about developing protected-mode software. Not only will the experience you gain help you expand your DOS applications today, it will give you a head start on the operating systems of the future.

Listing 19-1. PROT.ASM.
```
;****************************************************************
;*                                                              *
;* PROT - A 386 protected-mode DOS extender                     *
;* Copyright (C) 1989, by Al Williams                           *
;* All rights reserved.                                         *
;*                                                              *
;* Permission is granted for noncommercial use of this          *
;* software. You are expressly prohibited from selling this     *
;* software, distributing it with another product, or removing  *
;* this notice.                                                 *
;* If you distribute this software to others in any form, you   *
;* must distribute all of the files that are listed below:      *
;*                                                              *
;* PROT.ASM    - The main routines and protected-mode support.  *
;* STACKS.ASM  - Stack segments.                                *
```

DOS EXTENDERS

```
;*  GDT.ASM       - Global descriptor table.                     *
;*  INT386.ASM    - Protected-mode interrupt handlers.           *
;*  TSS.ASM       - Task state segments.                         *
;*  CODE16.ASM    - 16-bit DOS code (entry/exit).                *
;*  DLL.ASM       - Dynamic link code.                           *
;*  X386.ASM      - DLL driver.                                  *
;*  EQUMAC.INC    - Equates and macros.                          *
;*  DLLEQU.INC    - DLL equates.                                 *
;*  EXTERNAL.INC  - External definitions.                        *
;*  GOPROT.INC    - DLL mode-switching code.                     *
;*  PROTEXT.INC   - User's external definitions.                 *
;*  TSS.INC       - TSS structure.                               *
;*  FBROWSE.ASM   - Complete sample application.                 *
;*  FB.ASM        - Another sample application.                  *
;*  MULTI.ASM     - Multitasking example.                        *
;*  PROT.MAK      - Makefile.                                    *
;*  X386.MAK      - Makefile.                                    *
;*  PROTASM.BAT   - Compile driver.                              *
;*  _PROTASM.BAT    Used by PROTASM.BAT.                         *
;*                                                               *
;*  This file is: PROT.ASM, the main protected-mode code.        *
;*                                                               *
;*****************************************************************

; equates and macros
INCLUDE     EQUMAC.INC

PROT_FILE EQU       1
INCLUDE     EXTERNAL.INC

        PUBLIC      CRITSI,CRITBP,CRITDI,CRITAX
        PUBLIC      CRIT_SEG,CRIT_OFF,CRITICAL,CRIT_HANDLE
        PUBLIC      BREAKKEY,BREAK_HANDLE,BRK_OFF,BRK_SEG,_PSP
        PUBLIC      HINTFRAME,PINTFRAME,INTSP,_PC386
        PUBLIC      ST01,ST02,ST03,ST04,MULTI,MLOCK
        PUBLIC      DUMP_OFF,DUMP_CNT,DUMP_SEG,SAV_DS
        PUBLIC      SAV_ES,SAV_GS,SAV_FS,CURSOR,COLOR

IF      DLL
        PUBLIC      C_SP
ENDIF
```

DOS 5: A DEVELOPER'S GUIDE

```
; This is required to find out how large PROT is.
ZZZGROUP    GROUP       ZZZSEG


;********************************************************************

; 32-bit data segment
DAT32       SEGMENT
DAT32BEG    EQU         $

; 32-bit stack values
SLOAD       DD          OFFSET SSEG321
SSLD        DW          SEL_STACK

; This location will hold the address for the PMODE IDT.
NEWIDT      EQU         THIS FWORD
            DW          IDTLEN
IDTB        DD          0                   ; filled in at run time

; PSP segment address
_PSP        DW          0

; flag set to 1 if Intel Inboard 386/PC
_PC386      DB          0

; C program's SP
IF          DLL
C_SP        DW          0
ENDIF

; multitasking variables
; multitasking on
MULTI       DB          0
; multitasking lock counter
MLOCK       DW          0

; video variables for the OUCH and related routines
CURSOR      DD          0                   ; cursor location
COLOR       DB          7                   ; display color
```

DOS EXTENDERS

```
; temp vars for some nonreentrant interrupt routines
ST01        DD      0
ST02        DD      0
ST03        DD      0
ST04        DD      0
SAV_DS      DD      0
SAV_ES      DD      0
SAV_GS      DD      0
SAV_FS      DD      0

; Enables conditional breakpoints.
BPON        DB      0

; debug dump variables
DUMP_SEG    DW      0               ; If zero don't dump memory.
DUMP_OFF    DD      0               ; offset to start at
DUMP_CNT    DD      0               ; # of bytes to dump

; break and critical error handler variables
BREAKKEY    DB      0               ; Break key occurred.
CRITICAL    DB      0               ; Critical error occurred.
CRITAX      DW      0               ; critical error ax
CRITDI      DW      0               ; critical error di
CRITBP      DW      0               ; critical error bp
CRITSI      DW      0               ; critical error si

; address of user's break handler
BREAK_HANDLE EQU    THIS FWORD
BRK_OFF     DD      0
BRK_SEG     DW      0

; address of user's critical error handler
CRIT_HANDLE EQU     THIS FWORD
CRIT_OFF    DD      OFFSET DEF_CRIT
CRIT_SEG    DW      SEL_CODE32

; message for default critical error handler
CRITMSG     DB      'A critical error has occurred.',13,10
            DB      '<A>bort, <R>etry, <F>ail? $'
```

DOS 5: A DEVELOPER'S GUIDE

```
; Here is where vm86 int's stack up pl0 esp's.
INTSP       DD          $+PVSTACK+4
            DB          PVSTACK DUP (0)

; default VM86CALL parameter block
PINTFRAME VM86BLK     <>

; interface block for critical error handler
CINTFRAME VM86BLK     <>

; hardware interrupt vm86 block
HINTFRAME VM86BLK     <>

; storage for the original PIC interrupt mask registers
INTMASK     DB          0
INTMASKAT DB            0

DAT32END    EQU         $
DAT32       ENDS

;********************************************************************

; Begin 32-bit code segment.

SEG32       SEGMENT
            ASSUME      CS:SEG32, DS:DAT32
            PUBLIC      SEG32ENT,SEG32LEN
PCODE       PROC
SEG32BEG    EQU         $

; start of protected-mode code
; We jump here from inside CODE16.INC.

SEG32ENT:   MOV         AX,SEL_DATA     ; First order of business:
            MOV         DS,AX           ; load up segment registers.
            LSS         ESP, FWORD PTR SLOAD
            MOV         AX,SEL_VIDEO
            MOV         ES,AX
            MOV         AX,SEL_DATA0
            MOV         FS,AX
```

DOS EXTENDERS

```
              MOV       AX,SEL_GDT
              MOV       GS,AX
; Set up IDT.
              CALL32S   MAKIDT
IF            DLL
              XOR       EAX,EAX
              MOV       CURSOR,EAX
ENDIF
; Reprogram pic(s).
              IN        AL,21H
              MOV       INTMASK,AL
              CMP       _PC386,0
              JNZ       SHORT PICONIB
              IN        AL,0A1H
              MOV       INTMASKAT,AL
              MOV       AL,11H
              OUT       0A0H,AL
              OUT       20H,AL
              IDELAY
              MOV       AL,28H
              OUT       0A1H,AL
              MOV       AL,20H
              OUT       21H,AL
              IDELAY
              MOV       AL,2
              OUT       0A1H,AL
              MOV       AL,4
              OUT       21H,AL
              IDELAY
              MOV       AL,1
              OUT       0A1H,AL
              OUT       21H,AL
              IDELAY
              MOV       AL,INTMASKAT
              OUT       0A1H,AL
              MOV       AL,INTMASK
              OUT       21H,AL
              JMP       SHORT PICDONE
```

DOS 5: A DEVELOPER'S GUIDE

```
PICONIB:
; Inboard PC code
        MOV         AL,13H
        OUT         20H,AL
        MOV         AL,20H
        OUT         21H,AL
        MOV         AL,9
        OUT         21H,AL
        MOV         AL,INTMASK
        OUT         21H,AL
PICDONE:
        STI                         ; Enable interrupts.

; *** Start user code with TSS (req'd for vm86 op's, etc.).
        MOV         AX,TSS0
        LTR         AX
        JMPABS32    TSS1,0
PCODE   ENDP

;*** 32-bit support routines
;

IF      DLL
; packet dispatcher
; packet 0= call86 call--no segment return
; packet 1= call86 call--segment return
; packet 2= make descriptor + tablebase address (edx=offset)
; packet 3= make gate + tablebase address (edx=offset)
; packet 4= read break flag in ax
; packet 5= set break address
; packet 6= read critical error info
; packet 7= set critical address
; packet 8= multitasking off
; packet 9= multitasking on
; packet A= inc lock counter
; packet B= dec lock counter
DISPATCH PROC       FAR
        CMP         DWORD PTR ES:[EBX],1
        JA          SHORT NOTCALL
```

DOS EXTENDERS

```
; CALL86 calls
          JMP32S    GOCALL86
NOTCALL:  CMP       DWORD PTR ES:[EBX],2
          JNZ       SHORT NOTMAKSEG
; Make segment.
          PUSH      EDX
          MOV       EDX,DWORD PTR ES:[EBX+4]
          MOV       ES,WORD PTR ES:[EBX+8]
          POP       EBX
          JMP32S    GOMAKE_SEG
NOTMAKSEG:
          CMP       DWORD PTR ES:[EBX],3
          JNZ       SHORT NOTMAKGATE
; Make gate.
          PUSH      EDX
          MOV       EDX,DWORD PTR ES:[EBX+4]
          MOV       ES,WORD PTR ES:[EBX+8]
          POP       EBX
          JMP32S    GOMAKE_GATE
NOTMAKGATE:
          CMP       DWORD PTR ES:[EBX],4
          JNZ       SHORT NOTBRKCK
; Return break status.
          PUSH      DS
          MOV       AX,SEL_DATA
          MOV       DS,AX
          ASSUME    DS:DAT32
          MOV       AL,BREAKKEY
          XOR       AH,AH
          MOV       BREAKKEY,AH
          POP       DS
          RET
NOTBRKCK:
          CMP       DWORD PTR ES:[EBX],5
          JNZ       SHORT NOTBRKSET
; Set break address from packet--return old value in packet.
          PUSH      DS
          PUSH      SEL_DATA
          POP       DS
          ASSUME    DS:DAT32
```

DOS 5: A DEVELOPER'S GUIDE

```
            MOV         CX,BRK_SEG
            MOV         EDX,BRK_OFF
            MOV         AX,ES:[EBX+8]
            MOV         BRK_SEG,AX
            MOV         EAX,ES:[EBX+4]
            MOV         BRK_OFF,EAX
            MOV         ES:[EBX+8],CX
            MOV         ES:[EBX+4],EDX
            POP         DS
            RET
NOTBRKSET:
            CMP         DWORD PTR ES:[EBX],6
            JNZ         SHORT NOTCRREAD
            PUSH        DS
            MOV         AX,SEL_DATA
            MOV         DS,AX
            ASSUME      DS:DAT32
            MOV         AL,CRITICAL
            MOV         ES:[EBX+4],AL
            MOV         AX,CRITAX
            MOV         ES:[EBX+8],AX
            MOV         AX,CRITDI
            MOV         ES:[EBX+12],AX
            MOV         AX,CRITBP
            MOV         ES:[EBX+16],AX
            MOV         AX,CRITSI
            MOV         ES:[EBX+20],AX
            XOR         AL,AL
            MOV         CRITICAL,AL     ; Clear critical error flag.
            POP         DS
            RET
NOTCRREAD:
            CMP         DWORD PTR ES:[EBX],7
            JNZ         SHORT NOTCSET
; Set crit address from packet--return old value in packet.
            PUSH        DS
            PUSH        SEL_DATA
            POP         DS
            ASSUME      DS:DAT32
            MOV         CX,CRIT_SEG
```

DOS EXTENDERS

```
            MOV       EDX,CRIT_OFF
            MOV       AX,ES:[EBX+8]
            MOV       CRIT_SEG,AX
            MOV       EAX,ES:[EBX+4]
            MOV       CRIT_OFF,EAX
            MOV       ES:[EBX+8],CX
            MOV       ES:[EBX+4],EDX
            POP       DS
            RET
NOTCSET:
            CMP       DWORD PTR ES:[EBX],8
            JZ        SHORT MULTSET
            CMP       DWORD PTR ES:[EBX],9
            JNZ       SHORT NOTMSET
MULTSET:
            PUSH      DS
            PUSH      SEL_DATA
            POP       DS
            ASSUME    DS:DAT32
            MOV       AL,ES:[EBX]
            SUB       AL,8
            MOV       MULTI,AL
            POP       DS
            RET
NOTMSET:
            CMP       DWORD PTR ES:[EBX],0AH
            JNZ       SHORT NOTLK
            PUSH      DS
            PUSH      SEL_DATA
            POP       DS
            ASSUME    DS:DAT32
            CLI
            INC       MLOCK
            JNC       SHORT NMS1
            DEC       MLOCK
NMS1:       POP       DS
            STI
            RET
NOTLK:
            CMP       DWORD PTR ES:[EBX],0BH
```

```
            JNZ       SHORT NOTULK
            PUSH      DS
            PUSH      SEL_DATA
            POP       DS
            ASSUME    DS:DAT32
            CLI
            CMP       MLOCK,0
            JZ        SHORT NMS2
            DEC       MLOCK
NMS2:       POP       DS
            STI
            RET

NOTULK:
            RET
DISPATCH    ENDP
ENDIF

; This routine creates the required IDT.
; This is only a subroutine to keep from cluttering up
; the main code, since you aren't likely to call it again.
; Assumes that all ISR routines are of fixed length and in
; sequence. Of course, after makidt has built the table, you
; can still replace individual INT gates with your own gates
; (see make_gate).
MAKIDT      PROC      NEAR
            PUSH      ES
            MOV       AX,IDTABLE
            MOVZX     EAX,AX
            SHL       EAX,4
            ADD       EAX,OFFSET IDTBEG
            MOV       IDTB,EAX
            MOV       AX,SEL_IDT
            MOV       ES,AX
            XOR       AL,AL
; Make all interrupt gates DPL=3.
            MOV       AH,INTR_GATE OR DPL3
            MOV       CX,SEL_ICODE
            MOV       EDX,OFFSET IDTBEG
            XOR       SI,SI
```

DOS EXTENDERS

```
            MOV         EBX,OFFSET INTO
IDTLOOP:    CALL32F     SEL_CODE32,MAKE_GATE
            ADD         EBX,INTLEN
            ADD         SI,8
; loop form max # of interrupts
            CMP         SI,(TOPINT+1)*8
            JB          SHORT IDTLOOP
            LIDT        NEWIDT
            POP         ES
            RET
MAKIDT      ENDP

; This routine is just like the real-mode make_desc.
; EBX=base   ECX=limit   AH=ARB   AL=0 or 1 for 16- or 32-bit
; SI=selector (TI&RPL ignored) and ES:EDX is table base address
MAKE_SEG    PROC        FAR
GOMAKE_SEG:
            PUSH        ESI
            PUSH        EAX
            PUSH        ECX
            MOVZX       ESI,SI
            SHR         SI,3            ; Adjust to slot #.
; Shift size to right bit position.
            SHL         AL,6
            CMP         ECX,0FFFFFH     ; See if you need to set G bit.
            JLE         SHORT OKLIM
            SHR         ECX,12          ; Divide by 4,096.
            OR          AL,80H          ; Set G bit.
OKLIM:      MOV         ES:[EDX+[SI*8],CX
            SHR         ECX,16
            OR          CL,AL
            MOV         ES:[EDX+ESI*8+6],CL
            MOV         ES:[EDX+ESI*8+2],BX
            SHR         EBX,16
            MOV         ES:[EDX+ESI*8+4],BL
            MOV         ES:[EDX+ESI*8+5],AH
            MOV         ES:[EDX+ESI*8+7],BH
            POP         ECX
            POP         EAX
```

DOS 5: A DEVELOPER'S GUIDE

```
                POP     ESI
                RET
MAKE_SEG        ENDP

; This routine make gates.
; AL=WC if applicable
; AH=ARB    EBX=offset   CX=selector    ES:EDX=table base
; SI= selector (TI&RPL ignored)
MAKE_GATE       PROC    FAR
GOMAKE_GATE:
                PUSH    ESI
                PUSH    EBX
                SHR     SI,3
                MOVZX   ESI,SI
                MOV     ES:[EDX+ESI*8],BX
                MOV     ES:[EDX+ESI*8+2],CX
                MOV     ES:[EDX+ESI*8+4],AX
                SHR     EBX,16
                MOV     ES:[EDX+ESI*8+6],BX
                POP     EBX
                POP     ESI
                RET
MAKE_GATE       ENDP

; Routine to call BIOS/DOS. NOT REENTRANT (but so what? DOS isn't
; either).
CALL86          PROC    FAR
GOCALL86:
                PUSH    DS
                PUSH    GS
                PUSH    FS
RETRY86:
                PUSHAD
                PUSHFD
; Save new ebx.
                PUSH    DWORD PTR ES:[EBX+40]
                PUSH    EBX
                PUSH    ES
                INT     30H             ; Call PROT.
                PUSH    SEL_DATA
```

DOS EXTENDERS

```
            POP     DS
            POP     ES
            XCHG    EBX,[ESP]
            POP     DWORD PTR ES:[EBX+40]
            PUSHFD
            CMP     BREAKKEY,0      ; See if break occurred.
            JZ      SHORT NOBRKCHECK
            CMP     BRK_SEG,0       ; See if user has break handler.
            JZ      SHORT NOBRKCHECK
                                    ; Call user's break handler.
            MOV     BREAKKEY,0
            CALL    FWORD PTR BREAK_HANDLE
NOBRKCHECK:
            CMP     CRITICAL,0      ; See if critical error.
            JZ      SHORT NOCRITCK
; See if critical error handler.
            CMP     CRIT_SEG,0
            JZ      SHORT NOCRITCK
                                    ; Call critical error handler.
            PUSH    EAX
            XOR     AL,AL
            MOV     CRITICAL,AL
            CALL    FWORD PTR CRIT_HANDLE
            OR      AL,AL           ; AL=0? FAIL
            JNZ     SHORT RETRY?
            POP     EAX
            POPFD
            STC                     ; Make sure carry is set.
            PUSHFD
            JMP     SHORT NOCRITCK
RETRY?:     DEC     AL              ; AL=1? RETRY
            JNZ     SHORT CABORT
; To retry an error, we set up everything the way it was and
; redo the interrupt. This is cheating (a little), and may not
; work in every possible case, but it seems to work in all the
; cases tried.
            POP     EAX
            POPFD
            POP     DWORD PTR ES:[EBX+40]
            POPFD
```

```
                POPAD
                JMP         SHORT RETRY86
CABORT:         POP         EAX             ; ABORT
                POPFD
                LEA         ESP,[ESP+40]    ; Balance stack.
                MOV         AL,7FH          ; DOS error=7FH
                BACK2DOS
NOCRITCK:
                POPFD
                LEA         ESP,[ESP+40]    ; Balance stack.
                PUSHFD
; See if segment save requested.
                CMP         BYTE PTR ES:[EBX],0
                JZ          SHORT NOSEGS
; Load parameter block from static save area.
                PUSH        EAX
                MOV         EAX,SAV_FS
                MOV         ES:[EBX+28],EAX
                MOV         EAX,SAV_DS
                MOV         ES:[EBX+24],EAX
                MOV         EAX,SAV_ES
                MOV         ES:[EBX+20],EAX
                MOV         EAX,SAV_GS
                MOV         ES:[EBX+32],EAX
                POP         EAX
NOSEGS:
                POPFD
                POP         FS
                POP         GS
                POP         DS
                MOV         EBX,ES:[EBX+40]
                RET
CALL86          ENDP

; Directly clear page 0 of the screen.
CLS             PROC        FAR
                PUSHFD
                PUSH        DS
                PUSH        ES
                PUSH        EDI
```

DOS EXTENDERS

```
            PUSH      ECX
            PUSH      EAX
            MOV       CX,SEL_VIDEO
            MOV       ES,CX
            MOV       CX,SEL_DATA
            MOV       DS,CX
            CLD
            MOV       EDI,0
            MOV       ECX,2000
            MOV       AX,0720H
            REP       STOSW
            XOR       ECX,ECX
            MOV       CURSOR,ECX
            POP       EAX
            POP       ECX
            POP       EDI
            POP       ES
            POP       DS
            POPFD
            RET
CLS         ENDP

; Outputs message to screen.
; ASCIIZ pointer in ds:ebx--modifies ebx.
MESSOUT     PROC      FAR
            PUSH      EAX
NXT:        MOV       AL,[EBX]
            INC       EBX
            OR        AL,AL
            JNZ       SHORT SKIP
            POP       EAX
            RET
SKIP:       CALL32F   SEL_CODE32, OUCH
            JMP       SHORT NXT
MESSOUT     ENDP

; Performs CR/LF sequence to screen using OUCH.
CRLF        PROC      FAR
            PUSH      EAX
            MOV       AL,13
```

DOS 5: A DEVELOPER'S GUIDE

```
                CALL32F     SEL_CODE32,OUCH
                MOV         AL,10
                CALL32F     SEL_CODE32,OUCH
                POP         EAX
                RET
CRLF            ENDP

; Character and digit output routines
; hexout4 - print longword in EAX in hex
; hexout2 - print word in AX in hex
; hexout  - print byte in AL in hex
; ouch    - print ASCII character in AL
OUTPUT          PROC        FAR
; Print longword in eax.
HEXOUT4         LABEL       FAR
                PUSH        EAX
                SHR         EAX,16
                CALL32F     SEL_CODE32,HEXOUT2
                POP         EAX

; Print word in ax.
HEXOUT2         LABEL       FAR
                PUSH        EAX
                MOV         AL,AH
                CALL32F     SEL_CODE32, HEXOUT
                POP         EAX

; Print a hex byte in al.
HEXOUT          LABEL       FAR
                MOV         BL,AL
                AND         AX,0F0H
                SHL         AX,4
                MOV         AL,BL
                AND         AL,0FH
                ADD         AX,'00'
                MOV         BL,AL
                MOV         AL,AH
                CALL32F     SEL_CODE32, HEX1DIG
                MOV         AL,BL
```

DOS EXTENDERS

```
HEX1DIG:    CMP         AL,'9'
            JBE         SHORT H1DIG
            ADD         AL,'A'-'0'-0AH
H1DIG:
OUCH        LABEL       FAR
            PUSH        EDI
            PUSH        EAX
            PUSH        DS
            PUSH        FS
            PUSH        ECX
            MOV         CX,SEL_VIDEO
            MOV         ES,CX
            MOV         CX,SEL_DATA
            MOV         DS,CX
            POP         ECX
            MOV         AH,COLOR
            MOV         EDI,CURSOR
            CMP         EDI,2000        ; Rolling off the screen?
            JB          SHORT NOSCROLL
; Scroll screen if required.
            PUSH        DS
            PUSH        ES
            POP         DS
            PUSH        ESI
            PUSH        ECX
            PUSH        EDI
            CLD
            MOV         ECX,960
            XOR         EDI,EDI
            MOV         ESI,160
            REP         MOVSD
            POP         EDI
            SUB         EDI,80
            POP         ECX
            POP         ESI
            POP         DS
NOSCROLL:   CMP         AL,0DH
            JZ          SHORT CR
            CMP         AL,0AH
            JZ          SHORT LF
```

DOS 5: A DEVELOPER'S GUIDE

```
; Write to screen.
          MOV       ES:[EDI*2],AX
          INC       EDI
          JMP       SHORT OUCHD
CR:       PUSH      EDX
          PUSH      ECX
          MOV       EAX,EDI
          XOR       EDX,EDX
          MOV       ECX,80
          DIV       ECX
          SUB       EDI,EDX
          POP       ECX
          POP       EDX
          JMP       SHORT OUCHD
LF:       ADD       EDI,50H
OUCHD:    MOV       CURSOR,EDI      ; Update cursor.
          POP       ES
          POP       DS
          POP       EAX
          POP       EDI
          RET

OUTPUT    ENDP

          PUBLIC    OUCH,HEXOUT,HEXOUT2,HEXOUT4,CRLF,CLS
          PUBLIC    MESSOUT,CALL86
IF        DLL
          PUBLIC    DISPATCH
ENDIF
          PUBLIC    MAKE_GATE,MAKE_SEG
; default critical error handler
DEF_CRIT  PROC      FAR
          PUSH      ES
          PUSH      EBX
          PUSH      EDX
          MOV       BX,SEL_DATA
          MOV       ES,BX
          ASSUME    DS:NOTHING, ES:DAT32
; Load critical error handler's private stack.
          MOV       WORD PTR CINTFRAME.VMSS,CSTACK
```

DOS EXTENDERS

```
            MOV         CINTFRAME.VMESP,OFFSET CSTACK_1
            MOV         WORD PTR CINTFRAME.VMDS,DAT32
            MOV         CINTFRAME.VMINT,21H
            MOV         EBX, OFFSET CINTFRAME
            MOV         EDX,OFFSET CRITMSG
            MOV         AH,9
            PUSH        EBX
            VM86CALL                        ; Print message.
            POP         EBX
CLOOP:
            MOV         AH,7
            PUSH        EBX
            VM86CALL                        ; Get keystroke.
            POP         EBX
; Ignore function keys.
            OR          AL,AL
            JZ          SHORT CRITFNKEY
            MOV         AH,AL
            OR          AL,20H              ; Convert to lowercase.
            CMP         AL,'a'
            JNZ         SHORT CFAIL?
            MOV         AL,2
            JMP         SHORT CREXIT
CFAIL?:     CMP         AL,'f'
            JNZ         SHORT CRETRY?
            XOR         AL,AL
            JMP         SHORT CREXIT
CRETRY?:
            CMP         AL,'r'
            MOV         AL,1
            JNZ         SHORT CRITBAD
CREXIT:     MOV         DL,AH               ; Echo letter + CRLF.
            MOV         AH,2
            PUSH        EAX
            PUSH        EBX
            VM86CALL
            POP         EBX
            MOV         AH,2
            MOV         DL,0DH
            PUSH        EBX
```

DOS 5: A DEVELOPER'S GUIDE

```
            VM86CALL
            POP         EBX
            MOV         AH,2
            MOV         DL,0AH
            VM86CALL
            POP         EAX
            POP         EDX
            POP         EBX
            POP         ES
            RET
CRITFNKEY:
            MOV         AH,7
            PUSH        EBX
            VM86CALL                        ; Ignore fn key/alt-key.
            POP         EBX
CRITBAD:
            MOV         DL,7
            MOV         AH,2
            PUSH        EBX
            VM86CALL                        ; Unknown input--ring bell.
            POP         EBX
            JMP         SHORT CLOOP
DEF_CRIT    ENDP

SEG32END    EQU         $
SEG32       ENDS

SEG32LEN    EQU         (SEG32END-SEG32BEG)-1
            PUBLIC      SEG32LEN

DAT32LEN    EQU         (DAT32END-DAT32BEG)-1
            PUBLIC      DAT32LEN

; segment to determine the last memory address
ZZZSEG      SEGMENT
ZZZSEG      ENDS

            END         ENTRY
```

DOS EXTENDERS

Listing 19-2. CODE16.ASM.

```
;*****************************************************************
;*                                                               *
;* PROT - A 386 protected-mode DOS extender                      *
;* Copyright (C) 1989, by Al Williams                            *
;* All rights reserved.                                          *
;*                                                               *
;* Permission is granted for noncommercial use of this           *
;* software subject to certain conditions (see PROT.ASM).        *
;*                                                               *
;* This file is: CODE16.ASM, the 16-bit DOS entry/exit code.     *
;*                                                               *
;*****************************************************************

            INCLUDE         EQUMAC.INC
CODE16_FILE EQU     1
            INCLUDE         EXTERNAL.INC
CSEG        SEGMENT
            ASSUME CS:CSEG, DS:CSEG
            PUBLIC BACK16
            IF              DLL
            PUBLIC C_CS,C_DS
            PUBLIC ICA0,ICA1,PINTNO
            PUBLIC PENTRY
            ELSE
            PUBLIC ENTRY
            ENDIF
BEG16       EQU     $
IDTSAV      DF      0               ; space to save old IDT
XZRO        DF      0               ; constant to inhibit IDT

; area to save stack pointer
SOFFSAV     DW      0
SSEGSAV     DW      0

            IF              DLL
; save area for client's segment registers
C_CS        DW      0
C_DS        DW      0
```

DOS 5: A DEVELOPER'S GUIDE

```
CSIZE           DB      0               ; 0 for 16-bit 1, for 32-bit
; Save ICA.
ICA0            DW      ?
ICA1            DW      ?
; protected-mode interrupt
PINTNO          DB      ?
ENDIF


TEMP            EQU     THIS FWORD      ; space to load GDT
TLIM            DW      GDTLEN
TEMD            DD      0


; old keyboard interrupt vector--we have to catch reboots
KEYCHAIN        EQU     THIS DWORD
KEYOFF          DW      ?
KEYSEG          DW      ?


                IF      SPEEDUP
; timer interrupt vector
TIMECHAIN       EQU     THIS DWORD
TIMEOFF         DW      ?
TIMESEG         DW      ?
TICKS           DB      4
ENDIF


INTM            DB      0               ; interrupt mask - pic 1
INTMAT          DB      0               ; interrupt mask - AT pic 2

;psp
PSP             DW      0


PS2             DB      0               ; 1 if PS/2 w/ Microchannel
PC386           DB      0               ; 1 if Intel Inboard PC found
IBPC            DB      'INBRDPC%',0    ; device name for Inboard

; error messages
NOT386M         DB      'Error: this program requires an '
                DB      '80386 or 80486'
                DB      ' processor.',13,10,'$'
VM86M           DB      'Error: this program will not execute '
                DB      'in VM86 mode.'
```

DOS EXTENDERS

```
                DB      13,10,'$'

; 16-bit ss/sp for return to real mode
LOAD16          DD      OFFSET SSEG1
                DW      SEL_RDATA


;****** Begin program.
IF              DLL
PENTRY          LABEL   FAR
ELSE
ENTRY           LABEL   FAR
ENDIF

START           PROC    NEAR
                PUSH    CS              ; Set up DS segment; save PSP.
                POP     DS
IF              DLL
                MOV     CSIZE,AL        ; size of segments
ENDIF
                MOV     AX,ES
                MOV     PSP,AX          ; Save PSP.
                MOV     BX,DAT32
                MOV     ES,BX
                MOV     ES:_PSP,AX
; Check to see if we are running on a 386/486.
                XOR     AX,AX
                PUSH    AX
                POPF
                PUSHF
                POP     AX
                AND     AX,0F000H
                CMP     AX,0F000H
                JNZ     SHORT NOT86
NOT386:
                MOV     DX, OFFSET NOT386M
NOT386EXIT:
                MOV     AH,9
                INT     21H
                MOV     AX,4C80H
                INT     21H             ; Exit.
```

```asm
; here if it is 286 or better
NOT86:
                MOV     AX,0F000H
                PUSH    AX
                POPF
                PUSHF
                POP     AX
                AND     AX,0F000H
                JZ      NOT386

; If we got here we are on an 80386/486.
; Check PM flag.
                SMSW    AX
                AND     AX,1            ; Are we in protected mode?
                MOV     DX,OFFSET VM86M
                JNZ     NOT386EXIT

; OK...we are clear to proceed.
; See if we are on a Microchannel PS/2.
                MOV     AX,0C400H       ; Get POS address.
                INT     15H
                JC      SHORT TRYIB
                MOV     PS2,1
                JMP     SHORT ATSTYLE

; See if we are on an Intel Inboard/386 PC. If so, set flags in
; dat32 and in this segment.
TRYIB:
                MOV     DX,OFFSET IBPC
                MOV     AX,3D00H
                INT     21H             ; Try to open device driver.
; jump if AT-class machine
                JC      SHORT ATSTYLE
                MOV     BX,AX           ; Close device.
                MOV     AH,3EH
                INT     21H
                MOV     PC386,1
                MOV     ES:_PC386,1
ATSTYLE:
```

DOS EXTENDERS

```
; Set up new ^C, keyboard, and critical error handlers
; (keyboard catches ^Alt-Delete).
                MOV     AX,3509H
                INT     21H
                MOV     KEYSEG,ES
                MOV     KEYOFF,BX
                MOV     AX,2509H
                MOV     DX,OFFSET REBOOT
                INT     21H
                MOV     AX,2523H
                MOV     DX,OFFSET CTRLC
                INT     21H
                MOV     AX,2524H
                MOV     DX,OFFSET CRITERR
                INT     21H
IF              SPEEDUP
; Set up new timer handler and reprogram timer tick.
                MOV     AX,3508H
                INT     21H
                MOV     TIMESEG,ES
                MOV     TIMEOFF,BX
                CLI
                MOV     AX,2508H
                MOV     DX,OFFSET TICK
                INT     21H
                MOV     AL,36H
                OUT     43H,AL
                MOV     AX,16390        ; about 72.8Hz
                OUT     40H,AL
                MOV     AL,AH
                OUT     40H,AL
                STI
ENDIF

; * Create segments.
                PUSH    GDTSEG
                POP     ES
                MOV     EDX, OFFSET GDT
                MOV     EBX,CS
                SHL     EBX,4           ; Calculate segment base address.
```

```
            MOV     ECX,0FFFFH      ; 64K limit (don't change)
            MOV     AH,ER_CODE      ; read/exec code seg
            XOR     AL,AL           ; size
            PUSH    GDTSEG
            POP     ES
            MOV     EDX, OFFSET GDT
            MOV     SI,SEL_CODE16
            CALL    MAKE_DESC       ; Make code seg (16-bit/real).
            MOV     ECX,0FFFFFH
            XOR     EBX,EBX
            MOV     SI,SEL_DATA0
            XOR     ECX,ECX
            DEC     ECX             ; ecx=ffffffff
            MOV     AL,1
            MOV     AH,RW_DATA
            CALL    MAKE_DESC       ; Make data (4G @ zero base).
            XOR     EAX,EAX
            INT     12H
            MOVZX   ECX,AX
            SHL     ECX,10
; Get free memory segment.
            LOADFREE BX
            SUB     ECX,EBX
            DEC     ECX
            MOV     SI,SEL_FREE
            MOV     AL,1
            MOV     AH,RW_DATA
            CALL    MAKE_DESC
            XOR     EAX,EAX
            MOV     AH,88H          ; Get top of extended memory.
            INT     15H
            SHL     EAX,10          ; * 1024
            OR      EAX,EAX         ; Any extended present?
            MOV     ECX,EAX
            JNZ     SHORT EXTPRES
            MOV     ECX,1
EXTPRES:
            DEC     ECX
            MOV     EBX,100000H
            MOV     SI,SEL_EXT      ; 0 limit segment if no ext.
```

DOS EXTENDERS

```
            MOV     AL,1
            MOV     AH,RW_DATA
            CALL    MAKE_DESC
            XOR     EBX,EBX
            MOV     BX, SEG32
            SHL     EBX,4
            MOV     ECX,SEG32LEN
            MOV     AH,ER_CODE
            MOV     AL,1
            MOV     SI,SEL_CODE32
            CALL    MAKE_DESC       ; 32-bit code segment
            XOR     EBX,EBX
            MOV     BX,USERCODE
            SHL     EBX,4
            MOV     ECX,USERCODELEN
            MOV     AH,ER_CODE
            MOV     AL,1
            MOV     SI,SEL_UCODE
            CALL    MAKE_DESC
            XOR     EBX,EBX
            MOV     BX,USERDATA
            SHL     EBX,4
            MOV     ECX,USERDATALEN
            MOV     AH,RW_DATA
            MOV     AL,1
            MOV     SI,SEL_UDATA
            CALL    MAKE_DESC
            XOR     EBX,EBX
            MOV     BX,SS32
            SHL     EBX,4           ; Always para align stacks!
            MOV     ECX,SSEG32LEN
            MOV     AH,RW_DATA      ; Stack seg is data type.
            MOV     AL,1
            MOV     SI,SEL_STACK
            CALL    MAKE_DESC
; 16-bit data for return to real mode.
            XOR     EBX,EBX
            MOV     BX, SSEG
            SHL     EBX,4
```

```
; Real-mode limit (don't change).
            MOV     ECX,0FFFFH
            XOR     AL,AL
            MOV     AH,RW_DATA
            MOV     SI,SEL_RDATA
            CALL    MAKE_DESC
            XOR     EBX,EBX
            MOV     BX,GDTSEG
            SHL     EBX,4
            ADD     EBX,OFFSET GDT
            MOV     ECX,(GDTLEN)
            MOV     AL,1
            MOV     AH,RW_DATA
            MOV     SI,SEL_GDT
            CALL    MAKE_DESC
            MOV     AX,500H         ; Set video to page 0.
            INT     10H
            MOV     AH,0FH
            INT     10H             ; Get mode.
            MOV     EBX,0B0000H     ; monochrome
            CMP     AL,7            ; Check for mono.
            JZ      SHORT VIDEOCONT
            MOV     EBX,0B8000H
VIDEOCONT:
            MOV     ECX,3999        ; limit for text page
            MOV     AL,1
            MOV     AH,RW_DATA
            MOV     SI,SEL_VIDEO
            CALL    MAKE_DESC       ; Make video segment.
            XOR     EBX,EBX
            MOV     BX,DAT32
            SHL     EBX,4
            MOV     ECX,DAT32LEN
            MOV     AH,RW_DATA
            MOV     AL,1
            MOV     SI,SEL_DATA
            CALL    MAKE_DESC
            XOR     EBX,EBX
            MOV     BX,IDTABLE
            SHL     EBX,4
            MOV     ECX,IDTLEN
```

DOS EXTENDERS

```
              MOV    AH,RW_DATA
              MOV    AL,1
              MOV    SI,SEL_IDT
              CALL   MAKE_DESC
              XOR    EBX,EBX
              MOV    BX,ISR
              SHL    EBX,4
              MOV    ECX,ISRLEN
              MOV    AH,ER_CODE
              MOV    AL,1
              MOV    SI,SEL_ICODE
              CALL   MAKE_DESC
              XOR    EBX,EBX
              MOV    BX,TSSSEG
              SHL    EBX,4
; Create TSSs.
              MOV    ECX,TSSLEN
              MOV    AH,RW_DATA
              MOV    AL,1
              MOV    SI,SEL_TSS0
              CALL   MAKE_DESC
              MOV    AH,TSS_DESC
              MOV    SI,TSS0
              CALL   MAKE_DESC
              ADD    EBX,OFFSET TSS1BEG
              MOV    SI,TSS1
              MOV    ECX,TSSLEN
              CALL   MAKE_DESC
              MOV    SI,SEL_TSS1
              MOV    AH,RW_DATA
              CALL   MAKE_DESC
; PSP
              MOVZX  EBX,PSP
              SHL    EBX,4
              MOV    ECX,255
              MOV    AH,RW_DATA
              MOV    AL,1
              MOV    SI,SEL_PSP
              CALL   MAKE_DESC
```

DOS 5: A DEVELOPER'S GUIDE

```
; environment segment
            PUSH    ES
            MOV     ES,PSP
            XOR     EBX,EBX
            MOV     BX,ES:[2CH]
            MOV     AX,BX
            SHL     EBX,4
            DEC     AX
            MOV     ES,AX
            XOR     ECX,ECX
            MOV     CX,ES:[3]
            SHL     ECX,4
            DEC     ECX             ; Get limit from arena header.
            MOV     SI,SEL_ENV
            POP     ES
            MOV     AL,1
            MOV     AH,RW_DATA
            CALL    MAKE_DESC       ; Make environment segment.
IF          DLL
; Make client CS and DS.
            MOVZX   EBX,C_CS
            SHL     EBX,4
            XOR     ECX,ECX
            DEC     ECX
            MOV     AL,CSIZE
            MOV     AH,ER_CODE
            MOV     SI,SEL_CCS
            CALL    MAKE_DESC
            MOVZX   EBX,C_DS
            SHL     EBX,4
            MOV     AH,RW_DATA
            MOV     SI,SEL_CDS
            CALL    MAKE_DESC
ENDIF

; Turn on A20.
            MOV     AL,1
            CALL    SETA20
; no interrupts until prot mode
            CLI
            MOV     SSEGSAV,SS
```

DOS EXTENDERS

```
; Save sp for triumphant return to r/m.
            MOV     SOFFSAV,SP
            SIDT    IDTSAV
            LIDT    XZRO            ; Save and load IDT.
            XOR     EBX,EBX
            MOV     BX,GDTSEG
            SHL     EBX,4
            ADD     EBX,OFFSET GDT
            MOV     TEMD,EBX
            LGDT    TEMP            ; Set up GDT.
            MOV     EAX,CR0
            OR      EAX,1           ; Switch to prot mode!
            MOV     CR0,EAX
; Jump to load CS and flush prefetch.
            JMPABS  SEL_CODE16,PROT1

PROT1:                              ; GO!
            OPSIZ
            JMPABS32 SEL_CODE32,SEG32ENT

; Jump here to return to real-mode DOS.
; If desired AL can be set to a DOS exit code.
BACK16      LABEL   FAR
            MOV     BL,AL           ; Save exit code.
            CLI
; Turn off debug (just in case).
            XOR     EAX,EAX
            MOV     DR7,EAX
; Restore stack.
            LSS     ESP,FWORD PTR CS:LOAD16
            MOV     AX,SEL_RDATA
            MOV     DS,AX
            MOV     ES,AX
            MOV     FS,AX
            MOV     GS,AX
            MOV     EAX,CR0
; Return to real mode.
            AND     EAX,07FFFFFF2H
            MOV     CR0,EAX
```

DOS 5: A DEVELOPER'S GUIDE

```
; Jump to load CS and clear prefetch.
            JMPABS  CSEG,NEXTREAL
NEXTREAL    LABEL   FAR
            MOV     AX,CS
            MOV     DS,AX
            LIDT    IDTSAV          ; Restore old IDT 0(3ff).
; Reprogram PICs.
            IN      AL,21H
            MOV     INTM,AL
            CMP     PC386,0
            JNZ     SHORT PICIB386
            IN      AL,0A1H
            MOV     INTMAT,AL
            MOV     AL,11H
            OUT     0A0H,AL
            OUT     20H,AL
            IDELAY
            MOV     AL,70H
            OUT     0A1H,AL
            MOV     AL,8
            OUT     21H,AL
            IDELAY
            MOV     AL,2
            OUT     0A1H,AL
            MOV     AL,4
            OUT     21H,AL
            IDELAY
            MOV     AL,1
            OUT     0A1H,AL
            OUT     21H,AL
            IDELAY
            MOV     AL,INTMAT
            OUT     0A1H,AL
            MOV     AL,INTM
            OUT     21H,AL
            JMP     SHORT PICOUT
PICIB386:
            MOV     AL,13H
            OUT     20H,AL
```

DOS EXTENDERS

```
                MOV     AL,8
                OUT     21H,AL
                INC     AL
                OUT     21H,AL
                MOV     AL,INTM
                OUT     21H,AL
PICOUT:
; Clean up to go back to DOS.
                LSS     SP,DWORD PTR SOFFSAV
IF              SPEEDUP
; Restore timer and timer int.
                MOV     DX,TIMEOFF
                PUSH    DS
                MOV     DS,TIMESEG
                MOV     AX,2508H
                INT     21H
                POP     DS
                MOV     AL,36H
                OUT     43H,AL
                XOR     AX,AX
                OUT     40H,AL
                MOV     AL,AL           ; timing delay
                OUT     40H,AL
ENDIF
                STI                     ; Resume interrupt handling.
; Turn a20 back off.
                XOR     AL,AL
                CALL    SETA20
; Restore keyboard interrupt.
                MOV     DX,KEYOFF
                PUSH    DS
                MOV     DS,KEYSEG
                MOV     AX,2509H
                INT     21H
                POP     DS
IF              DLL
                CALL    FAR PTR DLLCLEAN
ENDIF
                MOV     AH,4CH          ; Blow this joint!
                MOV     AL,BL           ; Get return code.
```

DOS 5: A DEVELOPER'S GUIDE

```
            ; Return to the planet of MS-DOS.
                    INT     21H
    START           ENDP

    IF              DLL
                    PUBLIC  DLLCLEAN
    DLLCLEAN        PROC    FAR
                    PUSH    DS
                    PUSH    ES
                    PUSH    CS
                    POP     DS
                    ASSUME  CS:CSEG,DS:CSEG,ES:NOTHING
                    MOV     AL,PINTNO
                    PUSH    DS
                    MOV     AH,25H
                    XOR     DX,DX
                    MOV     DS,DX
                    MOV     ES,DX
                    INT     21H             ; Set interrupt unused.
                    POP     DS
                    MOV     AX,ICA0
                    MOV     ES:[4F0H],AX
                    MOV     AX,ICA1
                    MOV     ES:[4F2H],AX    ; Restore ICA.
                    POP     ES
                    POP     DS
                    RET
    DLLCLEAN        ENDP
    ENDIF

    ; routine to control A20 line
    ; AL=1 to turn A20 on (enable)
    ; AL=0 to turn A20 off (disable)
    ; Returns ZF=1 if error; AX destroyed (and maybe CX).
    SETA20          PROC    NEAR
                    ASSUME  CS:CSEG,DS:CSEG
                    CMP     PS2,0
                    JZ      SHORT NOTPS2A20
                    MOV     AH,AL
                    OR      AL,AL
```

DOS EXTENDERS

```
                IN      AL,92H
                JZ      SHORT PS2OFF
                OR      AL,2
                JMP     SHORT PS2SET
PS2OFF:         AND     AL,0FDH
PS2SET:         OUT     92H,AL
                XOR     CX,CX
PS2WAIT:        IN      AL,92H
                SHR     AL,1
                CMP     AL,AH
                JZ      SHORT PS2OUT
                DEC     CX
                JNZ     PS2WAIT
                RET
PS2OUT:         OR      AL,1
                RET
NOTPS2A20:
                CMP     PC386,0
                JNZ     SHORT A20IBPC
                PUSH    CX
                MOV     AH,0DFH         ; A20 on
                OR      AL,AL
                JNZ     SHORT A20WAIT1
                MOV     AH,0DDH         ; A20 off
A20WAIT1:
                CALL    KEYWAIT
                JZ      SHORT A20ERR
                MOV     AL,0D1H
                OUT     64H,AL
                CALL    KEYWAIT
                JZ      SHORT A20ERR
                MOV     AL,AH
                OUT     60H,AL
                CALL    KEYWAIT
                JZ      SHORT A20ERR
                MOV     AL,0FFH
                OUT     64H,AL
                CALL    KEYWAIT
A20ERR:         POP     CX
                RET
```

DOS 5: A DEVELOPER'S GUIDE

```
; A20 set for Inboard PC.
A20IBPC:
                OR      AL,AL
                MOV     AL,0DFH
                JNZ     SHORT A20SET
                MOV     AL,0DDH
A20SET:         OUT     60H,AL
                OR      AL,AL           ; Make sure ZF is clear.
                RET
SETA20          ENDP

; Wait for keyboard controller ready. Returns ZF=1 if time-out.
; Destroys CX and AL.
KEYWAIT         PROC    NEAR
                XOR     CX,CX           ; maximum time-out
KWAITLP:
                DEC     CX
                JZ      SHORT KEYEXIT
                IN      AL,64H
                AND     AL,2
                JNZ     KWAITLP
KEYEXIT:        OR      CX,CX
                RET
KEYWAIT         ENDP

; This routine makes a descriptor.
; ebx=base
; ecx=limit in bytes
; es:edx=GDT address
; al= size (0=16-bit, 1=32-bit)
; ah=AR byte
; SI=descriptor (TI & DPL not important!)
; Auto sets and calculates G and limit.
MAKE_DESC       PROC    NEAR
                PUSHAD
                MOVZX   ESI,SI
                SHR     SI,3            ; Adjust to slot #.
; Shift size to right bit position.
                SHL     AL,6
                CMP     ECX,0FFFFFH     ; See if you need to set G bit.
```

DOS EXTENDERS

```
                JBE     SHORT OKLIMR
                SHR     ECX,12          ; Divide by 4096.
                OR      AL,80H          ; Set G bit.
OKLIMR:         MOV     ES:[EDX+ESI*8],CX
                SHR     ECX,16
                OR      CL,AL
                MOV     ES:[EDX+ESI*8+6],CL
                MOV     ES:[EDX+ESI*8+2],BX
                SHR     EBX,16
                MOV     ES:[EDX+ESI*8+4],BL
                MOV     ES:[EDX+ESI*8+5],AH
                MOV     ES:[EDX+ESI*8+7],BH
                POPAD
                RET
MAKE_DESC       ENDP

; This is the routine that disables ^C interrupts.
; You could place your own code here if desired.
; NOTE: THIS IS VM86 CODE!
CTRLC           PROC    FAR
                PUSH    DS
                PUSH    AX
                MOV     AX,DAT32
                MOV     DS,AX
                ASSUME  DS:DAT32
                MOV     AL,1
                MOV     BREAKKEY,AL     ; Set flag.
                POP     AX
                POP     DS
                IRET
CTRLC           ENDP

; Reboot handler (VM86 code).
REBOOT          PROC    FAR
                STI
                PUSH    AX
                IN      AL,60H
                CMP     AL,53H          ; Delete key?
                JNZ     SHORT NOREBOOT
                XOR     AX,AX
```

DOS 5: A DEVELOPER'S GUIDE

```
                PUSH    DS
                MOV     DS,AX
                MOV     AL,DS:[417H] ; Get shift status.
                POP     DS
                TEST    AL,8         ; Check for ctrl/alt.
                JZ      SHORT NOREBOOT
                TEST    AL,4
                JZ      SHORT NOREBOOT
; If ^ALT-DEL detected, eat it and return.
                IN      AL,61H
                MOV     AH,AL
                OR      AL,80H
                OUT     61H,AL
                MOV     AL,AH
                OUT     61H,AL
                MOV     AL,20H
                OUT     20H,AL
                POP     AX
                IRET
; Not ^ALT-DEL; resume normal keyboard handler.
NOREBOOT:       POP     AX
                JMP     CS:[KEYCHAIN]
REBOOT          ENDP

IF              SPEEDUP
TICK            PROC    FAR
                ASSUME  CS:CSEG
; ticks--
                DEC     CS:TICKS
; If (ticks) return.
                JNZ     SHORT TICKOUT
; ticks=4
                MOV     CS:TICKS,4
; timechain()
                JMP     CS:[TIMECHAIN]
TICKOUT:        PUSH    AX
                MOV     AL,20H
                OUT     20H,AL
                POP     AX
                IRET
```

DOS EXTENDERS

```
TICK            ENDP
ENDIF

; critical error handler (always fail/ignore)
CRITERR         PROC    FAR
                PUSH    DS
                PUSH    DAT32
                POP     DS
                ASSUME  DS:DAT32
                MOV     CRITAX,AX
                MOV     CRITICAL,1
                MOV     CRITDI,DI
                MOV     CRITBP,BP
                MOV     CRITSI,SI
IF              DOS     LT 3
                XOR     AL,AL
ELSE
                MOV     AL,3
ENDIF
                POP     DS
                IRET
CRITERR         ENDP

LAST16          EQU     $
CSEG            ENDS
                END
```

Listing 19-3. INT386.ASM.

```
;******************************************************************
;*                                                                *
;* PROT - A 386 protected-mode DOS extender                       *
;* Copyright (C) 1989, by Al Williams                             *
;* All rights reserved.                                           *
;*                                                                *
;* Permission is granted for noncommercial use of this            *
;* software subject to certain conditions (see PROT.ASM).         *
;*                                                                *
;* This file is: INT386.ASM, the PM interrupt handlers.           *
;*                                                                *
;******************************************************************
```

DOS 5: A DEVELOPER'S GUIDE

```
; Peculiarities
; 1 - We don't emulate lock, IRETD, PUSHFD, and POPFD yet.
; 2 - When calling INT 25 or INT 26 from protected mode,
;     flags are destroyed (not left on stack as in VM86,
;     real mode).
; 3 - For now I don't support adding offsets to the return
;     address on your vm86 stack to change where IRET goes.
;     That could be fixed, but I don't know of any PC system
;     software that does that.

INCLUDE     EQUMAC.INC
INT386_FILE EQU     1
INCLUDE     EXTERNAL.INC

; fake segment for far ret interrupts
; (This segment has no descriptor in GDT/LDT.)
QISR        SEGMENT  PARA PUBLIC 'CODE16' USE16
            ASSUME   CS:QISR
; Push sacrificial words for IRET to eat.
; PL 0 stack controls return anyway.
QIRET:
            PUSH     0
            PUSH     0
            PUSH     0
            IRET
QISR        ENDS

; IDT segment
IDTABLE     SEGMENT
IDTBEG      EQU      $
            DQ       TOPINT+1 DUP (0)
IDTEND      EQU      $
IDTABLE     ENDS

;ISR segment
DEFINT      MACRO    N
INT&N       LABEL    FAR
            PUSH     &N
            JMP      NEAR PTR INTDUMP
            ENDM
```

DOS EXTENDERS

```
ISR        SEGMENT
           ASSUME     CS:ISR
ISRBEG     EQU        $
; This code defines interrupt handlers from 0 to TOPINT
; (TOPINT is defined in EQUMAC.INC).
; The interrupt code assumes these routines are the same
; size, even if the assembler tells you that some of
; them can be compacted with an override--don't do it.
; Also, don't let the assembler make multiple passes to
; compact this code automatically.
INTNO      =          0
           REPT       TOPINT+1
           DEFINT     %INTNO
INTNO      =          INTNO + 1
           ENDM

; Debug dump messages.
MESSAREA   DB         'INT=',0
STKM       DB         'Stack Dump:',0
TASKM      DB         '  TR=',0
RTABLE     DB         'G'
           DB         'F'
           DB         'D'
           DB         'E'
GTABLE     DB         'DISIBPSPBXDXCXAX'
MEMMESS    DB         'Memory Dump:',0

; All interrupts come here.
; We check for the interrupt # pushed on the stack and
; vector accordingly. This adds some interrupt latency
; but simplifies IDT construction.
INTDUMP    LABEL      NEAR
; Check for GP error.
           CMP        BYTE PTR [ESP],0DH
           JZ         NEAR PTR INT13H
NOT13:
; Check for vm86 pseudo-int.
           CMP        BYTE PTR [ESP],30H
           JZ         NEAR PTR INT30H
```

DOS 5: A DEVELOPER'S GUIDE

```
; Hardware interrupt?
        CMP         BYTE PTR [ESP],20H
        JB          SHORT NOTIO
        PUSH        ES
        PUSH        SEL_DATA
        POP         ES
        CMP         ES:_PC386,0
        POP         ES
        JNZ         SHORT INTIBPC
        CMP         BYTE PTR [ESP],2FH
        JMP         SHORT INTCONT
INTIBPC:
        CMP         BYTE PTR [ESP],27H
INTCONT:
        JA          SHORT NOTIO
        JMP         NEAR PTR HWINT
NOTIO:
; If we made it here, we have an unexpected interrupt
; so crank out a debug dump and exit to DOS.
        PUSHAD
        PUSH        GS
        PUSH        FS
        PUSH        DS
        PUSH        ES
        MOV         AX,SEL_VIDEO
        MOV         ES,AX
        MOV         AX,CS
        MOV         DS,AX
; Do dump.
        MOV         ECX,4
INTL1:
        MOV         AL,[RTABLE-1+ECX]
        CALL32F     SEL_CODE32,OUCH
        MOV         AL,'S'
        CALL32F     SEL_CODE32,OUCH
        MOV         AL,'='
        CALL32F     SEL_CODE32,OUCH
        POP         EAX
        CALL32F     SEL_CODE32,HEXOUT2
        PUSH        ECX
        MOV         ECX,6
```

DOS EXTENDERS

```
LSP1:       MOV         AL,' '
            CALL32F     SEL_CODE32,OUCH
            LOOP        LSP1
            POP         ECX
            LOOP        INTL1
            CALL32F     SEL_CODE32,CRLF
            XOR         ECX,ECX
INTL2:      CMP         CL,5
            JNZ         SHORT NOCRINT
            CALL32F     SEL_CODE32,CRLF
NOCRINT:
            MOV         AL,'E'
            CALL32F     SEL_CODE32,OUCH
            MOV         AL,[GTABLE+ECX*2]
            CALL32F     SEL_CODE32,OUCH
            MOV         AL,[GTABLE+1+ECX*2]
            CALL32F     SEL_CODE32,OUCH
            MOV         AL,'='
            CALL32F     SEL_CODE32,OUCH
            POP         EAX
            CALL32F     SEL_CODE32,HEXOUT4
            MOV         AL,' '
            CALL32F     SEL_CODE32,OUCH
            INC         CL
            CMP         CL,8
            JNE         SHORT INTL2
            MOV         EBX,OFFSET MESSAREA
            CALL32F     SEL_CODE32,MESSOUT
            POP         EAX
            CALL32F     SEL_CODE32,HEXOUT
            MOV         EBX,OFFSET TASKM
            CALL32F     SEL_CODE32,MESSOUT
            STR         AX
            CALL32F     SEL_CODE32,HEXOUT2
            CALL32F     SEL_CODE32,CRLF

; Stack dump.
            MOV         AX,SS
            MOVZX       EAX,AX
            LSL         EDX,EAX
```

DOS 5: A DEVELOPER'S GUIDE

```
                JNZ         SHORT INTABT
                MOV         EBX,OFFSET STKM
                CALL32F     SEL_CODE32,MESSOUT
                XOR         CL,CL
                MOV         SI,64
INTL3:          CMP         ESP,EDX
                JAE         SHORT INTABT
                DEC         SI
                JZ          SHORT INTABT
                TEST        CL,7
                JNZ         SHORT NOSCR
                CALL32F     SEL_CODE32,CRLF
NOSCR:          POP         EAX
                CALL32F     SEL_CODE32,HEXOUT4
                INC         CL
                MOV         AL,' '
                CALL32F     SEL_CODE32,OUCH
                JMP         SHORT INTL3

INTABT:
; Check for memory dump request.
                MOV         AX,SEL_DATA
                MOV         DS,AX
                ASSUME      DS:DAT32
                MOV         AX,WORD PTR DUMP_SEG
                OR          AX,AX
                JZ          SHORT NOMEMDUMP
; Come here to do memory dump.
                CALL32F     SEL_CODE32,CRLF
                PUSH        DS
                PUSH        CS
                POP         DS
                MOV         EBX,OFFSET MEMMESS
                CALL32F     SEL_CODE32,MESSOUT
                CALL32F     SEL_CODE32,CRLF
                POP         DS
                MOV         AX,WORD PTR DUMP_SEG
                MOV         ES,AX
                CALL32F     SEL_CODE32,HEXOUT2
                MOV         AL,':'
```

DOS EXTENDERS

```
            CALL32F     SEL_CODE32,OUCH
            MOV         EDX,DUMP_OFF
            MOV         EAX,EDX
            CALL32F     SEL_CODE32,HEXOUT4
            MOV         ECX,DUMP_CNT
DUMPLOOP:
            MOV         AL,' '
            CALL32F     SEL_CODE32,OUCH
            MOV         EAX,ES:[EDX]        ; Get word.
            CALL32F     SEL_CODE32,HEXOUT4
            ADD         EDX,4
            SUB         ECX,4
            JA          SHORT DUMPLOOP
            CALL32F     SEL_CODE32,CRLF
NOMEMDUMP:

            MOV         AL,20H              ; Send EOI signal.
            CMP         _PC386,0
            JNZ         SHORT NOTANAT
            OUT         0A0H,AL
NOTANAT:
            OUT         20H,AL              ; just in case hardware did it
            MOV         AL,7FH              ; Return 7f to DOS.
            BACK2DOS

; Here we check the GP fault.
; If the mode isn't VM86 we do a debug dump.
; Otherwise we try to emulate an instruction.
; If the instruction isn't known, we do a debug dump.
INT13II:
            ADD         ESP,4               ; Balance stack intno.
            TEST        [ESP+12],20000H
            JZ          SHORT SIM13A        ; Wasn't a vm86 interrupt!
            ADD         ESP,4
            PUSH        EAX
            PUSH        EBX
            PUSH        DS
            PUSH        EBP
            MOV         EBP,ESP             ; Point to stack frame.
            ADD         EBP,10H
```

DOS 5: A DEVELOPER'S GUIDE

```
            MOV         AX,SEL_DATA0
            MOV         DS,AX
            MOV         EBX,[EBP+4]     ; Get cs.
            AND         EBX,0FFFFH
            SHL         EBX,4
            ADD         EBX,[EBP]       ; Get eip.
            XOR         EAX,EAX
; When the emulation routines get control EAX is set like this:
; al = OPCODE byte
; ah = # of bytes skipped over
; bit 31 of eax=1 if OPSIZ prefix
; encountered
            JMP         SHORT INLOOP

; Set sign bit of eax if OPSIZ.
FSET:       OR          EAX,80000000H
INLOOP:     MOV         AL,[EBX]
            INC         AH
            INC         EBX
            CMP         AL,66H          ; opsize prefix
            JZ          SHORT FSET
; Scan for instructions.
            CMP         AL,9DH
            JZ          SHORT DOPOPF
            CMP         AL,9CH
            JZ          SHORT DOPUSHF
            CMP         AL,0FAH
            JZ          NEAR PTR DOCLI
            CMP         AL,0FBH
            JZ          NEAR PTR DOSTI
            CMP         AL,0CDH
            JZ          NEAR PTR DOINTNN
            CMP         AL,0CFH
            JZ          NEAR PTR DOIRET
            CMP         AL,0F0H
            JZ          NEAR PTR DOLOCK
; Whoops! What is that?
            POP         EBP
            POP         DS
            POP         EBX
```

DOS EXTENDERS

```
                POP         EAX
SIM13:
                PUSH        0                   ; Simulate error.
SIM13A:
                PUSH        13                  ; Simulate errno.
                JMP32S      NOT13

;******************************************************************
; The following routines emulate VM86 instructions. Their
; conditions on entry are:
; eax[31]=1 iff opsiz preceded instruction
; ah=count to adjust eip on stack
; al=instruction
; [EBX] next opcode byte
; ds: zerobase segment

; This routine emulates a popf.
DOPOPF:
                MOV         BX,[EBP]            ; Fix ip.
                ADD         BL,AH
                ADC         BH,0
                MOV         [EBP],BX
; Get ss*10H; add esp; fetch top of stack.
                MOVZX       EBX,WORD PTR [EBP+10H]
                SHL         EBX,4
                ADD         EBX,[EBP+0CH]
                MOVZX       EAX,WORD PTR [EBX]
                MOV         EBX,[EBP+8]         ; Get his real flags.
                AND         BX,07000H           ; Only preserve NT,IOPL.
                AND         AX,08FFFH           ; Wipe NT,IOPL in new flags.
                OR          EAX,EBX
                MOV         [EBP+8],EAX         ; Save his real flag image.
                MOV         EBX,2
                ADD         [EBP+0CH],EBX
                AND         [EBP+8],0FFFEFFFFH
                POP         EBP
                POP         DS
                POP         EBX
                POP         EAX
                IRETD
```

```
; routine to emulate pushf
DOPUSHF:
        MOV     BX, [EBP]       ; Fix ip.
        ADD     BL,AH
        ADC     BH,0
        MOV     [EBP],BX
        MOV     EAX,[EBP+8]     ; Get his flags.
; Get ss; add esp and "push" flags.
        MOVZX   EBX,WORD PTR [EBP+10H]
        SHL     EBX,4
        ADD     EBX,[EBP+0CH]
        MOV     [EBX-2],AX
; Adjust stack.
        SUB     DWORD PTR [EBP+0CH],2
; Mask out flag bits.
        AND     [EBP+8],0FFFEFFFFH
        POP     EBP
        POP     DS
        POP     EBX
        POP     EAX
        IRETD

; Emulate CLI.
DOCLI:
        MOV     BX, [EBP]       ; Fix ip.
        ADD     BL,AH
        ADC     BH,0
        MOV     [EBP],BX
        MOV     EAX,[EBP+8]     ; Get flags.
        OR      EAX,20000H      ; Set vm, clr RF and IOPL.
        AND     EAX,0FFFECDFFH
        MOV     [EBP+8],EAX     ; Replace flags.
        POP     EBP
        POP     DS
        POP     EBX
        POP     EAX
        IRETD

; Emulate STI.
DOSTI:
```

DOS EXTENDERS

```
            MOV     BX,[EBP]            ; Fix ip.
            ADD     BL,AH
            ADC     BH,0
            MOV     [EBP],BX
            MOV     EAX,[EBP+8]         ; Get flags.
            OR      EAX,20200H          ; Set vm, clr RF and IOPL.
            AND     EAX,0FFFECFFFH
            MOV     [EBP+8],EAX         ; Replace flags.
            POP     EBP
            POP     DS
            POP     EBX
            POP     EAX
            IRETD

; This routine emulates an INT nn instruction.
DOINTNN:
; Check for int15.
            CMP     BYTE PTR[EBX],15H
            JNZ     SHORT NORMDOINT
            PUSH    EAX
            MOV     EAX,[EBP-4]         ; Get interrupted eax.
            CMP     AH,87H
            POP     EAX
            JNZ     SHORT NORMDOINT
; Emulate INT 15 FN 87 for certain disk caches/ramdrives, etc.
; Get es from stack, flatten with si, and load selectors 1 and 2
; from that GDT to SEL_15S & SEL_15D.
            PUSH    DS
            PUSH    ES
            MOV     AX,SEL_GDT
            MOV     ES,AX
            MOVZX   EAX,WORD PTR [EBP+20]
            SHL     EAX,4
            MOVZX   ESI,SI
            ADD     EAX,ESI
            MOV     EBX,[EAX+10H]
            MOV     ES:[SEL_15S],EBX
            MOV     EBX,[EAX+14H]
            MOV     ES:[SEL_15S+4],EBX
            MOV     EBX,[EAX+18H]
```

```
                MOV     ES:[SEL_15D],EBX
                MOV     EBX,[EAX+1CH]
                MOV     ES:[SEL_15D+4],EBX
; Load ds/es, zero esi,edi (ZX CX) and movsw.
                MOV     AX,SEL_15S
                MOV     DS,AX
                MOV     AX,SEL_15D
                MOV     ES,AX
                XOR     ESI,ESI
                MOV     EDI,ESI
                MOVZX   ECX,CX
                CLD
                PUSH    ESI
                PUSH    EDI
                PUSH    ECX
                REP     MOVSW
                POP     ECX
                POP     EDI
                POP     ESI
                POP     ES
                POP     DS
; Restore state and return to caller with EAX=0 and CY=0.
                POP     EBP
                POP     DS
                POP     EBX
                POP     EAX
                ADD     DWORD PTR [ESP],2
; Clear carry.
                AND     BYTE PTR [ESP+8],0FEH
                XOR     EAX,EAX
                IRETD
NORMDOINT:
                PUSH    EDX
                PUSH    ECX
; Get ss.
                MOVZX   EDX,WORD PTR [EBP+10H]
                SHL     EDX,4
; Add esp.
                ADD     EDX,[EBP+0CH]
```

DOS EXTENDERS

```
; Move flags, qsir address to vm86 stack and correct esp.
; ... flags
        MOV     CX,[EBP+08H]
        MOV     [EDX-2],CX
        MOV     WORD PTR [EDX-4],SEG QIRET
        MOV     WORD PTR [EDX-6],OFFSET QIRET
        SUB     DWORD PTR [EBP+0CH],6
        MOV     CX,[EBP]          ; ip
; Adjust ip by # of bytes to skip.
        INC     AH
        ADD     CL,AH
        ADC     CH,0
        MOV     [EBP],CX
; Get tss alias (always directly above TSS in GDT).
        STR     DX                ; Get our task #.
        SUB     DX,8              ; Alias is one above.
        MOV     ES,DX
        MOV     DX,SEL_DATA
        MOV     DS,DX
        ASSUME  DS:DAT32
; Get pl0 esp from TSS and push to local stack.
        MOV     EDX,INTSP
        SUB     EDX,4
        MOV     INTSP,EDX
        MOV     ECX,ES:[4]        ; esp0
        MOV     [EDX],ECX
; Get int vector.
        MOV     DX,SEL_DATA0
        MOV     DS,DX
        MOV     ECX,ESP           ; Adjust stack for int 30H.
        ADD     ECX,60
        MOV     ES:[4],ECX
; Test for zero; if so, called from int 30H.
        OR      AH,AH
        MOVZX   EDX,AL
        JZ      SHORT FROM30
; Otherwise get int vector from CS:EIP stream.
        MOVZX   EDX,BYTE PTR [EBX]
        MOV     ECX,ESP
        ADD     ECX,24
        MOV     ES:[4],ECX        ; Adjust stack for non-int 30H.
```

```
FROM30:
; interrupt vector*4 = VM86 interrupt vector address
        SHL        EDX,2
; Try to clean up mess on stack.
        MOV        AX,SEL_DATA
        MOV        DS,AX
        MOV        STO2,EDX
        POP        ECX
        POP        EDX
        XCHG       STO2,EDX
        MOV        STO1,ECX
        MOV        STO3,EBP
        POP        EBP
        XCHG       STO3,EBP
        POP        ECX
        MOV        BX,SEL_DATA
        MOV        DS,BX
        MOV        STO4,ECX
        POP        EBX
        POP        EAX
        MOV        CX,SEL_DATA0
        MOV        DS,CX
; Copy segment registers and esp for vm86 int.
        PUSH       DWORD PTR [EBP+20H]
        PUSH       DWORD PTR [EBP+1CH]
        PUSH       DWORD PTR [EBP+18H]
        PUSH       DWORD PTR [EBP+14H]
        PUSH       DWORD PTR [EBP+10H]
        PUSH       DWORD PTR [EBP+0CH]
        MOV        ECX,[EBP+08]
; Push flags (with vm=1,iopl=0),cs, eip, rf=0.
        OR         ECX,20000H
; Clear iopl, rf, tf, if, and push flags.
        AND        ECX,0FFFECCFFH
        PUSH       ECX
; Read new cs/ip from 8086 idt.
; ... Push CS.
        MOVZX      ECX,WORD PTR [EDX+2]
        PUSH       ECX
```

DOS EXTENDERS

```
; ... Push IP.
        MOVZX     ECX,WORD PTR [EDX]
        PUSH      ECX
        MOV       CX,SEL_DATA
        MOV       DS,CX
        PUSH      ST04
        MOV       ECX,ST01
        MOV       EDX,ST02
        MOV       EBP,ST03
        POP       DS
        IRETD                        ; Go on to vm86 land.

; Emulate IRET instruction.
DOIRET:
; vm86 stack
        MOVZX     EAX,WORD PTR[EBP+10H]
        SHL       EAX,4
        ADD       EAX,[EBP+0CH]
        MOV       EBX,[EAX]          ; Get cs.ip.
; If top of stack=0:0, an RETF or RETF 2 was detected.
        OR        EBX,EBX
        JZ        SHORT FARRETINT
        PUSH      ECX
        XOR       ECX,ECX
; Compare return address with QIRET.
        MOV       CX, SEG QIRET
        SHL       ECX,16
        MOV       CX,OFFSET QIRET
        CMP       EBX,ECX
        POP       ECX
; If equal then "normal" IRET.
        JZ        SHORT NORMIRET

; If not equal, that vm86 jerk is faking an IRET to pass control.
; We must build a "fake" pl0 frame.
; Adjust sp.
        ADD       DWORD PTR [EBP+0CH],6
; Get ip.
        MOVZX     EBX,WORD PTR [EAX]
        MOV       [EBP],EBX
```

DOS 5: A DEVELOPER'S GUIDE

```
; Get cs.
        MOVZX       EBX,WORD PTR [EAX+2]
        MOV         [EBP+4],EBX
; Get new flags.
        MOVZX       EBX,WORD PTR [EAX+4]
        OR          EBX,20000H        ; Set vm, clr RF and IOPL.
        AND         EBX,0FFFECFFFH
        MOV         [EBP+8],EBX
        POP         EBP
        POP         DS
        POP         EBX
        POP         EAX
        IRETD                         ; Go on.

; This means qiret caught a FAR RET instead of an IRET.
; We must preserve our current flags!
FARRETINT:
        MOV         EAX,EBP
        POP         EBP
        POP         DS
        PUSH        EBP
        PUSH        EAX
        MOV         BX,DS
        MOV         AX,SEL_DATA
        MOV         DS,AX
        MOV         ST03,EBX
        POP         EBP               ; ISR's ebp
        MOV         EAX,[EBP+0CH]
        ADD         EAX,6             ; Skip pushes from qiret.
        MOV         ST04,EAX
; Get flags.
        MOV         EAX,[EBP+08H]
        MOV         ST02,EAX
        JMP         SHORT NIRET

; This handles the "normal" case.
NORMIRET:
        MOV         BX,[EAX+4]        ; Get flags.
        MOV         EAX,EBP
```

```
            POP       EBP
            POP       DS
            PUSH      EBP
            PUSH      EAX
            MOV       AX,BX
            MOV       BX,DS
            PUSH      SEL_DATA
            POP       DS
            MOV       ST02,EAX
            MOV       ST03,EBX
            POP       EBP              ; ISR's ebp
            MOV       ST04,0
NIRET:
            PUSH      ESI
            XOR       ESI,ESI
            OR        DWORD PTR [EBP+28H],0
; If CS=0 then int 30H asked for segment save.
            JNZ       SHORT V86IRET
            MOV       EAX,[EBP+14H]
            MOV       SAV_ES,EAX
            MOV       EAX,[EBP+18H]
            MOV       SAV_DS,EAX
            MOV       EAX,[EBP+1CH]
            MOV       SAV_FS,EAX
            MOV       EAX,[EBP+20H]
            MOV       SAV_GS,EAX
            MOV       ESI,8

V86IRET:
            MOV       WORD PTR ST01,CS
            POP       EBP
            XCHG      EBP,[ESP]
; Get tss alias.
            STR       AX
            SUB       AX,8
            MOV       ES,AX
            ASSUME    DS:DAT32
            MOV       EAX,ES:[4]       ; Get our current stack begin.
```

```
; See if we have to balance the VM86 stack.
        TEST    SS:[EAX+ESI+8],20000H
        JZ      SHORT STKADJD
        MOV     EBX,ST04
        OR      EBX,EBX
        JZ      SHORT ADJSTK
; Balance vm86 stack.
        MOV     SS:[EAX+ESI+0CH], EBX
        JMP     SHORT STKADJD
ADJSTK: ADD     DWORD PTR SS:[EAX+ESI+0CH],6
STKADJD:
; Get quasi flags.
        MOV     EBX,ST02
; Get real flags.
        PUSH    DWORD PTR SS:[EAX+ESI+8]
; Preserve flags.
        MOV     DWORD PTR SS:[EAX+ESI+8],EBX
LEAVEFLAGS:
; Only let 8086 part of flags stay.
        AND     DWORD PTR SS:[EAX+ESI+08],01FFFH
        POP     EBX             ; Load real flags into ebx.
; Save 386 portion of old flags + if.
        AND     EBX,0FFFFE200H
        OR      SS:[EAX+ESI+8],EBX
        POP     ESI
        XCHG    EAX,[ESP]
        PUSH    EAX             ; stack = ebx, new sp
        MOV     EBX,INTSP
; Get prior pl0 esp from local stack.
        MOV     EAX,[EBX]
        ADD     EBX,4
        MOV     INTSP,EBX
        MOV     ES:[4],EAX      ; Restore to TSS.
; Restore registers.
        POP     EBX
        MOV     ES,WORD PTR ST01
        MOV     DS,WORD PTR ST03
        POP     EAX             ; Restore "real" eax.
```

DOS EXTENDERS

```
            XCHG        EAX,[ESP]
            POP         ESP             ; Set up new top stack.
            XCHG        EAX,[ESP+4]
            OR          EAX,EAX         ; Test cs.
            XCHG        EAX,[ESP+4]
            JNZ         SHORT GOIRET
            ADD         ESP,8           ; Skip fake CS/IP from INT 30H.
GOIRET:
; Reset resume flag.
            AND         DWORD PTR [ESP+8],0FFFECFFFH
            IRETD

; Emulate lock prefix.
DOLOCK:

            POP         EBP
            POP         DS
            POP         EBX
            POP         EAX
            PUSH        0FFFFH
            PUSH        13              ; Simulate errno.
            JMP32S      NOT13

; This is the interface routine to allow a protected-mode
; program to call VM86 interrupts.
; Call with es:ebx pointing to a parameter block.
; +00 flag - if 1 then resave ES, DS, FS & GS
;            into parameter block after call
; +04 int number (0-255)   (required)
; +08 eflags
; +12 vm86 esp             (required)
; +16 vm86 ss              (required)
; +20 vm86 es
; +24 vm86 ds
; +28 vm86 fs
; +32 vm86 gs
; +36 vm86 ebp             (to replace that used in call)
; +40 vm86 ebx             (to replace that used in call)
;
```

```
; All other registers will be passed to vm86 routine.
;
; This routine depends on the dointnn routine.

INT30H:
        ADD       ESP,4              ; Remove intno.
; Check for exit dos.
        CMP       BYTE PTR ES:[EBX][4],20H
        JZ        SHORT EXTODOS
        CMP       BYTE PTR ES:[EBX][4],21H
        JNZ       SHORT NOTEX
        CMP       AH,4CH
        JZ        SHORT EXTODOS
        OR        AH,AH
        JNZ       SHORT NOTEX
EXTODOS:
        BACK2DOS
NOTEX:
        CMP       BYTE PTR ES:[EBX],0
        JZ        SHORT NOSEGSAV
; dummy CS/IP to signal IRET to save segments
        PUSH      0
        PUSH      0
NOSEGSAV:
; Stack up registers.
        PUSH      DWORD PTR ES:[EBX+32]
        PUSH      DWORD PTR ES:[EBX+28]
        PUSH      DWORD PTR ES:[EBX+24]
        PUSH      DWORD PTR ES:[EBX+20]
        PUSH      DWORD PTR ES:[EBX+16]
        PUSH      DWORD PTR ES:[EBX+12]
; Force VM86=1 in EFLAGS.
        XCHG      EAX,ES:[EBX+8]
        OR        EAX,20000H
        AND       EAX,0FFFECFFFH
        PUSH      EAX
        XCHG      EAX,ES:[EBX+8]
        PUSH      0                  ; Don't care cs.
        PUSH      0                  ; Don't care eip.
```

DOS EXTENDERS

```
          MOV       EBP,ESP
          PUSH      EAX
; Push vm86 ebx.
          PUSH      DWORD PTR ES:[EBX+40]
          PUSH      DS
; Push vm86 ebp.
          PUSH      DWORD PTR ES:[EBX+36]
          MOV       AX,SEL_DATA0
          MOV       DS,AX
; Get user's intno.
          MOV       AL,ES:[EBX+4]
; Set flag to dointnn not to check cs:ip for int #.
          MOV       AH,0FFH
; Go ahead...make my interrupt.
          JMP32S    DOINTNN

; Handle hardware int!
; This routine uses INT 30 to handle HW interrupts
; If interrupted in protected mode, a special stack
; is used. If in VM86 mode, the current VM86 stack is used.
HWINT:
          XCHG      EAX,[ESP]      ; Swap eax and int #.
          PUSH      DS
          PUSH      ES
          PUSH      EBX
          MOV       BX,SEL_DATA
          MOV       DS,BX
          MOV       ES,BX
          CMP       EAX,28H
          JB        SHORT IRQ07
          ADD       EAX,48H        ; vector IRQ8-F to INT 70-77
          JMP       SHORT IRQSET
IRQ07:
          SUB       EAX,24         ; vector IRQ0-7 to INT 8-0F
IRQSET:
; Set up special interrupt frame.
          MOV       HINTFRAME.VMINT,EAX
```

DOS 5: A DEVELOPER'S GUIDE

```
; Don't allow multitasker to switch.
        INC     MLOCK
        MOV     HINTFRAME.VMEBP,EBP
        POP     EBX
        MOV     HINTFRAME.VMEBX,EBX
        PUSH    EBX
; Set model flags.
        MOV     HINTFRAME.VMFLAGS,020000H
        MOV     HINTFRAME.VMESP,OFFSET SSINT1
        MOV     AX,SEG SSINT1
        MOV     HINTFRAME.VMSS,EAX
        MOV     EAX,[ESP+24]    ; Get flags.
        TEST    EAX,20000H      ; Check vm.
        JZ      SHORT NOTVMHW
        MOV     EAX,[ESP+28]    ; Get vm86's esp.
        MOV     HINTFRAME.VMESP,EAX
        MOV     EAX,[ESP+32]
        MOV     HINTFRAME.VMSS,EAX
NOTVMHW:
        MOV     EBX,OFFSET HINTFRAME
        PUSH    FS
        PUSH    GS
        INT     30H             ; Do interrupt.
        PUSH    SEL_DATA
        POP     DS
; Decrease multitasker's semaphore.
        DEC     MLOCK
; See if multitasking active.
        CMP     MULTI,0
        JZ      SHORT NOTASK
; Was interrupt a timer tick?
        CMP     HINTFRAME.VMINT,8
        JNZ     SHORT NOTASK
; Is multitasking locked?
        CMP     MLOCK,0
; Don't switch critical section.
        JNZ     SHORT NOTASK
; Is current task == TSS0?
        STR     AX
```

DOS EXTENDERS

```
            CMP       AX,TSS1         ; Don't switch root task.
            JZ        SHORT NOTASK
            JMPABS32  TSS1,0          ; Switch to root task.
NOTASK:
            POP       GS
            POP       FS
            POP       EBX
            POP       ES
            POP       DS
            POP       EAX
            IRETD


ISREND      EQU       $
ISR         ENDS

ISRLEN      EQU       (ISREND-ISRBEG)-1
IDTLEN      EQU       (IDTEND-IDTBEG)-1
INTLEN      EQU       (INT1-INT0)
            PUBLIC    ISRLEN,IDTLEN,INT0,INT1
            PUBLIC    IDTBEG,INTLEN
            END
```

Listing 19-4. GDT.ASM.

```
;****************************************************************
;*                                                              *
;* PROT - A 386 protected-mode DOS extender                     *
;* Copyright (C) 1989, by Al Williams                           *
;* All rights reserved.                                         *
;*                                                              *
;* Permission is granted for noncommercial use of this          *
;* software subject to certain conditions (see PROT.ASM).       *
;*                                                              *
;* This file is: GDT.ASM, the Global Descriptor Table           *
;* definitions.                                                 *
;*                                                              *
;****************************************************************
; See EQUMAC.INC for an explanation of the DESC macro.
```

DOS 5: A DEVELOPER'S GUIDE

```
INCLUDE     EQUMAC.INC
GDT_FILE    EQU     1
INCLUDE     EXTERNAL.INC
GDTSEG      SEGMENT
GDT         EQU     $               ; GDT space
            PUBLIC GDT
            DESC    SEL_NULL        ; DUMMY NULL SELECTOR
            DESC    SEL_GDT         ; GDT ALIAS
            DESC    SEL_CODE16      ; 16-BIT CODE SEGMENT
            DESC    SEL_DATA0       ; 4-GBYTE SEGMENT
            DESC    SEL_CODE32      ; 32-BIT CODE SEGMENT
            DESC    SEL_STACK       ; 32-BIT STACK
            DESC    SEL_RDATA       ; REAL MODE LIKE DATA SEG
            DESC    SEL_VIDEO       ; VIDEO MEMORY
            DESC    SEL_DATA        ; 32-BIT DATA
            DESC    SEL_IDT         ; IDT ALIAS
            DESC    SEL_ICODE       ; ISR SEGMENT
            DESC    SEL_TSS1        ; MAIN TASK BLOCK
            DESC    TSS1            ; SAME (MUST FOLLOW SEL_TSS1)
            DESC    SEL_UCODE       ; USER CODE
            DESC    SEL_UDATA       ; USER DATA
            DESC    SEL_PSP         ; DOS PSP
            DESC    SEL_FREE        ; FREE DOS MEMORY
            DESC    SEL_EXT         ; EXTENDED MEMORY
            DESC    SEL_ENV         ; ENVIRONMENT
IF          DLL
            DESC    SEL_CCS         ; CLIENT CODE SEGMENT
            DESC    SEL_CDS         ; CLIENT DATA/STACK
            DESC    SEL_86INT       ; DLL CALL GATE
ENDIF
            DESC    SEL_15S         ; INT 15 FUNC 87H SOURCE
            DESC    SEL_15D         ; INT 15 FUNC 87H DEST
            DESC    SEL_TSS0        ; DUMMY TASK BLOCK (may reuse)
            DESC    TSS0            ; SAME (MUST FOLLOW SEL_TSS0)
; SPARE ENTRIES
            DESC    SPARE0
            DESC    SPARE1
            DESC    SPARE2
            DESC    SPARE3
```

DOS EXTENDERS

```
                DESC    SPARE4
                DESC    SPARE5
                DESC    SPARE6
                DESC    SPARE7
                DESC    SPARE8
                DESC    SPARE9
                DESC    SPARE10
                DESC    SPARE11
                DESC    SPARE12
                DESC    SPARE13
                DESC    SPARE14
                DESC    SPARE15
                DESC    SPARE16
                DESC    SPARE17
                DESC    SPARE18
                DESC    SPARE19
                DESC    SPARE20
                DESC    SPARE21
                DESC    SPARE22
                DESC    SPARE23
                DESC    SPARE24
                DESC    SPARE25
                DESC    SPARE26
                DESC    SPARE27
                DESC    SPARE28
                DESC    SPARE29
                DESC    SPARE30
                DESC    SPARE31
GDTEND          =       $
GDTSEG          ENDS

GDTLEN          EQU     (GDTEND-GDT)-1
                PUBLIC  GDTLEN
                END
```

DOS 5: A DEVELOPER'S GUIDE

Listing 19-5. TSS.ASM.

```
;******************************************************************
;*                                                                *
;* PROT - A 386 protected-mode DOS extender                       *
;* Copyright (C) 1989, by Al Williams                             *
;* All rights reserved.                                           *
;*                                                                *
;* Permission is granted for noncommercial use of this software   *
;* subject to certain conditions (see PROT.ASM).                  *
;*                                                                *
;* This file is: TSS.ASM, the Task State Segment definitions.     *
;* If you are using TASM, you may have to change this file.       *
;* See below for more details.                                    *
;*                                                                *
;******************************************************************
INCLUDE         EQUMAC.INC
TSS_FILE        EQU     1
INCLUDE         EXTERNAL.INC
INCLUDE         TSS.INC

TSSSEG          SEGMENT
                ORG     0
; dummy TSS that stores the original machine state
TSS0BEG         TSSBLK  <>
TSS0END         EQU     $


; TSS to run the USER task


;******************************************************************
;*                                                                *
;* Attention TASM users!                                          *
;*                                                                *
;******************************************************************

; Set the next line to 0 if you can't get a working program
; with TASM.
; TASM has a problem initializing structures to external values.
IF 0
; You can use the following line for MASM:
TSS1BEG         TSSBLK  <>
```

DOS EXTENDERS

```
        ELSE
        ; To work around a bug in TASM use (this works in MASM too):
        TSS1BEG         EQU     $
                        DD      0
                        DD      OFFSET SSEG321
                        DW      SEL_STACK
                        DW      0
                        DD      0
                        DW      SEL_STACK
                        DW      0
                        DD      0
                        DW      SEL_STACK
                        DW      0
                        DD      0
                        DD      OFFSET USER
                        DD      200H
                        DD      0
                        DD      0
                        DD      0
                        DD      0
                        DD      OFFSET SSEG321
                        DD      0
                        DD      0
                        DD      0
                        DW      SEL_DATA
                        DW      0
                        DW      SEL_UCODE
                        DW      0
                        DW      SEL_STACK
                        DW      0
                        DW      SEL_UDATA
                        DW      0
                        DW      SEL_DATA0
                        DW      0
                        DW      SEL_VIDEO
                        DW      0
                        DD      0
                        DW      0
                        DD      $+2-OFFSET TSS1BEG
                        DB      8190 DUP (0)
                        DB      0FFH
```

```
ENDIF
; END OF TASM FIXES
TSS1END         EQU     $

TSSLEN          EQU     (TSSOEND-TSSOBEG)-1
                PUBLIC TSS1BEG,TSSLEN


TSSSEG          ENDS

                END
```

Listing 19-6. STACKS.ASM.
```
;****************************************************************
;*                                                              *
;* PROT - A 386 protected-mode DOS extender                     *
;* Copyright (C) 1989, by Al Williams                           *
;* All rights reserved.                                         *
;*                                                              *
;* Permission is granted for noncommercial use of this software *
;* subject to certain conditions (see PROT.ASM).                *
;*                                                              *
;* This file is: STACKS.ASM, which contains the stack segments. *
;*                                                              *
;****************************************************************
INCLUDE         EQUMAC.INC

; 16-bit stack segment (for CODE16)
SSEG            SEGMENT
SSEG0           DB      DOSSTACK DUP (?)
SSEG1           EQU     $
SSEG            ENDS

; 16-bit stack segment for vm86 int (both hardware & INT 30)
SSINT           SEGMENT
SSINT0          DB      VM86STACK DUP (?)
SSINT1          DB      ?
SSINT           ENDS
```

DOS EXTENDERS

```
; private stack for default critical error handler DOS calls
CSTACK          SEGMENT
                DB      CRITSTACK DUP (?)
CSTACK_1        EQU     $
CSTACK          ENDS

; 32-bit stack segment
SS32            SEGMENT
SSEG32          DB      PMSTACK DUP (?)
SSEG321         EQU     $
SS32            ENDS

SSEG32LEN       EQU     (SSEG321 SSEG32)-1
                PUBLIC  SSEG321,SSINT1,SSEG1,SSEG32LEN,CSTACK_1
                END
```

Listing 19-7. DLL.ASM.

```
;******************************************************************
;*                                                                *
;* PROT - A 386 protected-mode DOS extender                       *
;* Copyright (C) 1989, by Al Williams                             *
;* All rights reserved.                                           *
;*                                                                *
;* Permission is granted for noncommercial use of this            *
;* software subject to certain conditions (see PROT.ASM).         *
;*                                                                *
;* This file is: DLL.ASM, the real mode start-up for DLL entry.   *
;* All code in this file runs in real mode.                       *
;*                                                                *
;******************************************************************
INCLUDE         EQUMAC.INC
DLL_FILE        EQU     1
INCLUDE         EXTERNAL.INC

CSEG            SEGMENT
                EXTRN   ICA0:WORD,ICA1:WORD,PINTNO:BYTE
CSEG            ENDS
                EXTRN   DLLCLEAN:FAR
```

DOS 5: A DEVELOPER'S GUIDE

```
TSTACK          SEGMENT PARA PUBLIC 'STACK' USE16
                DW      256 DUP (?)
TSTACK          ENDS

IF              DLL
DLLSEG          SEGMENT PARA PUBLIC 'CODE16' USE16
_DLL            PROC    FAR
; X386 starts here....
ENTRY           LABEL   FAR
                PUBLIC ENTRY
                ASSUME CS:DLLSEG,DS:DLLSEG
                MOV     AX,CS
                MOV     DS,AX
; Find environment.
                MOV     AX,ES:[2CH]
                MOV     ENVS,AX
; Check command tail.
                MOV     STOPSP,ES
                MOV     STOPSP1,ES
                MOV     STOPSP2,ES
                MOV     CL,ES:[80H]
                OR      CL,CL
                JNZ     SHORT PARSECMD
NOTAIL:
                MOV     DX,OFFSET CPYMSG
                JMP     SHORT ERRABT

PARSECMD:
                INC     CL
                MOV     BX,80H          ; Point to cmd tail (es).
                XOR     CH,CH           ; cx=tail's length
                XOR     DX,DX           ; dot flag
                XOR     SI,SI           ; pointer into buffer
SKIPL:
                INC     BX
                JCXZ    NOTAIL          ; no actual tail
                DEC     CX
                MOV     AL,ES:[BX]
                CMP     AL,' '          ; space
```

DOS EXTENDERS

```
                JZ      SKIPL
                CMP     AL,9
                JZ      SKIPL
; Found start of filename.
GETFN:          JCXZ    ENDFN
                MOV     AL,ES:[BX]
                CMP     AL,' '
                JZ      SHORT ENDFN
                CMP     AL,9
                JZ      SHORT ENDFN
                CMP     AL,13
                JZ      SHORT ENDFN
                MOV     FNAME[SI],AL
                INC     SI
                CMP     AL,'.'
                JNZ     SHORT NOTDOT
                INC     DX
NOTDOT:         INC     BX
                DEC     CX
                JMP     GETFN
; end of filename
ENDFN:          OR      DX,DX
                JNZ     SHORT NOEXTEND
                MOV     AX,'E.'
                MOV     WORD PTR FNAME[SI],AX
                MOV     AX,'EX'
                MOV     WORD PTR FNAME[SI][2],AX
                ADD     SI,4
NOEXTEND:
                XOR     AL,AL
                MOV     FNAME[SI],AL    ; Terminate filename.
                DEC     BX
                MOV     ES:[BX],CL
                MOV     CMDBEG,BX
; Resolve path.
                CALL    SETFNAM         ; Let exec find errors.

; Take over a user int.
;
                MOV     AX,3560H
```

DOS 5: A DEVELOPER'S GUIDE

```
; Find unused interrupt.
INTSCAN:
            INT     21H
            MOV     CX,ES
            OR      BX,CX
            JZ      SHORT FOUNDINT
            INC     AL
            CMP     AL,68H
            JNZ     INTSCAN
            MOV     DX,OFFSET NOINTS
; no free interrupts...error
ERRABT:
            MOV     AH,9
            INT     21H
            MOV     AX,4C01H
            INT     21H

; Set up free interrupt.
FOUNDINT:
            MOV     AH,25H
            MOV     DX,OFFSET ISR60
            INT     21H
; Save vector # and ICA; write signature to ICA.
            MOV     BX,CSEG
            MOV     DS,BX
            XOR     BX,BX
            MOV     ES,BX
            ASSUME  DS:CSEG,ES:NOTHING
            MOV     BX,'PX'         ; X386 signature
            XCHG    BX,ES:[4F0H]    ; Swap signature and ICA.
            MOV     ICA0,BX
            MOV     AH,'='          ; remainder of signature
            PUSH    AX
            XCHG    AH,AL
            XCHG    AX,ES:[4F2H]
            MOV     ICA1,AX
            POP     AX
            MOV     PINTNO,AL
```

DOS EXTENDERS

```
; Free up DOS memory.
            MOV     AX,CS
            MOV     DS,AX
            ASSUME  DS:@CURSEG
            MOV     BX,ZZZSEG+1
; Calculate memory requirements.
            SUB     BX,STOPSP
            MOV     ES,STOPSP
            MOV     AH,4AH
            INT     21H
            MOV     DX,BX
; Load program from the command line.
            MOV     AX,CS
            MOV     ES,AX
            ASSUME  ES:@CURSEG,DS:@CURSEG
            MOV     DX,OFFSET FFNAME
            MOV     BX,OFFSET EXECBLOCK
            MOV     AX,4B00H
            MOV     SSSAV,SS
            MOV     SPSAV,SP
            INT     21H
            MOV     BX,CS
            MOV     DS,BX
            ASSUME  DS:@CURSEG
            LSS     SP,SSSPSAV
            PUSHF
            CALL    DLLCLEAN
            POPF
            JNC     SHORT GETRC
; Clean up int vect and ICA.
            MOV     DX,OFFSET UNMSG
            JMP     NEAR PTR ERRABT
GETRC:
; Get rc.
            MOV     AH,4DH
            INT     21H
            MOV     AH,4CH
            INT     21H

_DLL        ENDP
```

DOS 5: A DEVELOPER'S GUIDE

```
; Find file in current directory or on PATH.
SETFNAM         PROC    NEAR
FNAGN:
                MOV     DI,FFNAMP
                XOR     SI,SI
CPYLOOP:
; Append file name to ffname (initially blank).
                MOV     AL,FNAME[SI]
                MOV     FFNAME[DI],AL
                INC     DI
                INC     SI
                OR      AL,AL
                JNZ     CPYLOOP
; Try to open file.
                MOV     AX,4300H
                MOV     DX,OFFSET FFNAME
                INT     21H
                MOV     AL,1
; Found! Goto fnxit.
                JNC     SHORT FNXIT
; Not found. Get next path directory and place in ffname.
                XOR     AX,AX
                MOV     FFNAMP,AX
                CALL    NXTPATH         ; Get path element.
                JNZ     FNAGN
FNXIT:          OR      AL,AL
                RET
SETFNAM         ENDP

; Get path element in ffname[ffnamp].
NXTPATH         PROC    NEAR
                PUSH    ES
; Look at environment block (if 0 this is our 1st run).
                MOV     ES,ENVS
                MOV     BX,ENVP
                OR      BX,BX
                JNZ     SHORT PATHOK
; Find PATH env variable and set up pointers.
                XOR     DI,DI
```

DOS EXTENDERS

```
TRYNXTENV:
            MOV     SI,OFFSET PATHS
            MOV     CX,PATHL
            PUSH    DI
            CLD
            REPZ    CMPSB
; If zero then found.
            JZ      SHORT FNDPATH
; Not found. Skip to next variable or end of block.
            POP     DI
            XOR     AL,AL
            MOV     CX,0FFFFH
            REPNZ   SCASB
            CMP     AL,ES:[DI]
            JNZ     TRYNXTENV       ; more to go
; No PATH present; return.
            XOR     AX,AX
            POP     ES
            RET

FNDPATH:
            POP     AX              ; Discard saved di.
            MOV     ENVP,DI
            MOV     BX,DI

; Here, we have a pointer (envs:envp) to the current path
; directory.
PATHOK:
; Copy until ; or 0 --make sure 0 is last byte.
            MOV     DI,FFNAMP
            MOV     AL,ES:[BX]
            OR      AL,AL
            JZ      SHORT PATHRET
PCPYLP:     CMP     AL,';'
            JNZ     SHORT PMOVIT
            XOR     AL,AL
PMOVIT:
            MOV     FFNAME[DI],AL
            OR      AL,AL
            JZ      SHORT PATHFIN
            INC     BX
```

815

```
                INC     DI
                MOV     AL,ES:[BX]
                JMP     PCPYLP
PATHFIN:
; Ensure proper flag return.
                MOV     AL,1
; If last character isn't a \ or /, add a \.
                INC     BX
                CMP     FFNAME[DI-1],'\'
                JZ      SHORT PATHRET
; Some use / (like MKS toolkit).
                CMP     FFNAME[DI-1],'/'
                JZ      SHORT PATHRET
                MOV     AL,'\'
                MOV     FFNAME[DI],AL
                INC     DI
PATHRET:
                MOV     ENVP,BX
                MOV     FFNAMP,DI
                OR      AL,AL
                POP     ES
                RET
NXTPATH         ENDP

; data in code segment
NOINTS          DB      'X386: No free interrupt vectors.'
                DB      13,10,'$'
UNMSG           DB      'X386: Unable to execute program.'
                DB      13,10,'$'
CPYMSG          DB      'X386: Copyright (C) 1989,1990 '
                DB      'by Al Williams. '
                DB      'All rights reserved.',13,10
                DB      'Version 1.0',13,10
                DB      'Usage: X386 program',13,10
                DB      '$'
SSSPSAV         EQU     THIS DWORD
SPSAV           DW      ?
SSSAV           DW      ?
```

DOS EXTENDERS

```
; executable file name
FNAME           DB      80 DUP (?)

; resolved file name
FFNAME          DB      80 DUP (?)
FFNAMP          DW      0

; pointer to env
ENVP            DW      0
ENVS            DW      0


PATHS           DB      'PATH='
PATHL           EQU     $-PATHS

EXECBLOCK       EQU     $
                DW      0               ; Use my environment.
CMDBEG          DW      0
STOPSP          DW      0
                DW      5CH             ; 1st fcb in my psp
STOPSP1         DW      0
                DW      6CH
STOPSP2         DW      0               ; 2nd fcb in my psp

; This is the entry point to go to protected mode.
; Sometimes it will really be INT 60H, other times it
; will move.
ISR60           PROC    FAR
                ASSUME  CS:DLLSEG,DS:DLLSEG
                PUSH    DS
                PUSH    CSEG
                POP     DS
                ASSUME  DS:CSEG
                STI
                POP     BX
                MOV     C_DS,BX
; Get caller's CS.
                POP     CX              ; Gotta get IP first.
                POP     BX
```

DOS 5: A DEVELOPER'S GUIDE

```
                PUSH    BX              ; Replace stack data.
                PUSH    CX
                MOV     C_CS,BX         ; Save CS.
                MOV     CX,DAT32
                MOV     DS,CX
                ASSUME  DS:DAT32
                MOV     C_SP,SP
                JMP     PENTRY
ISR60           ENDP
DLLSEG          ENDS
ENDIF
                END
```

Listing 19-8. X386.ASM.

```
;******************************************************************
;*                                                                *
;* PROT - A 386 protected-mode DOS extender                       *
;* Copyright (C) 1989, by Al Williams                             *
;* All rights reserved.                                           *
;*                                                                *
;* Permission is granted for noncommercial use of this            *
;* software subject to certain conditions (see PROT.ASM).         *
;*                                                                *
;* This file is: X386.ASM, the user program that handles          *
;* dynamic loading.                                               *
;*                                                                *
;******************************************************************
INCLUDE         EQUMAC.INC
USER_FILE       EQU     1
INCLUDE         EXTERNAL.INC

IF              DLL

NODATA

PROT_CODE
USER            PROC    NEAR
; Create dispatcher CALL gate (AT SEL_86INT).
                MOV     AX,SEL_GDT
```

DOS EXTENDERS

```
                MOV     ES,AX
                ASSUME  ES:GDTSEG
                XOR     EDX,EDX
                XOR     AL,AL
                MOV     AH,CALL_GATE
                MOV     CX,SEL_CODE32
                MOV     EBX,OFFSET DISPATCH
                MOV     SI,SEL_86INT
                CALL32F SEL_CODE32,MAKE_GATE
; Load DS/SS.
                MOV     AX,SEL_DATA
                MOV     ES,AX
                ASSUME  ES:DAT32
                CLI
                MOVZX   ESP,C_SP
                MOV     AX,SEL_CDS
                MOV     SS,AX
                STI
; Get 32-bit return address from stack.
                XOR     EBX,EBX
                POP     BX
                CLI
                MOV     AX,SEL_TSS1
                MOV     ES,AX
                MOV     ES:[4],ESP
                MOV     AX,SEL CDS
                MOV     ES:[8],EAX
                STI
                PUSH    SEL_CCS
                PUSH    EBX
                MOV     DS,AX
                MOV     ES,AX
                MOV     FS,AX
                MOV     GS,AX
                RETF    4
USER            ENDP
PROT_CODE_END
ENDIF
                END
```

DOS 5: A DEVELOPER'S GUIDE

Listing 19-9. EQUMAC.INC.

```
;******************************************************************
;*                                                                *
;* PROT - A 386 protected-mode DOS extender                       *
;* Copyright (C) 1989, by Al Williams                             *
;* All rights reserved.                                           *
;*                                                                *
;* Permission is granted for noncommercial use of this            *
;* software subject to certain conditions (see PROT.ASM).         *
;*                                                                *
;* This file is: EQUMAC.INC, assorted macros and equates.         *
;*                                                                *
;******************************************************************
; EQUates the user may wish to change (one set for each mode)
IF              DLL
SPEEDUP         EQU     1               ; X4 clock speedup
DOSSTACK        EQU     100H            ; stack size for DOS start-up
VM86STACK       EQU     100H            ; stack size for VM86 int
CRITSTACK       EQU     30H             ; stack size for crit errs
PMSTACK         EQU     200H            ; stack size for p-mode stack
PVSTACK         EQU     260             ; pl0/vm86 pseudo stack size
ELSE
SPEEDUP         EQU     1               ; X4 clock speedup
DOSSTACK        EQU     200H            ; stack size for DOS start-up
VM86STACK       EQU     200H            ; stack size for VM86 int
CRITSTACK       EQU     30H             ; stack size for crit errs
PMSTACK         EQU     400H            ; stack size for p-mode stack
PVSTACK         EQU     260             ; pl0/vm86 pseudo stack size
ENDIF

; maximum protected-mode interrupt # defined
          TOPINT    EQU OFFH
; The critical error handler works differently for DOS 2.X than
; for other DOS versions. In 99% of the cases it won't make any
; difference if you compile with DOS=2....
; major DOS version number (2, 3 or 4)
          DOS       EQU 3

; parameter block to interface for int 30H (call86 & VM86CALL)
VM86BLK         STRUC
```

DOS EXTENDERS

```
        VMSEGFLAG       DD      0       ; Restore seg reg (flag).
        VMINT           DD      0       ; interrupt number
        VMFLAGS         DD      0       ; EFLAGS
        VMESP           DD      0       ; ESP
        VMSS            DD      0       ; SS
        VMES            DD      0       ; ES
        VMDS            DD      0       ; DS
        VMFS            DD      0       ; FS
        VMGS            DD      0       ; GS
        VMEBP           DD      0       ; EBP
        VMEBX           DD      0       ; EBX
        VM86BLK         ENDS

        ; access rights equates
        ; Use these with make_desc or make_seg.
        RO_DATA         EQU     90H     ; r/o data
        RW_DATA         EQU     92H     ; r/w data
        RO_STK          EQU     94H     ; r/o stack
        RW_STK          EQU     96H     ; r/w stack
        EX_CODE         EQU     98H     ; exec only code
        ER_CODE         EQU     9AH     ; read/exec code
        CN_CODE         EQU     9CH     ; exec only conforming code
        CR_CODE         EQU     9EH     ; read/exec conforming code
        LDT_DESC        EQU     82H     ; LDT entry
        TSS_DESC        EQU     89H     ; TSS entry

        ; Use these with make_gate.
        CALL_GATE       EQU     8CH     ; call gate
        TRAP_GATE       EQU     8FH     ; trap gate
        INTR_GATE       EQU     8EH     ; int gate
        TASK_GATE       EQU     85H     ; task gate

        ; dpl equates
        DPL0            EQU     0
        DPL1            EQU     20H
        DPL2            EQU     40H
        DPL3            EQU     60H

        .386P
        ; macro definitions
```

```
; Other macros use this to error-check parameters.
; Give an error if last is blank or toomany is not blank.
ERRCHK      MACRO   LAST,TOOMANY
IFNB        <TOOMANY>
IF2
            %OUT    TOO MANY PARAMETERS
ENDIF
            .ERR
ENDIF
IFB         <LAST>
IF2
            %OUT    NOT ENOUGH PARAMETERS
ENDIF
            .ERR
ENDIF
            ENDM

; Perform absolute 16-bit jump (in a 16-bit segment).
JMPABS      MACRO   A,B,ERRCK
            ERRCHK  B,ERRCK
            DB      0EAH            ;; absolute 16-bit jump
            DW      OFFSET B
            DW      A
            ENDM

; Perform absolute 32-bit jump (in a 32-bit segment).
JMPABS32    MACRO   A,B,ERRCK
            ERRCHK  B,ERRCK
            DB      0EAH            ;; absolute 32-bit jump
            DD      OFFSET B
            DW      A
            ENDM

; This generates a correct 32-bit offset for a proc call
; since MASM doesn't sign extend 32-bit relative items.
CALL32S     MACRO   LBL,ERRCK       ;; short call
            ERRCHK  LBL,ERRCK
            DB      0E8H
            DD      LBL-($+4)
            ENDM
```

DOS EXTENDERS

```
CALL32F         MACRO    SG,LBL,ERRCK  ; ; far call
                ERRCHK   LBL,ERRCK
                DB       9AH
                DD       OFFSET LBL
                DW       SG
                ENDM

JMP32S          MACRO    LBL,ERRCK     ; ; short jump
                ERRCHK   LBL,ERRCK
                DB       0E9H
                DD       LBL-($+4)
                ENDM

; jcc32 uses the condition codes used in the Intel literature.
; conditional jump macro
JCC32           MACRO    CONDX,LBL,ERRCK
                ERRCHK   LBL,ERRCK
                DB       0FH
IFIDNI          <CONDX>,<A>
                DB       87H
ELSEIFIDNI      <CONDX>,<NBE>
                DB       87H
ELSEIFIDNI      <CONDX>, <AE>
                DB       83H
ELSEIFIDNI      <CONDX>, <C>
                DB       82H
ELSEIFIDNI      <CONDX>, <NAE>
                DB       82H
ELSEIFIDNI      <CONDX>, <B>
                DB       82H
ELSEIFIDNI      <CONDX>, <BE>
                DB       86H
ELSEIFIDNI      <CONDX>, <E>
                DB       84H
ELSEIFIDNI      <CONDX>, <Z>
                DB       84H
ELSEIFIDNI      <CONDX>, <G>
                DB       8FH
ELSEIFIDNI      <CONDX>, <GE>
                DB       8DH
```

```
ELSEIFIDNI      <CONDX>, <L>
                DB      8CH
ELSEIFIDNI      <CONDX>, <LE>
                DB      8EH
ELSEIFIDNI      <CONDX>, <NA>
                DB      86H
ELSEIFIDNI      <CONDX>, <NB>
                DB      83H
ELSEIFIDNI      <CONDX>, <NC>
                DB      83H
ELSEIFIDNI      <CONDX>, <NGE>
                DB      8CH
ELSEIFIDNI      <CONDX>, <NL>
                DB      8DH
ELSEIFIDNI      <CONDX>, <NO>
                DB      81H
ELSEIFIDNI      <CONDX>, <NP>
                DB      8BH
ELSEIFIDNI      <CONDX>, <NS>
                DB      89H
ELSEIFIDNI      <CONDX>, <NZ>
                DB      85H
ELSEIFIDNI      <CONDX>, <O>
                DB      80H
ELSEIFIDNI      <CONDX>, <P>
                DB      8AH
ELSEIFIDNI      <CONDX>, <PE>
                DB      8AH
ELSEIFIDNI      <CONDX>, <PO>
                DB      8BH
ELSEIFIDNI      <CONDX>, <S>
                DB      88H
ELSE
                %OUT    JCC32: UNKNOWN CONDITION CODE
                .ERR
ENDIF
                DD      LBL-($+4)
                ENDM

; Override default operand size.
OPSIZ           MACRO   NOPARM          ; ; op size override
```

DOS EXTENDERS

```
                ERRCHK   X,NOPARM
                DB       66H
                ENDM

; Override default address size.
ADSIZ           MACRO    NOPARM       ; ; address size override
                ERRCHK   X,NOPARM
                DB       67H
                ENDM

; delay macro for interrupt controller access
IDELAY          MACRO    NOPARM
                LOCAL    DELAY1,DELAY2
                ERRCHK   X,NOPARM
                JMP      SHORT DELAY1
DELAY1:         JMP      SHORT DELAY2
DELAY2:
                ENDM

; BREAKPOINT MACROS

; MACRO to turn on NBREAKPOINTS
; If used with no arguments (or a 1), this macro makes NBREAKPOINT
; active if used with an argument > 1. NBREAKPOINT will break
; after that many passes.
BREAKON         MACRO    ARG,ERRCK
                ERRCHK   X,ERRCK
                PUSH     DS
                PUSH     SEL_DATA
                POP      DS
                PUSH     EAX
                IFB      <ARG>
                MOV      AL,1
                ELSE
                MOV      AL,&ARG
                ENDIF
                MOV      BPON,AL
                POP      EAX
                POP      DS
                ENDM
```

DOS 5: A DEVELOPER'S GUIDE

```
; Turns off NBREAKPOINT.
BREAKOFF    MACRO   NOPARAM
            ERRCHK  X,NOPARAM
            PUSH    DS
            PUSH    SEL_DATA
            POP     DS
            PUSH    EAX
            XOR     AL,AL
            MOV     BPON,AL
            POP     EAX
            POP     DS
            ENDM


BREAKPOINT  MACRO   NOPARM
            ERRCHK  X,NOPARM
            INT     3
            ENDM

; Counterbreakpoint--use BREAKON to set count control.

; BREAKPOINT with memory dump
; usage:    BREAKDUMP seg_selector, offset, number_of_words
BREAKDUMP   MACRO   SEG,OFF,CNT,ERRCK
            ERRCHK  CNT,ERRCK
            PUSH    EAX
            MOV     AX,&SEG
            MOV     DUMP_SEG,AX
            MOV     EAX,OFFSET &OFF
            MOV     DUMP_OFF,EAX
            MOV     EAX,&CNT
            MOV     DUMP_CNT,EAX
            POP     EAX
            BREAKPOINT
            ENDM

NBREAKDUMP  MACRO   SEG,OFF,CNT,ERRCK
            ERRCHK  CNT,ERRCK
            LOCAL   NONBP
            PUSH    DS
            PUSH    SEL_DATA
            POP     DS
```

DOS EXTENDERS

```
                PUSHFD
                OR      DS:BPON,0
                JZ      SHORT NONBP
                DEC     BPON
                JNZ     SHORT NONBP
                POPFD
                POP     DS
                BREAKDUMP SEG,OFF,CNT
NONBP:
                POPFD
                POP     DS
                ENDM

NBREAKPOINT     MACRO   SEG,OFF,CNT,ERRCK
                ERRCHK  CNT,ERRCK
                LOCAL   NONBP
                PUSH    DS
                PUSH    SEL_DATA
                POP     DS
                PUSHFD
                OR      DS:BPON,0
                JZ      SHORT NONBP
                DEC     BPON
                JNZ     SHORT NONBP
                POPFD
                POP     DS
                BREAKPOINT
NONBP:
                POPFD
                POP     DS
                ENDM

; Determine linear address of first free byte of memory
; (to nearest paragraph).
LOADFREE        MACRO   REG,ERRCK
                ERRCHK  REG,ERRCK
                XOR     F&RFG,E&REG
                MOV     &REG,SEG ZZZGROUP
                SHL     E&REG,4
                ENDM
```

DOS 5: A DEVELOPER'S GUIDE

```
; Set up PINTFRAME (uses eax).
; Loads vmstack & vmdata to the ss:esp and ds slots in pintframe.
; default ss:esp=ssint1
; default ds=userdata
PROT_STARTUP    MACRO   VMSTACK,VMDATA,ERRCK
                ERRCHK  X,ERRCK
IFB             <VMSTACK>
                MOV     AX,SEG SSINT1
ELSE
                MOV     AX,SEG VMSTACK
ENDIF
                MOV     PINTFRAME.VMSS,EAX
IFB             <VMSTACK>
                MOV     EAX, OFFSET SSINT1
ELSE
                MOV     EAX, OFFSET VMSTACK
ENDIF
                MOV     PINTFRAME.VMESP,EAX
IFB             <VMDATA>
                MOV     AX,SEG USERDATA
ELSE
                MOV     AX,SEG VMDATA
ENDIF
                MOV     PINTFRAME.VMDS,EAX
                ENDM

; Start PROT user segments.
PROT_CODE       MACRO   NOPARM
                ERRCHK  X,NOPARM
USERCODE        SEGMENT
USERCODEBEG     EQU     $
                ASSUME  CS:USERCODE, DS:USERDATA, ES:DAT32
                ENDM

PROT_DATA       MACRO   NOPARM
                ERRCHK  X,NOPARM
USERDATA        SEGMENT
USERDATABEG     EQU     $
                ENDM
```

DOS EXTENDERS

```
PROT_CODE_END  MACRO     NOPARM
               ERRCHK    X,NOPARM
USERCODEEND    EQU       $
USERCODELEN    EQU       (USERCODEEND-USERCODEBEG)-1
               PUBLIC    USERCODELEN
               PUBLIC    USER
USERCODE       ENDS
               ENDM


PROT_DATA_END  MACRO     NOPARM
               ERRCHK    X,NOPARM
USERDATAEND    EQU       $
USERDATALEN    EQU       (USERDATAEND-USERDATABEG)-1
               PUBLIC    USERDATALEN
USERDATA       ENDS
               ENDM

; Simplify programs with no data segment.
NODATA         MACRO     NOPARM
               ERRCHK    X,NOPARM
               PROT_DATA
               PROT_DATA_END
               ENDM

; mnemonic for call86 call
VM86CALL       MACRO     NOPARM
               ERRCHK    X,NOPARM
               CALL32F   SEL_CODE32,CALL86
               ENDM

; mnemonic for DOS return
BACK2DOS       MACRO     RC,ERRCK
               ERRCHK    X,ERRCK
       IFNB    <RC>
               MOV       AL,RC
       ENDIF
               JMPABS32  SEL_CODE16,BACK16
               ENDM

; variables and macro to create GDT/LDT/IDT entries
C_GDT          =         0
```

DOS 5: A DEVELOPER'S GUIDE

```
C_LDT           =       0
C_IDT           =       0

; Create "next" descriptor with name in table.
; If no table specified, use GDT.
DESC            MACRO   NAME,TABLE,ERRCK
                PUBLIC  NAME
                DQ      0
IFB             <TABLE>
                NAME    = C_GDT
C_GDT           =       C_GDT+8
ELSE
IFIDNI          <TABLE>,<LDT>
; For LDT selectors, set the TI bit to one.
                NAME    = C_&TABLE OR 4
ELSE
                NAME    = C_&TABLE
ENDIF
C_&TABLE        =       C_&TABLE+8
ENDIF
                ENDM

; segment defines
DAT32           SEGMENT PARA PUBLIC 'DATA32' USE32
DAT32           ENDS

SEG32           SEGMENT PARA PUBLIC 'CODE32' USE32
SEG32           ENDS

CSEG            SEGMENT PARA PUBLIC 'CODE16' USE16
CSEG            ENDS

TSSSEG          SEGMENT PARA PUBLIC 'DATA32' USE32
TSSSEG          ENDS

USERCODE        SEGMENT PARA PUBLIC 'CODE32' USE32
USERCODE        ENDS

USERDATA        SEGMENT PARA PUBLIC 'DATA32' USE32
USERDATA        ENDS
```

DOS EXTENDERS

```
SSEG            SEGMENT PARA STACK 'STACK' USE16
SSEG            ENDS

SSINT           SEGMENT PARA STACK 'STACK' USE16
SSINT           ENDS

CSTACK          SEGMENT PARA STACK 'STACK' USE16
CSTACK          ENDS

SS32            SEGMENT PARA PUBLIC 'STACK' USE32
SS32            ENDS

GDTSEG          SEGMENT PARA PUBLIC 'CODE32' USE32
GDTSEG          ENDS

ZZZSEG          SEGMENT PARA PUBLIC 'ZZZ' USE16
ZZZSEG          ENDS

ISR             SEGMENT PARA PUBLIC 'CODE32' USE32
ISR             ENDS

IDTABLE         SEGMENT PARA PUBLIC 'DATA32' USE32
IDTABLE         ENDS

ZZZGROUP        GROUP   ZZZSEG
```

Listing 19-10. EXTERNAL.INC.
```
;*****************************************************************
;*                                                               *
;* PROT - A 386 protected-mode DOS extender                      *
;* Copyright (C) 1989, by Al Williams                            *
;* All rights reserved.                                          *
;*                                                               *
;* Permission is granted for noncommercial use of this           *
;* software subject to certain conditions (see PROT.ASM).        *
;*                                                               *
;* This file is: EXTERNAL.INC, the common externals file.        *
;*                                                               *
;*****************************************************************
```

DOS 5: A DEVELOPER'S GUIDE

```
; EXTERNALS from PROT.ASM
IFNDEF          PROT_FILE
DAT32           SEGMENT
                EXTRN   CRITSI:WORD, CRITBP:WORD, CRITDI:WORD
                EXTRN   CRITAX:WORD, CRITICAL:BYTE, BREAKKEY:BYTE
                EXTRN   BREAK_HANDLE:FWORD, BRK_OFF:DWORD
                EXTRN   BRK_SEG:WORD,_PSP:WORD,_PC386:BYTE
                EXTRN   HINTFRAME:BYTE,PINTFRAME:BYTE,INTSP:DWORD
                EXTRN   STO1:DWORD,STO2:DWORD,STO3:DWORD,STO4:DWORD
                EXTRN   DUMP_SEG:WORD,DUMP_OFF:DWORD
                EXTRN   DUMP_CNT:DWORD,SAV_ES:DWORD
                EXTRN   SAV_GS:DWORD,SAV_DS:DWORD,SAV_FS:DWORD
                EXTRN   MULTI:BYTE,MLOCK:WORD
                EXTRN   CURSOR:DWORD
IF              DLL
                EXTRN   C_SP:WORD
ENDIF

DAT32           ENDS
                EXTRN   DAT32LEN:ABS
                EXTRN   OUCH:FAR,HEXOUT:FAR,HEXOUT2:FAR
                EXTRN   HEXOUT4:FAR,CRLF:FAR
                EXTRN   CLS:FAR,MESSOUT:FAR,CALL86:FAR
IF              DLL
                EXTRN   DISPATCH:FAR
ENDIF
                EXTRN   MAKE_GATE:FAR,MAKE_SEG:FAR
                EXTRN   SEG32ENT:ABS
                EXTRN   SEG32LEN:ABS
ENDIF

; EXTERNALS from TSS.ASM
IFNDEF          TSS_FILE
TSSSEG          SEGMENT
                EXTRN   TSS1BEG:BYTE
TSSSEG          ENDS
                EXTRN   TSSLEN:ABS
ENDIF

; EXTERNALS for the user's ASM (separate these out)
IFNDEF          USER_FILE
```

DOS EXTENDERS

```
USERCODE        SEGMENT
                EXTRN   USER:FAR
USERCODE        ENDS
                EXTRN   USERCODELEN:ABS
                EXTRN   USERDATALEN:ABS
ENDIF

; EXTERNALS from the GDT
IFNDEF          GDT_FILE
                EXTRN   GDT:ABS
                EXTRN   SEL_NULL:ABS
                EXTRN   SEL_CODE16:ABS
                EXTRN   SEL_DATA0:ABS
                EXTRN   SEL_CODE32:ABS
                EXTRN   SEL_STACK:ABS
                EXTRN   SEL_RDATA:ABS
                EXTRN   SEL_GDT:ABS
                EXTRN   SEL_VIDEO:ABS
                EXTRN   SEL_DATA:ABS
                EXTRN   SEL_IDT:ABS
                EXTRN   SEL_ICODE:ABS
                EXTRN   SEL_TSS0:ABS
                EXTRN   TSS0:ABS
                EXTRN   SEL_TSS1:ABS
                EXTRN   TSS1:ABS
                EXTRN   SEL_UCODE:ABS
                EXTRN   SEL_UDATA:ABS
                EXTRN   SEL_PSP:ABS
                EXTRN   SEL_FREE:ABS
                EXTRN   SEL EXT:ABS
                EXTRN   SEL_ENV:ABS
                EXTRN   GDTLEN:ABS
IF              DLL
                EXTRN   SEL_CCS:ABS
                EXTRN   SEL_CDS:ABS
                EXTRN   SEL_86INT:ABS
ENDIF
                EXTRN   SEL_15S:ABS
                EXTRN   SEL_15D:ABS
ENDIF
```

DOS 5: A DEVELOPER'S GUIDE

```
; EXTERNALS from STACKS.ASM
            EXTRN   SSEG32LEN:ABS
SSEG        SEGMENT
            EXTRN   SSEG1:ABS
SSEG        ENDS
SS32        SEGMENT
            EXTRN   SSEG321:FAR
SS32        ENDS
SSINT       SEGMENT
            EXTRN   SSINT1:FAR
SSINT       ENDS
CSTACK      SEGMENT
            EXTRN   CSTACK_1:ABS
CSTACK      ENDS
IFNDEF      DLL_FILE
IF          DLL
            EXTRN   ENTRY:FAR
ENDIF
ENDIF

; EXTERNALS from CODE16.ASM
IFNDEF      CODE16_FILE
IF          DLL
CSEG        SEGMENT
            EXTRN   C_DS:WORD,C_CS:WORD
CSEG        ENDS
            EXTRN   PENTRY:FAR
ELSE
            EXTRN   ENTRY:FAR
ENDIF
            EXTRN   BACK16:FAR
ENDIF

; EXTERNALS from INT386.ASM
IFNDEF      INT386_FILE
            EXTRN   IDTBEG:ABS
            EXTRN   ISRLEN:ABS
            EXTRN   IDTLEN:ABS
            EXTRN   INT0:FAR,INT1:FAR
            EXTRN   INTLEN:ABS
ENDIF
```

DOS EXTENDERS

Listing 19-11. TSS.INC.

```
;*****************************************************************
;*                                                               *
;*                                                               *
;* PROT - A 386 protected-mode DOS extender                      *
;* Copyright (C) 1989, by Al Williams                            *
;* All rights reserved.                                          *
;*                                                               *
;* Permission is granted for noncommercial use of this           *
;* software subject to certain conditions (see PROT.ASM).        *
;*                                                               *
;* This file is: TSS.INC. It defines a TSS structure.            *
;* Note that TSS.ASM gets certain defaults that a user program   *
;* doesn't.                                                      *
;*                                                               *
;*****************************************************************

; Define TSS structure.
; For more details, refer to the Intel documentation.
; Remember, the defined values are only defaults and
; can be changed when a TSS is defined.
        IFDEF           TSS_FILE
; definition with defaults required by TSS.ASM
TSSBLK          STRUC
BLINK           DD      0
ESPP0           DD      OFFSET SSEG321
SSP0            DW      SEL_STACK
                DW      0
ESPP1           DD      0
SSP1            DW      SEL_STACK
                DW      0
ESPP2           DD      0
SSP2            DW      SEL_STACK
                DW      0
CR31            DD      0
EIP1            DD      OFFSET USER
EF1             DD      200II
EAX1            DD      0
ECX1            DD      0
EDX1            DD      0
EBX1            DD      0
ESP1            DD      OFFSET SSEG321
```

DOS 5: A DEVELOPER'S GUIDE

```
        EBP1        DD      0
        ESI1        DD      0
        EDI1        DD      0
        ES1         DW      SEL_DATA
                    DW      0
        CS1         DW      SEL_UCODE
                    DW      0
        SS1         DW      SEL_STACK
                    DW      0
        DS1         DW      SEL_UDATA
                    DW      0
        FS1         DW      SEL_DATA0
                    DW      0
        GS1         DW      SEL_VIDEO
                    DW      0
        LDT1        DD      0
                    DW      0
        IOT         DD      $+2-OFFSET BLINK
        IOP         DB      8190 DUP (0)
                    DB      0FFH
        TSSBLK      ENDS
ELSE
; USER's version of definition
        TSSBLK      STRUC
        BLINK       DD      0
        ESPP0       DD      0
        SSP0        DW      0
                    DW      0
        ESPP1       DD      0
        SSP1        DW      0
                    DW      0
        ESPP2       DD      0
        SSP2        DW      0
                    DW      0
        CR31        DD      0
        EIP1        DD      0
        EF1         DD      200H
        EAX1        DD      0
        ECX1        DD      0
        EDX1        DD      0
        EBX1        DD      0
```

DOS EXTENDERS

```
ESP1            DD      0
EBP1            DD      0
ESI1            DD      0
EDI1            DD      0
ES1             DW      0
                DW      0
CS1             DW      0
                DW      0
SS1             DW      0
                DW      0
DS1             DW      0
                DW      0
FS1             DW      0
                DW      0
GS1             DW      0
                DW      0
LDT1            DD      0
                DW      0
IOT             DW      $+2-OFFSET BLINK
IOP             DB      8192 DUP (0)
                DB      0FFH
TSSBLK          ENDS
ENDIF
```

Listing 19-12. PROTEXT.INC.

```
;****************************************************************
;*                                                              *
;* PROT - A 386 protected-mode DOS extender                     *
;* Copyright (C) 1989, by Al Williams                           *
;* All rights reserved.                                         *
;*                                                              *
;* Permission is granted for noncommercial use of this          *
;* software subject to certain conditions (see PROT.ASM).       *
;*                                                              *
;* This file is: PROTEXT.INC, the user's version of             *
;* EXTERNAL.INC.                                                *
;*                                                              *
;****************************************************************
USER_FILE       EQU     1
INCLUDE         EXTERNAL.INC
```

DOS 5: A DEVELOPER'S GUIDE

Listing 19-13. DLLEQU.INC.

```
;*****************************************************************
;*                                                               *
;* PROT - A 386 protected-mode DOS extender                      *
;* Copyright (C) 1989, by Al Williams                            *
;* All rights reserved.                                          *
;*                                                               *
;* Permission is granted for noncommercial use of this           *
;* software subject to certain conditions (see PROT.ASM).        *
;*                                                               *
;* This file is: DLLEQU.INC, assorted macros and equates         *
;* for programs using X386.                                      *
;*                                                               *
;*****************************************************************

IFNDEF      BITS
            %OUT    YOU MUST DEFINE BITS AS 16 OR 32
            %OUT    BEFORE USING DLLEQU.INC
            .ERR
ENDIF
IFE         (BITS   EQ 16) OR (BITS EQ 32)
            %OUT    YOU MUST DEFINE BITS AS 16 OR 32
            %OUT    BEFORE USING DLLEQU.INC
            .ERR
ENDIF

; parameter block to interface for int 30H (call86 & VM86CALL)
VM86BLK     STRUC
VMSEGFLAG   DD      0           ; Restore segment registers.
VMINT       DD      0           ; interrupt number
VMFLAGS     DD      0           ; EFLAGS
VMESP       DD      0           ; ESP
VMSS        DD      0           ; SS
VMES        DD      0           ; ES
VMDS        DD      0           ; DS
VMFS        DD      0           ; FS
VMGS        DD      0           ; GS
VMEBP       DD      0           ; EBP
VMEBX       DD      0           ; EBX
VM86BLK     ENDS
```

```
; access rights equates
; Use these with make_desc or make_seg.
RO_DATA     EQU     90H             ; r/o data
RW_DATA     EQU     92H             ; r/w data
RO_STK      EQU     94H             ; r/o stack
RW_STK      EQU     96H             ; r/w stack
EX_CODE     EQU     98H             ; exec only code
ER_CODE     EQU     9AH             ; read/exec code
CN_CODE     EQU     9CH             ; exec only conforming code
CR_CODE     EQU     9EH             ; read/exec conforming code
LDT_DESC    EQU     82H             ; LDT entry
TSS_DESC    EQU     89H             ; TSS entry

; Use these with make_gate.
CALL_GATE   EQU     8CH             ; call gate
TRAP_GATE   EQU     8FH             ; trap gate
INTR_GATE   EQU     8EH             ; int gate
TASK_GATE   EQU     85H             ; task gate

; dpl equates
DPL0        EQU     0
DPL1        EQU     20H
DPL2        EQU     40H
DPL3        EQU     60H

; macro definitions

; Other macros use this to error-check parameters.
; Give an error if last is blank or toomany is not blank.
ERRCHK      MACRO   LAST,TOOMANY
IFNB        <TOOMANY>
IF2
            %OUT    TOO MANY PARAMETERS
ENDIF
            .ERR
ENDIF
IFB         <LAST>
IF2
            %OUT    NOT ENOUGH PARAMETERS
ENDIF
            .ERR
```

DOS 5: A DEVELOPER'S GUIDE

```
ENDIF
          ENDM

; Perform absolute 16-bit jump (in a 16-bit segment).
JMPABS    MACRO   A,B,ERRCK
          ERRCHK  B,ERRCK
          DB      0EAH          ; ; absolute 16-bit jump
          DW      OFFSET B
          DW      A
          ENDM

; Peform absolute 32-bit jump (in a 32-bit segment).
JMPABS32  MACRO   A,B,ERRCK
          ERRCHK  B,ERRCK
          DB      0EAH          ; ; absolute 32-bit jump
          DD      OFFSET B
          DW      A
          ENDM

; This generates a correct 32-bit offset for a proc call
; since MASM doesn't sign extend 32-bit relative items.
CALL32S   MACRO   LBL,ERRCK     ; ; short call
          ERRCHK  LBL,ERRCK
          DB      0E8H
          DD      LBL-($+4)
          ENDM

CALL32F   MACRO   SG,LBL,ERRCK  ; ; far call
          ERRCHK  LBL,ERRCK
          DB      9AH
          DD      OFFSET LBL
          DW      SG
          ENDM

JMP32S    MACRO   LBL,ERRCK     ; ; short jump
          ERRCHK  LBL,ERRCK
          DB      0E9H
          DD      LBL-($+4)
          ENDM
```

DOS EXTENDERS

```
; jcc32 uses the condition codes used in the Intel literature.
; conditional jump macro
JCC32           MACRO    CONDX,LBL,ERRCK
                ERRCHK   LBL,ERRCK
                DB       0FH
IFIDNI          <CONDX>,<A>
                DB       87H
ELSEIFIDNI      <CONDX>,<NBE>
                DB       87H
ELSEIFIDNI      <CONDX>, <AE>
                DB       83H
ELSEIFIDNI      <CONDX>, <C>
                DB       82H
ELSEIFIDNI      <CONDX>, <NAE>
                DB       82H
ELSEIFIDNI      <CONDX>, <B>
                DB       82H
ELSEIFIDNI      <CONDX>, <BE>
                DB       86H
ELSEIFIDNI      <CONDX>, <E>
                DB       84H
ELSEIFIDNI      <CONDX>, <Z>
                DB       84H
ELSEIFIDNI      <CONDX>, <G>
                DB       8FH
ELSEIFIDNI      <CONDX>, <GE>
                DB       8DH
ELSEIFIDNI      <CONDX>, <L>
                DB       8CH
ELSEIFIDNI      <CONDX>, <LE>
                DB       8EH
ELSEIFIDNI      <CONDX>, <NA>
                DB       86H
ELSEIFIDNI      <CONDX>, <NB>
                DB       83H
ELSEIFIDNI      <CONDX>, <NC>
                DB       83H
ELSEIFIDNI      <CONDX>, <NGE>
                DB       8CH
ELSEIFIDNI      <CONDX>, <NL>
                DB       8DH
```

```
            ELSEIFIDNI  <CONDX>, <NO>
                        DB      81H
            ELSEIFIDNI  <CONDX>, <NP>
                        DB      8BH
            ELSEIFIDNI  <CONDX>, <NS>
                        DB      89H
            ELSEIFIDNI  <CONDX>, <NZ>
                        DB      85H
            ELSEIFIDNI  <CONDX>, <O>
                        DB      80H
            ELSEIFIDNI  <CONDX>, <P>
                        DB      8AH
            ELSEIFIDNI  <CONDX>, <PE>
                        DB      8AH
            ELSEIFIDNI  <CONDX>, <PO>
                        DB      8BH
            ELSEIFIDNI  <CONDX>, <S>
                        DB      88H
            ELSE
                        %OUT    JCC32: UNKNOWN CONDITION CODE
                        .ERR
            ENDIF
                        DD      LBL-($+4)
                        ENDM

; Override default operand size.
OPSIZ       MACRO   NOPARM              ; ; op size override
            ERRCHK  X,NOPARM
            DB      66H
            ENDM


; Override default address size.
ADSIZ       MACRO   NOPARM              ; ; address size override
            ERRCHK  X,NOPARM
            DB      67H
            ENDM

BREAKPOINT  MACRO   NOPARM
            ERRCHK  X,NOPARM
            INT     3
            ENDM
```

```
; mnemonic for call86 call (assumes 32-bit segments)

CALLGATE    MACRO   NOPARM
            ERRCHK  X,NOPARM
            DB      9AH
IF          BITS    EQ 32
            DD      0
ELSE
            DW      0
ENDIF
            DW      SEL_86INT
            ENDM

VM86CALL    MACRO   NOPARM
            ERRCHK  X,NOPARM
            CALLGATE
            ENDM

GDT_CT      =       0

DESC        MACRO   NAM
&NAM        =       GDT_CT
GDT_CT      =       GDT_CT+8
            ENDM

            DESC    SEL_NULL        ; DUMMY NULL SELECTOR
            DESC    SEL_GDT         ; GDT ALIAS
            DESC    SEL_CODE16      ; 16-BIT CODE SEGMENT
            DESC    SEL_DATA0       ; 4GB SEGMENT
            DESC    SEL_CODE32      ; 32-BIT CODE SEGMENT
            DESC    SEL_STACK       ; 32-BIT STACK
            DESC    SEL_RDATA       ; REAL MODE LIKE DATA SEG
            DESC    SEL_VIDEO       ; VIDEO MEMORY
            DESC    SEL_DATA        ; 32-BIT DATA
            DESC    SEL_IDT         ; IDT ALIAS
            DESC    SEL_ICODE       ; ISR SEGMENT
            DESC    SEL_TSS1        ; MAIN TASK BLOCK
            DESC    TSS1            ; SAME (MUST FOLLOW SEL_TSS1)
            DESC    SEL_UCODE       ; USER CODE
            DESC    SEL_UDATA       ; USER DATA
            DESC    SEL_PSP         ; DOS PSP
            DESC    SEL_FREE        ; FREE DOS MEMORY
```

```
        DESC    SEL_EXT         ; EXTENDED MEMORY
        DESC    SEL_ENV         ; ENVIRONMENT
        DESC    SEL_CCS         ; C code segment
        DESC    SEL_CDS         ; C data/stack segment
        DESC    SEL_86INT       ; VM86CALL CALL Gate
        DESC    SEL_15S         ; INT 15 source
        DESC    SEL_15D         ; INT 15 destination
        DESC    SEL_TSS0        ; DUMMY TASK BLOCK (may reuse)
        DESC    TSS0            ; SAME (MUST FOLLOW SEL_TSS0)
        DESC    SPARE0
        DESC    SPARE1
        DESC    SPARE2
        DESC    SPARE3
        DESC    SPARE4
        DESC    SPARE5
        DESC    SPARE6
        DESC    SPARE7
        DESC    SPARE8
        DESC    SPARE9
        DESC    SPARE10
        DESC    SPARE11
        DESC    SPARE12
        DESC    SPARE13
        DESC    SPARE14
        DESC    SPARE15
        DESC    SPARE16
        DESC    SPARE17
        DESC    SPARE18
        DESC    SPARE19
        DESC    SPARE20
        DESC    SPARE21
        DESC    SPARE22
        DESC    SPARE23
        DESC    SPARE24
        DESC    SPARE25
        DESC    SPARE26
        DESC    SPARE27
        DESC    SPARE28
        DESC    SPARE29
        DESC    SPARE30
        DESC    SPARE31
```

DOS EXTENDERS

Listing 19-14. GOPROT.INC.

```
;****************************************************************
;*                                                              *
;* PROT - A 386 protected-mode DOS extender                     *
;* Copyright (C) 1989, by Al Williams                           *
;* All rights reserved.                                         *
;*                                                              *
;* Permission is granted for noncommercial use of this          *
;* software subject to certain conditions (see PROT.ASM).       *
;*                                                              *
;* This file is: GOPROT.INC, which contains macros to switch    *
;* to protected mode under X386.                                *
;*                                                              *
;****************************************************************
GOPROT16        MACRO
                LOCAL   PFFLUSH,INTPATCH,NOX386
                LOCAL   XIT,SETIP,NOXMESS,SETIP1
                PUSH    AX
                PUSH    ES
                XOR     AX,AX
                MOV     ES,AX
; Get first byte of sig.
                MOV     AX,ES:[04F0H]
                CMP     AX,'PX'
                JNZ     SHORT NOX386
; Get remainder of signature.
                MOV     AX,ES:[04F2H]
                CMP     AL,'='
                JNZ     SHORT NOX386
                POP     ES
                PUSH    BX
                CALL    $+3
SETIP:
                POP     BX
                ADD     BX,(INTPATCH+1)-SETIP
                MOV     CS:[BX],AH
                POP     BX
                POP     AX
; Flush prefetch.
                JMP     SHORT PFFLUSH
PFFLUSH:
INTPATCH        EQU     THIS BYTE
```

DOS 5: A DEVELOPER'S GUIDE

```
                INT     0
                JMP     SHORT XIT
NOX386:
                MOV     AX,CS
                MOV     DS,AX
                CALL    $+3
SETIP1:
                POP     DX
                ADD     DX, OFFSET NOXMESS-SETIP1
                MOV     AH,9
                INT     21H
                MOV     AX,4C01H
                INT     21H
NOXMESS         DB      'Error: X386 not loaded.',13,10,'$'
XIT:
                ENDM
```

; This is exactly the same code as above; however, the asm
; won't generate it properly in a 32-bit segment for DOS, so it
; is written as DBs. Actually, goprot32 will work for either
; type of segment. Both are included so it will be easier to
; read the code. Two segments could also be grouped, but that
; introduces other problems.

```
GOPROT32        MACRO
                DB      50H
                DB      06H
                DB      33H, 0C0H
                DB      8EH, 0C0H
                DB      26H, 0A1H, 0F0H, 04H
                DB      3DH, 58, 50H
                DB      75H, 1DH
                DB      26H, 0A1H, 0F2H, 04H
                DB      3CH, 3DH
                DB      75H, 15H
                DB      7
                DB      53H
                DB      0E8H, 0, 0
                DB      5BH
                DB      81H, 0C3H, 0DH, 0
                DB      2EH, 88, 27H
                DB      5BH
```

DOS EXTENDERS

```
            DB      58H
            DB      0EBH, 0
            DB      0CDH, 0
            DB      0EBH, 2FH
            DB      8CH, 0C8H
            DB      8EH, 0D8H
            DB      0E8H, 0, 0
            DB      5AH
            DB      81H, 0C2H, 0EH, 0
            DB      0B4H, 9
            DB      0CDH, 21H
            DB      0B8H, 1, 4CH
            DB      0CDH, 21H
            DB      'Error: X386 not loaded.',13,10,'$'
            ENDM
```

Listing 19-15. PROT.MAK.

```
########################################################################
#                                                                      #
# File: PROT.MAK                                                       #
#                                                                      #
# Description:                                                         #
# MAKE file for PROT. Change ASM  to reflect which assembler           #
# you use.                                                             #
#                                                                      #
# Microsoft MAKE and Borland MAKE are different.                       #
# For Microsoft MAKE use:                                              #
#    MAKE PROT.MAK                                                     #
# For Microsoft NMAKE use:                                             #
#    NMAKE -fPROT.MAK PROT                                             #
# For Borland use:                                                     #
#    MAKE -fPROT.MAK PROT                                              #
#                                                                      #
# **** IMPORTANT ****                                                  #
# If you use this MAKE file, never have a file named PROT              #
# (with no extension) in the current directory.                        #
# This is because of the method used to allow both makes to use        #
# the same MAKE file.                                                  #
#                                                                      #
########################################################################
```

```
# Change to tasm or masm.
# Microsoft definitions
ASM=MASM /A /DDLL=0
# Borland definitions
# ASM=TASM /A /DDLL=0

prot.obj : prot.asm external.inc equmac.inc
  $(ASM) prot.asm;

code16.obj : code16.asm external.inc equmac.inc
  $(ASM)  code16.asm;

int386.obj : int386.asm external.inc equmac.inc
  $(ASM)  int386.asm;

tss.obj : tss.asm external.inc equmac.inc tss.inc
  $(ASM)  tss.asm;

gdt.obj : gdt.asm external.inc equmac.inc
  $(ASM)  gdt.asm;

stacks.obj : stacks.asm external.inc equmac.inc
  $(ASM)  stacks.asm;

# the PROT line required by Borland/Unix/NMAKE
# Regular Microsoft MAKE will warn that PROT doesn't exist
# and echo the statement.
prot : stacks.obj gdt.obj tss.obj int386.obj code16.obj prot.obj
    echo PROT OBJs up to date
```

Listing 19-16. PROTASM.BAT.

```
@echo off
REM **************************************************************
REM *                                                            *
REM * File: PROTASM.BAT (for Microsoft w/MAKE)                   *
REM *                                                            *
REM * Description:                                               *
REM * Driver for assembling PROT programs.                       *
REM *                                                            *
REM * Requires DOS 3.3 or higher.                                *
REM *                                                            *
REM **************************************************************
```

DOS EXTENDERS

```
if %1.==. goto help
if exist #P#R#O#T.LNK erase #P#R#O#T.LNK
SET PROTERR=
:top
if %1.==. goto linkit
if EXIST %1.ASM goto asmit
echo %1.ASM does not exist
goto err
:asmit
call _PROTASM %1 PASSWORD
if NOT %PROTERR%.==. goto err
shift
goto top
:linkit
REM Make sure PROT files are up to date.

REM ***********************************
REM Use one and only one MAKE line.
REM This one is for Microsoft.
make /s prot.mak
REM This one is for Microsoft NMAKE.
REM nmake /s /fprot.mak prot
REM This one is for Borland.
REM make  -s -fprot.mak prot
if errorlevel 1 goto err

echo prot code16 int386 tss gdt stacks /m;>>#P#R#O#T.LNK

REM ***********************************
REM Use one link line.
REM for Microsoft
link @#P#R#O#T.LNK
REM for Borland
REM tlink /3 @#P#R#O#T.LNK

if ERRORLEVEL 1 goto err
goto end
:help
echo PROTASM - An assembly driver for the PROT 386 DOS Extender
echo usage: PROTASM progname,...
```

DOS 5: A DEVELOPER'S GUIDE

```
echo       Assembles the file(s) progname.asm into progname.exe.
echo       The PROT system is copyright (C), 1989, 1990
echo       by Al Williams. Please see the file "PROT.ASM" for
echo       more details.
:err
echo Assembly failed.
:end
if exist #P#R#O#T.LNK erase #P#R#O#T.LNK
set PROTERR=
```

Listing 19-17. _PROTASM.BAT.

```
REM ***************************************************************
REM *                                                              *
REM * File: _PROTASM.BAT                                           *
REM *                                                              *
REM * Description:                                                 *
REM * Used by PROTASM.BAT                                          *
REM *                                                              *
REM ***************************************************************
if %1.==. goto :help
if NOT %2==PASSWORD goto :help

REM ******************************
REM Use MASM or TASM as appropriate.
REM for Microsoft
masm /A /DDLL=0 %1;
REM for Borland
REM tasm /W2 /A /DDLL=0 %1

if errorlevel 1 goto err
echo %1 + >>#P#R#O#T.LNK
goto end
:err
SET PROTERR=X
goto end
:help
echo _PROTASM.BAT is used internally by PROTASM.BAT.
echo Please see PROTASM.BAT for details.
:end
```

DOS EXTENDERS

Listing 19-18. X386.MAK.

```
##########################################################################
#                                                                        #
# File: X386.MAK                                                         #
#                                                                        #
# Description:                                                           #
# MAKE file for X386. Change ASM and LINK to reflect which               #
# assembler/linker you use.                                              #
#                                                                        #
# Microsoft MAKE and Borland MAKE are different.                         #
# For Microsoft use:                                                     #
#     MAKE X386.MAK                                                      #
# For Borland use:                                                       #
#     MAKE -fX386.MAK X386.EXE                                           #
#                                                                        #
##########################################################################

# Change to tasm or masm and link or tlink.
# Microsoft definitions
ASM=MASM /A /DDLL=1
LINK=LINK
# Borland definitions
# ASM=TASM /A /DDLL=1
# LINK=TLINK /3

d_prot.obj : prot.asm external.inc equmac.inc
  $(ASM) prot.asm,d_prot.obj;

d_dll.obj : dll.asm external.inc equmac.inc
  $(ASM) dll.asm,d_dll.obj;

d_code16.obj : code16.asm external.inc equmac.inc
  $(ASM)  code16.asm,d_code16.obj;

d_int386.obj : int386.asm external.inc equmac.inc
  $(ASM)  int386.asm,d_int386.obj;

d_tss.obj : tss.asm external.inc equmac.inc tss.inc
  $(ASM)  tss.asm,d_tss.obj;
```

DOS 5: A DEVELOPER'S GUIDE

```
d_gdt.obj : gdt.asm external.inc equmac.inc
  $(ASM)  gdt.asm,d_gdt.obj;

d_stacks.obj : stacks.asm external.inc equmac.inc
  $(ASM)  stacks.asm,d_stacks.obj;

d_x386.obj : x386.asm external.inc equmac.inc
  $(ASM) x386.asm,d_x386.obj;

x386.exe : d_x386.obj d_dll.obj d_tss.obj d_gdt.obj \
           d_stacks.obj d_int386.obj \
           d_code16.obj d_prot.obj
  $(LINK) d_x386 d_tss d_stacks d_dll d_int386 d_code16 \
  d_prot d_gdt,x386.exe;
```

Listing 19-19. SIMPLE.ASM.

```
;*****************************************************************
;*                                                               *
;* PROT - A 386 protected-mode DOS extender                      *
;* Copyright (C) 1989, by Al Williams                            *
;* All rights reserved.                                          *
;*                                                               *
;* Permission is granted for noncommercial use of this           *
;* software subject to certain conditions (see PROT.ASM).        *
;*                                                               *
;* This file is: SIMPLE.ASM, the simplest PROT program.          *
;*                                                               *
;*****************************************************************

; include definitions
INCLUDE         EQUMAC.INC
INCLUDE         PROTEXT.INC

; no data segment
                NODATA

; code segment
                PROT_CODE
USER            PROC
```

DOS EXTENDERS

```
            BACK2DOS                    ; Return to DOS.
USER        ENDP
; end of code segment
            PROT_CODE_END
            END
```

Listing 19-20. PMDEMO.ASM and PMDEMO.DOS.

a. PMDEMO.ASM

```
;*****************************************************************
;*                                                               *
;* PROT - A 386 protected-mode DOS extender                      *
;* Copyright (C) 1989, by Al Williams                            *
;* All rights reserved.                                          *
;*                                                               *
;* Permission is granted for noncommercial use of this software  *
;* subject to certain conditions (see PROT.ASM).                 *
;*                                                               *
;* This file is: PMDEMO.ASM, a simple demonstration program.     *
;*                                                               *
;*****************************************************************

INCLUDE EQUMAC.INC
INCLUDE PROTEXT.INC

; Start data segment.
            PROT_DATA
MESSAGE     DB      'A protected mode message!',13,10,'$'
            PROT_DATA_END

; Start code segment.
            PROT_CODE
USER        PROC    NEAR
            PROT_STARTUP                 ; INITIALIZE PINTFRAME
            MOV     PINTFRAME.VMINT,21H
            MOV     EDX,OFFSET MESSAGE
            MOV     AH,9
            MOV     EBX,OFFSET PINTFRAME
```

DOS 5: A DEVELOPER'S GUIDE

```
            VM86CALL                    ; PRINT MESSAGE
            BACK2DOS                    ; RETURN TO DOS
USER        ENDP

            PROT_CODE_END
            END
```

b. PMDEMO.DOS

```
;**********************************************************************
;*                                                                    *
;* File: PMDEMO.DOS                                                   *
;*                                                                    *
;* Description:                                                       *
;* DOS equivalent of PMDEMO.ASM.                                      *
;*                                                                    *
;**********************************************************************

.MODEL      SMALL

.STACK      128

.DATA
MESSAGE     DB      'A real mode message',13,10,'$'

.CODE
USER        PROC
            MOV     AX,@DATA
            MOV     DS,AX
            MOV     DX,OFFSET MESSAGE   ; Point to message.
            MOV     AH,9
            INT     21H                 ; Print it.
            MOV     AH,4CH
            INT     21H                 ; Exit.
USER        ENDP

            END     USER
```

DOS EXTENDERS

Listing 19-21. FBROWSE.ASM.

```
;*********************************************************************
;*                                                                   *
;* PROT - A 386 protected-mode DOS extender                          *
;* Copyright (C) 1989, by Al Williams                                *
;* All rights reserved.                                              *
;*                                                                   *
;* Permission is granted for noncommercial use of this               *
;* software subject to certain conditions (see PROT.ASM).            *
;*                                                                   *
;* This file is: FBROWSE.ASM, a file browser.                        *
;*                                                                   *
;*********************************************************************

        INCLUDE   EQUMAC.INC
        INCLUDE   PROTEXT.INC

; If this equate is 0, use direct screen output; else use DOS.
DOSOUT     EQU       0

; This program displays a file. The file is stored as strings
; starting at the top of memory (the heap) and growing downward.
; At the start of memory is an array of pointers to lines in the
; heap. The strings are stored backwards and end with 0xa
; unless they are 80 characters long. If they are 80 characters
; long, they end with 0xd. Lines longer than 80 characters are
; split into multiple lines.

            PROT_DATA
BASE        DD        0               ; top screen line
PTRPTR      DD        0               ; pointer to end of lines[]
HEAPPTR     DD        ?               ; pointer to empty heap entry
FHANDLE     DW        ?               ; file handle
LBUF        DB        81 DUP(?)       ; line buffer
FBUFP       DD        0               ; pointer to character in fbuf
FBUFL       DW        0               ; # of char's in fbuf
FBUF        DB        512 DUP(?)      ; file buffer
; help message
UMSG        DB        'Usage: FBROWSE filename',13,10,'$'
; error messages
```

DOS 5: A DEVELOPER'S GUIDE

```
NFMSG      DB          'Can''t open file',13,10,'$'
FEMSG      DB          'File error!',13,10,'$'
OMMSG      DB          'Out of memory',13,10,'$'
; copyright message
CPYMSG     DB          'FBROWSE - Protected Mode File '
           DB          'Browser (C) 1989 by Al Williams'
IF         DOSOUT
; end of string for DOS function 9
           DB          '$'
ELSE
; end of string for PROT
           DB          0
ENDIF

; bios call frame
BINTFRAME  VM86BLK     <>

           PROT_DATA_END

           PROT_CODE
; This routine catches ^BREAKs and forces program termination.
ONBREAK    PROC        FAR
           MOV         AX,SEL_UDATA
           MOV         DS,AX
           JMP32S      USTOP0
ONBREAK    ENDP

; main program
USER       PROC        NEAR
; Enable break handling.
           MOV         BRK_SEG,SEL_UCODE
           MOV         BRK_OFF,OFFSET ONBREAK
; Clear the screen.
           CALL32F     SEL_CODE32,CLS
; Set up CALL86 parameter blocks (pintframe & bintframe).
           MOV         AX,SEG SSINT1
           MOV         PINTFRAME.VMSS,EAX
           MOV         BINTFRAME.VMSS,EAX
           MOV         WORD PTR PINTFRAME.VMDS,SEG USERDATA
           MOV         EAX, OFFSET SSINT1
```

DOS EXTENDERS

```
            MOV         PINTFRAME.VMESP,EAX
            MOV         BINTFRAME.VMESP,EAX
; Pintframe will be used for INT 21.
            MOV         PINTFRAME.VMINT,21H
; Get command line.
            MOV         CX,SEL_PSP
            MOV         FS,CX
            ASSUME      FS:NOTHING
            XOR         EBX,EBX
            MOV         BL,FS:[80H]
            OR          BL,BL
            JNZ         SHORT OPENFILE
; No command line  print usage message.
            MOV         AH,9
            MOV         EDX,OFFSET UMSG
            MOV         EBX,OFFSET PINTFRAME
            VM86CALL
            MOV         AL,1
            JMP32S      USTOP               ; back to DOS
; Open file for reading.
OPENFILE:
; Null-terminate file name.
            MOV         BYTE PTR FS:[81H+BX],0
            MOV         DX,_PSP
            MOV         PINTFRAME.VMDS,EDX
            MOV         EDX,80H
; Skip spaces.
SPACSKIP:
            INC         DX
            CMP         BYTE PTR FS:[EDX],' '
            JZ          SHORT SPACSKIP
            MOV         AX,3D00H
            MOV         EBX,OFFSET PINTFRAME
            VM86CALL                        ; Open file.
            MOV         WORD PTR PINTFRAME.VMDS,SEG USERDATA
            JNC         SHORT FOPENED
; Couldn't open file--print error.
            MOV         EDX,OFFSET NFMSG
            MOV         AH,9
            MOV         EBX,OFFSET PINTFRAME
```

```
                VM86CALL                        ; Can't open file.
                MOV             AL,1
                JMP32S          USTOP           ; back to DOS
; File opened OK.
FOPENED:
                MOV             FHANDLE,AX      ; Save file handle.
; See if extended memory present.
                MOV             AX,SEL_EXT
                LSL             EBX,EAX
                OR              EBX,EBX
                JNZ             SHORT USE_EXTMEM
; No extended memory present--use DOS memory.
                MOV             AX,SEL_FREE
USE_EXTMEM:
                MOV             GS,AX           ; memory segment --> GS
; Set heap pointer to top of available memory.
                LSL             EAX,EAX
                MOV             HEAPPTR,EAX
                MOV             EDX,EAX
                XOR             EBX,EBX
REREAD:
                MOV             EAX,EBX         ; Check for heap overflow.
                SHL             EAX,2
                CMP             EAX,EDX
                JB              SHORT HEAPOK
; No more memory--print error message.
                MOV             AH,9
                MOV             EDX,OFFSET OMMSG
                MOV             EBX,OFFSET PINTFRAME
                VM86CALL                        ; out of memory
                MOV             AL,1
                JMP32S          USTOP           ; back to DOS
HEAPOK:
; Put heap pointer in lines array.
                MOV             GS:[EBX*4],EDX
; Read line to heap in reverse order. Each line ends in CR.
                CALL            READLINE
                PUSHFD
; Point to next line in lines array.
                INC             EBX
```

DOS EXTENDERS

```
                POPFD
                JNZ         SHORT REREAD    ; not end of file?
; here at end of file
                MOV         PTRPTR,EBX      ; end of lines array
                MOV         AX,FHANDLE
                MOV         PINTFRAME.VMEBX,EAX
                MOV         AH,3EH
                MOV         EBX,OFFSET PINTFRAME
                VM86CALL                    ; Close file.
                MOV         DX,1800H
                CALL        SETCP           ; Set cursor position.
; Write copyright message.
IF      DOSOUT
                MOV         AH,9
                MOV         EDX,OFFSET CPYMSG
                MOV         EBX,OFFSET PINTFRAME
                VM86CALL                    ; Print copyright.
ELSE
; If not BIOS output then get rid of BIOS cursor.
                MOV         DX,0FFFFH
                CALL32S     DOSSETCP        ; Hide cursor.
                MOV         EBX,OFFSET CPYMSG
                CALL32F     SEL_CODE32,MESSOUT
ENDIF

; Inverse-video the bottom line.
                PUSH        DS
                MOV         AX,SEL_VIDEO
                MOV         DS,AX
                MOV         CL,80
                MOV         EDX,24*160+1    ; bottom line
INVLOOP:
                MOV         BYTE PTR [EDX],70H
                INC         EDX
                INC         EDX
                DEC         CL
                JNZ         SHORT INVLOOP
                POP         DS
; Skip over home-key processing.
                JMP         SHORT HK0
```

DOS 5: A DEVELOPER'S GUIDE

```
; home-key processing
HOMEKEY:  OR        BASE,0
; Don't do home if already there.
          JZ        SHORT KEYLOOP
HK0:
          MOV       BASE,0              ; Set screen start to 0.
; Come here to display a page starting at base.
PAGEDISP:
          CALL      DISP
; Read a key and act on it.
KEYLOOP:
          MOV       BINTFRAME.VMINT,16H
          XOR       AH,AH
          PUSH      ES
          MOV       BX,SEL_UDATA
          MOV       ES,BX
          MOV       EBX,OFFSET BINTFRAME
          VM86CALL                      ; Read a key.
          POP       ES
          CMP       AL,27               ; escape key?
          JZ        NEAR PTR USTOP0
          OR        AX,AX               ; break key?
          JZ        NEAR PTR USTOP0
          CMP       AL,3                ; break key
          JZ        NEAR PTR USTOP0
          OR        AL,AL
          JNZ       SHORT KEYERR        ; special key?
; Test for function keys.
          CMP       AH,48H              ; up arrow
          JCC32     Z,UPARROW
          CMP       AH,47H              ; home key
          JZ        SHORT HOMEKEY
          CMP       AH,4FH              ; end key
          JCC32     Z,ENDKEY
          CMP       AH,49H              ; page up
          JCC32     Z,PGUP
          CMP       AH,51H              ; page down
          JCC32     Z,PGDN
          CMP       AH,50H              ; down arrow
```

DOS EXTENDERS

```
            JZ         SHORT DNARROW
; Come here if you don't know what that key was!
KEYERR:
            PUSH       EDX
            MOV        DL,7                ; bell character
            MOV        AH,2
            MOV        EBX,OFFSET PINTFRAME
            VM86CALL
            POP        EDX
            JMP        SHORT KEYLOOP

; down-arrow processing
DNARROW:
            MOV        EAX,BASE            ; Don't go down if at end.
            ADD        EAX,24
            CMP        EAX,PTRPTR
            JCC32      AE,KEYLOOP
            INC        BASE                ; top of screen + 1
            MOV        AX,0601H            ; Scroll screen.
            CALL       SCROLL
            MOV        DX,1700H            ; Position cursor.
            CALL       SETCP
            MOV        EDX,BASE            ; Print bottom line.
            ADD        EDX,23
            CALL       PLINE
            JMP32S     KEYLOOP

; up-arrow processing
UPARROW:
            OR         BASE,0              ; Don't go up if at top.
            JCC32      Z,KEYLOOP
            DEC        BASE                ; Adjust top of screen.
            MOV        AX,0701H            ; Scroll screen.
            CALL       SCROLL
            XOR        DX,DX               ; Position cursor.
            CALL       SETCP
            MOV        EDX,BASE            ; Print top line.
            CALL       PLINE
            JMP32S     KEYLOOP
```

DOS 5: A DEVELOPER'S GUIDE

```
; end-key processing
ENDKEY:     MOV         EAX,BASE
            ADD         EAX,24
            CMP         EAX,PTRPTR
; Don't do end if already there.
            JCC32       AE,KEYLOOP
            MOV         EAX,PTRPTR      ; Get last line.
            SUB         EAX,24          ; Find top of screen.
            MOV         BASE,EAX
            JMP32S      PAGEDISP        ; Display page.

; page-up processing
PGUP:       MOV         EAX,BASE        ; Don't do pgup if at top.
            OR          EAX,EAX
            JCC32       Z,KEYLOOP
            CMP         EAX,24
            JBE         SHORT PGUP0     ; If near the top.. go pgup0.
            SUB         EAX,24          ; Find new line.
            JMP         SHORT PGUP1
PGUP0:      XOR         EAX,EAX         ; 1st line
PGUP1:      MOV         BASE,EAX
            JMP32S      PAGEDISP

; page-down processing
PGDN:       MOV         EAX,BASE        ; If at bottom, skip.
            ADD         EAX,24
            CMP         EAX,PTRPTR
            JCC32       AE,KEYLOOP
            MOV         BASE,EAX        ; Find new line.
            JMP32S      PAGEDISP

; Exit FBROWSE.
USTOP0:
; Clear screen.
            CALL32F     SEL_CODE32,CLS
            XOR         AL,AL           ; Zero return code.
            PUSH        EAX
            XOR         DX,DX           ; Home cursor.
            CALL        DOSSETCP
```

DOS EXTENDERS

```
            POP         EAX
USTOP:
            BACK2DOS

USER        ENDP


; Read a line from the file.
; Lines end in 0AH unless they are long, in which case they
; end in 0DH.
READLINE    PROC        NEAR
            PUSH        ECX
            MOV         CX,80
RLINE0:
            CALL        GFCHAR          ; Get character.
            MOV         GS:[EDX],AL     ; Store it.
            PUSHFD
            DEC         EDX
            POPFD                       ; end of line?
            JZ          SHORT RLINEXIT
            CMP         AL,0AH          ; end of line?
            JZ          SHORT RLINEEOL
            DEC         CX
            JNZ         SHORT RLINE0    ; 80-char line?
; Compare last character with 0ah--if true, pass it.
            CALL        GFCHAR
            CMP         AL,0AH
; If so, line exactly 80 chars.
            JZ          SHORT LONGLINE
            DEC         FBUFP           ; Unget character.
LONGLINE:
            MOV         AL,0DH
            MOV         GS:[EDX],AL     ; Save end marker.
            DEC         EDX
RLINEEOL:   CMP         AL,0FFH         ; Set NZ flag.
RLINEXIT:
            POP         ECX
            RET
READLINE    ENDP
```

863

DOS 5: A DEVELOPER'S GUIDE

```
; Scroll screen using BIOS.
SCROLL    PROC      NEAR
          PUSH      ES
          MOV       BX,SEL_UDATA
          MOV       ES,BX
          MOV       BINTFRAME.VMEBX,0700H
          MOV       BINTFRAME.VMINT,10H
          XOR       ECX,ECX
          MOV       DX,174FH
          MOV       EBX,OFFSET BINTFRAME
          VM86CALL
          POP       ES
          RET
SCROLL    ENDP

; Position the cursor.
DOSSETCP  PROC      NEAR
          PUSH      EBX
          PUSH      ES
          MOV       AX,SEL_UDATA
          MOV       ES,AX
          MOV       BINTFRAME.VMINT,10H
          MOV       BINTFRAME.VMEBX,0
          MOV       AH,2
          MOV       EBX,OFFSET BINTFRAME
          VM86CALL
          POP       ES
          POP       EBX
          RET
DOSSETCP  ENDP

SETCP     PROC      NEAR
IF        DOSOUT
          CALL32S   DOSSETCP
ELSE
          PUSH      ES
          MOV       AX,SEL_DATA
          MOV       ES,AX
          MOV       EAX,80
```

DOS EXTENDERS

```
                MUL     DH
                XOR     DH,DH
                ADD     AX,DX
                MOV     ES:CURSOR,EAX
                POP     ES
ENDIF
                RET
SETCP   ENDP

; Display a screenful.
DISP    PROC    NEAR
                MOV     AX,0600H
                CALL32S SCROLL          ; Clear screen.
                XOR     DX,DX
                CALL32S SETCP           ; Home cursor.
                MOV     CX,24
                MOV     EDX,BASE
DISP0:
                PUSH    EDX
                CALL    PLINE           ; Print lines.
                POP     EDX
                INC     EDX
                CMP     EDX,PTRPTR
                JZ      SHORT DISP00
                DEC     CX
                JNZ     SHORT DISP0
DISP00:
                RET
DISP    ENDP

; Print a line pointed to by [edx] going backwards to \n.
PLINE   PROC    NEAR
; Get line ptr.
                MOV     EDX,GS:[EDX*4]
PLINE0:
                MOV     AL,GS:[EDX]     ; Get char fm str.
                DEC     DX
                CMP     AL,0DH          ; long line?
                JZ      SHORT PLINE2
```

DOS 5: A DEVELOPER'S GUIDE

```
                CALL       OOUCH              ; Output character.
                CMP        AL,0AH             ; end of string
                JNZ        SHORT PLINE0
PLINE1:
                MOV        AL,0DH             ; Output CR.
                CALL       OOUCH
PLINE2:
                RET
PLINE           ENDP

; Get a character from the file.
GFCHAR          PROC       NEAR
                PUSH       EBX
                PUSH       EDX
                PUSH       ECX
GFSKIP:
                OR         FBUFL,0            ; buffer empty?
                JZ         SHORT FILLBUFF
                MOV        EAX,FBUFP          ; buffer used up?
                CMP        AX,FBUFL
                JNZ        SHORT FMBUFF
FILLBUFF:
                MOV        AX,FHANDLE         ; Read from file.
                MOV        PINTFRAME.VMEBX,EAX
                MOV        ECX,512
                MOV        EDX,OFFSET FBUF
                MOV        AH,3FH
                MOV        EBX,OFFSET PINTFRAME
                VM86CALL                      ; Read buffer.
                JNC        SHORT NOFERR
; file error here
                MOV        AH,9
                MOV        EDX,OFFSET FEMSG
                VM86CALL
                JMP32S     USTOP              ; back to DOS
NOFERR:         OR         AX,AX
                MOV        FBUFL,AX           ; Store buffer length.
                MOV        AL,0AH
                JZ         SHORT GFCEOF       ; end of file?
                XOR        EAX,EAX            ; Clear buffer pointer.
```

DOS EXTENDERS

```
            MOV         FBUFP,EAX
; This is where the character is read from a good buffer.
FMBUFF:
            MOV         EBX,FBUFP
            MOV         AL,FBUF[EBX]
            INC         EBX
            MOV         FBUFP,EBX
            CMP         AL,0DH          ; Skip CR.
            JCC32       Z,GFSKIP
GFCEOF:
            POP         ECX
            POP         EDX
            POP         FBX
            RET
GFCHAR      ENDP

; Output character in al.
OOUCH       PROC        NEAR
IF          DOSOUT
            PUSHAD
            PUSH        ES
            ASSUME      ES:DAT32
            MOV         BX,SEL_DATA
            MOV         ES,BX
            MOV         AH,2
            MOV         DL,AL
            MOV         EBX,OFFSET PINTFRAME
            VM86CALL
            POP         ES
            POPAD
            RET
ELSE
            CALL32F     SEL_CODE32,OUCH
            RET
ENDIF
OOUCH       ENDP

            PROT_CODE_END

            END
```

DOS 5: A DEVELOPER'S GUIDE

Listing 19-22. FB.ASM.

```
;****************************************************************
;*                                                              *
;* PROT - A 386 protected-mode DOS extender                     *
;* Copyright (C) 1989, by Al Williams                           *
;* All rights reserved.                                         *
;*                                                              *
;* Permission is granted for noncommercial use of this          *
;* software subject to certain conditions (see PROT.ASM).       *
;*                                                              *
;* This file is: FB.ASM, a file browser that uses X386.         *
;*                                                              *
;****************************************************************
.386P
BITS        EQU     32
INCLUDE     DLLEQU.INC
INCLUDE     GOPROT.INC

; This program displays a file. The file is stored as strings
; starting at the top of memory (the heap) and growing downward.
; At the start of memory is an array of pointers to lines in the
; heap. The strings are stored backwards and end with 0xa
; unless they are 80 characters long. If they are 80 characters
; long, they end with 0xd. Lines longer than 80 characters are
; split into multiple lines.

_DAT        SEGMENT    PUBLIC PARA 'DATA' USE32
BASE        DD         0              ; top screen line
PTRPTR      DD         0              ; pointer to end of lines[]
HEAPPTR     DD         ?              ; pointer to empty heap entry
FHANDLE     DW         ?              ; file handle
LBUF        DB         81 DUP(?)      ; line buffer
FBUFP       DD         0              ; pointer to character in fbuf
FBUFL       DW         0              ; # of char's in fbuf
; file buffer
FBUF        DB         512 DUP(?)
_PSP        DW         ?
; help message
UMSG        DB         'Usage: FB filename',13,10,'$'
; error messages
```

DOS EXTENDERS

```
NFMSG       DB          'Can''t open file',13,10,'$'
FEMSG       DB          'File error!',13,10,'$'
OMMSG       DB          'Out of memory',13,10,'$'
; copyright message
CPYMSG      DB          'FBROWSE - Protected Mode File '
            DB          'Browser (C) 1989 by Al Williams'
; end of string for DOS function 9
            DB          '$'

; packet for setting break handler
BRKPACKET DD            5
BRKOFF      DD          OFFSET ONBREAK
BRKSEG      DD          SEL_CCS

; dos interrupt frame
PINTFRAME VM86BLK       <>

; bios call frame
BINTFRAME VM86BLK       <>

; private stack for DOS calls
SSINT       DB          256 DUP (?)
SSINT1      EQU         $

_DAT        ENDS

_DAT16      SEGMENT     PUBLIC PARA 'DATA' USE16
; private stack for FB
STK         DB          512 DUP (?)
STK1        EQU         $
_DAT16      ENDS

; CODE SEGMENT
_COD        SEGMENT     PUBLIC PARA 'CODE' USE32
            ASSUME      CS:_COD,DS:_DAT
; This routine catches ^BREAKs and forces program termination.
ONBREAK     PROC        FAR
            MOV         AX,SEL_CDS
            MOV         DS,AX
            JMP32S      USTOP0
```

```
ONBREAK     ENDP

; main program
USER        PROC        NEAR
MAIN32:
            GOPROT32                    ; Switch to PM.
; Enable break handling.
            PUSH        DS
            POP         ES
            MOV         EBX,OFFSET BRKPACKET
            CALLGATE
; Set up CALL86 parameter blocks (pintframe & bintframe).
            MOV         AX,SEG SSINT1
            MOV         PINTFRAME.VMSS,EAX
            MOV         BINTFRAME.VMSS,EAX
            MOV         WORD PTR PINTFRAME.VMDS,_DAT
            MOV         EAX, OFFSET SSINT1
            MOV         PINTFRAME.VMESP,EAX
            MOV         BINTFRAME.VMESP,EAX
; Pintframe will be used only for INT 21.
            MOV         PINTFRAME.VMINT,21H

; Clear the screen.
            CALL32S     FB_CLS

; Get command line.
            MOV         CX,SEL_PSP
            MOV         FS,CX
            ASSUME      FS:NOTHING
            XOR         EBX,EBX
            MOV         BL,FS:[80H]
            OR          BL,BL
            JNZ         SHORT OPENFILE
; No command line--print usage message.
            MOV         AH,9
            MOV         EDX,OFFSET UMSG
            MOV         EBX,OFFSET PINTFRAME
            VM86CALL
            MOV         AL,1
            JMP32S      USTOP           ; back to DOS
```

DOS EXTENDERS

```
; Open file for reading.
OPENFILE:
; Null-terminate file name.
        MOV       BYTE PTR FS:[81H+BX],0
        MOV       DX,_PSP
        MOV       PINTFRAME.VMDS,EDX
        MOV       EDX,80H
; Skip spaces.
SPACSKIP:
        INC       DX
        CMP       BYTE PTR FS:[EDX],' '
        JZ        SHORT SPACSKIP
        MOV       AX,3D00H
        MOV       EBX,OFFSET PINTFRAME
        VM86CALL                        ; Open file.
        MOV       WORD PTR PINTFRAME.VMDS,_DAT
        JNC       SHORT FOPENED
; Couldn't open file--print error.
        MOV       EDX,OFFSET NFMSG
        MOV       AH,9
        MOV       EBX,OFFSET PINTFRAME
        VM86CALL                        ; Can't open file.
        MOV       AL,1
        JMP32S    USTOP                 ; back to DOS
; File opened OK.
FOPENED:
; Save file handle.
        MOV       FHANDLE,AX
; See if extended memory present.
        MOV       AX,SEL_EXT
        LSL       EBX,EAX
        OR        EBX,EBX
        JNZ       SHORT USE_EXTMEM
; No extended memory present--use DOS memory.
        MOV       AX,SEL_FREE
USE_EXTMEM:
        MOV       GS,AX           ; memory segment > GS
; Set heap pointer to top of available memory.
        LSL       EAX,EAX
        MOV       HEAPPTR,EAX
```

DOS 5: A DEVELOPER'S GUIDE

```
                MOV         EDX,EAX
                XOR         EBX,EBX
        REREAD:
                MOV         EAX,EBX         ; Check for heap overflow.
                SHL         EAX,2
                CMP         EAX,EDX
                JB          SHORT HEAPOK
        ; No more memory--print error message.
                MOV         AH,9
                MOV         EDX,OFFSET OMMSG
                MOV         EBX,OFFSET PINTFRAME
                VM86CALL                    ; out of memory
                MOV         AL,1
                JMP32S      USTOP           ; back to DOS
        HEAPOK:
        ; Put heap pointer in lines array.
                MOV         GS:[EBX*4],EDX
        ; Read line to heap in reverse order. Each line ends in CR.
                CALL32S     READLINE
                PUSHFD
        ; Point to next line in lines array.
                INC         EBX
                POPFD
        ; not end of file?
                JNZ         SHORT REREAD
        ; here at end of file
        ; end of lines array
                MOV         PTRPTR,EBX
                MOV         BX,FHANDLE
                MOV         PINTFRAME.VMEBX,EBX
                MOV         AH,3EH
                MOV         EBX,OFFSET PINTFRAME
                VM86CALL                    ; Close file.
                MOV         DX,1800H
                CALL32S     SETCP           ; Set cursor position.
        ; Write copyright message.
                MOV         AH,9
                MOV         EDX,OFFSET CPYMSG
                MOV         EBX,OFFSET PINTFRAME
                VM86CALL                    ; Print copyright.
```

DOS EXTENDERS

```
; Inverse-video the bottom line.
        PUSH        DS
        MOV         AX,SEL_VIDEO
        MOV         DS,AX
        MOV         CL,80
; bottom line
        MOV         EDX,24*160+1
INVLOOP:
        MOV         BYTE PTR [EDX],70H
        INC         EDX
        INC         EDX
        DEC         CL
        JNZ         SHORT INVLOOP
        POP         DS
; Skip over home-key processing.
        JMP         SHORT HK0
; home-key processing
HOMEKEY: OR         BASE,0
; Don't do home if already there.
        JZ          SHORT KEYLOOP
HK0:
        XOR         EAX,EAX         ; Set screen start to 0.
        MOV         BASE,EAX
; Come here to display a page starting at base.
PAGEDISP:
        CALL32S     DISP
; Read a key and act on it.
KEYLOOP:
        MOV         BINTFRAME.VMINT,16H
        XOR         AH,AH
        PUSH        ES
        MOV         BX,SEL_CDS
        MOV         ES,BX
        MOV         EBX,OFFSET BINTFRAME
        VM86CALL                    ; Read a key.
        POP         ES
        CMP         AL,27           ; escape key?
        JZ          NEAR PTR USTOP0
        OR          AX,AX
; break key
```

873

DOS 5: A DEVELOPER'S GUIDE

```
            JZ      NEAR PTR USTOPO
            CMP     AL,3            ; break key
            JZ      NEAR PTR USTOPO
            OR      AL,AL
; special key?
            JNZ     SHORT KEYERR
; Test for function keys.
            CMP     AH,48H          ; up arrow
            JCC32   Z,UPARROW
            CMP     AH,47H          ; home key
            JZ      SHORT HOMEKEY
            CMP     AH,4FH          ; end key
            JCC32   Z,ENDKEY
            CMP     AH,49H          ; page up
            JCC32   Z,PGUP
            CMP     AH,51H          ; page down
            JCC32   Z,PGDN
            CMP     AH,50H          ; down arrow
            JZ      SHORT DNARROW
; Come here if you don't know what that key was!
KEYERR:
            PUSH    EDX
            MOV     DL,7            ; bell character
            MOV     AH,2
            MOV     EBX,OFFSET PINTFRAME
            VM86CALL
            POP     EDX
            JMP     SHORT KEYLOOP

; down-arrow processing
DNARROW:
            MOV     EAX,BASE        ; Don't go down if at end.
            ADD     EAX,24
            CMP     EAX,PTRPTR
            JCC32   AE,KEYLOOP
            INC     BASE            ; top of screen + 1
            MOV     AX,0601H        ; Scroll screen.
            CALL32S SCROLL
            MOV     DX,1700H        ; Position cursor.
            CALL32S SETCP
            MOV     EDX,BASE        ; Print bottom line.
```

DOS EXTENDERS

```
                ADD         EDX,23
                CALL32S     PLINE
                JMP32S      KEYLOOP

; up-arrow processing
UPARROW:
                OR          BASE,0          ; Don't go up if at top.
                JCC32       Z,KEYLOOP
                DEC         BASE            ; Adjust top of screen.
                MOV         AX,0701H        ; Scroll screen.
                CALL32S     SCROLL
                XOR         DX,DX           ; Position cursor.
                CALL32S     SETCP
                MOV         EDX,BASE        ; Print top line.
                CALL32S     PLINE
                JMP32S      KEYLOOP

; end-key processing
ENDKEY:         MOV         EAX,BASE
                ADD         EAX,24
                CMP         EAX,PTRPTR
; Don't do end if already there.
                JCC32       AE,KEYLOOP
; Get last line.
                MOV         EAX,PTRPTR
                SUB         EAX,24          ; Find top of screen.
                MOV         BASE,EAX
                JMP32S      PAGEDISP        ; Display page.

; page-up processing
PGUP:           MOV         EAX,BASE        ; Don't do pgup if at top.
                OR          EAX,EAX
                JCC32       Z,KEYLOOP
                CMP         EAX,24
; If near the top.. go pgup0.
                JBE         SHORT PGUP0
                SUB         EAX,24          ; Find new line.
                JMP         SHORT PGUP1
PGUP0:          XOR         EAX,EAX         ; 1st line
PGUP1:          MOV         BASE,EAX
                JMP32S      PAGEDISP
```

```
; page-down processing
PGDN:       MOV       EAX,BASE        ; If at bottom, skip.
            ADD       EAX,24
            CMP       EAX,PTRPTR
            JCC32     AE,KEYLOOP
            MOV       BASE,EAX        ; Find new line.
            JMP32S    PAGEDISP

; Exit FBROWSE.
USTOP0:
; Clear screen.
            CALL32S   FB_CLS
            XOR       AL,AL           ; Zero return code.
            PUSH      EAX
            XOR       DX,DX           ; Home cursor.
            CALL32S   DOSSETCP
            POP       EAX
USTOP:
            PUSH      DS
            POP       ES
            MOV       AH,4CH
            MOV       EBX,OFFSET PINTFRAME
            VM86CALL

USER        ENDP

; Read a line from the file.
; Lines end in 0AH unless they are 80 columns long, in which
; case they end in 0DH.
READLINE    PROC      NEAR
            PUSH      ECX
            MOV       CX,80
RLINE0:
            CALL32S   GFCHAR          ; Get character.
; Store it.
            MOV       GS:[EDX],AL
            PUSHFD
            DEC       EDX
            POPFD                     ; end of line?
            JZ        SHORT RLINEXIT
            CMP       AL,0AH          ; end of line?
            JZ        SHORT RLINEEOL
```

DOS EXTENDERS

```
                DEC         CX
; 80-char line?
                JNZ         SHORT RLINE0
; Compare last character with 0ah--if true pass it.
                CALL32S     GFCHAR
                CMP         AL,0AH
; If so, line is exactly 80 chars.
                JZ          SHORT LONGLINE
                DEC         FBUFP               ; Unget character.
LONGLINE:
                MOV         AL,0DH              ; Mark long line.
; Save end marker.
                MOV         GS:[EDX],AL
                DEC         EDX
RLINEEOL:       CMP         AL,0FFH             ; Set NZ flag.
RLINEXIT:
                POP         ECX
                RET
READLINE        ENDP

; Scroll screen using BIOS.
SCROLL          PROC        NEAR
                MOV         DX,174FH
                JMP         SHORT SCR1
; Scroll entire screen.
SCROLLALL:
                MOV         DX,184FH
SCR1:
                PUSH        ES
                MOV         BX,SEL_CDS
                MOV         ES,BX
                MOV         BINTFRAME.VMEBX,0700H
                MOV         BINTFRAME.VMINT,10H
                XOR         ECX,ECX
                MOV         EBX,OFFSET BINTFRAME
                VM86CALL
                POP         ES
                RET
SCROLL          ENDP

; Clear screen.
FB_CLS          PROC        NEAR
```

DOS 5: A DEVELOPER'S GUIDE

```
                MOV         AX,0700H
                CALL32S     SCROLLALL
                XOR         DX,DX
                CALL32S     SETCP
                RET
FB_CLS          ENDP

; Position the cursor.
DOSSETCP    PROC        NEAR
            PUSH        EBX
            PUSH        ES
            MOV         AX,SEL_CDS
            MOV         ES,AX
            MOV         BINTFRAME.VMINT,10H
            MOV         BINTFRAME.VMEBX,0
            MOV         AH,2
            MOV         EBX,OFFSET BINTFRAME
            VM86CALL
            POP         ES
            POP         EBX
            RET
DOSSETCP    ENDP

SETCP       PROC        NEAR
            CALL32S     DOSSETCP
            RET
SETCP       ENDP

; Display a screenful.
DISP        PROC        NEAR
            MOV         AX,0600H        ; Clear text area.
            CALL32S     SCROLL
            XOR         DX,DX
            CALL32S     SETCP
            MOV         CX,24
            MOV         EDX,BASE
DISP0:
            PUSH        EDX
            CALL32S     PLINE           ; Print lines.
            POP         EDX
            INC         EDX
            CMP         EDX,PTRPTR
```

DOS EXTENDERS

```
          JZ        SHORT DISP00
          DEC       CX
          JNZ       SHORT DISP0
DISP00:
          RET
DISP      ENDP

; Print a line pointed to by [edx] going backwards to \n.
PLINE     PROC      NEAR
; Get line ptr.
          MOV       EDX,GS:[EDX*4]
PLINE0:
; Get char fm str.
          MOV       AL,GS:[EDX]
          DEC       DX
; long line?
          CMP       AL,0DH
          JZ        SHORT PLINE2
; Output character.
          CALL32S   OOUCH
; end of string
          CMP       AL,0AH
          JNZ       SHORT PLINE0
PLINE1:
; Output CR.
          MOV       AL,0DH
          CALL32S   OOUCH
PLINE2:
          RET
PLINE     ENDP

; Get a character from the file.
GFCHAR    PROC      NEAR
          PUSH      EBX
          PUSH      EDX
          PUSH      ECX
GFSKIP:
; buffer empty?
          OR        FBUFL,0
          JZ        SHORT FILLBUFF
; buffer used up?
          MOV       EAX,FBUFP
```

DOS 5: A DEVELOPER'S GUIDE

```
            CMP     AX,FBUFL
            JNZ     SHORT FMBUFF
FILLBUFF:
; Read from file.
            MOV     AX,FHANDLE
            MOV     PINTFRAME.VMEBX,EAX
            MOV     ECX,512
            MOV     EDX,OFFSET FBUF
            MOV     AH,3FH
            MOV     EBX,OFFSET PINTFRAME
            VM86CALL                    ; Read buffer.
            JNC     SHORT NOFERR
; file error here
            MOV     AH,9
            MOV     EDX,OFFSET FEMSG
            VM86CALL
; back to DOS
            JMP32S  USTOP
NOFERR:     OR      AX,AX
; Store buffer length.
            MOV     FBUFL,AX
            MOV     AL,0AH
; end of file?
            JZ      SHORT GFCEOF
; Clear buffer pointer.
            XOR     EAX,EAX
            MOV     FBUFP,EAX
; This is where the character is read from a good buffer.
FMBUFF:
            MOV     EBX,FBUFP
            MOV     AL,FBUF[EBX]
            INC     EBX
            MOV     FBUFP,EBX
; Skip CR.
            CMP     AL,0DH
            JCC32   Z,GFSKIP
GFCEOF:
            POP     ECX
            POP     EDX
            POP     EBX
            RET
```

DOS EXTENDERS

```
GFCHAR      ENDP

; Output character in al.
OOUCH       PROC        NEAR
            PUSHAD
            PUSH        ES
            MOV         BX,SEL_CDS
            MOV         ES,BX
            MOV         AH,2
            MOV         DL,AL
            MOV         EBX,OFFSET PINTFRAME
            VM86CALL
            POP         ES
            POPAD
            RET
OOUCH       ENDP

_COD        ENDS

; 16-bit code to do initial setup
_START      SEGMENT     PARA PUBLIC USE16
            ASSUME      CS:_START,DS:_DAT
;init DS/SS
SETUP:      MOV         AX,_DAT
            MOV         DS,AX
            MOV         SS,AX
            MOV         SP,OFFSET _DAT:STK1
; Save PSP.
            MOV         _PSP,ES
; Prepare for jump to 32-bit code.
            MOV         AX,_COD
            MOV         CS:WORD PTR [WHERE2+2],AX
; AX=0 for 16-bit or 1 for 32-bit code.
            MOV         AX,1
            JMP         DWORD PTR CS:[WHERE2]

; where to go for 32-bit entry
WHERE2:     DD          OFFSET MAIN32
_START      ENDS

            END         SETUP
```

DOS 5: A DEVELOPER'S GUIDE

Listing 19-23. MULTI.ASM.

```
;****************************************************************
;*                                                               *
;* PROT - A 386 protected-mode DOS extender                      *
;* Copyright (C) 1989, by Al Williams                            *
;* All rights reserved.                                          *
;*                                                               *
;* Permission is granted for noncommercial use of this           *
;* software subject to certain conditions (see PROT.ASM).        *
;*                                                               *
;* This file is: MULTI.ASM, a simple multitasking example.       *
;*                                                               *
;****************************************************************
            INCLUDE     EQUMAC.INC
            INCLUDE     PROTEXT.INC
            INCLUDE     TSS.INC

            PROT_DATA

; stack for new task
T1STK       DB          256 DUP (?)
T1STKE      EQU         $
            PROT_DATA_END

            PROT_CODE

USER        PROC        NEAR
            CALL32F     SEL_CODE32,CLS
; Set up pintframe.
            MOV         AX,SEG SSINT1
            MOV         PINTFRAME.VMSS,EAX
            MOV         AX,SEG USERDATA
            MOV         PINTFRAME.VMDS,EAX
            MOV         EAX, OFFSET SSINT1
            MOV         PINTFRAME.VMESP,EAX
            MOV         PINTFRAME.VMINT,16H

; Set up new task in TSS0.
            MOV         AX,SEL_TSS0
            MOV         FS,AX
```

DOS EXTENDERS

```
                XOR     EBX,EBX
                MOV     FS:[EBX].EIP1, OFFSET NEWTASK
                MOV     AX,SEL_UCODE
                MOV     FS:[EBX].CS1,AX
                MOV     AX,SEL_UDATA
                MOV     FS:[EBX].SS1,AX
                MOV     FS:[EBX].SSP0,AX
                MOV     FS:[EBX].ESPP0,OFFSET T1STKE
                MOV     FS:[EBX].ESP1,OFFSET T1STKE

; Turn on multitasking.
                MOV     AL,1
                MOV     MULTI,AL
; Delay 4,000 clock ticks.
                MOV     ECX,4000
SKED:
; Test keyboard for input.
                MOV     AH,1
                MOV     EBX,OFFSET PINTFRAME
                VM86CALL
                JNZ     SHORT KEYPRESS
; Switch to new task.
                JMPABS32 TSS0,0
; Execution resumes here when new task is preempted.
                DEC     ECX
                JZ      SHORT MULTIXIT
                JMP     SKED
; If a key was pressed, abort processing.
KEYPRESS:
; Read key.
                XOR     AH,AH
                MOV     EBX,OFFSET PINTFRAME
                VM86CALL
MULTIXIT:
                BACK2DOS
USER            ENDP

; New task--draw sliding bar at top of screen.
NEWTASK         PROC    NEAR
                MOV     AX,SEL_VIDEO
```

DOS 5: A DEVELOPER'S GUIDE

```
                MOV     ES,AX
                MOV     AX,07DBH
                XOR     EBX,EBX
TOPL:
                MOV     CX,0A000H       ; Delay counter.
; Waste some time so the display is not too fast.
DLOOP:          DEC     CX
                NOP
                NOP
                JNZ     DLOOP
; Store character.
                MOV     ES:[2*EBX],AX
; Look at next character.
                INC     EBX
                CMP     EBX,80          ; wrap-around?
                JB      TOPL
                XOR     EBX,EBX
                CMP     AL,' '
                MOV     AL,0DBH         ; block character
                JZ      TOPL
                MOV     AL,' '
                JMP     TOPL
NEWTASK         ENDP

                PROT_CODE_END

                END
```

APPENDIX A

Glossary

API	Applications programming interface
BCD	Binary coded decimal
BIOS	Basic input/output system
BPB	BIOS parameter block
BMR	Bit-mask register
CAD	Computer-aided design
CGA	Color Graphics Adapter
CPL	Current privilege level
CRC	Cyclic redundancy check
DMA	Direct memory access
DPL	Descriptor privilege level
DPMI	DOS Protected Mode Interface
DRR	Data rotate register
DTA	Disk transfer area
ECC	Error correcting code
EGA	Enhanced Graphics Adapter
EMS	Expanded Memory Specification
EOI	End of interrupt
EPL	Effective privilege level
FAT	File allocation table
FCB	File control block
Gbyte	Gigabyte
GD	General detect
GDT	Global descriptor table
GE	Global exact

GP	General protection
HGA	Hercules Graphics Adapter
HMA	High memory area
IDT	Interrupt descriptor table
IRQ	Interrupt request
ISR	Interrupt service routine
Kbyte	Kilobyte
LDT	Local descriptor table
LE	Local exact
LIM	Lotus-Intel-Microsoft
Mbyte	Megabyte
MCB	Memory control block
MCGA	Memory Controller Gate Array
MDA	Monochrome Display Adapter
MMR	Map-mask register
MMU	Memory management unit
MSW	Machine status word
NAN	Not a number
NMI	Nonmaskable interrupt
PDBR	Page directory base register
PDE	Page directory entry
PIA	Peripheral interface adapter
PFT	Process file table
PIC	Programmable interrupt controller
PL	Privilege level
PSP	Program segment prefix
PTE	Page table entry
RAM	Random-access memory
RGB	Red-green-blue
RMR	Read map register
ROM	Read-only memory
RPL	Requestor privilege level

GLOSSARY

SCSI	Small computer systems interface
SFT	System file table
SRER	Set/reset enable register
SRR	Set/reset register
TIGA	Texas Instruments Graphics Architecture
TSR	Terminate-and-stay-resident
TSS	Task state segment
UART	Universal asynchronous receiver/transmitter
UMB	Upper memory block
V86	Virtual 8086
VCPI	Virtual Control Program Interface
VGA	Video Graphics Array
WMR	Write-mode register
XGA	Extended Graphics Array
XMS	Extended Memory Specification
XOR	Exclusive *OR*

APPENDIX B

IBM PC Character Set

Decimal	Hex	Character	Decimal	Hex	Character
0	00		26	1A	→
1	01	☺	27	1B	←
2	02	●	28	1C	∟
3	03	♥	29	1D	↔
4	04	♦	30	1E	▲
5	05	♣	31	1F	▼
6	06	♠	32	20	
7	07	•	33	21	!
8	08	◘	34	22	"
9	09	○	35	23	#
10	0A	◉	36	24	$
11	0B	♂	37	25	%
12	0C	♀	38	26	&
13	0D	♪	39	27	'
14	0E	♫	40	28	(
15	0F	☼	41	29	)
16	10	►	42	2A	*
17	11	◄	43	2B	+
18	12	↕	44	2C	,
19	13	‼	45	2D	
20	14	¶	46	2E	.
21	15	§	47	2F	/
22	16	▬	48	30	0
23	17	↨	49	31	1
24	18	↑	50	32	2
25	19	↓	51	33	3

889

DOS 5: A DEVELOPER'S GUIDE

Decimal	Hex	Character	Decimal	Hex	Character
52	34	4	90	5A	Z
53	35	5	91	5B	[
54	36	6	92	5C	\
55	37	7	93	5D	]
56	38	8	94	5E	^
57	39	9	95	5F	_
58	3A	:	96	60	`
59	3B	;	97	61	a
60	3C	<	98	62	b
61	3D	=	99	63	c
62	3E	>	100	64	d
63	3F	?	101	65	e
64	40	@	102	66	f
65	41	A	103	67	g
66	42	B	104	68	h
67	43	C	105	69	i
68	44	D	106	6A	j
69	45	E	107	6B	k
70	46	F	108	6C	l
71	47	G	109	6D	m
72	48	H	110	6E	n
73	49	I	111	6F	o
74	4A	J	112	70	p
75	4B	K	113	71	q
76	4C	L	114	72	r
77	4D	M	115	73	s
78	4E	N	116	74	t
79	4F	O	117	75	u
80	50	P	118	76	v
81	51	Q	119	77	w
82	52	R	120	78	x
83	53	S	121	79	y
84	54	T	122	7A	z
85	55	U	123	7B	{
86	56	V	124	7C	|
87	57	W	125	7D	}
88	58	X	126	7E	~
89	59	Y	127	7F	⌂

IBM PC CHARACTER SET

Decimal	Hex	Character	Decimal	Hex	Character
128	80	Ç	166	A6	ª
129	81	ü	167	A7	º
130	82	é	168	A8	¿
131	83	â	169	A9	⌐
132	84	ä	170	AA	¬
133	85	à	171	AB	½
134	86	å	172	AC	¼
135	87	ç	173	AD	¡
136	88	ê	174	AE	«
137	89	ë	175	AF	»
138	8A	è	176	B0	░
139	8B	ï	177	B1	▒
140	8C	î	178	B2	▓
141	8D	ì	179	B3	│
142	8E	Ä	180	B4	┤
143	8F	Å	181	B5	╡
144	90	É	182	B6	╢
145	91	æ	183	B7	╖
146	92	Æ	184	B8	╕
147	93	ô	185	B9	╣
148	94	ö	186	BA	║
149	95	ò	187	BB	╗
150	96	û	188	BC	╝
151	97	ù	189	BD	╜
152	98	ÿ	190	BE	╛
153	99	Ö	191	BF	┐
154	9A	Ü	192	C0	└
155	9B	¢	193	C1	┴
156	9C	£	194	C2	┬
157	9D	¥	195	C3	├
158	9E	₧	196	C4	─
159	9F	ƒ	197	C5	┼
160	A0	á	198	C6	╞
161	A1	í	199	C7	╟
162	A2	ó	200	C8	╚
163	A3	ú	201	C9	╔
164	A4	ñ	202	CA	╩
165	A5	Ñ	203	CB	╦

Decimal	Hex	Character	Decimal	Hex	Character
204	CC	╠	230	E6	µ
205	CD	═	231	E7	τ
206	CE	╬	232	E8	Φ
207	CF	╧	233	E9	Θ
208	D0	╨	234	EA	Ω
209	D1	╤	235	EB	δ
210	D2	╥	236	EC	∞
211	D3	╙	237	ED	φ
212	D4	╘	238	EE	ε
213	D5	╒	239	EF	∩
214	D6	╓	240	F0	≡
215	D7	╫	241	F1	±
216	D8	╪	242	F2	≥
217	D9	┘	243	F3	≤
218	DA	┌	244	F4	⌠
219	DB	█	245	F5	⌡
220	DC	▄	246	F6	÷
221	DD	▌	247	F7	≈
222	DE	▐	248	F8	°
223	DF	▀	249	F9	·
224	E0	α	250	FA	·
225	E1	ß	251	FB	√
226	E2	Γ	252	FC	ⁿ
227	E3	π	253	FD	²
228	E4	Σ	254	FE	■
229	E5	σ	255	FF	

APPENDIX C

IBM PC Line-Drawing Characters

C9 ╔	CD ═	CB ╦	BB ╗	DA ┌	C4 ─	C2 ┬	BF ┐
BA ║				B3 │			
CC ╠	CE ╬	B9 ╣		C3 ├	C5 ┼	B4 ┤	
C8 ╚	CA ╩	BC ╝		C0 └	C1 ┴	D9 ┘	

APPENDIX D

IBM PC Scan Codes

Key	Scan Code	ASCII or Extended		ASCII or Extended with Shift		ASCII or Extended with Ctrl		ASCII or Extended with Alt	
	Hex	Hex	ASCII	Hex	ASCII	Hex	ASCII	Hex	ASCII
A	1E	61	a	41	A	01	^A	1E	NUL
B	30	62	b	42	B	02	^B	30	NUL
C	2E	63	c	43	C	03	^C	2E	NUL
D	20	64	d	44	D	04	^D	20	NUL
E	12	65	e	45	E	05	^E	12	NUL
F	21	66	f	46	F	06	^F	21	NUL
G	22	67	g	47	G	07	^G	22	NUL
H	23	68	h	48	H	08	^H	23	NUL
I	17	69	i	49	I	09	^I	17	NUL
J	24	6A	j	4A	J	0A	^J	24	NUL
K	25	6B	k	4B	K	0B	^K	25	NUL
L	26	6C	l	4C	L	0C	^L	26	NUL
M	32	6D	m	4D	M	0D	^M	32	NUL
N	31	6E	n	4E	N	0E	^N	31	NUL
O	18	6F	o	4F	O	0F	^O	18	NUL
P	19	70	p	50	P	10	^P	19	NUL
Q	10	71	q	51	Q	11	^Q	10	NUL
R	13	72	r	52	R	12	^R	13	NUL
S	1F	73	s	53	S	13	^S	1F	NUL
T	14	74	t	54	T	14	^T	14	NUL
U	16	75	u	55	U	15	^U	16	NUL
V	2F	76	v	56	V	16	^V	2F	NUL
W	11	77	w	57	W	17	^W	11	NUL
X	2D	78	x	58	X	18	^X	2D	NUL
Y	15	79	y	59	Y	19	^Y	15	NUL
Z	2C	7A	z	5A	Z	1A	^Z	2C	NUL

DOS 5: A DEVELOPER'S GUIDE

Key	Scan Code	ASCII or Extended		ASCII or Extended with Shift		ASCII or Extended with Ctrl		ASCII or Extended with Alt	
	Hex	Hex	ASCII	Hex	ASCII	Hex	ASCII	Hex	ASCII
1!	02	31	1	21	!			78	NUL
2@	03	32	2	40	@	03	NUL	79	NUL
3#	04	33	3	23	#			7A	NUL
4$	05	34	4	24	$			7B	NUL
5%	06	35	5	25	%			7C	NUL
6^	07	36	6	5E	^	1E		7D	NUL
7&	08	37	7	26	&			7E	NUL
8*	09	38	8	2A	*			7F	NUL
9(	0A	39	9	28	(			80	NUL
0)	0B	30	0	29	)			81	NUL
-_	0C	2D	-	5F	_	1F		82	NUL
=+	0D	3D	=	2B	+			83	
[{	1A	5B	[	7B	{	1B			
]}	1B	5D	]	7D	}	1D			
;:	27	3B	;	3A	:				
'"	28	27	'	22	"				
`~	29	60	`	7E	~				
.>	33	2E	.	3E	>				
,<	34	2C	,	3C	<				
/?	35	2F	/	3F	?				
|	2B	5C	\	7C	|	1C			
F1	3B	3B	NUL	54	NUL	5E	NUL	68	NUL
F2	3C	3C	NUL	55	NUL	5F	NUL	69	NUL
F3	3D	3D	NUL	56	NUL	60	NUL	6A	NUL
F4	3E	3E	NUL	57	NUL	61	NUL	6B	NUL
F5	3F	3F	NUL	58	NUL	62	NUL	6C	NUL
F6	40	40	NUL	59	NUL	63	NUL	6D	NUL
F7	41	41	NUL	5A	NUL	64	NUL	6E	NUL
F8	42	46	NUL	5B	NUL	65	NUL	6F	NUL
F9	43	43	NUL	5C	NUL	66	NUL	70	NUL
F10	44	44	NUL	5D	NUL	67	NUL	71	NUL

IBM PC SCAN CODES

Key	Scan Code	ASCII or Extended		ASCII or Extended with Shift		ASCII or Extended with Ctrl		ASCII or Extended with Alt	
	Hex	Hex	ASCII	Hex	ASCII	Hex	ASCII	Hex	ASCII
ESC	01	1B		1B		1B		78	NUL
BACKSPACE	0E	08		08		7F			
TAB	0F	09		0F	NUL				
ENTER	1C	0D	^M	0D	^M	0A	^J		
CONTROL	1D								
LEFT SHIFT	2A								
RIGHT SHIFT	36								
* PRTSC	37	2A	*			72	NUL		
ALT	38								
SPACE	39	20	▯	20	▯	20	▯	20	▯
CAPS LOCK	3A								
NUM LOCK	45								
SCROLL LOCK	46								
HOME	47	47	NUL	37	7	77	NUL		
UP	48	48	NUL	38	8				
PGUP	49	49	NUL	39	9	84	NUL		
GREY-	4A	2D	-	2D	-				
LEFT	4B	4B	NUL	34	4	73	NUL		
CENTER	4C			35	5				
RIGHT	4D	4D	NUL	36	6	74	NUL		
GREY +	4E	2B	+	2B	+				
END	4F	4F	NUL	31	1	75	NUL		
DOWN	50	50	NUL	32	2				
PGDN	51	51	NUL	33	3	76	NUL		
INS	52	52	NUL	30	0				
DEL	53	53	NUL	2E	.				

Notes: ASCII values of NUL indicate that DOS returns these keys as two bytes: a zero on the first call and the specified hex byte on the next call. The BIOS returns the hex byte as the scan code and zero as the ASCII code.

A ▯ signifies a space.

APPENDIX E

Annotated Bibliography

If you want to know more about a particular subject, the following books should be able to provide detailed information.

DOS, BIOS, and PC Hardware

Of course, the IBM technical references are the ultimate source of information on PC hardware. Their presentation, however, can be somewhat terse. They are also relatively expensive. Space prohibits a list of every document for every IBM machine and version of DOS, but a pamphlet called "Technical Directory" lists the available manuals and their prices. You can order the directory or IBM manuals by calling (800) 426-7282 in the U.S. or (800) 465-1234 in Canada. You can also write Intel at:

IBM Technical Directory
P.O. Box 2009
Racine, WI 53404-3336

We also won't cover the majority of the Intel manuals since there are so many. However, you can't beat them for detailed information on PC hardware. You can reach Intel Literature Sales by calling (800) 548-4725, or write:

Intel Literature
5200 N.E. Elam Young Pkwy.
Hillsboro, OR 97124

DOS 5: A DEVELOPER'S GUIDE

Microsoft Corp., *MS-DOS Programmer's Reference: Version 5.0*
Redmond, WA: Microsoft Corp., 1991

> This dense book is the official reference guide for DOS 5. It covers many DOS functions that haven't been officially documented in previous versions. This is not a tutorial—merely a reference.

Thom Hogan, *The Programmer's PC Sourcebook*
Redmond, WA: Microsoft Press, 1988

> This comprehensive reference guide contains only terse tables—not a good learning tool, but a great reference. However, the volume of information in this book sometimes makes it difficult to find exactly what you want.

Ray Duncan, *IBM ROM BIOS*
Redmond, WA: Microsoft Press, 1988

Ray Duncan, *MS-DOS Functions*
Redmond, WA: Microsoft Press, 1988

> These books are small, handy, and inexpensive. While they are lean on explanations, they are excellent as quick references.

Coprocessor Programming

John Palmer and Stephen Morse, *The 8087 Primer*
New York, NY: John Wiley and Sons, 1984

> Written by the principal architects of the 8087, this book gives some interesting insights into why the 8087 is the way it is. On the minus side, the book is dated—there is no coverage of the 287, 387, or 486's on-board coprocessor. Still, the book is useful, especially for those concerned with the esoteric issues regarding numerical precision.

ANNOTATED BIBLIOGRAPHY

Video Graphics

Roger Stevens, *Graphics Programming in C*
Redwood City, CA: M&T Books, 1989

Mouse Programming

Ray Duncan, *MS-DOS Extensions*
Redmond, WA: Microsoft Press, 1989

> This is another inexpensive quick-reference book. It also covers EMS, XMS, and CD-ROM.

EMS

Intel Corp., et al., *Lotus/Intel/Microsoft Expanded Memory Specification (Version 4.0)*
Hillsboro, OR: Intel Corp., 1987

Intel Corp., *The EMS Toolkit for C Developers*
Hillsboro, OR: Intel Corp., 1989

> This official specification document for EMS 4.0 and library of routines on disk for using EMS are available free of charge from Intel Literature (see above). The document number is 300275-005. The toolkit included with the specification provides C and assembly routines for managing EMS allocation.

Ray Duncan, *MS-DOS Extensions*
Redmond, WA: Microsoft Press, 1989

> This inexpensive reference book also covers mouse calls, XMS, and CD-ROM.

DOS 5: A DEVELOPER'S GUIDE

Protected Mode

Intel Corp., *80386 Programmer's Reference Manual*
Santa Clara, CA: Intel Corp., 1986

Intel Corp., *80386 System Software Writer's Guide*
Santa Clara, CA: Intel Corp., 1987

> These data books, being straight from the horse's mouth, are well worth having.

James Turley, *Advanced 80386 Programming Techniques*
Berkeley, CA: Osborne/McGraw-Hill, 1988

> This outstanding book on 386 techniques covers programming from the perspective of developing for a 386, non-DOS platform (perhaps an embedded system). Unfortunately, not a line of code in this book will run under DOS.

Extended Memory

Microsoft Corp., et al., *Extended Memory Specification Version 2.0*
Redmond, WA: Microsoft Corp., 1988

> This free specification from Microsoft completely documents the XMS protocol for using extended memory with an XMS driver. You may obtain the specification by writing to:

Microsoft Corp.
Box 97017
Redmond, WA 98073

Ray Duncan, *MS-DOS Extensions*
Redmond, WA: Microsoft Press, 1989

> This quick reference also covers mouse calls, EMS, and CD-ROM.

ANNOTATED BIBLIOGRAPHY

4 Gbytes under DOS

Thomas Roden, "Four Gigabytes in Real Mode," *Programmer's Journal*, November/December 1989: pp. 89–94.

Al Williams, "DOS+386=4 Gigabytes," *Dr. Dobb's Journal*
July 1990: pp. 62–71.

> Mr. Roden and I independently found the bug/feature in the 386 that allows SEG4G to work. Be sure to look up his article if you're interested in a different implementation.

DOS Extenders

Phar Lap Software, et al., *Virtual Control Program Interface*
Cambridge, MA: Phar Lap Software, 1989

Intel Corp., et al., *DOS Protected Mode Interface (DPMI) Specification*
Santa Clara, CA: Intel Corp., 1990

> These two papers document the two primary standards that allow DOS extenders and other protected-mode programs to coexist. VCPI is more mature, but DPMI is used by Windows 3.0 (which means many PCs already have a DPMI-compliant DOS extender installed). These documents are free of charge. You can obtain the VCPI specification from:

> Phar Lap Software, Inc.
> 60 Aberdeen Ave.
> Cambridge, MA 02138
> (617) 661-1510

> The DMPI spec is available from Intel Literature (see above).

Index

Note: A page number in boldface type indicates the beginning of a source-code listing.

A

A20 wraparound 25, 624
A20.C **197**
Aborts 615-616
Address calculation 17-19
Address translation 619
Addresses
    linear 600, 618-619, 622, 644
    logical 600
    physical 600, 619, 622
Addressing 9, 45-46, 601
Aliasing
    EMS 459
    memory 606
ANSI.SYS 60
Arena header 42-43
Arithmetic, floating-point 239
ASMFUNC.H **692**

B

Baud rate 222
BCD 244, 266
BIOS interrupts 37-38, 153-180
BIOS services
    clock 179
    disk 164
    equipment configuration 163
    keyboard 175
    memory size 163
    printer 177
    serial port 171
    video 153
BIOS variables 38, 180
BLKTEST.C **710**
Block drivers 466, 472
Boot record 474
BREAK386.ASM **647**
BREAK386.H **667**
BREAK386.INC **666**
Breakpoints 643, 646, 665, 668-669, 718, 731
BREAKS.ASM **274**
Buffer wrap 502
BUSY flag 143

C

$CALC.ASM **255**
CALC.C **255**
Call gates 610, 614-615, 725
CBRK386.ASM **678**
CBRKDEMO.C **686**
CEMS library 438
CEMS.C **439**
CEMS.H **438**
CEXT.C **634**
CEXT.H **633**
CGA
    see Video adapter, CGA
CGRAPH functions 339
CGRAPH.C **341**

905

CGRAPH.H **340**
Character drivers 466
Characteristic 241-242
CLI
    see Instruction, *CLI*
Clock, real-time 23, 212-213
Clusters 28
CMOS RAM 212-213
CMOUSE library 370
CMOUSEA.ASM **378**
CMOUSE.C **372**
CMOUSE.H **371**
CODE16.ASM **763**
.COM files, loading 31-32
COM port 221
COMATH.ASM **253**
COMLOOK.C **298**
Command line 39, 46-47
Commands, BREAK386 669
COMMAND.COM
    command execution 36
    loading 29
COMPAT.H **47**, 51, 53, 59
Controller
    display 26
    keyboard 24-25, 194-195
_control87() function 267
Control-Break 35, 37, 69, 70, 138, 272-273, 413, 455, 546-547, 715, 719
Control-C 35, 69, 70, 80-81, 138, 272-273, 413, 455, 546-547, 715, 719
Conventions 5
Coprocessor 239
    data types 241-242
    defaults 245
    emulation 251
COPROC.C **253**
CPL 609, 614-615
CRITERR.ASM 281
Critical error flag 143

Critical errors 36, 145-146, 273, 279-280, 546-547, 715, 720
CURLOCK.INT **540**
CURSIZE.C **542**

D
DBG386.C **672**
DBGOFF.ASM **676**
DD.ASM **479**
DDASM.BAT **485**
DDLIST.C **504**
DEBUG386.ASM **670**
Debugging
    drivers 504
    hardware 602, 616, 643-645, 673, 731
    PROT 731, 733
    TSRs 594
Denormal 243
Descriptor table
    global 603, 624, 630
    interrupt 603, 615, 624
    local 603, 624
Device drivers
    see Programs, device driver
    see also Drivers
Device header 462-463
Direct access
    graphics 317
    UART 223
    video 183
Direct memory access 24
_*disable()* function 59, 191
disable() function 59, 191
Disk information block 94
Disk transfer area 40
Disks 27, 28, 502-503
    clusters 28
    cylinders 27, 502-503
    sectors 27, 28, 502-503
    sides 27, 502-503
    tracks 27, 502-503

INDEX

Display controller 26
DLL.ASM **809**
DLLEQU.INC **838**
DMA
    see Direct memory access
DOS error codes 77-79
DOS extenders 628, 641, 713-714, 742
_dos_getvect() function 59
DOS interrupts 35, 36, 273, 279-280
    see also DOS services
DOS services
    date and time 118
    directory 115
    disk control 87
    FCB 102
    file operations 97
    handle I/O 102
    IOCTL 130
    memory 126
    miscellaneous 136
    process operations 120
    simple I/O 79
_dos_setvect() function 59
DOSSHELL 287
Driver
    block 34, 466, 493
    character 34, 466
    commands 462, 465-466, 472
    debugging 504
    device header 462-463
    EMS 10, 34, 36, 411-412
    listing 504
    loading 466
    mouse 33, 36, 357, 360, 391-393
    request packet 462
    status word 462
    UMB 43
    XMS 11, 25, 641
DTA
    see Disk transfer area

DUP.C **442**
Dynamic linking, PROT 724

E

EDISP.C **67**
EGA
    see Video adapter, EGA
EMS
    see also Memory, expanded
    aliasing 459
    code execution 455
    compatibility 437
    detection 414
    errors 416, 442
    page frame 412
    toolkit 411
EMSEXEC.C **456**
_enable() function 59, 191
enable() function 59, 191
environ variable 50
Environment variables 40-43, 50, 66, 508
EPL 609
EQUMAC.INC **820**
Error, critical 36, 546-547, 715, 720
Error codes
    386 616
    disk I/O 165
    DOS 77-79
    MMU 620-621
    page fault 620-621
ESCAPE.C **60**
ESKETCH1.C **394**
ESKETCH.C **379**
Exact bits 645
Exceptions
    coprocessor 245
    .EXE file
    loading 31-32
    processor 615-616, 624-625
EXE2BIN 461

907

Exponent 241-242
Extended error information 140-142
EXTERNAL.INC **831**

F

far keyword 45-46, 66
Faults 615
    general protection 617
    page 616, 620-621
FB.ASM **868**
FBROWSE.ASM **855**
File attributes 97-98
File handles
    see Handles, file
Flags
    see also Register, FLAGS
    BUSY 143
    critical error 143
Flow control
    see Handshaking
FP_OFF macro 46
FP_SEG macro 46
Functions
    hyperbolic 250
    PROT 721-722, 726-730
    transcendental 250

G

Gates
    call 610, 614-615, 725
    interrupt 617
    task 611, 617
    trap 617
GDT 603, 624, 630
GDT.ASM **803**
General protection fault 617
getch() function 272
getenv() function 41, 50
getopt() function 298, 315, 378
GETOPT.C **308**

GETOPT.H **313**
getvect() function 59
Global exact bit 645
GOPROT.INC **845**

H

Handles
    duplication 109
    EMS 412
    file 41-42, 102-115
    file predefined, 41
    redirection 109
Handshaking
    hardware 222
    software 222
    XON/XOFF 222
_harderr() function 286
harderr() function 286
Header
    arena 42-43
    .EXE 30-31, 43-44
HEXDUMP.ASM **288**
HGA
    see Video adapter, HGA
Hot keys 545

I

IDT 603, 615, 624
Indefinite 243
INDOS flag 544
inp() function 50
inportb() function 50
inport() function 50
Input 50
Instruction
    CLI 23, 59, 191
    F2XM1 250
    FABS 266
    FCLEX 246
    FLDENV 246

INDEX

FPREM 250
FSTSW 250
FSUB 266
FWAIT 240, 266
FXAM 250
IN 20
INT 616, 627-628, 675, 735-736
INTO 616, 675
IRET 20, 70, 538, 613, 627-628, 646, 735-736
LTR 626
OUT 20
STI 59, 191
string 19, 186
V86 735
Instruction emulation 628
Instructions
    coprocessor 247-249
    I/O 20, 609
    PL 0 608
    privileged 608
    real-mode 621
    string 19, 414
    V86 622, 714
INT 1 645
INT 5 37, 68-71
INT 9 191
INT 10H 37, 322, 544
INT 11H 37
INT 12H 37
INT 13H 37, 502, 544
INT 14H 37
INT 15H 37, 629-632, 639, 717
INT 16H 25, 37
INT 17H 37
INT 18H 37
INT 19H 37
INT 1AH 37
INT 1BH 273
INT 1CH 38, 509, 512

INT 1EH 38
INT 1FH 38
INT 20H 35
INT 21H 35
INT 22H 35
INT 23H 35, 273
INT 24H 36, 279-280
INT 25H 36
INT 26H 36
INT 27H 35
INT 28H 545
INT 2EH 36
INT 2FH 36, 509, 516, 523, 525
INT 33H 36, 357, 360
INT 60H 36
INT 67H 36, 412-415
INT386.ASM **781**
int86() function 53, 315
int86f() macro 53
int86fx() function 53
int86x() function 53, 455
INTASM environment 525
INTASM.BAT **537**
Interceptors 509
INTERCPT.ASM **527**
Interrupt descriptor table 603, 624
Interrupt functions 58
Interrupt gates 617
Interrupt request (IRQ) lines 21-22
Interrupt routine (device driver) 462
Interrupt service routine 20, 58
Interrupt vector table 59
Interrupts 18, 21-23, 51-53, 58-59, 70-71
    BIOS 37-38, 153
    clock 23, 38, 202, 209, 508-509, 512, 545
    coprocessor 245, 247
    critical error 145-146, 273, 279-280
    device driver 462
    DOS 35-36, 145-146, 152, 273, 279-280

functions 70
hardware 20-23, 188, 190-191, 512, 624, 631, 739
hooking 33, 58, 188, 508, 632
idle 152
keyboard 24-25, 190-191, 508
multiplex 36, 152, 509, 516, 523, 525
nonmaskable 23, 191, 245, 617, 625, 692
rules 188
timer 23, 38, 202, 508-509, 512, 545
TSR 508
UART 225
unexpected 718
user 188
V86 623
INTHOOK.CPP **189**
INTREGS macro 58
INTS macro 526, 537
IOCTL 130-136, 464
IOPL 609, 614
IRET
    see Instruction, *IRET*
IRQ
    see Interrupt request lines
ISR
    see Interrupt service routine

J
JOY.C **216**
JOYS.ASM **215**
Joysticks 212-214

K
Keyboard controller 24-25, 194-195
Keyboard scan codes 24-25, 175, 191, 272

L
Latch registers 324
LIST71.C **187**
LIST73.C **192**
LIST74.C **196**
LIST77.C **202**
Local exact bit 645
Logarithms 250
LPT port 217
LPTR type 633, 638, 706

M
Mantissa 241-242
MCB
    see Memory control block
MDA
    see Video adapter, MDA
Memory
    aliasing 606
    allocation 42-43
    allocation strategy 129-130
    conventional 10
    EMS 10-11, 410-412
    expanded 10-11, 410-412
    extended 11, 25, 629-631, 717
    protection 601
    types 10
    video 26
    XMS 11, 641
Memory control block 42-43, 199
Memory model 45-46
Mickeys 359
MK_FP macro 47
MMU 600, 618, 626
Mouse driver
    see Driver, mouse
Mouse
    events 358, 391-393, 408
    modes 358
    polling 358

INDEX

resolution 359
sensitivity 359, 391
MULTI.ASM **882**
Multiplex interrupt 36, 152, 509, 516, 523, 525
Multitasking 602, 611, 625, 644, 646, 734
Musical notes 210-211

N
NAN 243
near keyword 45-46
NMI
   see Nonmaskable interrupt
Nonmaskable interrupt 23, 191, 245, 617, 625, 692
Notes, musical 210-211
NUDISK.CFG **493**
NUDISK.CMD **501**
NUDISK.DRV **494**
Null selector 610
Numbers
   decimal 5
   hexadecimal 5
Numeric coprocessor 239

O
Offsets 10
Onion model 607
outp() function 51
outport() function 51
outportb() function 51
Output 50

P
Page
   directory 619, 621
   fault 616, 620-621
   frame 412
   table 619, 621

Paging 626
Palettes 335-338
Parallel port 217
Path names 97
Peripheral interface adapter 23
PFT
   see Process file table
PIA
   see Peripheral interface adapter
PIC
   see Programmable interrupt controller
PID
   see Process identifier
PIPE.CFG **487**
PIPE.DRV **488**
Pixels
   CGA 323
   EGA 324
   HGA 323
   VGA 324, 334
PMDEMO.ASM **853**
PMDEMO.DOS **854**
Pointers
   far 45-46, 66
   near 45-46
POPDIR.CFG **584**
POPDIR.CMD **587**
POPDIR.TSR **580**
Ports 19-20, 50
PRDEMO.C **220**
Print screen 37, 68-71
Printer port 217
Privilege 607, 719
   changing 610
   current level 609, 614-615
   effective 609
   I/O 609, 614
   V86 622
Privilege ring 607
Process 30
   identifier 44

protection 601
termination 36, 42
Process file table 41-42
Program segment prefix 38-47, 63-64, 546
    overlay 513
    parent 40
Programmable interrupt controller 21-22, 190-191
Programs
    .COM 30-32, 43-44, 509
    device driver 30, 34 (*see also* Drivers)
    .EXE 30-32, 43-44
    loading 29
    pop-up 33
    terminate-and-stay-resident 30, 33, 35-36
PROT.ASM **742**
_PROTASM.BAT **850**
PROTASM.BAT **848**
Protected mode 599, 624
PROTEXT.INC **837**
PROT.MAK **847**
PRTSC.ASM **75**
PRTSCRN.C **68**
PS.C **199**
_psp variable 46, 50
PSP
    see Program segment prefix
putenv() function 50

R

RAM, CMOS 212-213
Real mode 599, 621, 626
Real-time clock 23, 212-213
Registers 11
    32-bit 16-18, 601
    80386 16-18, 601
    coprocessor 246-247
    CR3 (*see* Registers, page directory base)

debugging 644-645
DMA page 24
EGA 324-325, 333
FLAGS 11, 18
general-purpose 11, 14, 17
index 11, 18
page directory base 619-620, 626
segment 11, 17, 44, 53
UART 224
VGA 324-325, 333
REGS union 51-52, 315
Relocation table 31
Rounding control 246
RPL 602

S

Scan codes 24-25, 175, 191, 272
SDUMP.CFG **590**
SDUMP.CMD **593**
SDUMP.TSR **588**
SEG4G library 706
SEG4G.C **693**
SEG4G.H **693**
SEG4GB.ASM **702**
Segmentation 9, 601-602, 618, 692
Segments
    fix-ups 31
    granularity 606
    overlap 10
    PROT 715-717
    real-mode 9
    selectors 602
SEGTEST.C 708
Selectors 602
    null 610, 616-617
Serial port 221
SERIO.C **226**
SERIO.H **238**
SETSPEED.C **524**
SETUP program 23

INDEX

SETVER 137, 139
SFT
    see System file table
signal( ) function 279
Significand 241-242
SIMPLE.ASM **852**
Software handshaking 222
Sound generation 23, 202, 209
SPACE.C **65**
SPYS.C **71**
SPYS1.C **73**
SREGS structure 53
Stack 18, 44, 512, 546, 609, 611, 615, 623, 719
    coprocessor 244
    EMS 459
    frame 685
    segment 610
    TSR 512
STACKS.ASM **808**
_status87( ) function 267
STI
    see Instruction, *STI*
Strategy routine 462
Switches, motherboard 23
System file table 41

T

Task gates 611, 617
Task state segment 611-615, 623, 625
Tasks
    busy 613
    execution 613
    nested 613
Temporary files 112
Terminal emulation 225
TIGA
    see Video adapter, TIGA
Timer 23

Timing 202, 209
    high-resolution 210
TONE.ASM **204**
TONE.H **208**
TONETEST.C **207**
Tracepoints 643
Trackballs 357
Transcendental functions 250
Transient 507
Trap gates 617
Traps 615
TSR
    see also Programs, terminate-and-stay-resident
    architecture 507
    coexistence 508
    common errors 595
    context management 545-547
    debugging 594
    DOS access 544-545
    hot keys 545
    INTASM environment 525
    interceptors 509
    memory consumption 508
    pop-up 544
    relocation 515
    removal 523
    signature 509
    transient portion 507
TSR.ASM **549**
TSRASM
    default commands 577
    environment 548
    user-defined procedures 579
TSRASM.BAT **575**
TSRCFG.INC **563**
TSRCMDS.INC **570**
TSRINTS.INC **564**
TSRMAC.INT **558**
TSRVARS.INC **560**

TSRVIDEO.INC **573**
TSS
   see Task state segment
TSS.ASM **806**
TSS.INC **835**

U

UART
   see Universal asynchronous receiver/transmitter
UMB
   see Upper memory blocks
Universal asynchronous receiver/transmitter 221
Unnormals 243
Upper memory blocks 43, 129-130, 199

V

V86 mode 599, 621
Variables
   BIOS 38, 180-182
   DDASM 486
   INTASM 539
   mouse 358-360
   PROT 721-722
   PROT configuration 723
   TSRASM 579
   TSRASM configuration 578
Verify flag 93
VGA
   see Video adapter, VGA
VIDDET.C **320**
Video 26, 317
   8514/A 317
   attribute 184
   buffer 183
   CGA 26, 317-318, 323, 335, 358
   EGA 26, 317-318, 324, 336, 358
   HGA 26, 317, 322, 323, 339, 358

MDA 26
modes 154, 318-319
pages 26, 183
snow 186
TIGA 317
VGA 26, 317-318, 334, 337-338, 358
XGA 317
Video_info structure 338, 340
Virtual memory 600, 606, 618
VM_DISK.C **453**
VM_EMS.C **451**
VM_EXT.C **639**

W

WASTE.ASM **516**
WASTE0.ASM **510**
WASTE1.ASM **513**
WASTEX.INT **525**

X

X386.ASM **818**
X386.MAK **851**
XGA
   see Video adapter, XGA
XMS
   see Memory, extended
XON/XOFF 222

M&T BOOKS

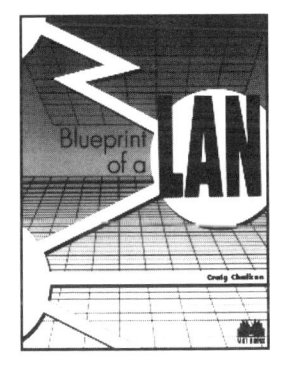

A Library of Technical References from M&T Books

Blueprint of a LAN
by Craig Chaiken

For programmers, valuable programming techniques are detailed. Network administrators will learn how to build and install LAN communication cables, configure and troubleshoot network hardware and more. Addressed are a very inexpensive zero-slot, star topology network, remote printer and file sharing, remote command execution, electronic mail, parallel processing support, high-level language support, and more. Also covered is the complete Intel 8086 assembly language source code that will help you build an inexpensive-to-install local area network. An optional disk containing all source code is available. 337 pp.

Book & Disk (MS-DOS)	Item #066-4	$39.95
Book only	Item #052-4	$29.95

LAN Protocol Handbook
by Mark A. Miller, P.E.

Requisite reading for all network administrators and software developers needing in-depth knowledge of the internal protocols of the most popular network software. It illustrates the techniques of protocol analysis—the step-by-step process of unraveling LAN software failures. Detailed is how Ethernet, IEEE 802.3, IEEE 802.5, and ARCNET networks transmit frames of information between workstations. Individual chapters thoroughly discuss Novell's NetWare, 3Com's 3+ and 3+Open, IBM Token-Ring related protocols, and more! 324 pp.

Book only	Item 099-0	$34.95

LAN Protocol Handbook Demonstration Disks

The set of seven demonstration disks is for those who wish to pursue the techniques of protocol analysis or consider the purchase of an analysis tool.

The analyzers will give you a clear view of your network so that you can better control and manage your LAN, as well as pinpoint trouble spots. The *LAN Protocol Handbook* demo disks are packed with detailed demonstration programs for LANalyzer® LAN Watch®, The Sniffer®, for Token-Ring and Ethernet, SpiderAnalyzer® 320-R for Token-Ring, and LANVista®. By surveying the demo programs, you will receive enough information to choose an analyzer that best suits your specific needs.

Requirements: IBM PC/XT/AT compatible with at least 640K after booting. Requires DOS version 2.0 or later. Either a color or monochrome display may be used.

Seven disks	$39.95

1-800-533-4372 (in CA 1-800-356-2002)

M&T BOOKS

A Library of Technical References from M&T Books

Internetworking
A Guide to Network Communications
LAN to LAN; LAN to WAN
by Mark A. Miller, P.E.

This book addresses all aspects of LAN and WAN (wide-area network) integrations, detailing the hardware, software, and communication products available. In-depth discussions describe the functions, design, and performance of repeaters, bridges, routers, and gateways. Communication facilities such as leased lines, T-1 circuits and access to packed switched public data networks (PSPDNs) are compared, helping LAN managers decide which is most viable for their internetwork. Also examined are the X.25, TCP/IP, and XNS protocols, as well as the internetworking capabilities and interoperability constraints of the most popular networks, including NetWare, LAN Server, 3+Open™, VINES®, and AppleTalk. 425 pp.

Book only   Item #143-1 $34.95

LAN Primer
An Introduction to Local Area Networks
by Greg Nunemacher

A complete introduction to local area networks (LANs), this book is a must for anyone who needs to know basic LAN principles. It includes a complete overview of LANs, clearly defining what a LAN is, the functions of a LAN, and how LANs fit into the field of telecommunications. The author discusses the specifics of building a LAN, including the required hardware and software, an overview of the types of products available, deciding what products to purchase, and assembling the pieces into a working LAN system. *LAN Primer* also includes case studies that illustrate how LAN principles work. Particular focus is given to Ethernet and Token-Ring. 221 pp.

Book only   Item #127-X $24.95

1-800-533-4372 (in CA 1-800-356-2002)

M&T BOOKS

A Library of Technical References from M&T Books

NetWare for Macintosh User's Guide
by Kelley J. P. Lindberg

NetWare for Macintosh User's Guide is the definitive reference to using Novell's NetWare on Macintosh computers. Whether you are a novice or an advanced user, this comprehensive text provides the information readers need to get the most from their NetWare networks. It includes an overview of network operations and detailed explanations of all NetWare for Macintosh menu and command line utilities. Detailed tutorials cover such tasks as logging in, working with directories and files, and printing over a network. Advanced users will benefit from the information on managing workstation environments and troubleshooting.
280 pp.

Book only   Item #126-1 $29.95

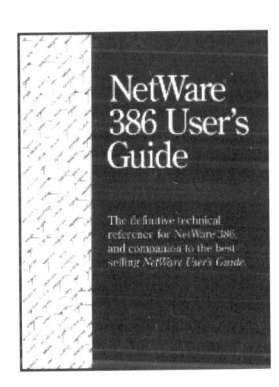

NetWare 386 User's Guide
by Christine Milligan

NetWare 386 User's Guide is a complete guide to using and understanding Novell's NetWare 386. It is an excellent reference for 386. Detailed tutorials cover tasks such as logging in, working with directories and files, and printing over a network. Complete explanations of the basic concepts underlying NetWare 386, along with a summary of the differences between NetWare 286 and 386, are included. Advanced users will benefit from the information on managing workstation environments and the troubleshooting index that fully examines NetWare 386 error messages. 450 pp.

Book only   Item #101-6 $29.95

1-800-533-4372 (in CA 1-800-356-2002)

M&T BOOKS

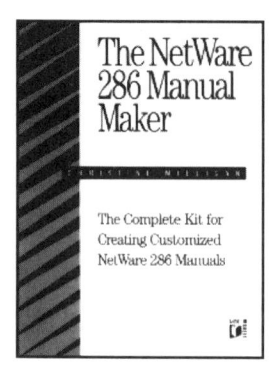

A Library of Technical References from M&T Books

The NetWare Manual Makers
Complete Kits for Creating Customized NetWare Manuals

Developed to meet the tremendous demand for customized manuals, The NetWare Manual Makers enable the NetWare supervisor and administrator to create network training manuals specific to their individual sites. Administrators simply fill in the blanks on the template provided on disk and print the file to create customized manuals and command cards. Included is general "how-to" information on using a network, as well as fill-in-the-blank sections that help administrators explain and document procedures unique to a particular site. The disk files are provided in WordPerfect and ASCII formats. The WordPerfect file creates a manual that looks exactly like the one in the book. The ASCII file can be imported into any desktop publishing or word processing software.

The NetWare 286 Manual Maker
The Complete Kit for Creating Customized NetWare 286 Manuals
by Christine Milligan
Book/Disk   Item #119-9 $49.95   314 pp.

The NetWare 386 Manual Maker
The Complete Kit for Creating Customized NetWare 386 Manuals
by Christine Milligan
Book/Disk   Item #120-2 $49.95   314 pp.

The NetWare for Macintosh Manual Maker
The Complete Kit for Creating Customized NetWare for Macintosh Manuals
by Kelley J. P. Lindberg
Book/Disk   Item #130-X $49.95   314 pp.

1-800-533-4372 (in CA 1-800-356-2002)

M&T BOOKS

A Library of Technical References from M&T Books

NetWare Programmer's Guide
by John T. McCann

Covered are all aspects of programming in the NetWare environment — from basic planning to complex application debugging. This book offers practical tips and tricks for creating and porting applications to NetWare. NetWare programmers developing simple applications for a single LAN or intricate programs for multi-site internetworked systems will find this book an invaluable reference to have on hand. All source code is available on disk in MS-PC/DOS format. 425 pp.

Book/Disk (MS-DOS)	Item #154-7	$44.95
Book only	Item #152-0	$34.95

Troubleshooting LAN Manager 2
by Michael Day

The ideal reference for network supervisors responsible for the maintenance of a LAN Manager 2 network. *Troubleshooting LAN Manager 2* builds a functional model of LAN Manager from the ground up, beginning with OS/2 and ending with fault tolerance and printer setup. Key components such as data structures, protocols, services, and applications are placed in a troubleshooting context, examining possible problems and providing hands-on solutions. More than basic hints and tips, this book lays a solid foundation upon which you can build a truly outstanding troubleshooting methodology. 337 pp.

Book only	Item #161-X	$34.95

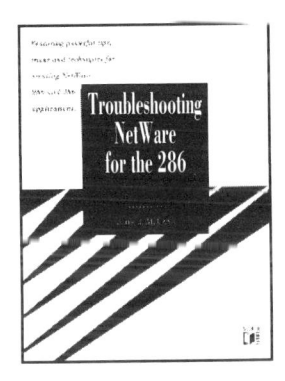

Troubleshooting NetWare for the 286
by Cheryl Snapp

The ideal reference for network supervisors responsible for the installation and maintenance of a NetWare 286 network. Contains a thorough overview of the NetWare 286 operating system plus step-by-step instructions for troubleshooting common and not-so-common problems. Detailed chapters emphasize the information most helpful in maintaining a healthy NetWare 286 LAN, including installation, file server and workstation diagnostics, printing utilities, and network management services. Covers NetWare 286 version 2.2. 350 pp.

Book only	Item #169-5	$34.95

1-800-533-4372 (in CA 1-800-356-2002)

M&T BOOKS

A Library of Technical References from M&T Books

Running WordPerfect on NetWare
by Greg McMurdie and Joni Taylor

Written by NetWare and WordPerfect experts, this book contains practical information for both system administrators and network WordPerfect users. Administrators will learn how to install, maintain, and troubleshoot WordPerfect on the network. Users will find answers to everyday questions such as how to print over the network, how to handle error messages, and how to use WordPerfect's tutorial on NetWare. 246 pp.

| Book only | Item #145-8 | $29.95 |

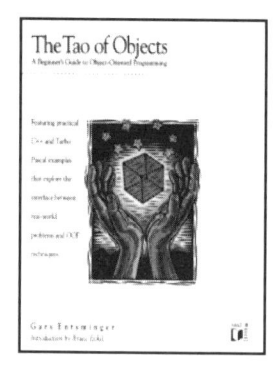

The Tao of Objects:
A Beginner's Guide to Object-Oriented Programming
by Gary Entsminger

The Tao of Objects is a clearly written, user-friendly guide to object-oriented programming (OOP). Easy-to-understand discussions detail OOP techniques teaching programmers who are new to OOP where and how to use them. Useful programming examples in C++ and Turbo Pascal illustrate the concepts discussed in real-life applications. 249 pp.

| Book only | Item #155-5 | $26.95 |

Object-Oriented Programming for Presentation Manager
by William G. Wong

Written for programmers and developers interested in OS/2 Presentation Manager (PM), as well as DOS programmers who are just beginning to explore Object-Oriented Programming and PM. Topics include a thorough overview of Presentation Manager and Object-Oriented Programming, Object-Oriented Programming languages and techniques, developing Presentation Manager applications using C and OOP techniques, and more. 423 pp.

| Book/Disk (MS-DOS) | Item #079-6 | $39.95 |
| Book only | Item #074-5 | $29.95 |

1-800-533-4372 (in CA 1-800-356-2002)

M&T BOOKS
A Library of Technical References from M&T Books

Fractal Programming in C
by Roger T. Stevens

If you are a programmer wanting to learn more about fractals, this book is for you. Learn how to create pictures that have both beauty and an underlying mathematical meaning. Included are over 50 black and white pictures and 32 full-color fractals. All source code to reproduce these pictures is provided on disk in MS-DOS format requiring an IBM PC or clone with an EGA or VGA card, a color monitor, and a Turbo C, Quick C, or Microsoft C compiler. 580 pp.

Book/Disk (MS-DOS)	Item #038-9	$39.95
Book only	Item #037-0	$29.95

Fractal Programming in Turbo Pascal
by Roger T. Stevens

This book equips Turbo Pascal programmers with the tools needed to program dynamic fractal curves. It is a reference that gives full attention to developing the reader's understanding of various fractal curves. More than 100 black and white and 32 full-color fractals are illustrated throughout the book. All source code to reproduce the fractals is available on disk in MS/PC-DOS format. Requires a PC or clone with EGA or VGA, color monitor, and Turbo Pascal 4.0 or later. 462 pp.

Book/Disk (MS-DOS)	Item #107-5	$39.95
Book	Item #106-7	$29.95

Graphics Programming in C
by Roger T. Stevens

All the information you need to program graphics in C, including source code, is presented. You'll find complete discussions of ROM BIOS, VGA, EGA, and CGA inherent capabilities; methods of displaying points on a screen; improved, faster algorithms for drawing and filling lines, rectangles, rounded polygons, ovals, circles, and arcs; graphic cursors; and much more! Both Turbo C and Microsoft C are supported. 639 pp.

Book/Disk (MS-DOS)	Item #019-2	$36.95
Book only	Item #018-4	$26.95

1-800-533-4372 (in CA 1-800-356-2002)

M&T BOOKS
A Library of Technical References from M&T Books

Programming in 3 Dimensions
3-D Graphics, Ray Tracing, and Animation
by Sandra Bloomberg

Programming in 3 Dimensions is a comprehensive, hands-on guide to computer graphics. It contains a detailed look at 3-D graphics plus discussions of popular ray tracing methods and computer animation. Readers will find techniques for creating 3-D graphics and breath-taking ray-traced images as, well as explanations of how animation works and ways computers help produce it more effectively. Packed with examples and C source code, this book is a must for all computer graphics enthusiasts! All source code is available on disk in MS/PC-DOS format. Includes 16 pages of full-color graphics.
500 pp. approx.

Book/Disk (MS-DOS)	Item #218-7	$39.95
Book only	Item #220-9	$29.95

Fractal Programming and Ray Tracing with C++
by Roger T. Stevens

Finally, a book for C and C++ programmers who want to create complex and intriguing graphic designs. By the author of three best-selling graphics books, this new title thoroughly explains ray tracing, discussing how rays are traced, how objects are used to create ray-traced images, and how to create ray tracing programs. A complete ray tracing program, along with all of the source code, is included. Contains 16 pages of full-color graphics. 444 pp.

Book/Disk (MS-DOS)	Item 118-0	$39.95
Book only	Item 134-2	$29.95

1-800-533-4372 (in CA 1-800-356-2002)

M&T BOOKS

A Library of Technical References from M&T Books

Advanced Fractal Programming in C
by Roger T. Stevens

Programmers who enjoyed our best-selling *Fractal Programming in C* can move on to the next level of fractal programming with this book. Included are how-to instructions for creating many different types of fractal curves, including source code. Contains 16 pages of full-color fractals. All the source code to generate the fractals is available on an optional disk in MS/PC-DOS format. 305 pp.

Book/Disk (MS-DOS)	Item #097-4	$39.95
Book only	Item #096-6	$29.95

Advanced Graphics Programming in Turbo Pascal
by Roger T. Stevens and Christopher D. Watkins

This new book is must reading for Turbo Pascal programmers who want to create impressive graphic designs on IBM PCs and compatibles. There are 32 pages of full-color graphic displays along with the source code to create these dramatic pictures. Complete explanations are provided on how to tailor the graphics to suit the programmer's needs. Covered are algorithms for creating complex 2-D shapes, including lines, circles and squares; how to create advanced 3-D shapes, wire-frame graphics, and solid images; numerous tips and techniques for varying pixel intensities to give the appearance of roundness to an object; and more. 540 pp.

Book/Disk (MS-DOS)	Item #132-6	$39.95
Book only	Item #131-8	$29.95

1-800-533-4372 (in CA 1-800-356-2002)

M&T BOOKS

A Library of Technical References from M&T Books

Advanced Graphics Programming in C and C++
by Roger T. Stevens and Christopher D. Watkins

This book is for all C and C++ programmers who want to create impressive graphic designs on their IBM PCs or compatibles. Through in-depth discussions and numerous sample programs, readers will learn how to create advanced 3-D shapes, wire-frame graphics, solid images, and more. All source code is available on disk in MS/PC-DOS format. Contains 16 pages of full-color graphics. 500 pp. approx.

Book/Disk (MS-DOS)	Item #173-3	$39.95
Book only	Item #171-7	$29.95

Graphics Programming with Microsoft C 6
by Mark Mallett

Written for all C programmers, this book explores graphics programming with Microsoft C 6.0, including full coverage of Microsoft C's built-in graphics libraries. Sample programs will help readers learn the techniques needed to create spectacular graphic designs, including 3-D figures, solid images, and more. All source code in the book is available on disk in MS/PC-DOS format. Includes 16 pages of full-color graphics. 500 pp. approx.

Book/Disk (MS-DOS)	Item #167-9	$39.95
Book only	Item #165-2	$29.95

The Verbum Book of PostScript Illustration
by Michael Gosney, Linnea Dayton, and Janet Ashford

This is the premier instruction book for designers, illustrators, and desktop publishers using Postscript. Each chapter highlights the talents of top illustrators who demonstrate the electronic artmaking process. The narrative keys readers in to the artist's conceptual vision, providing valuable insight into the creative thought processes that go into a real-world PostScript illustration project. 213 pp.

Book only	Item #089-3	$29.95

1-800-533-4372 (in CA 1-800-356-2002)

M&T BOOKS

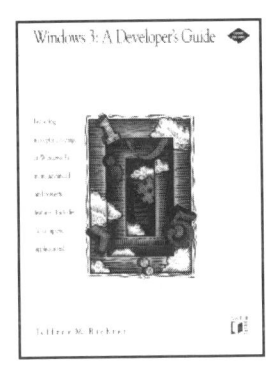

A Library of Technical References from M&T Books

Windows 3: A Developer's Guide
by Jeffrey M. Richter

This example-packed guide is for all experienced C programmers developing applications for Windows 3.0. This book describes every feature, function, and component of the Windows Application Programming Interface, teaching programmers how to take full advantage of its many capabilities. Diagrams and source code examples are used to demonstrate advanced topics, including window subclassing, dynamic memory management, and software installation techniques.
671 pp.

Book/Disk (MS-DOS)	Item #164-4	$39.95
Book only	Item #162-8	$29.95

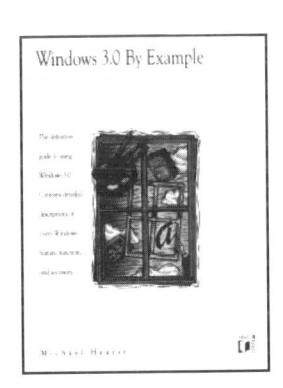

Windows 3.0 By Example
by Michael Hearst

Here is a hands-on guide to Windows 3.0. Written for all users new to Windows, this book provides thorough, easy-to-follow explanations of every Windows 3.0 feature and function. Numerous exercises and helpful practice sessions help readers further develop their understanding of Windows 3.0 398 pp.

Book only	Item #180-6	$26.95

The Verbum Book of Digital Typography
by Michael Gosney, Linnea Dayton, and Jennifer Ball

The Verbum Book of Digital Typography combines information on good design principles with effective typography techniques, showing designers, illustrators, and desktop publishers how to create attractive printed materials that communicate effectively. Each chapter highlights the talents of a professional type designer as he or she steps readers through an interesting real-life project. Readers will learn how to develop letterforms and typefaces, modify type outlines, and create special effects. 200 pp. approx.

Book only	Item #092-3	$29.95

1-800-533-4372 (in CA 1-800-356-2002)

M&T BOOKS

A Library of Technical References from M&T Books

Delivering cc:Mail
Installing, Maintaining, and Troubleshooting a cc:Mail System
by Eric Arnum

Delivering cc:Mail teaches administrators how to install, troubleshoot, and maintain cc:Mail, one of the most popular E-mail applications for the PC. In-depth discussions and practical examples show administrators how to establish and maintain the program and database files; how to create and modify the bulletin boards, mail directory, and public mailing lists; and how to diagnose and repair potential problems. Information on using the management tools included with the package plus tips and techniques for creating efficient batch files are also included. All source code is available on disk in MS/PC-DOS format. 450 pp.

| Book & Disk | Item #187-3 | $39.95 |
| Book only | Item #185-7 | $29.95 |

The Complete Memory Manager
Every PC User's Guide to Faster, More Efficient Computing
by Phillip Robinson

Readers will learn why memory is important, how and when to install more, and how to wring the most out of their memory. Clear, concise instructions teach users how to manage their computer's memory to multiply its speed and ability to run programs simultaneously. Tips and techniques also show users how to conserve memory when working with popular software programs. 437 pp.

| Book | Item #102-4 | $24.95 |

1-800-533-4372 (in CA 1-800-356-2002)

M&T BOOKS

A Library of Technical References from M&T Books

Clipper 5: A Developer's Guide
by Joseph D. Booth, Greg Lief, and Craig Yellick

An invaluable guide for all database programmers developing applications for Clipper® 5. Provides a quick introduction to Clipper 5 basics and discusses common programming needs such as designing data files, user interfaces, reports, and more. Advanced topics include networking, debugging, and pop-up programming. Code examples are used throughout the text, providing useful functions that can be applied immediately. All source code is available on disk in MS/PC-DOS format. 1300 pp. approx.

Book & Disk (MS-DOS)	Item #242-X	$44.95
Book only	Item #240-3	$34.95

DOS 5 User's Guide
A Comprehensive Guide for Every PC User
by Dan Gookin

Take control of the MS-DOS® operating system with this complete guide to using the world's most popular operating system. *DOS 5 User's Guide* contains clear, concise explanations of every feature, function, and command of DOS 5.0. Novice PC users will gain a quick start on using DOS, while advanced users will learn savvy tricks and techniques to maneuver their way quickly and easily through the system. Practical discussions and helpful examples teach readers how to edit text files, use directories, create batch files, and much more. Advanced topics include using EDLIN, the DOS text editor; configuring the system; and using the DOS shell. 771 pp.

Book only	Item #188-1	$24.95

1-800-533-4372 (in CA 1-800-356-2002)

M&T BOOKS

ORDER FORM

To Order: Return this form with your payment to M&T books, 501 Galveston Drive, Redwood City, CA 94063 or **call toll-free 1-800-533-4372 (in California, call 1-800-356-2002).**

ITEM #	DESCRIPTION	DISK	PRICE

Subtotal

CA residents add sales tax ___ %

Add $3.75 per item for shipping and handling

TOTAL

NOTE: **FREE SHIPPING** ON ORDERS OF THREE OR MORE BOOKS.

Charge my:
- ❏ Visa
- ❏ MasterCard
- ❏ AmExpress

❏ **Check enclosed, payable to M&T Books.**

CARD NO. _____

SIGNATURE _____ EXP. DATE _____

NAME _____

ADDRESS _____

CITY _____

STATE _____ ZIP _____

M&T GUARANTEE: If your are not satisfied with your order for any reason, return it to us within 25 days of receipt for a full refund. Note: Refunds on disks apply only when returned with book within guarantee period. Disks damaged in transit or defective will be promptly replaced, but cannot be exchanged for a disk from a different title.

8030

1-800-533-4372 (in CA 1-800-356-2002)

TIRED OF MANUAL FILE ENTRY? SAVE YOURSELF SOME TIME AND TROUBLE...

Order the
DOS 5: A Developer's Guide
Source Code Disk

Why bother manually typing in the book's source code when all the information you need is ready to use on disk? Code examples are used throughout the text, and this optional disk (PC/MS-DOS format) contains the source code for all the programming examples listed. Useful functions can now be applied immediately!

To order, return this postage-paid card with your payment to:
M&T Books,
501 Galveston Drive, Redwood City, CA 94063.
Or call **TOLL FREE 1-800-533-4372 (in CA 1-800-356-2002)**.

❏ **Yes!** Please send me the optional source code disk $20.00
    CA residents add applicable sales tax ___%
                                              Total _____

❏ Send me your latest M&T Books Direct Catalog.

❏ Check enclosed. Make payable to M&T Books.
Charge my   ❏ VISA   ❏ MC   ❏ AmEx
Card No. _____ Exp. Date _____
Name _____
Address _____
City _____ State _____ Zip _____

Note: Disks damaged in transit may be returned for a replacement. No credit or refund given.

7117

BUSINESS REPLY MAIL
FIRST CLASS MAIL PERMIT 871 REDWOOD CITY, CA

POSTAGE WILL BE PAID BY ADDRESSEE

M&T BOOKS
501 Galveston Drive
Redwood City, CA 94063-9929

NO POSTAGE
NECESSARY
IF MAILED
IN THE
UNITED STATES

————— PLEASE FOLD ALONG LINE AND STAPLE OR TAPE CLOSED —————